BIG WOLF

The Adventurous Life of Lieutenant Frederick G. Schwatka

DOUGLAS W. WAMSLEY

American History Press
Staunton Virginia

Copyright © 2022 Douglas W. Wamsley

All rights reserved. No part of this book may be transmitted in any form by any means electronic, mechanical or otherwise using devices now existing or yet to be invented without prior written permission from the publisher and copyright holder.

American History Press
Staunton, Virginia
Visit us on the Internet at:
www.Americanhistorypress.com

First Paperback Printing – February 2023

To schedule an event with the author or to inquire about bulk discount sales please contact American History Press.

The Library of Congress has catalogued the hardcover edition as follows:
Library of Congress Cataloging-in-Publication Data
Names: Wamsley, Douglas W., 1958- author.
Title: Big Wolf : the adventurous life of Lieutenant Frederick G. Schwatka / Douglas W. Wamsley.
Description: First edition. | Staunton, Virginia : American History Press, [2022]
Identifiers: LCCN 2021043094 | ISBN 9781939995391 (hardcover) ISBN 9781939995421 (paperback)
Subjects: LCSH: Schwatka, Frederick, 1849-1892. | Explorers--United States--Biography. | Yukon River (Yukon and Alaska)--Discovery and exploration. | Arctic regions--Discovery and exploration. | Franklin, John, 1786-1847. | John Franklin Arctic Expedition (1845-1851) | United States. Army. Cavalry Regiment, 3rd.
Classification: LCC G635.S39 W36 2021 | DDC 910.92 [B]--dc23/eng/20211005
LC record available at https://lccn.loc.gov/2021043094

Cover design by Rick Burkart; interior design by David Kane

Manufactured in the United States of America on acid-free paper. This book exceeds all ANSO standards for archival quality.

CONTENTS

Foreword	vii
Acknowledgements	x
Introduction	xv

CHAPTER ONE Pioneer Spirit	1
CHAPTER TWO First Call	23
CHAPTER THREE The Battle of the Rosebud	50
CHAPTER FOUR The Battle of Slim Buttes	76
CHAPTER FIVE Arctic Fever	101
CHAPTER SIX In the Land of the Midnight Sun	121
CHAPTER SEVEN To The North	147
CHAPTER EIGHT The Franklin Records Search	164
CHAPTER NINE King William Island and Return	185

Contents

CHAPTER TEN
The Traveler at Home   210

CHAPTER ELEVEN
New Horizons   226

CHAPTER TWELVE
Down the Yukon – Part I   249

CHAPTER THIRTEEN
Down the Yukon – Part II   272

CHAPTER FOURTEEN
To the Top of the Continent   290

CHAPTER FIFTEEN
Thro' the Wonderland   321

CHAPTER SIXTEEN
South of the Border   340

CHAPTER SEVENTEEN
The Last Journey   368

Conclusion   388

Chapter Notes   402
Bibliography   448
Illustration Credits   471
Index   473
About the Author   489

FOREWORD

The nineteenth century was a golden age for Arctic exploration. Few other regions of the earth were as yet uncharted, and none other presented such formidable perils. Would-be voyagers were obliged to winter their ships over for much of the year, and hope at best for a month or two in the summer to make progress where they could. If in need of rescue, there was no means of communication with the outside world. Any would-be rescuers that might be dispatched would face the same hazards, and often might need rescuing themselves. Their challenges were not limited to the natural world, but extended into a kind of cultural blindness. In a region where the Inuit hunted and thrived, travelling hundreds of miles by dog team, British and American explorers stuck to their ships. When they did travel by land, they clung to the practice of man-hauling their sledges, adding exhaustion to their long list of perils. Thoroughly unprepared for their Arctic journeys, they had poor and inappropriate provisions, lacked the skills to hunt effectively, and wore inadequate clothing, all challenges that the Indigenous people had long before learned to overcome.

The great drama of the age—the disappearance of Sir John Franklin's expedition while on a quest to find a Northwest Passage in 1845—dominated the public imagination for decades afterwards. More than any others, Franklin and his men had suffered from both natural and cultural limitations. The timing of their sailing coincided with a period of unusually cold winters, so cold that even the Inuit people suffered privation and death. Those who searched for Franklin labored with the same difficulties he had, and in the end, endured a decade of defeat. Finally, in the summer of 1859 Sir Francis Leopold McClintock went in search of Franklin. His only discoveries were a single written record, some scattered bones and a whaleboat laden with mostly useless material—"dead weight" as he put it—all of which only deepened the mystery of the explorer's disappearance.

Into this void, thanks to a set of unusual circumstances—the discovery of some spoons and forks associated with Franklin's men, the enthusiasm of the American Geographical Society, and the willingness of an American whaling concern to provide a ship and men – stepped a seemingly unlikely figure. Frederick Gustavus Schwatka, the scion of hardy immigrants who had travelled the Oregon Trail to establish a new home in the West, answered the call to undertake one last great search for Franklin. A man of seemingly irreconcilable contradictions, Schwatka had risen through the ranks of the U.S. Third Cavalry by fighting to defeat and contain the Indigenous people of the Great Plains. Still, more than any man before him, he trusted and worked alongside the Inuit, and followed their ways of travel and hunting. He was a clear-sighted, determined leader who quickly garnered friends, though at times he seemed to retreat into himself, struggling with addiction, first alcohol and then opiates. A word that was often applied to him – persistent - perhaps characterizes him better than any other. He was not the kind of person to stop short of his ultimate goal. And, unlike other men of his ilk, he extended his trust and enthusiasm to every person under his command; he gathered their spirits and made them one with his own.

The hardships he and his men faced were many. At times, even with plenty of ammunition and the most capable of hunters, they endured hunger and privation. Early on in their expedition, they had to make fateful decisions about which of the potential goals to pursue, and how best to prepare for the lengthy, unsupported journey required to reach them. That Schwatka succeeded and brought back the most complete eyewitness accounts of Franklin's fate yet known was largely due to his personal character. His Inuit companions, who worked so closely with him in supporting that mission, gained great respect for his skills, and their long work together made them intimate friends. In the long history of Arctic exploration, the parting of Schwatka and his fellow explorers from their Inuit colleagues was an uncommon event. All participants were moved to tears at the thought of the loss of such valued friendships.

History has perhaps been unkind to Schwatka. His accomplishments during the Franklin search and his later exploits in Alaska were eagerly followed by the American public, but as these frontiers receded so too did Schwatka's fame. His own struggles with addiction eventually brought his life to an untimely end at the young age of forty-three, and the public appetite for exploration shifted to the more abstract quest for the North Pole. Still, it is extraordinary that it has not been until now, nearly 130

Foreword

years after his death, that he has found an able biographer in the person of Douglas Wamsley. Wamsley's diligence in research—— already evident in his previous book, *Polar Hayes*—illuminates and clarifies many poorly understood chapters of Schwatka's career, and vividly brings to life this courageous yet complicated man. Today, with both of Franklin's ships now found, and the work of archaeologists now corroborating and extending many of Schwatka's discoveries, there could hardly be imagined a better time for his return to the Arctic stage.

Russell Potter
Professor of English
Rhode Island College

ACKNOWLEDGMENTS

According to Ada Brackett Schwatka, Frederick Schwatka's devoted but long-suffering wife, a veritable treasure trove of original documents was lost during the great catastrophe of the San Francisco earthquake of 1906. Seeking to preserve and protect Frederick Schwatka's journals, diaries, and personal papers while residing in the city after his death, Ada had thoughtfully deposited them in what was thought to be an impregnable location, a lockbox within a vault in a San Francisco bank. Amidst the tragic loss of life and devastation from the earthquake and attendant firestorm, Frederick Schwatka's papers were destroyed. With them, a valuable legacy was lost forever. Thus, the search for relevant primary material became a particularly difficult objective in and of itself, and an obsession, but ultimately a most rewarding experience.

As always, without the assistance of numerous individuals who were unflagging in their aid, this work could not have been completed. Without their dedication and encouragement, it would have been far from the comprehensive story of a man of such varied interests who accomplished so much in his brief but active life. Their support was particularly helpful during a time when many institutions were closed to the public due to the Covid crisis, and access was only available through countless email and digital image requests. Many thanks are due to their efforts.

In many respects, that this work was even started and has finally come to fruition, I must credit the polar historian David Stam, to whom I owe an inestimable debt of thanks. Many years ago, I had mentioned in passing my growing interest in Schwatka's life and my belief that Schwatka's influence on the course of not only northern exploration, but other aspects of American history, had been far from fully examined. From that moment, I was politely, but purposefully, questioned at every meeting or conversation, "How is Schwatka coming along?" David's enthusiasm for the project, as well as his encouragement, has served as a continual inspiration.

Schwatka's family and early education were particularly important influences, and institutions in Salem, Oregon, managed to provide helpful information as to both. From the outset of my research, several of those organizations, dutiful custodians of Oregon's pioneer history, served as useful repositories for details about his early life. Scott Daniels at the Oregon Historical Society and Kaylyn Mabey of the Willamette Heritage Center were extremely helpful. They located land and immigration records, donation claims, and a handful of surviving manuscripts documenting the arrival of the Schwatka family and their difficult early years of homesteading in the Northwest. Willamette University, the oldest educational institution west of the Mississippi, faithfully maintained records from its start in 1842, including during the period of Schwatka's attendance. Mary McRobinson ably assisted in locating appropriate records that provided insights into his schooling, activities, and budding interests. Steven Branting, Institutional Historian at Lewis-Clark State College, was particularly helpful in regard to offering biographical information and photographs of Frederick Schwatka's family which were gleaned during his own research.

The United States Military Academy, which closely monitors the progress of its cadets, maintains in its archives a wealth of information about Schwatka's performance, conduct and personal interests throughout his four years of attendance. Susan Lintelmann and Alicia Mauldin-Ware were untiring during my visits and through many follow up requests, especially during the period the library remained closed to the public. Following his graduation, Frederick Schwatka embarked on an eventful fifteen years of service with the U.S. Army. The military had a profound impact on the young man, opening doors and serving as the springboard for a professional career that stretched over the balance of his life. Schwatka's Appointment, Commission, Personal (ACP) file at the U.S. National Archives, a voluminous 500-page record, provides the most thorough record of Schwatka's commendable but largely unexamined military service, as well as his trials and tribulations within the senior military bureaucracy. A multitude of other service records held by the National Archives, such as post returns, agency correspondence, reports, and orders, only a few of which have been digitized, helped provide as complete a picture of his military career as possible. Katherine Vollen and Andrew Brethauer at the National Archives aided in providing ready access to this wealth of material. In addition, Marty Miller at the Nebraska State Historical Society assisted in locating materials that helped document the history of the posts at which Schwatka served in Nebraska, and life on the

Acknowledgements

Great Plains at the time. Early on, I reached out to Marc Abrams in Brooklyn, who maintains a large digital archive of newspaper articles gathered while conducting his own research on the Indian wars. I was quickly provided with dozens of helpful references to Lieutenant Schwatka.

Archivists at a number of institutions helped with various aspects of Schwatka's wide-ranging activities. Glenda Barahona at the Medical Archives and Special Collections of New York University, the repository of Bellevue Medical School records, helped to locate archival material regarding Schwatka's classroom and clinical experience while at Bellevue. Gary Barnhart at the Montana State University Library proved indefatigable in his efforts to locate relevant correspondence in the files of Yellowstone photographer Frank J. Haynes related to Schwatka's ill-fated Yellowstone trip and his falling out with Haynes. Tal Nadan at the New York Public Library helped direct me to the *Century Magazine* archives which offered insights into Schwatka's relationship with the editors of that publication and Schwatka's literary career. Those documents also helped shed a different light on Schwatka's strained relationship with Frank Haynes.

The few extant original diaries of participants in Schwatka's expeditions helped to provide another view of the personal dynamics and relationships during these journeys. At the Alaska Science Center of the U.S. Geological Survey, Elizabeth Drewes-Todd managed to relocate the rarely viewed diary of Charles Willard Hayes, geologist to Schwatka's final expedition to Alaska, as well as a series of high quality photographs from that same expedition. Sandra Johnson at the Alaska State Library furnished a copy of the journal of J. B. Mcintosh, a civilian member of Schwatka's Yukon excursion, whose dry humor and observations added color and insights to that journey. Through the diligent efforts of Andrew Dzaugis, science librarian at Clark University, the extensive glass slide collection of Professor William Libbey, scientist on Schwatka's Mount St. Elias journey, has now been catalogued, revealing a unique photographic record of that trip. At the New Bedford Whaling Museum, Mark Procknik located several logbooks documenting activities during Schwatka's 1878-80 Arctic journey.

A number of persons provided insightful comments on all or portions of the manuscript. Paul Hedren generously offered his time and expertise on the Great Sioux War and the many diverse aspects of frontier military service, as well as critical commentary on those facets of the manuscript. Paul also deserves special mention for providing the most memorable aspect of the entire project, a guided tour of the Rosebud Battlefield State Park. Russell Potter likewise deserves special mention for his review of

Acknowledgements xiii

the manuscript and his unflagging assistance and encouragement through the entire project. Dr. Todd Harburn offered valuable commentary as to the many physical and mental ailments that so plagued Schwatka during his lifetime.

David Pelly freely shared his knowledge of the history of the exploration of the Back River before and after Schwatka's trek. In addition, the oral history gathered by David through his interviews of the Ukkusiksalik Inuit provided an important Native perspective on Schwatka's Arctic work. Similarly, Kenn Harper gave freely of his time and expertise in matters of Inuit language and history. Douglas Stenton assisted in connecting Schwatka's nineteenth-century Franklin search with his own recent and important bioarchaeological studies of members of that ill-fated expedition. David Woodman provided knowledgeable insights into the wealth of Inuit testimony gathered by Schwatka's search expedition. Schwatka had many exploits in Alaska, and Christopher "Timo" Allan provided constructive comments on Alaskan history and Schwatka's varied Alaskan pursuits.

Robert Cronan, of Lucidity Information Design, did a fine job of preparing the maps tracking Schwatka's various whereabouts. His presentation provided a realistic depiction of the varied and unforgiving terrains through which Schwatka traversed. With a patient and steady hand, David Kane and Franci Ferguson at American History Press are also deserving of acknowledgement for their untiring efforts in guiding Schwatka to completion.

Schwatka's many visits, lectures and interviews were frequently covered by contemporary newspapers and periodicals, many of which were local publications of limited distribution. A substantial number are now available in digital form, and they filled important gaps in obtaining a thorough understanding of Schwatka's eventful life.

Other institutions that merit thanks for their assistance include the following: Alaska State Library and Archives, Juneau, AK; The American Geographical Society Library, UWM Gilda Meir Library, Milwaukee, WI; American Philosophical Society, Philadelphia, PA; Denver Public Library, Denver, CO; Gilder Lehrman Institute of American History, New York, NY; Johns Hopkins Libraries, Baltimore, MD; Lilly Library, Indiana University, Bloomington, IN; Manuscript and Archives Division, New York Public Library, New York, NY; Minnesota Historical Society, St. Paul, MN; Smithsonian Institution Archives and National Museum of American History, Washington, D.C.; Montana Historical Society Research Center, Helena, MT; G.W. Blunt Library, Mystic Seaport Museum, Mystic, CT; The National Cowboy & Western

Heritage Museum, Oklahoma City, OK; National Maritime Museum, London, England; New York State Newspaper Library, Albany, NY; Rock Island County Historical Society, Rock Island, IL; Scott Polar Research Institute, Cambridge, England; Smith College Special Collections, Northampton, MA; Tacoma Public Library, South Tacoma, WA; Union Pacific Museum, Council Bluffs, IA; The University of Illinois Rare Book and Manuscript Library, Urbana, IL; and University of Virginia Library, Charlottesville, VA; Yukon Archives, Whitehorse, Yukon; Yukon Native Language Centre, Yukon University, Whitehorse, Yukon.

As always, without the support, encouragement and patience of my own long-suffering family, Leslie, Matthew and Christine, this work would not have seen the light of day. To them, I owe a debt of thanks that I could not repay. I'm grateful to all of you.

Douglas W. Wamsley

INTRODUCTION

At 3:00 A.M., the witching hour, on the second of November 1892, a cool drizzle fell as a police officer made his regular rounds along First Street in the heart of the commercial district of Portland, Oregon. An early-morning stillness had settled over the otherwise bustling city, a metropolis of the Pacific Northwest. While passing a row of retail storefronts, the officer nearly stumbled over a burly middle-aged man, neatly dressed and sporting pince-nez spectacles, lying unconscious outside a doorway. A two-ounce vial of laudanum, an opium derivative, was found beside him, half empty of its contents.

Believing the man to be in a drunken stupor, vigorous efforts were taken to revive him and move him on, all of which had no effect. The insensible man was carried with some effort to the nearby St. Charles Hotel, where he was carefully placed in a chair in an attempt to make him comfortable and sober him up. But his condition worsened within the hour. A police wagon was called, and he was transported to the local jail. The city physician, aroused from his slumber by that wonder of modern technology, a newly installed telephone, quickly arrived to attend to the still unresponsive patient. Immediately recognizing that the man was suffering from a narcotic overdose, he was rushed to Good Samaritan Hospital. Despite the doctor's best efforts, the man, only forty-three-years-old, died at 5:00 A.M. Immediately following his death, rumors started circulating. Many said that in a discouraged and depressed mood, he had elected to take his own life. A few days afterward, a handful of close friends and family assembled to attend his funeral in his hometown of Salem, Oregon. A modest headstone was erected over his grave in the family burial plot, simply reading "Frederick Schwatka-Explorer."

Frederick Schwatka, one of the most well-known Americans of the time, had suffered an inglorious fate. In his prime, throughout the 1880s and early 1890s, he had been recognized as a famous explorer, popular writer, celebrity and household name. He was a mainstay at the morning breakfast table, his lively and entertaining features appearing in a wide variety of newspapers and magazines across the country. A proverbial bundle of energy and a brazen self-promoter, crisscrossing the country by rail through urban and rural America, he was a constant fixture on the lyceum lecture circuit that was so popular at the time.

Upon his death, Frederick Schwatka's fleeting popularity soon faded. An obituary telegraphed to newspapers nationwide carried only a brief biographical summary with a scant few memorable highlights, all within the tight character limits of the printed page. His faithful wife of ten years, and stoic widow for thirty-seven, would faithfully labor in vain to preserve his legacy.

His was an all too brief but adventurous life, filled with exploits as remarkable as the popular dime novels of the time. Today Frederick Schwatka's exploring achievements are hardly remembered, victims perhaps of subsequent and more publicly renowned geographical accomplishments such as the discovery of the North and South Poles. But Frederick Schwatka was far more than another forgotten American explorer, absent from textbooks and remembered by a few geographic place names. Born in 1849, as the spirit of Manifest Destiny captivated the country, Frederick Schwatka was an enthusiastic participant in its westward and northward expansion. He was the son of proud pioneer settlers in the Oregon Territory who forged a new beginning in the Northwest through self-determination and self-sufficiency. Like those pioneers, Schwatka's life embodied the restless spirit that moved a young nation, and like it, one that was prone to faults and growing pains. An expansionist at heart, in his own eyes, he had "seen two iron rails in a wilderness [grow] to a great country." He lived in a time of wide-open spaces that matched his own equally wide ambitions. In his short but eventful life, his inquisitive nature drove him to pursue a diversity of interests, fairly characterizing him as a renaissance man: soldier, explorer, naturalist, physician, lawyer, free-lance correspondent and prolific author; a man who made notable contributions in a number of those fields.

Schwatka's broad-minded personality was well suited to an understaffed post-Civil War military that by necessity served multi-faceted roles in the yet unsettled West. As a dutiful cavalry officer for more than a decade, he made a name for himself during some of the most hard-fought campaigns of the Indian wars before and in the aftermath of Custer's defeat at the Little Big Horn. He was an eyewitness to the subjugation of the American

Indian and the demise of the open prairie. He rubbed shoulders with western legends like Buffalo Bill and Calamity Jane. As a military man and pathfinder in his own right, he also carried on a tradition within the U.S. Army of contributing meaningfully to the investigation and exploration of the continent. All in all, Frederick Schwatka was an enthusiastic participant with a front-row seat in the American western experience, with an unshaded view that he was not hesitant to share. A careful examination of his life offers an informative and valuable window into our own country's history.

Frederick Schwatka was a man of marked contrasts. Despite battling debilitating physical ailments and addiction-related maladies, his outstanding career as an explorer was comprised of expeditions marked by splendid feats of endurance. Among them were the longest journey by sledge and the longest by watercourse, as well as an attempted ascent of what was then believed to be the highest mountain in North America. Frederick Schwatka also figures prominently in one of the greatest crusades and mysteries of the nineteenth century, the discovery of the fate of the lost explorer Sir John Franklin. Schwatka's journeys stretched from Hudson Bay and the Canadian Arctic to Alaska and the Pacific Ocean. To the nineteenth-century public, the phrase "Schwatka's Search" became synonymous with a long and burdensome task, conjuring up an Odyssean epic. For the general public and the armchair adventurer in an increasingly urbanized society, the stories of his travels and adventures brought widespread attention to unexplored lands, particularly the newly acquired territory of Alaska. His writings offered a safe and comfortable window through which to view an untamed American wilderness that was rapidly fading into history. While his explorations gained some publicity during his lifetime, his prolific literary legacy has been largely forgotten and his work and influence in the field of travel writing little examined.

Throughout his life Schwatka remained a contradiction in personality. To his detractors, he was headstrong, vain, and insufferable, but to his friends and companions he was open-minded, warm-hearted, and admired. He was frequently at odds with the political and military establishments, as well as the scientific community which marked him a rank amateur. However, laboring in the field and on the trail, where cooperation was vital, he could forge sound relationships and engender loyalty under the most trying of circumstances. Though he maintained a steadfast belief in the rightness and inevitability of westward settlement, he was sympathetic to its consequences. Historians have frequently pointed to his writings that reflect the flagrant cultural bias which was prevalent at the time. Despite those writings, Schwatka respected and learned from North America's first peoples. His personal interest in their wellbeing made a lasting impression on his Native counterparts. Privileged to be adopted into the Brulé Sioux tribe, the legendary chief Spotted Tail himself conferred upon Schwatka the name "Big Wolf." When news of Schwatka's untimely death reached them more than a decade after their last encounter, the grieving Sioux mourned Schwatka's passing with prayers and song. Following the completion of Schwatka's historic Arctic journey his Inuit companions of two years, who were not easily given to emotion, wept in sorrow upon his departure.

Surprisingly, no review of this seemingly contradictory man has ever been undertaken, a factor that no doubt has contributed to his status as an overlooked figure in American history. He may not have been judged poorly by history, but he has not yet received his true measure of attention. This works looks to shed the proper light on the remarkable life and accomplishments of Frederick Schwatka.

A NOTE ON USAGE AND SPELLING

To maintain consistency with historical usage, in quotations, the original spellings in printed or manuscript materials generally have been retained, including the terms Eskimo, Esquimau and Esquimaux. Elsewhere, the more appropriate terms, such as Inuk, Inuit, Kalaallit or Inughuit are used. Where Schwatka's spellings differ from those of others, such as in some names, his spellings are generally followed to avoid confusion. Temperature readings are given in degrees Fahrenheit and distances are in statute miles (5280 ft.), unless otherwise noted.

CHAPTER ONE

PIONEER SPIRIT

It is not surprising that Frederick Schwatka was a restless adventurer at heart, and a possessor of an independent and roaming spirit. His parents and grandparents epitomized the nineteenth century immigrant experience, pioneers who were prepared to endure difficult travels and hardships for the promise of an improved life and economic circumstances. Schwatka hailed from a strong-willed, working class family, with relatives engaged as highly skilled and hardworking craftsmen. According to one family chronicler, the explorer's ancestors hailed from Prussia along the southern coast of the Baltic Sea. His grandfather, August Schwatka, born in 1773, was a devout German Lutheran who labored as a blacksmith and ironworker near the commericial center and port city of Danzig (today Gdańsk, Poland), in a region undergoing a turbulent transition. Starting in 1772, a series of partitions of the Commonwealth of Poland by its more forceful neighbors, Prussia, Russia and Austria, ultimately led to the end of the independent political state of Poland in 1795 (not to be reestablished until 1918).[1]

Discouraged by the attendant political and economic upheaval, in 1796, at the age of twenty-three, August Schwatka took the bold step of emigrating to the New World, relocating to the city of Baltimore, Maryland. Baltimore would have been an attractive new homeland, a land of hope and opportunity, within which Schwatka could look to make a fresh start. At the end of the eighteenth century, the city was a boomtown. It had a growing industrial base that mirrored the manufacturing and shipbuilding capabilities of Gdańsk, and an incessant need for skilled labor. In 1798, George Washington referred to Baltimore as "the risingist city" in America, a competitor to the commercial centers of New York City and Philadelphia, and the second leading port of entry for immigrants after New York City. As a result, for many German professionals, tradesmen, merchants and artisans, Baltimore became a popular destination.[2]

A close-knit German community thrived in Baltimore and extended a helping hand to newcomers as they transitioned to the new country. Within this community, and by dint of hard work and determination, August Schwatka slowly prospered, establishing an iron forge and foundry on West Saratoga Street that specialized in high quality iron and metal products. Wielding a hammer and anvil under the scorching heat of the forge, blacksmiths were the linchpins that kept the eighteenth and nineteenth century economies humming. Their industry fabricated commercial products like nails, horseshoes, wagon wheels and axes, industrial goods and tools, and even workaday household wares such as kitchen utensils and sewing tools. Schwatka's long-time blacksmith business in Baltimore even holds a unique place in American history. His shop on West Saratoga Street, which was sold in 1830 by his children, is still operated at the same location by G. Krug & Son and is the oldest continually operating iron shop in North America.[3]

Assimilated into his new community and now comfortably settled in his business, in 1802 August Schwatka married Catherine Geissendörfer, a young woman who had emigrated to Baltimore from Bavaria in 1800. Married in Baltimore's Zion Lutheran Church, they became faithful members of the markedly German congregation. Even as newly arrived immigrants, they developed a strong allegiance to their adopted homeland. August Schwatka became a public-spirited citizen, active in both the city's affairs and the local German society. Having achieved a modicum of success, he gave back to the community by sponsoring young immigrants through apprenticeships and performing other benevolent activities.[4]

With patriotic zeal, August Schwatka and other Baltimore citizens of German descent took up arms in the city's defense during the War of 1812. Baltimore was the scene of a determined attack by the British in September 1814, following the burning of the U.S. Capitol. More than four thousand British regulars landed at North Point, just outside the city, but they were doggedly repelled by American forces shielded behind a hastily built three-mile-long earthwork defense. During the accompanying British naval bombardment, amateur poet Francis Scott Key, detained on a British warship in the city's harbor, penned a poem, "Defence of Fort M'Henry," that formed the lyrics for the young nation's national anthem. One historian remarked that Baltimore's German-American defenders rose to the occasion and marched "as American citizens and patriots, on the 12th of September, 1814, into battle against the English, and, by their valor, under the benign designs of Providence, warded off the murderous designs of the enemy."[5]

In the meantime, the Schwatka family expanded. Catherine bore her husband eleven children, among them, Frederick Gustave Schwatka, father of the explorer, born in Baltimore on March 27, 1810. Little is known of Frederick Gustave's early life, except that he would likewise become a skilled craftsman. Proficient as a carpenter and cooper, he shared a strong work ethic like his father, and was intensely proud of the fledgling democratic republic of his birth. In the early nineteenth century, most young men and women learned skilled trades through the traditional apprenticeship method, and Frederick Gustave's path was no exception. Following this customary practice, in 1825 Frederick Gustave was apprenticed an "oak cooper," binding himself for five years to a local Baltimore craftsman. Under the stringent terms of his indenture, in exchange for unpaid round-the-clock devotion to his master, he was fed, clothed, cared for and taught the trade. Apprenticeship also imposed a stringent social code that forbade "haunting ale houses, taverns or play houses," "playing cards, dice or any unlawful game," and "from contracting matrimony." In 1830, after completing his apprenticeship, and despite his extensive family connections to Baltimore, Frederick Gustave was not content to settle down within the confines of the prosperous city of his parents and siblings.[6]

To suggest that he was possessed of a migratory spirit would be an understatement, and it is no small wonder that his sense of wanderlust would be ingrained in his namesake son. The allure of the expanding American West of the mid-nineteenth century would eventually become all-consuming. Frederick Gustave's initial forays reflected modest and gradual steps in that direction until, at last, overcome by visons of unbounded prosperity, he could no longer resist its attraction. When he left Baltimore is unclear, but on October 24, 1833, in Wheeling, West Virginia (then part of Virginia), he married twenty-one-year-old Amelia Hukill, of Scottish-Irish descent.[7]

Amelia was an attractive woman with dark and deeply set eyes who bore a serious countenance, perhaps anticipating the more difficult times ahead. Shortly after their marriage, the couple relocated further west to the city of Cincinnati, Ohio. Poised on the edge of the frontier, it was often a debarkation point for prospective homesteaders migrating westward. Although the move was a significant undertaking, Frederick Gustave could take comfort in the fact that Cincinnati was more firmly established than its far western counterparts. The city was a bustling metropolis of some twenty-five thousand residents. Perhaps as importantly for the Schwatkas, Cincinatti had begun to attract a large number of German immigrants; nearly half its population between 1820 and 1860 was of German

Frederick G. Schwatka, Sr. and Amelia Hukill Schwatka, parents of the explorer.

descent, a factor easing the task of assimilation and employment. In fact, Cincinnati was a major city, the largest in population not located on the Atlantic Coast or the Gulf of Mexico. For the romantic poet Henry Wadsworth Longfellow, it was the "Queen of the West," or simply the "Queen City." "Porkopolis" was the much less flattering name by which it was known for decades, due to its prosperous meatpacking industry. Visitors marveled at the fleet of steamboats lining its wharves on the Ohio River, and its numerous churches, schools, libraries and other institutions rivaled those of the East. If Schwatka was looking for a frontier experience, he would have to look farther west.[8]

While in Cincinnati, Frederick Gustave's coopering was put to good use in a city where skilled craftsmen were in high demand. At the same time the family quickly expanded as the first of eight children were born—Catherine, Helena, and Amelia. His time spent in Cincinnati was also important for another reason, his association with the fraternal organization known as the "Independent Order of Odd Fellows." The uniquely named society had been officially charted in the United States in Baltimore in 1819, although its roots could be traced back to eighteenth-century England. By chance, as a nine-year-old boy, Frederick Gustave was introduced to the organization when he witnessed the first public procession of its initial thirty-five members in April 1819 as a youth residing in Baltimore. The grand ceremonial parade must have made a lasting impression, because in

1836 Frederick Gustave gained acceptance into the Cincinnati Odd Fellows Lodge at the age of twenty-six.[9]

The clandestine rituals and secret signs of the I.O.O.F. led to distrust and skepticism from detractors. But for the migratory population of the nineteenth-century United States, its mission served a practical purpose by providing a venue for social interaction and a support network for members, particularly among craftsmen and tradesmen. Beyond comradery and commercial networking, the organization's loftier principles advocated benevolence and charity to those less fortunate in the wider community. Schwatka became a life-long member of the Odd Fellows, over time, holding senior positions and representing his constituents at national gatherings. The most well-recognized aspect of Frederick Gustave's character, frequently recalled by those who knew him well, was his devotion to the work of the Odd Fellows.[10]

Despite their relative prosperity in Cincinnati, the growing Schwatka family again relocated, this time to the recently settled town of Burlington, Iowa Territory, where they resided from about 1839 to 1845. Burlington (named after the city in Vermont) was first settled in 1833 following the opening of a trading post there by John Jacob Astor's American Fur Company in 1829. Coincidentally, like Schwatka, Astor had been a German immigrant to Baltimore before moving to New York City and making his fortune in the fur trade business. By 1839 Burlington had become a small, but vibrant port city with approximately 1,200 inhabitants, and the designated territorial capital of the Iowa Territory (Iowa did not gain statehood until 1846). Situated on the west bank of the Mississippi, it carried on a prosperous business in lumber and meatpacking, while its residents built stately homes overlooking the river that added to its small-town charm. While in Burlington, the Schwatka family welcomed two more children, a fourth daughter, Laura, and a first son August.[11]

By 1845, several years after settling in Burlington, the peripatetic Schwatka had pulled up stakes and moved his wife, children and belongings to Galena, Illinois, some one hundred and fifty miles upriver. The move may have been driven by a combination of business and family related reasons, since at least two of his siblings had settled in the city shortly before their arrival. Galena was at the time a thriving community of approximately 2,500 residents, located in the northwest corner of the state of Illinois. As the busiest port on the Mississippi River between St. Louis and St. Paul, Galena also served as a launching point for settlers moving westward. Its history mirrored that of boom-and-bust mining towns of the West, as its fortunes were also tied to precious minerals. Deposits of lead ore (known as *galena*) had been widely known in the area for centuries, but in 1822, the War Department of the federal government stepped in to exercise control by issuing mining leases. When the Schwatka family arrived, the area was producing virtually all of the country's lead ore. However, a steep depression in lead prices soon thereafter triggered an economic downturn, followed by an enormous outflow of residents.

It was in Galena that a fifth daughter, Josephine, was born in 1847, and then Frederick Gustave Schwatka Junior, the subject of this work, on September 29, 1849. But Galena would hold few childhood memories for the future explorer. Shortly thereafter, Frederick Gustave, father of seven young children, was on the move once again. Perhaps the economic impact on his trade served as an impetus for Schwatka to join the hardy migrants whom he had longingly observed as they passed through the port city of Galena. No doubt, glowing reports of a new El Dorado in the wilderness stirred his own imagination, as it did many young men in 1849. On a spiritual level, the devout Schwatka may have considered it divine providence that his family would play an integral part in the American expansionism that was reaching across the continent in a spirit of Manifest Destiny. In any event, by the spring of 1850, five years after settling in Galena, the lure of westward settlement and the prospect of better economic opportunity had become so enticing that Frederick Gustave Schwatka secured an ox-drawn wagon and joined the growing procession of determined settlers making for the Pacific Northwest.[12]

After reports published in 1806 announced that explorers Captain Meriwether Lewis and Lieutenant William Clark had reached the Oregon coast, the westward path along the so-called "Oregon Trail" was blazed over time by ambitious trappers, merchants, and missionaries. The trail comprised several routes running from Independence, Missouri and other towns along the Missouri River, through what are today the states of Kansas, Nebraska, Wyoming, and Idaho, and then northwest to the Columbia River and Willamette Valley in the Oregon Territory. The earliest pioneers, a hardy group of less than one hundred, reached the Willamette Valley by wagon in 1841. After the "Great Migration" of 1843, in which a group of more than one thousand settlers made the crossing, a steady flow of migrants followed.[13]

By 1850, when Schwatka hitched his wagon and the cry of "Wagons Ho!" rang out, the trail was well-worn, but still a hazardous two-thousand-mile trek that required some five months of arduous travelling. One out of ten adult pioneers failed to survive the crossing; sadly, children fared even worse, as many as one in five succumbed along the way. The list of pitfalls was awful to even contemplate. Epidemics (cholera and dysentery among others) could ravage wagon-trains; rough terrain, river crossings and accidents could be just as deadly, as could bouts of severe weather. A trip that often started with such promising hope frequently ended in one of utter heartbreak. For his initial journey, Frederick Schwatka travelled without his wife Amelia and their seven children, all of whom remained in Galena. It proved to be a prudent decision. Soon there was an outbreak of cholera that took a considerable toll on settlers and wreaked havoc on the wagon trains.

Schwatka's destination was near the town of Astoria on the southern shore of the Columbia River at its outlet near the Pacific Ocean, west of the Willamette Valley. It may be more than coincidence that Schwatka gravitated toward another outpost originally established by the trader John Jacob Astor. Schwatka's former home in Burlington had likewise been located near an Astor trading business, a circumstance which offered potential commercial opportunities for the skilled tradesman.

Astoria had been established in 1811 as a fur-trading post by the ambitious Astor and was the first American settlement on the Pacific Coast. In 1813 the post was transferred to the British fur-trading firm, the North West Company, due to a decline in the fur trade and the imminent prospect of seizure by the British. It was then returned to the United States in 1846 after the execution of the Oregon Treaty which established the boundary between the United States and British North America at the 49th parallel. By then, American settlers were migrating to the expanding port city which also offered convenient access to the Willamette Valley via the Columbia and Willamette Rivers. In 1850, the year that Schwatka first arrived, the Willamette Valley had become the destination of the majority of the six thousand settlers to the Oregon Territory. The area had prospered due to several factors, one of which was its fertile soil, which was easy to cultivate, and its mild and perfectly suited climate.

Popular works of the period had romanticized the Pacific Northwest as a new "promised land." In 1836, at the behest of Astor, the highly acclaimed American author Washington Irving had immortalized the Northwest and its boundless opportunities with his dreamy narrative, *Astoria, or Anecdotes of an Enterprise beyond the Rocky Mountains*. Irving's tale of rough fur-traders, speculators, and adventurers foretold the immense commercial possibilities of the region and was considered among the most influential works in promoting settlement of the Pacific Northwest. Frederick Gustave Schwatka may have been drawn to the Oregon Territory by Irving's romantic tale of El Dorado beyond the Rocky Mountains, but there was another contributing factor to his decision—the Donation Land Act of 1850.

The act was passed by Congress to encourage settlement in the Pacific Northwest and to counter incursions by the British and Canadians. Settlers were enticed by the grant of free tracts of land—320 acres to an unmarried man and 640 for a married couple—to those who occupied and plowed their plots before December 1, 1851 (later extended until December 1, 1855 at half the original size). With 640 acres equal to one square mile, the original grant was particularly generous. To be entitled to outright ownership, settlers were required to work the land for a period of four years. That opportunity was all the enticement that Frederick Schwatka needed. He arrived in Oregon in August 1850, staking a 640-acre claim at Point Adams, a narrow peninsula on the southern edge of the Columbia River where it enters the Pacific Ocean, twelve miles from Astoria (currently the land falls within the confines of Fort Stevens State Park).

Point Adams is a low, narrow stretch of land, at the time covered by a thick growth of hemlock and pine, with a dense underbrush of alder, salmonberry, and blackberry. It is surrounded by a sandy beach, and the area experiences highly variable weather. The Columbia River off Point Adams could be treacherous, with its strong currents and shifting sand bars, making navigation a tricky affair for the unacquainted sailor. Captain Robert Gray, commanding the merchant ship *America*, has been credited with the discovery of the Columbia River in 1792, and the identification of "Adams Point" (later named "Point Adams" by the explorer George Vancouver). Gray's discovery opened up the lucrative fur trade industry in the region, and established relationships with the Indigenous communities while bartering for sea otter and beaver furs. While it was certainly a spectacular setting on the distant fringes of the continent, it was not the most auspicious location to stake a homestead.[14]

Frederick Gustave took his homesteading obligations seriously. He immediately set to clearing the land, tilling the soil, and erecting a home, all in expectation of eventual ownership. Within a year, the persevering homesteader had constructed a well-built home and harvested a full season of crops. Schwatka's work ethic was held in high regard. Butler P. Anderson, U.S. district attorney for the territory of Oregon, characterized him as an "industrious, hard-working energetic farmer and among the first immigrants to Oregon in 1850." Though ardent in his belief that he could achieve economic prosperity in the West, Schwatka was also a cautious man who was prepared to earn his reward over the long haul through homesteading. Despite the gold strike at Sutter's Mill in 1848, a circumstance that saw more than half of Oregon's residents lured to California by visions of quick riches over the next few years, Schwatka assiduously cultivated his property stake in a four-year effort to establish outright ownership under the Land Act.[15]

Schwatka's immediate neighbors were members of the Chinook-speaking Clatsop who lived on the extremity of Point Adams, scratching out an existence by fishing and fur trading. At one time, their Point Adams village was among the largest Indian communities in the Oregon Territory. Opportunely situated on the edge of the coastal waterway, their village, Niak'ilaki (meaning "pounded salmon place"), was an important gathering place for social and trading activities, a flourishing community of several hundred persons. An abundance of fish made the village an important resource center. Salmon is still revered as a divine gift from the wolf-spirit Talapus, believed to have saved the Clatsop at a time of starvation.[16]

For a time, the Clatsop community engaged in a thriving economic enterprise with European traders, serving as a vital hub in the maritime fur trade, furnishing furs and needed food and resources. Like many other Indigenous groups, however, they suffered from conflicts with incoming settlers, principally the ever-increasing hordes of ambitious traders who frequented their territory, as well as from devastating epidemics of disease contracted from their encounters.

One of the more egregious clashes was the shelling of Niak'ilaki by a gunboat of the Hudson's Bay Company in 1829. This followed rumors (that later proved to be inaccurate) that the Clatsop had murdered the survivors of the company's ship *William and Ann* which had foundered nearby. Although armed conflict contributed to loss of life, a full ninety percent of the deaths of Indigenous peoples in the Northwest, including the Clatsop, were attributed to the rampaging effects of disease. According to the 1853 U.S. Coast Pilot, at about the time Schwatka set down stakes, the Clatsop village consisted of a few ramshackle wooden lodges, the interior of which "resembled a miserably constructed ship's cabin, with bunks, &, etc., the only light being admitted from above, near the ridge and gable end." Around their site, the defensive-minded Clatsop had constructed a wooden stockade of planks to defend against attacks.[17]

Although displeased by the encroachment of white settlers who arrived under the Land Donation Act, the Clatsop maintained a peaceful attitude, a compliment to their tolerance in the face of an ever-increasing number of homesteaders. The Clatsop were also recognized for their integrity and honesty in their dealings with the newcomers, as well as their impressive craftsmanship skills. The Schwatka family members would become well acquainted with the Clatsop and gain a unique perspective of their lifestyle and manners. Pioneer recollections record that one of Schwatka's homestead neighbors, known as "medicine woman," had nursed several Clatsop children back to health when they suffered from severe fever. Another tells of a visit by one of the Schwatka girls to the Clatsop settlement. With both groups struggling manfully to maintain a foothold in the same harsh and wild environment, they would have developed a mutual respect for each other. And the Schwatka family would certainly sympathize with their plight, as both would soon share a similar fate at the hands of the federal government.[18]

Seeking to consolidate the Indians in the Columbia River basin onto reservations to enable further white settlement, in mid-1851 Anson Dart, the first director of Indian Affairs for the Oregon Territory, negotiated a treaty with the Clatsop. Its terms established a reservation on a portion of the Clatsop land at Point Adams, while ceding the balance of the land there to non-Indian settlement. Dart's reservation also encompassed the land under Schwatka's claim, and Schwatka was hastily ordered to vacant his land and homestead. However, the treaty was never ratified, since the territorial Indian Affairs office did not have the last word on the matter.[19]

With a commanding position on the river overlooking the Pacific, to the War Department, the Clatsop reservation and Schwatka's homestead property occupied a strategic location that was considered too valuable to surrender. By 1852, the department had different plans for Point Adams, as it looked to defend the Northwest and the newly defined border between British North America and the Oregon Territory. Unbeknownst to Schwatka, in February 1852, President Millard Fillmore had authorized the War Department to establish forts at the mouth of the Columbia River for just that purpose. In August of that year an army surveyor stepped onto Schwatka's homestead and broke the unexpected and unwelcome news that the U.S. government had claimed the property for use as a military post (Fort Stevens), with the understanding that the U.S. government would compensate him for his claim. For Schwatka, it was a bitter disappointment after his backbreaking work, only to be exacerbated later by the government's refusal to compensate him for its land grab. Only after an agonizingly slow-moving appeal did Congress finally acknowledge the government's obligation and authorize an award of $6,000 in February 1884, more than thirty years later. The recognition in the congressional debate that "Lieutenant Schwatka of Arctic fame" was the son of the claimant was likely a deciding factor in its approval at that late date. The Clatsop, who had suffered the same fate with the seizure of their land by the U.S. government, were either relocated to one of several reservations or made their way to nearby settlements. [20]

Perseverance was a hallmark of Frederick Gustave Schwatka, and despite not having settled the land matter, in 1853 he returned to Illinois to retrieve his family and escort them on another trek across the plains to the West. They left behind relatives and friends they had known for years in Illinois, as well as their firmly established position within their community. It was an emotional departure for the Schwatkas, as they pondered the daunting challenges ahead and their uncertain but hopeful future in the Oregon Territory. For Frederick and Amelia Schwatka, the long and arduous journey would be especially trying. Safely shepherding seven children across an unsettled continent posed its own obstacles, but Amelia Schwatka was expecting her eighth child when the family departed Galena. The Schwatka family would have comprised a considerable entourage; multiple wagons to simply transport nine family members, as well as additional wagons to carry their supplies, equipment, and household belongings, accompanied by numerous oxen, cattle and a number of horses. Like most westward caravans, the Schwatka family travelled as part of a larger group of settlers, some of whom would likely have been known to them.

Wagon trains typically departed in the spring, so that they might reach their destination before the harsh and deadly winter weather settled into the western mountain passes. Migrants were all too familiar with the dreadful fate suffered by the Donner Party during the winter of 1846-47. For Amelia Schwatka, even the most favorable travelling conditions while crossing the extensive grasslands of the prairie would have been extremely uncomfortable with the constant jarring and lurching of the wagons in the well-worn ruts of the earlier caravans. Ironically, the earliest childhood memory of young pioneer Frederick Jr. was that iconic symbol of the vanishing frontier, the buffalo, or American bison. At the time, the shaggy humped beasts still roamed the plains in vast herds that defied estimates, darkening the horizon for miles, but those numbers were fast diminishing with the westward tide. As his emigrant group stopped along the Platte River, Nebraska Territory, the wide-eyed boy, almost four years old at the time, sat perched on the edge of his wagon spellbound for hours at the sight of the limitless thundering herd. Indelibly etched in his mind, he recalled the event years later:

> My first encounter with buffalo was in the spring of 1853, which as a child I can just remember.... On the Platte River where the Loup Fork comes in, and where the city of Columbus, Nebraska, now stands, we were delayed for five hours and a half while such a herd was passing. The herd was estimated to contain all the way from one hundred thousand to ten million buffaloes, according

to the astonishment of the person hazarding the guess. We had to turn the rear of the wagons towards the approaching herd, persons with firearms leaning over the 'tail-gate,' and discharging their pieces to break the great throng right and left, to prevent them from smashing the wagons into splinters and trampling the inmates into mince-meat, as they have been known to do.[21]

But it was also a cultural eye-opener for the young traveler. Unmentioned by Schwatka, but ever present, were the numerous Indians observed throughout the journey, who warily watched the inexorable procession of settlers with their cumbrous wagons and boisterous animals encroaching on their longtime tribal homelands. The Schwatka family was fortunate to have crossed the Platte River basin during a peaceful hiatus in relations. Two years previously, the Fort Laramie Treaty of 1851 had been signed by several Indian Nations, which confirmed territorial rights on the part of the Indians while guaranteeing safe passage for travelers on the Oregon Trail. As a result, most encounters between the two cultures were nonviolent, often simply to barter for goods.

After crossing the Nebraska Territory into the more rugged and arid area that is now Wyoming, Schwatka's group reached Fort Laramie, a major stopping place on the trail. The fort was a hub of activity, with thirty-five thousand settlers passing through the area in 1853. Over the next three to four weeks, the Schwatka family would have traversed the Rocky Mountains and Continental Divide by the so-called South Pass (considered the easiest pass through the Rockies). Crossing the barren and desolate stretch west of the flat-running Big Sandy River, they likely reached Fort Bridger, another major outpost and the junction of the southern Mormon Trail. Following the Snake River to the northwest through what is now southern Idaho, they would have continued along the Blue Mountains and through the verdant valley of the Grande Ronde, ultimately arriving at the banks of the Columbia River, at The Dalles, the end of the overland route of the Oregon Trail.

For Amelia Schwatka her time came 175 miles short of their final destination. Under what must have been difficult and stressful circumstances, on October 16, 1853, she gave birth to a sixth daughter, Annie, on the side of the Oregon Trail in their covered wagon at The Dalles. The Schwatkas were part of a relatively larger migration that converged at The Dalles in the fall of 1853. At the time, The Dalles was considered "the eastern outpost of Oregon," but comprised only a handful of hastily constructed buildings, a number of traders' tents, and a larger tent city of settlers who staked out claims in the area. The trail could take its toll on weary travelers, many of whom would arrive destitute at The Dalles, literally trading the clothes off their backs for food.[22]

Amelia Schwatka was left with little time for recovery for the remainder of the journey, since winter was fast approaching. With a great sense of relief, the Schwatka family reached Oregon City, thankful to Providence for deliverance of their family intact. While in Oregon City, Frederick Schwatka wasted no time in filing a Donation Act claim on November 13, 1853, on a tract south of his Point Adams' claim, on the west side of the Lewis and Clark River, a minor tributary that snakes its way north toward its confluence with the Columbia River near Astoria. Schwatka had a knack for staking his claims in strategic areas. His new land claim was near Fort Clatsop, the encampment of Lewis and Clark's Corps of Discovery during the winter of 1805-06 at the mouth of the Lewis and Clark River.[23]

After finally reaching their new homestead, the hard work of clearcutting the trees and cultivating the land began anew. Although Frederick Schwatka succeeded in his farming efforts, the family ultimately relocated to Albany, Oregon Territory, in June 1855, some 150 miles southward, where Schwatka found his cooper trade more profitable. In 1857, when Frederick Jr. was eight years old, the family was on the move once again to the city of Salem, twenty-five miles north of Albany, to a residence on Commercial Street that would become the last and permanent home of Frederick and Amelia Schwatka.[24]

When Frederick Gustave and family arrived in Salem there were between 400 and 500 settlers in the modest but growing city in the heart of the Willamette Valley on the banks of the Willamette River. White settlement had only begun in 1837, with the establishment of a Methodist mission, but enterprising merchants, traders and farmers soon followed. With the harnessing of the Willamette River, mills, factories and foundries flourished, and with them an assortment of hotels, bars, and a variety of retail establishments. Salem's residents were an energetic group, pursuing the American dream. It was known as a place where "men beginning with a small capital in a few years raise themselves to independence."[25]

Designated the territorial capital in 1851-52, and state capital in 1859, Salem's citizenry included an educated crowd of lawyers, jurists and politicians. By 1860, its population reached one thousand residents, still a small town in many respects. Although homes, churches and businesses grew within its modest limits, outside the confines of the city the scenery quickly reverted to primitive woodlands and wetlands. Salem settlers adopted an egalitarian outlook, socially and economically. The Donation Act had inspired equality of opportunity by which homesteaders measured success and standing based upon individual effort rather than through birthright. But at the time it was an equality mostly enjoyed by whites.

The issue of statehood had become a hotly disputed matter over the issue of slavery, which delayed the territory's entry into the Union. Both sides struggled with whether Oregon would be designated as a free or slave state. In Oregon, the pro-slavery Democratic Party was the ruling party, overwhelmingly controlling state and local politics until the Civil War. Oregon ultimately entered the union in 1859, but not before its politicians had drafted into law some of the most restrictive rules against minorities. When the state's residents had voted on a new constitution in 1857, in advance of statehood, they had banned slavery. However, the voters also adopted, by an even greater number of votes, a prohibition on in-migration by Blacks. Those Blacks already in Oregon were prohibited from property ownership and from entering contracts or accessing the court system. (The exclusionary provisions were not enforced and were superseded by the ratification of the Fourteenth Amendment a decade later, which guaranteed equal protection to all.) Nothing would suggest that the Schwatka family held the prejudicial views reflected in those discriminatory prohibitions. Quite the contrary, egalitarian principles directed their course of conduct. They were known as "an old republican family who in earlier days were whigs." In contrast to the pro-slavery Democratic Party, the nascent Republican Party in Oregon with which the Schwatkas were aligned first began organizing about 1855, as the minority Whig Party dissolved. Its platform strongly mirrored the anti-slavery movement at the national level.[26]

During their early years in Salem, the family lived in cramped quarters under the religious guidance of Frederick Gustave and his wife Amelia. Like many Salem residents, the Schwatka family appears to have maintained farmland and domestic animals on the outskirts of the town that were cared for by family labor. Frederick Gustave continued his benevolent work through the Odd Fellows, and as members of the evangelical church, both Frederick Gustave and Amelia gave meaningfully of their time to charitable and civic causes.

For the Schwatka family, matters of local consequence had more life and death import than national events. As the Southern states formed a confederacy in 1861 and shots were fired at Fort Sumter, parts of Salem and surrounding towns suffered the worst flood in their history. The Willamette River overflowed in the winter of 1861-62, submerging homes, farms and businesses in its wake. Floodwaters ran so deep that old-timers recalled that a steamboat could have made its way up Salem's aptly named Ferry Street. The gruesome spectacle of a public execution,

Salem's first, a double hanging of two men convicted of murdering a wealthy farmer in 1865, attracted gawking spectators by the thousands from nearby counties. Before the sentence was carried out, the two men admitted the act, and a local newspaper published their confessions in pamphlet form, with the proceeds donated to their widows. Likely on behalf of the newspaper, fifteen-year-old Schwatka was spotted peddling copies at the hanging as the condemned men said their last.

The nation may have been one Union, but Frederick Gustave Schwatka, Sr. recognized that he and his family, some three thousand miles from the opposite coast, were of a distinctly different character than their eastern counterparts. A photo taken late in life reflects a modest, unassuming man, ill-at-ease with the formality of wearing a tie. By far, the most conspicuous feature is his ceremonial neck sash, proudly representing his association with the Odd Fellows, symbolically overlaying his more fashionable attire and the society it represented. When he died in 1888, his obituary highlighted the fact that he was affectionately known as "Father Schwatka," and "no man of the early pioneers was more beloved and held in more esteem." A pillar of the community with "an unblemished reputation," he was often turned to for his local experience and knowledge. Proudly, he could recite the smallest detail regarding the early history of the territory. After suffering the loss of both legs to amputation, he could still be seen navigating around town handing down advice from his wheelchair. [27]

His wife Amelia died in 1885 at age seventy-two. A strong woman who reared eight children, her obituary praised her successful efforts at raising a frontier family "bearing the impress of her Christian care and education." Of Frederick Jr.'s siblings, none achieved the level of fame as their explorer brother, but most were enterprising and successful. Catherine, the oldest, became a schoolteacher in Salem, and also operated a leading millinery and fancy goods store; Annie, born in the covered wagon at The Dalles, was a nurse and later a matron at Portland's Hill Military Academy. August C. Schwatka, older brother of the explorer, became a dedicated newspaper man. Initially based in Salem, he was the proprietor and editor of the *Agriculturalist and Plowman* and later foreman for the *Oregon Statesman*. Relocating to California, he worked for the *San Francisco Chronicle* and thereafter as a correspondent for the *New York Herald*. For a time, he also served as secretary of the Oregon State Agricultural Society. His wife, Annie Gaines Schwatka, achieved a minor level of local recognition as one of the first white women to descend the interior walls of Crater Lake to the shoreline. [28]

Amelia Schwatka Jr., the third daughter of Frederick and Amelia Schwatka, is however, deserving of recognition in her own right. After marrying Thomas Strang, she moved to Lewiston, Idaho, where she opened a photographic studio in 1864 at the age of twenty-six. Frontier wives enjoyed greater freedom of choice in economic pursuits, and in the case of Amelia, her business success was impressive. She may have been the first professional female photographer to operate in what was then Idaho Territory. In 1868, she moved with her husband and two children to Santa Cruz, California, where she was regarded as one of the finest children's portrait photographers in the region. She was also of an inventive mind, obtaining a patent for a new boot design in 1869. Tragically, her own son, Frederick (nephew of the explorer), died during a hazing incident in 1884 while a cadet at the U.S. Naval Academy.[29]

Other than Frederick Jr., they may not have achieved a national level of fame in their lifetimes, but the Schwatka parents were proud that their children were respectful and productive, and they could be most thankful that they had managed to raise eight children to adulthood, a highly unusual circumstance in nineteenth-century America, especially for homesteaders in the West.

For Frederick Jr., life as a youngster on the edge of the frontier naturally fostered an interest in vigorous outdoor activities and a love of adventure. A childhood friend recalled that as soon as the schoolbooks were laid down, Schwatka was out the door, with gun in hand, to the fields that surrounded Salem. That Schwatka was an avid hunter is obvious from the few memories he himself recounted from his youth. In an 1892 article entitled "Hunters' Lucky Shots," he boasted of his success as a teenager in taking multiple game birds with one shot, a feat repeated on several occasions in both the thickets and flatlands. But Schwatka was more than just an outdoor lover. His personality was marked by a profound curiosity, and in the Northwest, it was its Indigenous people to which he turned that curiosity.[30]

As a boy exploring the surroundings of Salem, Schwatka stood in a unique position by virtue of his intimate familiarity with the territory's Indigenous peoples and first-hand exposure to their cultures. By the mid-1850s, Salem was still in many respects a frontier outpost, notwithstanding its relatively rapid growth. In the Oregon Territory, some of the fiercest acts of violence between whites and American Indians occurred during that period. The opening of the Oregon Trail and the discovery of gold in California led to an influx of miners and settlers into the Rogue Valley in southern Oregon near the California border. Land and resources historically utilized by the Indigenous peoples were appropriated, sparking a series of confrontations. The so-called Rogue River Wars were particularly violent, with atrocities on both sides that ended with the defeat of the Indians in 1856 and their removal to reservations. Similarly, between 1855 and 1858, the so-called Yakima War, fought principally in southern Washington Territory for much the same reasons, ended in the defeat of the chief Kamiakin and the Yakama groups. Ultimately, resolution of all the conflicts in the territory followed a similar pattern to those elsewhere in the United States. Forced from their lands, where they had lived for millennia, the Indian people of the Willamette Valley were escorted to a miserable existence on reservations. With meagre economic opportunities on the reservations, some would return to Salem to perform menial tasks or to work as laborers on homestead lands.

Within the confines of Salem, Schwatka was familiar with the Indian members of the community who had attempted to assimilate into white culture. He also visited them on his own when hunting and exploring excursions took him to the reservations (including perhaps the displaced Clatsops who were acquainted with his father). His parents had taught him tolerance and fair treatment at an early age, combined with an open-mindedness that was unusual among settlers. Coupled with his own unbounded intellectual curiosity, and by virtue of his own inquisitive nature, he gained a first-hand understanding and appreciation of their culture, and a fluency in several Indian dialects.[31]

For Frederick Schwatka, the travels of Lewis and Clark, and the labors of traders, trappers and miners who followed them, were not events in some far distant land in a far distant time. Their explorations and discoveries were proud, local history, still fresh in the mind, a history that was indelibly impressed upon the imagination. Pathfinding in the backwoods of Salem, Schwatka could literally follow in those illustrious footsteps and envision his own discoveries. He certainly must have felt a level of pride in the fact that his own father had staked his homestead near Fort Clatsop.

The Northwest Coast of America could boast of great explorers, but among them the Dane Vitus Bering may have been the most relevant to our subject, Frederick Schwatka. In 1725, Bering led the first of two expeditions to determine the geography of the northern extremity of the Siberian mainland and its relationship to the coast of North America. On his first attempt, although the expedition managed to sail into the strait that bears Bering's name, fog obscured the American coast and his expedition returned with an inconclusive result. Beginning in 1733, Bering organized his second monumental expedition. That he managed to even set sail seven years later was itself an extraordinary achievement and a testament to his mental and physical endurance, qualities that would become a hallmark of Frederick Schwatka. In a backbreaking effort, over a period of years, most of the expedition's supplies and equipment were carted thousands of miles across Russia to Kamchatka on the Pacific coast. Following exasperating delays, the main expedition, consisting of two ships—one led by Bering, the other by A. I. Chirikov—set sail eastward towards America. Chirikov's ship reached the American coast first, touching in southeast Alaska before returning to Petropavlovsk, having achieved the first landing of Europeans on the Northwest Coast of America. For his part, Bering reached the Alaskan coast at Kayak Island, where a mere eight hours were spent in scientific work before returning. Bering's ship was shipwrecked off one of the Aleutian Islands, where Bering died. Nonetheless, he had demonstrated that Asia and America were not connected, and as importantly, sparked the beginning of the Alaskan fur trade after the discovery of plentiful sea otters in the area.

After-the-fact biographical sketches tend to reflect hindsight and embellishment as much as fact, especially when recounted by family members. Schwatka's nephew William Brackett, in a brief article published in the *Peoria Journal* following Schwatka's death, claimed that Vitus Bering served as the driving inspiration for Schwatka's future exploration endeavors, about whom Schwatka spoke with "admiration and reverence." According to Brackett, "the traditions of Bering's expeditions of discovery had been handed down for many generations" through Schwatka's ancestors on the southern Baltic Sea, close to the Dane's homeland. Brackett went so far as to claim that among Bering's crew there were "several stalwart men in whose veins flowed the ancestral blood" of Frederick Schwatka and that "the influence of heredity, and the achievements of Bering had much to do, in making Schwatka an explorer of the North." Whether we can believe that Schwatka's distant relatives served with Bering or that heredity somehow played a crucial role in Schwatka's inclination to follow in Bering's footsteps seems a bit farcical. However, Schwatka did hold the Danish explorer in high regard, and may have learned from him the lessons that organization, preparation and perseverance are keys to success. In 1889, Schwatka penned a glowing introduction to the biography of Bering that was authored by the historian Peter Lauridsen. Schwatka interjected his own opinion that "America has always respected Bering as a great explorer, and oftentimes heralded him as one of the highest of heroes."[32]

More objective recollections from those who knew Schwatka as a boy recall the youthful Schwatka as a gregarious, gun-loving, ruddy-faced boy with a streak of independence. He was noted for his boyish pranks (of which he was the recognized leader), and was not above self-deprecating humor, a trait later used to good effect in his writing. As a child, Schwatka attended one of the three or four recently established public schools. The schools were generally well regarded, and Schwatka likely gained more than the basic literacy and math skills. Opportunities for secondary education in the western territories in the mid-nineteenth century were more limited than those available in the East, with its more numerous and well-established public and private institutions. However, the adolescent Schwatka was fortunate that the Salem pioneers and missionaries had the foresight to quickly establish a prominent institution of higher learning on the fringe of the frontier, Willamette University. Officially chartered in 1853 and the oldest college west of the Mississippi, Willamette had operated since 1842 as the Oregon Institute. Initially, it had been run by the Methodist church as a mission school for Indians.[33]

The original mission was founded for the purpose of assisting the Indians who had suffered greatly from white settlement and disease. Its motto, "Non nobis solum nati sumus" ("not unto ourselves alone are we born"), from Cicero, harkened to its missionary and religious origins and its desire for its students to give of themselves for the benefit of others and "lead a life of achievement, contribution and meaning." The admonition echoed and reinforced a refrain already well known to the young Schwatka through family influence, and further instilled in him a sense of empathy and fair treatment. Although the school claimed to be a non-sectarian institution, its religious and moral influences were considerable. Students attended daily prayers and a Bible reading in the school chapel and were required to attend a Sunday service at a place of worship of their choice.

Besides a degree-oriented course of study, the institution offered a college preparatory department in the arts and sciences. The Willamette archives record that young Schwatka attended the school's two-year preparatory program, finishing in the spring of 1867 at the age of seventeen. Not surprisingly, Willamette offered a sizable measure of English grammar, composition, and reading, but the governing board of this pioneer school, emulating its elite eastern institutional counterparts, had introduced a nineteenth-century classical education, with a solid grounding in Greek and Roman studies. The ancient languages and cultures occupied a disproportionate status in the preparatory curriculum as required coursework in both academic years. Republican civic virtues articulated by the Cato, Cicero, and other men of antiquity, held special meaning for settlers in a territory that, in 1859, had just achieved statehood and representative government. Despite its frontier location, Willamette could boast a course of study that compared favorably to the more seasoned private schools of the East.[34]

The Willamette experience offered other influential features for its students, including literary and debating societies, which sought to improve the critical thinking skills of its members, as well as to develop persuasive writing and oral expression. Schwatka was remembered as an active participant in the school's Hesperian Society, meeting late on Friday evenings under the flickering light of oil lamps and candles to debate timely social and political issues, such as the merits of capital punishment, the abolition of slavery, and the justification of military warfare. The Hesperian Society offered its student members a more demanding venue than traditional student organizations. Its membership welcomed prominent lawyers, politicians and religious personages who elevated its discourse and challenged the intellectual abilities of its student participants. Rubbing shoulders with Salem's influential local leaders bolstered Schwatka's self-confidence and advocacy skills and opened his mind to civic responsibilities. Willamette life also included student writings. The February 1867 issue of the *Willamette Chronicle* could not fail to capture the attention of any Schwatka biographer. An anonymous student essay, published while Schwatka was in attendance, entitled "Latest by Telegraph—North Pole," tells the desperate plight of a polar traveler fighting to endure the extreme cold of the North.[35]

Schwatka made the most of the educational opportunities available to him. He was recognized for his interest in mathematics and poetry, both of which he excelled at, and his enthusiasm for the Hesperian Society. Schwatka's intellectual abilities had also made a strong impression on Thomas M. Gatch, the highly regarded president of Willamette University. Undoubtedly, the university looked to be a logical choice for post-secondary education for the promising young student. Close to home, Willamette would have offered distinct advantages and a fine education that would have adequately prepared him for a respectable position in his community. Nonetheless, as Frederick Schwatka considered his next academic challenge, he turned three thousand miles to the east in pursuit of a position at the U.S. Military Academy at West Point.

Perhaps the choice was not as curious as it looks on its face. To a young boy in Oregon with a pioneer mindset, volunteer and regular federal troops were among the most visible manifestations of expansionism. Stationed in forts throughout the state, Schwatka would have seen soldiers helping to forge the pathway to western settlement by scouting trails, escorting wagon trains, constructing roads and protecting settlers, miners, and Indians. Perhaps somewhat telling, upon his graduation from the Academy in 1871, Schwatka accepted a post in the U.S. Third Cavalry, a regiment that had served with distinction in protecting the Oregon Trail and the Willamette Valley. Also, at that time, Frederick Schwatka Sr., not generally disposed to writing, took up a pen on his son's behalf, petitioning the staunch Republican U.S. senator from Oregon, George H. Williams, to permit young Schwatka to return to Willamette as a professor of military science. Though unsuccessful, Frederick Sr.'s only known surviving letter, written in an unpracticed hand with manifold misspellings, reveals much about the distinct nature of the pioneer character of his son Frederick Schwatka. According to Frederick Sr., his young son, raised on the fringe of the frontier, was of a different breed from his counterparts on the opposite coast with what he termed their "eastern habits." He asserted that his son Frederick was the best suited candidate to teach Oregon's own because "he has been raised here in Oregon and [is] familiar with the Spirit of the Oregon People," meaning its frontier culture that fostered individualism, self-reliance, and a practical can-do attitude.[36]

Schwatka's strong desire for a cadetship at the Academy, and an early sign of a single-minded and ambitious nature, were plainly evident in his January 23, 1865 letter that the none-too-shy youth dashed off to Edwin M. Stanton, Lincoln's secretary of war. At the age of fifteen, still two years shy of the Academy's minimum admission age, Schwatka did not hesitate to advise Stanton that "knowing that you have the appointment of cadets, I thought I would try to get an appointment." An eager Schwatka urged Stanton that "if there is any chance to [gain an appointment] in the next five years please inform me."[37]

While Schwatka anxiously waited for his chance for an Academy appointment, Salem's newspaper business gave him his first opportunity to support himself by his own efforts. He managed a foot in the door working as a "printer's devil," in support tasks at his older brother's publication, the *Agriculturalist and Plowman*. The savings from his newspaper position also served as the means to pay his preparatory school tuition at Willamette. It is probably stretching the imagination to believe Schwatka's relative, William Brackett, when he stated that Schwatka was also a regular correspondent, a veritable Samuel Clemens, writing articles for "various newspapers on the Pacific Coast and for some years was a regular correspondent of several leading dailies published in California." At least, no record of any of Schwatka's West Coast writings have been identified.[38]

A rather contrasting viewpoint was offered by Asahel Bush, the editor of the *Oregon Statesman*, a Democratic paper, who recounted that young Frederick Schwatka also worked for a time at the *Statesman* as a mailing clerk. The most that the editor would venture about Schwatka's talents was that he was "adept" at addressing newspapers. According to Bush, young Schwatka did have a yearning for poetry, and his poetical aspirations led him to send his missives anonymously through the post to the *Statesman's* editor for publication, where "only a passing notice was accorded to them," and "while at his desk, the youth would, with inexpressible anguish, see his cherished poems unceremoniously pitched into the fire before his astonished gaze by the practical but unsentimental publisher." The *Statesman's* editor regularly wielded a sarcastic pen, and over the years Schwatka would be on the receiving end of any number of his jibes.[39]

Even if Schwatka was not the eager cub reporter, he gained a sound schooling in the newspaper business, with its aggressive hunting for news, the need for clear and concise reporting, and the usual scramble to meet deadlines. By virtue of his schooling or his newspaper experience, or a combination of both, an interest in writing was also nurtured, an interest that would lead Schwatka to become a prolific author during the course of his life. The newspaper enterprise also offered the young man a window into the wider world and its events, particularly during the tumultuous years of the American Civil War. As a teenager in Salem, Oregon, young Schwatka had been far removed the tragic battlefields of the war, but he certainly followed the political and military movements with deep interest as the latest dispatches were received from across the country and debated among pressmen and printers on the newsroom floor.

With the war's end and reconstruction in place, the country was turning its eyes to the west, as young Schwatka was still looking for his opportunity in the east. Notwithstanding Schwatka's application to the secretary and having met the Academy's age requirement, Schwatka had to count on the patronage of either a congressman or the president in order to gain entry to the Academy. According to a boyhood acquaintance, Schwatka's intelligence "attracted the attention of Salem's best citizens," including Oregon's governor, Addison C. Gibbs, and Willamette President Gatch. As a result of their influence, Schwatka ultimately secured an appointment through Oregon Congressman James H. D. Henderson, a one-term Republican and ardent abolitionist. Schwatka was accepted with the class beginning in July 1867 and could finally make that long-awaited journey eastward.[40]

CHAPTER TWO

FIRST CALL

SIXTY MILES NORTH of New York City, the United States Military Academy commands a stunning view overlooking the Hudson River. Its strategic location above a narrow turn in the river led the Continental Army of General George Washington to establish a military post there during the Revolutionary War. In 1802, over two decades after the war, the Academy was formally established on the site. Over the course of the next sixty years, it emerged as the leading military and engineering school in the United States.

West Point graduates served with distinction in the Mexican War and the Indian wars, and the Academy aptly demonstrated its effectiveness as a training-ground for commissioned officers during the American Civil War. Nearly all senior officers of both the Union and Confederate armies were graduates of West Point. Their skills were put to full use in organizing and leading the sizable armies of the North and South, and in applying and adapting those skills in an unprecedented scale and manner of warfare, all the while serving with professionalism, discipline and bravery.[1]

For a young man who had rarely journeyed beyond Oregon, the trip to the populous eastern United States offered an eye-opening view of the wider world and served as a testament to his commitment. Independent and resourceful at a young age, Schwatka had saved his hard-earned wages from his newspaper work to pay his fare to the opposite coast, booking passage on the so-called "Panama Route." Less well-known than the arduous Oregon Trail, the journey consisted of a 3,300-mile journey by ship from San Francisco to Panama City, a crossing of the forty-seven-mile Isthmus by train, and a two-thousand-mile ocean voyage from the Gulf Coast to the eastern seaboard. Although conceivably shorter in travel time, the route could involve extensive delays due to the unreliability of train service and the risk of tropical disease while detained in Panama. To a young man in a hurry, it was, however, the preferable alternative.[2]

With his appointment in hand, and after completing the roundabout eastward trip, young Schwatka was still not assured of admission. Candidates were first required to pass a physical examination and a basic proficiency test in English, math, geography, and history, all of which he easily accomplished. Although the proficiency test was not considered overly challenging, nonetheless a total of nineteen of seventy-four candidates in Schwatka's entering class of 1867 failed it. The rather high percentage reflected a stricter entrance examination that had been instituted in 1866. Schwatka's difficulty was not the test itself, but his actual presence on the scheduled test date. He arrived in Baltimore in June suffering from an undisclosed "protracted" illness (perhaps a tropical fever). Prevented from attending the scheduled meeting of the examiners, he ran the real risk of failing to qualify by his absence. However, a brief extension of time was granted to allow his recovery, and on June 20 he passed his examination.[3]

Arriving at the Academy in the summer of 1867, even the self-confident young Frederick Schwatka must have been impressed, and perhaps even a bit daunted, as he took his place among the long line of storied cadets who had passed through its halls. Schwatka adjusted to life as a "plebe" (or fourth-class cadet) as well as could be expected in an environment of constant oversight and near total control. The Academy's location, set apart from scattered villages of Orange County, New York, added to its isolation. The daily routine of cadets was one of strict discipline and hard work, especially for the newcomers. Upon their arrival, fourth-class cadets were drilled from morning to night, and spent several weeks in rigorous military training in the field.[4]

They returned to an attractive campus comprised of thirty or so buildings, all of which fully served the school's various objectives. These included the "Academy," a three-story building that held recitation rooms, engineering and drawing rooms, science labs, a large gymnasium, the riding building, the observatory, and a library. The most impressive building, the four-story cadet barracks, with its Elizabethan-style facade of red sandstone, housed both cadets and officers, and was equipped with hot water for bathing and heating, a luxury at the time. Schwatka shared a room with a fellow fourth-class cadet, which offered an opportunity to share common experiences, particularly in the first few stressful months as plebes navigated their unfamiliar setting. The demanding routine of the first semester could test the strongest of constitutions. Perhaps still suffering from his cryptic illness, or simply from the nervous strain of the military regimen, on July 15 Schwatka reported to the post hospital

Frederick Schwatka, USMA graduation photo, 1871.

complaining of severe stomach cramps. It may be speculating too much to suggest that this incident represented an early manifestation of what would later become a chronic, and at times, debilitating stomach ailment from which Schwatka would suffer.[5]

The Academy maintained a reputation as the principal school of engineering and mathematics in the United States, and as such its curriculum had been weighted toward these technical studies. The physical sciences—physics, chemistry, astronomy and geology—balanced these out, together with those associated with the science of war—infantry, artillery and cavalry tactics, gunnery, swordsmanship and military law. Literature, classical studies and languages, other than French and Spanish, had no place in this specialized curriculum. The course of study had long been established by Superintendent Sylvanus Thayer and Professor Dennis Hart Mahan. Both men maintained the Academy as a seat of military thought and training, despite significant reform movements in American colleges that urged a greater emphasis in the liberal arts. All told, a full 63% of academic points accounted for mathematics, science and engineering.[6]

Following field training, academic work occupied the bulk of the daily routine. In the classroom, cadets were challenged in each subject through a system of blackboard recitation. Its goal was to build confident and assertive decision-makers, who would be able to think quickly and logically on their feet while under stress. Following delivery of a lesson and assignment of a problem, a cadet would be called on to prepare an answer on the blackboard, and thereafter questioned orally. Bi-annual examinations for promotion followed the same approach but were far more exhaustive, extending for hours over a period of days. According to one commentator, recitations were "the dominant feature of an overall culture of examination," a teaching method intended to further critical analysis rather than simple rote memorization.[7]

Lessons in the art of war had a special significance when delivered by professors and assistants who themselves were battle-tested Union soldiers, some of whom were still convalescing from their wounds. In addition, seven of Schwatka's classmates had served during the Civil War and they freely shared their own experiences. The campaigns of Grant, Sherman and other Union officers were recounted from first-hand experience to a wide-eyed audience, many of whom must have been disappointed that a belated birthdate had left them too young to participate. Academic work was completed by 4:00 P.M., at which time cadets were drilled for about one and a half hours. This was followed by supper and a brief recreation period, after which was a final period of study and lights out at 10:00 P.M. Schwatka was fortunate that several minor changes had recently been introduced that helped make life more bearable for cadets. He was able to enjoy the refreshing privilege of walking off campus on weekends, and breakfast and supper were optional, thus freeing up time for baths, study or simply relaxation. In addition, cadets were granted one month leave for each of their first three years.[8]

In addition to coping with the stress of Academy demands, and despite regulations forbidding the practice, incoming plebes suffered from hazing (referred to as "deviling") during the war years, and particularly during Schwatka's tenure. Upperclassmen harassed fourth-class cadets by requiring them to perform servile tasks, such as running errands, cleaning their boots, or making their beds. Young Schwatka was perhaps spared the worst of the ordeal, as sons of distinguished personalities tended to receive harsher treatment from upperclassmen, and he did not fit into this category.

Surviving records from West Point provide documentary evidence of Schwatka's performance and offer insightful glimpses into his maturing interests. Based on the point system established at the Academy to determine a cadet's order of merit, Frederick Schwatka was ranked 20th overall in his graduating class of 41, a creditable performance. Interestingly, the subjects of his highest and lowest performance were in the languages, with a ranking of 7th in Spanish (by far his best overall rank) and 23rd in French. The French language had been taught from the time of the American Revolution, as French military and engineering methods were considered among the best in the world and talented French engineers had served in the U.S. Army Corps of Engineers. Spanish, a more recent introduction, came at the behest of the secretary of war in 1854, following the Mexican-American War. It was believed that it was a necessary language for the accomplished soldier due to the westward expansion of the country and intercourse with Spanish speaking peoples. The culturally minded and westward leaning Schwatka understood that reality more than his classmates, who devoted little time to its study and generally placed no importance upon the subject.[9]

According to his classmates, in addition to Spanish, Schwatka had a decided preference for mathematics and the sciences and an "especial aptitude for natural history." The Academy's mathematics and elementary science courses, and its modest collection of natural history specimens, certainly piqued his interest (he ranked 14th in mathematics and 18th in the sciences). Of particular interest would have been its spectacular, large-scale model of the rich silver mine in Valenciana, Mexico, which foreshadowed Schwatka's future interest in seeking his fortune in Mexico. In the military arts, Schwatka ranked 26th in artillery, 20th in cavalry and 20th in engineering.[10]

With discipline and obedience imperative to proper military order, the Academy also rated cadets on a daily basis through a "demerit" system which penalized them for infractions in their conduct. Demerits for individual offenses ranged on a scale from one to five, one being the least offensive. In his four years, Schwatka managed to compile a total of 332 demerits, slightly above the average total for most cadets. By way of comparison, the best performer, cadet James R. Wasson, scored a low of 107 demerits and the worst offender, cadet Frederick Dent Grant, son of the president, amassed 740.

Schwatka received a "five" on four occasions (profane language or allowing unauthorized visitors while sentinel), and a "four" on four occasions (absent at inspection or from class or visiting after hours). The balance was an accumulation for minor infractions (tardiness for parade, class or meals; inattention in class or on parade; and inspection lapses such as an untidy uniform, unpolished shoes or equipment, or arriving unshaven). While his demerits did not characterize him as a serious transgressor, he was prone to a degree of laziness, sloppiness, and a lack of attention to detail. There was even a hint of disregard for authority, an early display of a trait that would mark his later military career. It is worth noting that his demerits substantially increased each semester, from fourteen in his first, to eighty-six in his eighth and final. Such conduct may reflect a complacency marked over time or a maturing desire to follow his own path. It is tempting to believe that Schwatka's independent streak was rooted in his frontier upbringing, a culture that emphasized individualism and self-reliance. Perhaps most indicative of his lighthearted nature were the multiple instances he was flagged for "laughing" while at drill or parade.[11]

Besides the classroom regimen, the life of a cadet was an active one, and the physical demands at West Point set it apart from more traditional colleges. Military exercises played a prominent role; squadron drills, skirmishing, mock battles, swordsmanship and riding all occupied significant portions of the cadets' busy schedules. The strenuous nature of military training invariably led to occasional injuries, and young Schwatka accepted his share of sprains and strains in stride. He suffered his most severe injury during his third year. For many cadets, the art of riding and handling a horse was the most dreaded experience of plebe life, but to Schwatka it was second nature. It was during a cavalry exercise, when vaulting into the saddle while his horse was on a full run, that an overconfident Schwatka overshot his target and missed his steed entirely. Although suffering a badly sprained ankle, the worse bruise may have been to his ego. He could only bring himself to confess the affair to his parents well after his four-week convalescence. In a bid to downplay his own miscue, he likely left them more unsettled by revealing that it was not unusual for three or four cadets to be disabled in a single drill.

Recreationally, Schwatka enjoyed rowing and became a distinguished member of the crew team. He was highly regarded for his muscular strength and endurance. The highlight of his rowing prowess was the upset victory in his third year by his six-man crew team over the graduating class and the second-year class at the annual regatta held at the 1870 graduation ceremony. The brawny Schwatka was his boat's "stroker," the rower who sets the pace for the other rowers.[12]

During Schwatka's tenure, the Academy was managing its own growing pains. As part of its reconciliation efforts, during his second year in 1868, the Academy admitted its first cadets from former Confederate states. In 1870, Schwatka's senior year, the first Black cadet was admitted, followed by the second in 1873; both were subject to persecution and harassment. The Academy had long had its critics in the legislative bodies in Washington, D.C., reflecting concerns of patronage appointments, lack of competitive entrance exams, and objections to a standing army. Although somewhat tempered after the Civil War, this animosity continued to fester, finally rearing its head during Schwatka's senior year. Two plebes made an unauthorized trip off post while another lied to a member of the first (senior) class about their conduct. Members of the first class, exercising what they believed to be their duty under the honor code, voted to expel the three plebes and marched them out of the Academy. There is no evidence that Schwatka was directly involved with this incident. Congress was furious that the first class cadets had taken matters into their own hands, and ordered a committee to investigate their insubordination. Rumors circulated that the House of Representatives would move to expel the entire first class, Schwatka included. The expulsion did not happen, and the wayward plebes were reinstated, but the investigative committee ultimately recommended dismissal of the insubordinate first class cadets. The secretary of war, William W. Belknap, simply ignored the recommendations, as did a military Court of Inquiry.[13]

On June 8, 1871, Schwatka's graduating class was in high spirits after completing their final examinations. Spanning two weeks, averaging several hours per day, these were a grueling, comprehensive series of tests. In keeping with Academy tradition, Frederick Schwatka and the other successful members of the class were awarded their degrees amid lavish military exercises and ceremonies. Even President Ulysses S. Grant, himself a graduate (class of 1843) and the proud father of a cadet in the class of 1871, was on hand to attend the celebration. More at ease with the cadets than with the dignitaries, Grant mingled and talked freely with the graduates, even relating some amusing incidents from his time at the Academy. A co-ed "hop" completed the festivities, the young ladies for miles around having been invited, causing a frantic run on dress shops. Despite the celebration, all those present understood that even with the end of the War of the Rebellion, which had taken such a tragic toll on the lives of its graduates, service in the U.S. Army could be among the most hazardous career choices. In fact, two of Schwatka's own classmates would pay the ultimate price at a young age during the Indian wars of the 1870s.

Frederick Schwatka certainly left the Academy with a level of competence in military training and leadership. For a young man possessed of an inquisitive mind, the West Point experience was also a confidence builder; confidence to pursue a broad range of interests and activities in a quest for knowledge and self-improvement. Standing at six feet, two inches tall, he had a commanding physical presence that added an air of authority. By and large, the Academy life had appealed to this young westerner, but rankings and scores only shed a partial light on character. During their four years together a small class of cadets grew to know each other intimately, in all situations, and in good and bad times. The opinions of those who knew him best, his classmates and peers, offer the most insightful look into his character.

According to one classmate:

> He [Frederick Schwatka] will be best remembered, however, for his inexhaustible cheerfulness and good nature, which never seemed to forsake him under the severest trials or in the most distressing situations. There was no state of affairs, however distressing, in which he was not able to discover a ridiculous side, or out of which he was not able to deduce a humorous conclusion. He was always ready for a practical joke, in which he was quite willing to be accounted the principal sufferer, so long as it contributed to the general stock of amusement.[14]

In short, he was a friendly, likable fellow, with a good sense of humor under the most trying of circumstances. Those were traits that would serve him well over the next twenty years. Frederick Grant, who knew him well, echoed similar sentiments in 1880, but with some unusual insights: "Schwatka, while personally popular among his classmates, was regarded as an eccentric character. He appeared at the Academy in July, wearing a heavy overcoat and fur cap. He was extremely brusque of manner, and enjoyed a practical joke, but withal was tender-hearted and generous to his companions." Interestingly, Grant also remarked that Schwatka's classmates believed that Schwatka "hungered for fame," evidently a trait that Grant was not prepared to attest to himself.[15]

At his graduation in June 1871, Frederick Schwatka was commissioned as a second lieutenant along with his remaining forty classmates (of the fifty-five who had originally started). He was the fourth West Point graduate from the state of Oregon, a fact of which he was immensely proud. Although assignments upon graduation could include the Corps of Engineers, or positions with the cavalry, infantry, or artillery, all the newly graduated second lieutenants in Schwatka's class were ordered to report to the cavalry or infantry. Frederick Schwatka was appointed to the U.S. Third Cavalry, Company M, under the command of Captain Anson Mills. The Third Cavalry regiment to which Schwatka had been assigned was originally organized in 1846 as the Regiment of Mounted Riflemen, a distinctive unit of mounted soldiers with greater mobility and more effective firepower for dealing with frontier fighting. Its original purpose had been the protection of settlers along the Oregon Trail.

The biographical sketches of Frederick Schwatka that exist tend to pass lightly over his cavalry service. When they do mention that he played a part in the Indian wars, they seldom acknowledge his creditable role in the conflicts, as well as the importance of this service to his growth and maturity. Fully at home on the range, his military experience spanned the frontier far and wide, immersing him in diverse cultures. This time in his life was filled with exploits and adventures that read like the dime novels of the time.

With the combative struggle between the North and South now concluded, the nation shifted its focus toward the development of the West. When the golden spike was driven at Promontory, Utah in 1869, the transcontinental railroad unified the country. Its completion spurred the growth of the West, eliminating the long, hazardous wagon trains of previous decades. With the westward movement of an increasingly larger number of settlers, competition for land and resources inevitably led to a series of conflicts with the American Indians, who had lived on the land for centuries. In response, the post-war army that Schwatka had entered was shifting priorities, from preparing for large-scale engagements to fighting unorthodox campaigns with the Indians.

Rapid demobilization after the war had reduced the army from over one million soldiers to an authorized strength of approximately fifty-four thousand by 1866. With further reductions, it had been whittled down to about twenty-nine thousand by 1871. Corresponding reductions in volunteer units further disbursed the remaining Regulars, all of whom were called to do more with less. The principal occupation of the post-war army became the staffing of frontier outposts to help open the West, and the occupation and Reconstruction in the South.[16]

What became known as the Indian wars was played out in a vast area that knew no territorial borders, extending from the bordering Mexican states to Canada (then British North America), with the vast territory of the fledgling United States sandwiched in between. These engagements were fought over challenging and widely varying terrains, across deserts, plains, and mountains, under an equally unforgiving extreme of climates. Compounding the difficulties, the hard-pressed soldiers were squaring off against Indian opponents who commanded a mastery of the countryside. The small military outposts that dotted the west were like oases in the desert, outside of which the frontier remained unbounded and awe-inspiring. But civilization was fast approaching.

After graduation, Schwatka spent some well-deserved relaxation at home in Salem but the respite was all too short-lived. On October 16, he was ordered to report to Benicia Barracks, near Suisun Bay, in Benicia, California, a staging post for soldiers assigned to the Southwest. His first assignment was to conduct a detachment of new recruits to posts in the Arizona Territory, and join his Company M, Third Cavalry, at Fort McDowell. The task, a rather mundane first taste of command, was completed by the end of November 1871. Fort McDowell was a major outpost in the Arizona Territory in the land of the Apaches, some of the fiercest fighters in the Southwest. Schwatka's recruits supplemented the troops organized by Lieutenant Colonel George Crook, newly appointed commander of the Department of the Arizona, who was engaged in campaigns to pursue and subdue the Apaches who were causing unrest throughout the area.

For most of the soldiers guided by Schwatka, the trip was a tiresome exercise in scorching conditions across a dry desert landscape. For Schwatka, it was a cultural learning experience that he would later describe for readers of *Century Magazine*. He characterized it as his first visit to "Apache land," acknowledging the ancestral occupiers of the territory, and so began his practice of amateur scientific examination. He observed a harsh and severe setting where water was scarce and often tainted by alkali, where temperatures soared throughout the day and game was scarce. A keen observer offering a fair-minded assessment, he marveled at how the Apaches had "wrested a precarious existence" in that demanding environment. He noted how they had learned to take advantage of the indigenous plant life by surviving on the beans of the mesquite tree, the fruit of the saguaro cactus, and the prickly pear. He also offered lengthy descriptions of their dress, home life, practices and superstitions.[17]

Schwatka was awed by their physical stamina, noting that "some of their running feats of endurance are marvelous to relate, and are oftentimes made in a withering heat that makes life in the open field burdensome almost beyond bearing to the white man." An Apache courier sent ahead to announce the impending arrival of the cavalry reached the destination, ninety miles distant, in thirteen hours, a trip that took Schwatka's party a full three days. Not hesitant to admit their superiority, Schwatka even went so far as to conclude that "their endurance and rapidity of action are superior...to that of white men." The title of his *Century Magazine* article, "Among the Apaches," appropriately reflected Schwatka's vantage point, and from within their midst, he was sympathetic to their plight and understanding of their hostility. According to Schwatka, the artificial border established between Mexico and the United States "ran ruthlessly through the heart of their country, paying less attention to them than to the barren lands which it divided, and for which untold ages had been their home."[18]

Schwatka spent little time in the Arizona Territory, joining the main detachment and Captain Anson Mills, under whom Schwatka would serve the next seven years. Mills and companies of the Third Cavalry were preparing for their next assignment, Fort McPherson, a major outpost in central Nebraska. This entailed a tiresome and miserable journey of almost one thousand miles, spanning some six weeks, with a backtrack through San Francisco. Their journey to Fort McPherson may have been exasperating, but their departure from Arizona was viewed as a godsend. Mills later wrote that the officers were so disgusted with their Arizona experience, that upon leaving the territory "we took off our shoes and beat the dust of Arizona over the rail, at the same time cursing the land." The Southwest posting had also exacted a heavy toll on their physical wellbeing. Mills had lost thirty pounds while stationed in the territory; his wife, who had accompanied him, shed twenty. The post surgeon at Fort McPherson reported that a large number of the newly arrived troopers were suffering relapses of malarial fever contracted in Arizona. Frederick Schwatka was likely one of them, and the illness would plague him at inopportune times over the course of his lifetime.[19]

Captain Anson Mills was a remarkable man of many talents, and his relationship with Schwatka was fortuitous to the young lieutenant's career. Mills was a country boy, born on a farm in Thorntown, Indiana in 1834. Despite failing out of West Point in 1857 due to a deficiency in mathematics, Mills nonetheless excelled as a surveyor and engineer, planning the city of El Paso, Texas, for which he was recognized as "the Father of El Paso." Still determined to serve in the army, he procured a commission during the Civil War, never missing a day of service, even though his regiment, the Eighteenth Infantry, suffered some of the highest number of casualties in the regular army. From 1865 through 1893, he served largely on the frontier, rising to the rank of brigadier general. Easily recognizable by a distinctive Midwest accent, with a wide, dark moustache that overshadowed a narrow gray goatee, he was well regarded by his men.[20]

In frontier outposts, with time hanging heavy, the practical-minded Mills constantly tinkered with improving equipment for use in the field. His creative efforts were handsomely rewarded. He ultimately invented and patented a cartridge belt that became the standard in the U.S. and Europe, which made him a fortune. To the residents of El Paso, he is still known as the proponent of perhaps the tallest "reinforced concrete" building (skyscraper) in the world for its time, the eponymous "Anson Mills Building."

In the confines of the desolate outposts and in the field, comradeship was vital, and Mills grew to know Schwatka well over the course of their time together, helping to guide and mentor his development as a soldier and as a young man. Mills would come to place correspondingly greater responsibilities on Schwatka, and to rely on him for critical and dangerous missions. Mills found him a man after his own heart, resourceful and with a wide range of interests. He remarked in his autobiography that Schwatka was "one of the most interesting officers . . . I ever met," and that he "gained a national reputation in his search for the remains of the Franklin expedition."[21]

Arriving in mid-January 1872, troops of the Third Cavalry spent the balance of the winter at Fort McPherson, a location that may have stirred Schwatka's early memories, since it served as a resupply station on the Oregon Trail. Leaving Fort McPherson, companies of the outfit, including Schwatka's Company M, were assigned to the post at North Platte Station, fourteen miles to the west, a detail later regarded by Mills as the most important he ever held. Both North Platte Station and Fort McPherson fell under the oversight of the Department of the Platte, one of a handful of military districts spanning the country and administered by the War Department. The Department of the Platte covered a vast region that included Nebraska, Wyoming, Utah, and a corner of Idaho. The Department's initial mission was to protect settlers along the Oregon Trail to Salt Lake City, and subsequently safeguard construction of the Union Pacific Railroad from Indian threats as the line advanced westward.

North Platte Station was established in 1867 (the same year Nebraska achieved statehood), near the confluence of the North and South Platte Rivers on the west side of the town of North Platte. In 1867, the Union Pacific had established a depot in the town, and had constructed a railroad bridge crossing the North Platte River. The post's first commanding officer was Captain Arthur MacArthur, a Civil War hero in his own right, more widely recognized as the father of General Douglas MacArthur. Besides protecting railroad workers, scouting for Indians was the principal duty of soldiers who occupied the post. Troops might remain in the field for days or weeks on end, chasing a cunning foe that was only occasionally spotted, and less frequently overtaken, by the soldiers. But life in the saddle on the Plains appealed to Schwatka. He could happily endure miles on horseback, in all terrains and suffering under all conditions, while camping under the stars. The risk of Indian encounters only compounded his sense of excitement.[22]

The station at North Platte, a typical frontier outpost, comprised an eight-acre compound of basic pinewood-framed buildings. Soldiers found it generally comfortable to the extent that military posts on the Plains could somehow be considered satisfactory quarters. As a junior officer, Schwatka would have had the benefit of a room for lodging and kitchen accommodations. The proximity of the barracks to the

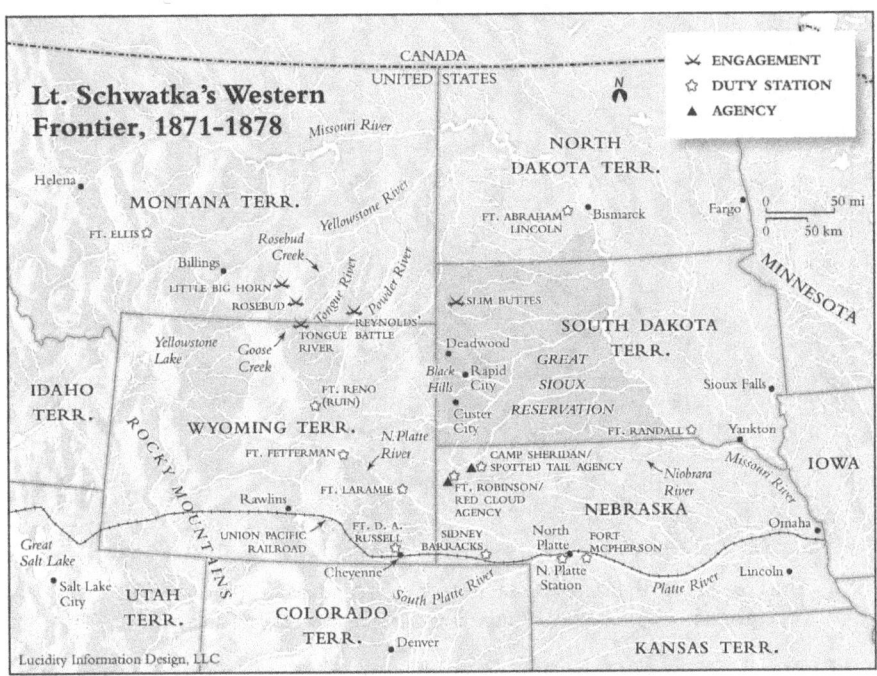

town made for mixed, but generally positive, relations with the 1,000 or so civilian residents. At the time, North Platte was a dusty prairie town, a smattering of modest homesteads and buildings and entirely devoid of trees. A few planks along the main thoroughfare served as a sidewalk. From time to time, emigrant wagon trains bound further west filled its streets, as did cattle driven on their way to the stockyards. The army added to the town's cultural life with Company M's musicians playing at local affairs. Less welcome were the occasional drunken incidents and brawls involving soldiers, especially following payday. For his own part, Schwatka settled comfortably near the army town, which saw rapid growth due to the adjacent railway. Displaying an entrepreneurial streak, at a cost of $3,000 he erected a two-story building downtown which he rented to retail establishments. Known as the "Schwatka" building, it also served as a community event facility, hosting lively parties and dance events. Looking to further profit from the town's growth, Schwatka and Captain Mills even speculated in some undeveloped land on its outskirts.[23]

The boundless plains of western Nebraska nonetheless offered Frederick Schwatka adventure and excitement that conjures up the Old West of legend. Prominent businessmen, politicians, and dignitaries looking for a "wild west" experience frequented North Platte and Fort

The Post at North Platte Station (L to R): guardhouse, storehouse, officers' quarters, duplex officers' quarters occupied by Lt. Paul and family.

McPherson for sport hunting due to ease of entry to the wide-open prairie and the relative abundant game. The army brass encouraged these excursions, recognizing that they could help enlist support in Washington for military funding. Hardliners, like Lieutenant General Philip Sheridan, also saw the extermination of the buffalo as the answer to the "Indian problem." As small war parties of Sioux frequented the area, troopers from the Third Cavalry regularly performed escort duties, and Lieutenant Schwatka rarely missed such opportunities.

In the fall of 1872, the young cavalry officer even had the good fortune to accompany the larger-than-life Plainsman hero, William F. "Buffalo Bill" Cody, on one such hunting excursion. Schwatka would get to know Buffalo Bill well, at work and at play, as Bill was serving as chief of scouts for the Third Cavalry stationed at nearby Fort McPherson. By 1872, he was already a legend in the West as a professional guide and hunter; his reputation as a showman and cowboy icon would begin later that year with his first stage appearance.

Schwatka's hunting party was comprised of several prominent Nebraskans, among them U.S. District Judge Elmer S. Dundy and several lawyers and politicians, all escorted by Schwatka and soldiers of the Third Cavalry and led by Buffalo Bill. Whether they truly expected to bag big game or simply desired a social jaunt on the Plains was a fair question. Among them, attorney James Neville was outlandishly attired during the course of the entire trip in a formal swallow-tail coat and high silk hat. According to one participant, as they galloped "pell-mell" across the prairie in pursuit of their quarry, Neville "presented a picture against the horizon that does not have its parallel in pioneer history." Buffalo Bill thought that the sight of the bounding Neville "was enough to make a 'horse laugh,'" and that his own mount, Buckskin Joe, had actually done so. According to one participant, the prominent Omaha lawyer John Lee Webster, the distinguished members of the party had an exciting time chasing game across the barren prairieland, somehow managing to stay out of harm's way, but the amateur hunters secured not one animal.[24]

Webster, who penned a recollection of the event years afterward, referred to the outing as "the last romantic buffalo hunt," a statement that sadly foreshadowed the ultimate demise of the animal from the Plains. Nonetheless, Buffalo Bill, the consummate showman, in keeping with his Plainsman persona, managed to lasso a large bull buffalo for the entertainment of the failed hunters. Schwatka, the twenty-two-year-old cavalryman, also received high marks for his escort work. The young lieutenant comported himself well among the dignitaries, competently handling an informal diplomatic role as representative of the U.S. government. John Lee Webster noted that Schwatka "at all times had been generous, courteous and polite to us, as well as an interesting social companion." Schwatka enjoyed the social aspects and camaraderie of the hunting excursions and would perform his diplomatic escort role on multiple occasions.[25]

The allure of the "wild west," with its sport hunting in an exotic locale, also attracted European nobility. In one celebrated excursion, in January 1872, immediately before Schwatka's arrival at Fort McPherson, Buffalo Bill had escorted the Grand Duke Alexis, son of Russian Emperor Alexander II, accompanied by Lieutenant General Sheridan and Lieutenant Colonel George A. Custer. The most regal dignitary Schwatka ever escorted was Windham Thomas Wyndham-Quin, 4th Earl of Dunraven and Mount-Earl, the rather long-titled member of a prominent Irish family, who were large landowners in County Limerick. The name alone conjures up visions of a Victorian sportsman attired in a tweed shooting jacket and breeks. As the son of a pioneer, Schwatka ranked individual initiative above hereditary birthright and was dismissive of nobility. He found the earl's peerage a fitting target for his humor, at a later date remarking that he once had a "distinguished personage with me loaded with so many titles that I was afraid if they should suddenly shift they might throw him out of the saddle he rode so poorly."[26]

Hardly a stuffy blueblood, the earl was a fine companion, if not an accomplished outdoorsman. He fully enjoyed the hardships of his elk hunt, ignoring his status and competing on equal terms with Buffalo Bill and Schwatka. Freed from social conventions, his efforts to secure a "good shot" were prodigious; even crawling on his stomach through dwarf cacti plants to silently approach his prey. Despite his noblesse, he was a firm supporter of the American "experiment" in government, curiously remarking that "the curse of my country is its nobility." It was on this excursion that Schwatka took down an antelope at five hundred yards, a shot that he recorded with some pride in his catalogue of "Lucky Shots." One aspect of Schwatka's well-to-do client did not slip by unawares. Financial independence allowed the earl unfettered discretion to do as he well pleased, enjoying complete freedom of action and freedom of choice. This stood in marked contrast to Schwatka's current station under harsh army discipline and humble pay.[27]

Conservation and protection of the buffalo had yet to fully take hold in the West, and it would be unfair to characterize Schwatka as an avid proponent. Nonetheless, like a true sportsman, he recognized that "to have an occasional day's sport with a hard ride here and there and to bring in a nice head of horns" was preferable to "wholesale slaughter for only the tongues and 'humps.'" Schwatka was himself an indefatigable buffalo hunter during his cavalry service on the Plains. Besides serving on escort duty, he also enjoyed hunting game for food stocks for the troopers and townspeople, once escorting a detail of twenty-nine men from the Third Cavalry over 476 miles in search of quarry throughout October and November of 1873. In later years, Judge Dundy, a regular hunting companion, remarked that Schwatka was a "devoted hunter," and that "when he was stationed at North Platte, the animal that could get away from him had to be a mighty smart one." Dundy's comments evidently ring true, as Schwatka noted that during the 476-mile outing, seventy-one buffalo were taken in what seems a rather excessive hunting display. However, Schwatka noted that his hunting forays, unlike sport excursions, "utilize[ed] every part of the beasts we killed, from the hoofs to the horns." Nonetheless, even as a newcomer to this open country, the young lieutenant could foresee the consequences of the encroaching inroads of eastern civilization. Within ten years, the cumulative effect of easy access to the Plains by railroads, sport and subsistence hunting, and an insatiable demand for leather for garments and accessories would lead to the virtual extermination of the American bison.[28]

One sensational hunting event in 1873 that holds a place in western hunting lore, in which Schwatka played a part, may have topped them all, William Frank "Doc" Carver's Champion Buffalo Hunt. Another in a line of colorful personalities to pass through the Plains, Doc Carver (a dentist by trade and one-time performer with Buffalo Bill), was an expert marksman, hunter, and plainsman and self-proclaimed "Champion Buffalo Hunter of the Plains." The brash self-promoter even claimed to have thirty thousand hides to his credit. When "Buffalo Curley," an all-around blackguard from Texas, had the nerve to challenge Carver for the title and a $500 purse, winner take all, word spread like wildfire throughout the territory. If the reports of witnesses are to be believed, a diverse assemblage of plainsmen, ranchers, soldiers, and Sioux and Pawnee warriors lined nearby Frenchman Creek to witness the spectacle of what was billed as the greatest buffalo shooting match in history. Schwatka and the soldiers of the Third Cavalry, arriving in company with a group of curious ladies, served to maintain order among the rival camps and between the Pawnee and Sioux, historic enemies. The rules were simple; the man who could kill the most buffalo on one run of his horse (meaning until the hapless animal dropped), was the winner. When the shooting was over, Doc Carver had killed a remarkable 160 buffalo and earned the undisputed title of champion buffalo hunter, although Buffalo Bill may have begged to differ. Following the much-heated contest, the outmatched Curley, evidently a sore loser, threatened the life of Doc Carver, a circumstance that was tactfully defused by Schwatka before any blood was spilt. According to one acquaintance of Carver, Schwatka's "sage advice" quelled this dispute and many others, earning the diplomatic young lieutenant the nickname "Peacemaker of the Plains."[29]

In the army's multi-faceted roles in the West, escort duty extended beyond simple sport hunting excursions. Sheridan had also approved the use of army resources to facilitate scientific investigation of the still partially unexplored and unexamined country. It was known that the region held a treasure of paleontological resources, including on and near Sioux treaty lands. In the 1870s, Professor Othniel Charles Marsh and Edward Drinker Cope were in the midst of the "great dinosaur bone wars," seeking to outdo each other in collecting and publishing their finds. North Platte and Fort McPherson served as convenient launching points for Marsh's excursions between 1870 and 1873. For the ever-inquisitive Schwatka, escort duty for Marsh's fossil hunting party may have been the scientific highlight of the 1873 summer season. As the territory to be explored fell near the hunting grounds of the Sioux, an armed escort was considered a wise precaution. The Third Cavalry extended quite a helping hand to the professor and his Yale student researchers. Captain Mills, Lieutenant Schwatka, and seventy-one enlisted men supported Marsh's effort, leaving

North Platte on June 17 and slowly worked their way across the Sand Hills region toward the South Dakota border. With their considerable discoveries securely packed and stored, the party returned on July 14, having covered four hundred miles in the process. In his report, Mills offered his opinion that these excursions, supported by the army, would dispel "the idea too prevalent that our army is a useless and idle institution by showing the vast extent of wild country for which we have to care."[30]

But it was not all fun and games in the West. It was a rough and dangerous place, where wanton killings were not uncommon. In early 1873, reports reached Fort McPherson of the murder of three leaders of the Oglala Sioux, named Whistler, Badger and Handsmeller. Their bodies had been found badly decomposed; two had been shot at close range, the third had his head split by an axe. Initially, suspicion focused on the Pawnee, based on the historical enmity between the tribes. At the time, emotions were running especially high, since the Sioux had recently stolen some twenty Pawnee ponies and a Pawnee had been killed in the scuffle. From Fort McPherson, Captain Charles Meinhold and fifty-seven men of Company B, Third Cavalry, left the post to prevent an outbreak of violence and bloodshed between the two groups and to more fully investigate the circumstances of the murder of the three Sioux. Meinhold was accompanied by Lieutenant Schwatka from North Platte Station, who was temporarily assigned to duty with Meinhold's company. Schwatka's role was to serve as a soldier-detective to help interrogate individuals with possible knowledge of the foul deed. The notion that Schwatka's selection, from outside Fort McPherson, may have been purposefully made based on a recognition of his intellectual prowess, is an intriguing thought. In any event, through his interrogation of a local farmer who had chanced to cross the path of two white men acting suspiciously in the vicinity of the bodies of the Sioux, Schwatka was able to produce sworn testimony and physical evidence that freed the Pawnee from all suspicion, which led to the likely conclusion that the three had been murdered by the hands of white men. Although no one was ever brought to justice, one of the suspects for the murder was identified as "Wild Bill" Kress, whose similarity in name to "Wild Bill" Hickok briefly caused some confusion as to whether the more recognized "Wild Bill" had committed the murders.[31]

Notwithstanding its episodic periods of activity, life at North Platte could be monotonous and uneventful for long stretches, particularly in winter when railroad construction was suspended, and outdoor activities subsided. Through mid-1874, post returns continued to record that Company M performed the usual garrison duties and scouting as the order of the day. Nonetheless, hostile and deadly activity could and did occur without warning. After Indian attacks were reported in the area of southeast Wyoming Territory, a major campaign under Captain Mills was organized in August 1874 to locate and punish the transgressors. The campaign was indicative of frontier activity. It was a cumbrous contingent that consisted of twelve officers (Schwatka included), scout Buffalo Bill, and more than 240 enlisted men comprised of companies of the Second Cavalry and Third Cavalry. Additionally, it was supported by a train of twenty-four wagons and seventy-four pack mules, all intent on locating a highly mobile Indian force. Shortly after their departure, the caravan was struck by an unexpected heavy snowstorm in the Rattlesnake Hills which buried them under two feet of snow in thirty-six hours. At times, poor maps led to unexpected detours in rough terrain, and heavy reliance was placed on the scouting skills of the guides. At one point Schwatka led the entire party out of a blind canyon through a steep and treacherous side trail. As for their primary objective, with the element of surprise virtually lost, only a few vacant Sioux encampments were encountered. In quite a testament to the spirit of his troopers, Mills reported that despite suffering from a bout of severe weather, the loss of twenty-three horses, and the death of one man in a vicious bear attack, his hardy men were "cheerful, pleasant and agreeable" during their six-week tour. To Mills and to his young lieutenant, Frederick Schwatka, more than anything else, the unsuccessful affair highlighted the weakness of travelling in large parties over difficult terrain in pursuit of a skilled and highly elusive foe.[32]

During that expedition, one humorous tale that involved Lieutenant Schwatka managed to pass its way into Buffalo Bill folklore. For a plainsman who was the epitome of the "crack" shot, it was perhaps Bill's finest exhibition with the use of a pistol. While in camp, Bill and Schwatka were bathing in the Sweetwater River when Schwatka spotted a grouse, a prime candidate for a tasty dinner. With one revolver between them, but both equally confident of their shooting acumen, Schwatka was permitted the privilege of the first shot. He duly missed. Grabbing the pistol, Bill scolded the young lieutenant, "You can't shoot for cold beans; I'll show you how to profit by this opportunity," and then proceeded to empty the chamber of its remaining five rounds, missing the lucky bird every time. Frustrated with his poor showing, Bill threw the pistol at the bird, and by chance, struck it and knocked it dead. Although the affair led to a good-natured ribbing in camp, fortunately, the humorous tale failed to diminish Bill's persona as an expert marksman.[33]

More excitement came to the North Platte area in late 1874 with the electrifying report that gold had been discovered in the Black Hills of the Dakota Territory, some two hundred miles away. The legendary Black Hills are a range of dark, pine-timbered hills sheltering lush grassy meadows and valleys, rising distinctly from the surrounding Plains. They held a special significance to the Indians both as a reliable hunting ground and as a spiritual abode. Rumors of gold-bearing ore had sparked an interest by Euro-Americans in the land, ever more so after the devastating Panic of 1873 and the attendant economic depression which followed. Lieutenant Colonel George A. Custer's Black Hills Expedition had explored the infrequently visited territory and civilian prospectors accompanying him made the discovery, quickly triggering a national gold rush.

With visions of another Sutter's Mill, and with it a massive influx of miners and a potential economic bonanza, North Platte politicians and businessmen rushed to position their town as the ideal staging point to the gold fields. Fueling their optimism, Captain Mills had been dispatched by the government to determine the feasibility of a route from North Platte to the Black Hills for transporting supplies. It is hard to overstate the frenzy that soon overtook the citizenry of North Platte. Reporters trailing Mills's party to the Black Hills pressed the captain and Schwatka over the feasibility of every mile of the proposed route. When word reached North Platte from back East that Buffalo Bill had promised to guide a group of wealthy Bostonians-turned-miners to the Black Hills, the townspeople offered to outbid competing towns for the privilege of conveying them. Gold mania swept numerous frontier towns within Nebraska and the Dakota and Wyoming Territories, and each brashly touted its location as the "best route" to this new El Dorado.

After the return of Captain Mills's surveying party, Lieutenant Schwatka, who had thoroughly mapped the proposed route, served as spokesman to describe its features before a hastily called town meeting of frenzied citizens. His favorable report that the road was feasible, but required some repairs, sent the town into a breakneck scramble to assemble a road crew for the improvements. Alas, much to the disappointment of its businessmen, North Platte's location left it too far east of other better approaches to the Black Hills. Ultimately, only Sidney, in western Nebraska, some 120 miles to the west of North Platte, a railway stop for the Union Pacific, could compete with the towns of Cheyenne, Pierre and Bismarck as favorably placed jumping off points.[34]

     At frontier outposts, intervals of downtime, sheer boredom, and perhaps loneliness and depression, led many officers and soldiers to turn to heavy drinking. In North Platte, the situation was exacerbated by the fact that the small town supported as many as twelve saloons. According to his friend Judge Dundy, while stationed at North Platte the one thing Schwatka enjoyed more than hunting was whiskey. Even then, Schwatka's drinking could be excessive. The concerned lawman strongly urged him to remedy his failing, a suggestion at which Schwatka "simply laughed." Another companion in the field, George Hopkins, noted that Schwatka's "social nature led him to indulgence in strong drink, and left him without power to resist. The demon got full possession of the better nature of the man."[35]

In light of his energetic personality, inquisitive mind and steady work ethic, it is hard to understand why Schwatka turned to drink as an outlet. The post at North Platte offered Schwatka intellectual pursuits that were unavailable at more isolated stations. Having made the acquaintance of the town's professionals, the intelligent and well-educated cavalryman learned to mix with ease among their company. With time on his hands, his active mind led him to pursue an apprenticeship with a local attorney with whom he had forged a friendship, and ultimately to obtain a law license in the state of Nebraska. Perhaps Schwatka was looking ahead to a future career or, more likely, merely acquiring knowledge for the sake of knowledge. The study of law was not an unfamiliar pursuit for the young cavalryman. As a student at West Point, he had been thoroughly schooled in military law and ethics, as well as their application. Moreover, he had already exercised police powers in the absence of civilian authority. The path to becoming a licensed legal practitioner in mid-nineteenth century was far less formal than today's standards. In Nebraska, to be admitted to the bar, a candidate was required to study in the office of a practicing attorney for two years, and then pass a bar examination (no law schools existed in Nebraska until the late 1890s). Schwatka satisfied the necessary apprenticeship and, after successfully passing his examination in Omaha, was sworn in to practice in Nebraska on May 21, 1875. Celebrating the accomplishment with his fellow legal associates, he outdid himself with a particularly "gigantic toot," according to one fellow officer. His errant behavior was the conversation piece the next morning among the boarders at his Omaha lodgings, as the pale, bleary-eyed lieutenant made his way to the breakfast table. That his degree was never put to use seems to confirm that his interest in the profession was merely an intellectual pursuit.[36]

At the time, Schwatka's convivial habits appear not to have negatively affected his professional duties. For the enlisted men though, the story was far different. North Platte Station was representative of the difficulties faced by commanders in the field. Alcoholism was one of many vices plaguing frontier posts, especially those adjacent to civilian settlements where all-too-eager merchants were more than willing to dispense strong spirits. Moreover, effective treatments for alcohol abuse were in their infancy, and nonexistent in the army. Soldiers were often left to dry out in hospitals or sick wards, without adequately addressing the underlying cause. The long-term damaging effects of chronic alcoholism on physical and mental health were not yet fully known. The army basically turned a blind eye unless it so interfered with the ability of a soldier to perform their duty. In that case discipline was applied, often harshly. Such was the case at North Platte Station. During November and December 1873 alone, eight soldiers were discharged by Captain Mills for "chronic and incurable alcoholism." [37]

To say that Schwatka possessed an inquisitive mind and was a man of many interests would be an understatement. In the late spring of 1875, he took clear-cut steps toward another professional pursuit. He requested a leave of six months from military service in June 1875, to be effective September 20, 1875, for what might seem an unusual goal for a line officer—enrollment in medical school in pursuit of a degree in medicine. Although the spartan frontier lifestyle held a certain appeal, it was obvious that the bright and scientifically minded Schwatka endeavored to look for a more satisfying career choice, well beyond garrison life on the Plains, and with a better chance of advancement.

The study of medicine presented a sufficient intellectual challenge to the inquisitive young man, but it also offered other distinct advantages to the independent-minded Schwatka. Assistant surgeons in the army had status; they held rank equal to that of first lieutenant, with opportunity for further promotion. Moreover, the Medical Department was organized as a separate branch within the army. As such, though subject to the orders of a post commander, regular army physicians operated with a greater level of autonomy than line officers. The position so appealed to Schwatka that he decided to pursue medicine as his chosen profession.[38]

Interestingly, Schwatka's request coincided with the May 1875 assignment of his Third Cavalry company to Camp Sheridan, south of the Black Hills. In stark contrast to North Platte Station, Camp Sheridan was precisely that, a frontier outpost of hastily erected buildings near the Spotted Tail Indian Agency. Spotted Tail Agency had been established under the Fort Laramie Treaty of 1868 as a permanent agency home for Chief Spotted Tail's Brulé Sioux. After a series of frustrating relocations of the Brulés, in 1874 the Spotted Tail Agency was established on Beaver Creek, twelve miles upstream from its junction with the White River, in northwestern Nebraska. This was some six miles from the Dakota boundary; Camp Sheridan was located within a mile of the agency. At the same time, Red Cloud Indian Agency, which accommodated Chief Red Cloud's Oglala Sioux, was established some forty miles west of Spotted Tail Agency. It had an adjacent military post, Camp Robinson (later Fort

Robinson), nearby. Both agencies would soon play an integral role in the Great Sioux War. Before the arrival of the Third Cavalry, the white Indian agents at Spotted Tail and Red Cloud Agencies had turned over their administrative authority to the War Department amidst flaring tensions sparked, in part, by Northern Indians from outside the agencies.[39]

During Schwatka's brief deployment at Spotted Tail Agency social activity was more prevalent than military action, and that was occasioned by the remarkable chief, Spotted Tail, namesake of the agency. In 1875, Spotted Tail was about fifty-five-years-old, and still actively involved in Indian affairs. In his younger days, he had been a fierce and skillful warrior, having fought heroically in the First Sioux War. He was at both the Grattan and Blue Water Creek fights, and was twice wounded in action. Finally captured and imprisoned at Fort Leavenworth, he became convinced of the futility of halting westward white expansion and turned his outlook to peace and negotiation. After learning the English language, he became an accomplished diplomat, striking hard bargains with presidents, generals and administrators. Brigadier General Crook's aide-de-camp, Lieutenant John Gregory Bourke, wrote in his diary that "'Spotted Tail' was one of the great men of this country, bar none, red, white, black or yellow." In contrast to other agencies, Chief Spotted Tail's conciliatory attitude maintained peaceful relations among his people. He became a good friend to Schwatka and Mills at Camp Sheridan, and both officers respected the chief.[40]

Through the summer of 1875, at Mills's direction, permanent accommodations were constructed for the post, with Schwatka tasked with overseeing the day-to-day details. Still a forlorn place even after completion of the new construction, one visitor recorded that "the perimeter of the ground-plan is strangely like a coffin." Lieutenant Colonel Richard Irving Dodge, visiting the post in 1875, was dismayed by the filth, remarking in his diary that it was a "miserable camp-water bad, filled with dead animals, refuse of Indian camps, &c." With peace now established at Spotted Tail Agency, Schwatka and the troops at Camp Sheridan were occupied in field duty outside the agency. These activities included deterring goldminers from entering the Black Hills, corralling poachers, and mundane scouting and escort assignments.[41]

Anson Mills took treaty compliance seriously, and in mid-May he and two companies of cavalry stopped one large group of one hundred and fifty miners and twenty-eight wagons from entering the Black Hills. The Third Cavalry companies, with the assistance of soldiers from Captain Fergus Walker's First Infantry, managed to surround the miners before dawn and disarm them at the point of a Gatling gun battery wielded by the Ninth Infantry. In strict compliance with Sherman's order, and to the dismay of the miners, all mining equipment and all nonessential supplies and weapons were destroyed. In June, it was Schwatka's turn to wield the heavy gun and present an overwhelming show of force. With Lieutenant Frederick W. Sibley, Second Cavalry, along with a detachment of some sixty men, accompanied by an infantry detachment manning the Gatling gun, they left Camp Sheridan to search for another sizable group of miners reportedly on their way to the Black Hills. A small contingent was tracked down, but this time Schwatka opted for a less heavy-handed seizure, sparing the destruction of their property.[42]

For the forward-looking Schwatka, medical school certainly looked like a more promising and challenging choice than continued garrison duty at an isolated outpost. He applied to Albany Medical College and Bellevue Hospital Medical College in New York City. His credentials were such that he was accepted to both. He elected to attend Bellevue. The medical school had been incorporated in 1861, the third such school in the city of New York (the school merged with the University Medical College of New York University in 1898). Bellevue's requirements for a medical degree required three years of study under the direction of a physician, completion of a course of lectures at Bellevue, a dissection course, and successful completion of a medical-related thesis and written examination.[43]

Schwatka was extremely fortunate that two of the physicians at the Nebraska posts where he was stationed generously offered to act as his preceptors—Doctor J. Burrows Gardiner and Doctor Adoniram Judson Gray. Both physicians served as acting assistant or "contract surgeons," civilians operating under contract to the government for specified lengths of time, without military rank or status. Private contracting was a common practice as medical officers in the army were in short supply across the frontier outposts. Schwatka's two sponsors had seen experience in the Civil War and Indian wars, and both were thoroughly knowledgeable regarding modern treatment methods. Under them, Schwatka would have learned basic first-aid, the methods used for compounding prescriptions, and the recording of patient treatments and outcomes.[44]

The harsh conditions of frontier service, often coupled with a poor diet, could take a toll on one's physical constitution, leading to a far higher incidence of illness among soldiers than the civilian population. Diseases could ravage a post in short order and accounted for far more fatalities and sick days than conflicts with the Indians. We can gain an accurate picture of the caseload that Schwatka observed under the guidance of his medical preceptors. The sick report for North Platte Station from 1870 to 1874 catalogued a wide range of complaints. Topping the list were 117 accidents and traumas, followed by 99 cases of bronchitis and catarrh (colds), 80 cases of fevers of all types, including typhoid and malaria, 51 cases of dysentery/diarrhea, and 16 cases of venereal disease. One must look at the very bottom of the list to find the 6 non-fatal gunshot wounds.[45]

Schwatka would have had a busy time of it through mid-1875, as he was concurrently studying under at least one attorney for his bar requirements and at least one physician for his medical degree, all this while attending to his regular garrison duties. In the four years of active service up until the time of his request for leave of absence, he had taken only seven days of leave. Schwatka received the first of his many extended leaves of absence from the military to take his place at Bellevue Hospital Medical College for the 1875-76 winter session, which ran from late September 1875 through mid-February 1876. Of the 159 students in his graduating class, Schwatka was the only student enrolled from the U.S. Army.[46]

In the nineteenth century, no standard medical curriculum was mandated by a central governing body, leading schools to develop their own program of instruction. The curriculum at most medical schools was heavily weighted towards formal lectures across a series of common medical subjects. Clinical instruction was much less defined. It was reliant, in part, upon the apprenticeship model to train physicians, and upon access to a nearby hospital or other healthcare institution while attending medical school. Schwatka's selection of Bellevue Hospital Medical College would prove to be an excellent choice. The school had early recognized the importance of clinical instruction as an integral part of medical studies and had assumed a leading position in connecting didactic (lecture) training with practical medical training. The medical school touted its proximity to Bellevue Hospital for clinical experience, together with the clinical opportunities made available to its students at other city operated charitable institutions.[47]

Bellevue Hospital was respected as one of the leading hospitals in the country. Its physicians and surgeons had accomplished any number of "firsts." It maintained the first maternity ward in the United States, and established the first emergency ambulance service in the country. Bellevue physicians were instrumental in the movement to improve public health, an effort that led ultimately to, among other things, New York City's first sanitary code. It also treated more than seven thousand patients in 1874, more than any other hospital in the country, and its affiliated institutions handled an additional several thousand cases among them. A medical student at Bellevue would be afforded a wide-ranging clinical experience covering all branches of medicine, and one that might only be matched in a handful of large cities in the United States.[48]

Attendance at lectures, to which students devoted much of their time, occupied five or six hours daily, each course typically meeting several times per week. Although many a student bemoaned the time spent in lecture hall, the scientific study would have appealed to the inquisitive young Schwatka. While it may not compare with today's instruction, Bellevue offered a course of lectures in medicine and surgery during the Winter Session, the completion of which (together with accompanying clinical components and thesis) would satisfy the degree requirements. The school's faculty included prominent and progressive individuals in the field of medicine who could inspire students with their accomplishments.

We are fortunate to know the identity of several of Schwatka's professors at the medical school. Schwatka attended lectures and clinical instruction delivered by Doctor Austin Flint Sr. (1812-1886), a world-renowned authority on internal medicine and the heart, who helped introduce the binaural stethoscope into general use in the United States. Flint's own highly regarded medical textbooks were recommended texts at Bellevue and many medical schools across the country, including his cornerstone "Principles and Practice of Medicine." Schwatka certainly benefitted from Flint's innovative approach that advocated diagnosis by a process of exclusion and thorough physical examinations. The surgical department at Bellevue was one of the best in the country. Schwatka received instruction from at least two prominent surgeons, Doctor Lewis A. Sayre, a leading orthopedic surgeon, and Doctor William Holme van Buren, a leader in urogenital surgery. Schwatka's professor in anatomy, Doctor Alpheus B. Crosby, was regarded as a fine educator, one commentator noting that he was "one of the most eminent practitioners and medical authors in New England." [49]

The final requirement for the medical degree was the completion of the thesis. Few students undertook original work of scientific recording and observations, relying on summaries of lectures and textbooks instead. The subject for Schwatka's thesis was diphtheria, an illness that would have special significance in the mid- to late-nineteenth century as a deadly epidemic disease with no known cure. It is a highly contagious bacterial infection affecting the mucous membranes of the nose and throat, and at times, the tracheobronchial tree, that can lead to difficulty in breathing, heart failure, paralysis and death. Historically, children and the elderly were more susceptible. The disease is now known to be caused by the *Corynebacterium diphtheriae* bacteria, which releases a toxin affecting the tissues, and is preventable by vaccine. Schwatka's work ran more than fifty neatly handwritten pages long, and provided a summary of the state of the disease in 1876, its potential causes, characteristics, symptomatology and treatment. No reference is made to actual cases, and no sources are cited in the write-up. Perhaps the most that could be said about Schwatka's thesis was that it spoke to the state of medicine in the United States, which had not yet gained widespread acceptance of the so-called "germ theory." Consistent with then current thinking, Schwatka's thesis pointed out that although there was some evidence of the infectious nature of the disease (caused by receiving the "sputa from affected persons"), that conclusion "still remains open for complete determination." It was not until 1883 that it was determined that diphtheria was caused by the *Corynebacterium*, by which time Dr. Flint's writings had accepted the approach.[50]

Frederick Schwatka was awarded his medical degree on February 21, 1876, at a ceremony held at the New York Academy of Music, with a dinner following at the fashionable Delmonico's Restaurant. From the surviving information regarding his performance at Bellevue Hospital Medical College, Schwatka left the medical school qualified to practice medicine. At the age of twenty-six, he had accomplished more than most persons would in a lifetime. If he had taken a few quiet moments to reflect on his progress as a young man, he had every reason to be proud of his achievements. That he hailed from a modest homesteading family from the Far West in the mid-nineteenth century, and had succeeded as a student, soldier, outdoorsman, lawyer, and physician, make these achievements even more impressive.

Just as important, however, Frederick Schwatka was an observant eyewitness to, and participant in, the country's westward expansion. Nurtured within an egalitarian frontier family, he was possessed of a solid sense of equality and tolerance, and valued self-reliance and hard work above social position. He had borne witness to inequities and maltreatment, particularly toward the Indians, and he would have reason to confront those inequities again.

Schwatka certainly had every desire to continue his medical career. He applied to the medical department of the U.S. Army for a position as a commissioned surgeon, but the department was itself in a state of transition. It had been reduced by substantial numbers following the close of the Civil War. More important, likely for the same reason that the army would not spare him for a teaching position at Willamette University, it was not prepared to lose a West Point officer, particularly one experienced in frontier fighting, at a time when tensions were rising in the West.[51]

CHAPTER THREE

THE BATTLE OF THE ROSEBUD

UPON HIS GRADUATION from Bellevue Medical College, Frederick Schwatka was left with little time for relaxation or a brief visit home. On March 21, 1876, duty once again called, and he was ordered to the army recruiting headquarters in New York City to escort a detachment of new recruits from the Fourteenth Infantry to the Department of the Platte. From there he was to rejoin his Third Cavalry company at Fort D. A. Russell near Cheyenne, Wyoming. Fort Russell was another spartan outpost which had been originally tasked with protecting workers for the Union Pacific Railroad. It was serving as a staging point in the Great Sioux War of 1876-77 when Schwatka arrived.[1]

Schwatka returned to the field at an unsettled time in Indian relations. Red Cloud's War, a series of conflicts initiated by settlers and miners moving along the Bozeman Trail through favored Indian hunting grounds in Wyoming and Montana (the Powder River region), had ended with the signing of the Fort Laramie Treaty of 1868 with the Northern Indians. The treaty established the "Great Sioux Reservation," an exclusive tribal area encompassing that portion of today's South Dakota west of the Missouri River (including the Black Hills region). In addition, in the "unceded Indian Territory" within the adjacent disputed Powder River Region, the Indians were granted travel and hunting rights. Military posts were ordered to be vacated and white settlers and miners were excluded.

With the discovery of gold in the Black Hills within the lands covered by the agreement, it was inevitable that the frenzy to extract valuable minerals would lead to government renegotiation or even outright disavowal of its stipulations. This all-too-obvious conclusion was plainly apparent to Lieutenant Schwatka while stationed in the midst of Sioux country adjacent the Black Hills. For a time, the army had served to maintain treaty obligations and had excluded prospectors and settlers from the region, a role in which Schwatka had played a part. As he turned his attention to the practice of medicine in the fall of 1875, he could sense the growing friction between the white men infiltrating the region and the Northern Indians intent on preserving their traditional way of life. In a remarkable attempt at reconciliation, Indian representatives, including Chiefs Red Cloud and Spotted Tail, had travelled to Washington, D.C. to meet with President Grant and other administration officials. Efforts on the part of the government to purchase the treaty lands outright were rejected by the tribesmen. In response, the government changed course, concluding that the desire for precious metals and settlement outweighed the interests of the Indians. Without any resolution of the matter, President Grant opened the region to prospectors and instructed the military to condone unrestricted access. Frustrated by the inability to coerce the Indians into surrendering treaty lands, the government lost patience and on November 1, 1875 issued an ultimatum.[2]

The Northern Indians were ordered to return to the Great Sioux Reservation by January 31, 1876; any who failed to comply by that date would be considered hostile. It was a futile order that was largely a pretext for action. Some tribes discussed the one-sided terms but decided that the need to procure game in advance of winter made compliance impossible even had they elected to do so. The Indians felt betrayed, and it was difficult to reconcile the government's action. Even Lieutenant John Bourke, aide-de-camp to Brigadier General Crook, commented that "[i]t is hard to make the average savage comprehend why it is that as soon as his reservation is found to amount to anything, he must leave and give up to the white man."[3]

The failure of the Northern Indians to comply led Crook, commander of the Department of the Platte, to commence his first action, a winter campaign. Crook was the logical choice to lead a sweeping offensive. His reserved and taciturn disposition often frustrated his subordinates, but he was possessed of a hard-driving and resolute will. Like many senior frontier officers, he was a West Point graduate who had seen extensive fighting during the Civil War and had even been captured and briefly held as a prisoner of war by the Confederate Army. Following the war, he made a name for himself as an Indian fighter during the Snake War of 1864-68, fought in portions of California, Nevada and the Northwest. He had also played a part in subduing the Apaches in the Arizona Territory in the early 1870s.[4]

A thoughtful Indian fighter, Crook had applied novel tactics in his successful campaigning; the extensive use of Indian scouts, winter campaigning, and increased mobility through the use of mule packs instead of unwieldy wagon-trains that slowed troop movements. In dress he was likewise unorthodox, shunning the military uniform of his rank for more comfortable civilian attire or that of a private, and often sporting a hunting jacket. He also held a firm belief in the humane treatment of the Indians.[5]

As Schwatka was being recalled by the army from the classroom in the early spring of 1876, the winter campaign had already opened on a disagreeable note. A large, but unknown number of well-armed warriors roamed the vast territory of the unceded region in the area of what is now northern Wyoming and southeast Montana. They remained resolute in their belief that they could successfully oppose or avoid the small frontier armies that had been assembled to confront them. Crook believed that a decisive blow on a large village in mid-winter would leave the occupants physically weakened, at the mercy of the elements and broken in spirit. Such a bold strike might also facilitate a quick change of heart on their part. On March 1, 1876, Crook advanced troops from Fort Fetterman to Old Fort Reno (a Bozeman Trail relic) in the Wyoming Territory, establishing it as a supply base. The weather was unbearably frigid, and the troops trudged through deep snow in heavy wool and furs, subsisting on meals of frozen bacon and beans served with lukewarm coffee. Proceeding along the Tongue River, they located a large Indian village near the Powder River in southeastern Montana Territory. Colonel Joseph Reynolds was dispatched by Crook with six cavalry companies and some 300 men to attack and destroy the village.[6]

At sunrise on March 17, Reynolds stormed the village, comprised largely of Cheyenne and a smaller number of Oglala Sioux, thus opening the Great Sioux War. Despite the element of surprise, the defenders managed to escape to safety outside the village. Reynolds succeeded in capturing several hundred horses and destroying the camp, its food and stores (except a solitary lodge which was left standing, housing an aged, blind Indian woman). Reynolds's victory was short-lived. He quickly retreated from the smoldering remains of the camp, enabling the Indians to recapture most of their horses. One wounded soldier, Private Lorenzo Ayers of Captain Mills's M Company, was abandoned on the field and suffered a dreadful fate at the hands of his captors, a callous decision for which both Reynolds and Mills bore a fair share of the responsibility.[7]

Casualties were high, not from fighting but from the weather. More than fifty soldiers suffered frostbite, while only a handful died of wounds. But it was the abandonment of the dead and the reality that one wounded comrade was left on the battlefield to a horrible death that had the most discouraging effect on the troops. Fear of capture and torture weighed heavily on the mind of soldiers on the frontier. Following the attack, according to Lieutenant Bourke, morale sagged and desertions increased as fellow soldiers declared that "they would not fight under men who would leave their dead and dying to fall into the hands of a savage foe."[8]

The incomplete action by Reynolds marked the end of any further winter campaigning. General Crook turned his attention to the upcoming summer operation, soon dubbed the Big Horn and Yellowstone Expedition. The army now adopted a three-pronged approach, using a total strength of some 2,400 men converging on the Northern Indians in the Powder and Tongue River country to push them back to the reservation or destroy them. Colonel John Gibbon from Fort Ellis, near Bozeman, would move east; Brigadier General Alfred H. Terry (with Custer's Seventh Cavalry) at Fort Abraham Lincoln, near Bismarck, would move west, and Brigadier General Crook (with Schwatka's Third Cavalry company) would start north again from Fort Fetterman. A desolate and forlorn frontier post, removed from any semblance of civilization or comfort, Fetterman was located on the south bank of the North Platte River, near present day Douglas, Wyoming. One reporter remarked that "it was a hateful post—in summer, hell, and in winter, Spitzbergen. The whole army dreaded being quartered there." Crook would muster one thousand soldiers and about one hundred packers and teamsters. Some two hundred and fifty Shoshone and Crow allies, considered a vital component to the overall force, were to join him later. Supplies, munitions and even a 1,000-head beef herd necessary to maintain the campaign were gathered. Under Crook, Lieutenant Colonel William B. Royall commanded fifteen companies of cavalry, including four companies of the Third under Captain Anson Mills (Companies A, E, I, and M, including First Lieutenant August C. Paul and Second Lieutenant Frederick Schwatka). Under Major Alexander Chambers two companies of the Fourth Infantry and three of the Ninth Infantry also joined the movement.[9]

Over a period of several months in the field, from May through October 1876, Lieutenant Frederick Schwatka, serving with the Third Cavalry, repeatedly proved his mettle and gained hard-earned experience during some of the fiercest and most protracted combat of the Indian wars. The nation had high expectations for the expedition while it awaited the opening of its newest El Dorado in the Black Hills. The public was kept well informed, with a number of newspaper correspondents imbedded with the troops, all vying for headlines and "scoops" while sharing the hardships and occasional dangers of the field.

John Finerty, a daring twenty-nine-year-old correspondent with the *Chicago Times*, travelled with the Third Cavalry, and would come to know Lieutenant Schwatka well during the campaign. A fiery Irish rebel who had left his native Ireland for the United States after incurring the wrath of the British government, Finerty proved his worth as a reporter on the campaign. Beneath that activist temperament was a classically educated scholar and talented writer whose dispatches would enliven the pages of the *Times*. Finerty first met Schwatka as the young lieutenant hastily approached on his mount "at break-neck pace," accompanied by an orderly, carrying an order for the captain with whom Finerty was travelling. Quickly sizing him up, Finerty's initial impression of Schwatka was that of an obedient and "stout young officer," fully committed to his duty. Upon delivering his message, Lieutenant Schwatka stopped only long enough to mop his brow, take a swig from his superior's canteen, and then "set out like a whirlwind" to fulfill another mission.[10]

Reuben Briggs Davenport, reporter for the *New York Herald*, would also come to know Schwatka, and would share with him the hardships and horrors of the campaign. Davenport was among the youngest of the reporters at age twenty-four, with roots in New York City. There was no mistaking his association with James Gordon Bennett Jr.'s widely popular *New York Herald*, which enjoyed the largest circulation in America. Davenport arrived with the words "NEW YORK HERALD" conspicuously emblazoned on his saddlebags, blankets, haversack and even his canteen, raising some eyebrows, and perhaps a few chuckles, among the hard-nosed veterans. Davenport had more significant difficulties during the expedition though, as he was universally abhorred by his fellow reporters and the soldiers for his irksome personality and reports criticizing the management of the campaign. He became the recipient of "tall tales" and "whoppers," to which his gullible newshound disposition frequently succumbed, making him a laughingstock. Schwatka would offer some support for the beleaguered and isolated reporter. Davenport would later write that in Schwatka he found a "rare geniality of nature, [and] a largeness of heart." That Schwatka could befriend Davenport bespeaks well of Schwatka's good-hearted disposition.[11]

Leaving Fort Fetterman on May 29, Crook's force, a colorful, four-mile-long procession of blue-shirted mounted men and infantry trailed by a fully stocked line of wagons and pack mules, set off for Fort Reno. Two weeks out, they soon passed the hillside where in December 1866, Captain William Fetterman and eighty soldiers under his command had been lured into an ambush, leading to their total destruction. At the time, it was the worst defeat suffered by the U.S. Army in the Indian wars, but today it is largely overlooked by the Custer defeat. Finerty referred to it as "a gloomy memorial of Indian warfare," and Bourke remarked that it is "hard to analyze the emotions to which the sight gave rise." It certainly disturbed even the hardiest of soldiers.[12]

It may be true that an army marches on its stomach, but it was equally true that it marched on its pack mules and horses. Although only a week out of Fetterman, traveling over poor and badly worn trails, steep hills, and numbing streams had severely taxed the heavily laden pack mules, and even some horses were lagging. Among the men, exposure to the elements contributed to rheumatism and other cold weather ailments. They were looked after by several physicians who had their hands full even before the fighting. As they neared the Montana Territory, at a camp at the junction of Prairie Dog Creek and the Tongue River (a tributary of the Yellowstone River), the first casualty of the campaign, Private Francis Tierney, succumbed on the evening of June 6. Tierney had accidentally shot himself on May 29 while incautiously tossing to the ground his gun belt holstering a loaded pistol. The poor boy had lingered for a week after suffering terribly. His solemn burial, attended by mournful officers and soldiers, was another melancholy circumstance that led Finerty to muse, "the interment of a soldier in the great American wilderness of that epoch was about the gloomiest of funeral experiences."[13]

The somber mood was quickly overshadowed by events of a more pressing nature, occurrences that heightened the expectation that an encounter was imminent. On June 8, fresh Indian tracks were discovered by a buffalo hunting patrol, as well as a lame, abandoned pony that was brought back to camp. Watchful soldiers now reported several possible Indian sightings, and jittery pickets of the Second Cavalry fired at what were thought to be some stealthily approaching Indians. That evening, upon a hill just outside the camp, words were briefly exchanged in the darkness between a scout from Crook's camp and an unidentified Indian.

At about 6:30 P.M. on June 9, pickets guarding the eastward approaches fired warning shots to arouse the camp. "At last they have come," reported Lieutenant James E. H. Foster. High above the bluffs to the north, across the river and overlooking their camp, several Indians began firing onto Crook's encampment while galloping to-and-fro and yelling wildly, seemingly taunting the soldiers. One or two attackers seemed to be directing the attack and serving as lookouts. Their rifle fire slowly gained a range on Crook's headquarters with its tents, horses and wagons. To one correspondent, the hail of fire was so rapid that "the air seemed alive with bees." The teamsters and soldiers returned fire until Crook ordered a cessation as their distance from the attackers was too far to be effective.

After assessing the situation, Crook moved to protect his flanks and to remove the threat from the bluffs. Three companies of the Ninth Infantry were ordered to guard the eastward approaches. In order to clear the heights, Crook ordered Mills's battalion of four companies of the Third Cavalry, including Schwatka's Company M, to cross the river, scale the ridge, and disburse the attackers. At the same time, a company of the Second Cavalry was ordered to advance to the left of Mills's battalion, edging along some thickets, to guard his approach. As Mills saddled his troops and gave the order "Forward!," his troopers were filled with a sense of anxious anticipation. They carried the standard .45 caliber 1873 Springfield carbine (with an effective range of about six hundred yards) and the .45 caliber 1873 Colt single action revolver. Under scattered fire, Mills's battalion managed "half wading, half swimming" to ford the swift-flowing Tongue River in good order, the water reaching as high as the horses' flanks.[14]

Reaching the base of the bluffs and the cover of a cottonwood grove, they dismounted, every eighth man holding the horses, as the balance of the soldiers scrambled up the ridge. The companies deployed with Troop I on the left, E in the left center, M in the right center and A on the right. Climbing the bluffs was no easy task as they were steep and slippery, and sporadic rifle fire continued to harass them. For Schwatka, even with an initial adrenalin rush, the prospect of facing an unknown number of enemy combatants must have generated some apprehension. Once the battalion had scaled about halfway up the bluffs, the Indians quickly moved to a higher crest about one thousand yards away which flanked Mills's battalion. With the four companies reaching the plateau almost simultaneously, the soldiers turned to face the attackers. They let off an initial discharge and advanced with a loud roar. The Indians, with the benefit of their horses, remounted and returned fire, which flew harmlessly over the heads of the battalion. Unflustered, they quickly regrouped on another crest further back. As the companies approached the next ridge in good order, the warriors again retreated well beyond the range of the battalion.[15]

Realizing the futility of further pursuit of their elusive foe, Mills broke off the engagement. Finerty had viewed about a dozen warriors through his field glasses but surmised that as many as fifty had been engaged in the skirmish. According to Finerty, the Indians were none the worse for the encounter and even took great delight in a conspicuous display of their equestrian skills. Though assumed to be Sioux, the attackers were actually Northern Cheyenne. Upon hearing shots to his rear, Mills moved his battalion back to the main encampment, arriving as the Second Cavalry drove off a group of the attackers who had attempted to stampede the

"The Indians attempting to surprise General Crook's Camp at Tongue River, June 9th."
From *Frank Leslie's Illustrated Newspaper,* August 12, 1876

horses. The entire engagement lasted an hour and resulted in minor wounds to three soldiers and possibly one Indian death. Mills's battalion had performed as an efficient, cohesive unit as many of the cavalrymen, including Schwatka, had been far from untested.

The action was a prelude to the more serious engagement a week later—the Battle of the Rosebud, a formidable action that tested the resilience of both sides. Following the skirmish at Tongue River, Crook moved his forces fourteen miles to a more comfortable camp on Goose Creek in the shadow of the Big Horn Mountains, where he anxiously awaited his Crow and Shoshone allies. Much to Crook's relief, they arrived on June 14. Both tribes made grand entrances, splendidly attired in colorful mantles and war bonnets. The Shoshones proudly circled Crook and his staff on horseback before dismounting, as boisterous yells and whoops filled the camp.

Crook had now concluded that this was the opportunity to strike a forceful blow that would weaken and demoralize his opponent and lead to their capitulation. According to Finerty, "Crook was bristling for a fight." Crook's scouts had obtained information that a large Indian village sat along Rosebud Creek, a tributary of the Yellowstone River, further inside the Montana Territory. An additional inducement for Crook was the fact that the legendary chief Sitting Bull, a fierce fighter and staunch enemy of westward expansion, was reported to be among the group encamped in the village. Only two weeks before, at an enormous gathering of his people, Sitting Bull had participated in a thirty-six-hour Sun Dance ceremony (later known as "Sitting Bull's Sun Dance"), during which he had a vision of the annihilation of the U.S. Army.[16]

Looking to advance quickly on the village, leaving his supply train, Crook had his troops leave their tents and carry only blankets, four days' rations, and one hundred rounds of ammunition. The infantry was forced to saddle and utilize the pack mules for transportation, a lively event that caused great amusement among the Crow and Shoshone Indians accompanying the troops. During the raucous "breaking-in" spectacle, the classically stubborn animals frequently threw their mounts, with more than one novice rider unceremoniously tossed into sage and prickly pear cacti. The soldiers somehow managed to gain the upper hand and impose their will. On June 16 Crook pushed the mobile force hard, covering thirty-five miles toward their objective in miserable, rainy weather. As large numbers of buffalo were now spotted, a potential harbinger of the presence of Indians, a sense of apprehension fell over the command. A random gunshot that rang out late in the day added to the tension, until it was learned that reporter Finerty had accidentally discharged his firearm, nearly shooting himself in the process.

Crook's troops approached Rosebud Creek, camping in its headlands, with low bluffs surrounding them forming a natural amphitheater. After an early start on June 17, the large force marched along the banks of the stream, the troops spanning both sides in an effort to keep the command more compact. A halt was made at about 8:00 A.M. when scouts returned with reports of Sioux further along the watercourse. From Mills's location near the head of the column, Rosebud Creek continued east about a mile, turned north, and flowed through the narrow cañon (known as Rosebud Narrows) that would become one of the many focal points in the subsequent encounter. Despite the knowledge that an engagement was imminent, mounts were unsaddled and set to graze. The soldiers generally relaxed in what shade was available under the rapidly warming day. The Third Cavalry was spread out along the south bank (right side) of the stream as follows: in advance, the First Battalion of Third Cavalry, four companies commanded by Mills; followed by Captain Guy V. Henry leading the Second Battalion of the Third Cavalry with four companies, and then a squadron of two companies of the Third commanded by Captain Frederick Van Vliet. On the opposite, or north side, were stationed the Second Cavalry Battalion under Captain Henry E. Noyes, and the Infantry Battalion (from the Fourth and Ninth Infantry). As the date, June 17, was the anniversary of the Battle of Bunker Hill, Finerty perceived it as an omen of good luck, and a bright, sunny morning seemed to confirm that omen.

The Rosebud battle differed from the more traditional hit-and-run Indian engagements that spotted the West due to the extraordinarily large number of combatants—some 1,300 men under Crook (including 250 Crow and Shoshone allies) against a fighting force of perhaps 1,000 Sioux and Cheyenne (Indian estimates are always difficult to assess). It was also unique due to the length of the battle, over six hours; the "stand and fight" attitude of the Indian warriors; and the wide theater of combat (about fourteen square miles).[17]

Captain Mills, who was perched on slightly more elevated ground on the right bank, claimed that he was the first to see the Sioux and Cheyenne initiate their charge from the north, some two miles away. Mills called out to Crook, interrupting his game of cards, with the startling news. The initial contact occurred when an advance party of Sioux and Cheyenne warriors clashed with the Shoshone and Crow allies scouting for Crook.

In some of the fiercest fighting of the day, the Shoshones and Crows managed to delay the more numerous attackers, giving Crook's troops time to assemble. Captain Azor H. Nickerson noted that "every hill appeared to be covered with their swarming legions, and up from every ravine, and out of every little vale, more seemed to be coming." In contrast with other engagements, the determined Sioux and Cheyenne pressed the advantage on Crook's main force. While the Crows and Shoshones tangled with one group of attackers, the infantry companies emerged from the left bank of the Rosebud as skirmishers. The Second Cavalry likewise pressed forward. Captain Mills quickly grasped the situation and wasted no time assembling his battalion on the opposite bank, shouting to "Saddle up, there – saddle up, there, quick!" After splashing his way across the muddy creek to confer personally with Crook, Mills was ordered to take and hold the bluffs directly ahead and secure Crook's right flank. Mills observed two sets of rock-strewn ridges, the first, one-half mile ahead, the second another one-half mile farther.[18]

Scrambling back to his command, Mills immediately ordered "front into line" and advanced three companies of the Third Cavalry behind the infantry. Companies A, E and M (some 179 men in total), sprang into action, and at Mills's command made a textbook mounted cavalry charge towards the first ridge, the riders side-by-side with revolvers drawn.[19] Finerty, buried in their midst, best describes the exciting scene, which he recalled had "passed like a flash of lightning or a dream":

> This order was executed with a brilliancy and celerity seldom equaled, under a sweeping hostile fire, which made a volcano of the plateau between the lower bluffs above our camp and the higher ones occupied by Sitting Bull. The battalion charged at a full gallop with fierce ringing cheers, halted for a moment to pour in a withering volley, and then galloped swiftly up the ascent to the crest of the ridge. Despite their great number and splendid position the Sioux centre broke and ran like a pack of wolves, taking shelter on other bluffs, 1,200 yards behind, for this battle-ground is a succession of ridges for miles on miles. The battalion then dismounted and deployed as skirmishers along the position they had carried.[20]

The cavalry maneuver was carried out with commendable skill and discipline under difficult circumstances. Besides facing a volley of enemy fire, maintaining the formation of the battalion was complicated by the fact that their course was marked by a steep and rugged incline. According to Finerty, the Sioux "were not idle." While scrambling about the ridge, in some instances their horses lost footing and fell on their riders, but no injuries were observed. As the battalion reached the base of the first ridge, the Sioux gave way, to the cheers of the troopers. The cavalrymen hastily dismounted, leaving the horses to each fourth man, with a field of large boulders offering protection for the mounts. The balance of the battalion worked its way forward in a skirmish line, advancing up the ridge, using smaller boulders for cover while engaging warriors close at hand.[21]

The mounted warriors presented a startling spectacle which was meant to instill fear in their opponents. According to Mills: "These Indians were most hideous, every one being painted in most hideous colors and designs, stark naked, except their moccasins, breech clouts and head gear, the later consisting of feathers and horns....Their shouting and personal appearance was so hideous that it terrified the horses more than the men and rendered them almost uncontrollable before we dismounted and placed them behind the rocks." Schwatka claimed that they faced an enemy of 400 Sioux, but Mills estimated the attackers at between 1,000 and 1,500 warriors. Even accounting for uncertainty in the heat of battle, the discrepancy is fairly wide and difficult to reconcile. In any event, acting swiftly in the face of spirited fire, Mills, Schwatka and the other troopers quickly "charged right in and through them [the Indian positions], driving them back to the top of the ridge." Mills had a healthy respect for their horsemanship and fighting skills, noting that they were "the best cavalry soldiers on earth." The Sioux made spirited runs at the battalion, and by adroitly hanging over the side of their horses, with one arm around the neck and a leg over their horse, they exposed little of their bodies, while firing from underneath the horse's neck. With Mills's force safe and secure behind the rocks, however, the attackers withdrew to the second ridge, about 600 yards back.[22]

On the second ridge, according to Finerty, the Sioux were "bold and impudent" and "slapping an indelicate portion of their persons at us, and beckoning us to come on." Finerty even imagined that Crazy Horse himself was directing the action of the warriors using a reflective device or pocket mirror. Mills's force remounted and advanced, applying the same tactics they had on the first ridge. The battalion charged the attackers, and again dismounted and used the boulders for cover, securing that ridge as the warriors withdrew to another to the west. At the same time as the warriors regrouped again on the third ridge, the greater part of the fighting had begun to shift away from the immediate area. However, a sizable number of warriors had assembled on the third ridge, still looking "as fresh, apparently, as ever," according to Finerty. Using the cover of a ravine, the warriors, now reinforced, approached and threatened Mills's front. In order to check the advance, Mills made yet another determined charge, and although under intense fire, managed to dislodge the attackers. Some sense of the intensity of the fight comes from Private Thomas Lloyd, Company E, in a letter to his cousin several months after the event:

> It was one of the hottest places I ever was in. Once, in the Rosebud fight I wouldn't give much for my scalp. The company was surrounded by Indians and only that we stuck together and [gave] them the best in the shop; they would have got away with our scalps. They stood and fought us within 100 yards, until we got 6 volleys into them and commence to drop them and their ponies. Then they took a tumble and fell back into the hills and trying to coax us to follow but we knew too much of Mr. Sitting Bull for that.[23]

During the encounter, one soldier was badly wounded. Trumpeter Elmer A. Snow of Schwatka's Company M was awarded the Medal of Honor for his heroics under particularly appalling circumstances. While charging the second ridge, Snow was shot through the right elbow and left wrist, rendering his hands useless. His now unrestrained horse continued to ride precipitously close to the attacking warriors, who were obviously bewildered by the escapade but maintained a steady fire.

Fortunately, by skill or by sheer luck, Snow's horse circled back to his companions and finally slowed as Snow managed to drop himself to the ground. The severely wounded trumpeter survived the ordeal but suffered severe impairment to both of his hands.[24]

As the battle raged on, Mills and his battalion were ordered to hold their positions on the ridge on the right side of the theatre. The engagement had become a series of individual actions scattered across the Rosebud valley. In the separate, heated engagements, including some hand-to-hand fighting, Crook's forces managed to repel the attackers. But they could not defeat them since they continually shifted their points of attack on the field. Finally, Crook looked to break the indecisiveness of the battle. He still believed that a large village, no less than that of Sitting Bull, sat somewhere down the Rosebud Narrows. Perhaps in Crook's mind, that explained the aggressive and continued tenacity of the Sioux and Cheyenne warriors, who uncharacteristically had stood and fought. Having fixed on its existence, the village offered a tempting target for Crook, a means to break the stalemate and deliver a crushing blow.

Crook ordered Mills to "take your battalion and go for their village away down the cañon." Schwatka's Company M, with two other companies of the Third Cavalry and five companies of the Second Cavalry, were ordered to withdraw and form a column to attack the village thought to be located at the far end of the Rosebud Narrows, ironically also named "Dead Canõn." Although the troops were still full of excitement over the day's struggle, some had apprehensions at the prospect of traversing the steep-walled valley. The narrow defile seemingly afforded distinct advantages to Indians who were surely concealed amidst the outcroppings and trees dotting its bluffs. Especially unnerving were thousands of hoof tracks, initially thought to have been those of buffalo, but found to have been made "by the thousands of ponies belonging to the immense force of the enemy here assembled."[25]

The threat of danger from warriors holding strategic positions on high ground quickly became a reality, as fire rang down on the column. A charge by Captain Alexander Sutorius of E Company promptly cleared the ridge. According to Bourke, through the cañon's straight, tapering walls, with the danger of ambush ever present, at the head of the column rode Lieutenant Frederick Schwatka and the reporter John Finerty. Filled with uneasiness, Finerty noted that "some of the more thoughtful officers had their misgivings" about the tight passage. Halting at a cross cañon, they tightened their girths and prepared for what was expected to be a desperate fight. As fate would have it, however, Indian tenacity may have spared Mills's force the tragic fate suffered by Custer's command a week later.

"The Sioux Charging Colonel Royall's Detachment of Cavalry, June 17th."
From *Frank Leslie's Illustrated Newspaper*, August 12, 1876.

Just as they were gearing for the advance, a buckskin-attired trooper galloped in, covered in dust, having made a daring run to reach Mills. Barely recognizable with his long brown beard turned ash gray, Crook's aide-de-camp, Captain Azor Nickerson, carried an urgent order from the general. To the surprise of Mills, Crook ordered Mills to return to the main theatre to support other detachments. The reason for the abrupt recall of Mills's battalion was that Lt. Colonel Royall and four of his companies, which were attempting to attack the Sioux and Cheyenne warriors along Kollmar Creek (a dry tributary of the Rosebud), about one mile west of Crook's position, had themselves become the focal point of action. In an attempt to withdraw to Crook's position, they would be subject to some of the most dangerous and deadly advances of the day by the Cheyenne and Sioux.

With the village supposedly in plain sight, some of Mills's officers pressured him to ignore the order to return and press an attack on the village. "We have the village and can hold it," they implored Mills, but the captain dutifully followed orders. Schwatka and the troops quickly turned about and emerged from the valley through a low side bluff, scrambling through rocks and trees. Orders were given by Mills to "Prepare to mount—mount!" and the soldiers dashed to Crook's assistance with a boisterous cheer. Royall's forces did manage to relieve the pressure on their own, and with timely and spirited support from Shoshone and Crow allies, and the sight of the approaching cavalrymen of Mills's battalion, Sioux and

Cheyenne warriors abruptly and finally retreated from the field.[26]

The Rosebud village, phantom or not, continued to occupy the thoughts of the soldiers assigned to destroy it. Lieutenant Schwatka, in a letter to his father written shortly after the Custer defeat a week later, noted that his column had nearly reached the village before doubling back, and that the Indians had felled trees at the far end of the camp to entrap them. Schwatka described a particularly dangerous situation awaiting the troopers, writing that he had learned that "from 2,000 to 4,000 Indians lined both sides of the cañon. Had we gone one mile farther our battalion of cavalry and one of the Second Cavalry would have suffered the fate that Custer met with six days later when he charged the same village, about twenty miles from our battle-field, on the Little Big Horn River." After Crazy Horse surrendered at Red Cloud Agency in May 1877, the chief played on that thought, informing Crook that at the moment that Crook ordered Mills's forces to cease their attack on the village, 2,000 warriors were hidden along the walls of the cañon poised to attack. Crazy Horse boasted that he could have crushed Mills's forces "as effectually and even more quickly than was Custer's regiment destroyed, and he yet wonders what led the great white chief [Crook] to make that fortunate halt." The notion that there truly was a legion of warriors prepared to prey on Mills's vulnerable battalion, who were for some reason held back from the main theatre, has been largely dispelled. In addition, Schwatka was misinformed about the location of Sitting Bull's village. His men were not bearing down on it through the cañon of the Rosebud. That village sat miles away, well beyond the Rosebud theater of action.[27]

The Battle of the Rosebud was a test of fortitude on both sides. Crook's men suffered nine or ten killed and approximately fifty wounded, mostly in the desperate struggle along the Kollmar Creek. For Schwatka, in the aftermath of the battle, his service was not yet complete. At a makeshift hospital, the medical staff, with his assistance, indefatigably tended the wounded all evening. Curiously, the expedition's medical director, Captain Albert Hartsuff, whose report was exceedingly complimentary of the skills of the medical staff, omitted any mention of Schwatka's name. It certainly was not based on Schwatka's qualifications, since he had graduated from one of the most prestigious medical schools in the country and had sufficient experience to treat or assist in the treatment of many battlefield injuries. Schwatka's service did not pass unnoticed by Lieutenant Bourke, however, who observed that "Doctors Hartsuff, Patzki and Stevens, assisted by Lieut. Schwatka, who has a slight knowledge of therapeutics, have been and are doing all that is possible to ameliorate the condition of the unfortunates under their care."[28]

Hartsuff's omission may have reflected a reality of the underlying makeup of the medical staff. Regular army medical officers were commissioned officers, like their fighting counterparts. They were generally well-qualified and well-trained, and had passed a rigorous examination before an army board of physician examiners. They considered themselves an elite group and, as such, tended to view their subordinates much differently. In contrast to commissioned medical officers, contract physicians were civilians hired for a stated term, with no official rank or opportunity for promotion. They were junior to medical officers, varied in their skills and at times poorly treated. There were, however, many occasions when commissioned medical officers and contract physicians worked well together in the western campaigns. Nonetheless, implicit bias did exist among the various medical staffs in the field. It is certainly possible that in the eyes of the commissioned medical officers, Lieutenant Schwatka stood even further afield than contract physicians. As a line officer, Schwatka's first priority was to fight and inflict injury rather than treat it, and as such he was not considered a member of the medical department. Hartsuff's omission could as easily have been an intentional snub rather than an unintentional slight.[29]

The most senior officer taken down during the engagement was Captain Guy Henry, gravely wounded by a bullet that passed through both his cheeks, breaking his nose and striking his optic nerve. Blinded in one eye, "throwing blood from his mouth by the handful" remarked Finerty, he was said to have continued to give orders for several minutes until collapsing. When Finerty offered condolences to the miraculously surviving Henry several hours later, the gritty officer simply replied, "It is nothing. For this we are soldiers!" He was carted three hundred miles to Fort D. A. Russell where he recovered and served with distinction throughout the Spanish-American War.[30]

Shoshone and Crow scouts, and Sioux and Cheyenne warriors, had also suffered casualties in the engagement. The Indian scouts suffered one dead and about seven or eight wounded; the casualties for the Northern Indians were largely unknown, but easily counted in the dozens. One of the more mournful scenes that touched even the hardened fighters among Crook's men was the funeral rite for a young Shoshone boy killed and scalped in the fighting. Tears poured down the faces of young and old alike. Finerty noted that "I had been led to believe that Indians never yielded to the weakness of tears, but I can assure my readers that the experience of that morning convinced me of my error."[31]

It was obvious that Crook's army had suffered a setback when he withdrew from the field, despite their heroic fighting. Doing so prevented

Crook from joining Terry's command, including Custer's Seventh Cavalry, ahead of their upcoming battle with the Sioux. In a fight that saw gallantry and heroics on both sides, Lieutenant Schwatka distinguished himself at the Rosebud. The report of Lieutenant August C. Paul expressly singled out two men of Company M of the Third Cavalry for special mention: disabled trumpeter Snow, for bravery while wounded, and Lieutenant Frederick Schwatka, who "throughout the entire fight acted very courageously." To his father, Lieutenant Schwatka admitted the reality of the encounter, writing that "we had quite a severe fight on the head of the Rosebud Creek, Montana Territory, with the Sioux and Cheyennes under Sitting Bull and Crazy Horse, numbering about two or three thousand."[32]

Crook quickly fell back to the forks of Goose Creek, in today's Sheridan, Wyoming, to resupply and regroup for the continued campaign against the Northern Indians. A forced calm fell over his forces. Campaign life became a monotonous routine through the month of July. Some men hunted buffalo, elk or bear, some read and reread out-of-date newspapers, and others idled away the time by sketching. As for Schwatka, according to Finerty, he had already set his course for the unknown North: "He [Schwatka] had no love for light literature, and he lay awake nights thinking of the North Pole and Sir John Franklin's bones." The recollection by Finerty, written in 1890, was likely a bit of hindsight. Schwatka may have had thoughts of the North on his mind, but Franklin's bones would not have been utmost. The events giving rise to the Arctic expedition that Schwatka would subsequently lead did not occur until a year later.[33]

Schwatka evidently was not the only scientifically minded soldier. General Crook was an avid hunter, fisherman and amateur naturalist, and would often, to the consternation of his men, ride off to stalk birds and butterflies. A captured prairie owl, dubbed "Sitting Bull," became a mascot for the headquarters detachment. Even more surprising, it was discovered that "Calamity Jane," Martha Jane Canary, desperate for work, had infiltrated the wagon teamsters dressed in male clothing. Her undoing was her profanity, which was less enthusiastic than that evinced by a stage driver, which she also claimed to be. Once her true identity had been revealed, she was arrested and forced to dress in woman's attire. Mills recounted that on the day of her arrest, while he was inspecting the wagon train, Calamity jumped up and shouted "'There is Colonel Mills, he knows me' when everybody began to laugh, much to my astonishment and chagrin, being married." Mills claimed that he had never met the celebrity, but ironically, years later, acknowledged that Calamity had been a cook for his next-door neighbor, Lieutenant John B. Johnson, and presumably ran into Mills frequently.[34]

As fate would have it, several days later, while Crook was stalking bighorn sheep, Mills and Schwatka undertook a hiking trek, scrambling up the northernmost peak of the Big Horn Mountains on a spectacularly clear day that they believed might offer some interesting views. Some thirty-five to forty miles in the distance they spotted smoke on the horizon. Believing it was the aftermath of a military engagement, they immediately advised Crook. It was not until June 30, however, that messengers from General Terry met Mills with news that Custer's immediate command had been killed to a man. Custer had been some thirty miles northwest of the Rosebud battlefield when he decided to advance on the Indian village at Little Big Horn. The outcome was disastrous. When the dispatch was read to the troops, Bourke noted that "the shock was so great that men and officers could hardly speak when the tale slowly circulated from lip to lip." Following Custer's defeat, despite the setback and its impact on the morale of Crook's command, the general was more determined than ever to mount a punitive expedition.[35]

During the lull, Thomas C. MacMillan, twenty-six-year-old correspondent for the *Chicago Inter-Ocean*, whose physical health was not fit for rough life on the trail, returned to civilization, as did several other correspondents travelling with the troops. MacMillan was soon working a more comfortable reporting position during an extended tour of Europe. He spent most of his professional career with the *Inter-Ocean*, with short terms in public office as an Illinois congressman and senator. It was not surprising that correspondents abandoned the campaign. Life on the trail was as hard on reporters as it was on soldiers. As Finerty noted:

> Let no easy-going journalist suppose that an Indian campaign is a picnic. If he goes out on such business he must go prepared to ride his forty or fifty miles a day, go sometimes on half rations, sleep on the ground with small covering, roast, sweat, freeze, and make the acquaintance of such vermin or reptiles as may flourish in the vicinity of his couch; and, finally, be ready to fight Sitting Bull or Satan when trouble begins, for God and the United States hate non-combatants.[36]

Marching with troops was not a new practice among journalists. During the American Civil War, travelling in the field and providing "on-the-spot" reporting had become common, with newspapers eager to meet the public's demand for timely information. All the major dailies employed staff reporters who closely followed the military campaigns and actions of the war. The *New York Herald* had as many as forty correspondents and reporters in the field at a time. War-related news was a hot commodity, especially for first or exclusive reports, and papers were prepared to compensate journalists prepared to assume the risks to ferret it out. Although there was a general spirit of camaraderie among the press corps, each reporter rushed to get the "scoop" for their paper, and exploits of reporters delivering dispatches under difficult circumstances and by extraordinary means became legendary. The intrepid reporting and tactics that had marked the Civil War coverage were applied equally to the Indian wars. Some of those frontier reporters even achieved celebrity status. Henry Morton Stanley, for example, first came to the attention of James Gordon Bennett Jr., manager of the *New York Herald*, with his reporting on the frontier Indian campaigns through dispatches to the *Missouri Democrat* and several other newspapers.[37]

With MacMillan's absence, the door opened for Frederick Schwatka to take a transformative professional step and embark on a career in journalism. Seizing his chance, he eagerly stepped forward to prepare dispatches for the *Inter-Ocean* in MacMillan's stead. For the former newspaper apprentice, nothing could have suited him more. Schwatka had practice before his new *Inter-Ocean* relationship. His somewhat self-serving account of the Battle of the Rosebud, highlighting his contribution, written as a letter to his father, was published in the *Willamette Farmer*, perhaps at his son's behest. We must assume that his superior, Captain Mills, approved of Schwatka's *Inter-Ocean* relationship, and the newspaper would have been thrilled to have a reporter so close to the action.

Schwatka was not the only soldier to assume double duty as a reporter in Crook's campaign. Lieutenant James E. H. Foster, Company I, Third Cavalry, who befriended Schwatka, served as an anonymous correspondent for the *Chicago Tribune* and *New York Daily Graphic*. During the remaining course of the Big Horn and Yellowstone Expedition, Schwatka submitted eight lengthy reports, dating from July 23 to October 22, and each labeled "correspondence" or "special correspondence" to the *Inter-Ocean*, without identification of Schwatka as the author.[38]

Schwatka's writings reflect a combination of campaign reporting and nineteenth-century travelogue. With little time devoted to actual fighting, Schwatka trained his observant eye on the people, places and events surrounding the campaign and delivered a descriptive narrative for an interested armchair audience. Raised on the frontier and driven by a spirit of Manifest Destiny, expansionism and commercial exploitation of the West were self-evident in his mind and common themes in his writings. The varied regions through which his Third Cavalry marched, the valleys of the Rosebud Creek, Tongue and Powder Rivers, the Big Horn

Mountains and Black Hills, were each viewed with an eye towards their potential for settlement and economic prosperity, whether it be through mining, cattle ranching or farming, with an ever present but unwritten thought on how he might make his own fortune.

Examples abound. Under the heading "Tongue River Valley for the Settler," Schwatka wrote that "...the Tongue River valley, where we struck it, is much finer than where we left it sixty miles south of here. Should the Northern Pacific Railroad ever be completed along the Yellowstone, it is perfectly evident that these smaller valleys will soon be occupied with stock ranches and farms, the country offering better facilities for grazing, protection and all other essentials of a stock farm...." In his September 16 communication, he wrote, "...the Little Missouri where we cut it, is, in fact, a beautiful stream, well wooded, with a fine surrounding country, and is no doubt destined to support a considerable population when the Indian question is fairly settled. The next few days marches through this unknown country did not shake our belief in its general fertility, for, to say the least, it will support innumerable herds of stock...." He reported that no "paying" quantities of gold had been found on the eastern slope of the Big Horn Mountains, but prospecting efforts were yielding dividends in Deadwood and its environs, news that certainly attracted the interests of a mineral-crazed public.[39]

Schwatka proved to have a flair for the written word, and his personal interest features delivered lively accounts for his *Inter-Ocean* readership. While idle at Goose Creek, his July 23 letter included an almost biblical sighting of a grasshopper swarm: "myriads of grasshoppers filled the air, appearing like an immense drifting snow-stream, trending towards the southeast." Another missive tells the melancholy tale of a "stray prospector," who had wandered from his mining comrades and was murdered and scalped, his unburied body interred by the Third Cavalry eight months after his death. Schwatka's reporting of the engagements, particularly the subsequent Battle of Slim Buttes, is matter-of-fact, objective, and without the overstatement or embellishment that might be expected from a soldier-turned-war-correspondent. Regarding the commendable conduct of Crook's Crow and Shoshone scouts, Schwatka was not the least bit hesitant to offer credit where it was due, particularly noting that those allies "saved us from a severe surprise in the canons of the Rosebud, at the Battle of the Rosebud Hills." Schwatka's reporting on the campaign painted a clear, unvarnished picture of both the expedition's privations and hardships, as well as the grandeur and prospects of the Big Horn, Yellowstone and Black Hills regions.[40]

Not surprisingly, what stands out prominently in his *Inter-Ocean* communiques, and separates him from his fellow correspondents, are his lengthy observations of Indian culture. Those observations include, among others, an extensive and vivid description of an elaborate scaffold grave of an important Sioux personage killed in the Battle of the Rosebud (visited after the fight), and detailed, graphic descriptions of two important rituals he was privileged to attend: a Shoshone scalp dance and a Sioux Sun Dance. The Sioux grave piqued Schwatka's curiosity as much for its contents as for its construction. He was particularly impressed with the skilled handiwork of a dexterous "housewife" who had fashioned the handsome patchwork blanket that wrapped the body. His Shoshone allies left him little time for examination though. The grave was immediately torn down and desecrated, and the dead man scalped.

Schwatka witnessed the scalp dance following the Rosebud fight as victorious Shoshone scouts returned to camp with two Sioux scalps, yelling war songs from the battlefield in a loud chorus soon taken up by the entire band. The affair failed to arouse the interest of the soldiers or the other correspondents. Upon learning that the boisterous commotion was the anticipated scalp dance, the inquisitive Schwatka, curious to view a ceremony that was "so seldom seen," gained permission to view it as a Shoshone guest in their camp. Schwatka's only companion for the visit was Dr. Charles Stephens, a citizen physician who had accompanied the command.

Schwatka's account of the dance, a ceremony performed mainly by women, follows the customary pattern of the celebration, and captures the Shoshone exuberance associated with victory in battle. The Shoshone warriors were gathered in a tight circle about fifty feet in circumference, two deep in places. Within the circle, five women stood in line, the second and fourth holding the captured scalps attached to long, slender poles which bent from the weight of the scalps. Five warriors stood opposite the women attired in black blankets with their faces blackened. The warriors began to sing the scalp song in a low cadence, slowly increasing and slowly joined in by the spectators, "to a fearful chorus that no pen, nor musical scales, with all its sharps and flats, could dare describe or portray," noted Schwatka. The women approached the warriors, keeping time to the music and the increasing intensity of the song, and lowered the scalps to touch the faces of the warriors. That touching served as a signal; the music abruptly ceased and every warrior in the camp gave the Shoshone war whoop in loud yells. The intoxicating ceremony was repeated multiple times until morning broke.[41]

In contrast to the scalp dance, where the women took a central role, the Sun Dance was a male-oriented ceremony, with many women in the community assisting. Schwatka viewed the spectacular event on location near Chadron Creek in Nebraska in June 1875 (near the site of the present Chadron, Nebraska airport), midway between the Spotted Tail Agency and Red Cloud Agency. The young lieutenant claimed that he was one of the few whites who had ever been privileged to witness it, and his account ran through most of his letter published in the *Inter-Ocean* on September 11, 1876 and was later reworked as an article for *Century Magazine* in 1890. That Schwatka would choose to chronicle an event that occurred more than a year previously displayed an earnest and genuine interest in the Indian ceremonies as well as an enthusiasm for journalism that went above and beyond the expected war-related dispatches.[42]

The ceremony would have been an awe-inspiring event merely by virtue of the sheer numbers involved. Schwatka estimated that some 15,000 Sioux were present over the course of the ten days during which the ceremony was conducted, although never more than 10,000 appeared at any one time. The numbers were quite likely an exaggeration on Schwatka's part, an early trait that would be reflected more frequently in his later writings. Participants included both Brulés from the Spotted Tail Agency and Oglalas from the Red Cloud Agency. Schwatka's account is a factual recital of events he witnessed, with little reference to the dance's religious underpinnings or its importance to the Indian participants. To the Sioux, the Sun Dance is their most important ritual, a spiritual renewal for the purpose of strengthening the ties among the individual and his relatives, the community and the universe, through vows and personal sacrifice. The ritual as witnessed by Schwatka followed traditional practice; it commenced with the selection of a "sun-pole," a thirty-foot cottonwood, selected by the maidens of the group. The selected tree was stripped of its bark and branches, and surrounding trees within 200-300 yards were cut close to the ground. On the following morning, Schwatka watched a group of imposing young warriors in battle-like formation gather a half-mile from the sun-pole on their mounts with rifles and bows and arrows at the ready.[43]

At the moment the sun broke the horizon, an elder gave the signal for a charge upon the sun-pole, and the young men rushed *en mass*, "with war whoops and hideous yells," firing bullets and arrows, in what must have been a chaotic and violent scene. One unfortunate warrior died when he was trampled after falling from his horse. Now, the limbless sun-pole, imbedded with thousands of rounds and arrows, was cut down and transplanted to the center of the dance site, where it was encircled

"The Charge of the Sun-Pole."
Painting by Frederic Remington for Schwatka's *Sun-Dance of the Sioux*.

by two rows of cottonwood poles (the inner ring being slightly higher), creating a sort of amphitheater for the onlookers. Partially covered with blankets, according to Schwatka, it appeared like a circus tent without a top. The diplomatic young cavalryman had won the confidence of a "fine old warrior named Whistling Elk," who invited Schwatka "inside the ring," a favored position that was seldom extended to a white man, Schwatka noted with some pride.[44]

Though music and dance played a significant role in the ceremony over several days, Schwatka offered little perspective as to their meaning or importance, remarking that they were no different from the ordinary songs and dances heard in any village and a mere "side show." On the designated day, young warriors stand facing the sun from an early hour, fists clenched and arms pressed against their chests, dancing and keeping time with their feet to music. Then, in groups of five or six, they advance to the sun-pole where a medicine man prepares them for the most physically demanding dimension of personal sacrifice. In Schwatka's words:

> When the self-imposed victim bares his breast to the medicine-man, the latter takes up from one side of the warrior's breast as

much of the skin and flesh as he can hold between his thumb and first two fingers; a slender knife is then inserted beneath, the cutting edge turned to the breast, and, when withdrawn, a long skewer of polished bone or hard wood is passed through the wound to take its place. Over this is passed an elk-skin thong in a figure of eight style over both ends, and the thong is tied to a long horse-hair lariat that is fastened to the top of the 'sun-pole.' A similar procedure is then gone through with on the opposite breast, this thong also tied to the same lariat and the young brave is ready for his dance. About three to six being thus prepared they commence operations, the whole object being to tear the thongs through the flesh and skin, and free themselves at one time from the 'sun-pole,' and the hated name of 'boys.' With fearful songs he relates how he will slay his enemies in the future, how he will kill buffalo and a thousand other promises to fill the assembled multitude with joy, at the same time with all the fortitude he can muster he bears his weight on his rope to free himself.[45]

The young warriors who endured the piercing ritual were now committed to fulfilling promises to themselves and the broader community, with the sun serving as the source of spiritual strength and power. Schwatka recognized that the sun played a part in the ceremony but offered only the simple remark that the Sun Dance was perhaps dedicated to the sun. Once freed from their lashings, the warriors knelt in silence facing the sun until it set, thus completing the ceremony. Schwatka recognized the event as "the grandest ceremony performed by these tribes," and a spectacular visual experience. He no doubt viewed the tribal ritual through a Victorian-age mindset common to nineteenth-century observers, and he was simply unaware of the full religious scope of the ceremony. In any event, like other white witnesses, particularly those with a military bent, his observations emphasized the ceremony's martial acts and physical harshness, more than its religious underpinnings, characterizing the dance as a "wild and barbarous rite," and the all-important piercing as an "ordeal of self-torture" on the part of the young warriors.[46]

For Schwatka, in his *Inter-Ocean* description, the Sun Dance was a manhood ritual, the young warriors who tore their thongs being freed of "the hated name of boys." Perhaps in hindsight one can fault Schwatka's lack of full comprehension of the nature of the ceremony, but he was a military man, not a trained anthropologist, simply recording an elaborate ceremony. In contrast to his war correspondent peers, however, Schwatka displayed a marked interest in American Indian life and culture, which was plainly evident by the space devoted to those matters and his diligent efforts to gather that information. Finerty, on the other hand, generally held a negative opinion of Indians, and other reporters directed their attention to the campaigns and the soldiers, faithful to their assigned role of war correspondent.[47]

Curiously, one of the few other reporters demonstrating an interest in the Indians was the disparaged Reuben Davenport. Young Davenport was no neophyte to the West and Indian culture, despite the ridicule he endured from his veteran campaign companions. Prior to Crook's summer expedition, Davenport had covered the Newton-Jenney Expedition sent by the U.S. Geological Survey in 1875 to survey the Black Hills to assess its gold potential. More importantly, after the expedition, Davenport made a dangerous and unescorted ride across the Black Hills to interview Chief Spotted Tail. His interview, with the aid of an interpreter, was reported in the *New York Herald* in English and Sioux, possibly a first for the *Herald* or any other newspaper.[48]

The June 1875 Sun Dance ritual that Schwatka had described in his field dispatch for the *Inter-Ocean* in September 1876 was reworked as an even more focused article in the *Century Magazine* in 1890 under the title "The Sun-Dance of the Sioux." *Century* was a widely popular magazine, finely illustrated, that sought to maintain high literary standards for an audience considered to be upscale and educated. Schwatka's *Century* piece, in contrast to his *Inter-Ocean* dispatch, highlighted and even more graphically sensationalized the eye-catching physical aspects of the ceremony for his readership, namely the tumultuous charge of the mounted warriors to the sun pole and the painful ritual of piercing and liberation. A full-page engraving of the thundering sun pole charge based on an oil painting by the highly regarded western artist Frederic Remington added a stunning visual aspect to the article. As but one example of the exaggerated narration of the corporeal aspects, the act of breaking free of the skewers was "generally accomplished in about half an hour" in the *Inter-Ocean* account but in *Century Magazine* that painful experience drags on far longer: "generally in two or three hours the victim is freed, but there are many cases where double or even triple that time is required." No doubt Schwatka sought to capture the attention and tug on the emotions of his readership with the more sensational copy. Certain aspects of the ritual identified by Schwatka in the *Inter-Ocean* dispatch were downplayed or omitted. For example, the all-important vows made by the tormented warriors, so central to the purpose of the ceremony, were omitted, and even Schwatka's own characterization of the symbolic purpose as a manhood passage was removed.

Scientific experts could be quick to find fault with Schwatka's writings. The anthropologist Alice Cunningham Fletcher, who made exhaustive studies of music, songs and rituals of the Plains Indians and critiqued Schwatka's *Century Magazine* version, opined that Schwatka's nonrecognition of the ceremony's religious character would have been a "fatal omission" in the eyes of the Sioux. As a vivid account of the ritual though, Schwatka's narrative in *Century Magazine* introduced the ceremony to a large audience and it remains a frequently quoted nineteenth-century description of the ceremony.[49]

Schwatka was never one to be deterred by his critics, and he relished his unique role as the fighting correspondent. Over the next two months, he would have more than enough fodder for his active pen.

CHAPTER FOUR
THE BATTLE OF SLIM BUTTES

> And thus when shades of evening fell
> The scene was calm and still.
> And Crook, he whispered, "all is well
> Since Burt has gained the hill.
> Our men will have their fill to-night;
> 'Tis just as heaven wills,
> All honor Crawford, boy, to you,
> To Schwatka, Bubb, and Mills."
>
> *- Jack Crawford*[1]

WHILE A SHOCKED NATION was still reeling from the news of the Custer defeat, Brigadier General Crook looked to shore up his own demoralized forces to improve his fighting capability against a numerous and determined foe. By August 3, 1876, his men had been reinforced by additional infantry companies—ten companies from Colonel Wesley Merritt's Fifth Cavalry, and several hundred Shoshone scouts—putting his total contingent at about 2,200. At the same time, Sherman had ordered the military to take control of the Sioux agencies to prevent sympathetic Indians from joining the northern camp. On his march to Crook, Merritt had intercepted several hundred Cheyenne warriors who had fled the Red Cloud Agency to join their companions, but Merritt managed to return them.[2]

Wasting little time, on August 5, Crook's reinvigorated Big Horn and Yellowstone Expedition immediately broke camp and headed for the Yellowstone, where General Terry's forces had withdrawn after Custer's defeat. Crook was a competent frontier fighter, among the best serving in the army. He understood that travelling light would be the only means of overtaking the Sioux, but this strategy almost backfired. In addition to the clothes on his back, each man carried an overcoat, a blanket, a poncho, four days' rations, eating utensils, and one hundred rounds of ammunition. A mule train carried another fourteen days' rations and one hundred and fifty rounds of ammunition per man. During the next six weeks, the men would ride or trudge more than eight hundred miles under constantly changing weather conditions. Bright sunny days could quickly transform into extended periods of rain, sleet and snow. The poor horses suffered severely, and as a result some eventually became food sources for the troops. Even before the column started, Finerty noted that the horses of the Second Cavalry and Third Cavalry, like most others, had had no grain since June and fully one-third "looked well fitted for the boneyard."[3]

The defiant Crook pressed north in his pursuit of Sitting Bull. On their way, his forces reached the Rosebud, camping eight miles downstream from the location of the heated engagement on June 17. According to Schwatka as *Inter-Ocean* correspondent, Crook's scouts could not resist a detour to the location of the now legendary village that Mills had been tasked to charge on that day. Having reached the village, as if to confirm the truth of their earlier reporting, the scouts remarked that the immense number of bare spots where lodges once stood confirmed "that [the village] must have contained a great many warriors." About a mile upriver, they found what was believed to be felled timber for the protection of the village. A mile further, they located the point at which Mills's battalion was ordered to turn away from the village on June 17, leading Schwatka to remark that "many conjectures naturally arise among us as to what would have been the fate of that cavalry charge had only that one mile been traversed."[4]

Crook's force finally met Terry's on August 11 farther down the Rosebud. The two forces travelled together to the Yellowstone and obtained limited supplies from the steamer *Far West*. On August 26 the forces once again separated. Shortly thereafter, sizing up the condition of his overtaxed command, a discouraged Crook was forced to concede that overtaking Sitting Bull was all but futile. He ordered a move two hundred miles southeast to Deadwood, both to resupply and to offer protection to mining camps in the area that he feared might suffer depredations at the hands of the Indians. As an eyewitness to the state of their condition, Finerty wrote that "so ragged, filthy, forlorn-looking a set of men as the soldiers of Crook's expedition I have never beheld."[5]

By September 5, there were but two and one-half days rations for each man for what would become a ten-day journey, leading to what has been called the "Starvation March" or "Horsemeat March." Many horses and mules had already begun to play out, simply dropping dead in their tracks as they plodded along. Pistol shots rang out as men mercifully shot suffering animals at Crook's order. The unnerving gunfire and death toll left a ghastly pall over the command. Davenport reported their situation as "a race against the lean, lank legs of starvation, with the odds against us." As many as two to three hundred cavalrymen without mounts were now reduced to walking along the flanks. To make matters worse, what remained of the rations ran out completely on September 7 during a downpour that seemed to have no end. Even the hardiest of soldiers were flagging.[6]

With nothing to eat aside from horse or mule, the troops started cutting steaks from the dead animals, killing as many each day as was necessary. Some men also split cacti for nourishment, suffering terribly from dysentery as a result. Morale was understandably low. Mills later remarked that "the men were about ready to mutiny." In a letter to his father, Lieutenant Walter S. Schuyler, aide to Crook, described his experience, "I saw men who were very plucky just sit down and cry like children because they could not hold out." Desperate to obtain food and supplies, Crook ordered one hundred and fifty "picked" men from the Third Cavalry under Captain Mills to make a desperate dash for the Black Hills' settlements with the best horses and sixty pack mules to rush back with provisions for the famished troops. With Mills were his officers, Lieutenants John W. Bubb, George F. Chase, Emmet Crawford, Adolphus H. Von Luettwitz, and Frederick Schwatka, the latter appointed adjutant to the detachment. The trek was considered particularly hazardous as large concentrations of Indians were known to be in the area.[7]

On the night of the September 7, Mills pushed his troopers hard, travelling through a raging rainstorm. Setting out again the next morning at 4:00 A.M., after only a few hours rest, they groped their way through a blanketing fog. That afternoon Frank Grouard, while scouting ahead, observed a number of ponies in the distance, a sure sign of a village in the vicinity. The village was below the heights known as Slim Buttes, named for the massive limestone and clay outcroppings towering almost perpendicularly hundreds of feet above the surrounding landscape of rolling prairie and scattered pines. In Finerty's opinion, the stunning geologic feature resembled an array of mammoth Norman castles. Indian lodges were pitched across the grassy bottomland astride what is known today as Gap Creek, at a junction of several smaller creeks. Sadly, the picturesque location would be the site of one of the most brutal confrontations of the Great Sioux War.[8]

While Mills and the soldiers secreted themselves and their horses in a nearby cañon about three miles from the village, Grouard crept forward to assess its size and exact location. In an interview years later, Mills recalled that Grouard initially refused to approach the village. This compelled Mills to join him, but together they could not get close enough to obtain an accurate count. The following morning, again scouting the village, Grouard returned with no helpful information. He did, however, return with a fresh horse he had corralled, by which Mills suspected he planned to make an escape if the situation took a turn for the worse. Mills had nothing but respect for Grouard's scouting abilities, but as to his character, Mills remarked that "I always regarded him as a coward and a big liar." In his autobiography, while referencing the village and his plans, Mills bluntly stated that "I did not know its strength, but was willing to take my chances in view of General Crook's positive orders," which Mills understood to mean to attack any hostile encampment encountered. Not surprisingly, the idea of attacking the village when its strength was unknown caused a high degree of apprehension among the soldiers. Davenport noted that there "was an anticipation of another disaster like that which befell Custer and his gallant Seventh," and Schwatka, who would be the first to enter the camp, would later echo that sentiment.[9]

Unknown to Mills at the time, the village was comprised of Indians of several bands, including Minneconjou, Oglala, Brulé, and Cheyenne. Many of these Indians were followers of the Minneconjou Iron Plume who were heading for Red Cloud Agency, having separating from Crazy Horse and Sitting Bull after the battle with Custer's Seventh Cavalry. After conferring with his lieutenants, Schwatka, Crawford and Bubb, Mills strongly pushed a plan of attack on the camp at dawn, even though he was still unsure of its size. Mills impressed upon his men the obvious fact that they would likely be spotted at daybreak in any event. With their reduced force and badly weakened mounts, Mills argued forcefully that they would surely be at risk in the inevitable engagement. His officers grudgingly agreed, no doubt with the Custer disaster still on their minds. Although a surprise attack at daybreak could be an effective strategy for overwhelming and destroying an unsuspecting enemy, when unleashed on a slumbering village, its indiscriminate nature could also inflict serious injury and death not only on combatants, but on women and children.[10]

Mills's plan was to have Lieutenant Emmet Crawford advance quietly from the north and slightly east of the village with fifty-three men, dismounted, with Lieutenant Von Luettwitz starting from the south and east with fifty-seven men, also dismounted. Mills selected Lieutenant Schwatka to perform the most dangerous task. He was to take twenty-five men, mounted, to stampede the Indian horses and then charge through the village yelling and firing revolvers to cause panic among the 200 or so inhabitants. Both Crawford's and Von Luettwitz's troops would follow Schwatka's charge and fire at the surprised and panicked occupants. To reduce the chances of a noisy distraction alerting the Indians, Lieutenant Bubb, with the remaining soldiers, pack mules and horses, would remain concealed in the rear, about a mile back from the village, until after the shooting began.

Mills and his men passed a miserable evening in a cold misty rain, nibbling on stale hardbread and a few bacon strips and sleeping on a layer of thick mud under wet blankets. According to Davenport, the small fires glowing in the heavy mist created a sublime setting in the gorge, producing "grotesque and unreal effects," and a troubled sleep for a group of already uneasy soldiers. For Schwatka, with the pressing thought of leading the charge, sleep was not his foremost consideration. A range of emotions rushed through his mind, a combination of fear of the unknown, mixed with a zest for personal glory. At about 2:00 A.M., during the uncomfortable night ("one of the ugliest I ever passed" according to Mills), his troops were formed into the three groups.[11]

In the field, plans seldom go off exactly as expected even under the best of circumstances, and the attack on the village at Slim Buttes was no exception. Considerable time was spent putting gear, weapons and ammunition in order, saddling the horses, and leading them slowly over muddy ground in the intense darkness. After some difficulty spotting the Indian ponies, the troops crossed a small creek and took a position on a ridge several hundred yards from the camp. At dawn, Schwatka and his men finally mounted and readied themselves to storm the village. As he prepared to face an uncertain enemy, Schwatka knew this was his moment to make a mark for himself. As his mounts approached to within seventy yards, however, the Indian ponies, sensing the intruders, broke and began stampeding through the camp. With the element of surprise now totally lost, the order to commence a charge was quickly given. Mills later recorded in his official report that "right gallantly did Schwatka with his twenty-five men execute it."[12] From here, we give Schwatka's spirited first-hand account of the charge, as written in a letter to his father:

> Just as we approached the crest of the bluff overlooking the village a small herd of ponies stampeded into it, and as for our plans nothing was left but for me to charge, and yelling at my men to draw pistols and charge, in I went. I must say that I felt a trifle uncertain as to what I might expect, for we knew nothing whatever of the size of the village and had been following the

trail four days before, of from 2,000 to 3,000 lodges that had split up, and probably the village ahead of me was the concentration of this splitting that Custer had so unluckily dashed into, two marches before on the Little Big Horn. There wasn't time for any great amount of reflection, however, and I was soon right into the village with my men, yelling and firing pistols smack into their lodges. The day and night had been very rainy and they had tied their lodges so closely that to untie them was not assisted by my charge. In fact, when broad daylight left us in charge of the village, we found nearly every lodge had been ripped open by knives to assist in their exit. I found but little trouble in getting away with their herd of 200 ponies and horses; for when twenty-five cavalry men make up their minds to create a fearful din, I will not hesitate to pronounce it the most perfect success on record.[13]

Schwatka was not only a key participant in the action; he also had the privilege of penning an account for the public as special correspondent for the *Chicago Inter-Ocean*. His dispatch offered a more modest account of the charge, omitting the reference to himself: "The mounted party, pistols in hand, yelling and firing into tepees, rushed through the little town and soon depopulated it of ponies, and gave the human population such a morning reveille as they did not have to awaken them at every daylight. The dismounted men followed up the mounted charge rapidly with a deadly fusillade into the village."[14]

As Schwatka charged through the camp with guns blazing, some of the thirty-seven lodges were knocked down and trampled. The dismounted soldiers closed on the camp and fired, while the warriors who had managed to cut their way out of their lodges returned fire. In the rushed commencement of the charge, Lieutenant Von Luettwitz could not complete his flanking maneuver from the southeast, and fleeing Indian women managed to hustle the dead, wounded and children across the stream and up the nearby bluffs to the south and west. In the meantime, Schwatka rounded up the better part of the horses after he had passed through the camp, with some falling back into the hands of the Indians. Most of the Sioux warriors had by now regrouped in the bluffs and maintained a steady fire upon any exposed soldier within the proximity of the camp.[15]

The charge by Schwatka on the village of unknown size was itself a daring act that took raw courage, but it was not his final valorous act. According to Davenport, who was present at the scene, Lieutenants Schwatka and Crawford "made repeated charges which drove the Sioux

"Lt. Schwatka's Charge at Slim Buttes."
Painting by Charles Schreyvogel.

from those points from which their fire was annoying. They both made rapid explorations of the hills to gather up stray ponies so that they should not be secured by the Indians. In these they had many pistol encounters with the Indians and forced them to retire repeatedly. The gallantry displayed by both of these officers was splendid." Jack Crawford, the so-called "Poet Scout of the Black Hills," and daring correspondent for the *Omaha Bee*, also recorded that he, Schwatka, and several soldiers dug field entrenchments in the face of a steady fusillade to provide cover for the wounded and the pack train which had advanced toward the village. The spadework was carried on at considerable personal risk. One soldier, Private James Quinn, Company E, Third Cavalry, was later awarded a Certificate of Merit by President Hayes at Schwatka's behest for his bravery in building the breastworks under the heavy fire and for his charge on the village.[16]

Mills quickly sent word by courier to Crook, who was some twenty miles distant, to immediately forward reinforcements. Word reached Crook by 9:00 A.M. Fearful that Mills would run short of ammunition, Crook quickly sent one hundred men from the Third Cavalry mounted on the best remaining horses, while he followed with the balance of the command. Although the majority of the warriors had regrouped on the bluffs after the initial charge by Schwatka, a small band of some twenty-five Indians, led by Iron Plume, had sought refuge in a deep ravine west of the camp. That group comprised a number of women and children who had also scampered into the ravine, including several wives of the chiefs. Ironically, the ravine had formerly been a playground for the children. Within that gorge, the entrance to which was sheltered by thick underbrush, the Indians had hastily thrown up dirt breastworks, using their bare hands and knives. The defenders were emboldened by the expectation that Crazy Horse, encamped with numerous warriors nearby, would soon arrive to turn the tide. Attempts made by Mills to dislodge the Indians from their formidable defensive position were unavailing, and his own troops began to suffer casualties during the attempt. With the arrival of Crook's column, a renewed attempt with greater force was made to break the stalemate. Crook positioned infantry and dismounted cavalry around the crevasse and opened up a steady wall of fire, the reports of their weapons reverberating loudly throughout the surrounding buttes.

As the Sioux took casualties, frightened women began to sing death chants and children were heard crying loudly, causing even the hard-nosed fighter Crook to declare a ceasefire. According to Finerty, before their wailing cries were heard, Crook, the disciplined soldier that he was, had no knowledge that the women and children had taken refuge in the ravine. Two scouts cautiously approached the ravine to coax the defenders to exit with the assurance of safety if they surrendered. The offer was taken up by one warrior, and some twelve women and seven children. All of them emerged shell-shocked and covered in dirt and blood, and most were met by Crook himself. One woman carried a dead child; another woman with a child strapped to her back was so traumatized that she refused to release Crook's hand. Despite any remaining women and children, the barrages then commenced again, continuing on for two more hours. A withering torrent of some 3,000 rounds poured into the gorge. Mercifully, in a break in the shooting, communication was established with the defenders, and a captive Indian woman managed to persuade one warrior to surrender, with assurances from Crook that the lives of the remaining fighters would be spared if they too surrendered.[17]

After further dialogue, the Minneconjou leader, Iron Plume, offered to surrender. Slowly the great chief emerged from the ravine, supported by another warrior. He was seventy-six-years old, but Finerty saw "a fine looking, broad-chested Sioux, with a handsome face and a neck like a bull." Within moments, Iron Plume summoned the two remaining warriors from the ravine. Iron Plume had suffered a painful wound; he held his protruding intestines in his hands. Crook's surgeon could do nothing for him, and he died several hours later without uttering as much as a moan.[18]

The fighting was not yet over. Chief Crazy Horse had responded to the plea for assistance, arriving with an additional 500 to 600 fighters. The warriors took positions largely among the buttes south and west of the camp and poured a rain of fire on Crook's troops. After taking precautions to protect the pack mules and horses, including the captured Indian herd, Crook disbursed his forces to meet the warriors. Slowly, in a wall of fire, Crook's soldiers worked up the slopes of the buttes, pushing the attackers back. A blanket of smoke hung over the area as both sides exchanged heavy fire, the loud reports creating an eerie rumble across the buttes. Although one attempt was made to break through the Third Cavalry line to the southwest, it was repulsed, and the Sioux retreated.[19]

In the overall engagement, Crook's men suffered three killed and some twenty-seven wounded; Indian casualties were not tallied but were undoubtedly heavier. One of the first soldier casualties was Lieutenant Von Luettwitz, who was shot through the knee at the commencement of the fight and collapsed into the arms of Mills. A career officer who had fought in the Prussian and Austrian armies and had survived the carnage of Gettysburg and other Civil War engagements without serious injury, he lost a leg by amputation at Slim Buttes. Most other deaths and injuries occurred while attempting to take the ravine. One such casualty was the respected scout Charley White, aka "Buffalo Chip," who, while attempting to sneak a shot into the gorge, was shot through the heart, holding on long enough to utter "My God, my God, boys, I'm done for this time!" before falling dead. Among the Indian deaths were at least one baby and three women killed in the ravine, several of whom had been ghastly mutilated by the barrage of fire that left the ravine a blood-soaked pit. In a particularly heartrending scene, an orphaned child brought to view the captives and the dead ran screaming to her mother, one of the dead Indians. In another dastardly and grisly act, unknown to Crook and the officers, a friendly Indian, "Ute John" and several soldiers, scalped some of the dead Indians, an act in Finerty's words, that was an "exhibition of human depravity [that] was nauseating."[20]

Mills succeeded in capturing a cornucopia of supplies—two-days' rations of dried meat and fruit, some fresh game, a large number of blankets, and some ammunition and arms—as well as about 175 ponies. In the midst of the carnage in the aftermath of the battle, the ravenous soldiers wasted no time in devouring the foodstuffs. A slight albeit minor feeling of retribution overcame the soldiers as among the trophies captured by Mills were souvenirs from Custer's fight: A Seventh Cavalry

Buckskin lodge, Sioux prisoners, Seventh Cavalry guidon captured at Slim Buttes. Lt. Schwatka is seated to the right, scout Frank Grouard is seated to the far left.

guidon, a glove belonging to Captain Myles W. Keogh of the ill-fated cavalry, several Seventh Cavalry saddles, a letter to a Seventh Cavalry private, and, somewhat surprisingly, several hundred dollars in cash. In recognition of his capture of the village, Mills retained an unusual souvenir, Iron Plume's lodge.[21]

Crook's exploits were not complete. His men and horses were still starving, some were injured, and all still desperately needed to reach Deadwood, not only for supplies and medical attention but for shelter. Aside from the poor weather, the men were showing signs of scurvy, that bane of sailors, a disease that could plague soldiers as well, particularly at western frontier outposts and during prolonged campaigns. Antiscorbutics like fresh fruit and vegetables did not travel well and outposts often failed to receive adequate quantities.[22]

Their departure from the battlefield was not without incident, as the warriors maintained a steady rearguard fire during the morning of September 10. The action was only halted by a determined response by the Fifth Cavalry, which suffered two men wounded. The same day, an

Officers of the Third Cavalry. Lt. Schwatka on the far right, Capt. Mills to Schwatka's lower right, and Lt. Augustus Paul to Mills's right.

early halt was made after fifteen miles over concerns as to the health of the injured men suffering from the rough trail and incessant rain. The injured were transported on litters pulled by mule teams, and they suffered badly from the carriage. Crook generously turned over the remaining dried foods to the invalids and the healthy were left to once again survive on horse and mule steaks.

A ghastly incident only added to the gloomy specter overshadowing the march and spoke to the emotional strain of the battle. Lieutenant Von Luettwitz had a vision of his amputated leg being unearthed and mutilated by the Indians. Coincidentally, a detachment sent back to Slim Buttes found that the graves of dead soldiers had been despoiled. On September 11, desperate for relief, Crook again sent Mills with fifty mounted men, including Schwatka, to make a dash for Deadwood to gather much needed supplies, while the main command struggled on in the cold, unrelenting rain.

The march on September 12 was, according to Bourke, one that "will always occupy a niche in my memory as the severest and most discouraging ever made." Schwatka echoed a similar sentiment when he wrote for the *Inter-Ocean* that "the march of the 12th was one long to be remembered in the sufferings of the American soldiery." The column endured a "long, long" march of thirty-five miles over alkali flats, in sheets of rain with no ponchos, with only horsemeat for sustenance, which in some cases was devoured raw by the starving men. Surviving horses sank in the mud, and men soaked to the skin had their boots stuck in the quagmire. A total of seventy horses dropped dead by the wayside.[23]

The injured suffered worst of all. As the travois mules struggled, the frantic animals tossed the wounded men, sending them screaming and writhing in pain. Through it all though, foot soldiers could find a little humor, wisecracking that "if [the infantry] only marched far enough they would eat all the cavalry horses." The procession stretched for miles as the stronger men trudged on and reached camp first, while stragglers fell in over the next twelve hours, with some so weary they did not arrive until the next morning. Schwatka noted in a rather prophetic statement that "many a man slept awful that night, as if he were but a drunkard in the slums of a city, prostrate on the wet ground." Another seven-mile march the next day finally brought them relief when the sound of wagons reached their ears. The supply train organized by Mills had arrived with fresh meat and vegetables. Having lived for more than a week on horsemeat, sagging spirits were immediately lifted as the ravenous men fell upon the boxes of food. A relieved Schwatka wrote that "the succor was like heaven itself to the starved command." From there the remaining thirty-two miles to Deadwood were made under better circumstances, with eager food purveyors from Deadwood riding out to satisfy a highly receptive audience in what became a circus-like atmosphere.[24]

The Battle of Slim Buttes represented the first victory for the U.S. Army following the defeat of Custer and the Seventh Cavalry at the Little Big Horn. It was also a moral victory, so it was hyped by the press. All the same, the victory involved the use of harsh and indiscriminate tactics that killed and wounded both warriors and non-combatants. For his part in the engagement, Schwatka achieved a modicum of acclaim. Finerty wrote that "Schwatka did his work in a thorough manner, and made a mark of which he may well be proud." The correspondent Jack Crawford, in a letter published in the *New York Herald*, remarked that "Lieutenants Crawford and Schwatkee [sic] deserve great credit for dashing charges and cool bravery." In his official report, Mills recommended the four officers in charge of the detachment for brevets, noting that:

> It is usual for commanding officers to call special attention to

acts of distinguished courage, and I trust the extraordinary circumstances of calling on 125 men to attack, in the darkness, and in the wilderness, and on the heels of the late appalling disasters to their comrades, a village of unknown strength, and in the gallant manner in which they executed everything required of them to my entire satisfaction will warrant me in recommending for brevet Lieutenants Bubb, Crawford, Von Luettwitz and Schwatka....[25]

An *Inter-Ocean* editor gave Schwatka more credit than Schwatka's own modest reporting of his actions as an unnamed "special correspondent." The *Inter-Ocean* reported that "our correspondent in the field with General Crook, his party under Colonel Mills, of the Third Cavalry, attacked and carried the village of American Horse's band, and killed the chief. It was in this fight that our correspondent 'corralled' 200 Indian ponies and held them against great odds, as his detachment was repeatedly assaulted by the Sioux...." For Lieutenant Schwatka, he had won the personal recognition and congratulations that he had so dearly sought. That brief glimpse of fame was a heady stimulant that left him desirous of more.[26]

But there was a darker side to the victory. The Indian wars could be particularly unpleasant and vicious affairs on both sides. The Battle of Slim Buttes, in particular, left a profound emotional mark upon its participants, even if they had not been physically wounded. Later in life, it was not uncommon for the participants to refuse to discuss the engagement, or if they did, to express remorse. The harshness and brutality left its own mark on Frederick Schwatka as well. Campaign correspondent Reuben Briggs Davenport, in a piece written after Schwatka's untimely and tragic death, remarked that the depravity of the 1876 campaign undermined Schwatka's sympathetic heart and genial personality and led to a depression that troubled Schwatka considerably later in life and led to his early death.[27]

Although better understood today, the stresses and hardships of combat have always been known to take their toll psychologically, as well as physically. Whether Schwatka suffered from post-traumatic stress disorder (PTSD), as we call it today, would be speculating. Certainly, Schwatka's psyche could have suffered from the strains of frontier service, negatively affecting his temperament and personality. The condition may have triggered self-destructive coping mechanisms as well, such as heavy drinking. Davenport's observation perhaps uncovered a hidden truth that may shed some light on Schwatka's progressively disconcerting conduct over the course of his life and offers some explanation as to how such a talented man could be so troubled.

Davenport had his own difficulties during and after the campaign. His published criticisms of the management of the campaign had irked both soldiers and officers. One of his most serious criticisms was the statement in the *New York Herald* that Captain Mills had considered a withdrawal from the field in the midst of the engagement. In response, Schwatka and two other officers were quick to publish refutations of Davenport's criticism of their superior's conduct. In a letter to the editor of the *Army and Navy Journal*, under the heading "A Munchausen Reporter Corrected," they responded that "these allegations are utterly without foundation in fact." Davenport later withdrew the allegation and apologized to Mills.[28]

Yet, the animosity towards Davenport continued unabated. Years later, in 1890, Davenport threatened a libel suit against Captain Charles King of the Fifth Cavalry. King, in his own memoirs, had labeled Davenport "a desperate coward" during the Big Horn and Yellowstone Expedition, specifically calling out Davenport's alleged fainthearted conduct at Slim Buttes. Davenport may have had personality flaws, but battlefield cowardice was not one of them. Throughout the campaign, the *Herald* reporter rode and stood side by side with the soldiers in the midst of harsh fighting and placed himself at serious risk of injury or death in his news gathering efforts. So outraged was Davenport that he requested Schwatka to offer a testimonial on his behalf as he marshalled others to support his position. One might have expected Schwatka to be inclined to back up his messmate King, a fellow officer. To Schwatka's credit, in support of Davenport, Schwatka took up his pen and offered a strong rebuttal against the claim of cowardice, which was forwarded by Davenport to the *Army and Navy Journal* for publication: "There was such a handful of white men in the Slim Buttes fight pitted against the villages of Roman Nose and American Horse that no one on our side could have acted with ordinary or even assumptive cowardice without having it known to all." Schwatka's response struck a conciliatory tone as well though, and offered an amicable solution, remarking that King was "an unqualified gentleman," and if advised of this inadvertent slip, he would "gladly right any wrong."[29]

King heeded Schwatka's advice. An unreserved apology was published by King in the *Army and Navy Journal* and in revised editions of his memoirs. Davenport would serve in various publishing roles for the balance of his life and authored several books. At the time of the libel threat, he was publisher and editor of the New Haven *Morning News*. Perhaps seeking an escape from a hypercritical earthly world, his investigative talents turned to the reputed clairvoyant powers of the spirit-rapping Fox sisters, one of whom, Maggie Fox, had been betrothed to the Arctic explorer Elisha Kent Kane. The feisty reporter's work, *The Death-Blow to Spiritualism*, debunked the Fox sisters' supernatural powers, at least to those who may have actually believed in them.[30]

Crook's forces finally reached Deadwood on September 15, to the welcome cheer of townsfolk and miners, exuberant to be at least momentarily relieved from the fear of Indian raids or assault. For days, the elated citizenry celebrated with dances, bonfires and drinking. The Starvation March has come to be remembered as one of the most difficult ordeals of any combat unit. In January 1877, Private Thomas Lloyd, Troop E, Third Cavalry, recalling the dreadful experience for his cousin, wrote:

> I don't mind the fighting part, but the hardships we had to go through and starvation. You would likely think it rather hard to sit down and eat horse meat for your dinner at home; where you would have plenty of bread and other articles with it, would you not? But, what do you think of me and everybody else there; as soon as you would get to camp, shoot an old sore back mule, so poor that he could hardly walk; take your butcher knife, cut as nice a slice as you could get and eat it raw. No salt, pepper nor anything at all, live on it alone for 8 days and travel from 20 to 40 miles a day. Well if ever you will experience it (that I hope you never will) you will know what it is.[31]

The campaign's deprivations of the preceding weeks were now behind them, as they celebrated and recuperated from their ordeal. Deadwood certainly had its respectable citizens, but it was a classic mining town with a main street replete with bars, gambling halls, seedy hotels, theaters, harlots and, according to Finerty, "other moral abominations." Some five thousand persons lived in the town and its environs in everything from log cabins, canvas tents and even the side banks of its streams. Those who were not involved in hunting for gold were conniving to steal it from those who did. For a time, gold dust had served as the settlement's currency. The town was almost as dangerous as the Indian campaign. Schwatka claimed that six people were killed in the seven days he was there. Only one month before, the gunman "Wild Bill" Hickok had been shot in the back by Jack McCall in a saloon and was buried above Whitewood Creek. Years later, Schwatka confessed as to his own misbehavior. One evening, still ravenous for food, he and a group of hungry men broke into the rear of a closed restaurant "to feast for some time on pickled pig's feet, the only thing ready for eating found in the place."[32]

That fall the components of the Big Horn and Yellowstone Expedition returned to their respective stations. Captain Mills and his Third Cavalry company returned to routine duty at Camp Sheridan. For Schwatka, the demands of the campaign behind him, he could look forward to a somewhat restful stay. At Camp Sheridan, it was a time to re-establish earlier friendships. Upon Mills's arrival, Chief Spotted Tail held a large "dog feast" in honor of Mills's wife, "Nannie," another of the chief's friends from prior acquaintance at the small post. The chief was not offended when Nannie hesitated to taste the main course, a decision she claimed she later regretted. Lieutenant Schwatka, a guest at the event, had an iron stomach and could tolerate just about any dish. In later years, he boasted that he had "eaten everything from beaver's tail to moose's tail; from warmed-over walrus hide to a ragout of rattlesnake." Although dog was generally no exception, the one meal he did pass on was the canine fare at Camp Sheridan. According to Schwatka, his friend, Minneconjou Sioux chief Touch-the-Clouds "had sacrificed an old mesozoic mongrel, boiled it for a day or two in a weak molasses water and then sprinkled it with sugar to serve as dessert."[33]

Returning the gesture, a more elaborate dinner was hosted for Spotted Tail by Mills at his Camp Sheridan lodging to which several leading chiefs were invited. Also present at the dinner was a visiting Sister of Charity from Kansas, as was Lieutenant Schwatka. The lieutenant was a polished guest at these events, who could contribute his own genial humor and hold polite conversation in any crowd. The highlight of the evening was Chief Spotted Tail, in full dress, dancing with the nun in her customary robe. So struck was the sister with the chief's daughter, Red Road, that Mills asked the chief if the daughter would like to return to the sister's convent in Kansas. The chief heartily agreed. But love was too strong a potion, and Red Road, fearing she would be separated from her lover, Lone Elk, eloped with the warrior the evening before her expected departure for Kansas. Nonetheless, relations among the officers and the Indians were generally friendly and Mills and his staff worked hard to maintain that rapport. Spotted Tail was a frequent guest at Camp Sheridan, often accompanied by lesser chiefs. Frederick Schwatka stationed at Camp Sheridan, as well as his counterpart John Gregory Bourke stationed at Camp Robinson, understood and appreciated the unique vantage point from which they could observe, and immerse themselves within, a rich Indian culture. According to Bourke, "Indian life was not only before us and on all sides of us, but we had also insensibly and unconsciously become part of it."[34]

Lieutenants Schwatka and Bourke epitomized the "soldier-scientists" of the nineteenth century, educated fighting men whose inquisitive nature led them to pursue a range of intellectual interests while serving within the military establishment. Open-minded enough to look beyond their primary soldiering roles, Bourke and Schwatka developed a respect for the American Indians they encountered. Despite confronting them at various times on the field of battle, they did not view their counterparts as mere impediments to westward expansion. Bourke was an 1869 graduate of the U.S. Military Academy and served his entire professional career in the Third Cavalry. For much of that time, he served as aide to Crook, who encouraged and permitted Bourke the freedom to pursue his personal interest in Indigenous peoples. Recruited by John Wesley Powell to assist the Bureau of Ethnology in the growing field of ethnography, Bourke continued his anthropological work until his death in 1896. During that time, his extensive studies and writings made major contributions in American Indian life and culture, and through Bourke the Indians had an ardent supporter.[35]

There was a special camaraderie between these two nonconformist soldiers that reveals itself in Bourke's diaries. Bourke clearly found Schwatka an intriguing character, a marked contrast to the typical frontier soldier, intellectually minded and inquisitive like Bourke, but also unconventional in an amusing manner. Those eccentricities made a lasting impression on Bourke, and he penned them in some detail in his diary. For example, he confirmed that cadet Schwatka did indeed report for duty at the U.S. Military Academy in the oppressive mid-summer heat wearing a fur hat and long tailcoat as had been reported by Schwatka's classmate Frederick Dent Grant. Bourke amusingly noted that Schwatka's fondness towards animals led him to maintain a menagerie of sorts while he occupied a large building at Spotted Tail Agency, complete with an owl, a pair of coyotes, a pair of wild cats, and several deer. Lieutenant William P. Clark, Second Cavalry, who had bunked there after a night of heavy drinking, was roughly greeted by a number of these denizens when he arose in the dark for a glass of water. Bourke was even amused by Schwatka's small peculiarities, like his calling card which was made of wood with his name scrawled in lead pencil. Notwithstanding Schwatka's jocular persona and despite his troubles with drink, Bourke admired him, and would later write with a strong sense of pride of his "bold courage" during his celebrated Arctic journey of 1878-80. About his fellow officer Frederick Schwatka, Bourke astutely noted that "he is very brave, very erratic, good-natured and hospitable, a hard drinker and very witty and intellectual."[36]

Likewise, Schwatka was clearly impressed with Bourke's assiduous attention to Indian culture and the wealth of ethnological material he had gathered. When Schwatka pitched his own Apache article to *Century*

Magazine, he stressed to *Century's* editor that the value of his article was its originality, as very little had been written about the tribe. In that regard, Schwatka added that his messmate John Gregory Bourke had been detailed by Crook to collect "all information regarding the Apaches," and that "the mass of information he has collected is simply enormous...." but is "held tightly" by the government.[37]

These two officers were clearly the exception; most soldiers took little interest in the plight of the American Indians or their wellbeing, but there were some sympathetic officers who were more understanding. Crook himself set a prime example, despite his hard campaigning and vigorous fighting in the field. Crook believed strongly in their fair treatment and became an ardent public advocate on their behalf. Taking a long-term view, he believed in setting them on their own footing by means of their own labor so they could achieve self-sufficiency. Curiously, within the Third Cavalry, several officers stood out for their sincere desire to aid their Indian companions. They include Lieutenant (later Captain) Emmet Crawford, Schwatka's companion on the Big Horn and Yellowstone Expedition, who had stood side by side with Schwatka in the fight at Slim Buttes, and Lieutenant Britton Davis, another close friend of Schwatka. Both Crawford and Davis would gain the trust and respect of the Apache while working as Indian scout commanders. They cared about their welfare, sought to improve conditions at the agencies and patiently undertook to aid the Apache in following a different path than warfare. In the case of Crawford, for example, he believed that teaching them farming might lead them down a potential road to economic independence. Schwatka likewise maintained his interest in Indigenous peoples, although he would ultimately pursue a different scientific agenda.[38]

In the biographical sketch prepared by his nephew Brackett, an account that is not above exaggeration and therefore lends itself to legitimate skepticism on some points, Brackett claimed that after the conclusion of the Big Horn and Yellowstone Expedition, Schwatka went among the Sioux as a "scientist and student and obtaining leave of absence for that purpose, lived with them in their lodges as one of them, just as he afterwards lived with the Eskimos in the Arctic. He acquired their language, studied their manners and customs and lived with them [in] their daily life." There is no record of any relevant leave of absence nor evidence that Schwatka lived in lodges with the Sioux, a circumstance which was likely to have been taken notice of by at least one person.[39]

Schwatka's inherent interest in the Indigenous people around him led him to an appreciation of the Sioux which was strengthened through ample opportunity for interaction by virtue of his proximity to the Spotted

Tail Agency. According to Brackett, through his conduct, Schwatka earned the "respect, confidence and affection" of the Sioux. The sentiment was so strong that three members of the tribe—Spotted Tail, Touch-the-Clouds and Good Will—who were "warm friends" to Schwatka, adopted Schwatka into their tribe, a claim that Schwatka himself acknowledged in 1891. During the initiation ceremony, Spotted Tail conferred upon Schwatka the name "Big Wolf." According to Brackett, the Sioux "had faith in him because they believed he respected their ways and methods."[40]

There were limits to Schwatka's attitude of mutual respect. Schwatka could wholly appreciate the customs and even the impressive skills and personal qualities of his Indian and Inuit counterparts. Unlike many of his peers, he was not hesitant to state so, but he also articulated harshly condescending views. His writings frequently identify them as "savages" and "savage races," and it is impossible to ignore this disturbing language. For example, he wrote that the Apache, of whom he was so impressed with their physical prowess, practice "the most barbaric forms of witchcraft," and are possessed of "a savage passion for finery."[41]

Schwatka was a man of his time in a day when the prevailing scientific opinion accepted theories of cultural differences that reflected Euro-American superiority. The sentiments he expressed were consistent with those of many other travelers, missionaries, and explorers who had contact with Indigenous people in this period. But Schwatka's attitude was by no means one-sided. Schwatka's intimacy with Indigenous people forced him to face this contradiction: If they were possessed of certain superior skills and admirable qualities worthy of respect, how could they still be deemed primitive? It was a position that he acknowledged without ever taking pains to explain. In his "Sun Dance" article for *Century Magazine*, for example, Schwatka pointed out this contradiction when he wrote that the Sun Dance he witnessed was "the greatest self-sacrifice of the greatest native nation within our boundaries. Within a year they had checked, at the Rosebud Hills in Montana, the largest army we had ever launched against the American Indians in a single fight; ...had wiped Custer's fine command from the face of the earth; had never lost a battle worthy of the name in the war which led to their subjugation; and had proved the utter worthlessness of victory to a savage race contending against civilization." Similarly, this contrast was apparent in his children's story, "How a Great Sioux Chief was Named." Schwatka described how his renowned friend Spotted Tail, whom Schwatka rightly viewed as a great leader and chief, had performed "countless deeds of personal valor" and "like all really great men, whether their lot be cast in civilized or savage life, this great Sioux chief was modest."[42]

In an 1883 article about the lifestyle of the Inuit, "Among the Natives of the North," Schwatka offered a clue into the basis of his understanding. He made the intriguing remark that the Inuit, like the American Indian, was "low on the ethnological scale—and here I believe he is placed by scientists, ..." a comment identifying Schwatka's own source of knowledge on the matter, that of prevailing scientific opinion. Schwatka may have echoed that opinion based on the weighty authority of its proponents and the then common belief in "hierarchies of culture." However, did his respect and admiration for the skills and personal qualities of Indigenous people, so openly expressed in his writings, at least suggest that he may have questioned scientific orthodoxy? In any event, Schwatka expressed those views fairly consistently over the course of his life. Interestingly though, his earliest writings, those of the *Inter-Ocean* dispatches in the midst of the Great Sioux War, struck a far less derogatory tone. For example, his original *Inter-Ocean* dispatch of the Sun Dance written from the field in 1876 avoided much of the condescending commentary included in his 1890 Sun Dance article in *Century Magazine*, and as was commonplace in his later publications.[43]

As an author, Schwatka learned over time how to read his audience. One gets the sense that he espoused a view to fit with the norm of the time, one as to which he believed his readership and his publishers (including *Century Magazine*) were receptive. In the late nineteenth century, such sentiments were prevalent in education, literature, and even public venues and forums like lectures, museums, and exhibitions. In that regard, publishers likewise had a hand in selecting and shaping their authors' content features. The editors of *Century Magazine* viewed their role as not simply wielding a blue pencil, but rather occupying a higher calling, influencing and directing social and cultural thinking by virtue of their offerings. *Century Magazine's* Editor-in-Chief, Richard Watson Gilder, brother of Schwatka's later Arctic companion William Gilder, was well acquainted with Schwatka and his several contributions to the magazine. Gilder maintained an active, hands-on role in selecting works for publication, and was reputed to have reviewed every manuscript submission to *Century* during his long tenure (1881-1901). Schwatka's "Sun-Dance of the Sioux" was a particularly prominent and impressive showcase piece for the magazine, with its inclusion of five attractive illustrations of works by the famous American artist and illustrator Frederic Remington. Schwatka's feature would likely have passed through the discerning eyes of Gilder, who served as the magazine's cultural compass.[44]

Besides his interaction with the Sioux and his other military duties, Schwatka had a busy time of it at Camp Sheridan. He was appointed post adjutant, quartermaster, commissary officer and treasurer, positions also previously held for a time at North Platte Station. These mainly humdrum administrative tasks were often passed off to junior officers at frontier posts. Nonetheless, they were important to efficient post operations and served as a management training regimen for those officers. In support of Captain Mills, Schwatka handled official correspondence, issued rations, clothing and equipment, assigned duties, conducted inspections, managed building and ground maintenance, and investigated acts of misconduct. From May 21 through October 27, 1877, Schwatka served as commanding officer of Company M in the absence of Captain Anson Mills (on leave) and First Lieutenant August Paul (absent sick). In that role, routine garrison duties were generally the order of the day for Schwatka, mixed with sporadic incidents of a more serious nature. In his May 1877 report, the frustrated agent at Spotted Tail Agency had declared the region of northwest Nebraska "entirely beyond the realms of law," with only the presence of the military providing any level of restraint. With an abundance of Indian ponies ranging the Spotted Tail Agency, horse thievery by whites, in particular, was a constant menace and one of the more time-consuming pursuits for Schwatka's command, with arrests few and far between. Perhaps taking advantage of the leadership change at the post, on May 24, just three days after Mills's departure, several deserters fled the post with five horses, but could not be immediately apprehended. The next month, Schwatka was on the trail for a hard eighty miles, this time successfully rounding up a gang of horse thieves and recapturing the stolen Indian stock.[45]

As part of his assignment, Schwatka personally investigated a dreadful tale of murder, and in doing so, identified and arrested the likely culprit. In a tale reminiscent of the legendary detective Sherlock Holmes, Schwatka's confidence in his Sioux companions and their exceptional skills solved the crime and freed one or more Indians from suspicion of murder.

As the story goes, Gilbert C. Fosdick II, a naïve, starry-eyed young dreamer, left the flourishing industrial "silk-city" of Paterson, New Jersey, and arrived in Kearney, Nebraska, amidst the gold-crazed hordes that were dashing to the Black Hills with far more enthusiasm than money. Flat broke, Fosdick managed to land a job as a driver on the newly formed Kearney and Black Hills Stage, a mail carrier operating between those two locations. Fosdick's route was a lonely twenty-mile circuitous stretch, a portion through heavily wooded hills, used only by the occasional miner and emigrant and by horse thieves escaping with Indian ponies stolen from the Spotted Tail Agency (the stage road skirted the southeastern corner of the agency). One day in mid-June, Fosdick saddled a mule and started his run even though he was advised that Indians were spotted on the line. He was last seen alive some ten miles from his destination, reportedly fleeing from Indians. The line's supervisor, a Mr. Hardenburg, claimed to have found and buried his body a week later, which he alleged had come to a gruesome end, suffering gun-shot wounds to the head and body and a horrible scalping. According to Hardenburg, Indians spotted near the scene led to the conclusion that a party of Northern Indians from outside the agency had committed the dastardly deed in their effort to steal his mule.

Charged with the investigation, Schwatka hesitated to jump to the conclusion that Indians had committed the act. Schwatka enlisted several Sioux guides to assist in an examination of the crime scene. One of them, Good Voice, a widely respected Brulé headman and trusted scout, was well known to Schwatka for his superior knowledge of tracking and pathfinding. Riding with Schwatka and Hardenburg to the remote location and closely examining the grounds, Good Voice quickly reconstructed the circumstances of the crime, first determining that there was no evidence of any Indian presence in the area and then showing Schwatka "how the mule had been led, where he [the murderer] had first attempted to kill him [Fosdick], and then led him up the cañon about 100 yards where the mule was found." The exhumation of Fosdick's body also confirmed that Fosdick had not been scalped as Hardenburg claimed. Good Voice then reached the firm conclusion that Hardenburg's horse was the same as used by the murderer, each was missing a shoe of identical size; Good Voice had made a point of measuring Hardenburg's horse while at the crime scene. Schwatka was equally impressed that Good Voice then remarkably managed to find and hold the trail of the murderer's horse over hard ground that bore few observable marks for more than ten miles in the direction of Pine Bluff Station, the post to which Hardenburg had returned after Fosdick's death.[46]

All suspicions now turned to Hardenburg, whose lucrative horse thieving enterprise was about to be exposed by the whistleblower Fosdick. Separately, a young man hired by Hardenburg to transport stolen ponies for sale in Kearney subsequently confessed to Schwatka the thievery ring and Hardenburg's motive for the murder. Though Schwatka arrested Hardenburg for Fosdick's murder, the disappointing conclusion to the tale was that Hardenburg was freed later by civil authorities too apathetic or too fearful of Hardenburg to pursue a conviction. Despite the failed conviction, Schwatka did not hesitate to credit his companion Good Voice, strongly recommending that he be made a first sergeant of one of the American Indian detachments, a promotion that was promptly approved. In addition, in another of Schwatka's short stories headlining Indian personages (entitled "Ho Wash-Tay"), Schwatka penned a complimentary account of his companion's prowess for the benefit of readers of *The Youth's Companion,* a popular magazine for young people.[47]

There were other important matters at the agencies affecting the course of the Indian wars to which Schwatka was witness. Chief Spotted Tail had successfully performed several acts of peacemaking on behalf of the army, convincing tribes to lay down arms and return to the reservations. On October 24, 1876, at Red Cloud Agency, Spotted Tail was anointed as Head Chief of the Sioux by General Crook in recognition of his diplomatic peacemaking efforts. In February 1877, General Crook visited Spotted Tail at Camp Sheridan to ask the chief to perform his most difficult feat of negotiation: to convince the chiefs of the various Northern Indians, including the chief's nephew, Crazy Horse, and his warriors, to surrender their arms, ponies and ammunition, in return for amnesty for their previous actions. Schwatka had full confidence that the venerable chief could succeed. Having heard from Spotted Tail directly, on February 5, Schwatka informed his father that "the Indian question is not nearer definitely settled but I think the Indians will come in, in the spring. Spotted Tail had a talk here today and I think will start out to bring Crazy Horse and the hostile Sioux, who are anxious to come in if they will not be imprisoned, and who are willing to give up their ponies and arms if they can be under Spotted Tail and not Red Cloud." About Sitting Bull, who had a reputation as the fierce leader of an army of warriors, Schwatka noted "he is a myth. There are about 75 to 100 chiefs who rank him. Most of the Indians here no [sic] nothing about him." He further advised his father that the more formidable enemy was Crazy Horse: "We have had thirty to forty killed and about one hundred wounded (leaving out the Custer Massacre), in fights with Crazy Horse who is the only war Chief of importance."[48]

Spotted Tail succeeded. A large number of Sioux, including Crazy Horse, surrendered at the Spotted Tail and Red Cloud Agencies that spring, leading to the close of the Great Sioux War. Crazy Horse spent a few tense months at Red Cloud Agency during the summer of 1877, during which time rumors abounded that he was planning to escape and return to the Plains to hunt freely and resume raiding. General Crook planned to meet with Crazy Horse and other chiefs to address the situation, until it was reported (incorrectly as it turned out) that Crazy Horse intended to murder him. Fearing matters would only worsen, General Crook ordered Crazy Horse's arrest. Ahead of the arresting soldiers, Crazy Horse and his wife fled to Spotted Tail Agency, where after discussions with Lieutenant Jesse Lee, the agent at Spotted Tail Agency, Crazy Horse agreed to return to Camp Robinson. On September 5,

Crazy Horse returned to the post only to be tragically stabbed and killed in a guardhouse scuffle. His body was ceremoniously wrapped and for two months it was scaffolded on a hill overlooking Camp Sheridan. Crazy Horse's death was a time of great mourning at the agencies. It also raised fears of an uprising, which only subsided over time by the conciliatory efforts of some of the more influential chiefs.

For the Third Cavalry, matters outside the agency occasionally took the forefront, notwithstanding the heavy events of the preceding few weeks. Brazen train robberies by masked gunmen were a mainstay in Hollywood western film genre, but they had an authentic counterpart on the Plains. On September 18, 1877, a gang of six heavily armed and masked men, the "Black Hills Bandits," held up a Union Pacific Railroad train stopped at Big Springs outside of Ogallala, Nebraska, some 175 miles southeast of Camp Sheridan. The audacious gang happened upon an unexpected jackpot, freshly minted $20 gold coins worth more than $60,000, together with more cash and other valuables, all of which was taken at gunpoint from the frightened passengers. As word spread of the robbery, the largest robbery ever of the Union Pacific Railroad, a widespread manhunt was quickly launched. From Camp Sheridan, troops of the Third Cavalry, commanded by Schwatka in Mills's continued absence, scoured the countryside south and east of the post in the direction of Big Springs, covering over one hundred miles in an unsuccessful effort to locate the bandits. Four of the gang members were ultimately captured or killed at locations outside of Nebraska; two were never heard from again.[49]

But there were changes coming to the Spotted Tail and Red Cloud Agencies that were more momentous in nature. Against their strenuous objections, the Oglalas and Brulés were relocated from their agencies in the White River Valley under orders of President Rutherford B. Hayes. In late October, they departed reluctantly *en masse* from both agencies, a long sorrowful procession eastward toward the Missouri River. In the same month, Colonel Nelson Miles captured Chief Joseph and four hundred of his Nez Perce followers just short of the Canadian border in Montana. They were moved through a series of locations to the Indian Territory (today's Oklahoma), where many died from malnutrition and malaria. Scattered actions still continued, but the Great Sioux War was slowly but inextricably drawing to a close.

Schwatka served a role in the removal of the Brulés from their agency location on Beaver Creek near Camp Sheridan. In November 1877, he was assigned detached duty to the relocated Spotted Tail Agency, some forty miles from Yankton, Dakota Territory, on the Missouri River. Schwatka and troopers of two companies of the Third Cavalry assisted the Brulés on their disheartening journey to their new agency and in their settling in over the winter of 1877-78. Already in low spirits with their removal, unseasonably mild temperatures and heavy rains during the march left the poorly equipped Indians completely demoralized. According to one reporter, "gumbo mud abounded in its perfection, pedestrianism was difficult and nasty, equestrianism nearly impossible, and wagoning entirely so." It was no wonder that some Indians simply left the main body before reaching their destination. The new location was similarly unimpressive. The agency buildings themselves, of cheap temporary construction, sat in low bottom land subject to flooding and mud.[50]

From the hastily built military post overlooking the agency buildings, Schwatka considered his prospects, and he envisioned a future of low pay, slim opportunities for advancement and even less excitement, all within a military bureaucracy. He later told a reporter that "the venturesome in my nature came to the surface on account of the very dullness of my surroundings while I was serving in the army. I was stationed at the Spotted Tail Agency on the Upper Missouri. The smaller frontier posts had been contracted to the larger garrisons and with this consolidation disappeared much of the exciting side of the service." After a hard driving eight thousand miles in the saddle over the preceding seven years, Schwatka was looking forward to a new adventure. Newspaper reports in the *New York Herald* that the American Geographical Society in New York City was planning a trip to the North reached him on the Plains, and as his fellow officer Charles King aptly noted, Schwatka "never lost a chance for adventure."[51]

In his years on the Plains, Frederick Schwatka was an eyewitness to the transformation of the West during the most turbulent of times. The frontier was the venue within which he had come of age. Despite the cruelty of the campaigns on both sides and the ultimate subjugation of the Northern Indians, he maintained an open-minded attitude toward, and genuine interest in, his erstwhile foe, a commendable trait for a military man who could as easily hardened his views in regard to his Indian counterparts. The frontier was also a classroom, an invaluable experience, where Schwatka learned how to live, travel and survive on the land. Lastly, Schwatka left a favorable impression on those who knew him, despite the hardships. Besides Davenport, who spoke of his kindly nature, the correspondent Robert E. Strahorn, who shared the field with Schwatka, fondly recalled that among the lieutenants "for whom I formed a great attachment, was the bright, witty and brave Schwatka, whose successes as an Arctic explorer have since made him world famous." Those successes had not come by mere chance, and Schwatka would need to apply all those lessons learned in the field as he readied for his next big adventure.[52]

CHAPTER FIVE
ARCTIC FEVER

FOR CENTURIES THE POSSIBILITY of a navigable waterway from the Atlantic to the Pacific Ocean had lured merchants and mariners with the tantalizing hope of a shorter passage to the treasures of the Orient (which at the time meant India, China and Japan). The reasons for achieving that objective may have changed over time, but the attraction was as strong in the mid-nineteenth century as it was in the fifteenth century. In his quest to find a shorter route to the Orient, Columbus discovered an unexpected obstruction in the American continents, and sparked a new period of westward discovery. Soon thereafter, Magellan succeeded in reaching India by virtue of a long southern voyage and the Spanish were claiming a large stake in the Americas.

Seeking to avoid competing directly with Spanish interests in the New World, the British pursued a different approach to the Orient, a so-called Northwest Passage, a navigable route from the Atlantic to the Pacific Ocean by way of the northern coast of North America. The search for the Northwest Passage would be largely a British endeavor, beginning with the voyage of John Cabot in 1497, who is believed to have landed at either Labrador or Newfoundland. In 1576, the English privateer and seaman Martin Frobisher sailed on the first of his three voyages to the northwest in search of the Orient. His discovery of a long, open strait, which he named Frobisher Strait on southern Baffin Island, gave hope for an unobstructed passage to the west. Frobisher's hope ultimately proved to be a dead end, the first of many false leads in the search for a Northwest Passage.

Other daring voyages are no less renowned than Frobisher's and significant in their own right. With a charter from Queen Elizabeth I to search for a Northwest Passage, between 1585 and 1587 John Davis sailed on three occasions north along the Greenland coast into the strait that bears his name, returning along what would become known as the Baffin Island coast. He "rediscovered" the landmass of Greenland, forgotten by mariners, and charted a portion of its west coast, as well as the entrance to Hudson Bay. Davis's voyages were premised on the persistent theory that at some point along the northern latitudes there existed an expanse of open water, or "Open Polar Sea," that would serve as a gateway to the Pacific or North Pole.

Davis's efforts sparked a series of successor expeditions. Within twenty-five years of Davis's third voyage, Henry Hudson had discovered the bay that takes his name and in which he lost his life to mutineers. In 1616, William Baffin and Robert Bylot (one of Hudson's forgiven mutineers) made a remarkable voyage besting Davis's farthest north (that is, the farthest north latitude he had reached) and discovered Baffin Bay and three sounds, named Lancaster, Smith and Jones, of which Lancaster Sound would prove to be the only practicable route for a Northwest Passage. Baffin's voyages were then all but forgotten. Between 1631 and 1632 Luke Foxe and Thomas James continued the search for a passage through Hudson Bay and effectively demonstrated that there was no practical route through the bay to the Pacific. James and his crew spent a miserable winter suffering from starvation and scurvy in the southern part of Hudson Bay. His somber narrative may have served as the inspiration for Samuel Coleridge's *Rime of the Ancient Mariner*.

Renewed efforts in the mid-eighteenth century coincided with the activities of the Hudson's Bay Company in North America. Having been granted exclusive rights to territory and trade in Hudson Bay and Strait, the company had made only feeble attempts at discovery while it exploited its commercial monopoly. In 1741, through the instigation of the colonial administrator Arthur Dobbs, who threatened to seek the termination of its charter unless the company acted on its promise to seek a Northwest Passage, the company was prodded into further discovery. Dobbs forced several expeditions which made important discoveries within the bay but reconfirmed that there was no practical route to the Pacific from the western end of the bay.

A financial incentive had been introduced in 1745 when the British Parliament had passed an act providing for a reward of twenty thousand pounds sterling for the discovery of a Northwest Passage through Hudson Strait. The reward was later modified to eliminate the Hudson Strait requirement, but it established that the route had to be above the 52nd degree of north latitude. In 1818, it was further modified to include rewards for a partial discovery of a Northwest Passage, based on crossing the 110th meridian west.

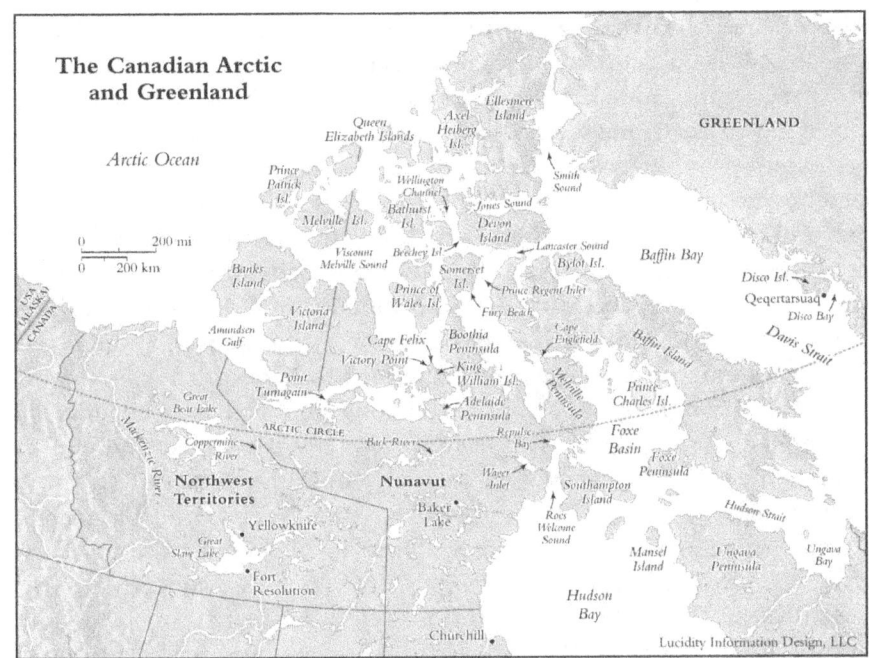

Since the search for the passage was largely a naval enterprise, most of the activity in the northern part of America had been focused on its eastern coastlines and Hudson Bay. The interior coast had remained largely unmapped. In 1770, following rumors of copper deposits along a large river running to a northern sea, the Hudson's Bay Company dispatched Samuel Hearne to investigate the truth of the claims. Though no significant mineral deposits were uncovered, with his guide, Matonabbee, Hearne traveled down the Coppermine River, reaching its mouth at the Arctic Ocean, the first European explorer to do so. In 1789 Alexander Mackenzie traveled down the other great river of the North, which now bears his name, until its terminus at the Arctic Ocean. With the exception of these two landings, the interior of the northern coast of the American continent remained largely a mystery. There the matter stood at the conclusion of the Napoleonic wars.

Following the defeat of Napoleon, a rapid demobilization and a peacetime navy left thousands of British officers and sailors on half-pay, many of whom sought distinction on special assignments such as exploration and surveying. The British Admiralty that had helped secure the high seas from the French threat looked with equal confidence at solving the question of a Northwest Passage, largely due to the efforts of Sir John Barrow, second secretary of the Admiralty. In 1817, it had been reported by whaling captains, in particular the scientific-minded navigator William Scoresby, that large quantities of ice had been drifting into the Atlantic, and that the coast of Greenland had been free of ice farther north than previously known. Scoresby brought these facts to the attention of Sir Joseph Banks, the influential president of the Royal Society, who forwarded them to Lord Melville, First Lord of the Admiralty, for consideration. Banks pressed Lord Melville to settle once and for all the issue of a Northwest Passage and the geography of the north part of America. As second secretary of the Admiralty, John Barrow, a strident advocate for geographic and scientific discovery on the part of the Royal Navy, firmly supported those renewed efforts to the north.[1]

Acting upon Scoresby's report, Barrow approved two expeditions by the Royal Navy to the Arctic in 1818. The first expedition, led by Commander David Buchan, was an overly optimistic attempt to sail to the Bering Sea and the Pacific Ocean via the North Pole following a passage between Greenland and Svalbard (a Norwegian archipelago). The expedition comprised two ships, HMS *Dorothea* and HMS *Trent*. Reaching Svalbard, determined efforts were made to push the ships through the ice; at times the men wearily hauled the ships by ropes tied to the foremasts. Invariably, both ships became entangled in the ice west of Svalbard and suffered severe damage. Battered by the unrelenting ice, the ship's bell of the battered *Trent* tolled ominously, ringing the death knell. After a series of powerful gales, Buchan managed to extricate the ships and they limped home in a badly leaking condition. The expedition had proved that an approach to the Pole from this route by ships under sail was impossible, a conclusion previously demonstrated by Captain Constantine John Phipps more than forty years before.[2]

The second expedition, under Commander John Ross, probed the three sounds believed to have been visited by William Baffin two centuries ago, a feat long since erased from modern memories. Passing north into Baffin Bay, Ross reached Cape York at the north end of Melville Bay. Ross made the acquaintance of his so-called "Arctic Highlanders" (the Polar Eskimos or Inughuit), their first encounter with Europeans. Their destiny would be forever changed by the future explorers to Smith Sound. After skirting the entrances to Smith Sound and Jones Sound, Ross entered the westward running Lancaster Sound. This course appeared to offer a better chance for a Northwest Passage. Those hopes were dashed however when Ross observed what he believed to be a connected chain of mountains blocking further passage. Ross proudly named his discovery the "Croker Mountains" after the first secretary of the Admiralty.

Ross's discovery of the imaginary Croker Mountains would be proven spectacularly wrong. The officers on board Ross's expedition, some of whom would go on to make their own mark in the North, silently disagreed with their senior officer's conclusion. Upon Ross's return, Lieutenant William Edward Parry, second in command, managed to convince Barrow that Ross had been woefully mistaken in his assumption regarding the Croker Mountains, and that Lancaster Sound offered a viable possibility for continued westward extension. With Barrow's support, in 1819-20 Parry proved himself correct, continuing through Lancaster Sound as far as Melville Island, where he overwintered, a first in the High Arctic. The ambitious Parry claimed the government's prize of £5,000 for the crossing the meridian of 110 degrees, a partial discovery of a Northwest Passage. Parry made two more attempts at a Northwest Passage but never equaled the geographical success of his voyage of 1819-20.

Parry's successful expedition of 1819-20 was one part of a two-pronged approach aimed at solving the question of a Northwest Passage and the mapping of the geography of the northern part of North America. In coordination with Parry's attempt, the persistent Barrow dispatched an overland expedition to the mouth of the Coppermine River to explore the north coast of America eastward to Hudson Bay. It was optimistically considered possible that the expedition could link with Parry's expedition approaching from the east. The command of that overland expedition was awarded to Lieutenant John Franklin.

Sir John Franklin was born on April 16, 1786 in the village of Spilsby, Lincolnshire, the ninth of twelve children of a fairly prosperous tradesman. An energetic but disciplined youth, his commendable and eventful Royal Navy experience has been largely overshadowed by his more recognized Arctic service. Like many British naval officers of the Napoleonic era, young Franklin began an adventurous life at sea at an early age. As a lowly first-class volunteer at the age of fourteen on the path to midshipman, Franklin commenced his professional career. He had his first taste of combat while aboard the HMS *Polyphemus* in Nelson's division during its bloody engagement with the Dutch at the Battle of Copenhagen. But it was exploration that became his passion, even at that young age. Calling on family connections, always useful for advancement or choice appointments, he gained a position as a midshipman on the discovery ship HMS *Investigator* commanded by his relative Captain Matthew Flinders. A patient mentor with wide naval and scientific competencies, Flinders served as a positive influence on the young man, then still only fifteen-years-old. For more than a year, Franklin was occupied in the

Portrait of Sir John Franklin, by Louis Haghe.

tedious task of surveying the coast of Australia (then New Holland). Along the way, he learned useful navigation and scientific skills, while building his resume for later exploratory assignments.³

By 1805 young Franklin was serving as signal midshipman on HMS *Bellerophon* in the midst of the Battle of Trafalgar. One biographer has penned a romantic image of Franklin dutifully receiving the timeless message from Nelson's *Victory* that "England expects that every man will do his duty," and running it to his superior. While the *Bellerophon* engaged in tight quarters with the *L'Aigle*, a 74-gun French ship of the line, several of Franklin's fellow officers and men fell dead at his feet. Despite a high number of casualties, Franklin managed to survive unscathed, but he did suffer a slight deafness in his ears from the fierce cannonade. During the War of 1812, he served aboard HMS *Bedford* during the Battle of Lake Borgne a month before the American victory at New Orleans, suffering a shoulder wound while engaging with American gunboats. In 1818, Franklin had gained his first Arctic experience as a lieutenant commanding HMS *Trent* in Buchan's unsuccessful North Pole expedition.⁴

Franklin would figure prominently in Barrow's endeavor to survey the unmapped stretch of the American continent. In July 1821, after an arduous voyage both on foot and by canoe, Franklin's party reached the mouth of the Coppermine River. Taking to the Arctic Ocean in their barely seaworthy bark canoes, they traveled eastward, charting a total of some 500 miles of rugged coastline, until they reached a location that Franklin named Point Turnagain. Unfortunately, the turn should have come sooner, as the worst part of the journey was still ahead. The headstrong, perhaps even foolhardy Franklin had failed to heed the advice of his guides, who had entreated him to head back earlier on account of the lateness of the season. Low on provisions, with a scarcity of game, the return became a classic tale of disaster as winter set in, filled with starvation, murder, and cannibalism as they crossed the aptly named "Barren Lands." After Midshipman Robert Hood was murdered by the voyageur Michel Terohaute, Michel was himself killed at the hand of surgeon and naturalist Doctor John Richardson. Of the original twenty members, eleven died on the harrowing retreat across the Barren Lands. If not for the exertions of Lieutenant George Back, who made a remarkable journey for relief, as well as the Indians who generously delivered food for the starving group, Franklin would certainly have died. Upon his return to England, Franklin was popularly referred to as the "man who ate his boots," an assertion that was undoubtedly true.

A near death experience would have discouraged less ambitious men, but undeterred by his previous ordeal, Franklin was off again in 1825 to the Canadian Arctic. During his brief return to England, he had married the poet Eleanor Anne Porden in August 1823. The marriage was short-lived, as Eleanor tragically died of tuberculosis in 1825, shortly after Franklin had departed on his second North American Arctic expedition. A self-sacrificing wife, she had implored Franklin not to forsake his career and his expedition on account of her failing health. On this expedition, Franklin's plan was to proceed overland to the Mackenzie River and travel westward along the Arctic Ocean to Icy Cape (the most northeastern point previously reached by Captain Cook in 1778). Separately, John Richardson was to travel eastward from the Mackenzie River. Captain Frederick William Beechey, approaching by sea from the Pacific, was to proceed through Bering Strait in the hope of meeting the westward-traveling Franklin. Beechey succeeded in reaching Point Barrow, but Franklin was unable to close the gap, reaching a point approximately 160 miles from Barrow. Franklin nonetheless charted an additional several hundred miles of coastline to the west and Richardson managed to map the Arctic coastline east to the Coppermine River. The conditions under which the parties labored were severe but not as life-threatening as Franklin's previous death march, and not one man was lost. Franklin and Richardson had accomplished another significant piece of mapping, and the northern part of the continent was slowly taking shape.

Returning to England, Franklin was lauded as a hero and subsequently knighted in 1829. He married the ambitious and talented Jane Griffin, who was destined to become as well-known as any Arctic explorer of the nineteenth century. From 1830 to 1834 Franklin was commander of HMS *Rainbow* during a lackluster assignment in the Mediterranean, far removed from the polar seas, more the diplomat than explorer. Meanwhile John Ross, through the financing of gin distiller Felix Booth, was redeeming himself in the Arctic. Ross, now fifty-one-years-old, planned another attempt at a Northwest Passage through Lancaster Sound, this time fitted with an auxiliary steam engine and paddle wheel (both of which would later prove useless). Ross was a progressive in many fields, including the popular but long-debunked art of phrenology (the study of the shape and size of one's head to determine character and mental abilities), as well as more practical pursuits, such as the use of steam power in navigation. John Ross was accompanied by his nephew James Clark Ross, who in the eyes of Jane Franklin was "the handsomest man in the navy." The younger Ross had already participated in five Arctic voyages and had developed an expertise in several scientific disciplines, including magnetism and natural history. Departing England in early August of 1829, they entered Lancaster Sound. With mixed emotions Ross passed beyond his imaginary "Croker Mountains" and into Prince Regent Inlet. Hugging the coast, he mapped 150 miles before entering a harbor (Felix Harbor) established on the Boothia Peninsula.

During the first winter, friendly relations were established with the Inuit who frequented the area and provided valuable geographical information. They rightly advised Ross that he had entered a dead end with no southern outlet. The expedition was now limited to land excursions. In the spring of 1830, James Clark Ross set off westward with several men and sledges, to link with Point Turnagain reached by Franklin. He traveled across the Boothia Peninsula and over a frozen channel to the north dotted with reefs, shoals and islands, the largest of which he named the Matty Island. Crossing the channel, he reached King William Land (at the time not known to be an island), and travelled along its coast to its northernmost point, named Cape Felix, about two hundred miles from the *Victory*. Little did Ross know that King William Island would figure so largely in the Franklin narrative and Frederick Schwatka's own travels. With few supplies, Ross and his companion, Thomas Abernathy, continued farther along the northwest coast of King William Island to Victory Point. Off the west coast of King William Island, Ross witnessed firsthand the large masses of ice pushed as much as one-half mile above the tide mark. Ross was unaware at the time that this stretch of ice had drifted south from its starting point in the Beaufort Sea to the north. At Victory Point, Ross was some two hundred and twenty miles northeast of

Point Turnagain. But with rations now running low, he could only retreat to the *Victory*.

The following spring, James Clark Ross, again accompanied by Abernathy, identified the position of the North Magnetic Pole to the northeast of King William Island. Now beset by ice, John Ross and his crew were forced to spend a third winter in the Arctic. The *Victory*, unable to extricate itself from its resting place at Felix Harbor, was abandoned, and consequently a retreat was made northward to a location known as Fury Beach, where a wearying fourth winter was spent. The following spring, after a difficult sledge journey, small boats were launched into Lancaster Sound. Ironically, the whaler *Isabella*, the ship employed by Ross on its 1818 voyage of discovery, found and rescued him and his crew. Ross's second expedition was a resounding success. His party had spent four consecutive winters in the Arctic, charted miles of newly discovered lands, and discovered the North Magnetic Pole. The irascible Ross had redeemed himself and was knighted, and Felix Booth was repaid by act of the House of Commons.

Several smaller land expeditions added to the mapping of the Arctic and have a bearing on the Franklin narrative. When no word had been heard from Ross's expedition, a privately funded expedition led by George Back was dispatched for a potential rescue mission. Word of Ross's safe return reached Back before his own departure, and the expedition became one of discovery rather than relief. Back turned his sights to a river fed by the Great Slave Lake that was rumored to empty into the polar sea. In a long and difficult journey, Back succeeded in traversing this river, later named the Back River, to its outlet at the Arctic Ocean. The Hudson's Bay Company, with several highly competent land expeditions, added further details to the Arctic coast that Franklin had been unable to complete. In 1837, Peter Warren Dease and Thomas Simpson descended the Mackenzie River, traveled west, and completed the unmapped coastline to Point Barrow. In 1838, they descended the Coppermine River, turned east, and passed Franklin's Point Turnagain. Crossing the strait separating King William Island from the mainland, they traveled along the coast of King William Island, passing the estuary of the Back River and continuing forty miles farther to the Castor and Pollux River. They came within sight of Rae Strait that separated King William Island from the Boothia Peninsula. All that was left in the symbolic mapping of the Northwest Passage was to link Franklin's Point Turnagain with Ross's Victory Point.

Through the efforts of Sir John Barrow and the Royal Geographical Society, the British Admiralty was persuaded to outfit a naval expedition to complete the last remaining gap of unmapped coastline along the northern part of the American continent and to solve the now largely academic question of a Northwest Passage. For the restless Barrow, having reached the age of eighty, it was to be the completion of a goal that he had pursued with few interruptions from 1818 through his retirement from public life in 1845. None, however, could have guessed that the proposed expedition would end in such tragic circumstances. In December 1844 Barrow delivered to Lord Haddington, the first lord of the Admiralty, a proposal to complete the discovery of a Northwest Passage. Having decided upon the expedition, the Admiralty sought a qualified commander. Sir James Clark Ross was the logical choice, but he flatly turned them down. Even though still a relatively youthful forty-four-years-old, he had served in no fewer than seven expeditions, several of which were as noteworthy for their length as they were for their accomplishments. Evidently, the overtaxed Ross had had his fill of polar service. Recently married after his most recent expedition, it was suggested that he had promised his bride that he would take no more polar commands. Regardless of the truth of the rumor, his health had not fully returned by late 1843 after four years on his Antarctic expedition.

With the first and best choice unavailable, the Admiralty turned to its senior Arctic officer, fifty-eight-year-old Sir John Franklin. Franklin had made it perfectly clear that he desired to lead the expedition, and his wife, Lady Jane Franklin, also made it apparent that she desired her husband command it. As early as 1836, Franklin had written to Captain Francis Beaufort that "You know, I am sure, that no service is nearer to my heart than the completion of the survey of the North coast of America, and to the accomplishment of a N.W. Passage." In 1845 he still held that conviction. Commenting on his qualifications for command, his friend Sir William Edward Parry advised Lord Haddington that, "he is a fitter man to go than any I know; and if you don't let him go, the man will die of disappointment!" Command of the expedition would also serve as a redemption for some frustrating years between 1836 and 1842, when Franklin served as governor of Tasmania, or Van Diemen's Land, as it was then known. Franklin's second in command was to be the experienced Captain Francis Crozier, who would command the HMS *Terror*, as he had in the Antarctic under Sir James Clark Ross.[5]

On May 14, 1845, the two ships of the Franklin expedition, the flagship HMS *Erebus* and its companion ship HMS *Terror*, with a total crew of 134 officers and men, sailed from the wharves of Greenhithe, England, a village on the Thames River outside of London. The expedition was the largest and most complete ever assembled for the purpose of navigating the fabled passage. Franklin's instructions were straightforward, at least on paper. He was to enter Lancaster Sound and Barrow Strait. Once he arrived at Cape Walker he was to proceed to the southwest and head toward the Bering Strait. If blocked by that approach, he was to attempt Wellington Channel to the north.

After a brief stop in Sheerness, the vessels crossed the Atlantic, reaching the Whale Fish Islands (near Disco Bay) in Greenland on July 4. Although five men had become sick and had to return home, the officers were generally optimistic about their prospects. Commander James Fitzjames optimistically believed they might accomplish their objective in one summer. Franklin sent a last dispatch on July 12 from the Whale Fish Islands. The last contact with Franklin was made at the end of July by two whaling ships in the latitude of Lancaster Sound. In his final conversation with the outside world, in what could be viewed as a pessimistic statement, Franklin advised the whaleman, Captain Martin, that his ships were provisioned for five years but might be able to last as long as seven. The Franklin expedition was never heard from again.

Since the ships were provisioned for five years, the Admiralty expressed no particular concern when no news arrived from Franklin during the first two years. By the spring of 1847, however, the silence had become cause for apprehension by the public. As anxiety mounted, the British government dispatched a series of expeditions, initially in the hope of rescuing Franklin and his crew, and later to ascertain their fate. The search began in earnest in 1848. Over the following decade it comprised more than thirty public and private expeditions.

The first clues were discovered in the season of 1850-51. Following the trail of the missing Franklin ships into Lancaster Sound, several British ships fell in with two American vessels that were also volunteering in the search for Franklin. In August 1850, at Beechey Island, the first winter encampment of Franklin's expedition was discovered, and with it the lonely graves of three of Franklin's men and the remnants of their brief stay. All evidence pointed to a hasty departure by the expedition, but where it was destined in the maze of islands and ice of the Canadian Arctic remained a mystery. We must follow the searchers to King William Island, where the answer to Franklin's fate was ultimately discovered, and to place Schwatka's own expedition in its proper context.

That the missing expedition had become a doomed one was first uncovered by the Scotsman, Doctor John Rae, of the Hudson's Bay Company. Rae was among the foremost of Arctic travelers, and the European who had the strongest claim to be the first to adopt Inuit methods to sustain himself in his Arctic travels. His success irked the class-conscious Royal Navy establishment. The veteran explorer, intensely loyal to the

Hudson's Bay Company and rightly proud of his accomplishments, had already conducted three expeditions surveying the Arctic coast between 1846 and 1851, including a search expedition for Franklin with Doctor John Richardson. By Rae's own reckoning, he had traveled more than ten thousand miles on foot and in small boats, many under exceedingly difficult conditions and hardships. In 1853-54, he had not been searching for Franklin, but rather conducting a survey on behalf of his employer on the west coast of Boothia, an unmapped corner of the northern coast of North America. In fact, Rae thought it so unlikely that he would cross Franklin's path that he went so far as to advise George Simpson, governor of the Hudson's Bay Company, that "I do not mention the lost navigators, as there is not the slightest hope of finding any traces of them in the quarter to which I am going."[6]

On March 31, 1854, Rae and four men set out from Repulse Bay on the west coast of Hudson Bay, man-hauling sledges due to a shortage of dogs. At Pelly Bay on his outward journey, Rae received news from an informative Inuk named In-nook-poo-zhe-jook that a party of white men ("Kabloonans") had died of starvation some distance to the west of where Rae was, and not far beyond a large river. Unable to act upon such imprecise information, Rae felt compelled to continue his survey, his primary purpose. Reaching the Castor and Pollux River and the cairn marking Dease and Simpson's farthest eastward progress, Rae continued his survey of the Boothia coast only slightly further before returning to Repulse Bay.[7]

At Repulse Bay, Rae obtained further details from the testimony of Innookpoozhejook and others, namely that about the year 1850, some forty white men were seen retreating southward on the sea ice along the west shore of King William Island, dragging a boat and sledges. All of them were suffering from starvation. The distressed men communicated by signs (not speaking Inuktitut) that their ship or ships had been crushed in the ice. Later the same season the Inuit had discovered the bodies of about thirty men on the mainland, and five bodies on a nearby island, at locations that Rae understood to be in the vicinity of Back's River (near Point Ogle on Adelaide Peninsula and Montreal Island). Some bodies had been buried, while others had not, and some were scattered under an overturned boat or in a tent. Rae learned from the Inuit the startling news that "from the mutilated state of many of the corpses, and the contents of the kettles, it was evident that our wretched countrymen had been driven to the last resource—cannibalism—as a means of prolonging existence." Rae's informants were not eyewitnesses to these events but had obtained their information from others who had met the white men and seen their bodies. Rae had also obtained numerous relics, including Franklin's Hanoverian Guelphic medal, that added physical corroboration to the story. Rae hastily returned to England in October 1854 with the first definitive news of the dreadful fate of the Franklin expedition.[8]

The news was received in England with a mixed response—satisfaction over the long-awaited discovery of the expedition's sorrowful fate, and outrage over the suggestion that British seamen had taken to the last resort. As prominent a figure as Charles Dickens weighed in on the controversy, claiming that "the vague babble of savages" should not condemn valiant British sailors. Attacks in the press, with no basis in fact, discounted Rae's second-handed "hearsay," which he felt duty bound to convey factually as it was provided. The truth was that Rae had accomplished more than all previous search expeditions bar none. Despite returning with evidence of Franklin's fate, Rae's decision to return to England rather than follow up the Inuit reports left him open to an additional criticism that he had squandered an opportunity to have discovered even more. His defense was certainly justifiable—the season was far too advanced to accomplish anything further without endangering himself or his men. It is tantalizing to speculate, but probably unlikely, that in 1854 written records of the lost expedition might still have survived.

Following Rae's return, the Hudson's Bay Company dispatched Chief Factor James Anderson and James Stewart by canoe to search the vicinity of the Back River in 1855. The two managed to locate some tantalizing clues at Montreal Island, including a piece of wood initialed "Mr. Stanley," surgeon of the *Erebus*, and a plank bearing the word "Terror," unmistakable evidence of the missing expedition. Lacking an interpreter, they gained only fragmented information from the Inuit to the effect that a number of white men had died from starvation and that the Inuit had collected relics from a boat. Because of the damaged state of their own canoes and heavy ice in the vicinity, Anderson and Stewart were unable to cross to Richardson Point and the location later known as Starvation Cove, locations that would figure largely in Schwatka's later search.

With the search area narrowed to the vicinity of King William Island, and the British government preoccupied with the war in the Crimea, it was left to a determined Lady Jane Franklin to organize a privately funded expedition to continue the search for her husband. Her object was to locate more conclusive evidence of the expedition's fate and possibly locate written records. Lady Franklin offered the command to the Irish explorer Francis Leopold McClintock, a Royal Navy veteran of several earlier searches who had fine-tuned the art of man-hauled sledges as a means of travel.

McClintock sailed from Aberdeen in the *Fox* in July 1857. Leaving West Greenland after acquiring a sled driver, Carl Petersen, and dogs, the *Fox* was locked in the ice of Melville Bay and drifted south the length of Baffin Bay. Released the following spring, McClintock proceeded through Lancaster Sound to the eastern end of Bellot Strait by way of Prince Regent Inlet but was blocked by ice in his attempt to reach King William Island. Sledge parties dispatched during the spring of 1859 encountered Inuit on the west coast of Boothia Peninsula at Cape Victoria. Evidently, Petersen, fluent in Kalaallisut (Greenlandic) could communicate sufficiently enough with the Inuit of the Canadian Arctic to learn that a ship had been crushed to the west of King William Island and that white men had died of starvation on an island to the southwest, corroborating the testimony received by Rae. McClintock bartered for numerous relics of the lost expedition, including a silver medal of Alexander M'Donald, assistant surgeon of HMS *Terror*. McClintock also learned that every scrap of wood in the possession of the Inuit had come from the sunken ship. During a later meeting of the same group of Inuit several miles north of Cape Victoria, McClintock learned of a second ship that had been forced on shore at a place they called "Oot-loo-lik" and that a body of a man with long teeth had been found on the ship. McClintock believed that Ootloolik was located west of King William Island.[9]

At Cape Victoria, McClintock and Lieutenant William Hobson separated their sledge parties. Hobson continued to march directly toward Cape Felix, and McClintock kept south along the east coast of King William Island. It was a magnanimous gesture on McClintock's part, as McClintock understood that Hobson's track was likely to come upon the stranded ship or other physical evidence of the lost expedition. Thus, Hobson might be the first to discover the expedition's fate (although as commander credit would go to McClintock). McClintock continued his circuit acquiring other relics along the way from Inuit familiar with the wreck. Through Petersen, McClintock learned that many white men had dropped as they moved toward the Back River. Some were buried and some not, and also "there had been *many books*..., but all have long ago been destroyed by the weather." They were told that the location of the stranded ship was distant, five days travelling on the west coast of the island, but it had largely disappeared, its remaining materials carried away by the Inuit. McClintock quite possibly learned of cannibalism at this point or elsewhere but omitted any reference to it in his accompanying narrative. Crossing to Montreal Island, McClintock found a few articles of European origin (portions of a meat tin, iron and copper fragments), and then moved back to King William Island. On King William Island east of Cape Herschel,

McClintock discovered the first skeleton, later identified as Henry Peglar, captain of the foretop, HMS *Terror*, by the papers on his person.[10]

After passing Cape Herschel, McClintock located a note left by Hobson to the effect that Hobson had located a written record of the lost Franklin expedition at Victory Point, the so-called "Victory Point record." The record (a completed standard Admiralty form), first briefly noted that the Franklin expedition had spent the winter of 1846-47 (actually 1845-46) on Beechey Island after circumnavigating Cornwallis Island, and ended with "All Well." Around the margin of the record, a second note scribbled along the margin dated April 25, 1848, told a different and more tragic story. The expedition ships had been "deserted" on April 22, 1848, having been beset off the northwest coast of King William Island since September 12, 1846. Sir John Franklin had died on June 11, 1847 and the total loss by death had been nine officers and fifteen men. On April 26, 1848 the survivors were headed for the Back River. Finally, here was conclusive evidence of the fate of Franklin, recovered fourteen years after the expedition's departure. Upon McClintock's return, this written record of Franklin's expedition, would be graphically reproduced in all the illustrated papers and became a fold-out of every edition of McClintock's narrative. (Hobson also found a second record near Victory Point, written prior to the ships' abandonment, with no additional information).

McClintock continued to follow in Hobson's tracks along the coast of King William Island. Near Cape Crozier, he discovered a ship's boat (previously discovered by Hobson), mounted on a heavy sledge and pointing to the northeast, which led McClintock to conclude that the men were attempting a return to the ships. Inside the boat were two human skeletons, and both inside and outside, an enormous quantity of sundry items, everything from useful items such as clothing and nails to completely useless items such as numerous small books, silk handkerchiefs, and chocolate, the "mere accumulation of dead weight" for sledge travelers, according to McClintock.[11]

On June 2, McClintock reached Victory Point. Here, he placed a copy of the Victory Point record, together with copies of his and Hobson's records in a prominently visible cairn. These would all be found by Schwatka twenty years later. (McClintock also buried another record ten feet true north of the cairn, which would not be located by Schwatka.) At this location, an enormous array of superfluous materials was strewn across the landscape, as if the crews had removed them from the ship and simply dropped anything not necessary for the retreat. Among the debris were four sets of stoves, pickaxes, shovels, a dip circle, iron hoops, a copper lightning conductor, curtain rods, a medicine chest, and even a heap of clothing piled four feet high. Completing their search, both McClintock and Hobson returned to the *Fox* and sailed for home by mid-August.

Much to his credit, McClintock had returned with enough information from which the fate of the Franklin expedition could be explained, but he had recovered no journals or written records besides the two documents recovered by Hobson. Could there still be survivors trapped in some remote ice-bound region awaiting rescue even at this late date? The desire to answer that question was to launch a quixotic search doggedly pursued by an eccentric printer from Cincinnati, Ohio.

On February 7, 1860, the *Daily Gazette* of Cincinnati announced that "a respected well-known citizen of this City starts to-day to New York," to meet Henry Grinnell and other distinguished countrymen, his purpose being a proposed American maritime expedition to Boothia and King William Island. That "respected well-known" citizen was Charles Francis Hall, a Cincinnati newspaper publisher and engraver, whose fascination with Franklin's fate would compel him to abandon his wife and son and lead his own search for survivors of the ill-fated expedition. Markedly enthusiastic about whatever captured his fancy at the time, Hall became obsessed with the rescue of potential survivors of Franklin's expedition, a possibility that was extremely unlikely by 1860. Speculation has abounded as to the reason for this newly found attraction. Perhaps his arctic fever was triggered by the outpouring over the death of Elisha Kent Kane, whose solemn funeral procession passed through Hall's hometown of Cincinnati on a journey unmatched in American history. Whatever the reason, there was no denying Hall's arctic fervor. Hall's expedition was launched on a "shoe-string" budget, a one-man operation, paid for by small contributions, largely in goods. His plan was almost too simple. Courtesy of the whaler, *George Henry*, Hall was to be transported to Baffin Island and from there, with Inuit companions, he would travel by sledge to King William Island.[12]

Unfortunately, after landing on Baffin Island, Hall's expedition boat was wrecked, and he was limited to excursions in the Frobisher Bay area. This setback had its silver lining, however. Hall made the acquaintance of two Inuit, who would become his loyal companions, Ebierbing (Ipiirvik) and Tookoolito (Taqulittuq). Over the course of several expeditions, Tookoolito served as interpreter for innumerable conversations, and Ebierbing served as trusty guide and competent hunter for both Hall, and later, Schwatka. Confined to Frobisher Bay, Hall made an excursion during which he made a noteworthy discovery unrelated to Franklin, relics from Martin Frobisher's expeditions of 1576, 1577 and 1578, whose voyages, like those of another sixteenth-century navigator, John Davis, had become mythical.

Tookoolito (Taqulittuq).

Ebierbing (Ipiirvik).

Two years later, in 1864, Hall managed to sail north again on board the whaler *Monticello*, with a similar objective and plan of action. Accompanied by Tookoolito and Ebierbing, Hall intended to establish his camp at Repulse Bay, adopt an Inuit lifestyle and visit King William Island. However, he was mistakenly landed on the coast of Hudson Bay more than one hundred miles south of Repulse Bay. Making the best of the situation, however, he learned from the Inuit the area where many years before two ships had sunk, and a great many white men had starved to death. Remarkably, to his great joy he learned that there were three or four who did not die. He was also informed that some of the survivors had lived on the flesh of their comrades.[13]

After a series of frustrating delays, it was not until the spring of 1866 that Hall was able to make a move toward King William Island. Although his Inuit companions proved unpredictable escorts, prone to hunting diversions and superstitious distractions, Hall managed to collect some intelligence regarding the lost expedition. From the Pelly Bay Inuit he gathered testimony as to the fate of the two ships, the disastrous retreat of Franklin's men and hard evidence in the form of discarded relics, silverware, and equipment. As far as the two ships, one had been crushed in the ice and sunk, and the other rummaged for valuables as it drifted south near Ook-joo-lik (which Hall believed was near O'Reilly Island). The Inuit also told Hall of the aggressive behavior of another group, the Nattilingmiut, who were prepared to kill and plunder any group that entered their region. The threat of bloodshed roused such fear among Hall's travelling companions that they refused to visit King William Island, so Hall was forced to retreat to Repulse Bay. The return trip was sadly marked by personal tragedy. "King William," Tookoolito's infant child, weakened and died while on the trail. It was only by tender coaxing that she finally surrendered the child for burial.

For the next two years Hall's excursions were limited to the area of Melville Peninsula, as he chased down (unsuccessfully) rumors that white men, perhaps the lone straggling survivors of Franklin's party, had been seen there. Hall was not deterred by the fact that it was a highly improbable place for Franklin's men to have been looking for rescue or relief. One rumor that a "monument," together with a lone white stranger, had been spotted near Cape Englefield on the far northwest corner of Melville Peninsula, sent Hall on a three-month quest to the location. There he found a stone monument (possibly an Inuit inukshuk), and a tenting place he believed was constructed by white men. Alas, there were no records. The far-fetched report was possibly a sighting of the cairn erected by John Rae twenty-five miles south of Cape Englefield during his 1847 excursion. The imaginative tale of Franklin's men stranded near Cape Englefield would also later figure prominently in Schwatka's expedition.

Hall returned to Repulse Bay, disgruntled with his Inuit travelling companions who had balked at continuing their journey out of fear of a hostile encounter with the Nattilingmiut. With the perceived need for several "armed white men as a guard," Hall sought out the services of several whaling men and convinced five to join him. Hall's relations with the whalers proved to be no better than they had been with the Inuit. Hall shot and killed one of them, Patrick Coleman, under suspicious circumstances. Hall claimed that he had been threatened by "mutinous conduct," but his behavior in returning to his tent to retrieve the gun with which he killed Coleman had the markings of a premeditated act. Hall was never prosecuted, due to the jurisdictional uncertainties within the regions of the north, but had anyone fully scrutinized the affair, Hall's leadership capacity would have been sorely questioned.[14]

In the spring of 1869, with a party of Inuit, the persistent Hall again attempted to reach King William Island. While en route to Boothia Peninsula, Hall met a group of Inuit at Pelly Bay, who possessed a number of Franklin relics taken from a large ship at King William Island: a stone jug, an Inuit lamp fashioned from copper, the edge of a sword, and a wooden snow shovel made from the plank of a ship. In getting wood out of the ship, the Inuit claimed that the ship had sunk after a hole had been bored. Hall was alarmed to hear tales suggestive of cannibalism among the remains found of white men: "arms, legs, &c., were found cut off to be eaten, and the cut of the bone had always showed this to have been done by a saw." At a further encampment on Boothia Peninsula, Hall encountered a group of Nattilingmiut who also possessed a number of Franklin relics, including a spoon bearing Franklin's crest. One individual whom Hall was pleased to see was Innookpoozhejook (previously known to Rae), who provided a wealth of information. The Inuk provided Hall with a sketch identifying a number of important locations: where a ship had sunk off O'Reilly Island; one of the Todd Islands off the southeast coast of King William Island where the remains of five bodies were found; a "boat-place" on the northwest coast of King William Island; and an island on the west coast of the inlet of which Richardson Point forms the east cape (later Schwatka's Starvation Cove), where a boat and the remains of a great many men could be found.[15]

As for the ship off O'Reilly Island, while boarding it the Inuit had found the body of a big man in a cabin with his clothes on, remarkable for his "long teeth," which made a strong impression, as well as the fact that five men could not lift him. The ship was well stocked and untouched; sails, rigging, and boats were still in place. The Inuit had stripped it of useful materials over time, but it was inadvertently sunk by the Inuit who had cut a hole in the ship to remove some planking. Of great interest to Hall were reports that the tracks of four men, "kabloonas," were seen on the land near where the ship sank.

Innookpoozhejook described the "boat-place" on King William Island (determined by Hall to be at the bottom of Terror Bay), separate from the "boat-place" found by Hobson, as a location where a tent and bones had also been found. A boat at Terror Bay contained bones and "a great many papers and books and written stuff were in it." Hall noted that "these are all trash to the Inuit; the winds and the weather had made destructive work of them. The Innuits [sic] would trample them under feet as if grass." Inside the tent were a large number of bones with the flesh removed. The Inuk also repeated facts suggestive of cannibalism: "some bones had been sawed with a saw; some skulls had holes in them." There were numerous relics within the tent: blankets, cups, spoons, forks, knives, pistols, and interestingly "papers and books written upon." According to Hall's notes, "as these last were good for nothing for Innuits [sic], the men threw them away," except for one book which was given to the children and ultimately torn to pieces.[16]

Hall's Inuit companions had advised him that four mutilated bodies (limbs severed and flesh removed) and one untouched corpse had been found on Keeuna (Todd Island); curiously, a tin can of meat had also been found there and was eaten by the Inuit. Hall quickly scouted Todd Island with Innookpoozhejook but found only one large thigh bone since the land was deeply covered with snow. While at Todd Island, an Inuit woman interviewed by Hall also confirmed that a boat and many skeletons were located on an inlet to the west of Richardson Point, evidently Starvation Cove, a location Hall was unable to visit. She also told Hall that many of the bodies had the flesh cut off as if "to eat." Crossing from Todd Island to King William Island near the Peffer River, a skeleton was uncovered (later attributed to Lieutenant Henry Le Vesconte of HMS *Erebus*), and a monument built.[17]

Hall also received reports of a meeting of Franklin's men when the Inuit were camped on the southwest shore of King William Island. The white men were dragging one large sledge with a boat and a smaller one with supplies. The leader, Ag-loo-ka (possibly Crozier, and known to them from Parry's expedition), had a telescope on his neck and was seen shooting several geese. He was also observed writing notes in a small book. The Inuit understood by sign language that the white men were heading toward Repulse Bay. The Inuit offered a rather interesting description of Franklin's men: one was "very fat," the others "all poor"; one was missing his front teeth; one man was cross-eyed, and another had marks on the saddle of his nose. Hall was furious to learn that the Inuit had left the white men to their fate. He was just as furious with his own Inuit companions who refused to travel further west along the coast of King William Island to Terror Bay. Once again fearful of an encounter with the Nattilingmiut, they sought the refuge of Repulse Bay.

Within the span of some four weeks, Hall had uncovered more information than he had in all of his previous four years. Hall's five-year quest had demonstrated the unlikelihood that any of Franklin's men had survived. There matters largely stood until 1877.

CHAPTER SIX

IN THE LAND OF THE MIDNIGHT SUN

FREDERICK SCHWATKA HAD SETTLED in for a quiet winter at the relocated Spotted Tail Agency. The pace of activity at the agency necessarily slowed during the winter months as snowstorms and frigid weather limited outdoor activity. For the time being, young Schwatka was resigned to routine matters within the agency, a discouraging state of affairs for this restless man of action. News from the outside slowly trickled its way to the remote location, however, and when the January 23, 1878 issue of the *New York Herald* reached his desk, an article immediately caught his attention, the subject of which stirred his ambition. The timing could not have been better.[1]

According to the *New York Herald*, the American Geographical Society in New York City was outfitting an expedition to the Far North for reasons connected with the lost explorer, Sir John Franklin. But why was this British explorer, the subject of an international manhunt played out some twenty years ago, suddenly newsworthy again? After all, Franklin's fate had been conclusively determined in 1859 when Sir Leopold McClintock discovered the written record of his lost expedition on King William Island and with it, confirmation of the death of Franklin himself. Even Charles Francis Hall, the eccentric and wildly optimistic searcher who visited King William Island as late as 1869, would have conceded that the likelihood of finding any survivors at this point in time would have been highly unlikely. However, it was not survivors, or even the bones of Sir John, that had sparked the most recent Franklin frenzy. It was his tableware, specifically a spoon bearing his family crest.

The improbable tale leading to this newfound interest first began while Captain Edwin Potter, second officer Thomas Barry, and the crew of the aptly named New Bedford whaler, *Glacier*, were passing the winter of 1871-72 in Repulse Bay, about five hundred miles distant from King William Island by sledge. The commercial hunt for whale oil and baleen had led resourceful whalemen like those of the *Glacier* to extend their range throughout the cold, icy waters of the North Atlantic Ocean, even to the far reaches of this remote northwestern corner of Hudson Bay. The fishery there had been initiated in 1860, after two adventurous American whaleships first overwintered in the bay and returned with lucrative bowhead captures. The productive whaling grounds were largely confined to a stretch of about four hundred miles in and below Roes Welcome Sound, from Repulse Bay and Lyon Inlet in the north to Marble Island in the south. Due to the presence of pack ice throughout most of the year, single season voyages were impracticable. Whaleships like the *Glacier* would only reach the region by mid-August, and by late September would be settling in for winter at one of several harbors: Repulse Bay, Fullerton Harbour, Depot Island or Marble Island. The following spring, whaling in small boats from floe ice was possible until whaleships were released by July, after which they would spend a month or two hunting before returning home. The number of ships engaged in the Hudson Bay whale fishery was always small, about 146 in total between 1860 and 1915, but after 1870 it numbered no more than six ships per year. The fishery was dominated by the Yankee whalers from New Bedford and New London, and according to one Inuit observer, "the first whalers here spoke American."[2]

The influx of American whalemen altered the traditional lifestyle and material culture of the Inuit and introduced infectious diseases, just as contact with Euro-Americans had transformed other Indigenous cultures. Inuit employment became integral to the whaling practice, with the Inuit hired to supply fresh meat for the crews, manufacture clothing and to assist in whaling activities. In exchange for their services, the Inuit would receive manufactured goods of use to them, such as guns and ammunition, and mainstays like matches, tobacco, sugar, and tea. The area of Roes Welcome Sound was historically occupied by the Aivilingmiut, whose hunting skill was of particular importance to the whalers. As a result of the relative permanence of the whaling stations, life became centered around the whaling stations for an extended portion of the year. Word of mouth of the availability of the American goods attracted other Inuit groups to the whaling stations, such as the Nattilingmiut of King William Island and the Adelaide Peninsula region. It was for just that reason that they were led to the *Glacier*.

According to Barry, during that long winter of 1871-72, several

Inuit built their snow huts at Repulse Bay near the *Glacier*, among them two Nattilingmiut families who had travelled from the region of King William Island. The Inuit were in desperate need of pots, kettles and cooking utensils, and Captain Potter and Thomas Barry supplied the needed kitchen items in exchange for what looked to be several elegant pieces of silverware (three spoons), more suited for a Victorian dinner party than the mess of a whaleship. While Thomas Barry was making entries in his journal one evening by the dim candlelight of the ship, one observant Inuk peering over Barry's shoulder remarked that the book Barry was writing in was similar to one in which he had seen white men writing in previously. Believing that the earlier white men were from Franklin's party, Barry (who claimed to be fluent in Inuktitut), inquired further and received a response from two of the Nattilingmiut, which he paraphrased as follows:

> Many winters previous a party of white men came to where their tribe was then passing the winter, all of whom died of cold and hunger, the winter being very severe; that during that winter there was neither game nor seals, and they had themselves to subsist on the skins of seals and other animals; that one of the white men, whom the Esquimaux called a *leader* or *father*, was a stout man, who wore a coat with three stripes of some kind on the lower part of the sleeve, who gave directions to the others; that the white men died one man after the other, those who remained burying those who died, wrapping up the body in a kepick or blanket with which the Esquimaux cover themselves while sleeping, laying it upon a rock near by, and covering it with stones to keep it from the wolves and bears, and that when the spring came all were dead; that after many had died the rest made a ketch (*cairn* or *cache*) and put under it something resembling the book in which Barry was writing.[3]

Evidently, the map-reading skills of the two Inuit were proficient enough to indicate where the white men were buried by tracing on a map supplied by Barry. Starting from Repulse Bay, they followed the coast of Melville Peninsula northwards to the projection of Cape Englefield at the entrance to Fury and Hecla Strait. From there they pointed out the location of an island not found on the chart not far to the northwest in the Gulf of Boothia. This island was identified as the location where the whites were buried and the site where the cairn was to be found. Though recognizing that this new tantalizing information may have been of great import, Barry claimed he was forestalled from journeying to the location by lack of equipment and supplies.

But Barry's story was not the only "buried treasure" tale brought home by the *Glacier*. Interestingly, in 1873, the *New York Herald* reported Captain Potter's version of a conversation with a visiting Nattilingmiut group while on the *Glacier* during the winter of 1871-72. Though Potter's version offered different facts that might suggest a contradiction with Barry's tale, on closer examination, Potter's version may simply have been a different conversation (Potter never claimed that Barry was present during Potter's conversation with the Inuit and vice versa). In Potter's telling of the tale, several Inuit had made their way to Repulse Bay and the *Glacier* that memorable winter of 1871-72. On route to the whaleship, one elderly, starving Inuk in the group met his demise on the journey. Evidently, the Inuk had been an eyewitness to the Franklin disaster. Upon reaching the *Glacier,* it was left to his Inuit companions to relate the deadman's story to the whaleman. Potter claimed that he was told that Franklin's men headed south toward the territory of Hudson Bay (and not north and east to Melville Peninsula) and that five men, all frozen to death, were found on an unidentified shore under an overturned boat. Potter's account fails to mention any books or records. However, Potter did specifically mention that he acquired four spoons and two forks, all of which were silver, of which one spoon and one fork were indistinctly engraved with Sir John Franklin's crest (a conger-eel between two branches). When asked by Potter how the formal tableware was obtained, he was informed by the Nattilik Inuk (whom he claimed could communicate in broken English), that "they belonged to Mr. Franklin." The tale told to Potter, though differing from that told to Barry, accurately described events recited to Charles Francis Hall and later to Frederick Schwatka. Curiously, the *Glacier's* logbook, largely a day-to-day account of routine ship-related activities, and a possible primary source record as to what occurred, notes only one relevant clue that offers little clarification of either the account told to Barry or to Potter. On August 17, 1872, a marginal notation simply states, "got today silver fork," with no mention of any spoons or any associated story.[4]

In any event, the topic resurfaced in 1877 while Thomas Barry was again on another whaling voyage to the same area of Hudson Bay. Barry's whaleship for this voyage, the *Ann Houghton*, while plying an icefield off Cape Fullerton, had the misfortune of striking a reef and sinking in June 1877. The crew spent a miserable week huddled on a large rock treading above high-water, with only a tent sail as shelter, until rescued by other whalers. The survivors ultimately returned to New York in September

1877. During Barry's voyage, in the fall of 1876 prior to the disaster that befell the *Ann Houghton*, Barry claimed to have obtained another silver spoon from an Nattilingmiut group at Whale Point, which he subsequently learned was engraved with Sir John Franklin's crest. Under questioning by Barry, the Nattilingmiut (three men aged fifty to sixty years, two of whom did most of the talking), offered the same details as those provided by the other Nattilingmiut in 1872, identifying an island to the northwest of Cape Englefield as the location where white men were buried and the location of the cairn holding the journals.[5]

Upon his return to New York City in the fall of 1877, Barry informed John C. Morison of the shipping firm of Morison & Brown (owners of the ill-fated *Ann Houghton*), of the Nattilingmiut encounter on board the *Glacier* in 1872, as well as his more recent meeting in 1876. Morison, a consummate businessman, was immediately taken with the story, not by virtue of the honors attached to the discovery of the long-lost records, but rather the potential for a pecuniary reward for their recovery. Although Lady Franklin's £20,000 reward for the fate of Franklin had been well publicized (and ultimately paid), less well known was that in early 1872, she had offered another reward of £2,000 for the recovery of records of the Franklin expedition. Not shy in the least on the subject, Morison corresponded with Rear Admiral William Gore Jones, naval attaché to the British Legation, to ascertain the status of any reward. The response was encouraging. He was informed that Lady Franklin's reward had expired, but the British government would undoubtedly tender a reward (although its amount was not stated) for the recovery of any records from the Franklin expedition.[6]

Motivated to outfit an expedition to retrieve the records, but lacking the funds with which to do so, Morison brought the matter to the attention of Judge Patrick Daly, president of the American Geographical Society. Morison had hit upon an opportune partner. By 1877, the society, which had been founded in 1851, had achieved a level of international recognition in the field of geographical science with the guidance of a handful of farsighted councilors. Arctic exploration had always been at the forefront of its interests, and it had advocated on behalf of the expeditions of Elisha Kent Kane, Isaac Israel Hayes and Charles Francis Hall, largely through the efforts of Henry Grinnell. In fact, the humanitarian quest to find Franklin on Grinnell's part served as an impetus to the founding of the society. From 1864, the society's activities had been directed by President Daly, who was obsessed with the science of geography and a competent geographer in his own right. Like his predecessor Henry Grinnell, according to the historian of the geographical society, Arctic exploration was "the subject he [Judge Daly] followed most closely." Not surprisingly, Barry's story of the lost Franklin expedition, an expedition that went to the heart of the society, completely piqued his interest. This led to his further consideration of the matter and a subsequent interview with Thomas Barry.[7]

Daly had also served as chief justice of the Court of Common Pleas in New York for more than twenty-five years and was one of the state's most competent judges. Although generally enthusiastic about exploration, he applied his inquisitorial judicial mindset to matters before the society and was reluctant to accept new theories or information without pragmatic scrutiny. Thus, it is not surprising that Daly personally conducted an interview of Barry, and after "a long and satisfactory conversation," came to believe in the truthfulness of Barry's story. Ever the jurist though, he had the entire conversation transcribed, and sought corroborative information to assess the story's veracity.[8]

Daly turned to Hall's companion Ebierbing, then residing in Groton, Connecticut, who was acquainted with Barry, the two having evidently crossed paths in Hudson Bay. On Daly's behalf, Ebierbing conducted an interview with Barry that proved to be a remarkable cultural turnabout for Inuit relations. Historically, Inuit testimony was simply dismissed as untrustworthy or intentionally misrepresented, as Dickens had claimed when faced with Inuit reports that Franklin's men engaged in cannibalism. Here, an Inuk was asked to assess the language skills of a white man, Thomas Barry, and the veracity of Barry's statements. Daly's open-minded fact finding seems more than simply a product of his judicial background. Daly recognized Ebierbing's skills and intelligence and held him in respect, even publicly hailing him as a savior of the castaway crew of the *Polaris*. Ebierbing was also a welcome guest at the Daly household, comfortable enough to visit unannounced when in New York City. Maria Daly, Judge Daly's wife, was so taken with Ebierbing's cordial deportment that she remarked in her diary that he is "more of a natural gentleman than many an [sic] one calling himself such." Evidently a good judge of character, in contrast, she confided that she found the explorer Charles Francis Hall, "a very ignorant man…. Under an appearance of great simplicity and honesty he is self-seeking and pushing and has an ugly, vindictive temper I should judge."[9]

In any event, following Ebierbing's interview with Barry, he advised Judge Daly that "I know Thomas F. Barry; speaks Repulse Bay Esquimaux… He speaks it pretty well; about as well as I speak English." "Repulse Bay Esquimaux," was Ebierbing's reference to "whalers' pidgin," a jargon developed by the whalers and the Inuit, principally the Aivilingmiut of that region, to communicate with sailors in the whaling trade. The jargon comprises Inuktitut vocabulary, mostly nouns with a few verbs and little grammar. In his affidavit, Barry claimed he had learned the "Esquimaux language" from the Aivilingmiut of Repulse Bay. However, his affidavit references a number of words and phrases in "whalers' pidgin," confirming that it was this vernacular that he had used to communicate and not Inuktitut. Barry's information was acquired from the Nattilingmiut, who travelled to Repulse Bay for work and trade, and who could also have understood the jargon. Ebierbing had confirmed that Barry could not speak in the language of the Nattilingmiut. In any event, the fragmentary means of communication via "whaler's jargon" could certainly be susceptible to misinterpretation or misunderstanding.[10]

Interestingly, Ebierbing did not offer an unqualified endorsement of Barry's story. He concluded that "I think it probable that what the [Nattilingmiut] told Barry at Marble Island, when he was with Capt. Potter, might be true," but he added a significant qualification that the Nattilingmiut "might fool the white men when talking to them" as they feared the white men might blame them for the death of Franklin's men. However, Ebierbing did add a weighty fact in Barry's favor gathered from his own experience in the vicinity of Cape Englefield, having visited the region with Hall. Ebierbing confirmed the existence of an island in the vicinity of the location identified by Barry to the northwest of Cape Englefield, an island that Ebierbing and Hall had seen but had been prevented from visiting due to heavy ice. (The low-lying island, also reported on by Hall, was named Crown Prince Frederik Island by Knud Rasmussen in 1922). Based on Barry's statements and Ebierbing's generally supportive testimony, and perhaps influenced by Daly's own wishful thinking, Daly convinced himself that there was some truth to Barry's story. The geographical society would endorse an expedition to attempt to locate the written records. The expedition, referred to hereafter as "The Franklin Records Search Expedition," would be the only exploring expedition actively supported by the geographical society through its own funds or through fundraising efforts between 1863 and 1890.[11]

Following Daly's efforts, Morison turned to the British Admiralty to assess the information thus far obtained. Morison's account was submitted to the renowned explorers Sir Leopold McClintock and Doctor John Rae for review. It was time for the "Arctic Worthies" to render their opinions. Fully knowledgeable of King William Island and the Inuit of the region, McClintock was rightly skeptical of any records being discovered since the efforts of Rae, Hall and McClintock would likely have known or heard of their existence. Though sounding a bit dismissive of whalemen as a rule, his observations carried a real ring of truth and may have pinpointed the crux of the matter. McClintock remarked that the possession by whalemen of "the mere smattering of the Esquimaux language, such as the whaling seamen are able to acquire, compels them frequently to put leading questions; hence arise mistakes and confusion, rendering any information obtained through them open to grave suspicion." McClintock's response also identified other questionable aspects of Barry's story, such as the inaccuracy of the locations mentioned and the improbability of Franklin's officers wearing dress uniforms while on the march. Nonetheless, McClintock did not foreclose the possibility of finding some further information as to the fate of Franklin's crews, but he remained highly skeptical as to Barry's interpretation of the Inuit communication.[12]

John Rae offered a more direct rebuttal and what he argued was a rather logical solution to the matter. Rae concluded that "the whole report brought home by Barry I believe to be a mistake in all its important particulars, and if the Franklin records are ever found, it certainly will not be anywhere in the neighborhood of Cape Inglefield [sic]." Rae was of the opinion that the supposed cairn on the island off Cape Englefield in Barry's report was in fact the cairn that Rae had built twenty-five miles to the south of Cape Englefield in 1847. Rae also believed that it was the same cairn that in 1868 Hall had also mistaken as one constructed by Franklin's men. Rae even went so far as to state that the Inuit visited Rae's cairn years later and had notified Rae of the cairn, not realizing Rae himself had built it.[13]

Not all British Arctic explorers sounded as pessimistic a tone as McClintock and Rae, veterans with a personal stake in the Franklin search. A more encouraging assessment was advanced by a naval officer of a younger generation, Captain Albert Hastings Markham, who was present at a geographical society meeting in New York while on a cross-country jaunt (which included a dignitary western buffalo hunt, courtesy of the U.S. Army). After speaking to Barry and Ebierbing, Markham weighed in with his own opinion, stating that the story sounded plausible enough that an attempt should be made to find the records. Undaunted by doubters, Judge Daly nonetheless proceeded to set about organizing the Franklin Records Search Expedition.[14]

A revealing side note to the British involvement in the American search for Franklin played out as Morison and Daly formulated their plans. In

December 1877, the initial newspaper reports of Thomas Barry's account had reached Sophia Cracroft, niece of Sir John Franklin and close confidant of Lady Jane Franklin. Understandably curious to learn more of the circumstances where the Inuit encountered Franklin's starving men and the location of the cairn, she wrote directly to Thomas Barry, politely requesting further details. Barry handed the letter to his employer, John Morison, who curtly brushed off Cracroft, refusing to disclose any details of the location of the cairn so as to avoid competition for its discovery. At the same time, Cracroft was also corresponding with Professor Joseph E. Nourse, a Presbyterian minister and professor of mathematics at the U.S. Naval Observatory, who volunteered to gather what little information he could about the matter. Their acquaintance had begun after Nourse took on the daunting task of organizing Hall's rambling writings from his 1864-69 expedition for publication. (Hall's papers had been purchased by the U.S. government in 1874). As Nourse went about that task, beginning in April 1877, he had dogged Sophia Cracroft for two journals that Hall had generously loaned to Lady Franklin before his death. Among the loaned materials was a quarto work, Hall's so-called "Franklin Record Book," containing Inuit oral testimony ("conversations") collected by Hall during his sojourn, copies of which Nourse evidently did not possess.

In early December 1877, eight months later and after multiple requests, Ms. Cracroft promised Nourse that she would return the requested journals within a few days. Her response came with some admonitions, however. First, she made the logical suggestion that Nourse communicate with Sir Leopold McClintock in preparing the Hall publication, as McClintock was certainly an expert on the region visited by Hall. However, her request went further, suggesting suppression of certain content within Hall's journals. She wrote to Nourse that "there are passages of these very interesting journals which will no doubt be omitted altogether, as resting upon authority which Mr. Hall discovered to be untrustworthy." Though she did not specify which particular aspects should be censored, the statements by the Inuit that they had seen many bodies with flesh cut off "as if some one or other had cut it off to eat," were likely areas of concern. Judging by her next request, that concern must have been palpable. She asked that proof sheets be sent for review before publication to an expanded group of prominent British participants in the search: Sir Leopold McClintock, Vice Admiral Sir George Henry Richards, Admiral Richard Collinson and Sir Allen Young. The anxious request strongly suggested that this group of British naval heavyweights had an interest in controlling Hall's narrative, and with it, Franklin's legacy. Some of them would have an outspoken say about Schwatka's expedition at a later date, and Schwatka would also be the recipient of a similar censorship request.

To Nourse's continued frustration, Hall's journals were not forthcoming. Two weeks later, on December 14, 1877, Ms. Cracroft backtracked from her promise to send them immediately, requesting permission to hold them for a few weeks longer. Her justification was that the breaking story of Barry's report necessitated a review of those journals by McClintock as to Hall's trip to Melville Peninsula, the area within which Barry had reported on the cairn housing the Franklin records. But the delay only continued. It was not until a further seven months later, in July 1878, after the Franklin Records Search Expedition had departed, that an exasperated Nourse finally obtained the materials from Sophia Cracroft. Their return followed a separate plea to Admiral William Gore Jones for their return and Nourse's not so subtle threat to publish the fact that the materials had been withheld.

※ ※ ※ ※ ※

When the January 23 issue of the *Herald* crossed his desk at Spotted Tail Agency, Frederick Schwatka was eager to embark on the next adventure in his life, and ready to take the bold step from that of brave and obedient junior officer to that of leader with absolute authority and full responsibility. Immediately upon reading the news about the supposed cairn and a proposed search, he hastily dispatched a letter to John Morison pleading his case. In the letter he enumerated the hardships he had undergone on the Plains, and offered to lead the expedition, concluding that he "was not deterred by the trials to be encountered in the Arctic Regions." Both Morison and Daly were intrigued by the young soldier's offer. Recognizing that a personal interview would be the best means to size up the cavalryman, they immediately sent for him to meet them in New York City. Hopeful and optimistic, Schwatka must have viewed his chances as fairly good when he was asked to leave his post and undertake the long cross-country journey by rail.[15]

As a twenty-eight-year-old lieutenant, with an excellent military service record, but no Arctic experience, Schwatka was still a relative unknown outside his immediate military circle. But Schwatka came well prepared for his interview. "Arctic Fever" had fully grabbed hold of him. He found the American frontier, as expansive as it was, rapidly trodden by the creeping footsteps of civilization. His dream had become one of making a name for himself in that untouched arena, later declaring in one magazine that "the great unexplored Arctic may now be said to be the only field that is left to satisfy a worthy ambition." While stationed at

Camp Sheridan in 1876-77, he had devoted himself to the study of the Arctic regions and its exploration to date, so much so that he arrived at his interview fully conversant in the subject. So enamored was Schwatka with the Arctic that, according to Brackett, Schwatka had filed a formal application with the government to accept any Arctic exploring detail that might become available.[16]

At the time, it was difficult not to be captivated by the Arctic regions. Tales of new lands, thrilling natural wonders and spectacular disasters made for exciting press, and there were certainly enough of them to capture Schwatka's interest. Following McClintock's determination of Franklin's fate in 1859 and the conclusion of Hall's own search between 1864-69, science and geography had become their own justification for further efforts in the Far North. There was no scarcity of opinions about the importance of exploration of the Arctic among an inquisitive Victorian society that sought to quantify the natural and physical world. Much of the Arctic and its natural resources remained unexplored and uninvestigated. This pursuit of discovery was not limited to England and America; an imperialistic spirit motivated other European nations to actively enter the polar arena, as they looked to solve the vexing questions of the Arctic regions and establish their own mark in the north. A field of endeavor that had been pursued with unrelenting vigor by the Royal Navy during the Franklin search was expanded by competition among several nations vying for polar firsts. By the 1870s, one of those great polar causes was the discovery of the North Pole, which had become an obsession in its own right. As the spirit of Manifest Destiny was rapidly taming the American frontier, an adventurous Frederick Schwatka turned his attention to the unsettled Arctic frontier, a place where one could still make a name as an "explorer."

Schwatka had certainly followed the news of the disastrous expedition to reach the North Pole sponsored by the U.S. Government in 1871-73 under the command of Charles Francis Hall. After the expedition ship, *Polaris,* had settled into winter quarters, Hall had died under suspicious circumstances, and rumors circulated that he had been murdered by Emil Bessels, his onetime scientific officer. Matters went from bad to worse. Half the crew was separated from the ship and spent six months drifting south on a melting icepan, exposed to the elements and suffering from starvation and cold until being rescued. Ebierbing and Hans Hendrik, two of the stranded crew, had managed to keep them alive only by their hunting prowess.

At the same time as the *Polaris* debacle, European countries, likewise suffering from "Arctic Fever," set their sights on the north. In 1872,

Austria-Hungary, an unlikely polar entrant bordering the Adriatic Sea, embarked on its first major Arctic expedition through the urging of Count Johann Wilczek. The expedition ship, *Tegethoff*, shared an all-too-common fate, beset in the ice, its crew forced to make a dangerous retreat by small boat to the west coast of Novaya Zemlya, where they were ultimately rescued.

More recently, Schwatka could not have missed the exploits of the British Arctic Expedition of 1875-76, which had returned from Smith Sound in the fall of 1876 after an unsuccessful attempt on the Pole. No expense had been spared for this venture, the largest in terms of both cost and its complement of men. The princely sum of £150,000 was allocated to its success. The two-ship expedition, which included the HMS *Alert* and HMS *Discovery,* was the highlight of the summer season. So numerous were the banquets feting the would-be conquerors that the weary officers had to decline a number of them just to continue the work at hand. A crowd of two hundred thousand spectators jammed Portsmouth harbor to cheer them on their departure on May 22, 1875. "Waiting to be Won" was the title of a jingoistic cartoon in the graphically illustrated magazine *Punch*. If sheer energy and enthusiasm was all that was necessary to assure success, the British Arctic Expedition should have cruised to the Pole with little effort. Alas, the rousing send-off may have been among the most eventful moments of the expedition. After a failed North Pole attempt and after suffering badly from scurvy, the expedition limped home in the fall of 1876. A glum Captain George Nares, the commander, informed the Admiralty the disappointing news that "Pole Impracticable. No land to the northward, otherwise voyage successful.... The impracticability of reaching the North Pole was proved."

Perhaps of more interest to Schwatka was the 1875 summer voyage of the yacht *Pandora* by Allen Young (previously second officer on McClintock's *Fox* expedition), that demonstrated that interest in the Franklin expedition still held a singular attraction. Young's objective was an ambitious transit of the Northwest Passage in a single season, and with it, a visit to King William Island to search for the records and journals of the Franklin expedition. The *Pandora* was blocked by ice in Peel Sound, before returning the same season without reaching King William Island. Although a second attempt at the passage the following summer of 1876 was planned by Young in *Pandora,* those plans were modified by request of the Admiralty in order to have the *Pandora* communicate with the British Arctic Expedition.

Frederick Schwatka had followed these developments and must have considered them carefully as he assessed his own qualifications. At the age

Second Lieutenant Frederick Schwatka, April 1878.
Pach's Photographic Studio, New York.

of twenty-eight, he stood in the physical prime of his life, a commanding figure standing over six feet tall at a brawny two hundred pounds, with broad shoulders and a barrel chest. Gone was the fresh face of a youthful adolescent. In its place was a hardened persona, the fair complexion now markedly weather-beaten. A chevron moustache and goatee (so-called "Royale" style), popular at the time, as well as a thinning hairline, served as symbols of masculinity and maturity. Invariably attired in a well-worn uniform, he played the part of a serious, no-nonsense military man, confident in his task. At some point in recent years, to correct severe near-sightedness, he had donned distinctive pince-nez spectacles that added an intellectual look. But it was no illusion; underneath that exterior was a keen scientific (albeit amateur) observer and a passionate and capable writer, with a sincere love for the outdoors.

Although relatively young, having served with Crook on the frontier, Schwatka had gained hard-earned experience that would have equal application in an unforgiving arctic environment. Crook was an open-minded commander who recognized that enlisting Indigenous peoples could be integral to the success of his campaigns, a lesson that Schwatka took fully to heart. They knew the land, and the best means for traveling, adapting, and surviving, far better than Euro-American visitors. When encountering unfamiliar peoples, local guides provided comforting reassurance of peaceful intentions to otherwise cautious and mistrusting people and facilitated communication and information exchange. Coupled with his own ability to build mutual respect with Indigenous peoples, and a genial personality capable of engendering friendship and loyalty, Schwatka was well positioned to succeed in enlisting their support.

Under Crook's command, Schwatka also understood the difficulties associated with traveling over long distances through unfamiliar territory. As a military officer, he understood the need for planning, organization, and discipline as a means to success. With his training as a medical man, Schwatka was attuned to the physical needs of travelers. He knew from first-hand experience during the hardship of the Starvation March the importance of proper nutrition to maintaining peak physical condition. But those were simply the practical qualifications for what would be an epic journey. No longer a young boy tramping in the woods of the Northwest, Schwatka nonetheless continued to possess a streak of romantic adventurism. The grand accomplishments of the great explorer Dane Vitus Bering continued to serve as his own northern inspiration. He must have also felt an enormous level of pride that the Arctic expedition in which he was seeking to enlist was inextricably linked with that singularly gallant and noble endeavor, the discovery of the fate of Sir John Franklin's expedition.

With this background, in his interview, according to Morison, Schwatka handled himself well, a combination of his depth of relevant knowledge and his reassuring manner, complimented by a "manly deportment," all suggesting that he possessed the character and fitness to handle the command. Schwatka's frontier experience was certainly a practical positive, and his background as a man of science had obvious appeal to Daly. One more factor in Schwatka's favor was Daly's concern that the Nattilingmiut were "a warlike people," and that a military man would be an appropriate choice to lead the expedition. Fully impressed with Schwatka's qualifications to lead the party, Daly nonetheless sought independent confirmation of his abilities. Logically, for a recommendation, Daly turned to the man who could best speak to the young lieutenant's skills and personal fortitude—Schwatka's former commander Anson Mills, recently promoted to major, Tenth Cavalry. When questioned, Mills was enthusiastic in his support of Schwatka, recommending him highly and remarking that "he could not speak well enough of the young lieutenant's bravery in the field and his other soldierly qualities."[17]

Much credit for the success of the expedition was due to Daly's ability to thoughtfully assess Schwatka's qualifications and to ultimately place his confidence in the young man. Initially, Daly and Morison had planned to install Thomas Barry as the commander of the expedition, a decision that seems foolhardy in retrospect. With the arrival of Schwatka, the decision to appoint Barry leader of the land portion of the expedition was quickly reversed. Barry would still serve as captain of the transport ship.

Schwatka was also fortunate that his patron, Charles Daly, had sufficient influence to assure that Schwatka would be released from military service. Having won Daly's and Morison's support, official leave from the army was still a necessary predicate. As an upright jurist, Daly did not generally seek the society of politicians, scrupulously avoiding even the appearance of impropriety in his conduct. Nonetheless, he possessed a civic-minded disposition, and was invariably familiar with the nation's prominent citizens and politicians, crossing paths at the innumerable charitable and social affairs. Both he and his wife, Maria, were personally acquainted with President Rutherford B. Hayes, having previously met at a breakfast recently organized by Edwin Morgan, formerly governor of New York, and attended by John Jacob Astor. On Schwatka's behalf, Daly undertook to solicit President Hayes to obtain the needed release from Schwatka's military obligations, and to make the same request directly to William Tecumseh Sherman, commander in chief of the U.S. Army. Daly's letter to Sherman has survived, and it reflects shrewd positioning on Daly's part, emphasizing the perceived martial nature of the Nattilingmiut as justification for the need of a military man to command the Franklin Records Search Expedition:

My Dear General,

Messrs. Morison & Brown, shipping merchants of this city & members of our Society, are about to send out a whaling vessel for general whaling purposes, which will have to winter in Repulse Bay which is about 400 miles from the spot where we believe the last of Franklin's expedition perished. They are willing to send a party to this part of the Gulf of Boothia to look for the cairn, but they wish to have some person who is a military man and in whom they can place reliance to take charge of it. As the Nechilla [sic] Esquimaux, who live in that part of the Arctic, are supposed to be hostile, as they frequently make raids upon the Esquimaux South of them, and it is therefore necessary that the exploring party should have arms and military organization and be conducted by a military leader if it should happen to be attacked. They wish very much to place it under the direction of Lieut. F. Schwatka of the U.S. Cavalry, who is willing to go, if the Government will allow him. . . It would certainly reflect great credit upon us, as a Nation, if through us, the final fate of this large Expedition should be ascertained, and their records brought back, which are not only of interest, as ascertaining its final fate, but of scientific interest from the large portion of the Arctic which they explored. They were the real Discoverers of the Northward [sic] passage... I earnestly hope that the Lieut. may be detailed for this service with whom I have conversed, and who I think is a very competent young officer to be entrusted with this delicate duty. Charles P. Daly[18]

The request was not necessarily a foregone conclusion when it reached Sherman's desk. Leaves of absence from military service for personal glory in private endeavors were not freely granted. The hard-nosed general, who was focused on pacifying the West, firmly believed that staffing what he believed were frivolous and extraneous scientific or exploring crusades was not the proper role of the military. When weather observations were tasked to the army's signal unit, he bluntly remarked, "But what does a soldier care about the weather? Whether good or bad, he must take it as it comes." Similarly, when the talented and highly qualified Lieutenant Gustavus C. Doane, Second Cavalry, who had previously assisted in exploring the Yellowstone region, applied for leave to command Captain Henry Howgate's one-year "Preliminary Arctic Expedition," in 1877 (part of Howgate's plan to establish a scientific colony at Lady Franklin Bay), Sherman objected to his appointment, remarking that Doane was "a Cavalry Officer of too great service to be banished to the polar regions." Fortunately for Doane, Sherman was eventually overruled by the secretary of war.[19]

In this case, Schwatka's favorable connections worked to his benefit. Upon receipt by President Hayes of a similar request from Daly, President Hayes, unsure how to proceed, turned to Sherman directly. The president asked Sherman if an order from Sherman granting Schwatka leave of absence would suffice to free Schwatka from his service obligation and enable him to join the expedition. Sherman balked at the request, claiming that army protocol would not permit him to issue such a command, perhaps a thinly veiled means of avoiding political repercussions on Sherman's part if harm possibly came to the young lieutenant. Sherman responded to his adjutant that "leave of absence will not answer. Lt. Schwatka is advised to see the President in person."[20]

Interestingly, Sherman's personal thoughts on the matter, hastily scribbled as an afterthought alongside his response, reflect a high level of respect and perhaps even a fondness for the young lieutenant. Sounding like the reluctant father opposed to his headstrong son's aspirations but not prepared to deter him, Sherman shared his feelings, writing that Schwatka "is at the head of the list of 2nd Lts., 3rd Cavalry, strong & very handsome, too good a man to sacrifice on such an errand. Still, he is old enough to judge for himself. I would not order him to go on such an errand as herein set forth by Judge Daly, indeed would advise against it, but on this North Pole folly and the search for the 'papers' of Sir John Franklin given up as lost, men are willing to risk life and everything, and I do not desire to undertake objection. Wm. Sherman." In the end, President Hayes tendered Schwatka an indefinite leave of absence sweeping in its scope, in military lingo, permitting Schwatka "to go beyond the sea."[21]

With the expedition now beginning to take shape, public interest in the venture was initiated through the tandem efforts of Chief Justice Daly and the manager of the *Herald*, James Gordon Bennett, Jr. (generally referred to as Gordon Bennett). In 1867, the eccentric Bennett had taken the reins of the *Herald* from his father, James Gordon Bennett, Sr., the newspaper's founder. Gordon Bennett was an enterprising newspaperman who had recognized that competent journalists dispatching sensational stories from exotic locales made for exciting copy and increased circulation. Never was that more apparent than in Bennett's association with Henry Stanley and his quest for Dr. David Livingstone in the jungles of Central Africa. When Stanley "found" and interviewed Livingstone on the banks of the Lake Tanganyika, Stanley became an international celebrity, and the *Herald's* circulation multiplied. No longer was the press simply reporting the news. Gordon Bennett and the *Herald* were creating it. Bennett soon realized that Equatorial Africa was not the only region from which exciting copy could be obtained, and he was among the earliest newsmen to send reporters to the equally mysterious and sublime North. In the summer of 1873, *Herald* correspondents had accompanied the naval relief ships dispatched to West Greenland to search for missing members of the *Polaris* expedition. Much as they had done during the Indian wars, their lively accounts set the standard for adventure reporting. Besides providing sensational copy, *Herald* reporters shared the hardships and dangers of the expedition.[22]

Bennett's interest in the Arctic as a news locale would lead him to support the Arctic voyage of Allen Young in the *Pandora* in 1875, even subscribing to the tune of at least £4000. Bennett's hand-picked *Herald* correspondent, Januarius A. MacGahan, accompanied the voyage and delivered exciting copy with a flair for the dramatic and with it, a substantial increase in newspaper sales. When Thomas Barry arrived in 1877 with his remarkable tale, Bennett saw the opportunity for the next great "discovery" story if there ever was one. As a result, he supported the expedition from the outset, and he made sure that a *Herald* correspondent would accompany it.[23]

From his geographical society pulpit, Patrick Daly also championed exploration and field work to an ever-eager press, helping to keep geographical activities prominent in the public eye. "Public advocacy" of geographic endeavors was one of Daly's most significant contributions to the society. With his strong personal interest in the nascent Franklin Records Search Expedition, Daly certainly had his hand in its promotion from its formation until its departure, particularly through his connection with the *Herald*. To a large audience in Cooper Hall in February 1878, Daly delivered his annual geographical society address, with a special emphasis on the upcoming expedition. With his own flair for the theatrical, Ebierbing was also present on the platform, outfitted in arctic attire. Daly recounted at length the history of Barry's discovery, his own active involvement, and his belief that sufficient information had been communicated to justify a search for the Franklin records, where indicated by the Nattilingmiut, "at a comparatively small expense." In Daly's words, "the record of his journey is the very last thing that an explorer will part with, …in the hope that at some future time it would be found by civilized man." Giving Daly's annual address lengthy coverage, the *Herald* recounted Daly's comments nearly in full.[24]

Additionally, through several interviews reported in the *Herald,* the proposed expedition maintained a prominent position in the public eye. In January 1878, a *Herald* reporter held a lengthy interview with John Morison discussing the objectives and plans for the expedition. Of greater significance was the *Herald* reporter's interview of the newly appointed leader, Lieutenant Frederick Schwatka. The young cavalryman and his accomplishments were the focus of the interview, highlighting his Indian fighting skills, particularly his participation "in the bloody fight of the Rosebud just before Custer was killed and in the later engagement of the Slim Buttes, not to speak of the numerous other affairs of the prolonged campaign which ended with the surrender of Chief Joseph." In advance of events of the expedition themselves, Gordon Bennett knew how to arouse interest in the subject with sensationalism even prior to its departure, specifically by headlining the potential for hostile confrontations with the "warlike" Nattilingmiut. To further underscore that danger, a copy of Daly's letter to General Sherman, with its expressed fear of the combative Nattilingmiut and its appeal for a military man to lead the expedition, was reprinted in full along with Schwatka's interview. Likewise, in his *Herald* interview, the martial nature of the Nattilingmiut immediately became the center of attention:

> Who are the Nachillas [*sic*]?
> *They are a warlike tribe of savages to the north of those tribes of Esquimaux with whom our navigators have had to do so far. The Esquimaux report*

them as fierce and very hostile, on which account the latter have not been able to penetrate to the country where the cairn is believed to be.

You will have an escort?
Not a large one. But we shall be heavily armed. I shall take about six white men and about twenty Esquimaux. Our only danger is from the Nachillas [sic].

Will your force be large enough to encounter such a tribe?"
There are only about 150 of the Nachillas [sic] to fight. They are armed with bows, while we shall have breech-loading firearms, and be more than a match for them.[25]

The threat of the Nattilingmiut would become an oft-repeated point of tension and excitement in the press, portraying them as bigger than life bogeymen. No longer was the expedition simply a manly struggle of man against the natural world. The *Herald* created a more dramatic cultural conflict, that of the white man against the savage. The import was clear. Lieutenant Schwatka, the cavalryman who had subdued the Indians of the Plains, was preparing to do battle with, and to subdue, the savage Inuit of the Far North. The interview played to classic Victorian racial characterizations, the superiority of the Euro-Americans and their implements of civilization, one in which white men would always prevail in struggles with "primitive" cultures.

Much of the frenzy over the warlike nature of the Nattilingmiut can trace its roots to Ebierbing, who had raised the matter in his testimony to Judge Daly, and likely spread the word in subsequent conversations. While discussing his first face-to-face encounter with the Nattilingmiut when accompanying Hall in 1869, Joe stated that "they showed fight when we first saw them, and had knives, and one of them the barrel of a rifle made sharp like a knife." Ebierbing bolstered that narrative, remarking to a reporter with the *New York Tribune* in a separate conversation that they are "much larger than the men of most other tribes and very warlike."[26]

The geographical society endorsement of the project and Daly's advocacy on its behalf have long credited the American Geographical Society with the success of the endeavor. As is often the case, however, without the efforts of unheralded individuals who painstakingly handle the necessary practical details, many endeavors never would have gotten off the ground. That was certainly true in the case of the Franklin Records Search Expedition. Without the efforts of John C. Morison, who both originated the expedition and was largely responsible for its outfitting, the project never would have happened. By necessity and by design the Franklin Records Search Expedition was modestly outfitted, a circumstance that, in the end, contributed to its overall success. But even the most modest of expeditions require substantial assistance, and Morison worked behind the scenes to make it so.

The most significant outlay for the proposed expedition was the purchase or charter of a vessel for transport to Hudson Bay. Morison's firm satisfied that requirement by offering to outfit their sloop, *Eothen,* for a whaling voyage to that region, while at the same time transporting the exploring party to Repulse Bay at no cost. The firm also took on the not insubstantial task of additional refitting of the *Eothen* for an Arctic overwintering upon its anticipated return from its South Pacific sealing voyage. In contrast to other private expeditions, which relied upon cash contributions and innumerable and exhausting fundraising activities, cash subscriptions on behalf of the Franklin Records Search Expedition were nominal, amounting to approximately $450, mainly coming from Daly and several other geographical society members. As a result, largely through Morison's connections, most of the necessary materials and goods for the expedition came by arm-twisting suppliers to the whaling industry to persuade them to donate everything from "prayerbooks to pistols and pig-lead, from fireworks to fish-tackle and finger-bowls, and all the other various Boreal bric-a-brac...."[27]

The "bric-a-brac" included six hundred pounds of tobacco supplied by the Lorillard Company and five casks of "Blue Ribbon" beer that were generously furnished by the brewery Feigenspan & Co., the "Pride of Newark" (P.O.N.). Though the exploring party's intent was to live off the land, a donation of canned fruits and vegetables was accepted from the Erie Preserving Company of Buffalo, New York, one of the first canning companies in the country (but the canned foods spoiled after thawing before the first sledge journey). The "warlike" Nattilingmiut assured that the expedition was amply provided with firearms donations from the major arms companies: Winchester, Sharps, Remington, Whitney, Smith & Wesson, along with thousands of rounds of ammunition. A few scientific instruments were contributed by Bennett, e.g. a chronometer, sextant and aneroid barometer, and six alcohol thermometers (Fahrenheit scale) were donated by the firm of C. J. Tagliabue. The meager medicine kit consisted of a bottle of opium and some eyedrops. Lastly, the exploring party would be well read. Schwatka was pleased to receive a contribution from the publisher Appleton & Co. of a copy of all their publications on the Arctic.[28]

There was one highbrow public appeal that prevailed upon New

York's cultured class for the benefit of the expedition. Sebastian Bach Mills, a well-known concert pianist and former "infant prodigy," delivered a command solo performance that captivated the audience at Steinway Hall on the evening of May 22. Regrettably, the event netted few dollars despite the appearance of Ebierbing in arctic garb, and a gaudy exhibition of the donated firearms. More unusual were the few words offered by Morison in support of the expedition, who crassly remarked that if the expedition didn't find records or relics it might at least locate "skeletons from the expedition."

The publicity campaign carried on. In his interview with the *Herald*, Schwatka laid out his plans (referred to as an "experiment" by the press), which mirrored Morison's official instructions to Schwatka. Departing in June 1878, the land party under Schwatka, with all of their supplies and equipment, would be ferried to Repulse Bay by the *Eothen*, where, like the whalemen, they would employ Inuit assistants and some thirty to sixty dogs. The use of Repulse Bay was a logical starting point for a small party seeking to reach Cape Englefield on the west coast of the Boothia peninsula, or even King William Island for that matter. In that regard, Schwatka modeled his approach after that of both John Rae and Charles Francis Hall, who had organized small parties with a few white men and Inuit companions to travel largely coastal or water routes from Repulse Bay to Boothia Peninsula, and from Repulse Bay to the vicinity of King William Island.

Both Rae and Hall had launched their excursions in the spring, and after traveling as far as possible, had returned generally along the same outbound route to winter at or near Repulse Bay. Although Schwatka intended to follow the now beaten track with Inuit assistance, his strategy differed in that he planned to start his journey in late fall when snow would permit sledge travel. Upon reaching the cairn site (expected to be by November), winter quarters would be established at that location in readiness to commence the search as soon as snow cover had lifted the following spring. Thus, Schwatka would have longer search time than was available to McClintock or Hall. Returning to Repulse Bay, the *Eothen* (or a replacement) would settle in winter quarters and ferry the party home the following summer. Like many a hopeful Arctic plan, circumstances in the field would dictate adjustment. Schwatka's official instructions from Morison added two further significant considerations. If Schwatka located the remains of Sir John Franklin or any of his party, he was instructed to "take the same, have them properly taken care of and bring them with you." The *Eotheon*'s carpenter was to construct boxes before the sledge journey commenced for transporting any remains. Secondly, if by chance, the original purpose of the expedition should fail, "you will do your best to make it a geographical success, as you will be compelled to travel over a great deal of unexplored country."[29]

As for volunteers, Schwatka said that he had received a multitude of applications, most seeking to serve in any capacity, which signified in his opinion, "the absence of any capacity at all." It was Morison however who had the guiding hand and the final selections, and his choices proved, for the most part, to be excellent. Keeping tightly to the plan, the list was short. Thomas Barry was selected captain of the *Eothen* for the whaling voyage and was responsible for transporting the party to Repulse Bay. William Henry Gilder, correspondent for the *Herald* and Bennett's protégé, was appointed by Morison as second in command. Heinrich (Henry) Klutschak, a civil engineer and competent draughtsman, who was well known to Morison, was selected due to his "two years' experience in the country for which you are about to sail." Frank Melms was likewise chosen due to his two years of experience with a whaler in the Arctic regions. Melms himself claimed that another factor in his favor was that he was acquainted with the "native languages." Ebierbing was retained as a unanimous choice in light of his extensive experience. Of course, the plan was to enlist obtain additional assistance from the Inuit at Repulse Bay.[30]

The limited size of the exploring party assured that the men would be working and living in close quarters. Fortunately, each was possessed of an agreeable nature that led to a close-knit and supportive unit, despite their varied backgrounds. William Henry Gilder was born in Philadelphia in 1838 and had been raised in a proper nineteenth-century literary family before embarking on a life of adventure. His father, a clergyman, published several literary magazines, and later operated a female seminary. His brother, Richard Watson Gilder, served as long-time editor of *The Century Magazine* from 1881 to 1909. His sister, Jeannette Leonard Gilder, was a prominent female author, editor and critic at a time when men dominated the publishing field. Despite the genteel family background, William Gilder was a hard-as-nails veteran. At the start of the Civil War, he enlisted in the Fifth New York Volunteers, later transferring to the Fortieth New York Volunteers (the so-called "Mozart Regiment" after its sponsor, the Democratic Mozart Hall Committee). His combat courage was unquestionable. His unit suffered heavy losses at Gettysburg—of the 431 soldiers in his regiment, 143 were killed or wounded. For his own conduct, he was brevetted for "gallant and meritorious service," having been wounded in both the arm and leg. After the war, his interests turned to journalistic pursuits, serving as managing editor of the *Newark Register*

Colonel William Henry Gilder. Kreuger & Co. Studio, New York.

from 1871 to 1877, founded by his brother. In personal appearance, Gilder hardly fit the image of the seasoned explorer, but he was a splendid traveling companion and gifted writer. In 1886, a reporter for the *Montreal Star* described Gilder as follows:

> Rather under, rather than over, medium height, but compactly, broadly and strongly built. He is fair, fat and forty. Wears short red mustache and small side whiskers. Altogether looks more like a bon vivant than anything else. Dresses well, and has a partiality for good jewelry. In his talk he is modest, but somehow carries with him a subtle atmosphere of complacency, as a man conscious of proved strength. A brilliant conversationalist, equipped with a fund of anecdotes, which he relates with humorous zest, even when, as not frequently occurs, the story is against himself.[31]

Franz (Frank) Melms has generally referred to simply as an "experienced whaleman," but his background proved to be a bit more colorful. His father, Carl T. Melms, was of Prussian descent and after immigrating to Milwaukee in 1843, had founded the city's first brewery. With the success of the beer business, Carl Melms became the first "beer brewer baron" of

Milwaukee (the brewery was subsequently sold in 1871 to the Phillip Best Beer Brewery, later known as Pabst Brewery). His son, Frank, one of seven children, was born in 1849 and attended the best schools in Milwaukee. He soon "developed a roving disposition and love of adventure," according to his hometown newspaper. At the age of nineteen, the scrappy, fair-haired young man, all of 5 feet, 6 inches tall, left home to roam the prairie of the western states in some unknown capacity. Returning east, he shipped as a greenhorn on board the whaler *Isabella*, in 1875-77, captained by Henry Palmer out of New London. Sailing to Cumberland Sound, the ship spent two years in the vicinity of Davis Strait, overwintering on two occasions. The endeavor proved unspeakably harsh, so Melms must have had a strong constitution. At one point the *Isabella* was abandoned for fear of being crushed, with the crew making a harrowing retreat several miles across an icefield in the dark of winter under frigid temperatures. Close contact with the Inuit gave him a proficiency in their language and some understanding of their culture and habits. Undeterred by the experience, he volunteered for Schwatka's expedition. Originally retained as expedition cook, a position shared with Klutschak, he would soon make himself useful in all manner of work.[32]

Heinrich (Henry) W. Klutschak was born on May 3, 1848, in the city of Prague, Bohemia, at the time under the domineering rule of the Austrian Empire. Family influence played a decided role in the young man's interest in foreign places and people. His father, Franz Klutschak, worked to preserve a Czech identity, and cultural diversity, in the face of German-Austrian societal dominance. The elder Klutschak was the owner and editor of the newspaper *Bohemia*, and also served for a time as editor of *Panorama des Universums* (Panorama of the Universe), a monthly focused on communicating knowledge and appreciation of foreign cultures. In Prague, Henry studied engineering at the technical school, Technische Hochschule, and attended the military academy there. After graduation, he served in the First Artillery Regiment of the Austria-Hungary military from 1866 to 1871. With ethnic culture under pressure at home, and curious to see more of the world, Henry joined a whaling expedition departing from the United States. Morison had stated that Henry's first Arctic experience was gained on board a New London whaler to Repulse Bay, where he may have gained some understanding of Inuktitut. Remarkably, what Morison did not state was that the New London whaler on which Klutschak served for two years just happened to be the *Glacier*, during its voyage of 1871-73. This was the same ship and the same voyage during which Captain Potter and Thomas Barry had obtained the famous spoon and the rumors of the now fabled cairn. Just

Frank J. Melms

Heinrich W. Klutschak

as remarkably, Klutschak made no mention of his service on the *Glacier* in his own published narrative of the Franklin Records Search Expedition. Subsequent facts may explain why Klutschak desired to distance himself from Barry and the story. After his service on the *Glacier*, his roving nature led him on a two-year whaling voyage to the South Georgia Islands in the southern Atlantic Ocean (arguably the first for an Austrian) and subsequently as a translator on trans-Atlantic Ocean liners before joining the Franklin Records Search Expedition. He joined Schwatka's expedition as artist, surveyor and cook.[33]

Schwatka had thoughts about adding more members, but size was a limiting factor. His erstwhile companion on the Plains, the gunfighter "Texas Jack" Vermillion, aka "Shoot-your-eye-out Vermillion," was "raring to go" and just the thought of his presence would have enlivened the affair. More practically, Schwatka had intended to enlist a photographer, but camera equipment proved too cumbersome. In addition, Spencer Fullerton Baird, secretary of the Smithsonian, offered to supply a scientist as he had for other expeditions, but a suitable individual could not be identified by Baird prior to departure.

Through Morison's indefatigable efforts, the expedition was in a position to depart on June 10 but was delayed by what was initially reported as a manpower issue, a shortage of crew members to work the *Eothen*. However, a week later, the *New York Times* was carrying a troubling report that Schwatka was unwell at the Sturtevant House with an ailment that was undisclosed to the press. The circumstance must have been some cause for concern among the supporters, Morison and Daly, who surely would have known the truth of the matter, good or bad. On June 19, the schooner *Eothen* was finally towed down New York Harbor by the tug *Fletcher* in a dead calm. Finally recovered from his ailment or at least well enough to depart, Schwatka, feeling far more optimistic and looking promisingly to the future, remarked that: "Friends and many interested spectators…gave us many a hearty God-speed on parting, and three times three rousing cheers as the cable was cut loose that separated us for almost three years from nearly all the signs and comforts of civilization."[34]

CHAPTER SEVEN

TO THE NORTH

As the *Eothen* navigated its way toward Hudson Bay in late July 1878, with fair weather on a largely uneventful sea voyage, Frederick Schwatka and the members of his "overland" party could finally enjoy some leisure time as passengers after their hectic weeks of preparation. Relaxation took the form of reading, whale and bird watching, and amusing themselves with target practice on the friendly "dolphins" (long-finned pilot whales) bounding alongside, gunplay which had little effect. On this, Schwatka's maiden Arctic cruise, like innumerable voyagers before him, he was mesmerized by the vast array of shapes and sizes of the passing icebergs, drawing on comparisons to familiar objects from home for perspective. For the anxious John Morison, however, the *Eothen* was not simply a leisurely transport ship in support of some noble enterprise. The fate of his business hinged on the success of this whaling venture. The ship's recently completed Antarctic voyage had been an unexpected and abject failure, to the tune of $15,000 (some $450,000 in today's dollars), stretching the modest partnership of Morison & Brown to nearly the breaking point. Another "clean" return would spell the end of the firm.[1]

Eyeing the parade of icebergs in wonderment from the deck of the *Eothen*, Frederick Schwatka, the landsman, had time to contemplate the future as he opened his personal journal and penned his thoughts. The existence of that journal has itself remained an unanswered question. It merits some mention here in regard to the surviving historical accounts of the expedition that form the basis of our understanding of the journey. Schwatka certainly maintained a day-by-day journal during the course of the expedition. Some fifty years ago, a 117-page manuscript in Schwatka's hand was acquired by the Marine Historical Association (today the G.W. Blunt Library of the Mystic Seaport Museum). Though uncertainty has existed as to the nature of that manuscript, it is in fact a draft of a lengthy article prepared by Schwatka and not his original journal, which is not known to have survived. That article was published in final, edited form by Schwatka in 1880-81 under the title *In the Land of the Midnight Sun*. Rarely viewed, the article appeared in the short-lived and virtually forgotten periodical, *Good Company*. A much-abridged version of that original 117-page manuscript was also published by the Marine Historical Association in 1968, entitled *The Long Arctic Search: The Narrative of Lieutenant Frederick Schwatka* (at that time, its editor was apparently unaware of the published version of the article). As a result, the original manuscript serves as the most complete record in Schwatka's hand of the expedition and the primary source of his account. As for the other participants, no original journals are known to have survived, but both Gilder and Klutschak published book-length narratives of the expedition, and of course Gilder delivered a series of dispatches to the *New York Herald*.[2]

Among other things, Schwatka's manuscript managed to capture a few personal insights and feelings of a man who only infrequently revealed his inner thoughts. For example, despite Schwatka's outward display of self-confidence that persuaded Daly to offer him the command, Schwatka, not surprisingly, suffered from some trepidations:

> I do not hesitate to state that I assumed the new responsibility with much diffidence. I had seen no Arctic experience whatsoever, and a careful perusal of the literature of those Regions showed me that the leaders had, in every case, served previously in subordinate capacities, and were thus placed in possession of that most valuable of information, the information of experience. True, an American cavalry officer's service is oftentimes that of much arduous field duty, and occasionally the severest of winter exposure; but these in my mind faded into picnics as I read of ice 400 feet thick (Munck 1619), hummocks 150 feet high (Nares 1875) and the thermometer so low that mercury froze and cast into bullets was fired through thick boards, and white men staggered around as if intoxicated as the[y] breathed the terribly cold atmosphere.[3]

As the *Eothen* pushed further to the remote north beyond the Grand Banks and he pondered the lives of the hardworking Newfoundland fisherman, Schwatka also shared a feeling of alienation and loneliness that briefly overcame him: "Their lives seemed dreary enough, absent three and four months at a time from all news of the busy world, but I really envied them their comparatively short solitary sojourn when I reflected that I was assuming a voluntary ostracism of as many years."[4]

While hugging the north part of Hudson Strait near the Savage Islands, along the route customarily followed by the whalers, Schwatka and the *Eothen* made their first contact with the Inuit. The location was a long-established waiting spot for the Inuit, who would embark from shore in a flotilla of kayaks and umiaks to trade for goods and to share information with passing whalers and Hudson's Bay Company ships. Taking stock of their physical attributes, Schwatka found them "generally of low stature, chunky build, small feet, flat noses - especially those of Hudson's [sic] Strait, high cheek bones and small slit eyes." His Victorian sensibilities were put off by their odor, which he claimed had "a wild racy originality of its own which defies comparison." For Ebierbing it was a reunion of sorts, as he recognized some as old acquaintances from Cumberland Sound. For Schwatka, it was an eye-opening encounter. An ardent believer in fair treatment of Indigenous peoples, he was shocked and disgusted at how the whalemen cheated the Inuit in their bartering. The callous whalers parted with inconsequential measures of powder and tobacco to obtain far more valuable goods from the Inuit, namely whalebone, seal and bear skins, and reindeer meat. For his own part, Schwatka raised the ire of the whalemen when he bartered goods on an equitable basis. The generous act astonished the Inuit, so much so that one overjoyed benefactor even insisted on rubbing noses with the slightly embarrassed Schwatka.[5]

At Whale Point, on the west coast of Hudson Bay, a brief conversation with the local Aivilingmiut provided the intelligence that greater numbers of Inuit, as many as fifty, were encamped on the mainland near Depot Island, some forty miles to the south. Since Inuit assistance was essential to Schwatka's success, he had little choice but to direct the *Eothen* to Depot Island. His planned disembarking point had originally been Repulse Bay, a preferred starting point as it was closer than Depot Island to King William Island and Cape Englefield. Schwatka received some assurance from the knowledgeable Inuit of a favorable route from Depot Island to the northwest to the Back River and King William Island if that was to be their ultimate destination. Alternatively, if Cape Englefield off the coast of Melville Peninsula to the north was to be their destination, Schwatka could move back to Repulse Bay during the winter. In any event, he had no choice but to make the best of the situation.

By now Schwatka had a growing suspicion that Barry's story was not all that he had so confidently asserted it to be before they left New York. Schwatka was pointedly disturbed that Barry was now expressing

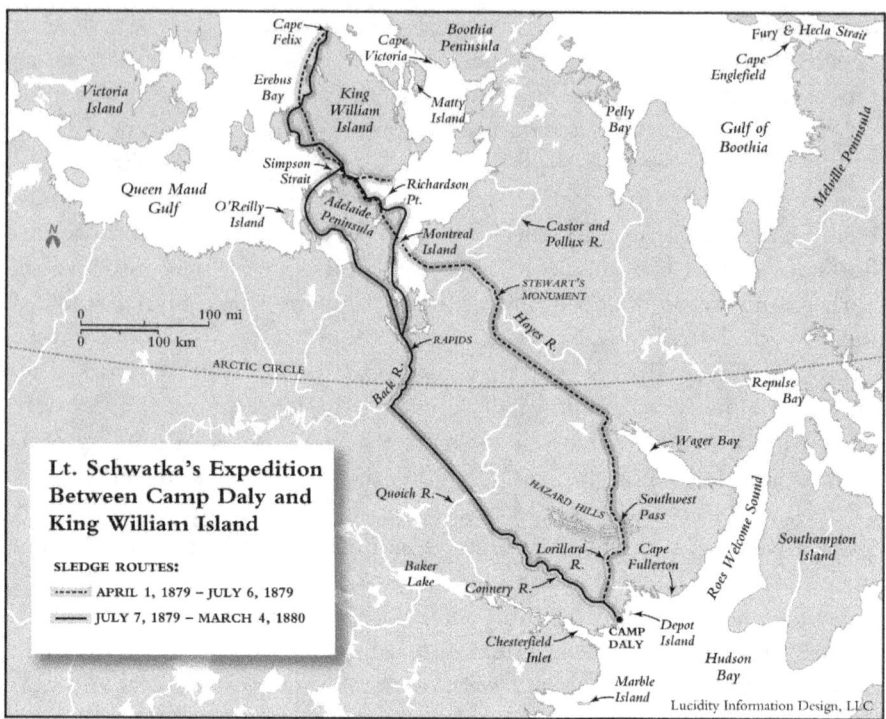

Lt. Schwatka's Expedition Between Camp Daly and King William Island

SLEDGE ROUTES:
- - - - APRIL 1, 1879 – JULY 6, 1879
———— JULY 7, 1879 – MARCH 4, 1880

confusion as to whether the cairn containing the records, the location of which had been communicated to him by the Nattilik men, was on King William Island or Cape Englefield. That doubt, on such a fundamental issue, certainty called into question what Barry understood in his conversation with the Nattilingmiut. The uncertainty also posed an enormous practical problem for an expedition which realistically could only reach one of those locations under the best of circumstances. The two places were located in different directions from Depot Island and separated by a distance of more than five hundred miles by sledge. Schwatka's hopes now rested with the Inuit located at the island who might shed light on the matter.

Depot Island served as a whaleship harbor and migration point for Inuit assisting the whalers. Upon their arrival on the mainland opposite the island, Schwatka's five-man party faced a treeless, bleak, and barren landscape marked by stark granite outcroppings, the only bright colors being scattered stretches of moss and an occasional wildflower. Their neighbors were a number of Aivilingmiut who had settled nearby, and who would generously assist the expedition over the next several months. They were well accustomed to Euro-Americans, having had contact with whalemen for more than fifteen years. Schwatka named

"View of Camp Daly from Observatory Point." Sketch by Heinrich W. Klutschak

their modest encampment "Camp Daly" after their benefactor Judge Charles Patrick Daly. It would serve as their home for the next eight months.

Having now set up camp, there was little time for reflection. Captain Barry and the *Eothen* were anxious to hunt for whales and an ominous gale looked to be approaching. Only a portion of the expedition's stores were hastily offloaded, with the understanding that the balance would be deposited when the *Eothen* wintered nearby. It was a decision that Schwatka's group would later regret. After a few hearty goodbyes and good wishes, the *Eothen* departed as the members of the Franklin Records Search Expedition watched in silence. It was a moment of mixed emotions that marked the real commencement of their endeavor. Despite the rush of activity, there was a sense of separation and alienation as they watched their connection to civilization sail below the horizon.

One of Schwatka's principal objectives was to *voluntarily* embrace the Inuit lifestyle in all respects, in their clothing, methods of travel, shelter, hunting, and diet. As Klutschak characterized it: "We knew only too well that a primary condition for the execution of our plan was that we should discard our mantle of civilized philosophies of life as much as possible, and acclimatize ourselves to their [Inuit] clothing, food, and style of accommodation, in accordance with the conditions of the country." It would not be fair to characterize the Franklin Records Search Expedition as the first to fully adopt Inuit methods, as was publicized at the time. Certainly, Charles Francis Hall had recognized the advantages to be gained in utilizing Inuit techniques for successfully living and travelling in the North. Dr. John Rae understood them as well, and put them to full use in his travels. But Hall and Rae were not simply the outliers. Even the most popular and widely known work on the Far North in the antebellum United States, Elisha Kent Kane's *Arctic Explorations*, had described how the Inuit lifestyle was the salvation of Kane's party. When the explorer Isaac Israel Hayes, a veteran of Kane's expedition, sought to extend Kane's work several years later, he adopted the same techniques.[6]

Even for veterans inured to hardships, adopting an Inuit manner of living was a difficult learning experience for men accustomed to their own lifestyles and habits. The first barrier to learning was simply communicating. Over several weeks, according to Klutschak, Schwatka's men managed to learn some basic words in Inuktitut to make themselves understood, but "whalers' pidgin" became the principle means of communication. Other adaptions took slightly longer. Gilder's first attempt at a multi-day hunting trip on foot with several Inuit companions left him completely spent and his feet badly lacerated. Too weary to hunt or even carry his firearm, he surrendered it to his Inuk companion, who appeared to have unbounded endurance and a knack for bagging game. He fared no better on another excursion, a one-hundred-mile trek to Marble Island to visit several whaleships at anchor. On the trail, having quickly finished his hard tack, he went without eating for four days as he was too stubborn to try the walrus meat which his travelling partners relished. Finally, faint from lack of food, he had no choice but to partake of it, and found that it provided both nutritional value and body warmth and did not taste half bad. However, matters went from bad to worse after a fall through the ice left him briefly submerged and completely soaked. In stiff and frozen clothing, and dangerously cold, he struggled the remaining distance to Marble Island. Physically wasted, it took him three weeks to recover twenty pounds lost from the ordeal, but he lost none of his zeal for the hardy, outdoor life of the Arctic.[7]

Schwatka had to cope with his own growing pains. He had learned from the Northern Indians that clothing fashioned from temperate zone animal furs and skins provided far more warmth and comfort in cold weather than government issue uniforms. Cavalrymen had incorporated buffalo and buckskin into their footwear, leggings, gloves and even bedding. But Schwatka found that as the temperature fell below -30°F at Camp Daly, his buffalo robes for sleeping (gifts of Chief Spotted Tail) became damp and frozen almost immediately. It took several cold nights before he switched to a caribou sleeping bag, after which the cold of the night was bearable. Schwatka and his men quickly learned that the switch to an Inuit style wardrobe was, according to Klutschak, "the only guarantee of effective clothing."[8]

The caribou had adapted to the harsh Arctic environment. Caribou hair provides superior insulation as air is trapped both between the hairs and inside its hollow strands, and is lightweight and water repellent. Given its importance to their survival, Klutschak's description of their caribou clothing is well worth noting:

> At home one wears an attigik, an over-parka with attached hood with the skin side against one's bare body. The pants (qarliiq) are wide, reach only to the knee, and are also worn skin-side inside: footwear consists of two pairs of stockings, the inner pair with the hair inside, the outer pair the reverse. Over the latter one wears a pair of boots of caribou if the weather is cold and completely dry. Otherwise one wears sealskin boots. For a sojourn outdoors, one wears a second suit with the hair side outside. All items of clothing are sewn with cords of plaited caribou sinew, which takes the place of our thread. Along the edges of the garments where the air can easily reach one's body are sewn fringes, also cut from caribou skin. On the one hand they break the wind; and on the other they permit air ventilation and make it impossible to become sweaty.[9]

Even their shelter at Camp Daly, initially a shabby canvas tent, a discarded relic from the 1877 wreck of the *Ann Houghton,* proved decidedly inadequate as the weather turned colder. As newcomers, Schwatka and the Euro-Americans laughed off as a mere novelty the replacement lodge built of ice blocks by the Inuit, but once snug in its warmth and comfort, they quickly realized their hasty misjudgment. Likewise, they marveled at the comfort of the snow hut that was constructed after the first sufficient snowfall. They rapidly learned by bitter experience the severity and extreme variability of the Arctic weather.

An attempted survey of the coast by whaleboat was almost their undoing. With short rations, Schwatka, Klutschak, and Melms spent three days on a small barren island during a raging storm confined to their useless sailcloth tent, soaked to the skin. Weak and dizzy from the experience, they luckily managed to return to Camp Daly during a break in the weather.

Through it all, Schwatka's lighthearted personality kept up their spirits, and the words "laughter" and "humor" on Schwatka's part are conspicuously present in Klutschak's narrative. According to Klutschak, Lieutenant Schwatka possessed a healthy humor "in inexhaustible measure." Even Frank Melms, who rarely had a voice in the various expedition narratives, wrote to his mother that in Schwatka "a kinder and fairer man would be hard to find." Melms did not publish a narrative, but his correspondence home reflected an enthusiastic and wide-eyed young man with a love of adventure, who got along well with his companions and had the time of his life. "You will be surprised that a person living in huts of snow or ice, can be contented, but in the company of such genial, refined gentlemen, as my three companions are, almost anyone would feel happy and contented," he wrote in his first letter. He proved to be a hardy and dependable participant, but in the end he received virtually no recognition. Like Schwatka, Melms also seems to have had a big heart. In his first letter, he also took great satisfaction in recounting how he had rescued a young Inuk girl who had fallen through the ice, returned her to shore, and "by the application of well-known means, restored [her] to life," much to the relief of her thankful mother.[10]

Through trial and error, and perhaps sheer discomfort, by late September Schwatka and his companions had managed to adopt Inuit style clothing, sleeping arrangements and eating; even raw meat, universally detested before, had become a dietary staple. In fact, Schwatka was one of the first to record the physiological effect of switching to a diet of raw meat. He noted that "when first thrown wholly upon a diet of reindeer meat, it seems inadequate to properly nourish the system, and there is an apparent weakness and inability to perform severe exertion or fatiguing journeys, but this soon passes away in the course of two or three weeks . . ." Schwatka's practical observations tracked what we now term "keto-adaptation," the process by which the body adapts over time to a low carbohydrate diet. Studies have demonstrated that exercise endurance, initially impaired upon the dietary switch, can generally recover over several weeks after a low carbohydrate diet is commenced and maintained.[11]

Organizational matters were Schwatka's strongpoint, but it took all of his skills to acquire the all-important dogs in sufficient numbers. A local scarcity of the four-legged workhorses upon his arrival at Camp Daly left him with deep apprehension. He was all too familiar with the lengthy delays suffered by Hall over several seasons due to the inability to find an adequate number of healthy animals. By barter, purchase and persuasion Schwatka slowly succeeded. Several long-distance trips by Gilder to Inuit encampments were critical to this effort. One of Gilder's journeys was a four-day sledge journey seventy miles to the northwest of Marble Island. There he established contact with an Inuit community whose members claimed to have never seen a white man. They generously shared caribou meat and fish with Gilder and supplied him with several dogs. During his one week stay, Gilder found himself immersed in their customs and lifestyle. Each evening within a large snow hut, in a communal gathering, the men would play a traditional drum, a deerskin stretched over a wooden hoop, while the women sang. Gilder provided few details of the performances other than the dismissive observation that they "would cause a sensation in New York, though I do not believe it would prove a lasting attraction to cultivated audiences."[12]

Over time and through mutual respect, Schwatka's relationships with his Aivilingmiut companions grew into genuine friendships. If their Christmas celebration was any indication, the feeling of mutual affection was strong. When Ebierbing asked if there would be stockings hung for gifts, Schwatka gave a decidedly Scrooge-like negative response, dampening the holiday spirit. However, on Christmas eve, Schwatka and Gilder surreptitiously filled boots and stockings with goodies: knives, matches, tobacco, and ammunition for the men; needles, thread and thimbles for the women. On Christmas morning, with Klutschak's assistance, Santa Claus made a boisterous arrival on a sled pulled by a dozen sledge dogs, admirable stand-ins for reindeer. The arctic Kris Kringle was none other than Ahmow, chief of the tribe, covered in a polar bear skin, who showered ship's biscuits and gifts upon the surprised and delighted Aivilingmiut. Even Schwatka was in for a holiday surprise. Shouting Schwatka's name in a booming voice, "Santa" pulled out a handsome, newly fashioned fur-costume, much to Schwatka's astonishment, and distributed the same to each of the Euro-Americans. The entire group then sat down to a Christmas dinner of salmon, caribou steak, pork and pancakes prepared by Klutschak. According to Gilder, "taken altogether there never was another such a Christmas Day in Esquimaux land."[13]

Although Schwatka's men were learning an Inuit lifestyle, Klutschak recognized that the Aivilingmiut likewise looked with piqued curiosity at the habits, routines, and customs of their Euro-American visitors. Unusual food items, like molasses and biscuits, were viewed with "special attention" by the Inuit, as were books, especially the illustrated periodicals of the day, and even articles of clothing adapted to a more temperate climate.

For Ebierbing, the stay at Camp Daly and meeting with the Aivilingmiut held special significance. Ebierbing was no stranger to Depot Island and was acquainted with some of the Aivilingmiut who were now visiting Schwatka's group. He had visited Depot Island with Hall in 1864-65 while wintering north of Whale Point and had wintered at Repulse Bay for several seasons thereafter. An Aivilingmiut man at Camp Daly named Ishoowark had previously accompanied Ebierbing and Hall on Hall's journey to King William Island in 1869. Ishoowark would also join the Franklin Records Search Expedition. At Camp Daly, Ebierbing also found a wife in an Aivilingmiut woman named Nipschark, the daughter of Ishoowark. Ebierbing's first wife, Tookoolito, a talented woman who had accompanied both Ebierbing and Hall on their three earlier journeys, had died two years before.

Schwatka engendered the trust and support of the Inuit with his willingness to embrace their demanding lifestyle, and by participating fully as an equal in their games, sports, and rituals. With his congenial but forceful manner, he became endeared, and eventually beloved, by his Inuit companions. Schwatka came to believe that he and his men "were considered one of their own," and "treated as brothers in blood." They even adopted an appropriate Inuit name for Schwatka, Igeark-too-aloo, meaning "the big one who wears spectacles." The well-traveled Schwatka had the honor of being perhaps the first and only explorer to hold names from both the Northern Indians and the Inuit. Gilder, by comparison, was known by "a less dignified appellation." Due to the similarity in Gilder's name as pronounced by the Inuit, "missergeeter," and the pesky biting insect, the Inuit referred to him by the Inuit word for "big mosquito," Keektoeyak-aloo. Schwatka likewise understood that a name can define an individual or group, and as such, he was sensitive to the feelings of his Inuit companions. Mindful that the word "Esquimaux" was viewed as derogatory by his Inuit companions, Schwatka accordingly adopted the term "Inuit" in its place in his dealings with them. It was a laudable show of respect and one we take for granted today; it was not until many years later that there was a movement to recognize the change.[14]

Convinced that the efficient weaponry displayed by Schwatka could ensure their needs, a few competent hunters, guides, and interpreters, men absolutely essential to his plans, were prepared to accompany the expedition. Most important was twenty-seven-year-old Toolooah, considered the best hunter and dog-driver, "a splendidly formed, handsome young fellow, lithe as a buck and a very successful hunter." Another important hunter, driver, and interpreter was the energetic Ikqueesik, "a fine-looking young man, with a big head and a shock of raven-black hair, as massive looking as a lion…." His Nattilik heritage would also prove important to averting potential hostility when meeting his countrymen. Lastly, Ishoowark was considered a "first-class hunter," and had the experience gained from

Hall's expedition. Their families, confident that they would fare better accompanying their husband-hunters, elected to join the party as well.[15]

With few instruments and no dedicated specialist personnel, scientific efforts were limited largely to geographical discovery and mapping. On a prominent hill overlooking Camp Daly, a large mound of rocks served as a baseline for triangulations and observations. Before departing, Schwatka and Klutschak completed a survey map of the coastline from Cape Fullerton to Marble Island. Their task was aided by the use of a whaleboat from the wreck of the *A. J. Ross,* which had been lost in the gale that occurred the day after Schwatka's party had landed at Camp Daly, its crew distributed among the remaining whalers in Hudson Bay. Schwatka claimed that the existing Admiralty charts were off by miles. This more accurate map was a matter of commercial importance to the whalers, who according to Klutschak, had lost vessels in the area due to the inaccurate charts. Captain Elnathan B. Fisher (*Abbie Bradford*), veteran of the Hudson Bay fishery, attested to the new chart's accuracy, and each of the whalers in the harbor at Marble Island gratefully accepted a copy.

Not until March 1, 1879, more than seven months after their arrival, would Schwatka boast that he had "all the dogs we could beg," a total of forty-four, enough to pull three sledges. His original planned departure date of November 1, 1878 had been exceedingly ambitious and had proved impossible, but with the dogs secured, he was optimistic that by April 1, with competent guides and hunters, he could make a start.

Having acclimated to the northern environ, the other all-important item for Schwatka was to verify the accuracy of Thomas Barry's story, to which he was already harboring serious doubts. Its resolution became a three-month arctic wild goose chase. Unfortunately, the two Nattilik men who had supposedly provided the details of the cairn to Barry in 1876 were non-existent. In Schwatka's words, the two men were "mythical," though it is not too surprising that after a lapse of time they might not be present at Schwatka's particular location in light of their nomadic lifestyle. One of the most knowledgeable of the Nattilingmiut at Depot Island was Ikqueesik, who had been retained by Schwatka as a guide. When questioned, Ikqueesik flatly stated that he "knew nothing of the Franklin Story except by hearsay, for none of which he could vouch." A second Nattilik man, supposedly with some knowledge of the event, was an elderly man known as "Monkey," but he had died the year before. According to Gilder, after learning that Ikqueesik had no first-hand knowledge and that "Monkey" had died, Barry remembered that it was "Monkey" who had given him the spoon and would talk with him about the cairn with books in it. According to Gilder that was highly improbable, as "Monkey" was a paralytic who could barely speak, and his wife denied he had ever been given a spoon. With Barry's credibility shattered in Schwatka's opinion, Schwatka chose to omit the frustrating efforts to corroborate Barry's tale from *Land of the Midnight Sun*. All that Schwatka published about the story was the terse statement that there was a "complete lack of confirmation of Captain Barry's statements regarding the two Netchilluk [sic] guides."[16]

The baffling tale of the Franklin records (and the now infamous spoon) would become an apocryphal "nine-lives" story that continued to live through false hopes. Near the start of the new year (1879), a Nattilik man of about forty-five, named Nu-to-k'-ec-ak, arrived at Depot Island and volunteered some tantalizing details about the Franklin expedition. He impressed Schwatka and Gilder with his knowledge as he recounted many facts that corroborated information previously reported by Rae, McClintock and Hall. Even though Hall's edited journal of his journey to King William Island was unpublished at the time of Schwatka's departure, Schwatka was not operating in the dark as to Hall's work. Before his departure, Schwatka was provided with several unpublished memoranda describing Hall's activities to aid him, and it is apparent from Schwatka's narrative that he had a fairly thorough knowledge of Hall's journey.[17]

But Nutokecak had some "new and important" information. When revealed, it captured the attention of Schwatka and Gilder and changed the focus of their search to King William Island. Years before, Nutokecak's father had located a cairn on the north side of Washington Bay on King William Island. After opening it, he found a tin box containing a piece of paper with writing on it. Nearby were the ruins of another white man's cairn which was set upon a large flat stone that the Nattilingmiut were unable to move. There was a belief that something was buried under the stone. Additionally, according to Gilder (but oddly, not mentioned by Schwatka), Nutokecak had brought a spoon from King William Island which fit the description of the one brought by Thomas Barry to the United States, i.e., it was broken at the bowl and mended by copper wire. Nutokecak claimed to have given the spoon to the wife of an Aivilingmiut man named Sinuksook, who had given it to Captain Potter. During the winter of 1878-79, Gilder fortuitously managed to locate Sinuksook's wife in the vicinity of Depot Island, and she confirmed giving the spoon to Captain Potter.[18]

So, by word of mouth, the story of the Franklin records had worked its way back to its original spokesperson, Captain Potter. By an astonishing coincidence, he just happened to be wintering aboard the *Abbie Bradford* at Marble Island at the time. Anxious to speak to him, Gilder and Klutschak quickly sledged a trail to Marble Island to interrogate the whaleman,

"Whaleships Wintering at Marble Island." Sketch by Heinrich W. Klutschak.

reaching their destination on January 15 (Schwatka followed later, arriving at Marble Island on February 18). Four whalers were frozen in at Marble Island—the *Abbie Bradford*, the *Abbott Lawrence*, the *Isabella*, and the *Eothen* with Captain Barry—as well as the shipwrecked crew of the *A.J. Ross*. In contrast to the robust health Gilder and Klutschak had experienced living with and adopting an Inuit diet, Gilder was surprised to find that several men from each ship were suffering from scurvy. Gilder was quickly welcomed on board the *Abbie Bradford* and located Potter, now serving as first mate, who was pleased to have an audience. Surprisingly, when Potter was asked if Barry had ever received a spoon, Potter claimed that he had never known Barry to have received a spoon and also asserted that the first he (Potter) had first heard about Barry's story was when he read about it in the newspapers. Potter did confirm that while on board the *Glacier*, he (Potter) had received a spoon from Sinuksook's wife, which had been stolen shortly thereafter. Moreover, the description of the spoon that had been stolen from Potter corresponded exactly to the one Barry said he had acquired from the Inuit. Potter also flatly rejected the assertion that Barry could understand the Inuit talking in their native tongue [Inuktitut] about books and records, which he called "supremely ridiculous" (an assertion that may have been true, though Ebierbing had testified that Barry could communicate in "whalers' pidgin").[19]

At this point, according to Gilder, "in this crucible of fact the famous spoon melted. So far as Captain Barry and his clews [sic] were concerned, we had come on a fool's errand." Remarkably, though the alluring tale of the Franklin records had dissolved, contrary to Gilder's lament over the melting utensil, the one confirmed bit of truth in this entire confounding story was, in fact, the spoon itself. On his arrival in New York City in October 1877, Barry had turned over to John Morison the distinctive spoon bearing Franklin's crest, immediately identifiable by the handmade rivet securing the bowl to the handle. Morison in turn presented the spoon to Sophia Cracroft through the assistance of Professor Nourse of the U.S. Naval Observatory. Today, it resides among the artifacts at the Scott Polar Research Institute.[20]

In the eyes of Schwatka and Gilder, Barry's story was simply not believable. Whether that was caused through a misunderstanding of the Inuit testimony, or a more deliberate fabrication to boost its interest as a potential Franklin search story, or perhaps elements of both, they did not definitively state. But what possible advantage could have been obtained by the now maligned tale? Although a motive was never definitively uncovered, Henry Klutschak, messmate of Barry for two years aboard the *Glacier*, intimated that the desire on the part of Barry and the firm of Morison & Brown to fit out a whaler to Hudson Bay, subsidized by the donations for the Franklin Records Search Expedition, was the undisclosed inducement driving their actions. It is an interesting possibility in light of Morison & Brown's precarious financial situation. In any event, Barry's conduct had set in motion a proposed enterprise of considerable effort and expense. As importantly, Judge Daly's judgment might be subject to question based on Daly's wholehearted acceptance of the story and his advocacy on behalf of the venture.[21]

Perhaps looking to avoid casting doubt over Daly's reasoning or quite possibly his own good sense, Schwatka simply omitted from *Land of the Midnight Sun* the troublesome details of the Potter interview elicited by the journalist Gilder, who no doubt saw it as good copy for the *Herald*. Klutschak took a similar approach as to the various shifting tales of the spoon, largely ignoring them in his published account altogether. However, irate over the frustrating matter, he remarked that Barry's stories "revealed themselves to be total falsehoods," evidently believing that Barry had purposely engaged in thoroughly deceitful conduct.[22]

Despite the disappointment that Schwatka had suffered, there was no doubt about the course that he would pursue. Having settled in back at

Camp Daly by mid-March, he knew this was still the potential chance of a lifetime; the opportunity to make a mark for himself as an explorer. There was no doubt that he would make a go of it. Morison's instructions left him with more than enough flexibility to proceed with a thorough reconnaissance of King William Island and the Back River, locations now deemed far more likely for finding any existing records than Cape Englefield. Such an endeavor could finally bring to an end the need for any further searches for Franklin or his fate.

A newcomer can sometimes bring a fresh perspective to a situation and offer a novel but effective solution. Schwatka knew all too well that "the unanimous opinion of Arctic authority on sledge travelling was to avoid land excursions as much as possible and to adhere rigidly to the vicinity of the coasts and great water courses; in fact some Polar explorers of undoubted reputation had pronounced land sledging absolutely impracticable for extended journeys...." Unburdened by preconceived notions of the best means for Arctic travel, Schwatka assessed the ability of sledges to travel on land with adequate snow cover and concluded that such an undertaking was conceivable. His experience with military travel by land, a practice with which he was thoroughly familiar and comfortable, provided inspiration and support for that decision. [23]

Ignoring the routes of Rae and Hall, which ran for stretches along the coasts and water courses to King William Island starting from Repulse Bay, or even approaches beginning at Wager Bay or Chesterfield Inlet (all three of which would involve a lengthy transport just to reach those respective starting points), Schwatka determined to make a beeline to King William Island from Camp Daly via an inland journey across the Kivalliq (Keewatin) barrens. It certainly was not lost on Schwatka that this course, or as he humorously referred to it, his "cannon-ball route," could yield new geographical discoveries and thereby entitle Schwatka to credit as a true "explorer." Modesty was not one of Schwatka's qualities. [24]

Additional support for that decision had come from Schwatka's vitally important sixteen-day reconnaissance journey led by Toolooah in early January 1879. That scouting trip covered one hundred or so miles in a northwesterly direction from Camp Daly in the direction of the western edge of Wager Bay (Ukkusiksalik). Schwatka's consideration of the route to King William Island recommended by Toolooah, and in lieu of a potential alternative route on the Connery River previously scouted by Gilder, reflected Schwatka's open-minded attitude and complete confidence in the young Inuk's judgment. Although no Euro-Americans had ever travelled the area, the Aivilingmiut of northwest Hudson Bay knew the land and were familiar with the Wager Bay region. Mobility was a necessary ingredient for their survival— pursuit of game had led Aivilingmiut families on extended inland journeys away from the bay in all directions, no doubt crossing the potential path advocated by Toolooah. Their familiarity with the region, though, led some of the knowledgeable Inuit to question the feasibility of such a potential route and to even advocate against it, due to the uncertainty of game. As a result, Toolooah served not only as a guide for Schwatka, but also as a representative of the Inuit who wanted to hear directly from their very best hunter whether they could adequately supply themselves with game through that region.

So, while Gilder and Klutschak had sledged to Marble Island in a quest to prove or disprove the veracity of Barry's story, Schwatka prepared for a winter trip as far as Wager Bay with Toolooah, his family, and a Nattilik boy, Milkolilluk. With one sledge and nine strong dogs from Camp Daly, the group travelled thirty miles in two days, reaching the Connery River, which flowed in a westerly direction, away from their intended destination. At this point, Schwatka still had intended to continue to follow the Connery River. However, Toolooah advised abandoning the river for an alternative course to the northward. He claimed that this would take them to a large river that ran in the direction of King William Island. Despite some apprehension on Schwatka's part, he nonetheless placed his faith in his pathfinder Toolooah.

The next day his trust was rewarded as they reached the river identified by Toolooah (named the Lorillard River by Schwatka after the cigarette magnate). After several days of travel along the Lorillard, averaging about fifteen miles a day, they reached their farthest point, a stretch of small but rugged hills reaching almost two thousand feet in height, named by Schwatka the "Hazard Hills." Scrambling to the highest point, which he named "Wheeler Peak," Schwatka had an unobstructed view of the horizon in all directions. The undulating hills extended westward, but as he gazed to the east he observed a more gentle grade extending far beyond the edge of Wager Bay. With this observation, he now felt confident enough to select this approach for his spring journey. Having travelled about one hundred miles to the Hazard Hills, Schwatka believed that he could accomplish the remaining distance across the unmapped territory to the nearest point of the Back River. This route would avoid a detour of several hundred miles along the coast to the entrance of Wager Bay. Just as important, plentiful traces of game observed along the proposed track eased the Inuit concerns that they could sustain themselves while traversing through the area.

Schwatka and Toolooah had only scouted a portion of the proposed route. However, the far edge of Wager Bay to the Back River was a known travel corridor utilized by the Inuit, particularly the Nattilingmiut migrating from King William Island. As important, the Aivilingmiut were aware that this region was occupied by the Utkuhiksalingmiut, a friendly people, who could serve as a potential source for resupply for Schwatka's party. As a result, with Toolooah's knowledge, Schwatka returned to Camp Daly confident in his approach to King William Island. Upon his return from the successful scouting mission, now fully inured to an Inuit lifestyle, Schwatka remarked that he "really enjoyed the whole trip," which was accomplished with temperatures as low as -53°F. He maintained that he had experienced relative comfort while clothed in caribou skins and sheltered in snow huts.[25]

During February and March, despite the cold winter weather, preparations for the long-anticipated journey were finalized with added enthusiasm now that the departure date was imminent. The months of acclimating had been successful, as the customary lifestyle of the Euro-Americans was forgotten and put aside. Looking forward to the impending start as the month of March closed, Schwatka's party was hopefully optimistic for the future.

CHAPTER EIGHT

THE FRANKLIN RECORDS SEARCH

WITH A CRACKING OF THE WHIPS, a howling of the dogs, and a hearty "Tavvautit! [farewell]" to their friends at Depot Island, Frederick Schwatka signaled the start of the Franklin Records Search Expedition on April 1, 1879. Although frequently described as a small party, the expedition was a rather sizeable community of seventeen participants, with several more added along the way. The initial members were as follows:

> Lieutenant Frederick G. Schwatka, commander
> Colonel William H. Gilder, second-in-command
> Heinrich W. Klutschak, scientist and artist
> Frank Melms, assistant
> Ebierbing, hunter and interpreter, and Nipschark, his wife
> Toolooah, twenty-seven-year-old hunter and chief sledge driver
> Toolooah's wife, Toolooahalek, and their young son Iyawkawauk
> Ikqueesik, chief guide and his wife, Kutcheenuark, and their young daughter, Koodleuk
> Ishoowark, and his wife, Karleko, and their son Koomawnah (about twelve)
> Ikqueesik's brothers, Milkolilluk (about eighteen), and Awanak (about fourteen)

In a most remarkable demonstration of leadership and personal trust established over eight months at Camp Daly, Frederick Schwatka had organized a group of thirteen Inuit (including four adult women and four minors). They were to accompany him on a trip of indefinite duration to a destination (King William Island) little known to his Inuit companions. They would carry just thirty days of food for the party, and two weeks' worth for the dogs. Schwatka's plan was to subsist entirely on food procured while in the field and to live and travel Inuit-style, a wholehearted extension of Brigadier General George Crook's approach to Native enlistment and living. Although Schwatka and his Euro-American companions professed that they had fully adopted Inuit methods for this venture, in reality it was more accurate to state that the Inuit had adopted the Euro-Americans. Schwatka and his men had taken on an Inuit diet, which included raw meat, and had discarded their temperate clothing for the more practical wardrobe of the north. However, for critical aspects of their journey, they were fully reliant upon Inuit skills that they neither fully learned nor put into use themselves.[1]

The clothing that they wore was painstakingly fashioned largely by Inuit women, who skillfully spent countless hours making suitable outfits from caribou for men and women over the course of the entire expedition. Gilder rightly noted that "[t]he dwellers in civilized cities can, therefore, scarcely appreciate the toil which all must share to secure the necessary garments to protect those who live in the highest latitudes."[2]

Schwatka marveled at the ability of the Inuit to build snow huts, so vital for long distance travel in cold weather, a skill that neither he nor the other Euro-Americans ever even attempted to master. Jokingly acknowledging his own ignorance, Schwatka remarked that "'[c]amping' in the Arctic à la Innuit, consists on the white man's part, of waiting until the natives have completed the igloo or snow house." That is not to say that Schwatka and his companions were idle by any means. At camp, they assisted in labor intensive chores such as loading and unloading sledges, setting up sleeping quarters, and drilling for water, a particularly laborious and time-consuming activity during most times of the year.[3]

All aspects of travel from start to finish were left in the hands of the Inuit, who managed the construction and maintenance of the sledges and masterly handled the dogs. The dog-driven sledge provided the mobility that was essential to the survival of the Inuit who were frequently on the move in search of game. Besides serving as a transport for game, the sledges transported a family and its belongings from one hunting locality to the next. Consequently, Inuit ingenuity had mastered a remarkable and highly effective sledge design with the modest raw materials on hand.

As they served a critical role in the journey, a note about their construction seems appropriate. Schwatka's three sledges were composed of runners two inches thick that ranged in length from 9-12 feet long and

8-10 inches high. The runners were attached to each other by wooden crosspieces (barrel-staves) that formed the bed of the sled. Not a single nail was used; tough, flexible hide thongs lashed the parts together. The lashings were strong enough to handle repeated shocks and poundings, and on uneven or broken ice the flexible lashings would stretch without breaking at the joints. The runners were shod with strips of whale bone, and these were iced every day with a layer of slushy snow and a mouthful of water that when spread over the runners immediately froze. Schwatka noted that sledging is an art "solely monopolized by the [Inuit]" and "it at once shows the great advantage of having them as allies, and the comparative folly of sledge journeys in rough Arctic countries without them."[4]

The dogs were each hitched to the sledge in a fan shape by leads of unequal length, with the lead dog (typically the most intelligent) on the longest lead. The ability to successfully manage a pack of recalcitrant dogs to pull a sledge with any semblance of control required patience and practice and an understanding of individual canine personalities. Arctic narratives are replete with humorous instances in which Euro-American explorers were ignominiously carried away by uncontrollable dog teams. Driving was itself a skill mastered at an early age, a complex combination of verbal and non-verbal commands and directions. Schwatka boasted that he was "adept" at driving dogs, but the accounts reflect that he and his men more often relied on their Inuit drivers, particularly in the many challenging situations they encountered.[5]

Although Schwatka's and Gilder's hunting supplemented their stores, Inuit hunters were largely responsible for satisfying the enormous food requirements for the party and its army of voracious dogs which were so vital to their survival. From his experience as a soldier and hunter, Schwatka understood the need for effective weaponry. The state-of-the-art firearms donated by the leading arms companies were his most valuable material contribution to the expedition and were treated as such. In the hands of a skilled hunter, the efficient repeating rifles and carbines performed well even in extremely low temperatures, when kept free from moisture. Their rapid fire could devastate a herd in quick succession, a necessary requirement when feeding so large a group. Schwatka had benefitted from marked advances in weaponry during the American Civil War and the Indian wars that had increased the effectiveness and range of firearms well beyond the shotguns and single shot, muzzle-loading weapons carried by Franklin's men in 1845 and McClintock's men in 1858-59. The Winchester repeating carbine used by Toolooah stored eight cartridges in a magazine which could be discharged speedily, faster than an astonished herd could beat a retreat after the first shot rang out. The rapid and steady firing of their weapons during the hunt led Schwatka to remark that "it sounded for awhile like a sharp battle, so rapidly and incessantly were the shots delivered." To Gilder, "it clearly illustrates the advantage of breech-loaders and magazine guns when game is plentiful and much is required." Schwatka neglected to identify the specific Winchester repeating model carried by his party, but the Model 1876 would have seemed well-suited for his purposes. By 1878, when Schwatka headed north, Winchester was producing its highly popular Model 1873, known as "The Gun that Won the West," as well as the more recent Model 1876, the so-called "Centennial Model." The Model 1876 was a version of the Model 1873, chambered for higher cartridge firepower and marketed for use in big-game hunting. Both reliable mainstays, as late as 1892 the explorer Robert Peary carried the Model 1873 on his Greenland ice-cap journey.[6]

A thoughtful leader, Schwatka gave much consideration to organization of the sledges and the teams assigned to each. The three sledges bearing their food supplies, guns, ammunition, and other bare necessities were loaded and equally distributed to render each sledge self-sufficient and equally balanced at about 1,500 pounds in weight. Conspicuously absent was one stock item—alcoholic drinks of any kind. Despite his personal fondness for the drink, a stronger sense of duty had prevailed, and intoxicating spirits were excluded, thus avoiding even the temptation to imbibe. According to Schwatka, and confirmed by Klutschak, during the entire sledge journey of almost a year, the Franklin Records Search Expedition did not carry any alcoholic drinks, an approach later praised by contemporary temperance societies. Both men were of the opinion that alcohol had only limited benefit as a restorative to raise body temperature when suffering from extreme cold or frostbite.[7]

To break down social barriers, the Euro-Americans were divided among the sledge parties. Schwatka and Gilder manned the first sledge with Toolooah, his family, and Milkolilluk; Klutschak with Ebierbing and Ishoowark and their families the second; and Melms, Ikqueesik, and his family the third. The sledge arrangements acknowledged what was already apparent, namely that Schwatka had placed his reliance on Toolooah for the physically demanding tasks of leading the sledge teams and the all-important task of hunting.

Ebierbing, dedicated guide for Hall for much of the 1860s, and a savior of the *Polaris* ice floe party in 1872-73, was no longer the Ebierbing of old. The passage of time had taken its toll. Although still a competent hunter, he was slowed by debilitating bouts of rheumatism and lacked the constitution of the younger and stronger Toolooah. His stamina was also impaired by a habit of heavy tobacco smoking. Nonetheless, he was a vital member whose skills were diplomatic in nature. His relationship with the Aivilingmiut of Depot Island was instrumental in organizing the expedition and gaining Inuit support. Ishoowark, whose family had joined the expedition, was Ebierbing's father-in-law, no doubt a persuasive factor in Ishoowark's decision to join, and Ebierbing's interpreting skills would prove essential to Schwatka's success in obtaining Inuit testimony.

With the weight of command hanging heavy, Schwatka contemplated the bold choice he had undertaken: "There is something peculiarly depressing in starting upon a long unknown venture, especially if a person has upon his mind all the care and duties of a commander to warn him that in case of misfortune, which he must avert, he alone does not suffer. And this was an expedition wherein misfortune might easily befall us." As an experienced leader, Schwatka was sensitive to the physical as well as mental demands posed by long journeys, especially as the fully stacked sledges posed a daunting challenge at the start.[8]

For the first few days the pace was slow as they adjusted to life on the trail. Not wishing to discourage morale with long, tiring treks to start, Schwatka let the Inuit travel at their own easy, meandering pace. From the outset, he was firm in his leadership when he believed it was necessary. With heavy sledge loads, the Inuit would have much preferred to shuttle the load from place to place by moving a portion at a time, rather than moving the entire load in one trip. Though the Inuit were particularly adamant, Schwatka was resolute and firmly rejected their request. Grudgingly they accepted the decision, and tacitly his leadership. Once he understood their routine and desire to camp in the early evening, he managed to impose a daily routine of six hours travelling time at an agreed pace, with a thirty-minute rest every ninety minutes, no matter what time they finished. During those brief idle moments, with drawing materials generously supplied by Judge Daly, the artist Klutschak would sketch expedition events and scenes.

Making camp was itself a time-consuming process of about two hours. It involved all hands in constructing shelters, unloading the sledges, preparing meals and feeding the dogs. After dinner, the final act was for all to disrobe and retire stark naked under a caribou robe, families sharing the same blanket. Schwatka and the Euro-Americans generally occupied the same hut as Toolooah and his family, with any cultural bashfulness long abandoned.

The initial part of their journey followed the route scouted by

"Down Hill, April 15, 1879." From *The Illustrated London News*, January 15, 1881.

Schwatka and Toolooah in January along the Connery River and northward to the Lorillard. A myriad of glacial lakes populated the rocky, rolling terrain of the Lorillard River region. Frozen waterfalls and small tributaries sparkled like crystal chandeliers or precious gems, depending on the observer, serving up a picturesque scene. The combination of fine weather and beautiful scenery kept spirits high. As they approached the Hazard Hills though, the landscape took on a steeper gradient with rough outcroppings.

The Hazard Hills mark the drainage divide which separates rivers and streams flowing northward to Wager Bay and those flowing southward to Hudson Bay and Chesterfield Inlet. These more mountainous conditions caused some anxiety. The crossing of the hills necessitated some challenging sledge handling, with dog teams double teamed, and at times triple teamed, to pull individual loads up the rough slopes. The slow travel led to several short travel days, much to Schwatka's frustration. There were at least a few brief moments when he questioned his choice of route. By April 12 they had managed to complete the crossing by navigating through a narrow gorge, deeply filled with snow (named by Schwatka "Payer Pass"). As they passed through the gorge, there was fear of an avalanche due to the inward pitch of its snow-covered canopy, but fortunately it never came.

For the first month, the group managed to travel an average of eight miles a day under Schwatka's direction. Their route continued to the northwest across a series of lakes and ponds separated by small ranges of slightly burdensome hills, with diversions along the way for hunting the

"Meeting the Ugjulingmiut on the Hayes River." From *Schwatka's Search*.

abundant caribou. The opportunity to bag the infrequently seen muskox was also a temptation much too great to pass up. On April 29, after a tiring six-mile chase, four were killed, the only time during the entire expedition that the shaggy-haired beasts were taken. As they passed to the west of Wager Bay, Schwatka noted that the bay had been incorrectly extended too far west on the Admiralty chart, and rightly surmised that from his location it had narrowed to a chain of lakes connected by rivulets. From April 29 through May 5, they encountered what was described by Klutschak as an "arctic desert," an elevated plateau (now known as the "Wager Plateau") that was devoid of animal life and limited in water, an uncomfortable stretch that tried the party's nerves. At the same time, Klutschak also described another uncomfortable phenomenon that troubled the group: the overcast skies left no shadows on the landscape, creating a monotonous white surface that "was painful to the eyes and unpleasant to the traveler." [9]

By May 9, as they marched toward the Back River, they reached the headwaters of a stream that offered smooth travelling. Schwatka named it the Hayes River, in honor of the president of the United States. Early on, Schwatka had adopted a practice of liberally assigning geographic place names, in part with an eye toward his own self-promotion. Assigning names was one means of seemingly bolstering his exploration credentials through "discoveries," and also garnering favor with the individuals so named. Although Canada had yet to formally annex the British claims to the territory of the Canadian Arctic, Schwatka's conduct was unlikely to be seriously considered an act of sovereignty, though it might irk some British and Canadian government officials.

In this remote location, Schwatka looked back with some emotion to his West Point association as they camped below a tall peak from which Toolooah spied by telescope the Back River valley. Capping the mountain peak was a geologically stunning attraction, a massive perpendicular wall of black granite that so moved Schwatka that he named it Stewart's Monument in honor of Lieutenant Reid T. Stewart, Schwatka's fellow cavalryman classmate who fell to hostile Indians in the Arizona Territory a year after West Point graduation.[10]

Meeting with the Ugjulingmiut

On May 15, as the Franklin Records Search Expedition rounded a bend in the Hayes River, they were startled to spot three snow huts dotting the horizon. They soon made their first contact with the unknown inhabitants. Following the usual Inuit custom, the men of Schwatka's party, some of whom were panicky, approached the snow huts as Ikqueesik shouted in a loud voice. Several men exited the shelter, but far from being hostile, their frightened expressions and physical trepidation surprised Schwatka's men. A somewhat astonished Gilder remarked that "these poor creatures were shaking in their shoes." Upon learning the identity of Schwatka's group, their fears subsided, and women and children emerged. These people were a small community of Ugjulingmiut, about twenty-five in number. To Klutschak, they represented man in the state of nature, the *noble savage*, "completely undebased and uninfluenced by civilization." From them, Schwatka and his companions would gather their first intelligence about the fate of the Franklin expedition. In addition, they would also be the first Euro-Americans to gain an understanding of how these people had come close to sharing a similar fate by virtue of the same expedition.[11]

Evidencing his appreciation of the Inuit culture, Klutschak noted that initially "our attention was drawn to the people themselves," and their story was indeed a tragic one. The Ugjulingmiut met by Schwatka's party were the beleaguered remnants of a once prosperous people who had previously resided on the northern and western coast of Adelaide Peninsula and the southern coast of King William Island near where the Franklin ships were lost. According to Gilder, their numbers had been reduced from fighting with the warlike Nattilingmiut. They were driven from their hunting grounds, and obliged to take refuge with the Utkuhiksalingmiut, a people who lived in this remote and desolate corner near the Back River, the two groups now living together. For Gilder, their testimony provided first-hand evidence of aggressiveness of the Nattilingmiut, at least towards other Inuit groups. Interestingly, Schwatka's account of their story provides a more historically complete basis for the plight of the Ugjulingmiut. To Schwatka, the Ugjulingmiut had been reduced to this remnant by virtue of a combination of "famine and inroads of neighboring bands."[12]

The tragic loss of the Franklin expedition is typically viewed as a disaster by Euro-Americans, but it had serious consequences for the Inuit of the region as well. Little did Schwatka know at the time that, ironically, it was the Franklin expedition itself that had contributed to the upheaval in the social and trading relationships among the peoples of King William Island and vicinity. The Ugjulingmiut had historically maintained a regular trading relationship with the Nattilingmiut of the Boothia Peninsula region, providing the Nattilingmiut with needed driftwood collected along the coasts that the Ugjulingmiut occupied. The abandonment of Ross's *Victory* and *Krusenstern* in 1832 in the Boothia Peninsula region had provided an unimaginable cornucopia of metal and wood which were invaluable to people struggling for survival in the north. Acquisition of the remnants of Ross's vessels had given the Nattilingmiut straightforward access to those materials and had disturbed the trading pattern between the Nattilingmiut and Ugjulingmiut, leaving the Ugjulingmiut without resources upon which they were dependent. The windfall of metal and wood bolstered the ability of the Nattilingmiut to subsist in a challenging environment, particularly in periods of climatic stress. The wreckage from Franklin's ships, the *Erebus* and *Terror*, in 1848, only compounded the situation of the Ugjulingmiut. The desire of the Nattilingmiut to acquire those resources led the Nattilingmiut to aggressively push into the lands occupied by the Ugjulingmiut, thereby displacing the Ugjulingmiut. But as Schwatka observed, famine may have already weakened and reduced the Ugjulingmiut, making them more vulnerable to the inroads by neighboring Inuit. More than forty years after Schwatka's encounter, the Ugjulingmiut told the explorer Knud Rasmussen of "that year of horror," a severe winter during which "a great many people died, however; some froze to death, others starved, and the bodies of the dead were eaten by the living—in fact many were killed to provide food," a circumstance that contributed to their reduced and beleaguered state. The Canadian Arctic climate during the years 1845 and 1859 has been characterized by scientists as "the culmination of a 50-year period of consistently unfavorable summers," marked by below normal temperatures and no break up of sea ice. The effects of the tail-end of the so-called "Little Ice Age" in this region was a circumstance that plagued Franklin and his ships, but also severely affected the subsistence of the Ugjulingmiut.[13]

To Schwatka, the hollow cheeks and sunken eyes of the Ugjulingmiut admitted to their starving condition even at this moment in time. With only their bows and arrows, they had been unable to procure sufficient caribou and musk oxen despite living in a region abundant in game, and their supplementary fishing efforts had failed. Remarkably, just the day before, Schwatka's group had left unmolested a herd of two hundred caribou well within rifle range because their sledges were loaded with more meat than they could carry. As a result, without fuel, the snow huts of the Ugjulingmiut were cold, dark and comfortless through the long winter. But as was their custom, they liberally shared their remaining food supplies with Schwatka's party, though hard pressed to replenish them until the spring. Moved by the gesture, Schwatka generously assured that he would provide them more in return.

One man in the party, Ik-kin-nil-lik Puh-too-rak (Puhtoorak), the senior man of the Ugjulingmiut, captured Schwatka's attention by providing some welcome information through Ebierbing as interpreter. In Puhtoorak, Schwatka had located a man who could speak from first-hand experience about meeting Europeans alive. The passage of time had not dulled his memory. He recounted that about forty-five years previously, as a boy, he met ten men in one boat on the Back River while fishing. They exchanged greetings; the men shook hands with the Inuit and the Inuit rubbed the back of their hands down the mens' breasts. The leader's name was Too-ah-de-ah-rak, which Ebierbing interpreted as Lieutenant Back, and Schwatka believed the event likely corresponded to George Back's expedition of 1833-35.[14]

Puhtoorak could also speak as an eyewitness observer of one of Franklin's ships. He recalled that when his son was seven or eight-years-old (about 1851-52), Puhtoorak was among the first to visit a ship stuck fast near an island that Schwatka understood to be about eight miles west of Grant Point on Adelaide Peninsula. The ship had four "sticks" pointing out and three standing up. Klutschak recorded that Puhtoorak and his people thought they saw white men on board in the fall; Puhtoorak believed that as many as four men had been present based on the footprints he observed in the snow. The following spring, when the men did not appear to be present any longer (perhaps moving on to the mainland), the Inuit gathered the courage to enter the ship. While exploring its dark interior, they unexpectedly came upon the body of a man in a bunk in the stern of the ship. They found meat in red tin cans, and recovered useful implements, knives, forks, spoons and plates. They saw books on board but left them untouched; according to Schwatka, some were later seen washed up on shore. He and his companions made a large hole in the ship's side, causing it to sink after the ice had melted. The ship was in shallow water such that when it sank, the masts stuck out of the water. After it sank, they saw a small boat near Wilmot and Crampton Bay and other items washed up on shore.[15]

Although the accounts of Schwatka, Gilder and Klutschak each reflected minor differences in the testimony, the intriguing story corroborated the tale as told to Charles Hall and Leopold McClintock in regard to a ship sunk near "Oot-loo-lik." Schwatka, who was fully confident of Inuit testimony throughout the journey, remarked that Puhtoorak's "replies were made in a frank, straight-forward-ready manner that carried the conviction of truth." Gilder noted that "truthfulness seems to be an inherent quality with them [the Inuit]." In this case, the Inuit testimony as told to Schwatka had accurately identified the area in shallow water where the wreck of the HMS *Erebus*, flagship of Sir John Franklin's last expedition, was ultimately located in 2014.[16]

The Franklin Records Search Expedition left the Inuit encampment but added three of the Ugjulingmiut to their party (Now-le-yout, his wife, and their five-year-old daughter), stretching its number to twenty. Before departing, Schwatka collected their first relics from the Inuit: tools and implements made from copper, tin and wood from one of Franklin's ships.

The four-day march along the course of the Hayes River to the Back River presented a marked change from the monotonous ice and snow-covered landscape, and buoyed their spirits. The banks of clay had eroded into imaginative shapes that reminded Schwatka of the "fantastic forms" of the Badlands, in another emotional look back to his former haunts. Schwatka could visualize church spires, rows of gabled houses and a Boston thoroughfare; Klutschak, the continental European, saw the Hippodrome and attractions in Europe.

The trek had recently been marked by an unrelenting weather pattern of stormy weather, forty-two consecutive days by Schwatka's count. Conditions had been so bad that at times they could not venture out of the safety of their huts, which began to collapse as the temperatures finally rose above freezing. Another troublesome aspect were vicious wolves in increasing numbers, which threatened the dogs. At night, flares were lit to keep the troubling animals at bay. Fortunately, food had not been a concern. With his Winchester repeating carbine, Toolooah, an indefatigable hunter in even the worst conditions, managed to secure sufficient numbers of caribou to satisfy both man and dog.

Meeting the Nattilingmiut

On May 21, the company camped at Montreal Island, a location where it had been reported by Puhtoorak's relative that a cairn had been spotted. However, after a diligent search, nothing of relevance was found. On the last day of May, after moving a few miles along the coast on the eastern side of the Adelaide Peninsula near Richardson Point, they came face-to-face with the long-perceived adversary—a Nattilingmiut group of about sixteen, a circumstance that caused serious trepidations on Ebierbing's part. Concerns were heightened during the approach, when the Nattilingmiut men, with bows and arrows in hand, formed "a line of battle" outside their snow huts. Schwatka wrote that the Nattilingmiut had mistaken his group for the "Kid-ne-liks" (today the Inuinnait or Copper Inuit of Victoria Island to the west), "with whom they are not on very peaceful terms." An old woman, whom they obviously considered expendable if Schwatka's group was hostile, was cautiously pushed forward. As a demonstration of strength, but certainly adding to the tension, Schwatka had his men fire a rifle. Whether the act had the intended effect is unclear, but contrary to their expectations, upon seeing the white men and recognizing their relative Ikqueesik, the Nattilingmiut were immediately friendly and accommodating, and quickly offered some intelligence regarding Franklin's fate. Word spread quickly among the Nattilingmiut of the arrival of these "Kabloona" (Qallunaat) which was quite a novelty to these people. Nearly one hundred inquisitive Inuit quickly descended on the camp, many of whom had never seen a white man before.[17]

The 'Boat Place' near Richardson Point - Starvation Cove

According to Schwatka, the Nattilingmiut were familiar with the Franklin story, a remark suggesting they were also all too familiar with the monotonous question-and-answer routine of white interviewers. Considerable effort was taken to assure the accuracy of their testimony. Two translators were utilized in interrogating the Nattilingmiut. Ebierbing would translate the English to his dialect, and then Ikqueesik would translate for the Nattilingmiut whatever Ebierbing had communicated to him. Klutschak believed this time-consuming process provided a more effective result, and he was impressed with the comprehension of the Inuit. Nonetheless, the accounts of the testimony as reported by Schwatka, Gilder and Klutschak vary at times from one another, mostly minor differences, but occasionally of more significance. With the cumbersome translation process, the large number of witnesses interviewed, and the repetitive questioning, it is not surprising that discrepancies occurred. In addition, the extent of an individual's recollection or recording of a topic or event could vary based on its relative importance to the particular individual.[18]

With one possible exception, the original notes from the interviews have not survived, and the respective narratives of Schwatka, Gilder and Klutschak are the only existing written records of the conversations. The one exception is the remarkable fact that during an interview of Lieutenant Schwatka by a reporter with the *New York Tribune* on October 5, 1880, just days after Schwatka's return to New York City, Schwatka "produced a tattered, weather-stained relic that at first sight looked like anything but a book." It was, in fact, Schwatka's notebook, within which "the dingy leaves told of entries made by the dim light of an Esquimaux lamp." Schwatka had introduced a clever device to bolster the truth of his narrative, a physical record authenticated by evidence of hard wear and use, and its association with the Inuit. He had returned from King William Island not just with the oral testimony of the Inuit, but with a genuine written record, whose contents held the answer. Shoring up his association with the ill-fated expedition, Schwatka also produced a small wooden box from which he carefully removed a few timeworn relics from the ill-fated expedition: a rusted tourniquet, tarnished brass buttons, an auger, a measuring stick, and a few rusty iron pieces.[19]

During the *Tribune* interview, Schwatka quoted brief entries for a handful of dates from his notebook, which were transcribed by the reporter and published in the *Tribune* within the context of the full Schwatka interview. The entries published in the *Tribune* pertain largely to Schwatka's interviews of Puhtoorak and three Inuit (Seotitecheung, Tuktoocheeah and Ahgekshewah), individuals who each provided information about the Franklin expedition books and records. The entries are more concise than the full details of the Inuit interviews as set forth in Schwatka's draft manuscript at Mystic but largely consistent. Of course, in the absence of the original notebook, it is uncertain if the quoted entries were read in full by Schwatka to the reporter or if they were transcribed accurately and fully.

Among the several Nattilingmiut who were interrogated over the course of the first week of June at various camps along the northern coast of Adelaide Peninsula, the first was the amiable elderly man named Seotitecheung who offered some profitable intelligence about the Franklin expedition. Seotitecheung was a link to previous Franklin search expeditions, having known Rae, McClintock, and Hall. To McClintock, he was remembered for having unsuccessfully attempted to steal a saw from the explorer, a tale which he recounted for Schwatka with "evident gusto as the perfect acme of a good joke." According to Schwatka, Seotitecheung told how he had seen a boat in the second cove west of Richardson Point about three miles away, and nearby were a number of skeletons and artifacts. Of particular interest to Schwatka was his statement that "there were also a great many papers of some sort scattered around the boat, but they are now all gone." Gilder similarly recorded that on a beach some three miles from their present camp several skeletons were observed, with books and papers strewn about the rocks along the shore and further back from the beach. There were other articles spotted, including a number of watches, some of which were silver and some gold. Klutschak was more selective in his reporting of the Inuit testimony in his published narrative. Klutschak only "quoted the most noteworthy" statements from his journal, by which he meant only "those given by several witnesses." Regarding Seotitecheung, Klutschak simply stated that Seotitecheung had seen a boat west of Richardson Point some years ago and found a skeleton. He (Seotitecheung) "cannot remember any details," noted Klutschak. Another Nattilik man (also named Toolooah), advised Schwatka and his men that he had also visited this location, named "Starvation Cove" by Schwatka, and nearly everything had been removed. Nonetheless, intrigued by the report of this boat place, a hastily assembled party consisting of Schwatka, Gilder, Toolooah, Seotitecheung, and Nattilik Toolooah, rushed to Starvation Cove the next day. Unfortunately, widespread snow cover limited their search at this location, evidently a dreary place of tragedy and death. No items of significance were found but Seotitecheung or Nattilik Toolooah pointed out where the boat had been located, and the location of the white men's tent and three "canoes" (Schwatka's term) that they were constructing. Schwatka planned to revisit the site on their return later that summer.[20]

To Schwatka and Gilder, Starvation Cove was the farthest point toward Hudson Bay, and salvation, that Franklin's retreating men had reached. Their surmise was largely correct, through the year 2018, the area surrounding Starvation Cove is the farthest location on the Adelaide Peninsula and the south shore of Simpson Strait where remains of members of the expedition have been found. In dramatic tones, Gilder offered a recreation of their pitiable circumstances for what would become an important location for the narrative: "The party was a small one, and had probably been sifted down to the few hardiest ones, whose anticipation of rescue from the horrible death that awaited them had not faltered under all their terrible sufferings while they had the continent in view. It probably seemed to them if only they could reach the mainland they would be comparatively safe. But even the bravest hearts must have sunk, and that there were many brave hearts among them cannot be doubted, when the awful desolation of this country forced itself upon them."[21]

As Schwatka's party continued westward along the Adelaide Peninsula, they met more of the Nattilingmiut and received or located artifacts of the lost expedition along the way. Of unusual interest was a pine board or plank covered with oil cloth and bearing the initials "L.F." embossed in nails. They were told this had been found on the east side of a peninsula near where the Inuit reported that one of the Franklin ships had sunk. Although speculation abounds to this day as to its connection with the Franklin expedition, like many of its intriguing aspects, its identity has never been firmly established (and the item itself, in fact, has disappeared). Another unique artifact obtained by Schwatka was the remnant of a sled, its length cut down by the Inuit, who advised Schwatka that it had been found in Erebus Bay on King William Island. Schwatka believed it was the one seen by McClintock in Erebus Bay with a boat mounted on it with several skeletons inside.[22]

The Nattilingmiut report of several graves and a white man's cairn near the Peffer River, an area that Ebierbing and Ishoowark claimed Hall had not visited, raised hopes that perhaps this was the long-sought cairn with the written records. (Neither Ebierbing nor Ishoowark had accompanied Hall to that location, which may explain their lack of knowledge). Goaded on with anxious enthusiasm, on June 5, Schwatka, Gilder, Toolooah and a Nattilik guide (named Ahdlekok) covered the twenty-five miles from Thunder Cove on the Adelaide Peninsula to the south coast of King William Island in under four hours. Schwatka spoke with anticipation when he stated, "I will not attempt to describe the many conflicting thoughts that rapidly ran through my brain, the suspense as I approached it." It was however "a double disappointment" when the monument proved to be one erected by Charles Hall on May 12, 1869, near the grave of two of Franklin's men. However, their efforts were not in vain. A third grave, unknown to Hall and covered with snow, was located.[23]

After returning to Thunder Cove, Schwatka's party travelled through a raging storm as far as Cape Geddes further west along the Adelaide Peninsula. Here two other Nattilingmiut witnesses interviewed on June 6 proved to be important for their recollections of Starvation Cove. They were Tuktoocheeah and her son Ahgekshewah. Tuktoocheeah, now between sixty-five and seventy years old, was originally from Pelly Bay, but had lived for many years with the Nattilingmiut. Both Hall and the

Ross's were acquainted with her.

Ahgekshewah was about forty years old and was the angakkuq, or medicine-man. Evidently, the discovery of the relics at Starvation Cove was an event indelibly imprinted on his mind. When he first came upon the Franklin relics at about the age of twelve or thirteen, he had found a can of gun powder, and inadvertently set it off by sprinkling it over a flame. According to Gilder, "he had never entirely recovered from the shock." That may perhaps explain his future erratic behavior. Schwatka noted that after the explosion "the parlor furniture and kitchen utensils [in his snow hut] were as badly mixed as some of his frothy gibberish." Despite his eccentricities, the fantastic story of the exploding can as told by Ahgekshewah was completely consistent with that told by his father, Pooyetta, to Hall in 1869.[24]

As for Tuktoocheeah, Schwatka believed that despite her age, her memory was not badly impaired. Gilder, on the other hand, thought that she was "so old that her memory was at fault, and she would wander about to different places and relate circumstances without explanation." In any event, both Schwatka and Gilder recorded that she had never seen any of Franklin's men alive but had seen six skeletons and no graves. According to Schwatka, four were found on Booth Point (on the south coast of King William Island), near longitude 95°, and two on a nearby island. Gilder noted that she remarked that four skeletons were found "on the main-land," and two on an adjacent island; this she pointed out on the "southern coast near 95° west longitude," presumably the southern coast of King William Island. However, Gilder went on to immediately add the confusing comment from Tuktoocheeah that "her husband was with her at the time and seven other Inuit. This was when she was at the boat place west of Richardson Point," i.e., Starvation Cove. Tuktoocheeah did not continue very long with her statement, as according to Gilder, she seemed mixed up as to the locations (Booth Point and Starvation Cove). According to both Schwatka and Gilder, the communicative Ahgekshewah stepped in to take up the narrative as his mother nodded along in agreement. (Klutschak did not identify the break in the testimony of Tuktoocheeah, and although not entirely clear, his account suggested that it was principally delivered by Tuktoocheeah).[25]

In any event, according to Schwatka, Ahgekshewah reported that his group was among the first to come on the scene, and at the boat place known as Starvation Cove they found a boat standing on its keel, and bones and several skulls inside and out. They evidently also found a compass or magnetic instrument because it stuck to any iron that it touched. Of most interest, they found a tin box full of books in the boat. The Inuit broke the box open, spilled out the books and kept only the box. To the supreme disappointment of Schwatka, after the box was broken open, the contents being of no value, they were taken by the children as playthings and scattered to the winds. Like so many birds, the loose papers fluttered around for several years and slowly disappeared. According to Schwatka, the story "dashed our highest hopes to pieces for it places beyond all doubt, the complete loss of the records of the lost party, that goal for which so many expeditions have strived and suffered, after all hopes of relieving the starving crews had passed."[26]

In light of the importance of the written records and their apparent destruction to the results of the Schwatka expedition, the relevant testimony bears on the subject. Gilder recounted that both handwritten and printed materials were shown to Ahgekshewah, to which Ahgekshewah responded that the books he had seen were "like the printed ones." Interestingly, in his draft *Midnight Sun* manuscript Schwatka wrote that "[b]eing shown writing and printed matter, *they* thought it was more like the latter [i.e., printed], but did not like to say positively as *they* did not examine them closely enough for that." (presumably "they" meant Ahgekshewah and his acquiescing mother). In the *Tribune* interview, quoting his original "notebook," Schwatka stated that "being shown writing and printed matter, *he* [Ahgekshewah] says they looked more like the latter [i.e., printed]," but Schwatka did not mention the qualification that they were not examined closely. At this point, it is unclear as to whether Schwatka chose to omit the qualification during his *Tribune* interview, or the reporter omitted it, or it was simply not stated.[27]

Klutschak, who presumably had the least interest in the fate of the records, provided the most definitive response. He recorded that in the boat there was a tin box "full of books *and written materials*," and thus Klutschak believed the testimony to mean that both books and manuscript materials were present. After visiting Starvation Cove in November, five months later, Klutschak would elaborate on the testimony he had heard about the box: "As far as anyone can place any faith in the Inuit's reports, the most significant importance of the site [Starvation Cove] lies in the fact that this was where the lead box of papers *and writings* [emphasis added] was once found." Klutschak's realistic appraisal aptly summarized the situation: "[I]n the interests of the success of our search we might have wished that we had found the relevant papers and writings. But there was no trace of them to be seen, although we visited the site three times, in spring, summer, and winter. Even from the Inuit we could extract only the assurance that the papers had been all destroyed. With the elimination of the documents...geography was robbed of an inestimable treasure."

Ironically, the expedition that sought the written records of the lost explorer, found their fate revealed in the spoken word of the Inuit.[28]

In his report to the geographical society in October 1880, Schwatka reported the justification for his assumption that the final records of the Franklin expedition had been conclusively lost at Starvation Cove:

> The most important information connected with this boat-place [Starvation Cove], which is evidently the farthest reached by any body of Franklin's men in 1848, is that concerning a SEALED *tin box*, about two feet long and about one foot square on the ends, which was *broken open* by the natives *and found to contain books* and a small piece of iron, to which all pieces of the same material would adhere when brought in contact. This tin box was retained by the Netchilluks [*sic*] and its contents emptied upon the ground, where they slowly perished.... That men thus placed should have burdened themselves with such a quantity of books, and the careful manner of their preservation, shows an importance which can only be attributed to the records of the expedition.[29]

Even Gilder reached the same conclusion—that these were the "more important records of the expedition"—as men in such condition would not have so burdened themselves with "general reading matter." Gilder added the additional support that because a number of gold watches had been found by the Inuit at Starvation Cove, this reflected the presence of officers and gave added weight to the conclusion that the records they carried were the "precious" records.[30]

Interestingly, additional bolstering of the Inuit testimony and destruction of the records comes from John Rae's expedition of 1854, more than two decades previous. In his official report to the Admiralty, Rae stated that the Inuit he had interviewed confirmed the death of some thirty men, graves, and an overturned boat at a location "on the continent, and five dead bodies on a small island near it," about one day's travel northwest of the Back River. Although not mentioned in his official report, in a letter to the editor of *The Times* (London) on October 23, 1854, Rae had revealed a few additional details, namely that at the location of the dead men "[a] large number of books were also found, but these not being valued by the natives had either been destroyed or neglected." In 1880, with Schwatka's conclusions about the precious records now a timely issue, in a letter to the *New York Herald* Rae sought to claim priority for confirmation of the destruction of the expedition's records. Rae wrote that upon being shown "blank manuscript and printed ones," the Inuit put aside the blank books

"The Last Franklin Search." Painting by Albert L. Operti.

and stated that "at least a dozen with 'markings' on them had been found where the many dead were." These were given to the children to play with and destroyed. For the same reasons as Schwatka and Gilder, Rae was convinced that the last survivors of Franklin's men who had traveled farthest south would have carried with them "the journals and records of their great work."[31]

Based on the overall thoroughness of the search of King William Island and the Adelaide Peninsula by the Franklin Records Search Expedition during the summer months of 1879, which found no "precious records" at any location, Schwatka believed that he could assert, beyond a reasonable doubt, that the important written records of the lost expedition had not survived. The added testimony of Seotitecheung, Tuktoocheeah and Ahgekshewah specific to the box, books and records apparently destroyed at Starvation Cove, which Schwatka accepted as trustworthy, enabled him to offer a plausible scenario as to the definitive fate as to the expedition's "precious" records and further confirmation of his expedition's success.

But Ahgekshewah had additional information to offer, and it caused more of a sensation. The angakkuq had claimed that at Starvation Cove, he had discovered a second tin box as large as the first, filled not with books, but with bones. Although Schwatka and Gilder both report this statement, Klutschak cautioned that statements about a box of bones "were reported variously and ambiguously." Klutschak makes no further comments about cannibalism, perhaps believing it was not worthy of further note or that it did not satisfy his requirement that it be corroborated by several witnesses. Both Schwatka and Gilder remarked that the Inuit were of the opinion that Franklin expedition members had been eating each other based on the sawed-off appearance of the bones. According to the angakkuq, bones that appeared to have been sawed off lay outside the boat, and two saws were found close to the boat. Gilder noted that the angakkuq opined that "they had been eating each other… because the bones were cut with a knife or a saw," and "what little flesh was still on the bones was very fresh; one body had all the flesh on."[32]

Gilder and Gordon Bennett knew when they had good copy. Despite its sensational nature, Gilder had no qualms reporting what he believed he had heard from the Inuit, and he had a reputation for accuracy in his reporting. Bennett first broke the story to the public when Gilder's letter to the *Herald* was published on September 25, 1880, with Gilder's electrifying statement that "there were almost unmistakable evidences of their being compelled to resort to cannibalism until at last they absolutely starved to death at this point." This was just the type of storyline that Bennett relished, and it would stoke the flames of controversy when it appeared in print, as it had some twenty-five years before.[33]

Washington Bay

Another story of interest came from an older Nattilik woman, Ahlangnyuck, who drew Gilder's attention with her jet black, shoulder length hair. She had visited Schwatka's camp on June 2 with a sad tale to tell as an eyewitness to the retreat of Franklin's crews. In contrast to the stories of Seotitecheung, Tuktoocheeah and Ahgekshewah, who recalled details regarding the circumstances of Franklin's men and their records at Starvation Cove on the Adelaide Peninsula, Ahlangnyuck offered details about the retreat as witnessed on King William Island. Schwatka learned from Ahlangnyuck that as she and her husband were traveling with several others along the east coast of Washington Bay on King William Island, they met a party of ten men dragging a sledge with a boat on it. The desperate men were looking starved and thin, with bleeding and black lips, possibly suffering from scurvy. They carried no food with them and wore no fur clothing; some slept in a tent, others in the boat on the sledge. During their brief encounter of some four days, they were supplied with seal meat by the Inuit who then departed to attempt to cross Simpson Strait before the ice broke up (which they failed to do). The Europeans followed but could not travel as fast, and were never seen again. The Inuit returned to the Matty Island near the eastern shore of King William Island later that summer. Ahlangnyuck mentioned the names of three of the Europeans, Too-loo-wug, the older leader, a big broad man, with a black beard mixed with grey; Ah-glook-tah, a younger leader with a reddish beard, and Doc-took, a short plump man with a long red beard. On the return to Terror Bay on King William Island the following season, the Inuit found a tent they cut into with "a great many" skeletons lying inside and outside, one body had flesh on but no stomach. One or two graves were located outside the tent. Ahlangnyuck stated that she also saw scattered relics and records, and according to Schwatka, a few "small books" which she thought were all destroyed, three of which were used as playthings by the children. Gilder believed that the few surviving members of this group reached Starvation Cove.[34]

The searchers were plainly moved by the tale of this eyewitness to the tragic events of the Franklin expedition. Following their return to the United States, Judge Patrick Daly, highly satisfied sponsor of the geographical society's endeavor, looked to fashion a lasting tribute. At Daly's urging, the artist Albert Operti was inspired to paint a "great" picture depicting a notable event from the expedition. The selection of the emotional interview of Ahlangnyuck by Schwatka and Gilder as their subject reflected due credit upon the Inuit to their success. Known for the exacting historical accuracy of his paintings, Operti spent countless hours under their guidance as he applied brush to canvas. Contrary to the typical depiction of the Native encounter trumpeting the Euro-American explorer, Operti's historically authentic imagery presents a largely Native-centric perspective. Within the confines of an Inuit snow hut, under the dim light of an oil lamp dutifully tended by an Inuit woman, Ahlangnyuck stands as the focus of attention of the scene. She recounts for the two captivated leaders her melancholy story, emotionally brought to tears as she recalls the scattered bones of the men she had seen the year before, now picked clean by scavenging animals. Schwatka and Gilder, captivated by Ahlangnyuck's tale, appear to hang on her every word, too spellbound to even scribble in their notebooks which rest loosely at their sides. As a work of art, "The Last Franklin Search," displayed at the offices of the American Geographical Society, stands as a fitting tribute to Ahlangnyuck and the strength of the spoken word of the Inuit.[35]

CHAPTER NINE

KING WILLIAM ISLAND AND RETURN

KING WILLIAM ISLAND is one of a myriad of islands that constitute the Canadian Arctic archipelago, one with special significance due to its association with the last expedition of Sir John Franklin. But the Inuit have known it far longer simply as "Qikiqtaq" (a big island). Legend has it that following the slow retreat of the glaciers, its first inhabitants were an unknown race, the Tuniit. Portrayed as gentle giants with superhuman strength, they had settled along its shoreline and taken advantage of its many abundant resources. With natural prowess, they stalked the caribou on land and hunted the seal in the coastal waters. For millennia, they led a peaceful and sheltered life while making Qikiqtaq habitable, marking caribou crossings with cairns and constructing stone dams to capture the plentiful fish in the area.[1]

At a more recent date, the Nattilingmiut discovered the island and may have driven out the more timid Tuniit. The Nattilingmiut similarly forged a hardy lifestyle in an unforgiving environment, guided by the seasonal wildlife migrations. In the winter, they hunted seals on the ice, and in summer they fished for salmon. When fall came, they tracked the great herds of caribou and prepared for the long, cold winter. And so it continued, year after year, before the white man arrived.

Few European visitors had touched its shores before Franklin arrived in 1846. Although the Inuit had lived in the region for many years, the first European explorer to reach the island was Commander James Clark Ross, who took possession in 1830 (thinking it a peninsula) and gave it the name King William IV after the reigning British monarch. In 1839, Thomas Simpson and George Dease, joint leaders of a Hudson's Bay Company expedition, discovered Simpson Strait and surveyed the island's southern shore.

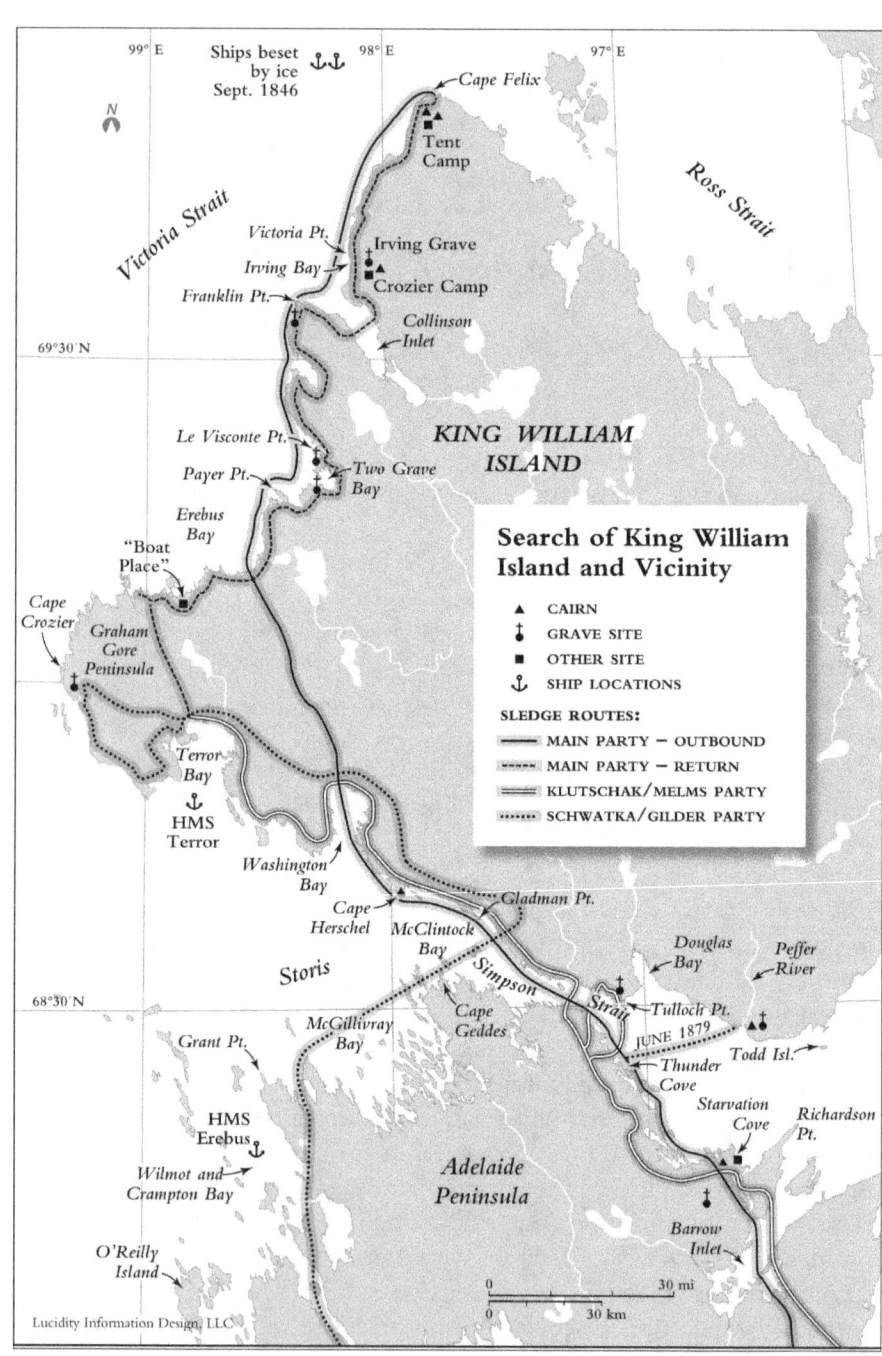

Relatively flat and featureless, the shores and adjoining mainland of King William Island consist of shattered and jagged limestone fragments that make for troublesome travelling on the part of the explorer and make the search for inconspicuous bones and relics problematic. During the most recent glacial period, it had been submerged; the post-glacial isostatic uplift produced a terrace-like effect along its shores. Ponds and small lakes dot its interior surface. Like most islands in the North, it is subject to frigid temperatures in winter, and cool, sometimes cold, temperatures during the brief summer. Despite low annual precipitation, fogs are frequent.

On June 10, 1879, Frederick Schwatka and members of the Franklin Records Search Expedition crossed the still frozen Simpson Strait and first set foot on King William Island. Schwatka offered no written expression of his emotions on reaching this noteworthy location, so important to his mission, but the words "U.S.F.S. (United States Franklin Search, June 10, 1879). All's well," indelibly carved in a large sandstone rock by members of his party announced their arrival and served to assure Schwatka's place among the most famous of Arctic explorers.[2]

Two marches later they reached Cape Herschel, which was identified by a partially demolished cairn erected by Dease and Simpson in 1839. Schwatka would have known that McClintock had previously examined the cairn and found it devoid of any records. On June 17, a smaller and more mobile group, consisting of Schwatka, Gilder, Klutschak, Melms, Toolooah and his family, and the fourteen-year-old Awanak, started for Cape Felix, the northernmost point on the island. Led by Ebierbing, the balance of the party was to hunt seals on the island or the mainland to secure blubber oil for the return trip to Camp Daly. In Klutschak's opinion, Schwatka's selection of Toolooah to accompany his party reflected Schwatka's undeniable respect for Toolooah's skills. In light of McClintock's efforts, Schwatka had little thought of locating the "precious records," but he held out hope that with a summer search they might locate graves and relics that had been overlooked. Schwatka's plan, an overly ambitious one in retrospect, was to conduct a four- to six-week survey of the north and west part of the island and cross back to the Adelaide Peninsula while Simpson Strait still remained ice-covered, and then head homeward for Camp Daly by autumn.

After reaching and traversing Washington Bay, Schwatka's party left the saltwater ice and started across the island directly for Collinson Inlet on the northwest coast. With the temperatures rising, they had a difficult slog wading through deep slushy snow and icy water. But as the weather warmed the air was filled with the cacophony of passing flocks of geese and ducks seeking their northern breeding grounds, as well as equally vociferous seals. These sounds of nature lifted spirits in the otherwise forlorn and barren country. Following his Admiralty chart, Schwatka expected his inland trek to Collinson Inlet would take him twenty-five miles east of Erebus Bay. However, Schwatka was surprised to find their march led his party directly to the shores of the bay and its chaotic icefield, a discrepancy he attributed to the position of Cape Herschel being some twenty miles west of its position on the Admiralty chart. Schwatka took a mild delight in identifying errors in his predecessors' charts. Such mistakes "are not infrequent in the hurried exploration of Arctic countries," he curtly remarked. He boasted that he could "write a volume descriptive of those I encountered in my two years Arctic surveying," which he evidently never did. Looking to avoid a long detour by following the land, the party struck directly across Erebus Bay. They were soon presented with what appeared to be an insurmountable obstacle for travel on the sea ice, massive floes of hummocky ice, interspersed with pools of water. Toolooah, the indispensable man, proved his skill as a dog driver, working his sledge "like a Trojan with his Herculean task, and we all owed it to his almost superhuman exertions that we placed ten miles between our morning and evening camp," wrote Schwatka. Even though the Euro-Americans had hitched themselves to the harnesses and had strenuously pulled, tugged, and pushed the sledge over the daunting icefield, Schwatka reserved his praise for the young man's energy and skill in sledge driving through the tortuous maze. The heavy, multi-year ice encountered by Schwatka's party had pushed through the wide channel of Victoria Strait onto the northwest coast of the island. Schwatka stared in awe at the ever-advancing ice, overwhelmed by this display of the force of nature. He understood that its unimpeded flow had sounded the death-knell for Franklin's ships. Surely, he recognized the contrast between the cumbersome self-contained, ship-based maritime expedition of Sir John Franklin which fell prisoner to the ice, and his own smaller, mobile party which successfully sustained itself off the land.[3]

In their search, Schwatka and his party went to great lengths to fully scour the ground for clues, while Toolooah and the Inuit manfully drove the sledge along the sea ice. The group continued to work their way north and west by means of a circuitous course hugging the coast, stopping near Franklin Point, where a possible grave and part of a skull were found nearby. Evidently, no consensus could be reached as to whether it was an Inuit or European. Near Franklin Point, Schwatka took some observations with the compass that suggested that the magnetic pole had shifted miles to the westward since 1831 when Ross first measured it. Not believing it would be so near his planned route, Schwatka despondently noted that

King William Island and Return

he had not carried a dip needle for more accurate measurement. Of more personal interest was the odd fact that neither he nor Gilder suffered from snow-blindness as badly as the others had, particularly the Inuit, which Schwatka attributed to his and Gilder's near-sightedness. They did however suffer badly from blistering wind and sunburn when the sun finally appeared, notwithstanding its low position on the horizon.[4]

On June 27, while Schwatka and Gilder searched Collinson Inlet, Klutschak and Melms walked along the coast toward Victory Point, where they found a campsite littered with decaying fragments of past use. Strewn about was a hodgepodge of stoves, kettles, bits of wood, clothing, blankets, ship's blocks, tackles and ropes, a surgeon's tourniquet, a sledge harness marked "T 11," a jug marked "R. Wheatley, Wine and spirit Merchant, Greenhithe, Kent," and a wooden brush with the name "H★ Wilks" cut in its side (Henry Wilks had been a Marine private on HMS *Terror*). One particularly sad relic showing the desperate state of the men was a blanket fashioned into a pair of crude stockings for a dubious attempt at warmth. Although Schwatka initially believed the site was a new find, this location was the temporary camp (known as "Crozier's Camp") used by Captain Crozier after the abandonment of the two Franklin expedition ships in 1848 and had been first spotted by McClintock's expedition in 1859. An important find nearby was a raised grave, not far from the waterline, made of flat slabs of limestone. It contained bones, moss-covered remnants of an English officer's uniform or overcoat, several gilt buttons, a silk handkerchief, and a telescope glass. A skull and several bones were found outside of the grave, which was believed to have been disturbed by the Inuit. Somehow, by the head of the grave, Klutschak spotted, perched upon a stone, a 2-1/2 inch silver medallion bearing a portrait of George IV on the obverse, and on the reverse, the notation that it had been "Awarded to John Irving. Midsummer 1830," as a second mathematical prize. That cherished memento of happier days led Gilder and Schwatka to immediately conclude that the grave was that of Lieutenant John Irving, third ranking Lieutenant on HMS *Terror*, the second of Franklin's two ship squadron.[5]

Though Schwatka's instructions from Morison called for him to bring back any remains of Franklin or his men that were located, only those attributed to Lieutenant Irving were collected and returned to England. Why Schwatka returned with only the remains of that one individual is puzzling. Perhaps an explanation can be found in Gilder's comment that Irving's remains were the only ones "sufficiently identified," though in the case of Irving one might argue that even that identification was far from certain. When unidentified remains of what were believed to be Franklin's

Monument over grave of Lt. Irving. From *The Illustrated London News*, January 1, 1881.

men were buried or reinterred, the location was generally marked by the erection of a monument, consisting of a pile of rocks, upon which a flat stone was placed horizontally, on top of which another handful of upright stones or a cross was placed.[6]

Lieutenant Irving had taken a roundabout course to his forlorn final resting place. With a propensity for science and navigation, Irving had entered the Royal Naval College in 1828 at the age of thirteen and had received his "second mathematical prize" in the year of his graduation in 1830. Disillusioned with his prospects for advancement in a peacetime navy, while a midshipman he resigned in 1837 to try his hand in greener pastures at sheep farming in Australia. After six hard years, his idyllic plans for a pastoral life had become a "losing concern." He made the fateful decision to return to the naval service in late 1843, and through family connections obtained a coveted, but in retrospect fateful, position on the HMS *Terror*. As snow cover prevented Schwatka's party from making a complete search of the location of the grave (referred to as "Irving Bay"), it was decided that a more thorough search would be conducted on their return from Cape Felix.[7]

Continuing the march, they reached the northernmost point of King William Island, Cape Felix, on July 3. To the west of Cape Felix, Franklin's ships were permanently beset in the ice. From that vantage point at

Cape Felix, all that was visible in that direction was a hopeless jumble of ice blocks of varying shapes and sizes, what would have been a most disheartening scene to those icebound sailors, their hopes fading with the passage of time. For nearly twenty months beginning September 12, 1846, as Franklin's ships drifted south along the island's coast, attrition slowly took its toll (including Sir John Franklin's death on June 11, 1847), until the fateful decision was made to abandon the ships. Near Cape Felix another significant Franklin campsite was found, one previously discovered by Hobson in 1859. The site was marked by a dismantled cairn surrounded by remnants of canvas, clothing, blankets, cups, broken pottery, red cans marked "Goldner's Patent," and even empty beer bottles, a sight that caused Klutschak to wryly remark that "men had once lived better here than we did now." Perhaps Klutschak's diet was the cause of his consternation, as he noted that by this time they were eating caribou almost exclusively, often raw, leaving him with a bad case of stomach discomfort.[8]

On July 4, in accordance with U.S. military tradition, the Franklin Records Search Expedition raised the Stars and Stripes at their camp. The custom thus dictated that the flag could not be lowered until sunset, which meant it flew for three days until their departure. Unbeknownst to Schwatka, the day held military importance of a more personal nature. Thousands of miles to the south, the U.S. Army had announced many long-overdue promotions, including Schwatka's advancement to first lieutenant effective March 20, an unknown field promotion of sorts. On July 5, Schwatka located a large cairn about two to three miles inland. It was set on a flat granite rock on a prominent ridge from which the coastline of the island was discernable to both east and west. At seven feet high, Schwatka surmised that it was a marker erected to measure the amount of drift of the ice-bound ships, or for some other scientific use. No record was found inside. In the debris of the broken cairn, a green bottle placed there by Schwatka on July 5, 1879, containing Schwatka's own note, was found on July 5, 1989, coincidentally 110 years later to the day, by a search group led by Stephen J. Trafton.

Schwatka left Cape Felix disappointed that Franklin's grave had not been located even though it was not a primary objective of their search. With Franklin's death occurring while the ships were beset off the coast, he logically believed "and confidently hoped" that Franklin would have been buried at this point if his body had not been consigned to the sea. But onward they pushed, and with the melting of the snow, their return trek down the west coast of King William Island was one of diligent search and numerous sundry finds.[9]

Hopes continued to rise, only to be dashed. Below Cape Felix, in yet another pile of stones, a paper was located with an image of a life-size hand. The hand was pointing to the southward, its bottom end disintegrated. An unusual find, perhaps from a signpost of earlier days. Ironically, it was the only original written record from the Franklin expedition recovered by the Franklin Records Search Expedition. The party went to great lengths to fully cover the nearby ground. With snow cover almost gone, starting from the low water mark and extending to the high tide line, the Euro-Americans formed a broad skirmish line, so as to maximize their coverage, while the Inuit continued to manfully drive the sledge along the sea ice. At each of their encampments, Schwatka remained an entire day and extended their search inland, in part, based on Hall's belief that records or other valuables would have been cached somewhere along the drift route of the ships, perhaps buried in a vault.

The tedious search had also become a torturous one on the rugged island. Sealskin boots repeatedly slipped on the flat rock surfaces and the numerous broken and sharp angular stones made walking a particularly painful affair. Moreover, as they plodded southward, a conspicuous trail of miscellaneous fragments of clothing, buttons, rags, and the like, evidence that they followed in the tracks of Franklin's retreating men, left them in a melancholy state of mind. One slightly hair-raising diversion from their more somber task was the discovery of a bear's den hollowed out in a snowbank. The inquisitive, and perhaps foolhardy, Gilder crawled in to gain a view of its interior, and to his relief found it unoccupied, but remarkably like a snow hut.

On July 11, they rounded Victory Point and returned to Irving Bay, the location of the grave of Lieutenant Irving, to find the snow entirely gone. They spent two full days in a diligent search, finding what Schwatka referred to as "many small articles visible that had been hidden during our last visit." For a brief moment, the excitement peaked when Toolooah's wife hurriedly rushed to Schwatka and Gilder while clutching a weathered piece of paper found in a pile of stones that had once been a cairn. Confident that it was a long-lost record from Crozier, somehow overlooked, an expectant Gilder carefully unfolded the document. Their disappointment was monumental when he discovered that it was merely a record left by McClintock in May 1859, reporting of McClintock's finding of Hobson's note, which had told of Hobson's finding the message of Crozier and Fitzjames. Shortly thereafter, with the knowledge that McClintock had buried a record ten feet true north of the cairn, a trench four feet wide by twenty feet was dug with some difficulty, but nothing was found. Nonetheless, it kept alive their hopes that perhaps some other

King William Island and Return   193

written testimonial might yet be located. Prior to leaving Irving Bay, a monument was finally erected over Irving's grave and a record buried with a copy of the McClintock note.[10]

On July 17, near Point Le Vesconte, at the entrance to a sheltered cove within the northeastern end of Erebus Bay, a number of disturbed bones and a shallow grave lined with small stones were found. The grave contained worn blue cloth and gilt buttons, leading Schwatka to conclude that it was of an officer from Franklin's expedition. Eyeing the construct of the grave, Klutschak was of the opinion that having reached this point Franklin's weakened men could only marshal the strength to cover the body with a few loose stones. A second rough grave was located some distance south of the first, containing a sailor's belt buckle and a musket cap, and within about four hundred yards, a badly decomposed skull believed to have been disinterred. Schwatka had praise for Toolooah's skill in spotting this grave: "had it not been for Toolooah's sharp eyes I doubt not but that we would have passed it without notice." About his Inuit companions' talents, Schwatka added, "I have already owed much to the keenness of their vision."[11]

Schwatka still believed, too optimistically in retrospect, that they could complete their search and cross Simpson Strait before ice break up, but that window was rapidly closing. On the evening of July 21, Schwatka's group arrived at the boat place first identified by McClintock in 1859 on the south side of Erebus Bay. Here, Klutschak noted "a sad sight presented itself." They discovered numerous skeletal remains and relics, including the prow and sternpost of a boat, a twenty-eight-foot plank from the boat, as well as the keel, and many discarded fragments and relics that stood as a mute testimony to the desperation of the brave men who had perished on its shores. A second boat noted by Hall was not located, but the Inuit later confirmed it had been removed and dismantled. It was a somber, tedious task of searching and finding, and in the case of bones, consigning them to a dignified burial and erecting a monument.

Without question, Erebus Bay was a place of despair and death. McClintock had surmised that based on the position of the boat he had found (facing Victory Point), a detachment had split from the main group retreating from Victory Point, opting to return to Franklin's ships. Schwatka and Klutschak concurred in that opinion, but Klutschak added that he believed that the men must have been in dire straits at that point, given the number of bones found at the location. A rather despondent Klutschak counted as many as seventy-six individual bones. Between 1982 and 2016, archaeological investigations at five sites at Erebus Bay located more than five hundred human bones from a minimum of twenty-one members of the Franklin expedition. More recently, by virtue of DNA analysis of these remains, it is now known that one of the men whose skeletal remains Schwatka had very carefully buried was Warrant Officer John Gregory, engineer of the HMS *Terror*. Gregory had joined HMS *Terror* from private industry rather than from the naval ranks. He was employed as an engineer at Maudslay, Sons & Field, a company specializing in the construction of marine steam engines, the firm that fitted the auxiliary engines for Franklin's ships. Presumably, he was brought on to work the problematic engines.[12]

On July 24 they were presented with a new challenge. The ice along the coast had begun to rapidly break up in great spasms during a gale, pushing massive blocks onto the shore and tossing the heavy sledge like a toy. From here on, their supplies would be backpacked and shuttled inland to Terror Bay some thirteen miles distant, a difficult and time-consuming means of travel that necessitated multiple trips. There were some occasional bright spots during their trek. Schwatka was struck by the mild climate of the interior of the island, which was covered in "perfect beds of gay and brilliant flowers, and whose bosoms were teeming with aquatic life, lured thither by the safety they presented for breeding. It seemed like visiting the beauties of the temperate zone once more so pleasant was the change."[13]

In addition, upon reaching Terror Bay in August, they did not want for food. Caribou were abundant and carried a thick layer of fat from having grazed mightily on the heavier vegetation. The Inuit collected several hundred pounds of this "interstitial fat" for the return journey, and Schwatka himself was said to have partaken of up to a pound at every meal, at times their only meal. For the moment, they had shaken the gloom associated with their heavyhearted project. Some amusement was even had at Schwatka's expense. The newly promoted first lieutenant interrupted his principal duties, and set off in an attempt to bag a large caribou, since he had spotted a trophy-size bull with an enormous set of antlers. He approached within range, but his first shot only wounded the sizable animal, which hobbled out to the refuge of the ice floes of the bay. A second shot took him down, but Schwatka had to wade waist-deep in the frigid waters to haul the carcass to shore. From a distance, the well-pleased hunter was spotted returning to camp with what appeared to be a red flag hanging from his rifle, but on closer inspection was seen to be his underpants hung out to dry.

On August 6, Gilder and Schwatka broke off from their group to commence a search of Terror Bay, and then proceed west to Cape Crozier to finish their reconnaissance of Graham Gore Peninsula, a prominent headland bounded by Erebus and Terror Bays. At the same time, at Schwatka's orders, the balance of the party travelling with Schwatka, i.e., Klutschak, Melms, Toolooah and his family, and Awanak, now headed by Klutschak, was to search the coast to the southeast. If the group headed by Ebierbing had not returned from the Adelaide Peninsula, Klutschak's group was to cross Simpson Strait and search Adelaide Peninsula. Separately, after effectuating the crossing to the Adelaide Peninsula, Toolooah was to return to King William Island to reconnoiter with Schwatka and Gilder.

Disappointingly, Schwatka and Gilder failed to locate the tent place of Ahlangnyuck, and found little else of interest on their extended excursion (over ninety miles during one busy week), except for a grave and partial skeleton near Cape Crozier. They later learned from the Nattilingmiut that the incoming tide had washed away any traces. Since Schwatka's visit, the waters of Terror Bay have revealed significant traces of the Franklin expedition. In 2016, the remarkably intact HMS *Terror* was located on the seabed at a depth of seventy-nine feet. Further examination of its remains may provide further clues to the Franklin mystery.

Four weeks later, Schwatka and Gilder were joined by the surprised Toolooah, with his family, Ikqueesik, Milkolilluk and Melms. Toolooah had feared for the health of Schwatka and Gilder, and according to Schwatka, had expected to find "such rash kabloonas as the Colonel and myself in a starved condition." Schwatka and Gilder had managed to secure more than enough caribou over a month to sustain themselves, although without the assistance of the Inuit women they were short of serviceable shoes and stockings. Throughout the entire length of the expedition, through good and bad, the two explorers got along famously and were rarely separated. About their four-week sojourn on their own, Gilder remarked that "this was altogether the pleasantest part of our experience in the Arctic."[14]

The hunting exploits of Schwatka and Gilder did not come near the success of Toolooah. The young hunter's skill kept the entire party, at times numbering twenty persons and some fifty dogs, fully nourished. Schwatka could add Toolooah's efforts to his list of "Lucky Shots," as Toolooah had on ten occasions killed two caribou with one shot, and in one case, three with one shot. Toolooah also managed to come out ahead in several exhilarating polar bear encounters. In one case, he became the hunted, finally downing the beast as it attacked. In a second instance without his gun, he came across a mother bear and cub. He drove the mother away with stones and killed the cub with just a knife blade. He had fully earned Schwatka's praise, who remarked that Toolooah was entitled to "due credit as a hunter in these inhospitable climes."[15]

Crossing to King William Island. From *The Illustrated London News*, January 8, 1881.

Schwatka and Gilder, now reunited with Toolooah's group, marched to their so-called "permanent camp" on the southwest coast of the island to await the freezing over of Simpson Strait. Along their course, they found no further evidence of Franklin's expedition except an oar at the head of Washington Bay. After having left Schwatka and Gilder, following instructions, Klutschak and his group had crossed Simpson Strait where they joined Ebierbing's party, all of whom returned to King William Island on September 17. This was accomplished by means of a makeshift raft made by lashing together four kayaks, in what was a nerve-wracking and a somewhat perilous three-mile voyage that took two trips to ferry seventeen persons and thirteen dogs. They had established a camp seven miles from Schwatka among a Nattilingmiut encampment to improve their opportunity to acquire game. Now reunited with Klutschak's group, Schwatka learned of the disappointing results of the search of Adelaide Peninsula and Starvation Cove that was conducted by Ebierbing and the Inuit. No records were located, but some bones of incomplete skeletons, one skull, and various uniform remnants, shoes, buttons, and relics had been found. The most interesting one was a commemorative medal of the launching of the steamer *Great Britain* in 1843, undoubtedly a token from the lost expedition. Ebierbing had been suffering badly through this part of the journey. When Schwatka caught up with him, the once proficient hunter was supporting himself with a cane, hobbled by another painful bout of rheumatism that troubled him for a month.[16]

By late September, frequent snowfall had so covered the ground that further searching was becoming fruitless. Based on Inuit reports of several skeletons in the vicinity of Hall's monument, a final search was conducted by Schwatka and Klutschak. At Tulloch Point, a cape on the west side of Douglas Bay on the southern coast of King William Island, they discovered some nineteen bones which they believed were of a Franklin expedition member. Schwatka was moved by the pitiable situation. In a doleful frame of mind, he noted that the grave, constructed of very small stones rather than larger ones nearby, pointed "unmistakably to the fact of the fast waning strength and energies of the starving sailors." (In the 1980s, however, analysis of the bones located at the site were determined to be Inuit.)[17]

With opportunities for search ended, trading for relics became the main pursuit. Klutschak bartered with the Nattilingmiut, who were eager to be compensated for authentic Franklin-related relics. As colder and stormy weather began to move in, Schwatka considered their options, now that their comprehensive search of King William Island had come to an end. In terms of the search, it had been diligent and thorough; of the one hundred and fifty days spent on the island, a full sixty had been engaged in the pursuit, substantially more than any previous searcher. For Schwatka, with the responsibility for the welfare of twenty men, women and children hanging over his head during the past seven months, while constantly on the move for food, the desire to reach Camp Daly and the safety and comfort of a permanent stop became his top priority. So much so, that rather than wintering on King William Island or Adelaide Peninsula, Schwatka elected to return to Camp Daly by again crossing the barrens. The plan was to stock as much game as could be carried on the sledges (which would only supply them part way), and hopefully look to supplement their stores on the trail. It was another bold choice requiring an inland traverse, and this time through the heart of the winter.

Establishing a favorably placed camp on a narrow stretch of Simpson Strait near Gladman Point, they watched in amazement at the seasonal migration of caribou crossing the newly formed ice to the mainland in immense herds ("a caribou hunter's Eldorado" said Klutschak), over a thousand on three consecutive days. The traditional pattern of the caribou migration was from the mainland to King William Island in the spring, and the reverse in the fall. The caribou frequently lined the southwest coast of the island in great numbers in autumn while awaiting Simpson Strait to freeze. Taking advantage of that circumstance, September 30 was a remarkable hunting day, with twenty-six killed, half by the joyful Toolooah, who kissed his rifle in thanks.[18]

On October 3, the ice had frozen over Simpson Strait, and large numbers of caribou crossed, leaving a few stragglers on the island. By October 7, the migration bonanza had abruptly ceased, an ominous sign for their future larder. Schwatka's experience along Simpson Strait, during the peak season for caribou numbers, was a far cry from that experienced by McClintock on King William Island. During the months of April and May, the same time that Franklin's men began their desperate retreat, McClintock found that no game was to be had.

The Nattilingmiut encamped nearby proved to be a cooperative and helpful people to the expedition, dispelling initial apprehensions as to their aggressive disposition. The industrious Inuit fashioned winter clothing and bedding for the return journey and supplied some badly needed dogs in exchange for caribou meat secured by Schwatka's men. The labor necessary to produce one suit—caribou coat, pants, and boots from start to finish—included skinning, drying, chewing, cutting and sewing. It was extremely time consuming, taking three to four days on the part of an accomplished Inuit woman, and each person typically required two suits.

Although Schwatka decried the Inuit's voracious appetites which devoured their food stocks, the mutually beneficial relationship provided a vital component to Schwatka's return trip in the dead of winter. From the Nattilingmiut, Schwatka also learned of a large inlet near Wilmot and Crampton Bay on the west coast of Adelaide Peninsula, which Dease and Simpson had apparently not examined. Geographical discovery still motivated Schwatka, and despite the desire to reach Camp Daly as quickly as possible, he was eager to explore and survey this extensive inlet.

In the meantime, Klutschak, who had great affinity toward the Inuit, managed to perform one diplomatic function involving the Inuit groups. Fully aware of the historical enmity between the Nattilingmiut and Aivilingmiut, carried through generations and involving "vendettas" that Klutschak claimed still occurred, Klutschak served as mediator for a reconciliation between the two parties. Assembling in a large snow house, the armed males of both groups ate heartily and held a two-hour conversation on the subject, finally putting their knives away and touching each other's chests, uttering the word "Ilaga (my relatives)." A communal entertainment followed, but Klutschak the peacemaker would not be present to see if the "treaty" would be honored.[19]

On November 1, the Franklin Records Search Expedition started its long-delayed march back to Camp Daly. Klutschak was not prone to exaggeration, and his remark that "this trip [to Camp Daly] probably stands alone in the history of Arctic travel," was no overstatement. At their onset the expedition was split into two groups: Schwatka, Gilder, with Toolooah, Ebierbing and their families manned one sledge for the side trip to Wilmot and Crampton Bay, while the balance of the party under Klutschak was to make a more direct run for the Dangerous Rapids near the Back River. On the way, Klutschak was to make a final visit to Starvation Cove to bury remains, erect a monument, and leave a record of the visit. If all went well, both groups would rendezvous at Dangerous Rapids on the edge of the Back River by November 15. Resembling a camel caravan trekking through the Sahara, the sledges were stacked "man-high" with caribou bodies (sans head and legs), and several hundred pounds of fat, the remaining sum of their successful hunting take.[20]

Despite his military training, Klutschak was a reluctant leader at best. Bellyaching as if he had drawn the short straw, he grumbled that Schwatka's group had the advantage in energy by virtue of Toolooah, whom Klutschak regarded as an Inuit exception "with regard to willpower and perseverance." Less forceful than Schwatka, Klutschak's Inuit companions followed their own schedule, leaving Klutschak to "experience many hours of vexation," and counting the days until he could surrender his command. His narrative of this particular portion of the journey is an extended gripe session in regard to his Inuit companions, and his frustration is almost palpable. For his part, Schwatka's party quickly headed south. They made slow progress to start, a combination of heavy sledges packed with meat and overfed dogs "being so fat that they were lazy." They encountered a large party of Nattilingmiut and Ugjulingmiut near the mouth of Sherman Inlet, some of whom they had met previously. The importance of the chance encounter was the receipt of additional confirmation of the earlier reports that one of Franklin's ships had been crushed in the ice near Grant Point. From the Inuit, they also received a piece of a boat from the ship lost near Grant Point and a block with the initials "10" or "OR" with the "R" defaced, which Schwatka surmised was from HMS *Terror* (though in point of fact their group was much closer to the location of the wreck of HMS *Erebus*).[21]

Repeating a pattern, the skittish Ebierbing was again in absolute fear of the murder of one of the men in the Schwatka party. The Inuit of the encampment wanted to engage in what Schwatka termed "gladiatorial contests," the two best men of each tribe exchanging blows. However, Schwatka abruptly cut off the amateur boxing match by advising the Inuit that he would give his own contest the next day with his magazine rifle, which "dampened all gladiatorial ardour." Schwatka correctly noted that family feuds among different tribes were far more common than unprovoked hostility, situations in which every male relation of the murdered man feels compelled to take vengeance on the perpetrator. Although Schwatka believed Ebierbing's fears were greatly exaggerated, through Ebierbing he told the Inuit that if anyone was harmed, they would pay the price. There was no conflict, but on their departure Ebierbing persuaded Gilder to make an overblown show of force by brandishing his pistol as they loaded the sledges. Shortly after leaving the encampment, Schwatka's party encountered a few Inuit returning by sledge, one of whom had been with the Inuit who initially found the boat and skeletons at Starvation Cove. According to Gilder, one woman named Toolooah confirmed "the testimony previously obtained in every essential particular," presumably as to both the destruction of "precious" papers and cannibalism, although Gilder did not elaborate.[22]

A rough survey of the extensive inlet (named Sherman Inlet), which ran more than fifty miles to the southeast, confirmed that Adelaide Peninsula was connected to the mainland by a rather narrow isthmus. Schwatka's party continued east across that narrow portion of this peninsula. For Schwatka's group, the long detour to map the inlet in the interest of science left them on a starvation march to the Dangerous Rapids. Since leaving King William Island, no caribou had been taken and temperatures were becoming numbingly cold; the average for November was -29°F, with a low of -49°F. On two occasions, with their supplies low, the dogs were forced to go eight days without food, an enormous testament to their fortitude. Schwatka rightly found that the endurance of these workhorses was "absolutely beyond comprehension." Travelling was slow, and the intense cold created a gritty effect on the snow that impeded travel. Whereas they could manage more than ten to fifteen miles a month earlier, now a good day was five to ten miles at best. At no point did they experience perpetual darkness through the entire day, but on the shortest of days, they gleaned only the briefest twilight, with the sunrise and sunset almost running into each other. Miraculously, they stumbled upon a cache of fish left by an unknown Inuit group which served to partially refresh the dogs. At the time, Schwatka was unaware that it had been stored there by the starving Ugjulingmiut they had met last summer. They were in better condition now and had taken the precaution of increasing their stock.[23]

Schwatka's party arrived in the vicinity of Dangerous Rapids on December 5, three weeks later than his planned arrival date of November 15. Schwatka was concerned by Klutschak's absence, since Klutschak's group had a far shorter distance to travel to the rapids. On December 7, two Ugjulingmiut boys who had followed Schwatka's tracks from the cache that he had broken into arrived at Schwatka's snow hut. To his relief, they explained that Klutschak's party was several miles away at the Ugjulingmiut encampment.

On December 10, the two parties of the Franklin Records Search Expedition were reunited, and no one was more pleased than Klutschak. Klutschak's frustrating story served to confirm Schwatka's command and leadership skills, the absence of which had led to a breakdown in order and routine within Klutschak's group. The plain truth was that the Inuit would pay no heed to Klutschak's weak admonitions to travel. Focused on safety and survival, they were content to remain with the food sources on their sledges or at the camps they encountered. When they did travel, the Inuit reverted to portaging their supplies, a practice forbidden by Schwatka, moving one sledge at a time, thereby tripling their travel distance and time, and forcing Klutschak and Melms to shepherd each leg.

By mere happenstance, Klutschak had reached the Ugjulingmiut camp near Dangerous Rapids as Schwatka also reached the rapids, learning of Schwatka's nearby presence upon his arrival. Klutschak's trek had not been difficult, with various encampments along the way, but for the stubbornness of the Inuit. Completely frustrated and dissatisfied with the duty of leading his group, Klutschak, the former military man, was "delighted to hand over to [Schwatka's] command again the detachment entrusted to my leadership." He was most satisfied that in the future he "would be spared the responsibility for constantly having to urge the Inuit along." Nonetheless, Klutschak had completed his principal task, the burial of the remains at Starvation Cove. With him at the time were some of the Nattilingmiut they had previously met and interviewed, who pointed out "precisely where the boat had been found and how and where the skeletons had been observed lying on the ground." The moving event led Klutschak to emotionally reflect that "Mother Earth could probably not produce a more desolate spot on this wide Earth than that where the last survivors of the Franklin expedition found their end." But that was not his last act regarding the Franklin expedition. About five miles south and east of Starvation Cove an Inuk located the remains of perhaps the last desperate survivor of the group who had perished at Starvation Cove. Manfully, this lone straggler had continued his forlorn journey, meeting his demise at this desolate location. The remains were buried, a monument was erected, and their search had come to an end.[24]

Reunited at their encampment, preparations were made for the challenging run from the Back River to Camp Daly on Hudson Bay. They rested the weary dogs and stocked up with a plentiful supply of kapisilik (round whitefish, a smaller salmon relative); some had been caught by bait and hook and some purchased from the Ugjulingmiut. Here, Schwatka was faced with another serious setback for the expedition. The competent hunter and guide Nowleyout, who had joined the group at the first meeting of the Ugjulingmiut in the spring of 1879, had decided to remain at this camp of his countrymen. His reasoning was simple and understandable. Nowleyout's daughter, at the age five or six, was already betrothed to a young man and Nowleyout was duty bound by Inuit tradition to abandon his daughter if he continued to Camp Daly, a circumstance that neither he nor his wife could bear.

To Klutschak, their trials and tribulations over the next few weeks "would only be boring in its monotony." During several weeks in December, they made slow and laborious progress down the Back River. The partially frozen river was bubbling with a multitude of rushing, open rapids that proved "Dangerous Rapids" an appropriate name, and an impossibility for sledge travel. Providing a visual representation, Schwatka noted that the rapids "look like titanic cauldrons of boiling water, huge dense black vapor, hanging over them often times obscuring the desolate scenery surrounding...." Klutschak believed that for "wildness and turbulence they are matchless." Forced onto the rugged riverbank, travel was hindered by a layer of ice formed from the steaming vapor that adhered to the sledges "with the pertinacity of set glue and to the snow beneath with a stubbornness worthy of an army mule." [25]

Temperatures hovered below -60°F. Christmas Day was celebrated with far less fanfare than the cheerful holiday the previous year, but Schwatka made sure they still made the best of it. Thirty-five caribou tongues and two salmon had been carefully tucked away for the event. In what Klutschak termed a "special dispensation," they cooked their holiday meal in a Franklin expedition kettle they had found, a rather ghoulish circumstance in light of the last extremity to which the Franklin members were driven. The dogs had finished the last reserves of their food and were weakening from lack of nutrition. Although spirits were momentarily revived, the reality of their situation left them in a gloomy state of mind that affected their emotional wellbeing. That evening, deep in thought, Klutschak stepped out and away from the comfort of his snow hut and pondered the utter loneliness he struggled with in the absolute silence of the Arctic night:

> Not a breath of wind, not a bird call, not a sound of any kind could be heard and an oppressive feeling lay on me like a mountain. The silence had become tangible, perceptible; it settled on the rock on which I sat; it settled on the river, on the ridges, and

everywhere. It had ceased to represent the negative significance of the non-presence of noise and, as the polar traveler Dr. I.I. Hayes had so strikingly commented, it had emerged as a positive force. It reflects the majestic scale and magnificence of this region; it embraces its desolation and loneliness; in the fullest meaning of the words it is the 'terrible silence of the polar night.' I felt alone and abandoned; as I stood up my first footstep on the hard snow rang out like an echo; I could hear something again. It sounded like life and the ghost was routed.[26]

Always a realist, Klutschak noted that "at the close of the year the prospects were far from bright for our party." The hunters had returned with no food and long faces. As the river drifted to the southwest and away from their destination, on the last day of the year Schwatka elected to abandon the Back River, taking his chances on a direct march for Camp Daly to the southeast. Schwatka again placed his trust in his Inuit guide, Toolooah, who had a general sense of the terrain across the barrens to Camp Daly. The course he plotted ran further south of their outbound track, and closer to Chesterfield Inlet. That return route would also bring them closer to contact with the Inuit visited by Gilder the previous summer, people who Schwatka hoped could extend a lifeline to his party. Spirits immediately brightened among the Inuit with the change of direction. A further boost was received in the form of the sun's rays which brought the slightest touch of light to the windows of the snow huts on the first day of the New Year. But daylight was still sparing, and much of the travel time was spent under a bright moonlight, which "shining upon the glistening snows converts the Arctic night into a broad twilight," wrote Schwatka. Despite the rise in hopes, the situation was still dire until Toolooah returned with four caribou, a godsend to the famished group. Though large numbers had migrated, the windswept landscape of the barrens had left bare stretches of relatively light snow cover that enabled some caribou to remain in the region through the winter while foraging for lichens and sedges.[27]

On January 3, the temperature reached an astonishing -71°F, one of the lowest temperatures ever recorded in the field at the time. The inland route of the expedition had taken them through the heart of the "cold pole" of the Canadian Arctic, a region of extremely low temperatures and wind chills. Just as remarkable were the consistently low temperatures during which they traveled; the mean temperature for the month of January hovered at -55°F.[28]

The chilling effect of the low temperatures posed difficulties beyond

The March in Cold Weather. From *Schwatka's Search.*

the obvious dangers of frostbite and hypothermia. "Don't tell secrets in the cold," is an apt but true adage that Schwatka and the hunters knew all too well. In the perfect stillness, when even the lightest of footsteps (muffled in fur) could be heard over a mile away, the difficulties of approaching the few elusive caribou they spotted posed a serious problem. To improve their chances of securing game, hunters frequently travelled in groups of two or three, often more than ten miles apart.[29]

Klutschak recorded other remarkable phenomena associated with the cold weather. A sledge travelling across even a flat snow surface made a whining sound (Gilder likened it to striking a steel bar), audible at more than two miles. The stunningly clear sky distorted distances. A snow hut at a distance of fifteen miles appeared to be as close as two miles. Remarkably, however, although there were frequent frostbites of a minor nature, remedied on the spot by the application of warm hands, no member of the expedition suffered any serious injury from frostbite. Ice-encrusted beards may typify the image of the valiant Arctic explorer, but Schwatka found that the congealed ice they collected was an undue hindrance.[29]

The poor dogs that had performed so valiantly and faithfully for almost twelve months were failing. Despite finding more game after crossing the divide between the Back River and Hudson Bay on January 15, the dogs were beginning to drop in their harnesses from what Klutschak attributed to a lack of nourishment, not a lack of food, but rather fat missing from the caribou. By January 17, eight had died. Everyone—men, women and children included—were now compelled to strap on the harnesses and assist hauling the sledges. Losing a dog at the rate of a one a day, by January 31 there were only nine weakening dogs on each of three sledges, so they had to consider abandoning one sledge and its contents. Schwatka was moved by the pitiful and "silent sufferings" of the overworked dogs, who in the worst of conditions never turned on their Inuit masters.[30]

The dogs' human counterparts suffered as well. The hunters often slept in snow huts without fire or bedding while in the pursuit of game. Women and children who were not exerting themselves physically particularly felt the biting cold. For Schwatka and Klutschak, who were firmly committed to an accurate calculation of their distances, chronometers were checked, and their course plotted with every start and stop, a particularly numbing experience with bare hands. There were undoubtedly some disparaging words cast about, but no dissension is reflected in the published narratives. In January they were forced indoors, but for eleven days in which they travelled only ninety-one miles, a frustrating period of inaction that delayed their progress. Away from the Back River, the terrain was noticeably more mountainous and rugged, with fewer scattered lakes and ponds. February fared little better, with thirteen travelling days and a mean temperature of -44°F.

A new plague descended in the form of ravenous wolves. The flares, which had been so effective before, were simply ignored by the single-minded beasts. On one occasion, marauding wolves killed four of the dogs and attacked Ikqueesik when he attempted to drive them off. On another, while Toolooah was hunting, a pack of thirty bloodthirsty wolves attacked him. He saved himself only by leaping upon a big rock and shooting one or two, thereby diverting the voracious animals to the dead carcass of their comrade. The Inuit had devised a particularly cruel means of wounding and killing them. Knives would be covered with caribou blood, and the handles buried in the snow with just the blades visible. The ravenous wolves would lick the blood not realizing they were slicing their own tongues in the process and slowly bleeding to death.

By mid-February, the entire group of men and dogs were reduced to a pitiful sight. As food was scarce, the remains of a dead caribou already ransacked by the wolves became a godsend. For Schwatka, the tortuous journey had become another Starvation March of 1876. With little blubber for use in cooking, they were reduced to scratching moss out from under the snow for fuel and eating frozen meat when fuel was lacking. The poor dogs had been reduced to an undernourished and exhausted crew of sixteen from the original forty-four.

Lying in the cold and darkness of their snow huts, the situation was rather bleak, made more depressing, according to Klutschak, by the monotone songs of the Inuit women. But February 19 was a day that brought euphoria to the entire group of weary and weathered travelers. From the top of a high ridge, they could plainly see the "water sky" of Hudson Bay about sixty to seventy miles to the southeast. Klutschak and Schwatka, both skilled in navigation and mapping, had been unable to check their dead reckoning against observations. They applauded themselves when they determined their location as latitude 64°23' N by observation on February 20, a difference of only two miles from Schwatka's dead reckoning over their course since December.

The real moment of relief arrived on February 25. While tracking a caribou, Toolooah made the startling discovery that the same animal was also being tracked by another Inuk. Upon spotting Toolooah, the frightened stranger darted back to his snow hut where he remained until Toolooah managed to establish contact. His name was Isedlak, an Inuk well known to Toolooah. He had been living with his wife and two children on their own for nearly a year. Once reassured of friendly intentions, he generously offered a supply of fish and the most welcome knowledge that Depot Island was only three marches distant.

After a two-day layover, on February 28, leaving their excess baggage behind, and dismantling the third sledge for fuel, the entire party headed for Camp Daly under far brighter circumstances. On their way, a most remarkable event occurred, one which was only recorded by Klutschak. While he was watching the Inuit men, who were diligently building their respective snow huts, they quickly stopped and hastily built a separate hut. Upon entering the new dwelling, Kutcheenuark, Ikqueesik's wife, gave birth to a baby boy after a twenty-mile march, a testament to fortitude if ever there was one. Klutschak expected a well-earned delay for the next few days for mother to recover, but the next morning, the newborn was wrapped in skins and placed on the sledge and another seventeen miles were accomplished without incident.

Their arrival at Depot Island was a joyful event for the Aivilingmiut community. With a welcome sigh of relief and with an overwhelming sense of satisfaction, Schwatka tried to record his feelings: "It is impossible to describe the emotions of a person who has been undergoing long continued absence amidst privations, labor and hardships, when some expected familiar place that heralds home looms upon the anxious vision, and tells in welcome words that all the privations, all the hardships are things of the past." Even the "non-emotional" Inuit were caught up in the moment, running and shouting as they arrived. Gilder was so taken with the excitement and the warmth of their greeting that he was running and shouting with them. Ahmow, guardian of Schwatka's stores at Depot Island, who came to meet them, gave Schwatka a hearty greeting, exclaiming "Ma-muk-poo am-a-suet suk-o!" (plenty good to see you). Tears were streaming down his cheeks.[31]

Then came the disappointing news. Thomas Barry had failed to leave the extra provisions (one thousand pounds of bread), trading materials, and stores that Schwatka had left on board the *Eothen* when they departed in June 1879. According to Gilder, Barry had "absolutely gone away with the food from us without a word of explanation." Schwatka was shocked at the dastardly act, which now left his party at risk of starvation. The Inuit at Depot Island were themselves extremely low on food, having suffered through a winter that saw them reduced to eating their own dogs and seal lines. The addition of eighteen mouths to feed, as well as the famished dogs, presented a real possibility of famine. Schwatka didn't mince words as regards to Barry's conduct: "I make no hesitation in stating that I was as totally unprepared to expect robbery as is usually the case where that crime is committed. Sufficient to say that that robbery deprived us of all our provisions, whose loss, had there been no ship within reach would have led to probable starvation, as after events seemed to prove."[32]

Matters turned from bad to worse, as a wintry storm confined them indoors and put an end to any hunting. After three days, despite their rationing, the food gave out; an emergency meal of a stiff walrus flipper sustained the camp on day four, tough walrus skin was the fare on day five. For the next five days, they endured "the fasting period," as Klutschak tactfully referred to their situation without food, as they anxiously awaited a break in the weather. All remained idle in their huts. The hungry children especially suffered, and their wailing added to their mental anguish. Rather than dwell on their misfortune, making the best of the situation, Schwatka learned that one unknown whaler remained at Marble Island, where Schwatka now pinned his hopes for supplies. Finally, with a break in the weather, Schwatka and two Inuit companions, named Eeglee-leock and Nanook, set off for Marble Island by sled pulled by the two best dogs. For Gilder, Klutschak and Melms there was little to do but anxiously await Schwatka's return.

At Chesterfield Inlet, their halfway point, Schwatka left the sled with Nanook and half the supplies and instructed him to return to Camp Daly (unknown to Schwatka the Depot Island group had secured a walrus to relieve their situation). In a remarkable feat of endurance and a testament to his concern for his companions, Schwatka and Eeglee-leock walked seventy-five miles in twenty-three hours to reach Marble Island. There, they found not the underhanded Barry, but a true gentleman and a generous whaleman, Captain Baker of the *George and Mary*. Captain Baker, who extended a warm greeting and provided much needed assistance, was astounded when a bedraggled white man dressed as an Inuk arrived at his ship on foot and delivered his remarkable tale of adventure. A sled with hardtack, pork and molasses was hurriedly sent back to Depot Island, with orders from Schwatka for the Euro-Americans to come join him. Gilder had already left Camp Daly and met the sled on its return run, and Klutschak and Melms quickly joined Schwatka on the *George and Mary*. There, they relaxed and actually lounged for several weeks, recovering from their ordeal. Schwatka and the Euro-Americans left Marble Island and their generous host, Captain Baker, on May 7 and settled back into camp on Depot Island on May 11, while patiently awaiting the whaling captain after ice break up. On June 7, their fortunes turned for the better as Captain Baker arrived, having just killed a whale. Its skin served as an epicurean staple until the Inuit could manage to secure additional food. After cruising Hudson Bay for whales, the *George and Mary* returned to pick up Schwatka and his men at Depot Island for the return trip home.

Gilder recorded an emotional farewell to their Inuit companions, with whom they had shared so much during the last twelve months. Many held hands with their white companions, "as if reluctant to let go," sad that their parting would likely be forever. Klutschak warmly recalled that "we had become very fond of the Inuit and vice versa." Gilder wrote, "[t]hat they were in earnest in the expression of their grief I have every reason to believe." His last remark perhaps captured their feelings best and acknowledged the reality of the situation: "They had, so to speak, adopted us as their children."[33]

As their boat left the island, Schwatka and Gilder sat in silence, their hearts filled with emotion, too moved to speak. Schwatka, the resolute military man, turned to Gilder and said "I was not prepared for this." "Prepared for what?" responded Gilder.[34]

Schwatka replied: "I was not prepared to feel the pain of parting from these people and this country as I feel it now. Even the near prospect of getting back to civilization, and of meeting friends and hearing news scarcely ameliorates the pang at this moment." Those emotions were extended most toward his close friend Toolooah, who could not bear an emotional farewell on board the *George and Mary*, and simply paddled round the departing ship in a small boat. Schwatka saw him in the small vessel, his face buried in his hands, weeping. "I can understand his feelings exactly," said Schwatka to Gilder. "He dare not trust himself to go through the ordeal, poor fellow. He knew he would break down when it came to that, and I am glad he didn't, for I am afraid I should too." Toolooah and his family had planned to return to the United States but declined at the last moment after pressure from the elders of the community.[35]

Schwatka and Gilder had nothing but praise for the enthusiastic and devoted young man, on whose judgment they had fully come to rely as an equal, and whose extraordinary efforts had been the salvation of the expedition on so many occasions. Simply as a matter of record, Toolooah had killed 236 of the total 532 caribou taken, together with numerous bears, seals and musk oxen. But the numbers do not come close to reflecting Toolooah's importance. At times on the verge of starvation, he was tireless in his efforts to secure food. When other hunters had given in and surrendered emptyhanded, hours or days later Toolooah could always be counted on to return with the much-needed game. Without his sledge driving abilities, the expedition could never have achieved what it did. Gilder stated "It is certain that to him more than to all the other natives with us combined is due the success of our enterprise." Ebierbing too remained. With his new wife, he too believed he would fare better here than in the destination where he had lost a wife and another child. Sadly, he died within a few years.[36]

Leaving Depot Island, the *George and Mary* stopped at North Bay in Hudson Strait, a regular rendezvous point for the local Inuit and passing whalers. Captain Baker may have been kind-hearted to Schwatka and his men, but whaling was a competitive business and Baker played every potential advantage. A resourceful whaleman, the captain would manage to take a whale without launching a harpoon. The whales had made a quick exit from Hudson Bay that season, a factor which explained the lack of success on the part of the *George and Mary*. But the Inuit near North Bay had managed to kill three cetaceans along Hudson Strait as they left the bay in April, storing the whalebone at Akkolear, a station about sixty-five miles northwest from North Bay. The successful Inuit crew was organized by an Inuk known to the whites as "Johnnie Bull," a talented young man who was well trained in whaling operations. For the *Herald*, Gilder simply reported that Captain Baker bought from the Inuit a head of whalebone, which was retrieved from Akkolear by the first officer of the *George and Mary*. Unwittingly though, the two explorers would become witnesses in a legal controversy that found its way into the courts of the United States. For now though, it was time for relaxing during the leisurely trip homeward.

CHAPTER TEN

THE TRAVELER AT HOME

WHILE CRUISING ALONG THE LABRADOR COAST two years before in 1878, Frederick Schwatka had been taken by the eagerness with which the returning Newfoundland fishermen sought news from the wider outside world. Now, as the *George and Mary* encountered several fishing barks, he and his men were the ones desperate for information. They were elated to receive current copies of the ubiquitous *New York Herald* from a passing schooner. With thoughts of home looming ever closer, on the evening of September 22 the *George and Mary* arrived at New Bedford. The subdued return of the expedition, not expected to call at this whaling port, was not momentous by any means. However, recognizing its import, a dogged news reporter for the *Boston Globe* elicited a few details, and the paper ran an "EXTRA!" in large font under the headline "Franklin's Fate. The Fate of Sir John's party clearly established," thus almost scooping even the *New York Herald*.

But with dramatic headlines introducing full page articles in the *Herald*, Gilder's breathtaking story of "Schwatka's Search," which ran across as many as ten issues over the next two-weeks in order to heighten the excitement, offered the complete thrilling story. In his correspondent role, Gilder furnished lively and colorful accounts of the day-to-day experiences of the expedition that filled the pages of the *Herald*. Never before had an on-the-spot reporter provided such extensive coverage of an Arctic adventure. With a circulation that was by far the largest of any newspaper in the United States, the Schwatka party's adventures reached a sizable audience, and was extended further by secondary coverage in numerous regional newspapers across the country. Gilder's reports graphically captured the hardships and sufferings of the overland party, while often humorously recounting his own trials and tribulations. The historian Beau

Riffenburgh noted that Gilder's sensational reporting was given more ink than President James Garfield's election the following month and lifted the circulation of the *Herald* and Gilder's own status to that of a celebrity.[1]

Through the extended press coverage, Frederick Schwatka, who had not expected a hero's welcome, had suddenly gained overnight fame. But the unanticipated public attention did not distract him from attending to more pressing business. His first thoughts turned to home. He telegraphed his anxious family in Salem, who were much relieved to hear of the good health of their absent son. His next step was to contact the U.S. Marshall's office. Schwatka could ignore Thomas Barry's shifting story of the Franklin silverware, but he was outraged by Barry's failure to leave the stores at Depot Island, conduct that left his expedition in peril, and reduced to surviving on a sealskin diet. Schwatka sought the long arm of the law for the arrest of Thomas Barry "for stealing on the high seas." Forceful when necessary, the typically reserved commander angrily asserted to a reporter that "the next time I see him [Barry], it will be in the United States Court."[2]

One step ahead of the law, Thomas Barry did make an appearance, not in court, but in the offices of the firm of Alexandre Brothers. The business of Morison and Brown had fared the worst from the expedition, collapsing after the *Eothen* returned with an empty catch on its whaling voyage. Alexandre Brothers had opportunely stepped in to become the new owner of the ship. At an interview conducted by Mr. Alexandre, to which a *Herald* reporter had been invited, Barry was pressed to explain his conduct. An indignant Barry vigorously denied that he absconded with the supplies earmarked for Schwatka's group. The whaleman asserted that he had left Depot Island in June 1878 with almost 1,400 pounds of bread that Schwatka's group had requested that Barry hold until their return. However, in January 1879, Barry claimed that Gilder, Schwatka, and a few Inuit visited his ship at Marble Island and the hungry group consumed virtually all the supplies that were left. Due to thick ice, bad weather, and a crew struck with scurvy, Barry was unable to unload these remaining stores at Depot Island later that season, so he had made for home. According to Barry, "I reached St. John's in September, sick, and was obliged to leave my vessel at that port in charge of my mate." Mr. Alexandre denounced Barry's conduct as "cowardly," asserting that Barry left Hudson Bay a month early, thus also explaining in part why the *Eothen* came up empty. Moreover, when the stores on board the *Eothen* were inventoried at St. John's after Barry had disembarked, his firm found enough food to last a crew fifteen months, all items that should have been left at Depot Island. Barry unconvincingly responded that those items must have been purchased after he had left the ship at St. John's. Refusing to answer further questions from a *Herald* reporter, an irate Barry stormed out of the office of Mr. Alexandre, never to be heard from again, a disagreeable footnote in Arctic history.[3]

Schwatka had other business to attend to: further leave from the military and an address on behalf of the American Geographical Society, which had so enthusiastically supported the expedition. Schwatka still held his position as an officer in the U.S. Army. With his leave of absence officially terminated on October 6, 1880, now First Lieutenant Schwatka requested a continuation from the army to tie up those loose ends. In response, Adjutant General Richard C. Drum assigned him "temporary special duty" in New York City, with the understanding that he would "repair to" Washington, D.C. as soon as convenient, a generous open-ended gesture on the army's part that it would soon come to regret. Following his return, Schwatka would begin to evince a marked indifference to his service obligations. His lack of commitment and conduct would soon become a source of friction with his superiors. Schwatka had always been a dutiful soldier who was proud of his service, but perhaps his unbridled freedom for more than two years had caused a change in attitude towards the strict discipline and structured bureaucracy of the military, or maybe his active mind and restless energy simply tired of garrison duty in the now-pacified West.[4]

In the meantime, the accolades for "Schwatka's Search," by which name the expedition was commonly known, came from both sides of the Atlantic. From England, British naval worthies, themselves Franklin searchers, were prepared to offer congratulations in remarkably identical, seemingly scripted, quotes. As reported by the *Herald*, they mentioned Schwatka's "perseverance" on his sledge journey, an achievement that, unlike the results of his search, offered no challenge to their own previous Arctic work. Sir Leopold McClintock, the discoverer of Franklin's fate, remarked that Schwatka "is entitled to great praise for his perseverance in the face of great difficulties." Sir Allen Young, who served with McClintock on the *Fox* was quoted, saying that "the reports of the expedition of Lieutenant Schwatka and his party to the shores of King William Land reflect the greatest credit on their energy and perseverance." Captain Sir George Nares, a participant in an earlier Franklin search with McClintock, "expresse[d] great admiration for the pluck and perseverance of Lieutenant Schwatka and his party."[5]

But underlying those congratulations was a reticence to concede too much credit to Schwatka in regard to the Franklin search so as to avoid diminishing their own legacy. The wider press coverage, which was more flattering of Schwatka's achievements, must have caused some angst among their ranks. The *Christian Herald* commented that "the mystery that baffled the exertions of the English searches has now been explained by the brave American explorer." An editorial in *The Times* (London) boldly asserted: "If it was given to M'Clintock to disperse the clouds which enveloped the fate of the vessels and their crews, Kane in the *Advance* helped to penetrate the darkness. Lieutenant Schwatka has now resolved the last doubts which could have been felt.... The [Schwatka] expedition adds the concluding link to the chain." Even renowned international Arctic authorities were offering their praise of Schwatka's work. The distinguished Austro-Hungarian explorer Karl Weyprecht remarked that "I believe that Mr. Schwatka's investigations have finally settled the question of the Franklin documents, and that further researches would be quite useless and superfluous."[6]

Once McClintock had an opportunity to read the *Herald* story in more detail, choosing his words thoughtfully so as not to appear the jealous defender of his own work, he penned a letter to Judge Daly on October 2. He positioned Schwatka's expedition as one that merely confirmed what McClintock had already discovered: "It affords me personally very great satisfaction to find that the results of my researches in the same region, and the opinions based thereon, have been so fully tested and borne out by [Schwatka's] laborious and careful explorations." Interestingly, the comment was not the first time McClintock's work was similarly defended from that of later searchers. In regard to Hall's 1865-69 expedition, Lady Franklin, drawing from a communication from McClintock, had advised Henry Grinnell that "in general, Hall's researches quite confirm those made by himself [McClintock]."[7]

McClintock's subordinate Sir Allen Young was even more outspoken, stating that "[t]he ground traversed by the American expedition had, however, already been travelled over by Sir Leopold McClintock (under whom I had the honor of serving as navigating officer) in 1859, when he and Lieutenant Hobson found the only authentic records that have ever come to light, telling us of the deaths of Franklin and of the officers and men in the ships up to the time of their being abandoned, and describing how and where the ships were left and the route taken by the retreating party." But that wasn't all; even McClintock's artifacts were portrayed as being superior to those of Schwatka, as Young went on to state that his expedition brought back the "most interesting of the various relics" and "heard the same stories" as Schwatka about the retreat of Franklin's men. Even Dr. John Rae, not one to be silenced when he felt the least bit slighted, penned a letter to the *Herald* declaring that in case anyone had forgotten, his 1854 expedition was the first to report on the retreat and death of Franklin's men, and that he too received reports from the Inuit that books, i.e., those with "markings," had been given to children as playthings and destroyed.[8]

The press offered the most believable assessment of the situation. The *Chronicle* reported: "No doubt attempts will be made, if they have not been made already, to lessen the value of the task performed by the American crew and undervalue the results of their arduous labors; but there can be no just grounds for such depreciation of very valuable services." William Parker Snow, a British civilian Franklin searcher, put it more bluntly: "Again is England disgraced by another brave flag—the gallant Stars and Stripes successfully accomplishing what was our bounden duty to have done in reference to the above ill-fated expedition."[9]

There was not universal acclaim for all Schwatka's actions. Gilder's reporting of "unmistakable evidence" of members of the Franklin expedition resorting to cannibalism, highlighting the touchy topic in his September 25, 1880 *Herald* dispatch, fired the first salvo in what would become a short-lived, but nasty exchange. Exacerbating that point was an editorial in the same paper that even went so far as to suggest that Franklin's men were reduced to committing murder of their weaker comrades in order to sustain themselves. Another crass *Herald* editorial went so far as to state that the "American method" which was adaptable and not above using Inuit assistance, was superior to the "English method," which operated with a "robust self-sufficiency." All of these articles were deliberately forwarded by Bennett to the attention of Clements R. Markham, honorary secretary of the Royal Geographical Society, goading Markham to respond. Markham, a strong proponent of British polar exploration, was himself a Franklin searcher in 1850-51 as a midshipman on HMS *Assistance* commanded by Captain Erasmus Ommanney. Markham bristled at the *Herald*'s scathing discourse, confiding to McClintock that "it would have been in much better taste if these Yankee ghouls had left the bones alone?"[10]

As the historian Janice Cavell has noted, Bennett's and the *Herald's* mean-spirited stance ran counter to Bennett's cordial relations with Lady Franklin and his support for Sir Allen Young's 1875 voyage of the *Pandora* in search of the Franklin records, a circumstance that may be explainable by Bennett's desire to sell newspapers. The first public comment of displeasure on the part of the British was directed to a *Herald* reporter by Sir Leopold McClintock, now the sixty-two-year-old commander in chief of the North America and West Indies Station, and perhaps the most prominent Arctic authority on the Franklin search. On September 28, an aggressive *Herald* newsman managed to corner McClintock at his command in Halifax upon Schwatka's return. Raising the cannibalism issue, the reporter remarked that information received by Schwatka from the Inuit "points to the conclusion of Rae," to which McClintock responded: "I should be very sorry to have any controversy raised in the matter; it is an unpleasant subject, and any discussion of it must be harrowing to the relatives of the missing men. I do not think any reliable information can be obtained on the subject, and the less said about it the better. I am disinclined to talk of it at all." In the same *Herald* article as the McClintock interview, Gilder himself spoke in his defense about the cannibalism claims, noting that "the natives made most positive statements of the fact and it only remains for each individual to form his own conclusion." He did offer a qualification however, remarking that "it is a common thing, however, for the Esquimaux to make such charges against white men, if not, indeed, a habit of all savages."[11]

At times, lost in all the press coverage was the reality that the Franklin expedition had been a human tragedy that still touched the hearts of numerous loved ones and friends some thirty years later. Sparing them further grief was certainly a legitimate concern. McClintock was an intimate friend and advisor to Lady Franklin. Although she had died, he would have felt a special interest in avoiding the release of any morbid facts that could serve to tarnish the legacy of Sir John Franklin or his late expedition. The enduring emotional consequences of that tragedy were on full display at the funeral of Lieutenant John Irving, HMS *Terror*. The remains of Lieutenant Irving, believed to be those recovered by Schwatka on King William Island, were sent to Scotland at the request of his brother, Major Alexander Irving. In an outpouring of sympathy, thousands lined the streets of Edinburgh on a bitterly cold January 7, 1881, to pay their last respects to Lieutenant Irving. The casket, drawn by gun carriage and draped with the Union Jack, was led by a party of Royal Marines and a military band, followed by officers of the Royal Navy and Royal Army, representatives of the Royal Society and Royal Geographical Society, city and university officials, and a long line of dignitaries and civilians. Although there was some carping over Schwatka's return of Irving's remains, in his defense, Morison's orders called for him to do so, and Irving's family was certainly grateful for the act. Sadly, in contrast to Lieutenant Irving's final burial in the family plot, Schwatka could do little to offer solace to Lady Fairholme, whose brother James Walter Fairholme, third ranking lieutenant on HMS *Erebus*, had also met his fate on the lost expedition. Unable to locate Fairholme's final resting place, Schwatka had collected a few wildflowers from an unidentified grave on King William Island as a memento and sent them to Fairholme's bereaved sister.[12]

Recognizing that by now the *Herald* had gone too far, while still in New Bedford Schwatka reached out to McClintock personally, hastily dispatching a succinct but graciously worded telegram to him. Schwatka respected the veteran explorer and had no desire to create any animosity with McClintock or with his British counterparts. Schwatka almost apologized on behalf of the *Herald*, expressing his regrets to McClintock over the newspaper's reporting. Adopting a deferential attitude, he added that "your expedition did better than mine." In light of the frightful acts of murder and cannibalism circulated by the *Herald,* as a show of respect, Schwatka declared that the Englishmen whose tracks he had followed "died like men." McClintock offered a candid reply, one over which he must have labored, given the extensive corrections in his draft. He offered his hearty congratulations on Schwatka's "successful exploration" and safe return, but reiterated his position that Schwatka's expedition served as a confirmation of his own work. He cautioned Schwatka not to spread tales of cannibalism, but interestingly, he acknowledged that there may have been cannibalism among Franklin's men:

> I greatly rejoice that no rumour of their being reduced to eat human flesh reached me. As the natives have not our extreme repugnance to cannibalism they would more readily assume it as a fact on much more slender evidence than would satisfy us. I hope you may see your way to omit any illusion whatever to this subject, its publication could not fail to cause very great pain to the surviving relatives & friends; & could do no possible good & might even do positive harm in similar cases of extreme privation. Lastly, it is now impossible either to prove or disprove what is at best only a suspicion.... I think it sufficient merely to direct your attention to the painful nature of this subject, without discussing it further. We know that instances are not wanting of starving men when in a state of despair bordering on madness having broken through all restraint, eaten the flesh of their deceased comrades, and some such may possibly have been amongst these lost one hundred & five men.[13]

McClintock informed Schwatka that he was particularly disturbed by the *Herald* article which suggested that the stronger of Franklin's men had murdered and eaten their companions. For his part, Schwatka had no need or desire to create a frenzy over the fact or to drive newspaper sales and overemphasizing this ghoulish topic might diminish his legitimate accomplishments. But as a faithful researcher he believed he was compelled to report the information he had received from the Inuit, in whose testimony he had confidence. In that regard, he found himself in the same place as Doctor John Rae had stood twenty-six years before, as the recipient of oral testimony from the Inuit about the Franklin expedition. Schwatka was his own man and confidently prepared to stand by the Inuit statements on the subject. In an interview with the *Tribune* on October 5, just days after his admonition from McClintock, Schwatka turned open his field notebook and, on the issue of cannibalism, he simply read the relevant entries: "Outside the boat [the angakkuq] saw four skulls. There were some in the boat and a tin box full of bones.... He thinks the men had been eating each other, as some of the bones were sawed in two." Later in the interview, Schwatka added his own commentary: "Why, they were so reduced that, from the native's account, they must have resorted to cannibalism, for some of the bones had been sawed in two, so as to extract the marrow." To support the Inuit testimony, Schwatka added that without exception the natives seemed remarkably truthful, and that he had taken pains to avoid leading questions or to put questions in such a form as to suggest an answer. Later that month, Schwatka's address to the geographical society offered the same brief details, but he knew where to draw the line. Schwatka made no further comment on the matter in *Land of the Midnight Sun*.[14]

But the British naval complaints continued unabated. Sir Allen Young and Admiral Edward Inglefield disputed the allegations in letters to the *Herald*, with Inglefield claiming that a review of Hall's journals (copies of which had been sent to Lady Franklin) showed that Inuit statements demonstrated that at least one party of Franklin's men met a violent death at the hands of the Inuit. Evidently, for Inglefield, Inuit testimony was completely trustworthy only when it bolstered his position. The pleas from the British officers evidently had their effect though. Even the *Herald* recognized the moral repugnance of pursuing the matter and called for a halt to the discussion. In an editorial the same day titled, "A Deplorable Discussion," the *Herald*, which had crassly fanned the fire, now declared a truce, pointing to the British officers' claim of a lack of evidence, writing "we most heartily deprecate any further dispute about the question of cannibalism. The evidence is so meagre that it does not justify a dreadful aspersion upon the brave dead. For the sake of decency and humanity the subject should be dropped."[15]

A further plea came from Professor Joseph E. Nourse, into whose hands Hall's papers had been placed on behalf of the U.S. Government. The professor had completed the daunting task of organizing Hall's rambling writings, publishing an edited version of his journals and some interviews in 1879 under the title *Narrative of the Second Arctic Expedition made by Charles F. Hall*. The pious clergyman sought to quell the tempest, but in the end only served to confirm the narrative. In a letter to the *Herald,* he advised Schwatka to treat the cannibalism statements "as the gossip of the old Esquimau woman...." Nourse knew better however, as there were several suggestive references in Hall's *Narrative*. In fact, a close reading of the Hall publication reflected multiple persons commenting on acts of cannibalism. After publication of a further British response from Vice Admiral Sir George Henry Richards along the lines of Inglefield's complaint, the matter largely dropped from the *Herald* and *The Times* (London) where the controversy had been mostly played out.[16]

Despite the running polemics of the press, however, Judge Daly, proud of the society's backing of the expedition, was quick to fete its leader on the society's stage. On the evening of October 28, an enormous gathering of more than one thousand five hundred patrons filled every seat of the spacious Chickering Hall to hear Lieutenant Frederick Schwatka relate his story. The event was as much a military "Stars and Stripes" celebration as a geographical society event. Arriving in full military dress, in one of his proudest moments, Schwatka greeted the numerous West Pointers and senior military men who "literally besieged" their fellow officer. The American flag flown at Cape Felix was draped over the hall's concert piano. To the press, Frederick Schwatka still presented an effective combination of "the man of action and the man of thought"; possessed of a bronzed visage and powerful physique, and with his spectacles, that of the intellectual educator. When Schwatka was formally introduced, there was "a perfect hurricane of applause" that lasted several minutes. Judge Daly presided in the chair, flanked by Schwatka's mentor Major Anson Mills, Tenth Cavalry, and officers of Schwatka's Third Cavalry and the Seventh Cavalry. The U.S. military looked to bask in the positive acclaim. With the anxiety over the continued absence of the U.S. Navy's missing *Jeannette* expedition, Schwatka's return after a two-year disappearance held a special significance and hopeful optimism for the *Jeannette's* crew.[17]

With the recovered Franklin relics displayed as mute testimony to that expedition's sad fate and as a symbol of Schwakta's great accomplishment, Lieutenant Frederick Schwatka delivered his lecture in a direct and straightforward manner, describing in detail the trials and tribulations of the expedition and its accomplishments. He would leave the sensationalism to Gilder and the *Herald*. He first emphasized his most widely recognized accomplishment, the longest sledge journey ever accomplished in the Canadian Arctic, both measured by time away from a "permanent" camp and by sheer distance. By defying convention, the pragmatic explorer managed to travel some 3,251 miles (or 5,232 km) over a continuous journey of eleven months and twenty-one days, living almost entirely off the land. Those distances seem exceptional based on a direct line to Cape Felix at the tip of King William Island, and back. The thoroughness of Schwatka's search, including many coastal forays along the finger-like inlets of King William Island, as well as numerous detours, added substantial miles. Schwatka used a dead reckoning calculation while on the trail, stopping to plot his distance and direction at every sledge break, about every 1-1½ hours, or two to five miles. Klutschak, a fastidious and competent observer, corroborated Schwatka's calculations, double-checking Schwatka's data and reached virtually the same conclusion.[18]

It was an unconventional journey. The well-established practice of his predecessors had been to accomplish as much as possible during a brief window during a few favorable months and return (often times on the same trail) to an adequately stocked and relatively more comfortable "permanent" winter camp. Both Rae (1846-47; 1853-54) and Hall (1865-66; 1868-69), had set out from Repulse Bay on their expeditions towards Boothia Peninsula and King William Island, and returned in the same season to a winter camp near Repulse Bay, their starting point. But Camp Daly, Schwatka's starting point, was located more than two hundred and fifty miles to the south of Repulse Bay. From Camp Daly, Schwatka took an unorthodox approach, striking to the interior directly across the Kivalliq barrens, with considerable sledging by land. Rather than establishing a "permanent" camp for winter, his most daring and significant achievement was his successful return journey through the barrens in the heart of winter, braving excruciatingly low temperatures, stormy weather and scarce game.

Previous explorers certainly deserve credit for successfully embracing the Inuit lifestyle in their travels, particularly Doctor John Rae. In his address to the society, Schwatka claimed that his "was the first Arctic expedition whose sole reliance for the subsistence of itself and draft animals has been premeditatedly placed in the game of the locality...." If true, it was by a matter of degree. Schwatka departed Camp Daly with only thirty days of food and two weeks of walrus meat for the dogs for what became almost a twelve-month journey. During Rae's first Arctic journey between 1846-47 to Melville Peninsula, after starting from York Factory, Rae's party of twelve men carried four months of food and supplies, travelled for fifteen months, and returned with one month of supplies, having lived off the land for most of the expedition. Similarly, during his 1853-54 expedition to Boothia Peninsula from Repulse Bay,

Rae was away for thirteen months and survived on his own for eleven months. In the end, it is probably fair to conclude that both Rae and Schwatka can be credited with having successfully lived off the land in their journeys.[19]

There were more significant differences in their travels that make comparisons less meaningful. John Rae generally traveled in very small parties of young able-bodied men, and as a result was capable of rapid travels over extensive distances, often exceeding well over twenty miles per day. Although Schwatka's expedition was distinguishable from the larger, ship-borne parties like Franklin's, with its many men and self-contained supplies, Schwatka's party was by no means small. He was responsible for a party of up to twenty persons, including women and children, and more than forty-four dogs. His travels necessitated much slower sledging speeds, and far fewer miles traveled per day. His much larger food requirements also necessitated extensive time devoted to hunting, and his Inuit hunters were frequently so occupied, particularly on the return journey.

One explorer who profited from Schwatka's methods was the Canadian Vilhjámur Stefansson. Over the course of three expeditions to the Canadian Arctic between 1906 and 1918, Stefansson adopted an Inuit lifestyle and travelled extensively, living off the resources of the land. Stefansson was greatly impressed with Schwatka's methods, remarking that Schwatka was "a brilliant exponent of living off the land" and in the course of his "great sled journey" in the search for the Franklin records "helped to develop the technique of sled travel." In 1885, when Robert Peary first began to formulate his first plans for polar travel (the crossing of Greenland), he likewise pointed to Schwatka's methods: "The new plan of a small party depending largely on native assistance, inaugurated by Schwatka, deserves to be recorded as the American plan...." Peary gave too much credit to Schwatka, however, as others had already formulated such approaches. Moreover, in Peary's case, the explorations of Doctors Elisha Kent Kane and Isaac Israel Hayes may have had a greater influence. They had relied on an Inuit lifestyle and utilized the aid of the Inughuit (Polar Eskimos) at the settlement at Etah, North Greenland, the location from which Peary would later recruit his assistants. In addition, the concept of "living off the land" would be less relevant to explorers like Peary, Nansen and others, when attempting geographic objectives such as the North Pole or the crossing of Greenland, where rapid advance was necessary, and game was far less abundant.[20]

Although his geographical additions were not monumental, Schwatka could legitimately claim that he had added to the geographical knowledge of the North, an important achievement for himself. His expedition mapped the unknown region of the Kivalliq tundra along their course to the estuary of the Back River, identifying the Hazard Hills, Southwest Pass, Stewart's Monument and several rivers, including the Hayes, Lorillard, and Connery. On Adelaide Peninsula, Schwatka mapped the length of Sherman Inlet (now Sherman Basin) and delivered a survey of the coast from Grant Point to the base of the inlet. Schwatka and Klutschak also improved the maps for the coast of Hudson Bay from Marble Island to Cape Fullerton.

Through the end of the nineteenth century, Schwatka's route from Camp Daly to the Back River had never been retraced by European explorers. Joseph B. Tyrrell of the Canadian Geological Survey conducted surveys in the Barren Lands to the south and west of Schwatka's track in 1893 and 1894, as did David T. Hanbury in private expeditions in 1899 and 1901-02. James W. Tyrrell, who joined his brother Joseph in 1893, noted that the Barren Lands was an area of *terra incognita*, stating that "of almost this entire territory less was known than the remotest districts of 'Darkest Africa.'" In 1902, Hanbury surveyed a route from Baker Lake to the Arctic coast and onto Great Bear Lake, which paralleled Schwatka's journey in certain organizational respects. In addition to Inuit guides, for extended portions of his journey, he was accompanied by their wives and children. Hanbury acknowledged that the white man was a "novice in the experience" of travelling in this land compared to the Inuit. Like Schwatka, his Inuit companions were adept at sledge travel, hunting, snow hut construction, making and mending clothes and footgear; in general, helping to facilitate his successful journey. In contrast to Schwatka, however, Hanbury specifically waited for winter to break before travelling through the Barren Lands in order to be assured of sufficient game. He understood the exceedingly difficult task of feeding a party of any size on the barrens, especially during winter, cautioning that: "In undertaking a journey without carrying sufficient supplies to keep the party alive, one assumes a great risk, especially if the journey is in winter…it is exceedingly difficult to travel over the barren ground in summer if deer [caribou] are scarce, and in winter, or rather, during the cold months, it is impossible."[21]

It was only well after the Schwatka expedition that Euro-American commercial interest and missionary activity came to utilize a stretch of Schwatka's outbound route to the Back River, namely the corridor from the western edge of the Ukkusiksalik region (Wager Bay) to the Back River. In the 1920s, the two rival fur trading companies, the Hudson's Bay Company and Revillon Frères, were still actively engaged in a bitter power struggle. With its control over Hudson Bay, the Hudson's Bay Company extended its posts along the northern portion of the west coast of the bay to meet the challenge. In the summer of 1925, a small HBC post was constructed at Tasiujaq, on the far western end of Ukkusiksalik, for purposes of initiating trade with the interior and thwarting its competitor's activity operating from Baker Lake. Located within one hundred and sixty miles of the Back River, Tasiujaq offered a shorter land route to the Utkuhiksalingmiut and Nattilingmiut lands than that undertaken by Schwatka from Camp Daly. In February 1926, setting off with two sleds, Hudson Bay traders, guided by the Inuk, Iqungajuq, reached the Hayes River (east of the Back River) and greeted a group of Utkuhiksalingmiut just as Schwatka had done almost fifty years previously. A month later an Utkuhiksalingmiut man travelled the corridor in reverse to Tasiujaq for trading, the first such occasion recorded by the Hudson's Bay Company, and in May of the same year the first Nattilik trader arrived at the post from the Back River. Of course, the route had long been known to the Inuit as a hunting corridor. The post, which eventually became unprofitable for the company, closed some twenty years later.[22]

Interestingly, the logbook at the Tasiujaq trading post records a mystifying entry that perchance touches on the Franklin expedition and its "precious records." On November 8, 1929, an Inuk from the Back River recounted for the benefit of an HBC trader the deathbed confession that was communicated to him:

> Eelanak (from nr. mouth Back River) stated a native who was dying told his relatives how he came across a beacon [rock cairn] a few years ago. He looked into the base of same and found some books which he tore apart and practically destroyed them all, his guilty conscience must have worried him, as this was absolutely the first time he ever mentioned anything to any natives about his find. I asked Eelanak to try and bring some of the pieces if he could get any into the post when he comes in, in the spring.[23]

Curiously, the historian Dorothy Eber collected an oral account of a strikingly similar event. An Inuit interpreter, Thomas Anguttitauruq, was told by Matthew Tiringaneak, who had lived in the Back River region, that Tiringaneak had learned from his grandfather that Tiringaneak's great-great-grandfather had located a cairn while hunting caribou east of Chantrey Inlet (which is at the mouth of the Back River), and that "in this cairn was a lot of white and brownish-coloured material wrapped in a leather pouch—that was paper for sure. There were a lot of strange markings. That's writing. They were brownish colored papers, not dark brown but light brown. He [Tiringaneak's great-great-grandfather] figured they were cursed by a strange spirit who had left them there and he took them and destroyed every last one of them." Eber collected some additional facts directly from Tiringaneak at a later date as to the motive for his action. Sadly, Tiringaneak's relative believed that if the papers were not destroyed, that he and his family would turn sick and die. Therefore, he tore them all to pieces and completely tore down the cairn.[24]

Through a methodical search conducted during the summer months, and with the assistance of Inuit testimony, as to the expedition's primary objective, Schwatka confirmed to a reasonable certainty the loss of the "precious records" of the expedition, thus marking the nineteenth-century end to the search. The numerous relics (more than one hundred) recovered by Schwatka were tendered to the British Admiralty. Nearly all that survive are now housed in the National Maritime Museum in Greenwich, London. A hodgepodge of commonplace useful items, such as bottles, pens, pencils, buttons, clothing fragments, nautical implements of various sorts, including the partial keel and stempost recovered by Schwatka, which had been viewed by McClintock. The Inuit oral testimony solicited by Schwatka, besides providing additional details as to the fate of the expedition and its records, more precisely placed the location of HMS *Erebus* previously communicated to Hall. Though not its primary objective, Schwatka's expedition also located a number of sites where human remains were recovered. Recognizing the human sacrifice on the part of the Franklin expedition, Schwatka provided a dignified interment of the skeletal remains, in addition to the removal of what were believed to be the remains of Lieutenant John Irving. Schwatka's monuments to their memory served as markers for more recent bioarchaeological investigators. In 2018, researchers located the grave first identified by Schwatka at the location known as Two Grave Bay, leading to additional skeletal and artifact finds, confirmation of a Royal Navy officer's grave and a revision of the history of the grave's disturbance.[25]

At least one historian has agreed with Klutschak's assessment that "the Schwatka expedition acquitted itself well and that in the light of its achievements and logistics it must be placed among the most prominent searches for Franklin remains or relics." Carried off at a modest cost with military precision and without loss or serious injury, the venture was an achievement that reflected well not only on Schwatka, but also helped promote the stature of the American Geographical Society internationally within the scientific community. By not falling victim to disaster or grim suffering though, Schwatka's expedition has failed to attract the same public fascination associated with the more spectacular and recognized disasters such as the Greely, De Long and Hall (North Pole) expeditions, all of which have enjoyed numerous modern retellings. The explorer Vilhjámur Stefansson summed up the situation: "My favorite thesis is that an adventure is a sign of incompetence.... If everything is well managed, if there are no miscalculations or mistakes, then the things that happen are only the things you expected to happen, and for which you are ready and with which you can therefore deal."[26]

Schwatka's success flowed directly from his organizational and leadership skills. His closest companions through the trials and tribulations of the expedition were in the best position to judge. Gilder and Klutschak were nothing but complimentary. Gilder noted that "Lieutenant Schwatka's thorough fitness for his position as commander of such an expedition may be attributed to its successful conduct through all the various stages of its experience," and "Schwatka's strong will helped the travelers to live while the dogs were falling exhausted and dying by the way." Klutschak, who knew all too well the difficult demands of leadership, noted that Schwatka understood that "strict discipline can be achieved if one knows how to lead a command without giving too may orders," and that the expedition's "success is largely to be ascribed to [Schwatka's] wide knowledge, good judgment, energy and correct handling of his men." Fittingly, in his closing remarks to the geographical society, Schwatka fully offered credit where credit was due: "To my subordinates, officers and men, white and native, is due the fact that such an undertaking was made possible, not only by their untiring energy in their several departments, but also to their cordial co-operation and harmonious working as a whole." But it was Schwatka who had set the example of cooperation, and his ability to lead was more than simply giving orders. Schwatka knew how to engender loyalty and support through mutual respect, particularly in regard to his Inuit companions.[27]

Schwatka's search was by no means the last word on the fate of the doomed expedition of Sir John Franklin. Though no written records have ever been located beyond the Victory Point record, since the close of the nineteenth century an ambitious array of private and government supported searchers have added to our knowledge of the circumstances surrounding the disaster. By one count, more than sixty discrete expeditions of varying sizes and means have been engaged in the search, a testament to the enduring fascination with the lost expedition as well as an overwhelming desire to resolve its unanswered questions. Since the 1980s a combination of painstaking archaeological work and the application of modern technology have aided in a more accurate reconstruction of events, including details about the locations visited by Schwatka and previous searchers, the health and causes of death of Franklin's men, and the circumstances of their retreat. More recent technology has also revealed the identification of one member of the Franklin expedition with a high degree of reliability, Engineer John Gregory. The discovery of both the HMS *Erebus* and HMS *Terror* by Parks Canada, both remarkably intact and housing a wealth of artifacts, certainly offers a completely new window into many aspects of the expedition. These latest finds may help further shape and perhaps reshape our understanding of the fate of the lost expedition.[28]

CHAPTER ELEVEN
NEW HORIZONS

IN LONDON, THE MATTER of the Franklin Records Search Expedition was still much unsettled, at least for Clements Markham, who was outraged over the *Herald* reporting. Writing to McClintock, he complained that the expedition had failed in locating the Franklin records, and so for that reason "it, therefore, became necessary for the interest of the sensational newspaper to spin out columns of nauseating rubbish about every fragment of old stocking or preserved meat tin they found. It is garbage of the most disgusting kind, and the revival of Rae's story of cannibalism is of a piece with the rest." It was not just gruesome stories of cannibalism that had put him on edge though. Closely scrutinizing Schwatka's enterprise with great care, he assured himself that McClintock's work was not in the least bit threatened. Having done so, he offered the same reassurance to McClintock, writing to him that "nothing has been discovered of the slightest importance, in addition to what you ascertained and reported. You discovered the history of Franklin's expedition in all its main outlines." Although outwardly confident in his expressed viewpoint, Markham could not dismiss a lingering concern that Schwatka's expedition had captured the limelight and might thus diminish McClintock's work in the public eye. "There is quite enough of Schwatka in the *N.Y. Herald*; they have spun their story out to the utmost," he told McClintock. Markham's calculated response was to urge McClintock to bring out a new chapter to his popular work, *The Voyage of the 'Fox,'* to lay bare "all that is worthy of serious attention" in Schwatka's work. To Markham, that meant reiterating that Schwatka's work simply confirmed McClintock's findings and had added "a few bones and Irving's medal. That is all...." Both Markham and McClintock had a stake in retaking control of the narrative. In their opinion, the resolution of Franklin's expedition had been conclusively determined by the British, principally by McClintock, and they had every intention to keep it that way.[1]

McClintock was pleased to oblige Markham. In late 1881, he delivered a revised edition of *The Voyage of the 'Fox,'* that had passed through the guiding hand of Markham. A supplemental chapter was appended for the purpose of preserving McClintock's position as the undeniable discoverer of the fate of Franklin and marking his expedition as the definitive search expedition. McClintock's approach was consistent with his prior statements to the press, and those of British naval officers involved in the search. To McClintock, Schwatka's sledge journey was itself a remarkable endeavor and entitled to due credit as such, but as a Franklin search effort it had added nothing. McClintock's new chapter was also somewhat dismissive of Hall's noteworthy expedition, invaluable for its Inuit oral testimony in augmenting the history of the ill-fated expedition. As for Hall, McClintock opined that except for the reports of a large tent filled with the remains of many men, "no important fact has been added [by Hall] to what was previously known; but several interesting details are afforded; two other boats were found, and the place where one ship sank defined." Notwithstanding the short shrift given Hall's work, the wealth of that oral testimony, even in McClintock's summary (a full three pages), speaks emphatically to its importance.[2]

In his new chapter, regarding Schwatka's search, McClintock offered a factual recital of what had been found. This included Irving's grave, the other graves (all despoiled) and artifacts, and a summary of the Inuit testimony about the events at Starvation Cove (but omitting any cannibalism stories), the ship off Grant Point, and the men seen at Washington Bay, as well as a summary of the search of King William Island. Most of this was old news to McClintock, information he claimed was largely known by his own or Hall's expedition. About Schwatka's diligent search on King William Island and the Adelaide Peninsula for the Franklin records, all McClintock could muster was that "[w]e must all feel the greatest regret that the exhaustive and final search which Lieut. Schwatka has so very ably carried out has been unrewarded by the recovery of a single scrap of writing or any new or important fact," an exaggeration, but one that certainly maintained McClintock's position. McClintock was again thankful to Schwatka for "the confirmation of some previously received reports," and because Schwatka's "minute examination" confirmed facts obtained by McClintock and already published in *The Voyage of the 'Fox.'*[3]

However, concerning Schwatka's sledge journey, which did not threaten his own achievement, McClintock was more generous with praise, but even then with some qualifications. As for Schwatka's return to Camp Daly in the dead of winter, McClintock concluded his commentary with the statement that "undoubtedly the most arduous part of Schwatka's brilliant achievement was his return winter march. To have accomplished so much, and to have brought back his party safe and well through so many dangers and privations, and thus to have conducted his little Expedition to a happy termination, reflects the highest credit upon him, and upon those who so ably supported him to its close." In terms of specifics though, McClintock felt the need to compare Schwatka's trek with others to place it in proper perspective, and a few of those comparisons are revealing. McClintock correctly pointed out that Dr. John Rae and his party were the first white men who sustained themselves in the Arctic regions by their own efforts. That statement properly gave credit to Rae, and likely was intended to address Schwatka's claim that Schwatka's expedition was the first Arctic expedition whose sole reliance for their subsistence was off the land.[4]

McClintock could be fastidious in his detail when it served his purpose. In particular, he spent considerable time assessing Schwatka's low temperature readings, which were taken by Klutschak through spirit (alcohol) thermometers. Although McClintock did not outright challenge those readings, a strong sense of skepticism is evident in McClintock's analysis. However, Klutschak defended the thermometers as "very fine instruments" which at low temperatures made accurate measurements within a variation of about 1-1½°C. McClintock thoughtfully compared the lowest mean monthly temperatures experienced by Schwatka's expedition with Arctic expeditions viewed as near Schwatka's position, namely those of Parry (1821-22: -24.1°F), Rae (1846-47: -29.4°F) and Ross (1829-30: -29.9°F; 1830-31: -32.5°F), which reflected a lowest mean for any month of -32.5°F (Ross 1830-31). Separately, McClintock referred to the British Arctic Expedition of 1875-76 as having experienced the "lowest *well-authenticated* [italics added] mean monthly average" of -40.64°F in December 1875. McClintock did acknowledge that Schwatka's party was inland and above sea level as they crossed the barrens, a factor which could have contributed to lower temperatures than his comparables, which were taken along the coast. According to McClintock, all four of his examples experienced far less severe mean monthly temperatures than Schwatka's lowest mean monthly of -53.2°F in January 1880. Casting further doubt on Schwatka's readings, McClintock added that it was unusual that Schwatka's party experienced such stormy weather along with these extremely low temperatures. McClintock found that low temperatures typically occur during calm weather.[5]

Interestingly, Schwatka's lowest mean monthly temperature for the winter of 1878-79, while at Camp Daly, a coastal location comparable to McClintock's locations, was -29.2°F for January 1879. This was nearly the same as Rae at Repulse Bay in 1846-47, but not as low as those of Ross during the winters of 1829-30 and 1830-31. Whether Schwatka's interior location during January 1880, the so-called "cold zone," accounted for his substantially lower monthly mean remains an unanswered question. However, Gilder claimed that after the doubts were raised as to the temperature readings of the Schwatka party (presumably McClintock's doubts), the thermometers were "tested and found to be curiously exact." Interestingly, in terms of mean daily lows, Schwatka's lowest daily mean temperature of -68.8°F on January 3, 1880, had some similarities to other Canadian Arctic wintering parties. For example, George Back's expedition of 1833-35, an expedition that spent the winter of 1834-35 at Fort Reliance on the edge of the barrens on Great Slave Lake, recorded a lowest daily mean temperature of -60.35°F on January 16, 1834. By way of further example, the British Arctic Expedition of 1875-76, cited by McClintock, similarly experienced a lowest mean daily temperature of -69.68°F on March 4, 1876 and an astounding mean weekly temperature of -60°F for the week ending March 4. Curiously, none of these lows were identified by McClintock.[6]

McClintock pointed to other aspects of Schwatka's expedition that may have benefitted from previous explorers and Inuit assistance. He noted, for example, that Rae had previously travelled the Quoich River towards the Back River delta, reaching a point that he claimed was about half the length of Schwatka's outward trek. In addition, he noted that Rae was told by the Inuit that there were routes to the polar sea from Wager Bay and Chesterfield Inlet. Rae was also told of an abundance of game during the winter to the southwest of Repulse Bay, arguably including the area through which Schwatka travelled. These facts, which would have been known to Schwatka, were intended by McClintock to place Schwatka's work in proper perspective with earlier searchers, but tended to downplay the level of unknown risk associated with the endeavor. On the other hand, the one obvious omission on McClintock's part that would have the effect of greatly highlighting the expedition's importance, and distinguish it from all earlier Arctic sledge journeys, including those of McClintock, was any reference to the sledge distance travelled by Schwatka's expedition. In Schwatka's geographical society address, the first and most significant geographic accomplishment highlighted by him was his journey of 3,251 miles, an achievement that he touted as "the longest sledge journey ever made." Ironically, there was no more accomplished expert on sledge travel than McClintock; according to Clements Markham, McClintock was "the great master of Arctic sledge travelling." In fact, in 1875, four years before Schwatka's journey, McClintock himself was holding out his 1853 sledge journey of 1,400 miles as the longest Arctic sledge journey ever made. In light of McClintock's meticulous critique of Schwatka's journey, his utter silence on the length of Schwatka's extraordinary distance is puzzling. In fact, in a letter from Dr. John Rae to McClintock dated July 26, 1881, as McClintock's revised edition neared public release, Rae expressed doubts as to Schwatka's claim based on his own calculations of Schwatka's track. McClintock, however, understood the obvious dilemma that by questioning or even addressing this aspect of Schwatka's journey, and placing it in proper perspective, might only serve to greatly diminish McClintock's own accomplishment. Evidently, McClintock could be selective in his comparisons when it best suited his narrative.[7]

It is unfortunate that Schwatka's published narrative, *In the Land of the Midnight Sun*, has passed unnoticed, both then and now, as it would have provided Schwatka with an opportunity for wider and more significant recognition. The abridged version of Schwatka's manuscript brought out by Mystic in 1968, *The Long Arctic Search*, reported the sober day-to-day aspects of the original manuscript, with a focus on the primary purpose of the expedition, the Franklin records and the search. That abridged version omitted many of the entertaining and descriptive features of the complete original manuscript that also appeared in *the Land of the Midnight Sun*, which had as its primary purpose the publication of an engaging story that would appeal to the public eye. *In the Land of the Midnight Sun* ran serially in four installments over the course of 1880-81 in *Good Company*. This monthly magazine, originally titled *Sunday Afternoon, a Magazine for the Household*, was the brainchild of Edward F. Merriam, son of George Merriam of dictionary fame. It had but a short life, running from 1878 to 1881, with a limited circulation, accompanied by persistent financial difficulties. Fortuitously, Schwatka managed to publish the last installment of *In the Land of the Midnight Sun* just prior to the magazine's demise in September 1881.[8]

The obscure and underfunded magazine, *Good Company*, served as the only source of a popular account of the Franklin Records Search Expedition by its leader. The circumstances regarding Schwatka's arrangement with Merriam's publication, and the reasons for its selection, remain an unanswered question. Schwatka's contribution was a welcome boost to the struggling publication, and certainly met its editor's literary standards. Like many travel narratives of the time, *In the Land of the Midnight Sun* highlighted the exotic aspects of an unfamiliar region. Schwatka's detailed descriptions of the natural history and natural wonders of the Arctic that he observed first-hand were seamlessly woven into the ongoing narrative. Similarly, Schwatka introduced the lifestyle and habits of the Inuit with whom he lived and travelled for almost two years. His descriptions of their (and his) day-to-day struggle in all aspects of life, such as constructing snow huts, cooking, hunting, fishing, and travelling were all the more compelling given his close contact and familiarity with them. Schwatka's straight-forward manner of expression presented clear and revealing descriptions that captured the essence of his subjects. As would be expected from a soldier-author, his prose was true to life and generally avoided the waxing romantic and poetic charms more commonly evoked by the earlier Arctic travel narratives of his explorer-author counterparts, specifically Drs. Elisha Kent Kane and Isaac Israel Hayes. For example, his unvarnished picture of the bloody end of a musk-ox hunt captured its stark, but graphic conclusion:

> We arrive just in time to see the grand finale as the last of them sink to earth. They present a most formidable looking appearance as they stand with their rumps together; and great blood-shot eyeballs glaring like red-hot shot and plunging and pawing at the circle of dogs that encompass them while the rapid blazing of magazine guns, right in their faces so close as to burn their long hair, makes up a scene that will impress one for life if once encountered.[9]

Life and death struggles certainly had their place, but even commonplace experiences, such as the troublesome nature of persistently fogged eyeglasses or the annoyance of loose reindeer hair from clothing and bedding, did not escape Schwatka's observant eye and were depicted in gritty detail with a true sense of unpleasantness. Although *In the Land of the Midnight Sun* suffers at times from the prevailing condescending attitude towards Indigenous peoples, its underlying premise, to fully adopt an Inuit lifestyle, rightly recognized Inuit skill and ingenuity in surviving and thriving in the Far North. Schwatka was not shy in offering praise for his Inuit companions who earned his respect and lasting admiration. His own knowledge of Arctic history is also on display with the addition of a comprehensive chapter on the earlier fruitless struggles to locate the missing British explorer, Sir John Franklin, as well as an informative background section leading to Schwatka's own expedition.

In any event, the recognized expedition chronicler was William Henry Gilder, whose reporting from the field and his later full-length narrative captured the attention of the American reading public. Gilder parlayed his own reports into a book-length narrative published in December 1881 under the title *Schwatka's Search, Sledging in the Arctic in Quest of the Franklin Records*. His timing was opportune as books of travels to exotic lands were exceedingly popular. According to the *New York Times,* Gilder's work was among the newly published travel books "in greatest demand." The title of Gilder's narrative aptly placed credit where it was due, as well as subtly reflecting Gilder's admiration for his commander. In fact, that succinct title, *Schwatka's Search,* became synonymous in the late nineteenth century for a long, trying journey. In his introduction Gilder was not shy in stating that his point that Inuit testimony confirmed that Franklin's crews were reduced to cannibalism "provoked more criticism than all the rest." Taking an approach that readers should decide for themselves, he noted that "this is set down just as it was heard, being worth neither more nor less than any testimony on an event which happened so many years ago," and there he left the matter. We now know cannibalism likely did occur on the Franklin expedition, a fact which tends to support the truth of the Inuit testimony recorded by Schwatka and Gilder. But evidently, Clements Markham, with a long memory, was not prepared to let it go. In November 1880, he did offer a glowing tribute to Schwatka's journey in general terms, noting that it was "most remarkable and in some respects his journey is without a parallel. It reflects the highest credit on the commander and on those who served under him so admirably." However, when Markham published his own glowing biography of McClintock in 1909, his enmity toward the work of Hall and Schwatka was all too apparent, remarking that they "added nothing of importance." Moreover, in Markham's comprehensive history of the exploration of the Arctic and Antarctic Regions from the voyage of Pytheas through Scott's expedition of 1912, entitled *The Lands of Silence* (published posthumously), silence was indeed apropos, as Markham managed to remain completely silent as to both Frederick Schwatka and the Schwatka expedition in this voluminous work.[10]

The other contemporary account of the Schwatka expedition by a participant was that of Heinrich Klutschak. Published in German under the title *Als Eskimo unter den Eskimos* (As an Inuk among the Inuit), its title emphasized Klutschak's adoption of Inuit techniques and its basis as a means to the success of the expedition. For Klutschak, emulating the lifestyle of the Inuit also served his other stated purpose, to make a scientific study of the Inuk in his own environment "in seinem unumsormten Zustande als Kinds des Nordens" (in his wild state as a child of the North). The most important features of Klutschak's work are his descriptions of the Inuit, namely the Aivilingmiut, Nattilingmiut and the Ugjulingmiut. Over the course of the narrative, Klutschak offered a description of the day-to-day lifestyle of the Inuit during their journey, along with their superstitions and myths, with a concluding separate but brief factual summary of their vocabulary, religion, and communal life. As the European "outsider" among three Americans, Klutschak's account also provided a separate viewpoint and perspective that largely corroborated the accounts of Schwatka and Gilder. Like Schwatka, Klutschak also suffered from a Euro-American bias that viewed the Inuit as uncivilized and spiritually deficient. Klutschak, however, possessed a more quixotic belief in the indisputable benefit of religious conversion than Schwatka, who was more skeptical as to its benefit or even its success, likely because of his frontier experience.[11]

Missionaries and explorers from Germany and Austria-Hungary had ventured to the North in the years before Klutschak. Their publications were received with considerable interest by German-speaking audiences, as were German language editions of British explorers such as Scoresby, Ross, Parry, Back and Franklin, and even a German language narrative of Hall's North Pole expedition published by its scientist Dr. Emil Bessels. Klutschak's work also enjoyed wide popularity upon its release, and he followed it up with a triumphant return to his homeland which included a lecture tour about his Arctic experiences. The Emperor Franz Joseph was so taken with Klutschak's work that he awarded Klutschak the Cross of Honor, perhaps the pinnacle of achievement in his promising young career. As an English language translation did not appear until 1987, Klutschak's most widespread influence on the English-speaking public however was through his drawings, since they were reproduced as lithographs in Gilder's book, as well as in multiple issues of the *Illustrated London News* and *Harper's Monthly* in 1881. The full and half-plate scenes in the widely popular *Illustrated London News,* in particular, reinforced stereotypical images of the Inuit and Inuit life, replete with kayaks, sleds, dogs, and Arctic wildlife, with the most frequent illustration being the iconic snow hut or "igloo," which made an appearance in every issue of the *Illustrated London News* mentioning the expedition. The all-too-common nineteenth century depiction of the Inuit as simple-minded and childlike features prominently on the front page of the supplement to the January 1, 1881 issue of the *Illustrated London News*. This well-known image features six Inuit gaping in wonder and astonishment at the nearly full-page image of a mounted soldier in the Second Afghan War. The accompanying text informs the reader that "these simple folk" were amused by the illustration and equally bewildered by a conjuring trick by Gilder, a "specimen of the ingenuity of the civilized man." Unfortunately, the lithographs failed to adequately capture the true character of Klutschak's field sketches, which offer a more accurate portrayal of Inuit life and avoided the Euro-American cultural bias. For example, as one historian has noted, Klutschak's original drawing of the Inuit eyeing the *Illustrated London News* shows a much different image, not a perplexed group of Inuit, but rather an image of Schwatka as the recipient of information or instruction from the adult Inuit.[12]

The Schwatka expedition paved the way for more important anthropological contributions. In the fall of 1882, as the pioneer anthropologist Franz Boas shaped his plans for a research sojourn to Baffin Island to study the Inuit groups of the Central Arctic, he closely studied the published accounts of the predecessor expeditions of Hall and Schwatka. He ultimately modeled his own approach on the Schwatka expedition by fully adopting an Inuit lifestyle. During 1883-84, with one companion, he immersed himself fully in Inuit society on Baffin Island. Writing to his fiancé while in the Arctic, he proudly wrote of his success: "As you see my Marie, I am now truly just like an Eskimo; I live like them, hunt with them, and count myself among the men of Anarnitung [an Inuit winter settlement]. Moreover, I scarcely eat any European foodstuffs any longer but am living entirely on seal meat and coffee." Besides emulating the Schwatka expedition, Boas made use of the earlier observations of Hall, Gilder and Klutschak when preparing his own influential work, *The Central Eskimo.* Over time, his observations and theories would ultimately lead to the rejection of hierarchal racial classifications.[13]

Among the publications by the participants in the Franklin Records Search Expedition are several others by Schwatka that have been overlooked in their importance. Those works testify to a far greater interest by Schwatka in his Inuit companions and their culture than he has been given credit. In 1883, Schwatka contributed a series of six lengthy articles under the title "Among the Natives of the North" in *Frank Leslie's Sunday Magazine.* The articles touched on a wide range of Inuit societal topics, including their home life, manners, and customs, and their moral and religious beliefs, coupled with an assessment of the motivations supporting their lifestyle. By living closely with the Aivilingmiut and Nattilingmiut for almost two years, literally under the same roof, and consciously participating in their activities as one of their own to further earn their trust, Schwatka gained a unique and unshaded perspective in regard to their social relations, including those between husband and wife and parent and child. Few, if any, Euro-Americans had observed the Inuit family unit as intimately. His thoughtful opinions and conclusions were generally positive and supportive. He found that "good nature prevails in their households," and although wives perform much labor, they were treated kindly, and cases of abuse were far less "than the cruel wife-beatings that are so commonly paraded before us through the medium of inferior criminal courts." He observed the patriarchal role of the elder family members, the practice of arranged marriages and even how divorces were permitted within certain limits. Hesitant to condemn practices that ran contrary to Euro-American values, he understood that they could serve a practical purpose in a singularly harsh environment. For instance, Schwatka did not cast a negative judgment on the practice of polygamy, a practice considered morally repugnant to a civilized society, as the Mormons knew all too well. With the Inuit men bearing the greater risk of life, at times, their society faced a disproportionate number of females; polygamy served as a means of support. He also admired their sense of duty and respect of their elders. Although perceived as harsh and unfair to the Victorian eye, he also understood that the young male hunters were most favored with food during starvation times, while the elderly and children were left unfed at times, much to their detriment. He could even defend their "uncleanliness," one of the most severe blights on their moral character, according to genteel society. Having lived two winters with the Inuit, he understood that "extenuating circumstances," contributed to the situation: "they are housed in their almost hermetically sealed *igloos*, or snow-huts; and with the low temperature, which forbids washing; the handling of seal and walrus blubber and smoking from the little stone lamp, it is easy to imagine their condition as to cleanliness."[14]

As for children, although Schwatka observed that the male child receives the larger share of attention, he was complimentary of their child rearing habits and believed that few peoples "have such a true affection for children" than the Inuit. Their tolerant approach to misbehavior, he believed led to obedience far better than "equally ignorant people at home." Patient guidance by their parents in necessary life skills, coupled with appropriate praise, made them accomplished "Nimrods" early in life. Schwatka was impressed with their concern for the welfare of their children and their willingness to adopt an orphan child. On the subject of infanticide, which he had been told was practiced by the Nattilingmiut, he did express disdain for the practice, but believed it had become obsolete.[15]

Schwatka did not limit himself to those Inuit with whom he was intimately acquainted, principally the Aivilingmiut and Nattilingmiut. He also included Inuit manners and habits across the Arctic from Greenland, Canada, Alaska through to Arctic Russia, drawing from the works of others such as Hans Egede and Henrik Rink for Greenland and William Hooper for Alaska. Schwatka's wide-ranging overview of the characteristics of the

Inuit of the North provides interesting comparative perspectives among different groups, and highlighted for the general reader the fact that, spread across thousands of miles, the Inuit comprised numerous subgroups with marked differences in lifestyles and habits.

Not a deeply religious man himself, Schwatka was no ardent promoter of missionary work, although he believed missionaries could improve spiritual well-being and dispel the dominant, and at times adverse, influence of the shaman. But Schwatka was a practical man. He had seen with his own eyes how the Inuit "were unmercifully bled by unscrupulous dealers." For him, the missionary could do a far greater benefit to the Inuit by implementing "a system of fair dealing in his trade." Schwatka embraced the classic concept of the "noble savage" in his outlook; his Inuit companions exhibited "inherent nobleness of nature in their character." Schwatka offered a generally praiseworthy account of their character. In fact, Schwatka's sympathies led him to express his fondness for his companions, remarking that "I feel kindly toward these poor isolated people, with their many comparative virtues and few vices." The few vices had been acquired through the corrupting influence of the so-called civilized men, such as whalemen and sailors. In contrast to many writings of the time, Schwatka did not offer a negative, one-sided picture of the Inuit. His companions exhibited truthfulness, honesty, and integrity in their dealings, were free with their hospitality, and could be generous to a fault.[16]

No doubt, Schwatka did not escape the ethnocentric attitude of the time, and could, at times, expound a painfully obvious bias in his opinions. He remarked, for example, that some of the Inuit groups in Alaska "are the most vicious, debased and unchristianlike of all the Esquimaux tribes." Similar to the approach taken regarding the defeated American Indians, Schwatka advocated a paternalistic approach recommending fairer treatment and justice on their behalf. He wrote for the masses with a purpose; his writings were intended to educate an uninformed audience on the diversity of Indigenous cultures, believing that understanding brings with it appreciation and respect. Of course, not all of it was romantic, and some writings were offensive to Victorian sensibilities, but he recognized that those cultures were being exploited and under risk of destruction.[17]

Schwatka's rather prolific expedition-related output included another series of well-illustrated articles in the magazine *Science*, focused on the Inuit construction of snow houses, Inuit tools and implements, and the characteristics of the Nattilingmiut. One scholar went so far as to conclude that the best materials on anthropology related to the Schwatka expedition are the articles by Schwatka that appeared in

Science. The largely overlooked articles provide a thorough discussion of the subjects and reflect Schwatka's close attention to detail. Schwatka also contributed an anthropological document that was only recently donated to the Smithsonian. In 1880, Director John Wesley Powell had printed several hundred blank schedules to be used by traders, missionaries and explorers in the field to document Indigenous languages. In his schedule, Schwatka dutifully collected an Aivilingmiut vocabulary of 500-800 words with accompanying brief ethnographic notes.[18]

Perhaps most appropriately though, Schwatka's most influential and enduring published work was one that captured his boyish, young-at-heart nature, a book written for a juvenile audience entitled *Children of the Cold*. Like many Victorian-era stories, *Children of the Cold* initially appeared as a series of seven articles in the popular and highly respected children's periodical, *St. Nicholas Magazine,* before being turned out in book form. The appearance of *Children of the Cold* coincided with the rapid growth in youth-oriented novels and periodicals during the late nineteenth century, which was driven by improved literary rates in juvenile audiences and reductions in production costs. Fictional works of adventure, with often fanciful and unrealistic tales, became mainstays with the likes of Jules Verne, Robert M. Ballantyne, and William Gordon Stables. As a work of non-fiction, however, *Children of the Cold* was cast in a different mold, offering an accurate and enlightening view of Inuit children and their life in the Far North, among the earliest full-length accounts of the life of the Inuit child.

In contrast to educational textbooks and "geographical readers" that offered the usual hackneyed and stereotypical descriptions of northern life to young and impressionable minds, *Children of the Cold* offered an authentic and engaging look at how their northern counterparts actually lived, worked and played. Based on Schwatka's patient and careful observations, its strengths and obvious appeal to young readers are its full and lively descriptions and numerous illustrations of Inuit children engaged in, and fully enjoying, games, toys, amusements and sports as much as the young readers themselves. It was an intimate portrait that could only have been completed by becoming one of their own, living among them and playfully joining in their activities, once again as a child. In easy-to-read detail, Schwatka explained how boys learn useful skills through play activities, such as shooting toy bows and arrows, engaging in mock muskox and polar bear hunts, and learning the basics of sledge driving with toy harnesses on puppies; similarly, young girls learn how to sew garments, boots and shoes by fashioning dolls dressed in the same materials as themselves, and how to perform domestic chores like lamp-wicking and cooking.

"Eskimo boys playing at hunting the Musk-Ox." From *Children of the Cold*.

Indeed, Schwatka may have been at his best in children's writing. His instructional style was particularly suited to a school-age audience. Remarkably successful, *Children of the Cold* ran through numerous editions as late as 1931. Beyond its popular appeal, the book became a mainstay for primary education purposes and was referenced in numerous teaching primers across the United States as an authoritative work on the northern lands, recommended both as reading for young children and for instructional use by teachers. One teaching guide stated of *Children of the Cold*: "This book is one of the "must haves" in every primary school. The teacher finds nothing better to interest the children in cold countries, and the little folks themselves will read and re-read the book almost before they can manage its vocabulary." In the teaching guide for the city of Boston, the work was recommended reading for fourth, fifth and sixth graders for geography and travel, and for reading by teachers to third graders. Illustrations could be as persuasive as text, and the numerous factually accurate depictions in *Children of the Cold* introduced a generation to such iconic images as the snow house (igloo) and dog sled and helped shape young people's impressions of the Far North. *Children of the Cold* piqued the curiosity of its young readers and led to many questions of Schwatka as to the character of their arctic peers. That interest led Schwatka to publish an insightful response in the *New York Independent* to the often-asked question in 1887, reflecting a more progressive opinion than he had previously shared. Recognizing their acumen, Schwatka reiterated that at a young age, his Inuit youth showed marked talent and maturity by which they successfully adapt to their particular condition. He had "no hesitation in saying they are far brighter and intelligent looking than the world believes." To Schwatka, the distinguishing feature between his Arctic "Nimrods" and his temperate zone youngsters was not their intellectual capacities, but rather the vastly different physical environments within which they live. He posited that though many factors may affect intellectual development, such as heredity or the absence of intellectual challenges, if his Inuit nimrods were afforded the same opportunities as their temperate zone peers, he believed that their intellect might progress similarly.[19]

The Franklin Records Search Expedition, as chronicled by the written narratives of Schwatka, Gilder and Klutschak, offered a Euro-American-centric account of the expedition, reflecting its members' cultural biases and prejudices, as well as a factual emphasis on the expedition's principal objective, the Franklin records or more broadly the Franklin expedition itself. Moreover, the small, tightly knit group of Euro-Americans controlled the written narrative and offered a consistently positive account of their own interpersonal relations over a two-year period, which at times faced challenging hardships and difficulties that could break the strongest of men. We are led to believe that those hardships and their interactions were handled without as much as a single disagreement or even a critical comment hurled by its participants. On the other hand, Inuit history and traditions, much like that of the Plains Indians, have been passed on by virtue of the spoken word rather than the written word. For example, the oral testimony supplied by the Inuit has offered critical facts respecting the fate of the Franklin expedition, and has served to fill in many important pieces of that mystery. Besides accurately identifying the location of the *Erebus*, that testimony provided crucial details as to the circumstances of their retreat and the failing condition of the men, and ended with the knowledge of the destruction of the written records. Without that testimony, most of which was gathered within the span of thirty years after disaster befell the expedition, and while it was still fresh in the minds of the storytellers, the Franklin story would be far from complete.

Similarly, the Schwatka expedition was an undertaking of much consequence for the Inuit who comprised most of the party. Its organization and execution constituted a community effort and affair. The Inuit who relocated to Camp Daly generously supplied their dogs, food, sledges, and clothing, and twelve of their members even volunteered to participate on the epic journey itself. But what was also remarkable was the hospitality and generosity offered by the various Inuit groups—the Aivilingmiut who supported the expedition from before its start until its finish, and the Nattilingmiut, Ugjulingmiut and Utkuhiksalingmiut encountered during the journey. For the Aivilingmiut of the party, the expedition to the Back

River, King William Island and the homeland of the Nattilingmiut was a journey of import, an inaugural enterprise to an unknown land occupied by a forceful and potentially hostile group. It was a once-in-a-lifetime event for the Inuit as much as it was for the Euro-Americans. Its history was carefully retained through Inuit oral testimony, and remarkably, even more than one hundred years later, the basic story could still be accurately retold. For the Schwatka expedition, the Inuit voices add some historical facts, additional perspective and even some color. They also offer a different perspective, one that logically emphasized interactions with the various Inuit groups encountered, and one that offers an "outsider's" view of the Euro-Americans and the interactions among themselves.

Over a period of years, starting in 1996, the historian David Pelly interviewed a number of Inuit from the Wager Bay region (Ukkusiksalik) to form a remarkable collection of their history, memories and impressions. One participant was seventy-one-year-old Tuinnaq Kanayuk Bruce, whose relative (identified as Ujaralaaq), was a participant in the Franklin Records Search Expedition. The salient points of this oral testimony passed on through two generations were remarkably accurate and perceptive. Bruce admitted that she was unfamiliar with the story of the Franklin expedition (and even Franklin's name), its route, or what it was searching for; rather she understood generally that ships were lost in the North and people would search for them. With a decided focus on the Inuit participants, however, Bruce had no hesitation accurately recalling that a Nattilik man travelled with the party and that his name was named "Ikusik" (spelled "Ikqueesik" by Schwatka). On the other hand, Schwatka would be disappointed to learn that Tuinnaq Kanayuk Bruce was not familiar with the name of the Euro-American leader of the party. She recalled that the Schwatka party left Cape Fullerton (actually Camp Daly), travelled close to Ukkusiksalik lands and continued north.[20]

The brief encounter with the timid but generous Ugjulingmiut was actually well remembered. She noted that the Ugjulingmiut were friendly, and that the Schwatka party traded for food with the impoverished group, then left to go farther north to look for ships that were lost. A cache with fish was well remembered for the fact they were cleaned "very neatly, even the cheeks of the fish were skewered," a reference to the Ugjulingmiut cache that helped restore them on the return trip. Her recollections of the Nattilingmiut were detailed, and the sense of outright fear on the part of the Schwatka party was clearly apparent even two generations later. So concerned were they that even the women were carrying weapons. However, the facts of the encounters are more combative than actually reported by the Euro-Americans, perhaps colored by the hostility towards the Nattilingmiut. Tuinnaq Kanayuk Bruce recalled that after the parties made the usual approach upon their initial encounter, a member of the Schwatka party and one Nattilik man engaged in a fight, with the Nattilik man repeatedly slashing the other such that "caribou hair from the fur parkas would fly off...."[21]

Although she was uncertain about the identity of Schwatka, one man made a distinct impression, and even his name was correctly remembered—"Henry," who served as the cook. This, of course, was Henry Klutschak. Her relative claimed to have accompanied the sledge that was led by Klutschak. Interestingly, she made the perceptive comment that Henry wore caribou clothing all the time "and didn't want to get rid of them," no doubt reflecting Klutschak's desire to fully live like the Inuit. Bruce also recalled that Henry "walked all over the place looking for something," and that he found a grave, although it was wrongly placed near Gjoa Haven. According to Bruce:

> Apparently, someone made a cairn, an inuksuk, beside the grave and put papers in the rocks. Henry found them. When he found the papers, they said that the doctor of the ship had died from sickness. Henry and the others walked around to search all the time. Henry found some coins that were stashed away. He was always talking very loudly. When he found the grave with the letters and the money, the others could hear him shouting from quite far away because he was so happy.[22]

Henry did in fact locate the grave of Lieutenant John Irving and a "coin," Irving's mathematical award medallion, was located at the base of the grave. The reference to the papers mentioning the sickness of the doctor, near Irving's grave by Bruce, may very well be the copy of the Victory Point record left by McClintock, which recorded the death of Franklin. Klutschak's vociferous manner of expression had made quite an impression on the Inuit and was mentioned on several occasions. Even after they arrived back at the ship, the boisterous Klutschak was still "taking very loudly as usual, and was very excited, and still wore his caribou clothing all the time." Bruce stated that the leader (Schwatka) "seemed to be embarrassed about Henry's actions and his loudness." Evidently, there was discussion of the fate of the sailors whose bones they found and a veiled reference to cannibalism. Bruce noted that while searching they found a human shoulder bone in a pot, but "they couldn't figure out whether it was the skeletal remains of a person that died from hunger or whether the guy was murdered." The statement strongly suggested that the Inuit believed that the men engaged in cannibalism but remained unsure of how the ill-fated sailor had met his doom, by natural causes or by murder.[23]

Tuinnaq Kanayuk Bruce was not the only Inuk to recite oral testimony regarding the Schwatka expedition. Jean-Marie Ananguaq, an Inuk who lived in the region of Repulse Bay and had guided members of the Fifth Thule Expedition from Repulse Bay to Wager Bay in 1922, also recalled the Schwatka expedition through testimony provided to him by his mother, Ujaralaaq. Ananguaq relayed this information in 1961 to Father Guy Mary-Rousselière, a missionary priest and anthropologist. Both Tuinnaq Kanayuk Bruce and Jean-Marie Ananguaq shared the same original source for their facts (Ujaralaaq), and Ananguaq largely corroborated the tale of Bruce, but in far fewer words. Ananguaq simply noted that "it was up there at Natsilik, it is said, that they lived, and that in the spring or summer, they found the remains of the whites who had starved to death." Fear of the Nattilingmiut and encounters with them overshadows Ananguaq's narrative as well. About the Nattilingmiut, Ananguaq remarked that "when the whites were up there among the Natsilingmiut there appears to have been times when they did not sleep but remained on guard and on the lookout while the Inuit slept." Ananguaq did provide some additional details regarding the arrival of the famished Schwatka party at Camp Daly in March 1880, and documented Schwatka's apparent anger at Gilder in regards to the stores supposed to have been left by Barry:

> Misikila [Mister Gilder] however had told the ship's captain [Thomas Barry], who had unloaded their supplies, to come back to set the barrels on land and to bring their food. As this last had done nothing of the sort, when they arrived in Pikiulik [Camp Daly], Misiuwakka [Mister Schwatka] got very angry. It is said that he was very tired and that he got angry at Misikila [Gilder], as nothing had been done. The Whites were hungry for White food and had nothing to eat but Inuit food.... But that captain had played a dirty trick on them when he failed to unload their food even though he had been ordered to do so. He had put them in a dangerous situation.[24]

The Inuit testimony by Tuinnaq Kanayuk Bruce and Jean-Marie Ananguaq added additional perspective, from a human-interest level, in regard to the interaction among Schwatka and his Euro-American members. As importantly, as far as the expedition itself, the testimony of Bruce did add one fact, potential corroboration of the cannibalism narrative from a participant other than the Euro-Americans. As the explorer Knud Rasmussen remarked, Inuit oral testimony demonstrates that "many, many years afterwards, they [the Inuit] preserve the traditions of their experiences with unblemished and sober reliability."[25]

Finally able to relax after his return, Schwatka was enjoying his time off in New York City. The few loose ends with respect to his Arctic venture were finished: the completion of his written report for the society, coordinating the sendoff of the remains of Lieutenant Irving to his family, as well as transmitting the numerous relics collected to Sophia Cracroft, and even presenting his various supporters with boreal tokens of appreciation, with Judge Daly the recipient of a fine specimen of a polar bear. Looking to extend his enjoyment in Gilded Age New York City, Schwatka petitioned and received a further extension of his leave from Adjutant General Drum, ostensibly "to write up the results of his sledge journey and travels." Residing at the luxurious Sturtevant House on 29th Street and Broadway, frequented by officers of the army and navy, he mixed with ease among his fellow military men. Steps from his hotel, he strolled down fashionable Fifth Avenue and looked upon America's high society, amidst the city's affluent uptown palatial mansions and beautiful churches, theatres and parks, a marked contrast to the packed tenements of the Lower East Side with its toiling immigrants, and a saloon for every twenty-five families. Inseparable from Gilder in New York City, the two were taken notice of in the society pages of local tabloids.[26]

But the Arctic bug had gotten a secure hold on both Gilder and his companion Melms. When Gordon Bennett eyed a *Herald* reporter to join the relief ship U.S.S. *Rodgers*, commanded by Lieutenant Robert Berry, searching for the missing *Jeannette* in late 1881, Gilder was his choice. The man was more than willing to go. Frank Melms, now a hardened Arctic veteran, also volunteered from his home in Milwaukee. The expedition served as a stark reminder of the hazards of Arctic service. While in winter quarters in St. Lawrence Bay on the eastern Siberian coast, the rescue ship *Rodgers* caught fire and burned, but with no loss of life. Lieutenant Berry dispatched the experienced Gilder on a 2,500-mile trek to a Russian telegraph station at Irkutsk to transmit the disastrous news to the United States. On route, while travelling by dog and reindeer sledge, Gilder learned details of the loss of the *Jeannette* and obtained copies of confidential dispatches from one of the survivors, Chief Engineer George Melville. Gilder cabled both stories to the *Herald* in a major scoop, and became embroiled in a major controversy as a result of his actions. Gilder later had his own designs for a North Pole expedition by way of York Factory to Fort Conger, Greely's quarters, but the unrealistic plan was aborted. For several more years he continued to serve as a correspondent for the *Herald*. He died in 1900.

The hardy Melms seems to have suffered some difficulties adjusting to life on the home front. After returning from the *Rodgers* expedition, his third wearying Arctic endeavor and the second to imperil his life, he settled into a much less hazardous position as a packer at a glass factory in Milwaukee. Shortly thereafter, according to a local paper, the young man suffered from an unknown "inflammation of the brain which threatened to either cost his life or unseat his mind." The illness sent him to the Milwaukee Asylum for the Insane, though his family vehemently denied the diagnosis of insanity. He evidently had several bouts requiring hospitalization over the years. Nonetheless, in a testament to the compelling attraction of the Arctic, in 1894 he volunteered for another expedition to the North being organized by a civilian Robert Stein, that ultimately failed to materialize. Despite his recurring illness, the plucky Melms, who talked continually about his "desire to go back on the ocean," managed to survive until 1916. He would outlive all his Euro-American companions on the Schwatka expedition by sixteen years.[27]

Klutschak's remaining life story was also a sorrowful tale. After Schwatka's expedition, he remained in New York City assisting Schwatka with lectures and completing the reports and maps for the expedition publications. Thereafter, he made a brief return to his homeland for his lecture tour. Surprisingly, Klutschak returned to New York City taking odd jobs as a clerk, private secretary, and errand boy, mainly through the kindness of John Morison. Klutschak was a true Bohemian, shirking more lucrative positions suited to his educational background and artistic talents. He advised Morison that he needed little money to live and "preferred to follow his own method of obtaining money." Stricken with tuberculosis, he resisted efforts by Morison and Daly to remove to the Sailor's Snug House in Staten Island, a retirement home for sailors managed by Captain Thomas Melville, brother of the famous author. Finally relenting, he started for Snug Harbor in a heavy snowstorm, but suffered a relapse and was forced back to his bedroom on Broome Street, in Manhattan's Bowery. He died penniless a week later on March 26, 1890. The local German community took up a collection for his burial at All Faith's Cemetery in Queens, New York.[28]

In New York City on the evening of November 1, 1880, Schwatka was the featured speaker at the regular meeting of the New York Academy of Sciences, a meeting that was unusually large due to Schwatka's address. Continuing his scientific focus, on November 17, at the special session of the National Academy of Sciences at Columbia College, he delivered an address to a packed house on "Ice and Icebergs in the Polar Regions," and "The Darkness of the Arctic Winter." To a friendly audience at the New York branch of the Naval Institute at the Brooklyn Navy Yard, on December 1 he delivered an address on his recent expedition.

Schwatka was enjoying his time off in Gotham City, maybe enjoying it too much. During the approaching holiday season, the merriment was brought to a crashing end. On the evening of December 23, after dinner with some friends, while alighting from his carriage upon the snow-covered pavement at the Sturtevant House, his foot slipped and he came down heavily on his right leg, causing a fracture. The break was serious, a fracture of both the tibia and fibula, an extremely painful experience. The irony was not lost on Schwatka that having dodged the perils of ice and snow during two years in the Arctic, he suffered his most serious accident upon a slippery street in New York City. Two of the best surgeons in New York City, Drs. Lewis Sayre and Edward Janeway, both associated with Schwatka from his days at Bellevue Medical College, tended to the emergency. His fracture was treated non-surgically, the standard of care for such injuries at the time. Once stabilized, concern was expressed that he might not recover the full use of his leg. Anxiety filled his mind, as he feared that he might not ever do hard travelling again, and that his chances of further exploits had come to an end. Overwhelmed by well-wishers, his doctors recommended peace and quiet. He was gingerly removed to the military post at Governor's Island, courtesy of General Winfield Scott Hancock, Civil War hero and commander of the Division of the Atlantic. To his concerned family, who had received little news of the injury and had many questions, he sent a letter that projected his usual upbeat, comical attitude and made light of his injury as he convalesced:

> I am now doing finely, and hope to be out in a few days on crutches, and will probably have a perfectly sound leg by the end of March. In fact I did well, considering that I have had eleven doctors–not one after another, but all the time since I have been hurt. Anybody less strong and healthy would probably have lost, not only his foot, but his head, and would have been dissected by this time. My attendants are old friends, my professors and army surgeons. In fact, I look at this ankle as a kind of blessing in disguise. While I was at the Sturtevant House, I found it almost impossible to make any headway in writing up a book relative to my expedition, for which I have got a contract with Harper Bros., owing to the constant calls in my room; and which book I might add, is the principal thing that is keeping me anchored in the east....You can write father and mother that it will be a very short

time before I see them and all the folks at home.[29]

For Schwatka, the work for *Harper's* appears to never have been written for various reasons, a victim of the accident, a busy lecture schedule, and numerous magazine requests. The lengthy *Midnight Sun* article in *Good Company* could have easily been converted to a book-length narrative, but never was. Schwatka's optimism about his recovery was also a bit misplaced. It was not until mid-February that he had recovered enough to make his way around on crutches. The accident had its silver lining of sorts though. Having received a four-month sick leave through mid-April 1881, he was prepared to do anything but return to the humdrum life at Fort D. A. Russell, the military post that beckoned. To Schwatka, the widespread adulation and attention associated with the numerous public events and press coverage were themselves an intoxicating mixture of a different sort. Like the military glory earned through his battlefield exploits, these actions simply fueled his desire for more. The spotlight had held some attraction for the thirty-one-year-old explorer turned celebrity and he set his sights on the lecture circuit, contracting for a West Coast tour with the Oregon and Washington Lyceum Bureau. On March 16, Schwatka had another disappointing setback to his plans, however—a refracture of his right fibula caused by a tumble out of his bed (so it was reported), which laid him up on crutches again for another month. The sudden clumsiness on the part of the normally stalwart explorer must have struck his friends as unusual and perhaps a symptom of a more significant underlying cause. In any event, the injury led Schwatka to request an additional four months' sick leave from the army. By now, both Adjutant General Drum and General Sherman were losing their patience with the persistently absent Schwatka. According to Drum, it was no secret he told Sherman that "Schwatka had fallen onto evil ways, and was said to be drinking very hard." Drum recommended that he be ordered to his post and active duty. Concurring with Drum's recommendation, Sherman refused Schwatka's request and ordered him to report to Fort D. A. Russell by May 14 before considering any further leave.[30]

Nonetheless disappointed with the decision, but resigned to it, Schwatka made the best of the situation. On his way to his post, he made several lecture stops at friendly venues, still preparing for his now belated West Coast tour. Returning to his old haunt at Fort D. A. Russell on May 11 was a rewarding homecoming of sorts. Brigadier General Crook still held command of the department, but with the cessation of the Indian wars, his duty was largely a mundane peace-keeping mission with isolated skirmishes and incidents. Although Schwatka was pleased to relive his exploits for the benefit of his Plains comrades, the thought of extended garrison duty and a body weakened by his leg injury left him somewhat morose. He took to his immediate commander, Colonel Albert Gallatin Brackett, a fifty-two-year-old career cavalry officer who had served with distinction in the Mexican War, the Civil War, and the Indian wars and had authored the first definitive history of the U.S. Cavalry. As a colonel for the Third Cavalry, Brackett had been engaged in Indian fighting for the previous thirteen years. But there was a silver lining to Schwatka's return to this frontier outpost. Schwatka made the acquaintance of Colonel Brackett's attractive young niece, Ada Josephine Brackett, who was travelling to the Rocky Mountains with her father Joseph Warren Brackett, a well-regarded lawyer from Rock Island, Illinois. By happenstance, Ada and her father made a brief stop at Fort D. A. Russell to visit her uncle, Colonel Brackett. The meeting, brief as it was, would not soon be forgotten by either Frederick or Ada.

The post surgeon at Fort D. A. Russell who examined Schwatka's leg concluded that his right leg "remains so weak that he is unfit for duty." The very accommodating surgeon recommended at least three months sick leave, and at Schwatka's urging, "a change of climate to the Pacific Coast to which he is desirous of proceeding." Through the chain of command, Schwatka's request was received by the now-exasperated Adjutant General Drum. Forwarding the request to General Sherman, Drum urged denial of the request, noting that "Schwatka's broken leg can be cared for as well in the Dept. of the Platte as any other dept." Sherman was deeply disappointed with Schwatka, the former daring young cavalry officer who had so forfeited his once promising military career. The normally tough-as-nails cigar-smoking general granted Schwatka his detached leave to travel to the West Coast, sadly concluding that Schwatka was a lost cause to the army, a victim of the misguided search for Franklin that Sherman had opposed from the start. Sherman thoughts were scribbled on the verso of Drum's note: "Of course Schwatka's services to the army are lost forever. He will never do duty again. That is manifest and is the natural and necessary result of his bad habits and wayward life, begotten of his Expedition in search of Sir John Franklin's remains."[31]

Released from duty on June 4, Schwatka was on the road again by mid-June, lecturing at Denver, San Francisco, Portland, Seattle, and Olympia through mid-September. In San Francisco, in particular, he was in demand by scientists, reporters, army officers and even the distraught relatives of missing whalers. On the evening of July 29, an audience of one thousand squeezed in, and more were turned away, to listen to his lecture at the California Academy of Sciences, San Francisco. As an Arctic expert, he was frequently called upon to hazard an opinion on the missing *Jeannette* expedition. Whereas he had previously sounded an optimistic tone in Emma De Long's presence, by mid-1881 he took "a gloomy view of the situation." If the ship had been nipped by the ice, the vessel would certainly be lost, he stated, and its crew stood little chance of reaching safety on the mainland. Speaking of his own plans, Schwatka claimed that it was "extremely likely" that within the year, he would be organizing a "hearty gang of men for the purpose of invading the icebound regions of the North." Was this wishful speculation or did he have a new adventure already in mind?[32]

CHAPTER TWELVE
DOWN THE YUKON
PART I

BY THE FALL OF 1881, Frederick Schwatka had finally worked his lecture tour to his home in Salem, where he was welcomed by a group of admiring family and friends. It was a homecoming that was a long time coming, after an absence of ten years. He had indeed enjoyed an eventful and arduous life since he left the Northwest to start his military career as a tenderfoot plebe at West Point. Proud of their local Oregonian son, he was greeted like no previous speaker had been at several lecture venues in the Northwest. To them, Schwatka's accomplishments reflected honorably on the entire state of Oregon and proved that this modest frontier settlement on the far edge of the country was no backwater, but could produce men of merit and brilliance on par with the most accomplished men of the East. Schwatka's stature was such that a petition signed on September 14 by the most prominent of Oregon's politicians and citizens, including its governor, William W. Thayer and twenty others, was telegraphed to Robert Todd Lincoln, secretary of war, requesting the favor of leave for Schwatka through January 1, 1882. The stated purpose of the leave was "to afford him time to remain with his aged parents, and to meet many of the citizens of Oregon (his native state) who desire the pleasure of his acquaintance."[1]

By now the military brass had reached their limit with the dallying lieutenant. When apprised of the request, a frustrated Adjutant General Drum turned to General Sherman for an iron-fisted response, advising Sherman that "Schwatka's is a case requiring very positive action, and I respectfully recommend it." Sherman exercised some restraint and struck a middle ground, tersely replying to give Schwatka one month's leave "with the notice that the General thinks it time he should rejoin his regiment proper command." But before the expiration of the latest absence, fate intervened on Schwatka's behalf. On October 7, Brigadier General Nelson A. Miles, commanding the Department of the Columbia, headquartered at the Vancouver Barracks, Vancouver, Washington, telegraphed General Sherman requesting that Schwatka be appointed Miles's aide-de-camp.[2]

The extent to which Miles and Schwatka had crossed paths during the Indian wars is unclear, though for at least one brief period the two had been in close proximity in the fall of 1876 near the Yellowstone River. More recently, with Schwatka on the Northwest Coast riding the fame associated with his successful Arctic venture, Miles saw an opportunity to discuss his own developing plans for the exploration of Alaska with the now highly regarded soldier-explorer. Evidently, the two saw eye-to-eye, and Miles wasted no time in making his personnel request for Schwatka directly to Sherman. A perplexed Sherman was surprised that any senior officer would be soliciting Schwatka's services but was nonetheless thankful that a solution to the disagreeable matter had presented itself. Sherman advised Drum that "if Genl. Miles wants Lt. Schwatka as aide, that will be the best disposition of him. If as reported his habits are bad-General Miles will soon discern the fact and apply a speedy remedy-Approved. W.T. Sherman, General." With Sherman's acquiescence, the lingering prospect of mundane garrison duty on the Plains was suddenly lifted. For Schwatka, much as the military had become a distraction as he followed his own agenda, it was the military that had given him the freedom to pursue those personal fancies, and it was the military that now opened the door to his next great adventure.[3]

Moreover, Vancouver Barracks was a desirable posting. As the headquarters for the Department of the Columbia, it was a well-established and comfortable duty station located on the north bank of the Columbia River one hundred miles from the ocean. In operation during the Mexican War and the U.S. Civil War and for the protection of settlers to the Northwest, it had been a springboard for rising senior officers, with more than seventy officers stationed there later attaining the rank of major, including Grant, Sheridan and Crook.

Schwatka's new commander, Brigadier General Miles, was a self-taught military man, who had left his position as a storekeeper to volunteer for the Union cause, rising from first lieutenant to major general of volunteers by the war's end. He was a decorated combat veteran, wounded on at least four occasions, and a recipient of the Medal of Honor for his courageous actions at Chancellorsville. Politically astute as well, his advancement followed his marriage to Mary Hoyt Sherman, General Sherman's niece. Active through the Indian wars, Miles was an energetic and dogged campaigner who brought Chief Joseph and the Nez Perce to surrender, as well as the Lakota and Northern Cheyenne, and later Geronimo. In 1880, Miles was promoted to brigadier general and given command of the Department of the Columbia, responsible for the vast territories of Oregon, Washington, Idaho, and Alaska. Of those outlier territories, Alaska was the most recent acquisition, the least well known and the one that captured Miles's progressive thinking.

By a vote of 37-2, the United States Senate had ratified the purchase of Alaska in 1867 and with it an extension of the country's Manifest Destiny. The unfortunate characterization of the Alaska purchase as "Seward's Folly" overlooks the reality that congressional and public support for the nation-building acquisition was considerable. Through that one action, the United States had acquired an Arctic presence by virtue of a territory more than twice the size of Texas for the price of $7,200,000, or mere pennies per acre.[4]

Although Congress had authorized the funds for the purchase, when the United States formally took possession, the legislature was reluctant to open its purse strings to administer the new territory (its governmental designation was "the Department of Alaska" until renamed the "District of Alaska" in 1884). As with the westward expansion, the U.S. Army was tasked with the role, but suffered from a shortage of troops, supplies, and funding. Its responsibilities were limited to maintaining peaceful relations between the Indigenous peoples and newcomers, and enforcement of customs and Indian trade laws. In 1877, budget tightening went so far as to force the withdrawal of troops from Alaska, leaving only a handful of weather stations manned by the U.S. Army Signal Corps. For a time, Treasury Department revenue cutters patrolling the coast and a naval force stationed in Sitka served as the government in Alaska, literally doing so from "the deck of a man-of-war." Such was the state of affairs in Alaska when Frederick Schwatka was posted to Vancouver Barracks. The army was largely on the outside looking in.

With an active mindset and an independent streak, Miles recognized the economic potential of Alaska, with its wealth of natural resources. In his mind, the military was best positioned to lead the effort to gain an understanding of the region and to open the land for settlement and development as it had previously done in the West. Of course, Schwatka was Miles's choice to implement that plan. Schwatka was certainly not the only competent soldier for the task, but he did have more name recognition than most. As an advocate for the exploration of Alaska,

Miles recognized that Schwatka's association with the endeavor could foster wider public interest in the undertaking as a "discovery" quest, elevating it beyond simply an undistinguished military exercise. For Frederick Schwatka, the ever-inquisitive adventurer, it was more than he could have hoped for, an all-encompassing exploratory mission to examine the geography, resources, climate, and peoples of the region.

Cognizant that an appropriation would be necessary to assemble an expedition on a scale suitable for Miles's ambitious plans, Schwatka was tasked by Miles to work up a cost estimate. Wasting little time, Schwatka delivered a comprehensive proposal for an expedition of two years, totaling $68,000 (about $1,700,000 in 2021 dollars). The lion's share of the cost, $30,000, would cover the purchase of one small vessel and several river boats for transportation. With its scientific-minded purpose in mind, $15,000 was allocated to pay for what looked to be a robust scientific corps. With Schwatka's plan in hand, in November 1881 Miles proposed to his superior, Major General Irvin McDowell, commander of the Division of the Pacific, that the military conduct the sweeping examination of Alaska's territory. McDowell wasted no time in approving Miles's request and forwarding it to Secretary of War Lincoln, and at the same time, potential funding bills were introduced in the U.S. Senate and House.[5]

In the meantime, publicity from the *New York Times* played precisely to Miles's renown as a soldier and Schwatka's recognition as an explorer, remarking that "it would be hard to point out in the entire Army, or outside of the Army, two persons whose organization and superintendence would give to such an expedition greater promise of success. General Miles, the conqueror of Sitting Bull and Chief Joseph, who rose from the volunteer ranks to his present high position by soldierly merit and prowess, is the very type of indomitable energy, while Schwatka's fame in arctic exploration is world-wide." Miles was buoyed by the editorial support, and Schwatka reveled in the public limelight.[6]

The focus of attention for Schwatka was not entirely consumed by the proposed expedition as he awaited final action by the government, a sluggish bureaucratic process that could span weeks, if not months. Life as a personal aide to a senior officer was dictated by the disposition of that particular commander. In Schwatka's case, Miles purposely adopted a relaxed posture. Combining military service with personal matters, Schwatka traveled on several occasions with Miles to San Francisco and to posts within Miles's command. Recognizing that Schwatka's popularity could aid his own project, Miles gave Schwatka the freedom to lecture in various cities on the Pacific coast. Schwatka was also not shy about offering interviews for Pacific newspapers. As matters stalled with the Alaska venture, personal matters moved to the forefront. On Christmas Eve 1881, the *Cleveland Leader* reported the rumor that Lieutenant Schwatka would soon marry Miss Ada Brackett, the daughter of Colonel Brackett, Third Cavalry. The newspaper had incorrectly identified Ada's father as Colonel Albert Brackett (he was her uncle), but the rumor was not too far-fetched. Finally, on January 4, Ada's hometown *Rock Island Argus* officially announced the engagement of Lieutenant Frederick Schwatka and Miss Ada Josephine Brackett. Beyond an active romantic correspondence, how the pair managed a long-distance courtship after their brief introduction at Fort D. A. Russell in June of 1881 remains a mystery. Evidently, it was a true case of love at first sight.[7]

Ada Josephine Brackett, born August 1, 1854, came from a prominent and highly regarded family. Her grandfather, James Brackett, originally from New Hampshire, had settled in Rock Island, Illinois in 1849, and built a successful legal practice. James Brackett had been a classmate of the American statesman Daniel Webster and a fellow investor in Webster's speculative land deals. Joseph Warren Brackett, one of seven sons of James Brackett, and Ada's father, was also a respected lawyer in Rock Island. The Brackett family members were public-spirited and staunch Unionists. Several took up arms on behalf of the North in the Civil War. Joseph Warren Brackett and his brother, Colonel Albert Gallatin Brackett, had served in cavalry units during the war. Colonel Albert G. Brackett continued active service after the war and had been Schwatka's Third Cavalry superior at Fort D. A. Russell in May and June 1881. Ada Brackett, one of three daughters, was an attractive, strong-willed, and intelligent woman, and "one of the loveliest girls in this city [Rock Island]," according to one local newspaper. The Brackett family's prosperous circumstances allowed for a cultured upbringing: a quality education at private schools, music lessons, homemaking, and ladylike pursuits. Male visitors, typically status conscious officers from the nearby Rock Island army post and arsenal, gathered for tea at their stately ivy-draped Italianate residence on First Avenue, with a prime location overlooking the Mississippi River. The refined Brackett daughters were likewise entertained by the officers who escorted them on riverside drives. Two of them had already married military men. But Ada Brackett did not fully embrace the role of the conventional nineteenth-century woman. She had been a bit of a tomboy when younger, who attracted gossip for her barebacked riding. Possessed of an independent streak and capable of a sharp tongue, she was still unmarried at the age of twenty-eight, waiting to select a suitable mate on her own timetable. There had been something special and exhilarating

Ada Josephine Brackett Schwatka.

First Lieutenant Frederick Schwatka.

about her chance encounter with Frederick Schwatka and their whirlwind courtship on the open prairie that had so charmed her. Perhaps it was his independent streak that mirrored her own. The tall, handsome, and now acclaimed cavalryman, with a jovial manner and infectious sense of humor, who was so different from her uninspiring and traditional military suitors, had completely captured her heart.[8]

Although both were exceedingly anxious to conclude the nuptials, Frederick Schwatka felt honor bound to his fiancé to attend to one matter of great importance to their future financial security. With yet another leave from the army in hand, in March, Schwatka left Vancouver Barracks to petition members of Congress for an award of full pay for the period of his service on his Arctic expedition. The extra pay totaled $2,226, more than enough to set the couple off on the right foot. General Sherman had authorized Schwatka to receive half-pay during the expedition, but his hands were tied by regulation from awarding any further compensation. Oregon congressmen were eager to help. Prior to Schwatka's departure from Vancouver Barracks, Senator La Fayette Grover and Representative Melvin George introduced corresponding bills for full pay in the Senate and House, respectively. Prospects for success were not good. Private bills fell into the category of personal favors for constituents, and were generally frowned upon and a low priority, especially those for military personnel who were paid established rates.[9]

Shortly after his arrival in Washington, D.C., Schwatka's attention turned to a more serious matter, a bout of malarial fever that was severe enough to confine him to Providence Hospital. Malaria was only one of many diseases that were prevalent throughout the country through the late nineteenth century, and malarial fevers were a leading cause of death. Although the soggy wetlands that permeated the District of Columbia served as ripe breeding grounds for mosquitoes, the disease was so widespread that Schwatka could as easily have been infected while on the frontier. Coincidentally, just several months before, Doctor Albert Freeman Africanus King had argued to a skeptical audience at the Philosophical Society of Washington that the pesky mosquito was the carrier of the malaria parasite. His solution was considered more preposterous, that it could be prevented by an ambitious plan that called for installing netting around the nation's capital. The disease could remain dormant for years, and as in Schwatka's case, serious relapses could occur periodically, often at inopportune times, with debilitating episodes of fever, shivering chills, and profuse sweating. Quinine, isolated from *Cinchona* bark, was an effective treatment for malarial fever, and known to have been used by Schwatka. Fortunately, over the course of several days, his symptoms slowly subsided.[10]

Despite his recovery, so principled was Schwatka that no preparations were made for the wedding pending resolution of the congressional action. The wheels of government moved slowly, and as the back pay bill languished, Schwatka was forced to extend his leave at monthly intervals. Now back at Rock Island, on August 6, a despondent Schwatka penned a personal appeal to Adjutant General Drum requesting yet another extension. Schwatka's anxiety was palpable as he pleaded for one additional month, advising Drum that his marriage "depends" on settling his accounts in Washington. The typically unyielding adjutant general acceded to the request ("but no more" he chastised Schwatka). Fortuitously, the next day, August 7, President Chester A. Arthur signed the long-awaited bill approving the full pay for the two-year period of his Arctic endeavor. Unfortunately, unimaginable trouble followed, and Schwatka never received the full payment. Schwatka had given his lawyer, William Hanscom, a power of attorney to collect the $2,226 of back pay from the paymaster-general in Washington, D.C. However, the unscrupulous Hanscom misappropriated the money. Following his arrest, only $1,009 was recovered, dealing an extremely disheartening blow to Schwatka. To make matters worse, under the prevailing law Hanscom could not be charged with any criminal offense for his reprehensible conduct.[11]

Nonetheless, the scandal didn't tarnish the joyful wedding ceremony on

September 6, 1882. The private affair was performed at the Brackett home by Reverend A. B. Allen of the Trinity Episcopal Church and attended by family and a few close friends. A hasty departure by the bride and groom was made to the city of Peoria, "the gem of Illinois," a larger city with a theatrical heritage (hence the phrase "Will it play in Peoria?"). By chance, the newlyweds were among the celebrated guests at the opening of the city's fabulous Grand Opera House. The elegant three-story red brick theatre in Queen Anne style was still receiving its final touches on opening night. In its time, the Peoria Opera House was considered one of the most beautiful theatres in the country, accommodating nearly 1,800 guests, with grandiose décor, multi-tier seating, and lavish box seats. The arrival of the stylishly dressed dignitaries, including Lieutenant and Mrs. Schwatka, was a show in itself. For almost an hour elaborate carriages and handsome horses arrived amidst a gawking crowd as the governor, officials and even local whisky barons made their grand entrances. The Schwatka's were entertained by "King for a Day," a rather appropriate operetta for the occasion. Returning to Rock Island, the newly married couple prepared for their hasty departure to the West Coast and Frederick's post at the Vancouver Barracks as their friends and family wished them well in their new life together. We know little of their married relationship, but joyous as the moment had been, the pair would suffer through some difficult times. Their first few months together though were delightful, as they settled in at their new residence. In comparison to many western duty-stations, Vancouver Barracks offered a pleasant level of comfort, recreation and a lively social life with theatricals, picnics, dinners, all within a backdrop of views of Mt. Hood and Mt. St. Helens. Despite peacetime stretches of dull monotony, Ada and Frederick Schwatka would have enjoyed their stay, occupying quarters in the married officers' row.[12]

The approval for the proposed Alaska reconnaissance mission was proving to be more problematic. Neither Secretary of War Lincoln nor General Sherman had any enthusiasm for the project, and both flatly disapproved Miles's request. Lincoln and Sherman counseled Miles that he would be better served by policing the territories of Idaho and Washington and protecting railroad employees than he would be in running exploratory jaunts across Alaska.

In Congress, the Alaska proposal became embroiled in a political turf battle and was roundly stifled. When the army had withdrawn from Alaska in 1877, the president's order prohibited the army from exercising further control over the region, a provision that had been invoked by political opponents and competing agencies when it suited their agenda. As Miles's supporters pushed the appropriation through Congress, the

Interior Department intervened and objected on the grounds that any "scientific survey" of Alaska's resources fell within the purview of its agency—the United States Geological and Geographical Survey of Territories. The position was certainly not well received by the Alaskan citizens looking for support, or the commercial interests who had eyes on its resources. Likewise, the eager Schwatka was particularly embittered by the bureaucratic stonewalling.[13]

By April 1883, an impatient Miles could wait no longer. Justifying the expedition on the basis of the army's responsibility to maintain order, Miles believed he could skirt a claim of noncompliance with the president's order. Funding a more modest expedition from his own department budget, he pressed forward, issuing his revised and final orders to Schwatka. Highlighting the need for a reconnaissance given the danger of hostilities with the Indigenous peoples, he advised Schwatka: "In view of the frequent reports of the disturbance of the peace between the whites and Indians in Alaska, and the indications that the present condition of affairs must lead to serious hostilities between the two elements in the near future, you are hereby directed to proceed to that Territory for the purpose of gathering all information that can be obtained that would be valuable and important, especially to the military branch of the Government." Though there was, in fact, no serious threat, Schwatka was ordered to assess the number, character and disposition of the Indigenous peoples, their disposition toward the whites entering the territory, their mode of life and weapons of war, the character of the country and the best means of sustaining a military force there, if necessary. Miles admonished Schwatka to "impress the natives with the friendly disposition of the Government."[14]

Miles still harbored legitimate concerns that opponents might still thwart his plans. Accordingly, Schwatka was instructed by Miles to "consider this duty especial and confidential," and to report directly to Miles. As with most of Schwatka's endeavors, the participants were a handful of thoughtfully selected members:

Dr. George F. Wilson, assistant surgeon U.S. Army, surgeon and ethnographer
Charles A. Homan, U.S. Engineer Corps, topographer and photographer
Sergeant Charles A. Gloster, Company K, First Cavalry, artist
Corporal William H. Shircliff, Company G, Second Infantry, assistant
Private John Roth, Company I, Twenty-first Infantry, assistant

J. B. McIntosh, miner, and private citizen with knowledge of the country.[15]

The inability to take on professionals covering a range of scientific disciplines was a frustrating setback to Schwatka and to the commercial interests, who advocated the inclusion of at least a geologist or mineralogist. Nonetheless, both Wilson and Homan would prove competent scientific observers in the roles assigned to them, as would the practical-minded McIntosh. Charles Augustus Homan was a long-serving army engineer, having enlisted during the Civil War and afterwards deployed in western outposts. While stationed at Vancouver Barracks, Homan was fortunate to have conducted topographic work in Washington Territory under the brilliant engineering officer George Washington Goethals (later chief engineer of the Panama Canal), work that led to his selection on Schwatka's expedition. He remained in the army until his retirement, while also serving briefly as surveyor of the city of Vancouver, Washington in 1889-90. For Schwatka's expedition, Homan was fully occupied with navigation and astronomical observations (a role which he shared with Schwatka), as well as the survey work, and even managed to capture a photographic record of prominent topographic features.

Doctor George Wilson had served ten years as an army surgeon (most recently at Vancouver Barracks) before his selection to Schwatka's expedition. In the years after the return of the expedition, Doctor Wilson became a prominent physician and surgeon in Portland, and served as president of the Oregon State Medical Association. He was also a professor of surgery in the medical department of the University of Oregon, and was generally instrumental in the advancement of medical practice in the state. Besides his medical responsibilities for Schwatka's expedition, Wilson was also responsible for preparing that portion of the report in Schwatka's instructions calling for a description of the Indigenous peoples encountered.

Unfortunately, little is known about the miner J. B. McIntosh, but he was surely no naive prospector who signed on solely for purposes of striking it rich. At the time of the expedition, he was married with several children, and was living in Portland. He was recruited based on his prior experience in Alaska. His diary, the only surviving original account besides those of Schwatka's published works, reflects an outdoorsman's practical knowledge of Alaskan wilderness travel. Actively engaged in assessing the mineral prospects of the territory traversed, McIntosh served an informal role as geologist. He proved to be an intelligent and perceptive individual, thoroughly familiar with the geology of the region. He also possessed a keen knowledge of the flora and fauna and maintained an inquisitive and generally respectful attitude toward the peoples they encountered.

Schwatka's instructions did not identify the traverse of the Yukon as the object of his expedition, but it is unlikely Miles would have dispatched him without a verbal understanding of his plans. As a small group seeking to cover as much territory as possible, traveling down the Yukon River, an important and only partially surveyed waterway, presented one obvious choice. One of the longest rivers on the North American continent, and the longest that empties onto the western coast of North America, the Yukon is one of the great rivers of the world. Its course runs more than two thousand miles from the northern British Columbia mountains to the Bering Sea. To Schwatka, this so-called "Nile of Alaska" was divided into three segments (based on his estimates): The upper course from its source to Fort Selkirk, a five hundred mile stretch to where it joins with the Pelly River; the middle stretch of about five hundred miles from Fort Selkirk to Fort Yukon; and lastly, the lower Yukon, a run of more than one thousand miles from Fort Yukon to the Bering Sea and Norton Sound. For half its course, it runs northwesterly, before turning 90° near Fort Yukon and flowing on a west and southwest course to the sea. The middle and lower portions of the river were fairly well known due to the efforts of the Russians, the Western Union Telegraph Company, and the Hudson's Bay Company. The less-travelled upper portion of the river, from the Chilkoot Pass to Fort Selkirk, was known mainly to the Indigenous inhabitants, some Hudson's Bay traders, and a handful of venturesome prospectors who closely guarded their knowledge of the country.

Assessing the best means to tackle the project, Schwatka recognized that it would be far easier to traverse the Yukon downstream from its source, letting the river do the work. With only the short summer for exploration, that approach would also enable him to map the largely unsurveyed portion of the river from its origin to Fort Selkirk. From there, he would continue to the coast in time to meet the last steamer leaving St. Michael in Norton Sound by the end of August. Always the efficient army officer, he considered the best means of travel and believed that constructing a large raft would enable a small party to make the descent in one season with all their effects. It would be a highly economical operation, operating on a shoestring budget, much like his sledge journey of 1879-80.

The members of the little exploring party left Portland, Oregon on May 22 on board the steamer S.S. *Victoria*, one of several vessels supplying the canneries along the coast. According to Schwatka, fear of governmental recall led to clandestine preparations for departure. The expedition left under cover of darkness at midnight, and "stole away like a thief in the night." Their departure was a poorly kept secret though, as the local

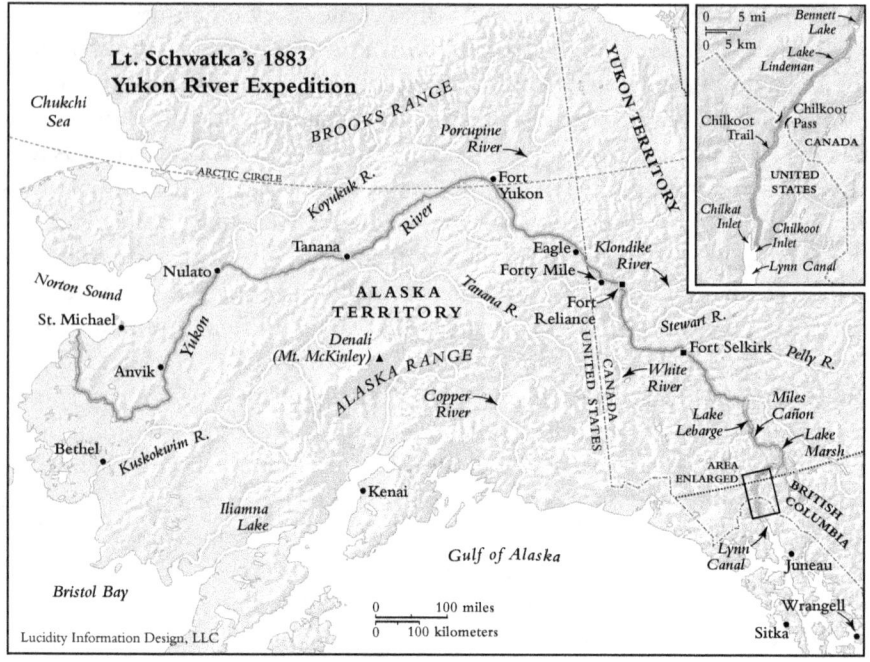

papers, pleased that any government action was afoot for Alaska, quickly broadcast the news. But by the time this reached anyone with authority, they were beyond the point of recall.[16]

Once again off on another journey, and with hasty preparations completed, Schwatka could enjoy a pleasant cruise along the Inside Passage to Alaska, a popular eco-tourism destination even then. For Frederick Schwatka, the trip was especially gratifying as Ada, his young bride, had accompanied her husband from his post to share the experience as far as the Presbyterian mission at Chilkat Inlet, the terminus of the *Victoria*'s voyage. It was a rapturous voyage for the two, a belated honeymoon they never had the full opportunity to share during their hasty departure from Rock Island. Because of it, Alaska would always hold a special fondness in Ada's heart. Standing on deck, the two watched the spectacular natural scenery in wondrous awe—alpine flowers and lush grasses along the shore, old-growth timber stretching up steep slopes towards the peaks of shrouded, snow-capped mountains, and spectacular waterfalls running from deeply set glaciers. For Frederick Schwatka, the cruise was also particularly uplifting, as he reveled in the freedom from the authority and officialdom of the military.

After passing through the former Russian settlements at Wrangell and Sitka, the *Victoria* stopped briefly to assist a disabled steamer bearing the optimistic name of *Eureka*, its luck evidently having run out. While awaiting repairs, Frederick and Ada stretched their legs with a walk along the tree-lined shore, followed by a demanding hike up a nearby summit that offered a breathtaking view of the Alexander Archipelago and myriad unnamed islands and channels. Re-embarking, they steamed up Lynn Channel to the convergence of the Chilkat and Chilkoot Inlets, proceeding up the Chilkat Inlet to the cannery operated by the Northwest Trading Company. Mr. Carl Spuhn, manager of the company, one of the two canneries in the inlet, generously offered his company steamer to ferry Schwatka's party and its supplies up the Chilkoot and Taiya Inlets to the Chilkoot Trail, the true departure point of the expedition.

As with most of Schwatka's expeditions, local assistance from Indigenous peoples was instrumental to his success. In this case, it was the Tlingit who occupied the Alexander Archipelago and portions inland. Until recently, the enterprising Tlingit had positioned themselves as the middleman in a material trade network, controlling the flow of furs outbound from Indigenous groups in the interior and incoming trade goods from Europeans. Reluctantly convinced to permit access to the interior through the Chilkoot Pass by other parties, the industrious Tlingit found a lucrative alternative business in packing goods and supplies over the pass. Some were also employed at the canneries.

Schwatka held the common view at the time that assimilation was the proper means by which to resolve the "Indian Question." In Southeastern Alaska, he pointed to what he believed were beneficial steps forward for those Tlingit who gained employment through "the new industries springing up in this coast-water strip." Schwatka estimated their numbers at approximately one thousand, the majority of whom were living in villages within Chilkat Inlet (near Pyramid Harbor) and Chilkoot Inlet. Schwatka's party had coincidentally arrived at the same time as the funeral and cremation of a Tlingit chief, to be followed by a sacred "potlatch" attended by every Tlingit in the area. Potlatches were important ceremonies honoring the dead and intended to acknowledge ties between the living and dead, with songs, ceremony, and feasts which could span as much as a week. Although Schwatka was extended an invitation and an honored vantage point, he surprisingly suppressed his usual curiosity for such ceremonies in his desire to keep to his tight timetable. With Spuhn's indefatigable assistance, Schwatka managed to induce thirty-five to forty Tlingit to agree to carry their effects from the head of Taiya Inlet and thence along the thirty-three miles of the Chilkoot Trail to Lake Bennett.[17]

The expedition's supplies, weighing approximately three tons, were unloaded and packed on the company's steamer. Unlike the Franklin Records Search Expedition, this expedition would not be reliant on their own hunting prowess for survival. Instead, they carried less appetizing government rations, enough to last five months, which they intended to augment with game taken in the field. On June 7, Schwatka departed, with a picturesque flotilla of nine or ten canoes towed along by the company's steamer. Ada Schwatka had said her goodbyes to Frederick, remaining as a guest of the family of Reverend Eugene Willard at the Haines Mission which the Willard family charitably managed for the benefit of the Tlingit community. As an army spouse from a military family, Ada was emotionally prepared to handle the separations, but this first parting left her in a melancholy mood. She soon returned East to take comfort with family in Rock Island until the return of her beloved.[18]

Hemmed in by steep timbered hills, the flotilla made its way up Chilkoot Inlet through the Taiya Inlet, about ten miles, to the mouth of the Taiya River. As the channel narrowed, a series of swampy mud flats within a wide delta marked the stopping point of the steamer. By dint of hard work, the fully loaded canoes were tracked upstream fifteen miles through a serpentine course by working a combination of ropes and poles, to the head of navigation. From there, it was left to the hardy packers, only tipping the scales at about one hundred forty pounds each, to each carry one-hundred-pound bundles of supplies. Guided by the packers along the eastern side of the river, they followed the Chilkoot Trail, passing the Nourse River, entering from the west, and the immense Baird Glacier, that straddled several mountains, flanking the left course of the river. Their crude pathway was littered with fallen trees and limbs, boggy swamps and stretches of fragmented boulders before finally reaching the base of the Chilkoot Pass. Always observant, Schwatka found the Tlingit to be both inexhaustible packers on the trail and good-natured under the most trying of circumstances. However, he was surprised at their "selfishness," or outright indifference, to helping each other. Those with empty canoes had refused to ferry their companions travelling on foot across streams and even declined to help their sick comrades unless paid for their assistance. Despite the daily toil hauling the packs, every evening without fail Schwatka watched in amazement as the Tlingit played one or more gambling games, at times wagering the clothes off their backs, a vice which Schwatka believed they had learned from contact with civilization.

Throughout the journey, Schwatka and Wilson recorded the characteristics of the many Tlingit and Athabaskan (mainly Tagish, Han and Tutchone) peoples who were generous in their desire to aid the expedition. From the Chilkoot Inlet through to Fort Selkirk, they encountered small groups of Tagish, whom they found friendly and accommodating. At a small camp near the trail, several Tagish, referred to by Schwatka as "Tahk-heesh," or "Stick," were hired as packers and proved to be quite capable. Schwatka's official report provided one of the first published descriptions of the Tagish based on personal observation. The enterprising Tlingit had maintained the contact and trade with the Tagish, making inland excursions to gather furs from the Tagish and selling them at a hefty profit to outside European traders. The Tagish had little contact with white men until recently when excursions had begun to be made to the trading stores at Pyramid Harbor. In fact, according to Schwatka, while the Tlingit ruled with an iron-hand over the Chilkoot Pass, they also acted "as self-appointed masters over the docile and degraded 'Sticks.'" Schwatka estimated that at most fifty Tagish lived along the Yukon as far as Fort Selkirk, and he observed them spread out in small family groups. Schwatka passed through their territory in summer, by which time they had scattered in their search of game. Like many groups they encountered, at the time, the Tagish still maintained a traditional hunting and fishing pattern. With a few dated Hudson Bay flint-lock muskets and pistols, they certainly posed no threat to anyone. Overall, Schwatka was impressed with the peaceful nature of the Tagish and found their "reasonable and humane conduct to each other" to be commendable.[19]

Of the three year-round passes crossing the coast range and leading to the headwaters of the Yukon, the one selected by Schwatka, the Chilkoot Pass, was the shortest, but not necessarily the lowest in height. In 1880, after the Tlingit monopoly on the pass was broken, a few adventuresome prospectors had dared to venture into the Yukon region using this access route. As much as Schwatka would hate to admit it, those early prospectors, with visions of riches in their sights, had been a step ahead of him along the length of the Yukon, obviously pursuing a different agenda.[20]

Schwatka had arrived thirteen years before a remote stretch of the Yukon River and its tributary, the Klondike River, would capture the attention of the world and fundamentally alter the region. Schwatka's pioneering work would play a role in that momentous event. In August 1896, prospectors discovered gold on what came to be known as "Bonanza Creek" in the Klondike region, located some six hundred miles from the end of the Chilkoot Trail. When stories reached the outside world of pure gold nuggets as big as walnuts, more than forty thousand "stampeders," prospectors who hoped to become rich beyond their wildest dreams, flocked to the Klondike region beginning in 1897. Many of them crossed the Chilkoot Trail surveyed by Schwatka. Coming in the midst of a devastating depression, the news of unimaginable wealth for the taking created an even greater attraction. More than twenty-two thousand stampeders used the Chilkoot Trail at its height during the winter of 1897-98.[21]

During the rush, the prospectors came to know every inch of the rough pathway. Multiple tiresome trips over the pass were made in dreadful conditions to transport the one ton of supplies mandated by the Canadian authorities to avoid starvation on the part of unprepared sourdoughs. Although a lucky few did strike it rich, most arrived to the Klondike only to find that the best spots had been staked and that claims had been exaggerated. In the process, the newly established town of Dawson City at the convergence of the Klondike and the Yukon rivers became a "boom town." Exploding to more than thirty thousand residents, all elements of society looked to make a quick buck—storekeepers, prospectors, saloonkeepers, prostitutes and gamblers. Within three short years though, the "rush" had abruptly ceased. But hope sprang eternal, and many of the undeterred moved on quickly to the next big strike in Nome in 1899. But all this was more than a decade to come after Schwatka's nascent survey expedition.

To Schwatka, his line of sixty or so climbers roped together along the Chilkoot Pass, "made one of the prettiest Alpine sights that I have ever witnessed." To those scrambling up the steep, nearly perpendicular grade in places, it was a fatiguing climb of five hours that left them crawling on hands and knees, reaching for rocky outcrops and scrub spruce for leverage and cutting steps in glacial ice and snow. A dizzying rise of 1,000-feet through the last half mile to the summit made the ascent particularly trying. Schwatka marveled at the superhuman climbing power of his hardy packers. After descending the snow-covered slopes, they continued on, making camp that evening after a difficult trek of thirteen miles, at which time the majority of the packers suddenly dropped their packs and demanded immediate payment for completing their task. Under the light of the midnight sun, Schwatka made good the fees, and they quickly departed, one not even stopping during a raging storm until he reached the Haines Mission.[22]

Two packers, partially Tlingit by descent, remained with Schwatka for the length of the journey. "Billy" Dickinson, according to Schwatka, was a "good-looking young fellow" about twenty-five-years-old, and "strong as two or three ordinary men of his build." Schwatka was objective in his assessment of the young man, remarking that in difficult situations "he put all his strength to use and proved invaluable," but on routine tasks he could be outright lazy. "Indianne," a fifty-year-old man, whose mother was Tagish, would serve as a valuable interpreter and had some knowledge

"In the Chilkoot Pass." Drawing by Charles A. Gloster.

of the Tagish locale. With their assistance, he fulfilled his official objective to assess the country and its people from a purely military standpoint.[23]

The following day, northeast of the summit of the pass, they reached Lake Lindeman, a ten-mile-long body of water that Schwatka took to be the head of the Yukon (named by Schwatka after Dr. Lindeman of the Bremen Geographical Society). Today, the headwaters of the Yukon River proper are generally considered to begin near Atlin Lake. Schwatka learned after his return that the country up through Lake Lindeman had already been surveyed by Drs. Aurel Krause and Arthur Krause, on behalf of the Bremen Geographical Society. Therefore, Schwatka's original work commenced at this point. Here, Schwatka's plan for navigating the Yukon took shape. When he had proposed to construct a raft to traverse the full length of the river, he wryly noted that "the idea was laughed at by the few white men of the country, as evincing the extreme of ignorance, and the Indians seemed to be but little behind them in ridicule of the plan." But work it did, and Lake Lindeman would later become an important destination on the Chilkoot Trail where thousands of vessels were constructed from the thick pine and spruce by prospectors looking to reach the Klondike mining camps. In 1898, during the height of the stampede, more than seven thousand vessels were built, deforesting the once picturesque landscape.[24]

Schwatka's raft, constructed under Homan's skillful guidance, was composed of the largest spruce logs available, joined at the corners like a log cabin and set with wooden pins. After some initial refitting after its first run, it measured about sixteen by forty-two feet. An oar was set in each of the bow and stern, where two slightly elevated decks were constructed, separated by a lower central space amidships, where two side oars were rigged. Perhaps harking back to his previous adventure, Schwatka christened the vessel *Resolute,* the same name as a Royal Navy vessel engaged in the fruitless search for Sir John Franklin. Although unwieldy, but drawing less than two feet of water, the raft could be rowed at a rate of one mile per hour, and a tent raised as a sail allowed some additional speed. Nonetheless, the makeshift vessel would successfully cover about 1,300 miles and save untold hours of labor hauling the supplies by land. The raft was masterful in its simplicity, and one that conjures up visions of runaway Huckleberry Finn and Jim floating down the storied Mississippi River.

In their newly built craft, the party crossed a barren region, sparsely populated by stunted pines, and a chain of lakes flanked by steep glacier-clad summits, with those on the east interspersed with striking red colored rocks and ridges. Schwatka could not resist naming the lakes for his colleagues, James Gordon Bennett, Jr., Captain George Nares, and Professor Othniel C. Marsh. Their tent-fashioned sail ferried them along at impressive speeds but occasionally sent waves dashing the raft's sides and putting it and their nerves to the test. Many of the lakes in the Yukon could be dangerous during periods of high winds.

As Schwatka's group left the lakes and entered the fast-moving river current, progress did not come without effort. Simply steering the ungainly vessel required the continuous work of at least two men, an oarsman on each end. Sand, mud and gravel bars, submerged obstructions, boulders, and rapid currents were regular perils and required constant vigilance and labor. Often, hours were spent standing in frigid waters prying the raft loose from bars or snags in swift currents. The appearance of tree-lined banks posed problems, with their overhanging limbs that could sweep the decks, and maneuvering to land for camp for the evening was a particularly tricky proposition.

Mindful of their need to reach St. Michael before the last steamer departed, little to no time was left for any exploring beyond the riverbanks traversed by the raft. There were certainly disagreeable moments associated with the day-to-day aspects of the trip, but few outright dangers. The marauding swarms of mosquitoes, gnats, and biting flies, which were incessant, posed the greatest annoyance. For a man inured to hardship, Schwatka's misery over the relentless bugs was remarkable even for him.

"Prying the Raft off a Bar." Drawing by Charles A. Gloster.

On the return from one hunting trek, Schwatka noted that "my fight back to camp with the mosquitoes I shall always remember as one of the salient points of my life." So thick were they that he doubted his ability to shoot, as he could not see clearly to take aim. Not that it mattered at all as they saw only two moose and several mountain goats and bears the entire trip, and none were taken. Schwatka was disappointed to learn from the Tagish that the game would only return to the river when the mosquitoes had ceased their onslaught. For a promoter of the last frontier, it was surprising to hear discouraging words from Schwatka, who stated that "the Yukon Valley is not held up as a paradise to future tourists." Counter to the Arctic climate, temperatures often reached 100°F in the shade and the sun could be blistering.[25]

On July 2, to the outright alarm of his hired companions, they faced their biggest challenge, the descent into the dangerous and terrifying grand cañon of the Yukon (named Miles Cañon after Schwatka's commander). The only cañon on the Yukon, no better description of it and its attendant rapids exists than from Schwatka's pen:

> The walls of the cañon are perpendicular columns of basalt, not unlike a diminutive Fingal's cave in appearance, and nearly a mile in length, the center of this mile stretch being broken into a huge basin of about twice the usual width of the stream in the cañon, and which is full of seething whirlpools and eddies where nothing but a fish could live for a minute... Through this narrow

shoot of corrugated rock the wild waters of the great river rush in a perfect mass of milk-like foam, with a reverberation that is audible for a considerable distance, the roar being intensified by the rocky walls which act like so many sounding boards. Huge spruce trees in somber files overshadow the dark cañon, and it resembles a deep black thoroughfare paved with the whitest of marble. At the northern outlet of the cañon the rushing river spreads rapidly into its former width, but abates not a jot in its swiftness, and flows in a white and shallow sheet over reefs of bowlders [sic] and bars thickly studded with intertwining drifts of huge timber, ten times more dangerous for a boat or a raft than the narrow cañon itself, although not so in appearance. This state of things continues for about four miles further, offering every possible variety of obstacle in turn, when the river again contracts, hemmed in by low basaltic banks, and becomes even narrower than before. So swift is it, so great the volume of water and so contracted the channel, that half its water ascends the sloping banks, runs over them for nearly a score of yards, and then falls into the narrow shoot below, making a veritable horseshoe funnel of boiling cascades, not much wider than the length of our raft, and as high at the end as her mast.[26]

Having revealed its dangers, Schwatka provided a particularly exhilarating account of shooting the rapids that provided perhaps the most action-packed escapade of the expedition. According to Schwatka, "our resolution formed, in the forenoon of the second of July, we prepared to 'shoot' the raft through the rapids," and the wooden vessel was cast loose and shoved off. Quickly entering the raging cañon, the raft careened dangerously off the western wall, tearing off two side logs as it disappeared out of sight in the bubbling foam. Now steering its own course, it rapidly traversed the four-mile obstacle course while being badly bumped by a dozen or more hazardously situated logs. Running through the cascades "like a charge of fixed bayonets," the bow of the wooden vessel was lifted by a wave to a steep angle and its nose plowed into the seething foam, abruptly emerging at the end of the cascades. According to Schwatka, "those on board of the raft now got hold of a line from their friends on shore," and after taking stock of the raft, found it had suffered a few broken logs but was otherwise unscathed.[27]

This was certainly a real hair-raising feat and the most dangerous undertaking of the entire trip, but according to McIntosh it was not the real story. As reported by the matter-of-fact miner, no one had the courage to ride the raft, and it was floated unmanned through the treacherous foaming whitewater. Billy navigated his more maneuverable canoe through the cañon to its midpoint where he landed and gained the raft as it passed, riding only the lower portion of the cascades on the raft. Schwatka's remark that a line was thrown to the men on board, while omitting that the adroit Billy gained the vessel later, had created the impression that the daring voyagers had manned the craft the full length of the cañon and its corresponding raging rapids.[28]

Schwatka, the emerging travel writer with a growing penchant for the tall tale, had added a sensational twist to make his story more exciting to his armchair audience. His more eye-popping account of "shooting" the rapids was reserved for his popular account, *Along Alaska's Great River*, and has become widely repeated adventure fodder in Alaskan literature. The challenging rapids later became known as the "White Horse Rapids," for their resemblance to the mane of charging white horses. The nearby town of Whitehorse, established during the gold stampede in 1896, takes its name from the rapids. During the Klondike Gold Rush, a fateful few miners breathed their last while shooting the Miles Cañon and rapids in makeshift crafts. A dam built in 1958 swallowed the rapids, but Schwatka's nail-biting tale was instrumental in bestowing the name of "Schwatka Lake" to its reservoir.

After a much more tranquil crossing of the lengthy Lake Lebarge, and after passing several large rivers coming in mainly from the east, the Yukon widened to over half a mile and became dotted with small islands. Several long stretches of heavy timber along the banks and inland that were smoldering and sending up thick black clouds of smoke across the horizon made for a slightly unnerving state of travel ("as if the whole world was on fire," noted Schwatka). One extraordinary natural wonder, if Schwatka is to be believed, was a blazing tree that had fallen in the river, its exposed branches still burning above the waterline. Equally unexpected, on July 9, two dispirited and starving miners, almost barefooted, who had faced the harsh reality of prospecting in the Yukon, staggered into the Schwatka camp attempting to return to Chilkoot on foot. Carrying little food, they had attempted, badly as it turns out, to live off the land. Schwatka later learned they had reached the Haines Mission in desperate condition, saved only by the charity of the Tlingit.[29]

July 10 was a remarkable day, with fifty-nine miles covered on the raft, their longest run in one day. It had been done along an open country interspersed with dense spruce and pine that reminded Schwatka of the gentle hills of the Lake District of England. On July 12, a treacherous set of rapids that rushed through several channels formed by an array of

"View in Miles Cañon from its southern entrance." From *Along Alaska's Great River*.

pointed trap rocks, named by Schwatka the "Rink Rapids," for the Danish geographer Heinrick Rink, marked the end of the most difficult river passages (today they are the "Five Finger Rapids"). Schwatka opined that a steamer fitted with a windlass could ascend these rapids, in which case the head of navigation on the Yukon could be the Miles Cañon, making the river navigable for more than one thousand miles from the coast. That vision actually came to fruition in 1898 when steamer traffic began between Dawson City and Whitehorse. As Schwatka envisioned, upstream travel through the Five Finger Rapids could be done by means of a cable attached to a rock so that steamers could winch upstream in fifteen to twenty minutes.[30]

On July 12, they reached the convergence of the Pelly River with the river they just descended. To Schwatka they had come down the Yukon, but historically the stretch from Lake Lindeman to the Pelly River was known as the Lewes River. Schwatka looked upon scenery that was "very grand," as he eyed a mountainous landscape shaped by powerful natural forces, marked by weather-beaten basaltic cliffs formed from cooling volcanic matter (now known as the Fort Selkirk volcanic field). Along the steep bank of the river an equally fascinating phenomenon had marked their watercourse for several days which left Schwatka pondering the nature of the universe. About two feet below the surface of the cut bank on one side ran a white stripe between two to three inches wide. Upon closer inspection, they correctly determined it to be a layer of volcanic ash from an exceptional eruption from "ancient times." Not quite ancient in geologic terms, Schwatka offered the first published account of the ash fall from a particularly violent mega-eruption of the Churchill-Bona massif (compact group of mountains) within the Wrangell Mountains about one thousand years before, an event widely disruptive to both human and wildlife in the region.[31]

Fort Selkirk was reached on July 13, where they found nothing but the crumbled remnants of three chimneys of what had previously been the Hudson's Bay Company trading post. The post was initially established by the pioneering trader Robert Campbell at the convergence of the Pelly and Lewes Rivers in 1848 and was relocated to the present site below the convergence in 1852. Trading activity by the Hudson's Bay Company with the Athabaskans aroused the ire of the enterprising but jealous Tlingit. Fearful of losing their trade monopoly, they surprised Campbell and looted its stores on August 1, 1852. The post was burned to the ground and blackened embers still littered the area during Schwatka's visit. At Fort Selkirk, Schwatka had reached what he claimed was "land familiar to the footsteps of white men who had made maps and charts, that rough and rude they were, were still entitled to respect, and accordingly at this point I considered that my explorations had ceased, although my surveys were continued to the mouth of the river; making the distinction that the first survey only is an exploration, a distinction which I believe is rapidly coming into vogue." In other words, the exploration of the upper course of the Yukon by virtue of his survey (about five hundred miles from Lake Lindeman) constituted a geographical "prize" that had been snagged by Schwatka. To him, it was a feat noteworthy in its completion and logically deserving of personal acclaim, but it would not come without some controversy.[32]

CHAPTER THIRTEEN
DOWN THE YUKON
PART II

MOTIVATED BY A DESIRE TO enhance his own accomplishments and always with an eye toward his own continued fame, Schwatka had cleverly elevated a moderately strenuous rafting adventure into a larger feat of exploration. By extending the Yukon by hundreds of miles simply through a name change (renaming the Lewes River the Yukon), he delivered an eye-catching claim of an end-to-end traverse of what was now one of the continent's longest rivers. Schwatka's excessive acts of renaming of geographical features served to further bolster that narrative of the "explorer" and "discoverer." Schwatka was not at all shy about his accomplishment, remarking in his official report that "geographical science is under obligations to this reconnaissance, for mapping a region worse than unknown...." Schwatka did, however, credit Homan with the thorough survey and map work, noting that "the credit for the same belongs to him." Perhaps personal motivations led Schwatka to overlook the most obvious consideration when travelling the Yukon River from Chilkoot Inlet to Fort Selkirk, namely that its course runs almost completely through British North America (Canada), a circumstance calling into question the necessity, and perhaps legality, of a branch of the U.S. government undertaking such an endeavor in the first place.[1]

In any event, neither Miles nor Schwatka had made any effort to obtain approval from the British government. For an expedition that had little internal U.S. government support, and in fact had provoked outright opposition, an international dispute added another unnecessary complexity. Fortunately, Lionel Sackville-West, British envoy to the United States, who had subsequently contacted U.S. Secretary of State Thomas F. Bayard to call attention to the oversight, concluded that the British government "do not attach any importance to this fact, and that no doubt had their acquiescence been asked it would not have been refused." Sackville-West did not want Schwatka's delineations to prejudice the British in their negotiations over the unresolved boundary between Alaska and Canada.[2]

The embarrassing affair placed Miles in an awkward position when called by his superiors to explain his reasons for a survey of British territory. Looking after his own reputation, Miles shifted the blame to Schwatka, responding that traversing British America "was not called for by the letter of instructions." The response was certainly disingenuous as it had been well publicized before Schwatka's departure that Schwatka would travel the Chilkoot Trail and down the Yukon. Within Canada though, concerns were raised by House member David Gordon (British Columbia) when word reached him that "an American armed expedition, under Lieutenant Schwatka, had traveled a thousand miles into British Territory, east of Alaska...." The actions of Schwatka served as the impetus for Canada to undertake a definition of the international boundary, along with their own investigations of the area.[3]

From Fort Selkirk, Schwatka followed a known path to the coast that posed few difficulties beyond the variable weather, which was marked by protracted rains and occasional downpours. No longer "explorers," Schwatka and his companions would continue their survey to the coast, thus completing the first survey of the entire length of the Yukon River. Although there are no personal diaries of the trip beyond McIntosh's unvarnished journal, the group seems to have been cohesive and mindful of their various responsibilities, and Schwatka's leadership and guidance seemed steady throughout. Although staffed principally by military men and subject to its corresponding discipline, even the assistance of Billy and Indianne appears to have been friendly and cooperative. Throughout the expedition, McIntosh, who was thoroughly in his element, spent considerable time in the quest for gold. Perhaps reluctant to admit that Schwatka himself was caught in a rush of gold fever, Schwatka only mentions the search for the precious mineral on one occasion, but McIntosh recorded that Schwatka eagerly accompanied him on several prospecting excursions. Prior to departure, one newspaper had inopportunely labelled the expedition as a "prospecting party," a designation Schwatka was careful to avoid, as it would characterize his expedition as simply a disguised mineral hunt, one similar to Custer's 1874 excursion in the Black Hills.

The upper course had not revealed any significant mineral finds. Near a river named the D'Abbadie River (after M. Antoine D'Abbadie, a French explorer), just above Fort Selkirk, Schwatka observed enough signs to recognize that he was entering a region offering more promising prospects. Schwatka remarked that "from the D'Abbadie almost to the very mouth of the great Yukon, a panful of 'dirt' taken with any discretion from almost any bar or bank, will when washed give several 'colors,' to use a miner's phrase." Similarly, near Fort Selkirk, McIntosh recorded his "usual inspection around the banks of the river for auriferous sands and for the first time on this trip found that I had a fine color of gold after washing the first pan." On the grounds of the old fort, he found "a dozen colors of gold to every pan but think this is too small" to offset the short season and distance from supplies. Schwatka and McIntosh had discovered what the early prospectors had already learned—that this section of the river held out better opportunities for gold in paying quantities.[4]

As they continued, they also found the river populated with greater numbers of Athabaskan peoples. About twelve miles below the Pelly River convergence, they encountered a village filled by an exuberant group of more than one hundred Northern Tutchone lining the banks to receive them, many swarming about them in canoes, shouting and screaming. Judging by their reaction, McIntosh surmised that most of them had never seen a white man. Although Robert Campbell had established Fort Selkirk in 1848, after its destruction in 1852, traders did not venture into Tutchone territory until the 1870s, and contact had been sporadic. At the time of Schwatka's visit, the Tutchone still maintained a semi-nomadic life and a fishing-hunting economy. The typical cycle was marked by fishing for salmon and freshwater fish in warm weather months, and in advance of winter hunting for moose and a variety of other game, while living off stored food in the coldest winter months. Their summer encampment, consisting of a collection of approximately twenty lodges of spruce brush walls covered by moose or caribou skins, was the largest seen by Schwatka's party on the Yukon. The large, boisterous crowd of 175-200 raised some concern on Schwatka's part for their safety, and guns were placed in the ready simply because of their sheer numbers. They posed no harm, and quite the contrary, after shaking hands, honored Schwatka's party by forming a line and paying tribute with joyful singing and dancing. McIntosh, quite impressed by the group, found them friendly and delighted by the impromptu visit, and remarked that they "have more life and energy among them than any we have met with on this particular trip." Homan found them fidgety as well, so much so he could not settle them down long enough for a photograph. To Schwatka, their low brush huts were simple, and their clothing worn, but he was greatly impressed with their skill in canoe construction. Their birch-bark canoes, with which they made extensive journeys, were both lightweight and durable. A keen observer, Schwatka believed that they could travel as fast as any canoe men in the world. Though he found their household utensils primitive, Schwatka was also impressed by their well-tailored traditional clothing.[5]

Back on the river, Schwatka was enthralled by the wondrous one-hundred-mile stretch from Fort Selkirk to the Stewart River that evoked the awe-inspiring grandeur of the Yellowstone or Yosemite, a mountain landscape rising to a plateau as much as three thousand feet above the riverbank. At their Camp 32, located more than one hundred miles below Fort Selkirk, Schwatka recorded the matter-of-fact observation that "we camped at the mouth of a swift fair-sized river coming in from the east which we afterwards ascertained of the traders to be Deer River and is so marked on the map." The Han who populated the area knew it as "Tr'ondëk," or as pronounced by Euro-Americans, "Klondike." Schwatka's inconspicuous campsite at the confluence of the Klondike and Yukon rivers would later be the location of the boom town of Dawson City.[6]

The Klondike River and its surrounding tributaries would bear witness to the Klondike stampede, starting in earnest in 1897. Though Schwatka's group preceded the gold rush, they did meet some of the soon-to-be legends of the Klondike. One was the enterprising merchant Joseph Ladue, "Jo" to Schwatka, who tagged along with Schwatka's party in his own scow for several days. The pushy trader sought unsuccessfully to peddle a replacement boat and supplies, rather energetically attempting to convince Schwatka that their raft was a deathtrap. Ladue and Schwatka must have shared some common experiences in the old west. Ladue was nineteen when he went west in 1876, laboring in a gold mine in Deadwood, Dakota Territory as Schwatka arrived from the Starvation March. Ladue had crossed the Chilkoot Pass to prospect in 1882. A man of foresight, when gold was struck in the Klondike, he bought much of the land that would become Dawson City and, along with several other land claims, struck it rich. Schwatka also made the acquaintance of the trader Jack McQuesten, the so-called "Father of the Yukon." Among the most successful of the early traders, he also made millions on claims in the Klondike gold region. Schwatka was evidently taken by the McQuesten's engaging personality and humorous, sometimes farfetched, tales.

Eight miles below the mouth of the Klondike, opposite the abandoned trading post Fort Reliance, Schwatka's group encountered the first of several Han bands. As they passed the village of Noo-klak-ó (or Nuclaco), with its approximately one hundred and fifty inhabitants, Schwatka was surprised to receive an extended salute by the friendly Han of seventy-five to one hundred rounds from their shotguns and rusty Hudson's Bay muskets, a custom harking back to their communication with Russians traders, but one which Schwatka believed was simply a useless waste of

"Near Entrance to the Klondike on the Yukon River."
Drawing by Charles A. Gloster.

ammunition. Leaving their Camp 33 a day later, they passed "a good sized river coming in from the west," which Schwatka named Cone-Hill after a prominent conical shaped hill at its mouth. Cone-Hill River, later renamed Fortymile River (forty miles from Fort Reliance), would become famous in 1886 as the location of the first gold strike in the Yukon, later overshadowed by the more spectacular Klondike gold strike.[7]

Further downstream, at the village of Klat-ol-klin, or Johnny's Village (its Americanized name, after its chief), near Belle Island, they found another group of approximately one hundred Han, the first settlement they considered "permanent," in that it maintained six ramshackle log cabins year-round. The Han were the last of the Athabaskan people to establish contact with white men, but by the date of Schwatka's arrival, they had conducted regular trading business with traders since the 1870s. As evidence of that trade, they wore European clothing almost exclusively, and possessed a variety of manufactured goods. Like other Indigenous peoples of the Yukon, their culture was in a state of transition. At the time, salmon were an important component of their diet, and spruce poles drying an ample supply of salmon attested to their proficiency. After the gold strikes in the region in the late 1880s, their culture and economy would change drastically, supplying furs and meat to the Euro-Americans and placing greater reliance on occupations supporting the

Euro-Americans' presence. Along with cultural change, with the gold rush and an influx of Euro-Americans, came disease and epidemics which would reduce their population. The Han suffered even more than other Indigenous peoples along the Yukon as the gold strikes and stampede were centered in their traditional homeland. As was the case of his Inuit companions, Schwatka was not shy about offering praise of the skills of the Han. He was particularly impressed with their ability to spot and catch salmon in the muddy, opaque waters of the lower Yukon, witnessing what he termed the "most wonderful and striking performance given by any natives we encountered." He watched in marvel as a young man in a canoe thrust a net to a depth of nine or ten feet and snagged his prey simply by detecting the slightest movement of the water.[8]

Shortly after leaving the Han settlement, they passed an abandoned trading post at Belle Island and a distinctive hill rising from the surrounding flatlands. Believing the hill to be located on the Alaskan side of the then International Boundary between Alaska and British territory, Schwatka named it Boundary Butte (now known as Eagle Bluff, outside the current town of Eagle). In 1887, the Canadian dominion surveyor, William Ogilvie, was sent to determine the boundary line utilizing astronomical observations and spent the winter of 1887-88 on the Yukon near Fortymile, placing the International Boundary eleven miles to the eastward of Schwatka's location.

Below a village (Charley's Village), comparable to Johnny's Village, the country fairly opened up after leaving the more mountainous region, and the group entered what Schwatka termed the "Yukon-Flats," a wide, level basin he viewed as flat as the Great Plains of the West. The miner McIntosh also proved to be an excellent observer of the country, peppering his diary with knowledgeable details. On July 23, he remarked that "timber, spruce and cottonwood is noticeably disappearing or getting smaller. Rosebushes, although their blooming time is over, grow in abundance on the islands. The common switch-willow grows thick. Yellow birch, of which the Indians build their canoes, grows plentiful up the side streams." For Schwatka, the plentiful wild rosebuds offered a tasty change of fare from canned foods, and perchance brought to mind memories of the momentous struggle on the Plains seven years before.[9]

On July 27, they reached Fort Yukon located at the junction of the Porcupine River, eight miles above the Arctic Circle. The once bustling trading post of the Hudson's Bay Company was found to sit within Alaska Territory after the purchase (falling west of the 141st meridian) and had become the domain of American traders. More important, at Fort Yukon the steamer *Yukon* had just arrived under the command of Captain

Petersen of the Alaska Commercial Company. The generous captain offered Schwatka's party his smaller twelve-ton schooner, docked three hundred miles downstream at the village of Nuklukayet, to replace their raft, and offered some provisions, which had been hard to procure off the land and water. The *Yukon,* which was on route upstream, even offered to pick up Schwatka and his men on its return trip to the coast wherever they met and tow the schooner to St. Michael. For McIntosh, the change in vessels couldn't come fast enough, as he complained that "all are getting very much disgusted and worn out with the progress we are making with the old craft." The frustratingly slow progress left them extremely uneasy about making the steamer at St. Michael. On the positive side though, Homan checked his dead reckoning with his sextant and chronometers, and concluded that in over one thousand miles since Chilkat Inlet, the error was less than six miles.[10]

With accurate maps supplied by Raymond's survey, they were prepared for the ramparts of the lower Yukon, which they passed without incident. On August 6, Schwatka's party crossed the Tanana River, the largest tributary of the Yukon, a largely unexplored river of several hundred miles, perhaps worthy of his later attention. At the trading station of Nuklukayet near their confluence (the current location of the city of Tanana), they stopped at the furthest inland trading post of the Alaska Commercial Company. They discarded their unpretentious vessel, which had dutifully served its purpose for some one thousand three hundred miles, for a ten-ton schooner or 'barka,' which oddly remained unnamed. Coincidentally, their durable raft *Resolute* shared the same fate as its namesake Arctic vessel, which was likewise abandoned. In a slightly melancholy state of mind, Schwatka remarked that their raft would likely become "kindling-wood for the trader's stove," and "seemed to deserve a better fate." With the wearily slow progress of the raft as they coasted towards St. Michael, the crew felt differently. McIntosh remarked that "nearly all rejoiced and were glad of the opportunity" to leave "our THUD of a raft." The balance of the journey was uneventful but filled with a few minor diversions and an overwhelming desire to reach the U.S. Revenue Cutter *Thomas Corwin* before its departure. Smoking, reading old novels, spinning yarns or simply sunning on the deck helped pass the time when not occupied in prying the boat off the occasional mudflat or sandflat, all the while suffering from wet, miserable weather. A femur and a tooth of a mastodon stumbled upon during a stroll near camp momentarily lifted the monotony.[11]

The search for Sir John Franklin was not on the top of Schwatka's mind when they stopped at the village of Nulato, noteworthy as the furthest permanent trading post of the Russian American Company.

Here however, Schwatka found not Franklin, but in this remote corner of the world, a grave and headboard marking the site of a Franklin searcher. The tragic story of this British officer reveals itself in the narrative of Captain Richard Collinson of HMS *Enterprise,* searching for Franklin by way of Bering Strait between 1850 and 1855. Stopping at St. Michael, *Enterprise* put ashore Lieutenant John Barnard and two other seamen to track down a rumor that white men were seen on the Yukon River in the Alaska interior, perhaps missing men from Franklin's expedition. That Franklin's men could have travelled as far as Alaska without relief or notice seems far-fetched, but rumors abounded between Point Barrow and Norton Sound during the summer of 1850. Leaving no stone unturned, the diligent Lieutenant Barnard accompanied several Russian traders to Nulato on their annual visit to track down the truth of one report of white men spotted in the interior. Unfortunately for Barnard, in the bitter cold dawn of February 15, the post was violently attacked by about eighty Koyukon, an Alaskan Athabaskan people. Unprepared and unprotected, more than fifty inhabitants were massacred, including Barnard, who suffered several severe stab wounds and died the following day. Reports surmised that harsh dealings by the Russian traders left the Koyukon angered. In any event, when Schwatka arrived at Nulato, Barnard's forlorn and weathered headboard was fast decomposing and disappearing into obscurity.[12]

At Anvic, their spirits were lifted that they might not be "frozen up in this HORRID COUNTRY," asserted McIntosh, when the steamers *Yukon* and *St. Michael* were spotted. Their little schooner was quickly hitched behind the *Yukon,* enabling them to make better time. On August 30 they finally reached St. Michael on the coast, a small village of twelve to fifteen buildings, principally those of the Alaska Commercial Company. To their great dismay however, the *Corwin* had already departed. Their last remaining hope for a return before winter rested with the trading steamer *Leo,* expected to arrive shortly. The all-consuming topic of conversation for the next several days was whether the *Leo* would reach St. Michael or whether it might be wrecked or otherwise diverted. Whiling away the time, Schwatka spent two eventful evenings as a guest at the nearby Inupiac village comparing his current experiences with the Inuit of Hudson Bay. Retaining what little Inuktitut he could from the Arctic expedition, he was surprised that he could carry on a limited conversation with the Inupiac, who spoke an Inuit language.[13]

During one evening, as part of a large group of more than fifty men, women and children, Schwatka and McIntosh attended a grandiose performance by an important shaman at their barabara, a semi-underground communal dwelling. Through a series of tricks and sleight-of-hand designed to impress his audience, Schwatka and the guests were foretold of the impending arrival of the *Leo* by the next moon. The shaman had a favorable track record, as he had previously foretold of the loss of the *Jeannette*. To their relief, he was proven correct again. The *Leo* did in fact arrive on September 8. McIntosh's bold and capitalized diary entry for that date spoke for all the men: "there's the SCHOONER, THE SCHOONER, THE SCHOONER IS IN SIGHT!!!" Although overloaded with members of the U.S. International Polar Year expedition, commanded by Lieutenant Patrick Henry Ray, who had returned from Point Barrow, Schwatka's men were unwilling to remain no matter how uncomfortable the return. Ray's expedition had been one of two stations established by the United States as its contribution to the First International Polar Year, a program of simultaneous scientific observations from multiple sites across the Arctic supported by a number of nations. The other polar observation station supported by the United States was the expedition of Lieutenant Adolphus W. Greely to Lady Franklin Bay on the Ellesmere Island coast, one that that would end in disaster.[14]

It had been a difficult run for the *Leo*. She had been nipped at Point Barrow, and her stem had split, causing her to leak badly. Schwatka's small band squeezed on board the already tight ship. He made the best of the crowded situation, sharing a berth with Homan beneath the dining room table. Determined nonetheless to make San Francisco, the *Leo* left with the Schwatka party, expecting to make repairs at Unalaska in the Aleutians if necessary. In fact, *Leo* did land on the remote island for repairs, a noteworthy stop of several days where Schwatka observed a temperate climate warmed by the so-called "Kuro-Siwo," a Pacific gulf stream, producing "luxuriant" grasses upon which a head of cattle kept by the Alaska Commercial Company for butter and milk were seen to graze. That observation would soon give rise to Schwatka's ambitious plan for prospective stock-raising on these remote islands. From Unalaska, the expedition made an uneventful return to San Francisco, and from there Schwatka boarded the "Queen of the Pacific" for a truly leisurely cruise to Portland.

Although disappointed that his large-scale plans failed to come to fruition, the ever-resilient explorer had made the best of the situation. Not only did he satisfy Miles's military objectives to scout the territory and its peoples, but he also achieved some other not insignificant results. Contrary to expectations regarding hostilities, Schwatka believed that an overall friendly feeling existed among the whites and the Indigenous peoples that he had encountered. Always objective in assessing those relations, he was not reluctant to admit the sad truth that if there occurred any conflict, "it will more than likely be the fault of the whites...." Obviously playing to his congressional readership, but truly of the same opinion, Schwatka found a "sincere desire" for a reoccupation of Alaska by the military, not to quell any potential hostilities but simply to provide some permanent form of law and order. His recommendation calling for the establishment of a system of military posts equipped with steam-powered transport to move rapidly within the interior was finally implemented in 1898.[15]

In light of the limited resources and time available, his traverse of the full length of the river during the summer of 1883 was an inventive piece of planning and execution, and the first actual survey of the Yukon River. George M. Dawson, noted surveyor and assistant director of the Canadian Geological Survey, who was critical of other aspects of Schwatka's conduct, was magnanimous in his praise for Schwatka's Yukon survey, noting that "to Lieutenant Schwatka is, however, due the credit of having made the first survey of the river, a survey which Mr. Ogilvie's work of 1887, has proved to be a reasonably accurate one, in so far as its main features are concerned." More than one hundred years later, in 1987, a report by the U.S. Geological Survey concluded that Schwatka's survey "has only in very recent years been superseded by better work." Schwatka might have taken some consolation from the fact that the U.S. Geological Survey, the agency that had stalled his original plans in 1882 and 1883, now expressed such praiseworthy compliments. Much of the credit for the geographical accomplishments belongs to Charles Homan, whose many diligent observations and topographic sketches provided its basis.[16]

On a practical level, Schwatka's survey offered meaningful assistance to the intrepid sourdoughs in the field. The route surveyed by Schwatka became one the principal transportation routes to the goldfields in 1897 and 1898. To the thousands of uninformed and inexperienced stampeders who descended on Alaska en route to the Klondike goldfields, many with no idea of where they were going or how to get there, Schwatka's report and map proved invaluable and likely saved lives. Among them, his work was not forgotten. In 1919, one old-time prospector, when asked who Frederick Schwatka was, the man "so frequently mentioned in Alaskan literature," he responded that "his trip over the [Chilkoot] Pass and voyage down the river was most graphically described in his report to the government and a copy of it was carried by most every man who went over the [Chilkoot] Trail into the Klondike in 1898. And it was this that placed the name of 'Schwatka' in every traveler's mouth."[17]

In contrast to the survey itself, there was however considerable consternation voiced by knowledgeable geographers for what they viewed as Schwatka's breach of the explorers' unwritten code. During the entire journey through what Schwatka considered the "unexplored" upper stretch of the Yukon to Fort Selkirk, Schwatka freely and unreservedly named rivers, streams, mountains, valleys, islands, and even secondary features such as rapids, buttes, and headlands, after a litany of his esteemed scientific associates. To Schwatka, it was the prerogative of the first recognized surveyor to designate place names, and name he did, beginning with "Perrier Pass" in place of the well-known "Chilkoot Pass" (a change which never came into use). Ignoring place names adopted by Indigenous peoples and, in some cases, the Hudson's Bay Company and even miners, left Schwatka open to criticism by George Dawson. Some was justified and some was not. For example, the stretch of river that Schwatka's expedition descended from the Chilkoot Pass to Fort Selkirk had been known by the Hudson's Bay traders and miners as the Lewes River for more than thirty years, Schwatka renamed the Yukon, thereby extending the length of the river. On that issue however, the Board of Geographic Names in Ottawa later sided with Schwatka, discontinuing the name of the Lewes River in place of the Yukon River. However, in an extremely magnanimous act, notwithstanding his frustration over Schwatka's naming flurry, Dawson retained many of Schwatka's names on the Canadian maps in light of the distinguished personages adorned by Schwatka. Ironically, despite the grumbling, Schwatka holds the remarkable distinction for having bestowed the most place names in Canada by a United States citizen.[18]

Beyond the nomenclature controversy, both Dawson and the noted Alaska explorer and geographer William Dall were rightly critical of the exceedingly harsh and outright inflammatory remarks in Schwatka's popular account, *Along Alaska's Great River*, in regard to the accuracy of earlier Yukon maps and the work of his predecessors. In a sweeping proclamation, Schwatka declared that "there is not an official or government map of Alaska, that, taken as a whole, is worth the ink with which it is printed." To make matters worse, Schwatka's rash criticism specifically referenced the U.S. Coast Survey prepared by Dall, as well as the map included in Dall's seminal work *Alaska and its Resources*. The only exclusions from Schwatka's ire were the survey maps produced by military surveyors like those of Lieutenant Patrick Ray, Captain Charles Raymond and Lieutenant George Stoney, which Schwatka found to be "undoubtedly excellent, second to none in the world made under similar circumstances...."[19]

Schwatka's remarks were certainly unnecessary and indefensible, motivated in part by a desire to inflate the value of his own work. The vehemence with which he launched his attack, and his defense of the military surveys, suggests another underlying purpose: to demonstrate to a politically motivated bureaucracy the foolishness of excluding the army from Alaska's affairs, a decision that had frustrated his own plans. Responding to the attack on his work, Dall remarked that Schwatka is "like many militarymen, preferring to ignore or affect contempt of any work done outside military circles." Dall believed that Schwatka should do justice to his predecessors, not hold them in contempt.[20]

Beyond the issue of the survey, Schwatka's reconnaissance accomplished significant results in other fields. Aside from his topographic work, Homan also served as amateur photographer for the expedition. Although the camera was of "cheap character," he managed to produce forty-seven plates providing a documentary record of the expedition using the dry-plate process. Unfortunately, the original plates were badly damaged and produced images that were heavily toned and largely unfit for publication when processed. In their place, Schwatka introduced lithograph engravings based on the photographs when he prepared his official *Report of a Military Reconnaissance* and in *Along Alaska's Great River*. Nonetheless, overlooked by later, more high-quality images, such as those of William Ogilvie during the boundary survey of 1887, Homan's images are among the earliest known photographs of the interior of Alaska and Alaskan glaciers. These include the glaciers known as Baird Glacier and Saussure Glacier, beyond the end of canoe navigation in Taiya Inlet north of Skagway, as well as images of locations of importance, such as Miles Cañon and the ruins of Fort Selkirk. Homan's efforts led Schwatka to emphasize the value of a camera for expedition photography. Separately, Sargent Gloster fulfilled his artist role. Twenty of his rough, on-the-spot watercolors of peoples and places have survived, some of which were the basis for engravings in Schwatka's works.[21]

As a dedicated physician, Dr. George Wilson viewed the health and welfare of the members as his first and foremost priority, a task which weighed heavily upon him. Recounting his service on behalf of the expedition, he prided himself on their safe return without the loss of human life, or even a serious injury. At the same time, Dr. Wilson succeeded in recording descriptions of numerous Indigenous peoples they encountered. His report is far from comprehensive, but the descriptions of the Tagish, Tutchone and Han are considered among the first systematic descriptions of these peoples and have only more recently been given credit they deserve. One historian went so far as to conclude that "Schwatka's ethnological report is a landmark in the study of Alaska's native peoples." With limited time among the various tribes, Wilson's information was gathered through personal observation and with the aid of their interpreters and others with whom he could communicate. Below Selkirk, traders such as McQuesten and Harper supplied ethnographic information, especially about the groups with whom Schwatka's expedition had very little contact. A strong element of Wilson's bias runs through his report though. In *Along Alaska's Great River*, Schwatka also described the Indigenous peoples harshly at times, mirroring some of the comments in Wilson's report. However, as in the case of his Inuit companions, Schwatka could acknowledge their varied skills and ingenuity in manners of hunting, fishing, canoeing and craftsmanship, as well as positive moral traits (aspects rarely viewed favorably by Euro-Americans). In addition, and rather uniformly, Schwatka reserved much criticism for the shamans or medicine men he encountered in the Yukon and elsewhere. Schwatka's position was not premised solely upon a cultural superiority that viewed their ceremonial practices as superstitious foolishness. Ignorance of the spiritual meaning of those beliefs may have led to intolerance. But Schwatka was possessed of a sense of fairness, and he also believed that the shamans exercised undue and unfavorable influence over their subjects by exploiting and accentuating superstitious fears to maintain a position of status and for personal gain.[22]

News of Schwatka's return fanned out quickly from San Francisco, and not all of it was agreeable or even accurate. A dreadful tale of murder splashed across the papers. The *New York Times* and numerous others reprinted a sensational report that during the course of the journey, when Schwatka and his companions were faced with the prospect of shooting the treacherous rapids of Miles Cañon, their Tlingit companions balked and attempted to commandeer the raft and force it ashore. In response, "Schwatka, in order to suppress the mutiny, opened fire on the Indians, killing three, when the others submitted and the rapids were run." Before it was even verified, the shocking news hurriedly ran in reports throughout the states, bringing notoriety and public attention to the expedition, and no doubt questions of the leader who had been tasked with assuring the Indigenous peoples of the military's friendly intentions. The false scandal was ultimately dismissed for what it was, but this kept the expedition squarely in the spotlight.[23]

At the same time, Schwatka, certainly a self-promoter and seeking to boost his own fame, began to do what he did best—publish a number of popular works for the general public. Schwatka's adventure fell squarely within the readership of *Forest and Stream*, a magazine geared towards a growing metropolitan audience of outdoor enthusiasts and recreational hunting and fishing devotees, who saw the outdoors as an escape and rejuvenation from an increasingly urbanized society and industrialization. With serialization commonplace among periodicals, amidst his military duties Schwatka penned his exciting story, *Down the Yukon on a Raft,* in ten installments between December 1883 and April 1884. Limiting his story to the first third of his journey, the "unexplored" upper reaches of the Yukon, the series offered Schwatka's practiced formula of travel narrative mixed with colorful descriptions of people, places, and events. Playing to his readership, it was told in a relaxed and informal style, sprinkled with self-deprecating humor that made light of their dangers and misfortunes. For example, he spoke directly to the outdoor novice in a lively manner about the travails of travelling by raft along a heavily tree-lined waterway:

> To the inexperienced man who has never had his hair combed by a whole timber district in a brief minute these remarks may seem absurd, but to the old veteran raftsman it will awaken many a sigh of sympathy from his breast as he picks splinters three inches long out of it and digs the moss, driftwood and leaves out of his eyes to look at his hat dancing on a limb a mile back, and takes an inventory of stock to see if that is all that is lost.[24]

For the armchair adventurer, the story offered a safe and comfortable window through which to view life in this remote wilderness. On its heels, Schwatka placed another abridged account in four issues of the magazine *Science,* modified to reflect the scientific, mainly geographical, accomplishments of the journey. In a similar vein, he delivered the results of his reconnaissance and extolled the natural resources of Alaska in person for the benefit of the American Geographical Society on the evening of December 12, 1884.

Commercial enterprises on the West Coast, San Francisco in particular, had looked with interest at Alaska and Schwatka's expedition. On January 20, 1884, with Schwatka's assistance, the *San Francisco Chronicle* published a lengthy report of his Yukon reconnaissance. Running several columns, the report was an abridged but detailed draft of the principal points of Schwatka's not-yet-completed official report to Miles, including a precisely scaled topographic map of the first part of the journey from Chilkoot Inlet to Fort Selkirk, together with a running narrative of the survey. Taking full advantage of the West Coast media attention, Schwatka even offered an exclusive interview to an all-to-eager reporter from the *San Francisco Examiner* who cornered Schwatka in Portland. Although declining to offer the reporter any "extracts" from his as of yet unpublished government report, he nonetheless proceeded to tout the commercial possibilities of the newly acquired territory, highlighting the opportunities for fishing, mining, and even a suggestion of cattle ranching in the Aleutian Islands, a novel idea born from his brief visit. All this publicity placed Miles in an awkward position. For his own sake, Miles was compelled to officially distance himself from his subordinate's press-mongering, as it ran ahead of any official report to be delivered to the secretary of war and expressly violated Schwatka's confidentiality instructions. Miles went so far as to advise his superior, Major General John Pope, that he "disapproved" of the details appearing in articles and magazines before delivery of Schwatka's report.[25]

Ironically, the perturbed congressional bureaucrats, who had flatly refused to support the expedition, now faced widespread public interest due to Schwatka's publicity, and clamored for the publication of Schwatka's official report, even requesting extra copies to be printed. Highlighting that interest, Senator Joseph Roswell Hawley (CT), in support of his resolution calling for its publication, remarked that "considerable public attention was directed" to Lieutenant Schwatka's military reconnaissance of Alaska, and that "the Secretary of War and Lieutenant General strongly recommend the printing of the report. I believe it is a matter of considerable public interest and value." The resolution, which was ultimately approved, provided for 5,400 copies, which included an additional 3,500 copies to be printed for Congress and the War Department. By comparison, the total number printed exceeded that of Lieutenant Ray's expedition to Point Barrow (3,900 copies). With a strong degree of sarcasm and disappointment, Schwatka bitterly remarked that the $8,350 appropriated by Congress to publish the final report exceeded the entire cost of the expedition.[26]

Through his connections at *Century Magazine*, in September and October 1885, Schwatka published a two-part travelogue titled *The Great River of Alaska* for the benefit of its educated and upscale audience. *The Great River* and the value of the resources of Alaska played to the magazine's nation-building theme advanced by its editor Richard Gilder, brother of William Gilder, which was widely prevalent in exploration narratives at the time. Additionally, unlike his Arctic sojourn, Schwatka managed to publish a full-length narrative, *Along Alaska's Great River,* by the firm of Cassell & Co. Expanding on his more staid official report and earlier articles, *Along Alaska's Great River* offered a popular account of the full story to the public that included more descriptive pieces, such as characteristics and encounters with Indigenous peoples, the difficulties and unpleasantries of the trip, as well as astute natural history observations. *Along Alaska's Great*

River was well received and later editions were brought out in 1891 and 1893 under the title *A Summer in Alaska*. The 1885 review in the *Christian Union* summed up the common theme that applied to all Schwatka's Alaskan writings: "All that Lieutenant Schwatka has written of his varied and extended experiences in northern latitudes is marked by the same ease of narrative and skill in presenting ethnographical and geographical facts in a popular way, mingling scientific observations with light and entertaining talk about the country, the people and daily incidents of the journey."[27]

Though a significant number of Alaskan-related scientific reports and features had been generated following the 1867 purchase, literature extolling life in Alaska for the general public had yet to come fully of age in the United States. Frederick Whymper published his own travelogue of his adventures in 1868, *Travel and Adventure in the Territory of Alaska*, that offered a readable and lively narrative that received positive acclaim at the time, but it recounted an earlier time during the sun-setting of the Russian presence and the transition from Russian America to the United States. The standard and most frequently cited work on the subject became Dall's 627-page tome *Alaska and its Resources*, published in 1870. The seminal reference work helped introduce Alaska to the American public, with half devoted to Dall's travels and observations in the newly acquired territory and half an encyclopedia, offering a multitude of facts and figures. There were other more focused works, such as those by the missionary Sheldon Jackson and the environmentalist Henry Wood Elliott, as well as magazine articles debating Alaska's value and offering suggestions for its best use. But by the mid-1870s, as Congress stalled on efforts to send scientific parties to explore the interior of Alaska, at least one editorial decried the lack of popular works on Alaska.[28]

The environmentalist John Muir, already renowned for his work in California, first visited Alaska in 1879 with the Presbyterian minister S. Hall Young to study its glaciers along the Alexander Archipelago, returning again in 1880. On a canoe trip in 1879 with Young, he discovered Glacier Bay and the magnificent Muir Glacier. Muir's visit to Alaska became a spiritual journey through an unspoiled virgin landscape, the handiwork of the Creator and a reflection of the Divine. Muir described its beauty and magnificence in a series of letters to the *San Francisco Bulletin,* reprinted in multiple newspapers. Schwatka could also marvel at Alaska's natural beauty and his writings reflected a perceptive eye that captured its exquisiteness. But Schwatka was constrained by a more material mindset, and his admiration did not invoke a spiritual awakening by being in one with nature as it did for the wilderness writer John Muir.[29]

Just as important, Muir's writings brought attention to the relative ease of travel in southeast Alaska along the Inside Passage. By 1884, tourists on Muir's heels were beginning to view a narrow window into Alaska, one that offered stunning beauty, but one whose accessibility by pleasure cruise via steamship stood in sharp contrast to the more remote, lesser-known interior that Schwatka had traversed. As late as 1892, Schwatka himself pointed out this striking difference, writing that "one of the peculiar features of this southwestern section of Alaska, and one that can only be appreciated by the explorer or hardy prospector or trapper, is the picnic-like pleasure with which [summer tourists] can travel the coast and its estuaries, only to plunge into the roughest of 'roughing it' as soon as salt water channels are left and the Alpine interior is essayed." Similarly, the traveler Ella Rhoades Higginson noted the contrast:

> Every year, from June to September, thousands of people "go to Alaska." This means that they take passage at Seattle on the most luxurious steamers that run up the famed "inside passage" to Juneau, Sitka, Wrangell and Skaguay…. However, the person who contents himself with this will know as little about Alaska as a foreigner who landed in New York, went straight to Niagara Falls and returned at once to his own country, would know about America.[30]

It was this lessor known Alaska that Schwatka publicized, and with it, a vision of a boundless economic future. Schwatka's most enduring contribution from his lengthy Yukon traverse, from one end of Alaska to the other, was the rich body of literature he produced over several years, which together with his lecturing brought widespread publicity and interest to the prospects of the territory and firmly fixed Alaska in the American conscience. As one reviewer put it, *Along Alaska's Great River* "…is well calculated to excite interest in this great possession and its future main artery of commerce…." Similarly, a *New York Times* editorial wrote that "it is not until regions as remote as Alaska have been brought to the notice of the public by explorers whose motive is an adventurous disposition or a scientific curiosity that the commercial 'prospector' is stimulated to see what can be done toward developing the resources that are thus made known."[31]

Schwatka's popular works reached a wide audience that included not only the general public, but also interested sportsmen and conservationists, businessmen, scientists, government officials and the wealthy, educated elite, all of whom had an interest and influence in its future. Whereas

Muir lamented the coming footsteps of civilization to unspoiled Alaska, Schwatka looked with excitement at the prospect of a commercial bonanza that was ripe for the taking. While he recognized and appreciated Alaska's beauty, his vision of Alaska was an extension of Manifest Destiny; one of exploiting Alaska's natural resources, fisheries, furs, forests and mineral deposits, and even its tourism value. However, he also recognized that exploitation came with the caveat that proper management was necessary to avoid destruction of the commercial value of those resources. Schwatka's Alaska was a rugged, untamed country, a different type of frontier, less suited to the sodbusters and farmers of the American West who arrived in prairie schooners. Schwatka had rubbed shoulders with Alaska's pioneers; they were weather-beaten prospectors, rugged trappers, enterprising traders, and capitalists willing to invest in nascent commercial opportunities. Over the next ten years, Schwatka's view of Alaska would shape our perceptions of this northern landscape. With an imperialistic flourish, he unhesitatingly remarked that "Alaska will ultimately become a great empire and a prolific source of wealth to the United States."[32]

CHAPTER FOURTEEN

TO THE TOP OF THE CONTINENT

WHILE FREDERICK SCHWATKA bided his time with routine and unadventurous duties, Brigadier General Miles continued to actively push his Alaska agenda in the face of political opposition. Schwatka's expedition had been an important first step for Miles. It had opened the door and established a precedent of government tolerance for U.S. Army participation in Alaska, if not its formal approval. The 1883 Yukon reconnaissance became the first in a series of explorations that would establish the army as a meaningful contributor to the territory's road to statehood. With the Yukon excursion firmly under his belt, no doubt Schwatka believed he was the obvious choice for the next Alaska assignment, but Miles had other plans.

Although the circumstances surrounding the decision to bypass Schwatka are unclear, it is not difficult to conclude that the independent-minded and outspoken Frederick Schwatka had rendered himself persona non grata among military and government officials. In Schwatka's place, Lieutenant William Abercrombie, a twenty-seven-year-old Indian wars veteran, was Miles's choice for an expedition in June 1884 up the unexplored Copper River and its tributaries. The disappointment over Abercrombie's selection could not have fallen harder on Schwatka. He was somewhat heartened by the fact that Abercrombie's expedition completely failed to ascend the Copper River. It was not for lack of trying. Abercrombie's attempt was particularly hair-raising, marked by treacherous ice conditions in frail canoes, dangerously fast currents, and neck-deep ice water. A beaten and disgusted Abercrombie pronounced it "impractical" to ascend the menacing river, but he would later be proven spectacularly wrong.

With Abercrombie's appointment, Schwatka was no longer necessary for Miles's purposes. He was officially relieved as his aide-de-camp on May 8, 1884. Unsure of Schwatka's next assignment, Miles turned to Lieutenant

General Philip Sheridan (successor to Sherman as Commander of the Army), who immediately ordered Schwatka to make a long overdue return to his Third Cavalry company, then stationed at Fort Thomas, Arizona Territory. Schwatka's reassignment to the Arizona Territory was particularly painful since it represented an unofficial and humiliating demotion to line status and garrison duty. Moreover, the order physically removed Schwatka from the Northwest, a place where he was connected to family and friends. Personal matters also weighed heavily upon him. His father, Frederick senior, at age seventy-four, had already lost one foot to amputation. As his son prepared to depart, the elder Schwatka faced another difficult surgery for the removal of the other foot.

Recognition from circles outside the United States served as a lone bright spot. Schwatka was the recipient of the La Roquette gold medal, awarded by the Geographical Society of Paris every two years for achievement in Arctic exploration. Schwatka had been the selection over the renowned Swedish Arctic explorer Adolf Erik Nordenskiöld, who had already been ennobled with the title of baron and granted a life annuity for his work. According to one reporter, whose sentiments were shared by Schwatka, "the only order Schwatka had conferred upon him by a grateful Republic was an order to join his regiment." A year later, the Imperial Geographical Society of Russia also awarded Schwatka a gold medal.[1]

Relieved of duty under Miles, Schwatka prepared for his return to his company at Fort Thomas, the regimental headquarters for the Third Cavalry. The post there could not have been more different than Vancouver Barracks. The post had a reputation as the "worst army post in the West." Built of adobe huts, and simmering in sweltering heat, it was rife with malaria and other diseases. The adjacent town reflected the worst of frontier settlements with its brothels, saloons, and rough characters. Its one highlight was that Schwatka could reconnect there with companions from the Big Horn and Yellowstone Expedition.[2]

The Indian wars had been slowly drawing to an inexorable conclusion, but for the persistent and warlike Apaches. In September 1882, General Crook, along with most of the Third Cavalry, had been assigned to the post to restore order at the agencies and to subdue Geronimo and several hundred of his followers roaming at large in the Sierra Madre. The problematic task was finally brought to a conclusion with Geronimo's surrender in 1886. The "Apache problem" was a long simmering conflict brought on by a variety of factors—expansionists creeping westward and unscrupulous Indian agents and traders who mistreated and cheated the Apaches. The Apaches had also been confined to unsustainable reservations, fearing that Indian self-sufficiency would end the traders' lucrative commercial business with the reservations.³

Despite his brief service in the Arizona Territory, Schwatka was knowledgeable of its Indian affairs. He formed his opinions based on his own experiences, at times ignoring conventional attitudes towards the Indians. Schwatka had witnessed the obvious injustices against the Apaches at the hands of the whites. At a later date, when no longer part of the military establishment, he would express his views publicly. In the *Brooklyn Times Union* of February 1886, he would articulate his strongly held belief, that the "Apache problem" was in large part the making of the whites, and might have been prevented "if the Indian Bureau had not done so offensive and unjust a thing as to remove the Chiricahua Apaches from the high Sierra and Arizona Mountains, where there was hunting, and compel them to live in the barren Gila Valley, where the thermometer stands at 112° in the shade and where there is no game, but tarantulas and lizards." The tribal country of the Chiricahua Apaches had been prosperous lands that were tempting to Euro-Americans, many of whom believed that the Indian presence should be no bar to entry and settlement.⁴

Following the removal of the Apaches to the San Carlos Apache Indian Reservation, a blistering hot, unhealthy, and malarial-infested location, many elected to take their chances off the reservation rather than settle. They formed, in large part, the belligerent elements confronting Crook. A year later, in his article "Among the Apaches" in *Century Magazine,* Schwatka was still sympathetic of the plight of the Apaches, who had faced outside conquerors since the time of the Spanish conquest. Now they faced the combined energies of Mexico and the United States, which Schwatka saw as "the humiliating spectacle of two civilized nations, claiming rank among the nations of the world, sitting in solemn conclave to devise a common plan that would annihilate a batch of breech-clouted bandits, whose numbers would not have made the hundredth city in either land."⁵

At the moment though, he was struggling with his own issues. Despite his new assignment to Fort Thomas, Schwatka's inevitable restless spirit, having been unbound for so long, could never accept a return to a soldier's life on the frontier. Faced with what he perceived as a broken career with the army, Schwatka was looking at a professional occupation, hopefully lucrative, beyond the military. Melding his plans into shape, on May 16 Schwatka made a presumptuous request to the adjutant general's office for six months leave of absence "to conduct explorations in Alaska under citizens of Portland, Oregon." At the end of that period, his resignation would become effective. Schwatka's rather vague mission sounded more like an undefined idea, arguably supported by local Oregonians, that was nothing more than a thinly veiled excuse to remain in the Northwest. To the press, he provided no further details. He simply noted that the citizens of Portland desired that he make another trip to Alaska "to get some definite idea of what the country contained" and to "see what the resources of the country were."[6]

To believe that the U.S. Army would permit a soldier leave to pursue a private venture was completely unrealistic. The response was as immediate as it was predictable. On May 27, Lieutenant General Sheridan flatly disapproved the request, stating "the Lieut. General cannot see any reason why Lieut. Schwatka should be given leave in the interests of a private party thereby obliging other officers to perform his duties." Schwatka was ordered to his company without delay. Reluctantly, he packed his outfit and started for Arizona Territory, but he had not yet given up hope of a more suitable alternative.[7]

Before leaving Vancouver Barracks, Schwatka had approached the prominent Portland capitalist and banker, William "Scotch" Reid, with an unconventional business proposition that may have served as the undisclosed basis for his requested leave. Reid was an enterprising and astute businessman who was a leader in the commercial development of Oregon. The successful capitalist had established several profitable banks, mortgage companies and manufacturing businesses, and had advanced the construction of railroads in Oregon.

Schwatka approached Reid with a plan that might appeal to his more speculative nature. The natural resources of the West had made millionaires of risk-takers adventuresome enough to take a chance. Here was the opportunity for Schwatka to make the financial fortune that had so far eluded him on the government pay scale. Convinced that the relatively mild climate and extensive grasslands of the Aleutian Islands were suitable for cattle grazing, Schwatka's scheme was to import and raise cattle on the islands. Reid and his financial backers would supply the capital, and Schwatka would serve as resident superintendent. Reports had even claimed that Reid, with strong Scottish ties, had travelled to Scotland to obtain those "slathers of capital" to fund the project and that Schwatka had already lined up $35,000 of the $50,000 of the needed funding. The obvious difficulty with Schwatka's scheme, and perhaps its death knell, was the transport of the animals to local markets, both because of the cost and the possible effect on their health. Schwatka had proposed to overcome the economic disadvantage by purchasing a ship but hadn't resolved the heath issue. As one highly skeptical critic put it, "the sea is rough, and a good deal of meat would be shaken off the cattle's bones before they got here." Another critic sniped that if Schwatka pulled it off, he would no longer be a "mere lieutenant," but the "major general 'cowboy' of the world."[8]

The cattle plan was not a completely far-fetched idea, as scattered attempts had previously been made to raise stock in the Aleutians. The Russians had imported cows, sheep, and hogs to Alaska as early as the 1790s to raise at local trading posts. In the Aleutians, several communities had raised cattle and hogs for subsistence in the 1830s. After the American purchase of the territory in 1867, traders to Alaska had also experimented with bringing beef cattle to the Aleutians. Shipped in the spring from San Francisco, the cattle fattened over the summer and were slaughtered after their return in October.

At the time Schwatka was seeking funds for his project, the latest intelligence reported that maintaining cattle herds through the winter months proved more difficult. Severe weather could leave the cattle weak and reduced in numbers; small flocks of sheep managed only slightly better. Nonetheless, in April, Schwatka could be heard talking up the prospects of cattle ranching in the Aleutians, an oasis warmed by the mild Japan Current, the so-called Kuro-Siwo (today the Kuroshio Current). With his own eyes, Schwatka had seen cattle on those islands "fatter than any grass-fed cattle that I have ever seen in the United States proper." To anyone who would listen, he was heard to say that "there is no doubt in my mind but that these islands will be well populated in the cattle interests within a reasonably short time." Since Schwatka's time, cattle grazing on the Aleutians has been tried with varying degrees of success, and today a commercial enterprise operates on the islands of Umnak and Unalaska, maintaining a herd of several thousand beef cattle.[9]

Behind his bold facade, Schwatka's emotional and physical wellbeing were slowly unravelling. Ada had left Frederick in San Francisco as she travelled back to her sometime-home in Rock Island while he proceeded to Fort Thomas. On June 1, during a stay at the Occidental Hotel in San Francisco en route to Arizona, Frederick stumbled over the rocker of a chair attempting to answer a knock at his door, fracturing the radial bone in his right forearm from the fall. It was probably no mere clumsy, isolated foot fault, but rather one of a series of alcohol-fueled incidents.

Shortly thereafter, having reached his station at Fort Thomas, Schwatka was admitted to the nearby post hospital at Fort Grant on both June 10 and July 5, in both cases for "inebriation." One physician even went so far as to characterize his illness as "acute alcoholism." His second spree (perhaps an overdone Independence Day celebration) found him absent from his post without leave on July 5, the first official record of professional dereliction attributable to his drinking. Conceding to the lack of effective alcoholism treatment in the frontier army, Schwatka was discharged in each case within one or two days, with the dubious resolution, "cure completed." Schwatka's chronic alcohol dependence was getting the better of him. At age thirty-five, heavy drinking had left him looking at least a decade older. His condition was further impaired by his unhealthy weight of 255 pounds, which left him, as several papers politely framed it, "bulky in appearance."[10]

By the 1880s, alcoholism was viewed by some as a disease, and treatment facilities were on the rise, but effective therapies for substance abuse were in their infancy. Schwatka's drinking had reached a terrible stage of alcoholism. At some point, Schwatka had begun to suffer from chronic, and at times debilitating, stomach pain. Whether caused by his drinking or whether he turned to the bottle for relief from the ailment is unclear. Schwatka would have known from his medical studies that gastritis is a common cause of stomach pain in alcoholics, but prolonged drinking can lead to more serious conditions, such as peptic ulcer disease.[11]

Shortly after his arrival at Fort Thomas, on June 21, Schwatka did not hesitate to make another brazen demand of his superiors. By telegram fired off to the adjutant general's office, he requested one year's leave, with permission "to cross the seas" on very important private business that required him to be in New York City by July 17 to embark to Liverpool on the luxury liner *City of Rome*. His resignation would be effective at the end of that one-year period. That business overseas is unclear, but reports were that he was entering into undisclosed special service for a foreign power. More likely, it was simply a meeting with potential foreign investors for the Alaska cattle project. On the heels of his June 21 telegram, the anxious and headstrong Schwatka issued a further ultimatum to his superiors, requesting to change his requested leave to six months instead of one year; otherwise, he "would offer [to] resign unconditionally. Would like to get rid of Army in three days." It was a rash request, and no one was more surprised to learn of his resignation than his wife Ada, who could only conclude it was a dreadful mistake, an impetuous outburst of an incoherent mind distorted by heavy drinking. After some weighty soul-searching, Ada made the extraordinary decision to intervene in her husband's professional affairs. Upon learning of his request, on July 11, from Rock Island, she took the extraordinary step of dispatching an impassioned plea by telegram directly to Adjutant General Drum claiming that "Lieut. Schwatka is delirious please do not accept his resignation." Ada also mustered the courage to raise the issue with her father, the prominent lawyer Joseph Brackett.[12]

Calling on his political connections, Brackett sent a hurried telegraph to U.S. Senator John Logan (Illinois) in Washington, D.C., asking Logan to "please see Secretary of War and get few months leave of absence for Lieutenant Frederick Schwatka who is now sick at Ft. Thomas. This is important." In the interim, Ada hastened to Fort Thomas to assess the situation. Their meeting and the course of their conversation can only be imagined. Ada was raised within a close-knit military family. Her father had served in both the U.S. Navy and U.S. Army, and her uncle, Colonel Albert Gallatin Brackett, whom she adored as much as her father, was a career officer with a brilliant reputation. She recognized that the military had its disadvantages, especially in a frontier army with its low pay, lack of promotion, long stretches of inactivity and boredom, isolation, and ruinous outposts, among other downsides. However, it did offer one very important lifeline to a young family—job security. Now, Frederick was throwing it all away for what looked to be a highly improbable venture (it never did come to fruition).[13]

Somehow, through what must have been a strained and highly emotional conversation, the headstrong Frederick argued persuasively that he knew better. Ada grudgingly accepted his decision, not that she would have had much choice. Despite her unconditional affection, marriage had failed to have a stabilizing influence on her husband. Having yielded, she telegraphed Adjutant General Drum from Fort Thomas on July 17, to "countermand" her previous telegraph, which was "incorrect," and to accept Frederick's resignation at the end of six months leave.[14]

Unknown to Ada Schwatka, on July 10, Major General John Pope, commanding the Division of the Pacific, had already internally approved Schwatka's request and had forwarded his recommendation for final approval. Secretary of War Robert Lincoln ultimately approved the six months leave, subject to Schwatka submitting his resignation, to be effective on January 31, 1885, which Schwatka duly tendered. This looked to be the end of Frederick Schwatka's military career, or was it? Not surprisingly, in the midst of his impulsive decision-making, Schwatka had overlooked another possible option, retirement. In December 1884, having burned his bridges with the army brass, Schwatka once again turned to his Oregonian connections for a potential change to his planned resignation, requesting their assistance in re-characterizing his departure as a retirement due to poor eyesight caused by his military service, an apparent attempt to qualify for a pension.

The Oregonians were tied together by a common bond of shared pioneer experiences. They would move mountains for the benefit of their own. On December 16, 1884, Senator Joseph Dolph (Oregon), together with Senator John Logan (Illinois), informed Lieutenant General

Sheridan that Schwatka desired to be placed on the retired list "believing himself to be entitled to the same on account of his eyesight having been greatly impaired while in the service." The senators requested to hold his resignation in abeyance until the retirement board could review his case. Looking to avoid a political miscue, Sheridan pushed the high-level request to Secretary of War Lincoln. By now, the military and political establishments had had enough. Lincoln wasted no time denying it on the basis that "Lieutenant Schwatka received the indulgence of a long leave of absence, based upon the tender of resignation, and that it is now too late for him to withdraw the resignation...." The resignation of a military man might not be newsworthy on its own, but Schwatka had made a name for himself, and his departure was broadcast widely. [15]

Embarrassed by press reporting that he had sought political pressure to reclassify his resignation as a retirement, Schwatka had no qualms about twisting the truth of the matter. He summarily denied the reclassification reports in letters to the editors of the *New York Times* and the *New York Tribune*. Quick to anger, Schwatka's emotions could get the better of him, as he blamed the army for driving him to resign. He told a *Times* reporter that the army did not "want to bring [Abercrombie's] results into competition with those of a civilian's expedition, such as mine would have been.... I didn't like the way I was treated by the department and I tendered my resignation from the service. It was not accepted until Jan. 31 last. I thought there was an effort on the part of the department to keep me out of Alaska."[16]

After seventeen years, almost half of his thirty-five years and his entire adult life, with mixed feelings, Frederick Schwatka retired his military uniform, and quietly returned to private life. With over eight-thousand hard miles in the saddle and as an eyewitness to western expansion, as he plainly put it, he had seen "two iron rails in a wilderness [grow] to a great country." It was an emotional parting, notwithstanding the circumstances, but one he was fully convinced was the right course. Certain of his next career move, he would make a go of it as a freelance writer and lecturer. Moving forward, his only uniform would be the polar dress donned during his lecture appearances, in keeping with an image of the manly explorer, and in many respects the showman and self-promoter. To Schwatka, his newly adopted profession would maintain his all-important independence as well as satisfy his fervent desire for celebrity and fame, even if the financial return would be unpredictable. History was not necessarily on his side. Dr. Isaac Israel Hayes, who also had wide name recognition for his Arctic exploits, had embarked on a professional lecturing and writing career a decade earlier, but could barely make ends meet. He ended his life penniless.[17]

Studio portrait of Frederick Schwatka playing the part of the Arctic explorer.

In an age of more limited entertainments, the public lecture was an immensely popular element within the framework of American culture at the time. Audiences of all ages and backgrounds filled lecture halls to gain an understanding of the wider world around them. They listened to everything from the latest achievements in science, exploration, history, literature, foreign peoples and cultures, and even pressing political and social issues, all in a spirit of self-improvement and self-enlightenment. According to Walt Whitman, in 1855 the lecture system had reached its peak, "then it was a perfect furor." Even by the 1880s it was still going strong. In large cities and innumerable small towns, across the entire fabric of society, evenings were set aside for travelling lecturers at lyceums and other institutions, their words often enhanced by stunning visual extravaganzas like lantern slides and "stereopticon" views. Adventurous explorers could generate excitement and were often attractive draws for a metropolitan society removed from the ever-dwindling wilderness.[18]

By the end of 1884, following his lecture to the American Geographical Society in December, Schwatka was lecturing regularly on Alaska and the Yukon, closing with words that sounded like a promotional tour for the territory as much as descriptions of his explorations. He touted to large and uninformed audiences throughout the East that "there is a grand future for Alaska…. It is a great possession for this great country," and "Alaska will ultimately become a great empire and a prolific source of wealth to the United States." His clever use of hyperboles that magnified the territory's enormity captivated his listeners and became oft repeated clips in the press: "Alaska is larger than all that portion of the United States east of the Mississippi"; "there is good grazing there for cattle to feed ten San Franciscos"; and the Yukon "is so long that its head waters might be in Salt Lake City and its mouth here in New York." His lectures served a purpose though, as one Alaskan missionary observed: "through the lectures of Lieutenant Schwatka, and the letters of officials of the Territory, Alaska seems to be brought more and more prominently before the public."[19]

On the circuit, "The Search for Sir John Franklin," a retelling of his geographical society address of several years before, served as additional lecture fodder. Five years later, his monumental sledge journey and life with the Inuit could still capture the interest of the public. Schwatka never had any hesitation referencing the last resort to which the Franklin party was driven. He would matter-of-factly state that "human bones were found sawed in two to get the marrow out, showing to what extremity the party was driven." Within the context of Schwatka's lectures, the morbid topic seems to have passed largely unnoticed, perhaps simply because of the passage of time. It was old news compared to the more recent sensational charges of cannibalism associated with the expedition of Lieutenant Greely, the few survivors of which had returned in mid-1884. "EATING DEAD COMRADES," and "WERE THEY CANNIBALS?" were just two of the ghoulish headlines splashed across the pages of prominent newspapers that riveted the attention of the American public.[20]

Lecture reviews were generally favorable, praising Schwatka's delivery and his humor: "Mr. Schwatka gave a very interesting description of his explorations.... Some of them were very funny, in fact there was a time during his lecture that the lecturer's listeners were fairly beside themselves with laughter." His words may have enthralled his audiences, but he was not exactly projecting the image of the robust explorer: He "conveys to one the idea upon looking at him of a prosperous commercial man rather than an author and explorer," noted one observer. One reviewer even found a comparison to Arctic wildlife appropriate, noting that Schwatka had "a pleasant face and a head as big as a walrus's." Schwatka soon discovered that lecture tours provided uncertain returns, undercut by competing events, bad weather, or his own illness. After sharing receipts with venues and agencies and accounting for travel costs, he frequently pocketed just a few dollars. A two-day lecture tour to Indianapolis in February 1886 was just one of several that was a complete financial failure.[21]

Through 1885 and 1886, while not lecturing, writing occupied much of his time, and his output was prodigious. Schwatka had gathered enough life experiences from his western and northern travels to fill volumes on a host of subject matters, including the exotic and out of the ordinary. Schwatka had also mastered the art of repurposing his words for different publishers, be they newspapers, magazines or books. He became adept at targeting his works to different audiences to expand his financial opportunities. His contributions to *Forest and Stream* appealed to recreational sportsmen and outdoor enthusiasts, as did *Nimrod in the North*, a full-length work published by the New York publishing house Cassell in mid-1885. It described the varied and exceptional opportunities for game in the Arctic regions, from pursuing or being pursued by the polar bear, bagging the prehistoric muskox or landing the cantankerous walrus. Through Schwatka's own adventures during the Franklin search and while in Alaska, he told of the trials and tribulations faced by the Arctic hunter and fisherman. Reviewers found *Nimrod*, like many of Schwatka's writings, "not of the literary guild. His style is crude; his sentences are often hopelessly involved, but he is bright and spirited, and writes with a swing that keeps the reader awake and interested from beginning to end." One critic, the scientific-minded William Dall, bemoaned the lack of a trained naturalist to assist in preparation of the work, a failing that he believed limited the work's value within the scientific community.[22]

In January 1885, pitching the business-oriented reader, in *Bradstreet's: A Journal of Trade, Finance and Public Economy* Schwatka delivered a fair assessment of Alaska's mineral potential as well as the practical difficulties of extraction, remarking that "in no place in the world is prospecting carried on with greater difficulties." Nonetheless, as if anticipating the great Klondike Gold Rush of 1897-99, he concluded that "it is fair to presume that many valuable mines are yet hidden in the less accessible parts." His juvenile work, *Children of the Cold*, published in several issues of *St. Nicholas Magazine* in the spring of 1885 and later in book form, was directed to the youth market, as well as to the classroom as an educational work.[23]

Of course, popular works by Schwatka were the most frequent. Schwatka delivered two lengthy articles on his exploration of Alaska in the popular *Century Magazine* during the fall of 1885, entitled *The Great River of Alaska;* and a full-length work, *Along Alaska's Great River*, published in early 1886. Although pursuing his own purposes, Schwatka had managed to maintain Alaska in the public eye. In addition, he peppered daily newspapers and magazines with descriptive short pieces, ranging from several sentences to several paragraphs, on an assortment of northern topics: their peoples, places, natural history, natural wonders, unusual episodes and adventures. He also wrote opinion pieces on subjects such as the best means of reaching the North Pole. He closely followed activities of all kinds in the North, keeping scrapbooks filled with hundreds of clippings from around the world, particularly Alaska. For the prolific Schwatka, on any given day, at least one of his features could be found in a newspaper or magazine published somewhere. But Schwatka was not satisfied with maintaining public interest in Alaska with merely his pen. He was formulating plans to offer another first-hand look from the top of its highest mountain.

Viewed from the Gulf of Alaska, Mount St. Elias rises vertically in spectacular fashion for almost three miles, the highest and most majestic peak in an impressive semicircle of snow-capped mountains that comprise the Wrangell and St. Elias Mountain Ranges. Straddling the Alaska-Yukon border, at a height of 18,008 feet, Mount St. Elias holds the position as the second highest mountain in Alaska and the fourth highest in North America. These formidable ranges include fourteen of the twenty tallest peaks in North America and a remarkable assemblage of glaciers, ice fields and volcanoes. Recognizing its lasting importance, in 1980 the region was established as the Wrangell-St. Elias National Park and Preserve, the largest national park in the United States.[24]

Mount St. Elias was first sighted by Europeans on July 16, 1741, by the great explorer Vitus Bering who was sailing in the *St. Peter* during his Great Northern Expedition (Velikaya Severnaya Ekspeditsiya) of 1733-43. Cautiously navigating through a heavy and persistent fog, the misty veil slowly lifted for Bering and his crew, presenting a panoramic range of mountains commanding the horizon, with one prominent volcanic peak rising dramatically above the others. Reports that Mt. Elias was erupting added a sublime effect, though it was later surmised that smoke and dust from falling rocks and debris caused the illusion. It was a spectacular introduction to the New World. The mountain and a nearby cape were given the name St. Elias, their discovery having fallen on the saint's feast day. Many later celebrated explorers, such as Cook, La Perouse, Malaspina, and Vancouver, had also sighted the mountain from the sea. But few attempts, if any, had been made to reach the mountain and no one had ever made a determined effort to set foot on its summit. For just that reason, it captured the attention of Frederick Schwatka.[25]

As a media property, the *New York Times* was a latecomer to the business of exploration sponsorship. In early 1886, at Schwatka's instigation, it was prepared to make a calculated move from simply reporting news to actually creating it through the backing of an expedition of discovery. Its rival,

Bennett's *New York Herald*, had achieved smashing successes and increased sales with Stanley's meeting with Dr. Livingstone in Africa (1872), as well as Gilder's reporting of Schwatka's Search (1880) and the *Jeannette* relief expedition (1882). By no means was the *Times* delinquent in expedition coverage though, even at times resorting to sensationalism in its expedition reporting. When news of cannibalism broke out following the return of the survivors of Greely's expedition in the summer of 1884, the *New York Times* provided particularly gruesome coverage in its pages.

The *Times* contended not only with rival newspapers like the *Herald* for readership, but with an expanding magazine industry that could attract readers with lavish illustrations and more diverse literary, artistic and scientific subject matter and talent. As one thoughtful editor put it, to effectively compete, the newspaper industry "must have a broader conception of news as meaning not merely the events of the day, but the intellectual, social and moral movements of the time." More relevant to Schwatka's purposes however, the editor also opined that "if new regions are to be opened up to commerce, [the newspaper] may send the explorers whose investigations will decide the line of investment." The *Times,* enviably eyeing the success of the *Herald* under Bennett, and fully attentive to the business side of journalism, was prepared to take these more aggressive steps.[26]

Sensing an opportunity, Schwatka, now an enterprising freelance author, pitched the *Times* with the idea of visiting Alaska for the purpose of "tell[ing] the world something of its Indian races, of its forests, its soil and its glaciers." *Times* editor George Jones was convinced that Schwatka was the right man at the right time for the newspaper to back for such a trip. With a carefully cultivated persona of the daring explorer who pushed the limits, and who could deliver exciting copy with a touch of embellishment just as good as any correspondent, Schwatka offered a combination sure to increase readership.[27]

An initial relationship between the *New York Times* and Schwatka played out over the summer of 1885. Schwatka contributed a series of in-depth features focused on the lifestyle of the Inuit that highlighted their complimentary traits, such as truthfulness, honesty, and faithfulness in their dealings. As human-interest stories, they went beyond the normal scope of daily news reporting and offered the potential for an expanded audience. Evidently pleased with the results, the two parties concluded a more significant agreement by which the *Times* would sponsor Schwatka on an expedition to Alaska. He would, in essence, create the story, a first on the part of the *Times*. Schwatka's objective would be to explore and perform scientific work among what were known as the "St. Elias Alps," a title that

Schwatka felt greatly underrated the grandeur of the Wrangell-St. Elias ranges. Though not its primary purpose, in Schwatka's words, "it would be considered no small victory to crown the king of the American continent, Mount St. Elias, with shoe leather of American make." For Schwatka, the ascent of Mount St. Elias would be an act of conquest and dominion, a classic struggle of man over nature.[28]

His view echoed a common refrain in the nineteenth century Euro-American climbing world, an aspect of a colonial expansionist attitude toward foreign places and people. Geographic prizes like the attainment of the North or South Pole, or similar climbing achievements, also sparked public interest. Undertaken amidst high risk and daring, the ever-present threat of disaster could also heighten any storyline. At the time, Mount St. Elias was thought by many to be the highest peak on the continent. With its relative proximity to the coast (approximately forty to fifty miles from tidewater), it was a tempting target for a significant mountaineering first. Even the *Times's* competitors offered favorable commentary, concluding that a scientific expedition to Alaska made more sense than "sending men to die terrible deaths in vain attempts to reach the North Pole." Schwatka took great satisfaction in the expedition, knowing that he was following in Bering's footsteps, an explorer whose determination and fortitude had earlier served as his inspiration.[29]

But this departure would be more emotionally trying than previous separations. On April 16, Ada and Frederick celebrated the birth of a first child, a daughter, Frederika, born in New York City. Clearly proud of his first and only child, for two months he played the role of the doting father. A scene of domestic tranquility briefly filled his normally bachelor-like existence. On June 5, Ada, Frederick and Frederika returned to Rock Island, and Frederick departed the following morning for the West Coast.

Professor William Libbey, the son of a wealthy New York city merchant, constituted the complete scientific corps of the expedition and was the only member recruited before departure. A request to Yale Professor Othniel C. Marsh to supply a naturalist went unfilled. Following his usual practice, Schwatka's expectation was to bring on a handful of local assistants in Alaska. Libbey had studied under the eminent Swiss geologist and geographer Arnold Henry Guyot. Succeeding Guyot as professor of physical geography at Princeton University, Libbey earned the first American professorship in the field of geography. He was a thoughtful choice on Schwatka's part, and his selection would lead to legitimate scientific results from the expedition. Libbey also possessed an adventurous nature and was attracted to far flung locales, having already participated in field work in dangerous and unsettled portions of the West. He was the first scientist to scale the 14,400-foot Mount Princeton in Colorado (named after his alma mater). He would go on to study an active volcano in Hawaii in 1893, serve as geographer on Robert Peary's Auxiliary Expedition to Northwest Greenland in 1894, and lead a scientific team on a Peary support expedition in 1899. An expert marksman, his shooting prowess would earn him medals in rifle competitions at the 1912 and 1920 Olympics. However, his most recognized and lasting contribution to Princeton was his introduction of orange and black as the "Princeton colors."[30]

Leaving New York City, Schwatka took his role as correspondent seriously, and was not content to limit his reporting to the expedition. Although his first letter remarked that his cross-country route would be uninteresting to my readers, he would soon pen as many articles and offer as many facts about the American West as the Alaskan expedition itself. Personally invested in its growth and settlement, he had travelled extensively through the deserts of the Southwest, the great plains of the Midwest, followed mountain ranges to its northern border and trekked through the Northwest coast and Alaska. Few could have offered the history or the insights into the growth of the West as Schwatka.

His dispatches are not only filled with details of its most magnificent features, like the grandeur of the Yellowstone, but also its smallest treasures shared only among locals, like a favorite fishing hole hidden among the ten thousand lakes region of Minnesota. His dispatches painted a sentimental journey, reflecting his own migration on the Oregon Trail as a boy and the mixed consequences of rapid progress and civilization. The city of Fargo, for example, was now the beneficiary of electric lights and street railways, in a country "where twenty years ago the wild Indian roamed alone and little dreamed that he would be fed on Government rations, wrapped in Government blankets and sent further west to grow scarce with the Buffalo." He lamented the inroads of civilization and the consequent demise of the Sioux, writing, "But the [Lakotas] of the Dakotas will in a few decades be heard of only in history as the greatest Indian nation in our borders with a few representatives here and there."[31]

With the completion of the transcontinental railroad, cross-country travel had become comfortable and convenient, a point emphasized by Schwatka, so much so that his letters read like free publicity for the railroad. His travel by the Northern Pacific Railroad from St. Paul to Tacoma, and his continual favorable references to the railroad in his articles, were no mistake. Coinciding with the *Times's* expedition, the railroad was pitching western sightseeing excursions by rail. Schwatka and the author John Hyde had just produced a flashy publicity booklet (commonly labelled a "travel guide") for the Northern Pacific Railroad. Entitled "Thro' Wonderland with Lieut. Schwatka," it featured a celebrity endorsement by Schwatka, trumpeting the picturesque sights to be had by train from St. Paul to Puget Sound, and a description of the Inside Passage to Alaska. Ephemeral though the piece was, the illustrated cover, with its visual representation of the pathfinding explorer blazing a trail through rough, broken country, served to bolster Schwatka's own intrepid image in the public eye, and with it his future marketability.

Departing the train in Tacoma, on their next leg Schwatka and Libbey travelled to Sitka by steamer, a three-week journey during which they made a worthwhile introduction to a British traveler, Heywood Walter Seton-Karr, coincidentally on his own way to the "Alps of Alaska" in an attempt to reach the summit of Mount St. Elias. Seton-Karr possessed a persuasive personality. The impromptu shipboard meeting led Schwatka to extend an invitation to him to join the *Times's* expedition, which was readily accepted. In retrospect, one wonders how Seton-Karr could have managed to climb St. Elias on his own if he had not joined with Schwatka.

With lineage from two distinguished families and an education at Eton and Oxford, the thirty-two-year-old Seton-Karr represented the aristocratic sportsman and traveler of the type escorted by Schwatka on the Plains. Typically unimpressed by gentleman adventurers of high-class breeding, Schwatka looked beyond Seton-Karr's ancestry and found a common bond. The two shared a keen passion for hunting and adventure and a constitution willing to endure hardships in the process. Seton-Karr had been trained at Sandhurst and had spent several years stationed in Egypt and Gibraltar. With an inquisitive nature much like Schwatka's, on a diversion from his military duties, he uncovered the legendary flint mines of ancient Egypt and important Stone Age implements in Somaliland. Independent wealth and a passion for big game had led him to all corners of the earth in the hunt. He even had a stake in the American West with his ownership of a cattle ranch in Wyoming. He would have raised a few eyebrows, though, with his firmly held belief that he could communicate with the dead. Seton-Karr was a fortuitous acquisition to the otherwise inexperienced climbing group. Schwatka noted that Seton-Karr already had seen considerable Alpine experience in Switzerland and the Tyrol. His attempt on Mount St. Elias was for the purpose of gaining acceptance in the prestigious and exclusive Alpine Club of London.[32]

They docked at Sitka, the former Russian trading post which was well known to Schwatka. The far-flung settlement brought back mixed memories, one of a pleasing Yukon trip and the other of an unpleasant departure from the military. Schwatka was a welcome guest of Alfred

Swineford, governor of the district of Alaska. In Sitka, the expedition took shape. Schwatka's original plan had been to ferry his party some two hundred miles by Indian war canoe to Yakutat Bay, a method that could have proved unpredictable and dangerous in the open water with a full load of supplies. Fortunately, Schwatka's military service again opened doors for him. William Collins Whitney, secretary of the Navy, offered the services of the U.S.S. *Pinta*, an aged steam tug that served as the police for the district, principally patrolling the seal fisheries. Seton-Karr believed it a good omen that their westward exploring ship was named after a discovery ship of Columbus to the New World. The *Pinta* was commanded by Lieutenant Commander Henry Ezra Nichols, an 1865 U.S. Naval Academy graduate. Nichols was thoroughly familiar with the southeast coastal waters of Alaska, having commanded the *Pinta* since September 1884, and for three summers previously had completed survey work along the coast for the U.S. Coast and Geodetic Survey.

At Sitka, several additional members were retained, among them the Alaskan pioneer John "Jack" Dalton, and Joseph Woods, a miner, as well as a Tlingit youth from the Presbyterian mission named Ker-Sunk (Kersunk). With a command of the English, the seventeen or eighteen-year-old Kersunk, better known as "Frederick," served as interpreter and packer. Dalton was one of those colorful Alaskan characters, like others that Schwatka met in the district, who would become legendary during the upcoming Klondike Gold Rush. Like many early Alaskan pioneers, he was an enterprising fellow. Hardworking, rough, prone to a hot temper and the occasional violent altercation, he was a jack-of-all trades, having tried his hand at ranching, sealing, and logging, always on the move for one reason or another. Perhaps looking to gain a sense of the country and take some measure of the recent mineral diggings in the Yakutat Bay area, he assumed the role of cook and campkeeper for Schwatka's expedition. In 1890 and 1891, the adventuresome Dalton participated in two expeditions, traversing sections of southeast Alaska. He later established a toll-based trail (the so-called Dalton Trail) and maintained a supply and pack horse business along the route to the Klondike Gold Fields from Pyramid Harbor to Ft. Selkirk. Together with other business interests, these made him a wealthy man.[33]

Leaving Sitka behind, on July 12 Schwatka's party entered the landlocked harbor of Yakutat Bay, with Mount St. Elias and the dramatic mountain range forming a spectacular backdrop. Under broad daylight at 2:00 A.M., Schwatka painted a scenic view of St. Elias, noting that "as we were entering Yakutat Bay, Mount St. Elias burst into full view, a most glorious Alpine spectacle, covered to the very base with ice and snow and

The *Times*'s expedition (L to R): Frederick(?), Seton-Karr, Libbey, Woods, Dalton, Schwatka.

raising his glistening white head for nearly 20,000 feet." Natural beauty notwithstanding, as Schwatka eyed possible approaches to its summit from a distance his expectations were quickly tempered by the daunting problem that all practical routes to the summit looked altogether unpromising.[34]

Distant from the far larger town of Sitka, the Yakutat Tlingit settlement at Yakutat Bay was less frequently visited through the time of Schwatka's arrival. That aspect, surmised Schwatka, would offer an opportunity for an examination of the Yakutat Tlingit culture and habits. The Yakutat Tlingit were by no means naïve and unacquainted with non-Native visitors; they were adept in their dealings, as Schwatka would soon find to his consternation. Following Bering's discovery of the Alaskan coastline and the initiation of the Pacific maritime fur trade, commercial exploitation of the sea otter had attracted Russian traders to southeast Alaska and Yakutat Bay. Sporadic trading with the Yakutat Tlingit continued under American auspices, but it was the lure of gold that attracted eager prospectors to work the enticing mineral-rich black sands near Yakutat in the early 1880s. In 1884, the Alaska Commercial Company had tried its hand at a trading post at Yakutat but had given it up as unprofitable the following year. In their place, Schwatka's party was surprised to find two adventurous Swedes who had taken over the post.[35]

At Yakutat Bay, Schwatka's group encountered the Yakutat Tlingit community and their chief, Yen-at-set'l, who would prove to be a formidable negotiator. Always open to reshaping his plans, at Yakutat Schwatka decided to continue by boat some sixty miles to the northwest in order to establish a land base of operations closer to Mount St. Elias.

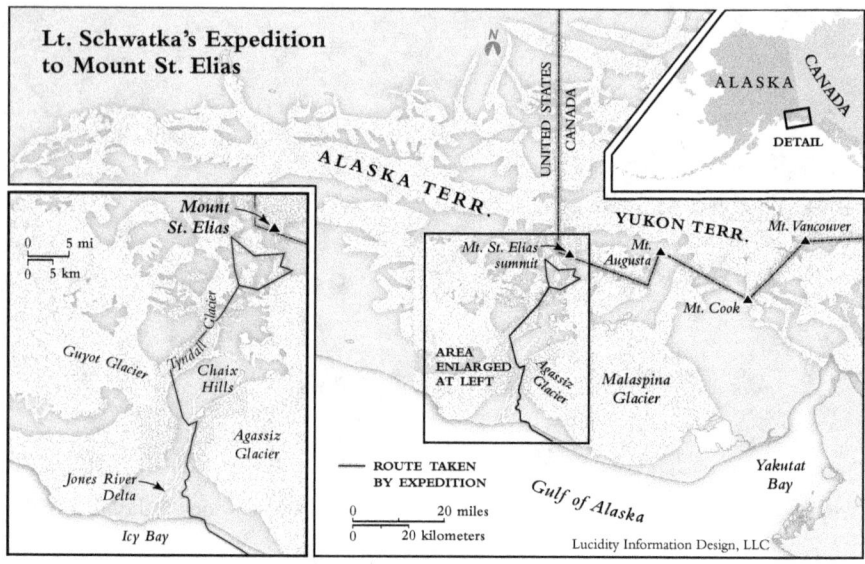

After introductions had been exchanged, bargaining for a war canoe transport and four or five packers to assist in this attempt tested Schwatka's patience to the utmost. The acquisition of a suitable transport was stymied by a series of delays and excuses on the part of the Yakutat Tlingit, viewed by Schwatka as intentional. Hiring packers proved equally difficult.

The Yakutat Tlingit balked at an ascent of Mount St. Elias out of what Schwatka characterized as an inordinate fear of the mountain, believing disaster would befall the expedition. Writing for the *Times,* Schwatka was astute enough to recognize that their trepidation was not based on cowardice, rather the Yakutat Tlingit held "in reverential awe" the "Big Mountain," or "Shaa Tlein," as a sacred site. To their Yakutat Tlingit companions, Mount St. Elias was viewed in a far different light than that of the Euro-Americans intent on the physical challenge and conquest. Dominating the landscape, the omnipresent specter of the prominent peak loomed large over the life of the Yakutat Tlingit, ever maintaining a watchful eye from aloft, assuming an almost lifelike presence and a situs of spiritual power. The Yakutat Tlingit had formed a special bond with the mountain, a connection which Schwatka understood. Regarding Schwatka's depiction of the Yakutat Tlingit in his writings, the noted anthropologist and Yakutat Tlingit scholar, Frederica de Laguna, commented that although writing for a general audience that "want to hear about the Indians as wild, superstitious, blanket-clad savages, there is a nevertheless real ambivalence in the attitudes of [Schwatka, Seton-Karr and Libbey] towards the Yakutat people."[36]

Chief Yen-at-set'l. Photograph by William Libbey.

Nonetheless, over several days Schwatka pushed hard for packers to accompany him to at least the base of the mountain. Overblown assertions by the Tlingit as to the impossibility of completing the trek from Icy Bay to the mountain itself were simply negotiating tactics to justify exhorbitant fees. Holding all the cards, the Yakutat Tlingit would only agree at rates Schwatka claimed were four or five times above standard. The stalemate was broken when the *Pinta* arrived in Yakutat Bay and offered an alternative means of transport, several Tlingit from Sitka, setting off a competitive rivalry for packers and shifting the bargaining power. The new arrivals were prepared to take on the task at more favorable rates, compelling the Yakutat Tlingit to underbid their competition for the task.

While concluding arrangements for packers, at the same time, the Yakutat Tlingit were extremely anxious to make the most of the trading opportunity that had fortuitously presented itself with the arrival of Schwatka's group. The unexpected trade negotiations produced the most significant ethnographic results of the expedition, a valuable collection of Yakutat Tlingit artifacts. The treasures did not come easy though. An exasperated Schwatka found that their acquisition also called for interminable "haggling" or "chinmusic." Collecting anthropological curiosities was an avid Euro-American pursuit during the late nineteenth century. In the remote confines of Yakutat Bay, the competition took on a spirited bidding when Lieutenant George Thornton Emmons, executive officer on the *Pinta*, joined the fray with Professor Libbey and Seton-Karr.

Emmons, an 1874 graduate of the U.S. Naval Academy, was first appointed to the Alaskan station in 1882. His father was Rear Admiral George Foster Emmons, who had served on the monumental U.S. Exploring Expedition of 1838 to 1842 with Lieutenant Charles Wilkes. With his own growing interest in Tlingit culture, Emmons had struck up a friendly relationship with Professor Libbey, who may have offered Emmons guidance on the collection and cataloguing of specimens.

A number of colorful baskets, charms and carved pieces were obtained by the group in a mutually acceptable exchange with the Tlingit. However, the "great find," according to Seton-Karr, was the discovery of an untouched grave of a shaman. In a secluded corner of the bay, the sacred burial place was surreptitiously looted by Emmons and Libbey in their eagerness to obtain high-quality pieces. One item deemed particularly attractive, a copper war dagger, was literally snatched from the clutches of the dead man's hand. Returning to the *Pinta* with two stuffed sacks, the gleeful discoverers spread the find across the floor of Emmons's cabin and the amateur collectors gaped at elaborate painted masks, a highly decorated shawl, an elaborate ceremonial baton and several carved crowns of goat horns. Perhaps troubled by the grave robbing, Seton-Karr justified the conduct on the grounds that the treasures would be "left to rot if not rescued as curios, as no Indian will touch them." For Schwatka's part, the items he had bartered or collected on the *Times's* expedition were reportedly donated to Libbey for Princeton's collection. Schwatka did not seem to possess the same zeal for artifact collecting that was so enthusiastically pursued by Libbey and Emmons and other Euro-Americans in the late nineteenth century. Perhaps his interaction with Indigenous peoples and respect for their burial rights may have led him to respect their property as more than mere exotic curiosities. [37]

After several days, now with three hired Yakutat Tlingit (bringing their group to nine), Schwatka's group prepared to move on to Icy Bay, courtesy of the *Pinta*. In retrospect, Schwatka could not know it at the time, although Icy Bay was a closer starting point to Mount St. Elias, the approach from Icy Bay would prove far more difficult than had the group started from Yakutat Bay. Several obstacles presented themselves from Icy Bay, the first and most dangerous being the large swells and roaring breakers on their approach to their landing spot. The bay itself was a mere coastal bight, fully exposed to the sea. After four trips by the *Pinta's* whaleboat, the supplies and instruments were safely landed by its dauntless sailors after a terrible struggle. In contrast to the tribulations of the *Pinta's* crew, a Tlingit war canoe that Libbey had managed to buy was likewise beached by the efforts of one Tlingit who literally surfed in on a gnarly wave.

A camp was established on the flat, sandy beach, surrounded by dense thickets of spruce, cedar and cottonwood stands. Those softwoods quickly gave way to scattered brush and a profusion of berry bushes, and then the ice-covered rocks, rubble and moraines of the imposing glaciers that formed the backdrop. At the time of the landing of Schwatka's party, a spectacular glacier almost three hundred feet high projected right into the sea (named the Guyot Glacier after Libbey's mentor), forming the west side of the bay. Viewing their surroundings, Professor Libbey correctly observed that many of the glaciers along the southeast coast of Alaska were "only the relics of their former greatness."[38]

To the blasts of its screaming horn, the *Pinta* sailed away, leaving the whaleboat and the *Times* expedition to its uncertain fortunes. The *Pinta* carried a last dispatch from Schwatka intended to build excitement for the upcoming ascent, a table listing the highest peaks in the United States, "designed to aid the reader who follows the movements of The *Times's* Expedition." Mount St. Elias boldly topped the list, exceeding its closest competitors by 4,000 feet.[39]

In this mysterious land, in a setting reminiscent of a Jules Verne novel, the party feasted upon unnaturally large strawberries and warily observed ominously large bear prints, more than fifteen inches long. According to Schwatka, they were tracks of the legendary St. Elias grizzly, "a monster among that monstrous kind." On July 19, the expedition got under way, leaving Dalton to man the base camp. For the first day, the party was split into two groups, one camp apart, so that measurements could be taken every thirty minutes to record the difference in barometric height. Schwatka's group left first, followed by Libbey's group a day later. Collectively, they carried rations for two weeks, together with blankets, sleeping bags, some "esquimaux clothing" for the ice, three rifles, two tents and Libbey's scientific instruments: barometers, thermometers, a hypsometer (a device for measuring altitudes) and a prismatic compass. Several ice axes and two hundred feet of rope constituted their modest climbing equipment. Although Seton-Karr boasted of having some alpine experience, he himself admitted that "our combined *alpinism* was insignificant." That weakness would contribute in part to their undoing. Schwatka envied Seton-Karr's apparent fitness, finding him to be "physically in very good trim." Schwatka could not make the same boast. At a hefty 255 pounds, he was no lightweight, and was too hefty and out of shape for an arduous and extended climb.[40]

After a half mile in canoes, their first march along the eastern shore of the bay and across a lush grassland, with its profusion of wildflowers, ripe strawberries, and scattered stands of timber, brought them to what

"Mount Saint Elias (20,000 feet) from Yakutat." Sketch by H. Seton-Karr.

Schwatka characterized as a large river emptying into Icy Bay, a "second Mississippi in appearance." That inflated description of this waterway would later prove to be a testy bone of contention. To Schwatka, its immense size, at a mile-and-a-half wide, came as a great surprise; half its width was water, the balance mud, sand and gravel. Schwatka claimed, with no real basis, that its size confirmed it was not simply runoff from the St. Elias glacier system, but rather a major river with its headwaters far beyond the mountain range, the glacial runoff mixing with the river until it ran miles out to sea. Never shy about naming, Schwatka bestowed the name of Jones River after George Jones, editor of the *Times* (ignoring the Tlingit name Yas´ei Héen (Yahtse River), by which it is still known). Highlighting the discovery for readers of the *Times*, he added that "geographically [it] was one of the most important discoveries of the expedition." Seton-Karr regarded it simply as the drainage of the snow and ice on and around the mountains, but Libbey would later defend it as a significant, unmapped river. As a result of glacial retreat since Schwatka's visit, the region of Icy Bay, and with it the Jones River, have been so substantially altered that the appearance in Schwatka's time is no longer known.[41]

The party trekked northward along the bank of the river, wading through a veritable quicksand of thigh-deep mud and icy cold water from numerous channels and streams that numbed the feet. A switch to higher ground and the heavily wooded forest and thickets proved no better, as the trail was nearly impassable. The fifteen-mile trek the first day ended at the spot where the Jones River emerged from under two great glaciers named by Schwatka, the Guyot Glacier to the west, and the second, to the east, named the Agassiz Glacier, an arm of the sprawling Malaspina Glacier, the largest piedmont glacier in the world.

With the Tlingit packers now extremely weary, Schwatka elected to rest the following day while awaiting Libbey's party. On July 22, after consolidating the two groups, by means of a difficult scramble they managed to climb several hundred feet onto the seam of the two glaciers. Travelling across the glaciers, switching from one to the other as conditions warranted, they encountered a rough road of rock and ice, slippery with mud, that left them struggling to maintain their balance. By now, the fatigued packers had worn through their footwear and were flagging under their 65-to-75-pound packs. Keeping with Euro-American tradition, Schwatka and Seton-Karr left the heavy lifting to the Yakutat Tlingit. Schwatka and Seton-Karr each carried a rifle, while one also held a barometer and the other the ice-axes.

Blocked in their approach to the mountain by branches of the Jones River, on July 23 the party was split in two to search east and west for a favorable path across the river. Behind the river sat a large glacial lake, upon which Schwatka bestowed the name Castina Lake after the president of the Italian Geographical Society, though his name was actually Onorato Caetani. A minor alarm was raised when Libbey was lost for more than a day on the Agassiz Glacier while the party was separated; he returned late on the evening of July 24 with a slightly sprained ankle after spotting a signal fire. A more serious concern was raised after Schwatka began to look "seriously ill" according to Seton-Karr, suffering from a sharp fever, chills, and chest pains. Karr's diagnosis as "ague" suggested perhaps a recurrent bout of malaria. His account, highlighting Schwatka's illness, was described in Karr's self-serving 1887 narrative, *Shores and Alps of Alaska* and was repeated for newspaper reporters. Despite the debilitating illness, for the moment, a determined Schwatka had decided to continue on.[42]

All the while, to Schwatka, Mount St. Elias seemed as far away as ever, as their slow progress began to dim his hopes that they would have enough supplies for the climb, even if they reached its base. Swinging around some small tree-covered hills isolated amongst the glaciers (the Chaix Hills), on July 25 they finally managed to span the river and reach another glacier that ran down the southwest flank of Mount St. Elias (named the Tyndall Glacier). More modest in size than the Agassiz and Guyot Glaciers, Schwatka still found it immense enough to bury the city of New York. After easier travelling along the glacier, they stopped at an isolated green spot that offered a fairly comfortable camp, with stunted willows, coarse grass and moss. The Tlingit avowed that this oasis in a sea of ice had never been visited by their people, and "had no place in the traditions of their race." Schwatka believed that in all his travels, this isolated haven was the "loneliest place in the United States." In a frank admission, he acknowledged that it was the only place where he could legitimately claim that the footsteps of Indigenous peoples had not tread before him. Their location, their fifth camp, near the base of the mountain offered Schwatka a glimmer of hope, as the summit appeared to be reachable via a direct course along the Tyndall Glacier. The camp became completely shrouded by fog and snow, creating a sublime effect that reminded Schwatka of a region as desolate as the polar regions and which caused some uneasiness among the Yakutat Tlingit. A heavy frost overnight raised some concerns as to the conditions on the higher elevations on the mountain. As Schwatka and Karr prepared to move forward on Mount St. Elias, the packers refused to proceed further out of "superstitious dread," noted a dismissive Seton-Karr.[43]

In a bid to achieve some amount of height on the mountain, on the morning of July 26 Schwatka, Seton-Karr, Woods and the boy Frederick, with only one days' provisions for each in twenty-pound packs, set off on a dash for the summit. Their plan was simple, but adventurous; make a bid for the summit and return within a continuous span of forty hours. They left in high spirits, as climbing conditions were ideal, "clear as a proverbial crystal," noted Schwatka, with not a cloud surrounding the peak. They made a long detour around the Tyndall Glacier to the west, finally scrambling up the edge of the glacier until the center was reached. As it became more difficult to distinguish the fissures on the ice surface as the ascent began, at about 8:00 A.M., the party was roped, with Woods in front, followed by Schwatka, the boy Frederick and then Seton-Karr, the most experienced climber. Schwatka, with his usual self-deprecating humor, remarked that he needed an inordinate length of rope as he "has an extremely unfashionable waist that requires about three yards of rope to go around it and make the necessary ties and knots." Not looking to jeopardize the life of young Frederick, the young boy was quickly sent back to their base camp.[44]

The climb along the glacier towards the summit was slow, marked by fragile snow bridges and widening crevasses, which required circuitous detours. Playing on the danger, Schwatka noted that they "walked as on the comb of a roof or a small log thrown over a stream." Seton-Karr feared for their safety, as Schwatka and Woods had no experience with ropes or axes. From their vantage point, Schwatka could see every glacier on the mountain and the prospect was daunting. Insurmountable ice cascades several hundred feet in height appeared to block all potential routes. At about 2:00 P.M., for that reason, they exited the Tyndall Glacier. The only possible course that approached the summit ran across a precipitous stretch of rock ridges and crags protruding through the ice. They placed their faith in the alpine veteran Seton-Karr, who carefully directed their course. According to Seton-Karr, at 3:00 P.M., a narrow ridge was reached where an hour rest was taken as Schwatka "was now in such an alarming condition," continuing to suffer from fever. Seton-Karr, now playing the hero in his own dramatic narrative, remarked that he feared for Schwatka's life if Schwatka was forced to overnight on the mountain.[45]

Leaving Schwatka at 5,800 feet, Seton-Karr proceeded with Woods until reaching an altitude of 6,800 feet, at which time a concerned Seton-Karr sent Woods back to nurse Schwatka. Seton-Karr continued alone until about 6:30 P.M., reaching 7,200 feet (measured by aneroid barometer). The inability to locate a safe route to the summit made further progress impracticable. From his vantage point, Seton-Karr looked downward and gained a magnificent panorama of the expansive St. Elias glacier basin. To his north, Seton-Karr viewed an unexplored mountainous region, "a galaxy of snow peaks, a sea of glittering glaciers, a collection of huge pinnacles." The daunting prospect of traversing that country left him "doubtful if anyone will ever penetrate any long distance." Most certainly, Seton-Karr would never have believed that his overweight and thoroughly fatigued companion, Frederick Schwatka, huffing and puffing 1,400 feet below, would prove him wrong five years later.[46]

Turning his back on the mountain, Seton-Karr rejoined Schwatka and Woods, and a hasty retreat was made by all three to their base camp by midnight. The next morning, reunited with the packers, they hustled to their preceding camp number four. That evening, as they rested in their tents, according to Seton-Karr, the jittery Yakutat Tlingit exclaimed that "they felt the ground 'moving and shaking.'" An exaggerated Seton-Karr remarked that "if it was not mere imagination, the lieutenant was shivering and shaking from chills and fevers with almost sufficient violence to convey the sensation of an earthquake to the acute senses of the Indians." Schwatka confirmed Seton-Karr's report that on the mountainside he had suffered from chills, but reported that it was due to perspiration. However, driven by vanity, to the *Times* readership, Schwatka downplayed his illness on the mountain, claiming, perhaps not very convincingly, that the shivering and chills he suffered there were merely the result of heavy sweating and from sitting in snow and ice amidst the dense condensation of the fog. Upon return to the camp number four, he had suffered another severe chill and perspiration and was running a slight temperature at 100°, for which he took some quinine. Failing to recover that evening, an additional dose the following day remedied the situation, so he claimed.[47]

Having completed the attempt on the mountain and trekked back to the beach, the entire party made a hasty return to Yakutat Bay. There Seton-Karr left on the trader's schooner for Kodiak, while Schwatka and Libbey awaited the return of the *Pinta*. For an expedition that sought lively dispatches sure to stoke the public's interest, the *New York Times* expedition certainly managed to capture its attention, but not for the reasons originally contemplated. Upon their return to Sitka, Schwatka and the *Times* pulled out all stops, running with the front-page headline "Success of the '*Times*' Expedition to Alaska," which featured "Lieut. Schwatka's perilous ascent of St. Elias to the Highest Point Ever Reached," together with the discovery of the Jones River, "not thought to be rivaled by any Alaskan River emptying into the Pacific Ocean." When Schwatka's report in the *Times* claimed the glory for the newly discovered Jones River, its rival newspaper, the *Sun,* excited at the prospect of embarrassing its competitor, immediately responded. The *Sun* produced a U.S. Coast Survey map showing an unnamed river flowing to Icy Bay, the same river "discovered" by Schwatka. The *Times,* stung by the criticism responded:

> And the great point is that, whatever guesses may have been made about Jones River, Lieut. SCHWATKA was the first to describe it and give it a name. This honor cannot be stolen from him by any such methods as *The Sun* has adopted. For it cannot be said that a man who merely guessed at a river and inserted it upon his map was its discoverer...."[48]

The *Sun* countered with a rebuttal attack, namely that Castina Lake, "discovered" by Schwatka, was also disclosed on an existing map. That charge was quickly dispelled by the *Times:* "This is a gross blunder or a self-exposing falsehood," snapped the *Times*, as Schwatka's lake is "some forty miles, probably, from the location of the small lake shown on the *Sun's* map....We have no use for the lake which the *Sun* has attempted to palm off upon its readers as Castina Lake....We propose that it be called Spleen lake, in honor of the editor of The *Sun*." The wordy controversy raged for several weeks, the *Sun* continuing its claim that the Jones River had already been discovered, writing "it must be a melancholy reflection to Mr. George Jones that an expenditure of sixty cents for a copy of chart 527 of the United States Hydrographic Office would have saved him all the cost of Lieut. Schwatka's travelling expenses to Alaska and back."⁴⁹

The *Times* went so far as to track down an officer at the U.S. Hydrographic Office, B. A. Colonna, who asserted that since no chart reflected a name for the Jones River, and ignoring the Tlingit name of the river, Schwatka was perfectly entitled to the honor. The *Times* vehemently requested a retraction of the *Sun's* "misstatements" and an apology to Schwatka, but the *Sun* continued its criticism. On October 23, Schwatka finally joined the fray, snagged by a reporter as he changed trains on his way to New York. He defended his position, stating that "the Jones River is a new discovery, that I followed it for thirty miles, that it is not down on any record or map, but that it will be on every official map of this country and be recognized the world over." The controversy finally ran out of steam and ink in mid-November.⁵⁰

However, the media spotlight on the Mount St. Elias expedition ended on another more tragic circumstance, one which reflected badly on its members. Wholly omitted from the reports of the *Times's* expedition, three Yakutat Tlingit had died by poisoning, a troubling story that was only brought to light by a Sitka correspondent to the *St. Paul Globe* (and republished by the *Sun*). Only after the *Globe* report did Schwatka acknowledge the incident, buried within an article on the habits and customs of the Yakutat Tlingit of Alaska. As Schwatka described it, while at Icy Bay, fearing that wolves might menace the camp when the expedition was in the field, Dalton had placed arsenic (intended for preserving specimens) in a can labeled yeast powder and set it outside the confines of the camp. During Libbey's return to the camp in advance of Schwatka and Seton-Karr, a Tlingit named Kernuk (not their young Tlingit interpreter), picked up the can but was told by Libbey of its contents and to throw it away; he was subsequently found with the can again, and again instructed to discard it. Unknown to Libbey, Kernuk returned to Yakutat with the can and its poisonous contents. While Kernuk was away on a hunting trip, a Yakutat Tlingit woman found the can, and unaware of its deadly ingredients, used it to bake some bread, sickening six persons, sadly, largely from one family: "Bear Hunter," who had been an expedition member, his wife and their three children, and a Tlingit from Sitka.⁵¹

Upon learning of the poisoning, Professor Libbey tended to them. All were given hot coffee, three of the suffering Tlingit were induced to vomit with an eagle feather and recovered (two of the children and the Sitka man). As for the other three, one child died; Bear Hunter and his wife were placed into the care of the medicine man, who refused to permit Libbey's medical treatment, preferring to use his own remedies and denied food by their family out of fear. The unfortunate adults died several days later.

In a carefully crafted summation of the affair, Schwatka not so subtly shifted the responsibility largely to the Yakutat Tlingit, noting that it was their habit to pick up discarded items, and once they understood that Kernuk had retrieved the forbidden poisonous material, they "unhesitatingly placed the blame on the man Kernuk" and viewed the conduct of the white men as "insignificant." Although Schwatka's characterization of the matter as "a family affair," served, in his opinion, to largely absolve his expedition of the responsibility for the deaths, Schwatka did acknowledge that the *Times's* expedition was "not wholly devoid of carelessness." The *Sun*, ever ready to fault the *Times*, rightly remarked that the responsibility for the three deaths did not rest altogether with the Tlingit, and demanded a report from Libbey. The following day, Professor Libbey delivered a detailed report in the *Times* that mirrored Schwatka's telling of the story, but under the disingenuous leading headline, "Superstitious Neglect-Killed by the Treatment of the Medicine Man." There the controversy ended in the papers.[52]

Schwatka's St. Elias expedition had focused a spotlight on Alaska, and more particularly Mount St. Elias, as a geographic prize. The first step, admittedly modest, by a group of novices led by Schwatka towards the summit of the "King of the Continent," was a pioneer Alaskan climb. This sparked an alpine interest in the mountain and laid the groundwork for the benefit of future climbers. Schwatka's account of the ascent reached enthusiasts in the *Alpine Journal*, and Seton-Karr's lively book, *Shores and Alps of Alaska*, similarly attracted interest in the climbing community, especially in Europe. In 1888, a group organized by the British Topham brothers and George Broke, citing Seton-Karr's book as their inspiration, ascended to 11,483 feet before running short of supplies. In 1890, a joint expedition by the National Geographic Society and the U.S. Geological Survey, under the charge of Professor Israel C. Russell, failed to reach Topham's highest, but another attempt by Russell in 1891 had reached 14,500 feet. Tragically, Russell's group suffered an accident on landing at Yakutat Bay in which several men were drowned.[53]

A far more prepared and experienced team commanded by Luigi Amedeo di Savoia, the Duke of the Abruzzi, reached the summit on July 31, 1897. Although Mount St. Elias was not the most technically difficult mountain, the duke, himself a noted mountaineer, retained the services of four Italian Alpine guides, recognizing that no major climb had succeeded without them and that both Schwatka and Seton-Karr had recommended their utility. Seeking to avoid the shortage of supplies and the logistical difficulties that plagued Schwatka's team and the other failed attempts, the duke carried 6,600 pounds of food on four sledges, sufficient to supply his party for fifty days. Lastly, the duke (and previous expeditions) listened to Karr's suggestion to access the base of the mountain from Yakutat Bay, rather than Icy Bay. Although still a difficult traverse across several glaciers by sledge, including the lengthy Malaspina Glacier, the duke managed to transport his men and supplies safely to the base and was well positioned to reach the summit.[54]

Schwatka claimed that "it will require a book to chronicle [the expedition's] accomplishments in full," something he never managed to do, and certainly an overstatement. Beyond the dispatches for the *Times*, Schwatka penned a two-part series for *Century Magazine* that repurposed his dispatches to the *Times*. Seton-Karr, a talented artist, completed a series of more than one hundred sketches that feature a stunning array of peoples along the Alaskan coast, including the Yakutat Tlingit who assisted the expedition. Libbey secured a set of approximately one hundred photographs (some of which were made into commercial lantern slides), and also collected a substantial number of Tlingit artifacts, all currently held by the Princeton Art Museum. Libbey's paper to the American Geographical Society offered a vivid description of the region, together with the only scientific analysis flowing from the expedition, a geologic survey of the area. According to one scientist with the U.S. Geological Survey, Libbey's survey was the "first written description of the complex glacier systems now known as the Bering, Guyot, and Malaspina Glaciers."[55]

To the members of the Royal Geographical Society at a meeting on March 14, 1887, Seton-Karr stepped forward and offered his own account of the climb, an account that was generally objective and matter of fact. In terms of his summit bid, a combination of threatening weather, shortage of food, and the impracticability of surmounting a steep ridge that led to the summit, all stifled his final ascent. That account did emphasize Seton-Karr's legitimate concern with Schwatka's health, and also expressed his anxiety over Schwatka's great weight. Seton-Karr volunteered the unflattering remark that Schwatka's "great weight - eighteen stone - would have made it very difficult for us had any of the snow bridges over the crevasses given way...." At the meeting, the accomplished climber Douglas Freshfield weighed in on the matter, remarking that to take a man of eighteen stone up a 19,000-foot mountain was "a Quixote enterprise," although he believed that Seton-Karr had nothing to fear in lifting the hefty Schwatka out of any crevasses. Schwatka himself acknowledged his weight as an obstacle, noting that "I was altogether too heavy for a long-continued climbing, and this was evident at every step we made up the slope of St. Elias." But defending his stamina, Schwatka went on to claim that "it must be said in my favor (and I must say it myself, as no others will) that my full capacity for endurance and muscle was not in anywise reached that day, as it was clearly the cloudy weather that put a stop to our contemplated ascent…." Notwithstanding Seton-Karr's and Freshfield's comments, Schwatka must have been a man of tremendous stamina to have travelled as far as he did in his condition.[56]

What was the most enduring result of the party's efforts? The expedition and its associated Jones River controversy did succeed in providing the *Times,* and the district of Alaska, with enormous publicity for its efforts, and proved to be well worth the modest price of its sponsorship. One newspaper appropriately noted that "[t]he *New York Times* is getting a tremendous boom of free advertising because it aroused the jealousy of its local rivals by successfully prosecuting through Lieutenant Schwatka an exploration of the hitherto unknown parts of Alaska." Schwatka's publicity, although self-serving at times, did hold Alaska, its spectacular beauty, and potential resources in the limelight of the general public. An editorial in the *Times* made the bold, but overstated assertion, that "the expedition of Lieut. Schwatka may be said to have done more to realize the expectations which Mr. Seward founded upon his purchase of Alaska than any other event that has happened since the purchase itself."[57]

CHAPTER FIFTEEN
THRO' THE WONDERLAND

Before the ink had dried on his first dispatch to the *New York Times*, Schwatka was parlaying his popularity and journalistic talents into a sponsorship with another major metropolitan newspaper. Schwatka did not hold a position as a staff correspondent with any particular publication, leaving him with the freedom to chase his own opportunities and to pursue his own course. The style suited his free-spirited nature but made for unpredictable prospects, and always left him on the lookout for his next assignment.

With the commitment from the *New York Times* in hand, Schwatka pitched the *New York World* with a proposition to raise the profile of Joseph Pulitzer's newspaper. When Pulitzer had purchased the *World* from Jay Gould in 1883, the paper was a losing proposition, hovering near bankruptcy. Under Pulitzer, the newspaper was entirely revamped and refocused, adding sensational, graphic, and human-interest features, just the type of story that Schwatka could deliver.

The enterprising and forward-looking Schwatka managed to conclude an arrangement with the *World* to sponsor a winter trip through Yellowstone National Park. For Schwatka, now an attractive media property, the trip featured another opportunity for image building—the stalwart Arctic explorer tackling one of America's most prized national parks in the dead of winter, a symbol of the untamed West. For Pulitzer, it was an adventure well-suited to his tastes, one that would excite curiosity and interest in his readership. Pulitzer cared little for quixotic feats of discovery, once telling his business manager that he "could do anything on behalf of the paper except hunt for the North Pole, or back the invention of a flying machine." Fascinating jaunts, like those of Nellie Bly retracing Phineas Fogg's quest around the world in eighty days, one of Pulitzer's staged exploits, captivated his audiences and were more his style.[1]

During the Big Horn and Yellowstone Expedition in 1876, Schwatka had travelled through the Wyoming Territory, but he does not seem to have visited the confines of the park. More important, he had no firsthand knowledge of the park's winter conditions. Schwatka claimed to have obtained some details about the park in 1871 from the legendary army scout and wilderness guide, Jim Bridger, who knew Yellowstone well and was fond of boasting of its spouting geysers, hot springs and boiling caldrons. Perhaps so, but Bridger had retired in poor health to Missouri by 1868, while Schwatka was still a cadet at West Point. While Schwatka travelled cross-country with the *Times's* Alaska expedition in the summer of 1886, time had not permitted a detour to Yellowstone. However, as Schwatka passed near the park on the Northern Pacific Railroad, his July 5 dispatch, headlined "The Yellowstone Park-The *Times's* Alaska Expedition in 'Wonderland,'" offered his readers a picturesque description that highlighted the park's magnificent features based on accounts of third parties. Schwatka closed with a preview of exciting things yet to come: "I have determined to see the Yellowstone National Park in the dead of Winter (this Winter too), on snowshoes, and see its most arctic and beautiful side."[2]

In addition to his arrangement with the *World*, Schwatka had negotiated with Clarence Buel, associate editor of the *Century Magazine*, to deliver one or more articles for the popular publication. Schwatka had good success with the *Century* as a forum, already having published several articles that espoused the possibilities of the district of Alaska and westward expansion that appealed to its editors' own nationalistic views. In October 1886, Schwatka made his latest pitch to Buel, announcing big plans, as usual, and playing up the uniqueness of the endeavor: "I have a fine chance to take a splendidly equipped expedition into the Yellowstone Park this mid-winter, on snow-shoes....The scenic and artistic matter that such an expedition could secure I think I have already laid before you, and it would certainly be radically different from anything ever before written and especially illustrated."[3]

If paid an advance and given fees consistent with his Mount St. Elias article, Schwatka offered to "willingly give *Century* credit of the expedition, if they cared for it." At the same time, Schwatka needed transport to Yellowstone, and logically turned to the Northern Pacific Railroad. He had already established a relationship with the railroad through his contribution to its marketing brochure, a piece that featured the ease of access to Yellowstone. The main line of the Northern Pacific Railroad passed through the town of Livingston, Montana, and from Livingston a branch line ran south to Cinnabar, a smattering of hastily erected buildings located six miles from the hotel at Mammoth Hot Springs, the park's northern entrance. From Cinnabar, coaches and carriages shuttled tourists to Mammoth and the park.[4]

Schwatka contacted passenger agent Charles S. Fee of the railway to arrange for the transportation for his party from St. Paul. Recognizing that Schwatka's plans could also benefit the railroad, agent Fee recommended that Schwatka hire the photographer, Frank Jay Haynes. The "Official Photographer" for the Northern Pacific Railroad, Haynes was one of the finest photographers of the era. Born in 1853 in Saline, Michigan, during the 1870s Haynes had travelled west with his camera and equipment, working initially as a portrait photographer in several western cities and later as a landscape photographer. His big break came when he was hired by the Northern Pacific Railroad to photograph the scenic and breathtaking features along its line for use in marketing publications, even making use of a customized railway car for his photographic studio. Yellowstone National Park, with its spectacular natural wonders, was an obvious locale for Haynes's work for the railroad. Exploring its environs for the best views, the resultant photographs did much to attract interest in the park. Thoroughly familiar with its attractions, he would ultimately prove to be the backbone of the expedition, though his relationship with Schwatka would end on an acrimonious note.

Schwatka understood that the addition of Haynes's photographs could enliven his contemplated *Century* article. As Schwatka and Fee worked to finalize the terms of Haynes's participation in the venture, Schwatka pushed Fee for up to twenty of Haynes's best images to illustrate the article. He also negotiated with Fee for "the privilege of buying at cost" several sets for himself, as well as several sets for Joseph Pulitzer and the *World*. Fee agreed to that request as well. Fee was shrewd enough to realize that the railroad stood to acquire some of Haynes's images for its benefit, but Schwatka cautioned Fee that *Century* would insist on exclusive rights to any images that the magazine published. Unfortunately, unbeknownst to either Fee or Schwatka at the time, each had come away with a different understanding of the terms under which Schwatka would purchase photographs taken by Haynes.[5]

Schwatka had recruited Henry P. Bosse, a draftsman in the Rock Island office of the U.S. Army Corps of Engineers and an accomplished photographer in his own right, as the expedition's artist. While Haynes was making a name for himself documenting the distinctive features of the Yellowstone on behalf of the railroad, Bosse was capturing stunning cyanotype images of the dramatically different Mississippi River and making a name as one of the first important photographers of that storied watercourse.

Two experienced snowshoers were recruited from among the many snowshoe clubs that had sprung up around the country. Snowshoeing, once a vital means of travel and survival, had become a popular recreational pastime, a means of rejuvenation in the great outdoors for a society undergoing rapid urbanization. James G. Ross, vice president of the Montreal Snow Shoe Club, and Henry C. Wadsworth, president of the Buffalo Snow Shoe Club, elected to join the expedition. Four other members were hired near the park—guides J. W. Coho, W. W. West, C. J. Baronette and Ed Wilson. Four others—Charles A. Stoddard, David Stratton, Charles H. Taylor and James A. Blakely—were retained as assistants. The oldest participant was the spry seventy-two-year-old Joseph Brackett, Frederick Schwatka's father-in-law, who would prove to be a hardy traveler, more fit than his hefty son-in-law.[6]

The choice of Yellowstone National Park for a winter expedition was well timed to coincide with the rapidly expanding interest in the public attraction. The first explorers to the region were American Indians who had roamed its expanse for more than ten thousand years. Later-arriving explorers had also recognized the region as a breathtaking natural assemblage of geysers, falls, hot springs, and cañons that was fundamentally unique and worthy of protection from commercial interests and exploitation. After explorations and surveys had returned with eye-opening reports of its stunning natural beauty, as well as its diverse fauna and flora, Yellowstone was established by Congress as the country's first national park in March 1872. At 3,400 square miles, it is almost larger than the combined states of Delaware and Rhode Island.

By 1883, the grandeur of the park was firmly imbedded in the American psyche, with more than one thousand newspaper articles attesting to its magnificence during the preceding decade. When the Northern Pacific branch line from Livingston to Cinnabar was opened in the same year, tourism exploded as the railroad widely promoted its accessibility. A tour of the park by President Chester A. Arthur in 1883 also contributed to increased public awareness. In 1886, the railroad further cemented its tie with the park by acquiring the lavish four-story Mammoth Hot Springs Hotel. The railroad's snazzy publicity brochure exuded an air of elegant comfort: "conveyed by an excellently equipped Concord coach from the terminus of the railroad to the hotel at Mammoth Hot Springs, six miles distant, the tourist finds himself surrounded by all the conveniences of modern hotel life."[7]

As fate would have it, Schwatka's trek in Yellowstone coincided with

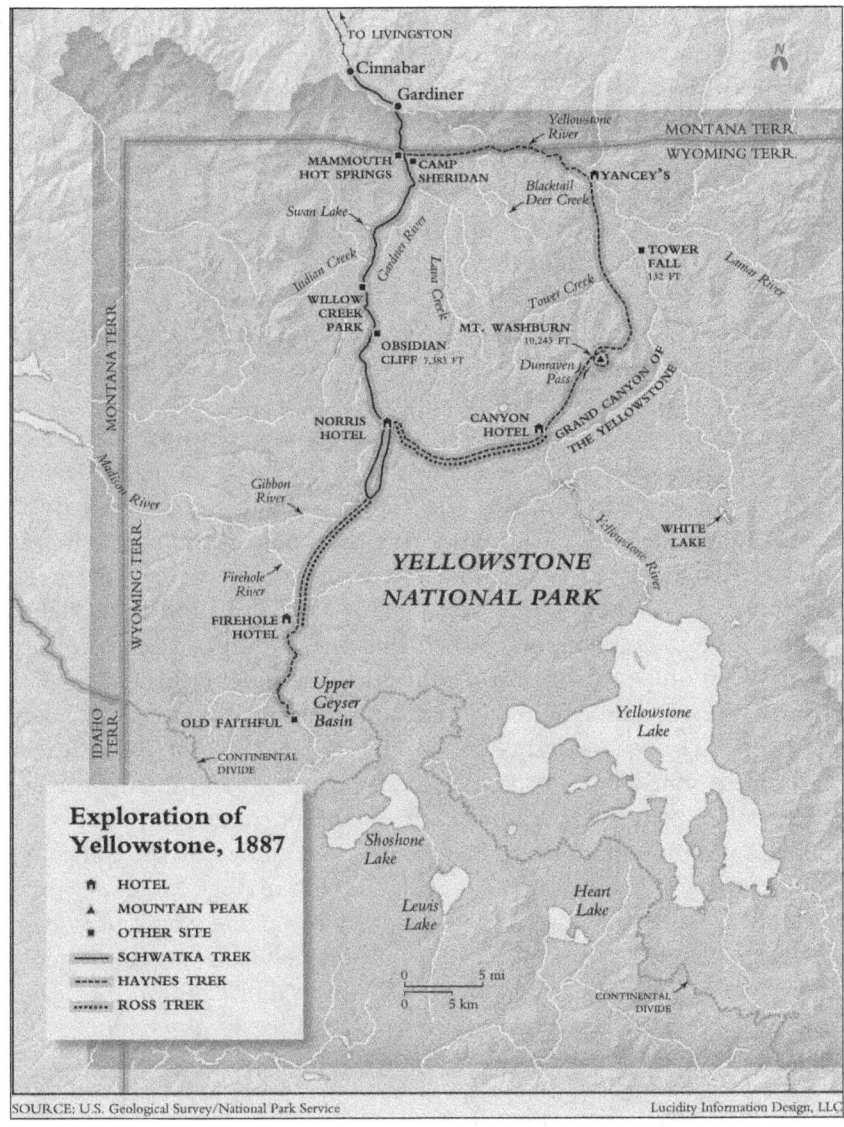

the severest winter weather in the region during the past decade, marked by a combination of prolonged bitterly cold temperatures, at times as low as −40°F, and continuing heavy snowfalls and blizzards. Relief parties had been sent to rescue stranded stagecoaches, and limbs were lost to frostbite. The cattle industry in the territories of Montana and Dakota suffered considerably. A drought over the preceding two years had already left grass sparse, and cattle were simply left to their fate owing to the cold and inability to feed in the deep snow. It was reported that in the Montana Territory ranchers lost more than 60 percent of their cattle over the winter. Such were the conditions that Schwatka's group faced as they prepared with eager anticipation for their excursion.[8]

Schwatka's plans were ambitious, too ambitious in retrospect. The proposed route was the "old trail" from Mammoth, thence east by wagon road to Yancey's Hotel and south to Tower Fall; continuing from there to Mt. Washburn, the highest mountain in the Park at 10,243 feet, and thence to the Grand Canyon of the Yellowstone and geyser regions, and finally back to Mammoth Hot Springs. The total distance would be approximately 175 miles, covered in about two weeks while using park hotels for shelter.[9]

Although Schwatka claimed knowledge of the area from his frontier days, his inexperience in winter travel in the region was plainly evident in his suggestion, early on, that the absence of snow might negate the need for snowshoes. For pack transport within the park, Schwatka initially considered engaging a few mounted Crow Indians, and making use of their lodges as shelter. Once acquainted with the more experienced recruits while in St. Paul, he learned the true nature of park conditions with its deep and drifting snow. Schwatka was quickly dispelled of the folly that the Indians would willingly travel under those conditions. In their place, Schwatka sought two teams of six dogs, but that idea was also dropped when both dogs and drivers became too difficult to come by. Schwatka's plan fell victim, in part, to the upcoming St. Paul winter carnival, a monumental outdoor extravaganza attended by thousands, that by unfortunate coincidence had tapped all the sled dogs and experienced drivers for miles. Ironically, Schwatka, now a big-name Arctic personality, had been extended the honor of leading the festival's dazzling opening ceremony, a grandiose entrance by dog team to deliver the regal head of the festival, King Boreas. However, his tight Yellowstone schedule would not permit the diversion.[10]

Schwatka's Yellowstone excursion would ultimately be made with Canadian snowshoes and skis. However, of the men recruited for the expedition, only two had any experience on skis. Cross country skis, at the time known as "Norwegian snowshoes," are an excellent choice for Yellowstone with its plentiful, but light and fluffy snow. However, it was rather comical to believe that the inexperienced members could gain any expertise with the heavy and ungainly ten-foot skis based on a handful of training runs. Haynes, a witness to the spectacle, confided to his wife about his troubling doubts regarding the lack of proficiency of some members of the party. In another ominous sign, those not acclimated to the higher altitude (almost 8,000 feet) suffered from shortness of breath and heart palpitations in the process.[11]

Schwatka was not planning to travel lightly, another factor that would seriously plague his expedition. His father-in-law served as quartermaster and was responsible for a quantity of supplies and equipment that would prove far too heavy for the excursion. Besides an assortment of bulky winter clothing, including an extra "reserve supply" for additional warmth, a wide variety of sleeping bags of different makes were freighted: sheepskin, buffalo robe, wolf, and reindeer. The party was also saddled with a profusion of climbing gear, ice-axes, ropes, and alpenstocks, as well as multiple firearms. Admitting that the quantity of food provisions carried would be burdensome (no "Sunday-picnic"), following his routine from his Arctic trip, Schwatka planned to have on board a condensed high-fat diet, presumably canned. To haul all this baggage, Schwatka harked back to his days on the Indian campaign by seeking a mule team and teamsters. The naive plan would prove wholly impracticable in Yellowstone's deep snow.

Notwithstanding his animosity towards the army, his military service continued to open the door to certain courtesies. The army had recently been tasked with administration of the park, and in 1886 a post (Camp Sheridan) was established at Mammoth Hot Springs. Just as the navy had furnished transport on the Mount St. Elias expedition, the army, namely Lieutenant Herbert Tutherly, First Cavalry, generously supplied several soldiers, a mule team, and a wagon. At the same time, since no roads connected Yancey's Hotel to points south, Schwatka's original route was now reversed. It was to run from Mammoth Hot Springs south to Norris Hotel, then to the geyser basins and Old Faithful, and then to the canyon region, returning by way of Yancey's.[12]

Flush with eager anticipation as he readied to start, Schwatka penned his first missive for the *World,* building upon the uniqueness of his off-season excursion. He added the prescient remark that Pulitzer and his newspaper would be repaid handsomely for their money, time and effort with some unanticipated discoveries at this time of year, unless the venture suffered a complete failure by some unforeseen accident.[13]

The expedition set off on the morning of January 5 with the party of thirteen hitched to their ten-foot-long Norwegian skis, five of whom pulled sleds fitted with pairs of four-inch runners. The accompanying military mule team hauled their prodigious assemblage of gear and supplies. It was an inauspicious start. A heavy snowfall, six foot drifts in some places, had made the road impassable for the struggling pack animals. After a wearying four miles, at Swan Lake the floundering and exhausted mule

The Schwatka Yellowstone Expedition passes Obsidian Cliff. Photograph by F. J. Haynes.

team was halted. The equipment was hastily removed from the wagon and placed on the sleds. Wishing them well, Lieutenant Tutherly and the troopers beat a swift retreat back to Camp Sheridan.

By the end of their first day, man-hauling the supplies, the Schwatka party had reached Indian Creek, some eight miles from their starting point. Because the men had trouble dragging the overloaded sleds, which tended to run badly off course, a frustrated Schwatka elected to drop almost all their baggage at a barn at Indian Creek and carry necessary items in packs while hauling two sleds with lightened loads.

Although the first day had been no picnic, according to Schwatka, in a later dispatch to Ada, the next day was "a severe test of the endurance of the men." Only several difficult miles were advanced to Willow Creek Park. Visibility had been reduced to almost zero in the windswept falling snow. Common landmarks and mountain peaks were obscured, making pathfinding difficult. With the temperature dropping below -22°F, those not accustomed to the cold suffered badly and a tent was quickly erected to provide some warmth and shelter. Disgusted with the sleds, which sank like anchors in the deep snow, at Willow Creek, the sleds, tent and bedding were abandoned. Photographic equipment and a limited supply of provisions were carried in knapsacks on the participants' backs. A few disgruntled members were later heard to complain that the "explorers" in the group, presumably including Schwatka, carried no packs or gear.[14]

The next day, after accomplishing about nine or ten miles by skis, the party reached the Norris Hotel at 10:00 P.M. It had been an exhausting ordeal. Clearly, not everyone in the group was fit for winter travel. Among the less adventurous travelers, morale was dropping rapidly. According to Haynes, some of the "leaders" returned two or three miles to encourage the stragglers along. One of those laggards was Bosse, who collapsed on the snow and refused to go on. Only after a guide callously remarked that "he's going to die, let's go on," did the prostrate artist pull himself up and plod along after the group. Schwatka was the last to arrive, but whether he was a straggler or a leader is unclear.[15]

At the Norris Hotel, they were welcomed by the winterkeeper, named Kelly, who maintained the lodge in the off-season. Kelly had also assisted the stragglers in Schwatka's party and would later assert that some of the stronger members had refused to help their struggling comrades. It was likely not lost on any of the Schwatka party, that as they were trudging through the snow, winterkeepers, some with their wives and children, were living in relative comfort and warmth at the various hotels. Their relaxed presence dispelled any thought that the excursion was anything more than a poorly executed alpine club event. Hotels may seem a bit misplaced in what was touted as a pristine wilderness. Yellowstone's hotels and its concessions, such as Haynes's photographic studio, were commercial enterprises that operated under lease arrangements with the government. With Yellowstone National Park, the Department of the Interior sought to frame an acceptable balance between the potentially competing policies of conservation and preservation on the one hand, and that of public comfort and recreation, on the other.[16]

One day was spent sightseeing around the Norris Geyser Basin, one of the most geologically volatile locales within the park, replete with numerous active geothermal features. Though a chilly -30°F, the mood improved as Haynes and Bosse managed to fulfill their original desire to capture with camera and sketchbook, respectively, the sublime spectacle of nature, a dreamlike scene of fantastic ice formations fashioned by steaming water and vapor. To Haynes, as the sun broke through the clouds, the entire basin "presented the appearance of a very busy manufacturing city, with its ten thousand smoking chimneys; where a hundred thousand wheels might be revolving, in the production of all that a complex civilization requires." [17]

The next day, January 9, strapping on skis and shouldering the heavy backpacks, Schwatka led the party towards the lower geyser basin.

Members of the expedition outside of Norris Hotel. Photograph by F. J. Haynes.

Before they had gone four miles Schwatka fell ill. Although reports as to his illness vary, he appears to have had respiratory trouble from the start. He now suffered from what Haynes referred to as a hemorrhage of the lungs and was evidently bleeding quite profusely. The exact cause of his symptoms is unknown. Whatever the cause, the disorder differed markedly from his ailment on Mount St. Elias. Fearing that to proceed further would endanger his life, Schwatka made an ignominious return to the Norris Hotel with his father-in-law and J. W. Coho, along with C. J. Baronette. Haynes and the balance of the party continued without incident to the Firehole Hotel, some fourteen miles distant. With telephone service available from the Norris Hotel to the Mammoth Springs Hotel, a communication from Schwatka made its way to his wife Ada. Downplaying his illness so as to avoid alarm, at the same time shielding his wounded pride, he advised her that he and Brackett had suffered severe colds, from which they were now fully recovered.[18]

Perhaps regretting their decision to leave their leader, or simply hopeful that the lieutenant had recovered sufficiently to continue, the experienced Ross led Wadsworth, Bosse and most of Schwatka's recruits back to Norris Hotel the following day, January 10. Ross had his hands full shepherding back the weaker members of the group, especially Bosse, "who lingered long and faithfully in the rear." Thoroughly frustrated with the progress of the expedition, Haynes was not prepared to sit idly and watch his chance at photographic opportunities fade. With Schwatka's blessing, Haynes decided to continue the winter trek as originally contemplated with the two best men, Stoddard and Stratton. He also telephoned Ed Wilson at Mammoth Hot Springs to join them at Old Faithful and the Upper Geyser Basin. Wilson's unaccompanied trek to Old Faithful was evidently made without incident and served to reinforce the notion that winter travel in the park was not an overly adventuresome exercise for an experienced traveler.

Haynes's party achieved Schwatka's original goal of visiting both the Upper Geyser Basin and the canyon area. After reaching Old Faithful, they were snowbound for five days, camped in a tent under the warmth of the immortal geyser, but forestalled from any photographic activity. The weather finally cleared on January 16, enabling an ecstatic Haynes to capture a series of magnificent photographs, including eruptions of Old Faithful, Giantess, Grand, Beehive and Castle. The Haynes party worked back to Norris, then onto the Canyon Hotel and on through the canyon area, where Haynes obtained some stunning views of the Grand Canyon of the Yellowstone and the Lower Falls. Leaving the canyon at below zero temperatures, with no tent or blankets, and a handful of biscuits and some chocolate, his group made a daring, perhaps foolhardy, twenty-mile trek to Yancey's across the Washburn range. While on the ascent of the mountain, a two-day blizzard forced them into an improvised backcountry snow shelter the first night, and the second was spent fully awake struggling to find their way. With a break in the storm the next morning, they managed to finally reach Yancey's. From there it was an easy trek to Mammoth Hot Springs.

On January 16, as Haynes was waylaid at Old Faithful, a group comprised of Ross, Wadsworth and several others left the Norris Hotel in in an attempt to reach Canyon Hotel. Schwatka's own self-pride, when combined with a sense of commitment to his recruits, compelled him to join them. However, after only a few miles the indefatigable explorer was

Henry Bosse in the sub-zero cold of the Norris Geyser Basin. Photograph by F. J. Haynes.

forced to quickly retreat to the Norris Hotel after his health once again began to fail. Those of Schwatka's group who had reached the Canyon Hotel remained a day and then returned to Norris. Physically beaten and emotionally demoralized, Schwatka mustered the strength to lead his group back to Mammoth Hot Springs on January 18, leaving the field for Haynes and his party. Interestingly, the ailing Schwatka and his party had their best day travelling in the park on the return to Mammoth, covering some twenty-two miles. The anticipation of exiting the park had evidently become a strong motivator, but even that presented its own difficulties. The heavy snow required the work of three Northern Pacific engines and one plow to clear the tracks between Livingston and Cinnabar. Once cleared, Schwatka made a quick exit from the park to limit any further expenses for his party. By doing so, he also avoided crossing paths with the adventuresome Haynes, an encounter Schwatka much preferred to sidestep.

For Schwatka, the Yellowstone trip had been an unmitigated failure, one for which he was largely responsible. Poor planning and an overburdensome load of equipment, clothing and supplies had hindered the progress of the party from the onset. Moreover, several members of the party recruited by Schwatka were entirely ill-suited for such a trip, either because they were not fit enough or lacked the experience to handle skis and snowshoes. However, Schwatka's failing health marked the end for

Lower Falls of the Grand Canyon of the Yellowstone. Photograph by F. J. Haynes.

Schwatka and his group. With Schwatka down, the recruited party lost its spirit. Anxious over Schwatka's health, the group was wracked with indecisiveness as to whether to continue or return, ultimately remaining with their now invalid leader. Certainly, some of the more accomplished snowshoers, like Ross and Wadsworth, could have completed the tour with Haynes's group.

Unfortunately, what had been a disappointing adventure among the geysers which Frederick Schwatka looked to put behind him erupted into an even more disagreeable falling out. On that account, Haynes bears some portion of the blame. Haynes recognized that his winter trek through the Yellowstone and his accompanying photographs opened a window of opportunity for both fame and profit. Behind the scenes, he worked his newspaper connections to his benefit and at Schwatka's expense. George Legg Henderson, reporter for the *Helena Independent*, who interviewed Haynes upon his return, crafted a story for the February 6 issue of the *Helena Independent* that portrayed Haynes as if he were the conqueror of the North Pole, slightly maligning Schwatka in the process. According to Henderson, Haynes's trek was "a feat of daring that had never before been accomplished in midwinter." Building the drama in regard to Haynes's return trek, Henderson wrote, "[Haynes's] party were all brave men. They knew their danger and met it in silence. They knew also that a time would soon come when they must lie down exhausted and join the innumerable host who had preceded them. Such was not to be their destiny." About Schwatka's seventy-two-year-old father-in-law, Joseph Brackett, the *Helena Independent* reporter went out of his way to remark that Brackett deserves special mention for "enduring hunger, cold and fatigue, and performing his share of the duties incident to the expedition. This royal son of Neptune came out as fresh as any of them," surely a dig at the younger Schwatka whose constitution had failed him. An editorial in the paper added the snide remark that Haynes had demonstrated "the difference between modest western pluck and immoderate eastern gall." After its publication, Henderson, now the self-perceived journalistic "kingmaker," boasted in a letter to Haynes: "I send you the *Independent*. Have received some very flattering comments on the article. You are the head and front of the Schwatka expedition. D. Stratton is satisfied that justice has been done to you and your party."[19]

Henderson's friendship with Haynes was enough to explain the reporter's overdone account of Haynes's winter trip, but Henderson's own close association with the park may have played a part in the mean-spirited commentary directed at Schwatka. Henderson was enamored by the park; he freely admitted that the park "had become part of his existence." Henderson considered himself the expert on Yellowstone, and for good reason. In 1882, he was appointed assistant superintendent; in 1883, he constructed and operated the Cottage Hotel at Mammoth Hot Springs. He was soon publishing his own tour guide, running tours by means of his own stagecoaches and buggies, and making a name for himself by penning numerous articles, lecturing, and serving as the most well-known "interpreter" of the park. Schwatka, the brash outsider and interloper, and his widely publicized winter excursion, may have simply triggered some resentment on the part of Henderson, the park's resident expert.[20]

Elated with his sudden status as conquering hero, Haynes wrote his own self-serving account of the expedition to another reporter-friend at the more widely circulated *Chicago Tribune,* also embellished by comments that belittled Schwatka and his party. Published on March 5, Haynes wrote that "I undertook the trip with Lieut. Schwatka of Arctic fame and a party of Eastern gentlemen, who soon found that the 'Great National' was much larger than Central Park, and that snowshoeing at 6,000 to 10,000 feet was a new experience." Haynes left the Schwatka party after he "saw the folly of having to do the park with an outfit that used three days in traveling twenty-two miles—the distance from the [Mammoth Hot Springs] to Norris."[21]

A large part of Haynes's frustration, as well as that of Charles Fee, with the Northern Pacific Railroad, had been an expensive misunderstanding over the purchase of Haynes's photographs. Schwatka was flabbergasted when Fee delivered an invoice to Schwatka for several hundred dollars for Haynes's photographs, which he flatly refused to pay. Schwatka claimed that Fee (an appropriate name in light of events) would only receive payment if the *Century Magazine* accepted the photographs and an accompanying article. This conditional arrangement was the same that Schwatka had negotiated with the magazine for his Apache and St. Elias articles. Agent Charles Fee and Haynes no doubt understood the arrangement differently. Incensed by what Fee believed was backtracking by Schwatka on the commitment, Fee wrote to Haynes that "there is no use 'crying over spilt milk,' and I shall have to stand up and make the best of it, but if I ever get an opportunity to even up there is a man [Schwatka] in Rock Island, Ill. that will know it, whether it is one or twenty years from now. I have got a pretty good memory myself." Nonetheless, Schwatka was just as adamant in his position, and his customary practice with *Century Magazine* did tend to support him. In a letter to editor Buel, Schwatka claimed that at the outset, when asked by Fee if *Century Magazine* would pay for the photographs, Schwatka had advised Fee and Haynes that *Century* editor Clarence Buel "would do nothing until all were submitted together, MS, sketches and photos, and then [the magazine would] reject or offer a definite price." As Schwatka wryly told Buel, "they may know how to run a railroad, but not a magazine."[22]

Making matters worse, Haynes sought to reap for his own benefit the financial arrangement that Schwatka had envisioned with the *Century Magazine*. Haynes contacted editor Buel directly, offering to sell his photographs to *Century*. Bolstering his case that Buel should purchase his photographs, Haynes asserted that his group of four were "the only explorers" in the entire party (having completed the full park circuit), and that Haynes was <u>the</u> photographer of the expedition. Not surprisingly, when Schwatka learned of Haynes's letter to Buel, he was livid over Haynes's slight to his exploring prowess, and what he viewed as Haynes's exaggeration as to his role as the only photographer. In response, Schwatka bluntly informed Buel that "I never care intentionally to elevate myself by pulling others down, and shall certainly resent their doing the same with me, as this case appears to be." Interestingly, in his response to Buel, Schwatka claimed that Haynes was one of three photographers, the other two being Ross and Bosse, thus disputing Haynes's claim to be the only photographer (a claim which Schwatka dismissed as "an exaggerated self-appointment of his [Haynes's] own."). Schwatka added that he had already received several photographs from Ross and was awaiting others. If so, none besides Haynes's are known to have survived. In his letter to Buel, Schwatka took some liberties as well, ridiculing the value of Haynes's spectacular mid-winter photographs, remarking that though Haynes may have obtained the best geyser photographs because he "lingered" in the park longer, those photographs were simply no different than those taken in summer (other than the Monarch Geyser which "gave winter effects"). Schwatka even put a spin on his own misadventure, telling Buel that even though he had suffered "a slight hemorrhage," he elected not to visit the Upper Geyser Basin because "one geyser basin was varying from another as a two-quart basin of water varied from one of a half-gallon." In the end, it all didn't matter, as *Century Magazine* elected not to publish either an article or photograph of the trip. Despite his stinging public criticism of Schwatka, the ultimate beneficiary of the Yellowstone excursion initiated by Schwatka was the photographer F. Jay Haynes. Orders for his portfolio of "Mid-Winter Views of Yellowstone National Park" (thirty-five views in total) were well received and affirmed his status as the park's official photographer.[23]

The final humiliating act in what was an already an embarrassing failure for Schwatka's Yellowstone expedition came from another winter visitor to the park only a few weeks later. On behalf of the outdoor magazine *Forest and Stream*, Thomas Elwood Hofer, a local guide and occasional correspondent, and his companion, Jack Tansey, undertook a winter survey of its wildlife. Hofer was the right man for the trip, fully acquainted with the park and competent on skis, as well as a lively travel writer. Properly equipped and prepared, over seven days the two followed a longer route than the Haynes party, covering about 225 miles, without suffering privation or hardship, and even "enjoying" the trek. They succeeded in their principal purpose of tallying an impressive list of winter wildlife in the park. In light of Hofer's untroubled success, the editors of *Forest and Stream* could not resist a snide poke in regard to Schwatka's dismal fate, which it told with a bit of glee:

> It is perhaps fitting that, with assurances of distinguished esteem, we proffer to the *New York World* our sympathy for it for the mysterious disappearance of its widely heralded mid-Winter Yellowstone Park Exploring Expedition, which, with Crow scouts, Esquimau dogs, Arctic clothing and bottled ammunition, we are apprehensive has been snowed under. The *World* will hail with a pulse of faint joy,

the relic of the party which our Commissioner [Elwood Hofer] sends us.[24]

The "relic" of Schwatka's party recovered by Hofer was a glass bottle spotted hanging from a tree twelve feet above the ground at Schwatka's first camp. Intrigued by the unusual placement, Tansey managed to climb the tree and bring it down. The two were surprised to find a note tagged to the outside of the empty bottle stating: "Placed on the level of the snow, Ther. -51°F" and signed "Schwatka Jan. 7." As the snow had never been higher than three feet at that location and the thermometer never below -31°F, Elwood recognized the absurdity of the comment. With his own dry humor, he concluded that "the whole thing was a misstatement and that the high winds had blown and lodged the bottle in the tree,.... Strange things happen in the Park."[25]

◊∾◊∾◊∾◊∾

Leaving the Yellowstone expedition behind and out of mind, Schwatka settled back to his recently acquired residence with Ada in Chicago. For the peripatetic Schwatka, now, even as a married man with home ties, he was still only homebound long enough to arrange his next adventure or lecture tour, and free-lance activities filled his short stays. According to a visiting reporter, the Schwatka's lived in a modest home on Michigan Avenue suited to Frederick's temperament, "one of the few unostentatious but very cozy and comfortable homes of the aristocratic thoroughfare." Schwatka's literary output for 1888 was prodigious, with more than thirty articles, their lengths ranging from several sentences to an extensive and informative ten-installment series "About Alaska" for a syndicate of Kansas newspapers. His prolific output and widespread syndication continued to make Schwatka a household name across the country, and he carved out a niche with his popular brief Arctic features. Fine-tuned with an informal, folksy writing style, he delivered lively, and often humorous, content pieces on out of the ordinary northern topics that offered pleasant sidebars to the more mundane journalistic news. For newspapers across the country, the shorter eye-catching one-off items addressed such matters as Inuit endurance, polar bears on ice floes, the quality of snow, ballooning in the Arctic, the ingenuity of snow houses, the possibility of reaching the North Pole, Alaskan forests, and even more diverse topics such as housekeeping practiced by Inuit wives (entitled "Good Housekeeping") and the "rights" of Tlingit women. For the *Century Magazine*, he contributed "An Elk Hunt on the Plains," an entertaining sport hunt while with the Third Cavalry. For the *North American Review,* an objective platform for discussion of timely current affairs, he penned a thoughtful review of the Alaska Fur Seal dispute, presenting both sides of the controversy without taking a position.[26]

Schwatka had raised his profile among literary circles and gained hard-earned recognition as an author. According to the editors of the *Chicago Inter-Ocean,* in 1888 Frederick Schwatka was held out as one of eight "famous and valued" American authors in the field of travel, an elite group that included Henry Stanley and Bayard Taylor. Schwatka maintained his fond interest in juvenile works, promoted as an "eminent contributor" to the *Youth's Companion,* a widely popular magazine with an audience of 430,000 families and 2,000,000 readers. He contributed a heartwarming story of an orphaned antelope turned pet on the frontier in *Harper's Young People,* and another tale of Inuit children, "Wintering in the White Zone," for *Cosmopolitan.* His works maintained the Arctic as a topic of interest through his own experiences; somehow, he also found time to edit *The Geographical News, the World Gazette of Geographical Information.*[27]

Writing provided some welcome income, but lecturing was his passion. During the summer, Schwatka was actively engaged in the Chautauqua circuit in both the northern and southern states. The Chautauqua was part of the larger movement towards self-improvement and education that was prominent in the post-Civil War period, an outgrowth of the booming lecture movement. First initiated in Chautauqua Lake in upstate New York in 1873, the open-air summer forums attracted distinguished speakers and educators in a relaxed setting of concerts and entertainment in rural America. At the popular resort of White Bear Lake, Minnesota, Schwatka was received with an enthusiastic "Chautauqua salute," the waving of colorful handkerchiefs by attendees. His lectures about Alaska and the Arctic received high marks.

Schwatka made a more noticeable but disagreeable appearance at the Piedmont Chautauqua, held in Salt Springs, Georgia. The Piedmont event was the brainchild of Henry Grady, editor of the *Atlanta Constitution,* and Grady took the Chautauqua concept to a new level of carnival spectacle. In July and August 1888, its first year, more than thirty thousand flocked to the resort village of Salt Springs and the Sweetwater Park Hotel outside Atlanta, Georgia. Over one hundred lectures were featured on a range of topics. These were all delivered in its spectacular Moorish temple seating six thousand, set among lavish Italian gardens, "a fairy scene" illuminated by electric lights and Japanese lanterns. A headline lecturer, Frederick Schwatka, delivered "Wonders of the Polar World," and "Perils of the Polar Sea." The Chautauqua itself was a "great success," but word reached the

Philadelphia Times, that the affair "was a good deal marred by the failure of Ex-Lieutenant Schwatka, of the army, to carry himself properly as a lecturer." Evidently, his old habits with the "flowing bowl" got the better of him. The *Times* pointedly remarked that his conduct made him "a decidedly inconvenient person to employ as a public lecturer." Building a positive public persona that was in-demand as a speaker, and that could financially support Schwatka's lifestyle, was itself a challenge. Schwatka's self-destructive missteps only exacerbated that task.[28]

CHAPTER SIXTEEN

SOUTH OF THE BORDER

For Frederick Schwatka, maintaining a presence in the public eye meant long weeks on the lyceum circuit, rehashing tales and anecdotes that had been told a hundred times, hopefully adding some degree of freshness each time. Night after night, town after town, the unvarying routine could be monotonous and downright wearisome. Dinner afterwards with an old friend or acquaintance was always a welcome happenstance.

Such was the case after Schwatka delivered a lecture at the local Y.M.C.A. on a wintry night in January 1889 in La Crosse, Wisconsin, an industrious lumber town adjacent to the Mississippi. On this night, Schwatka was not settling down for a meal and a drink with just anyone. An evening with the legendary Buffalo Bill was always a lively event not soon to be forgotten. Since 1883, "Buffalo Bill's Wild West Show," a circus-like western spectacular, had swept the country, making the cowboy-turned-entertainer an enormous success and celebrity. Joining the now famous Plainsman was Dr. David Franklin Powell, a La Crosse physician and a western legend in his own right. Raised on the prairie, where he learned his profession in the Nebraska Territory, Powell had earned the name "White Beaver" for saving the life of an Indian child. As an expert marksman in Cody's shows, in western folk parlance, he could "shoot a cork from a man's head with a pistol." A promoter and wheeler dealer of the first kind, besides practicing medicine, he pedaled all sorts of health elixirs and tonics ("Yosemite Yarrow" was his rheumatism cure) and also engaged in speculative land deals across the states.[1]

Powell had plans for more land deals on the horizon. At dinner that evening and at a follow-up meeting at the Leland Hotel in Chicago on February 20, Schwatka, Powell, and Cody discussed a plan to recruit five hundred "colonists" per year to Mexico within the confines of an immense land grant covering approximately 2,500,000 acres in northern Mexico (the so-called "Palomas Tract"). It was reported that a syndicate of well-heeled Chicago and Nebraska investors was looking to acquire the Palomas Tract from its owner, Luis Hüller, a German immigrant and entrepreneur. Schwatka, Cody and Powell were apparently working to populate the land covered by this tract, a condition imposed by the Mexican government. For Schwatka, it was another speculative scheme in his long desire to make the fortune that had so far eluded him. The project in which the three were involved coincided with a booming commercial interest in Mexico. This included massive land grants and railway concessions from the Mexican government to foreign investors at bargain prices. As part of a broader effort to spur economic growth, the favorably disposed Mexican government under President Porfirio Diáz was actively encouraging American investment. Venturesome capitalists, particularly railroads and mining enterprises, were looking to gain a hold in northern Mexico. There was a strong belief that Mexico was "one magnificent but undeveloped big mine" and that all it would take was sufficient capital to tap these mineral riches, the next El Dorado. The mines themselves were set deep within the recesses of the Sierra Madre mountain range and required mule teams to carry the ore hundreds of miles to market, a circumstance that could be improved with an efficient railway system. Hüller had acquired a number of these concessions from the Mexican government, including the Palomas Tract, named after Hüller's newly established town of Las Palomas, thirty-seven miles south of Deming, New Mexico.[2]

After the dinner meeting, Mexico took precedence among Schwatka's varied interests. Fortunately, the Yellowstone debacle had not tarnished his marketability as an adventuring journalist. Taking advantage of that reputation, he persuaded the *Chicago Inter-Ocean,* a progressive Republican newspaper that catered to the business class, to take a chance on a publishing angle likely to appeal to its commercial side. The *Inter-Ocean* agreed to sponsor Schwatka on a visit to northern Mexico with pen and sketchbook, and to deliver as many as fifteen articles between March and July 1889. Certainly, it was no mere coincidence that the region to be visited by Schwatka was the same as that covered by his proposed colonization plans with Powell and Cody. His correspondent role would provide him with the ideal opportunity to assess, and perhaps even advance, those plans. Now that the Apaches, who had once roamed lawlessly over the area, had been subdued, Schwatka believed that this "practically unexplored country" would make an interesting subject for *Inter-Ocean* readers. Offering his audience a tantalizing preview of what they might expect, Schwatka wrote that he had received reliable reports of large ruins of unknown origin that were far more extensive than similar ruins in Arizona and New Mexico. Reports of those ruins had been communicated to Schwatka by members of the Third Cavalry while chasing Geronimo through the Sierra Madre.[3]

While in La Crosse, Schwatka retained the young but talented studio artist Samuel (Sandor) Leopold Landeau to make sketches and take photographs during the Mexican journey. Landeau would serve as Schwatka's only companion from start to finish. Born in Hungary in 1864, Landeau's family had moved to Cincinnati while he was a child. After displaying artistic talent, he was sent to La Crosse for drawing lessons at the age of fifteen. He was operating a studio in La Crosse when Schwatka made his acquaintance, most likely offering art lessons and painting portraits of well-to-do locals. At times struggling to make ends meet, his paintings served as currency to satisfy his debts. At the age of twenty-five, anxious to see more of the world and acquire more varied subjects for his brush, he jumped at the opportunity to join Schwatka's expedition, leaving the comfort of his rented Main Street studio behind.[4]

On March 1, 1889, Schwatka's Palomas colony partners—Dr. Frank Powell and Buffalo Bill—sailed to Paris with Bill's Wild West Show for a featured tour of Europe, with thoughts of also gaining funds for their colonization project from an untried audience. At the same time, Frederick Schwatka stepped off the train in the town of Deming, New Mexico on his Mexican journey. Deming, Schwatka's jumping off point, was a true railroad town, its prosperity emanating from its connection to the transcontinental railway. A symbol of westward expansion, the "silver spike," linking the Southern Pacific Railroad with the Atchison, Topeka and Santa Fe, had been driven in Deming in 1883, thus completing the second transcontinental railway. When Schwatka arrived in March 1889, Deming was looking to reap the bonanza from the proposed railways that would run south to Mexico, ones with which Hüller's companies were closely involved. The town was abuzz with activity. Schwatka noted that "every stranger is thought to have something to do with [the railroads]." Everywhere he turned he rubbed shoulders with well-heeled investors, both American and European, who had come to assess business opportunities.[5]

Since the "vexing Indian question" had been settled in the Sierra Madre, as it had been in the American West, energetic development in northern Mexico could commence. Much of Schwatka's philosophizing in the *Inter-Ocean* during his Mexico trek stressed the inherent right of the United States to commercially control the regions he visited and the immense possibilities of those regions. Ever the expansionist, he advocated an aggressive economic imperialism, boldly asserting that "Mexico by right of contiguity belongs to us financially and commercially so long as foreign capital and enterprise must predominate at all in that country, and this fact we are just beginning to fully realize.... [I]t is indirectly to our benefit to predominate commercially in Mexico...." Even the name of his expedition—"America's Expedition"—heralded the coming of the eager capitalists from the north. That Schwatka, the reporter, may have had at least an appearance of a conflict of interest due to his business interest in attracting colonists did not seem to concern him in the least. Nearly every paper that mentioned Schwatka's excursion had him hard at work making preliminary surveys for the railroads, and his route did in fact coincide with Hüller's proposed railway route from Deming, New Mexico to Chihuahua, Mexico.[6]

Love of travel invigorated Schwatka as he and Landeau arranged their departure by mule-train, a slow but steady means of transport. He was not travelling lightly. At any one time, his caravan would have up to sixteen hired assistants and as many as forty-seven riding and pack mules. After crossing the Mexican border on March 6, their trail paralleled the rugged Sierra Madre Oriental, the eastern range of the Sierra Madre or "Mother Mountains" that formed the backbone of Mexico. Contrary to their expectations, against a backdrop of beautiful snow-covered mountains feeding innumerable rivers and creeks, they found lush and fertile grasslands along its foothills supporting large cattle ranches, markedly different from the desert landscape that lay to the east. Camping on the high plateau of the Sierra Madre at four thousand feet, the warm midday sun quickly turned cool after sundown with a firm breeze running off the mountain range.

A brief stop for a customs inspection was made in the town of Las Palomas, also the home of Hüller's recently completed fourteen-room palatial mansion and headquarters. Nearby, two newly established Mormon settlements, Colonia Diáz along the Casas Grande River and Colonia Juarez along the Piedras Verdes River, greatly impressed Schwatka. Both communities, beginning with Diáz in 1885, served as a refuge for displaced Mormons seeking to avoid enforcement of polygamy laws in the United States. Expressly avoiding a touchy discussion of their religious beliefs but recognizing that the polygamy issue had overshadowed everything else about them, Schwatka's writing highlighted what he viewed as their most impressive characteristic, that "they have no peer in pioneering among the Caucasian races." [7]

Schwatka's hosts along the way, wealthy landowners and businessmen, offered hospitable accommodations at their haciendas, large estates catered to by many servants. Though he was a welcome guest of these prominent personages, as an advocate of fair treatment Schwatka did not overlook the plight of Mexico's people. Schwatka was disturbed by the common practice of providing credit to the local Indian laborers, who quickly overdrew their accounts. They became "slaves" to the owners, who, according to Schwatka, "can do as they please with the poor creatures, and work them whenever and wherever they see fit." Many local farmers had been displaced through Porfirio Diáz land reforms which negated existing claims and concentrated land holdings in foreign investors, causing those displaced to move to haciendas for employment on any terms.[8]

In the Peidras Verdes region, his party was escorted to nearby ancient ruins by Mr. MacDonald, the business manager of the Juarez settlement. Although Schwatka was unaware, the area he visited encompasses archaeological sites attributed to Mogolian culture. Today this is the well-known and larger World Heritage Site of Paquimé, Casas Grandes, which encompasses the remains of more than two thousand adobe living areas, stores, and workrooms. The Mogollan civilization had thrived by successfully adapting to the northern Mexican desert environment. As active traders, they had established trading links and cultural ties with the Pueblo of the southwestern United States and northern Mexico. However, the culture suddenly disappeared about 1450 CE for reasons not yet fully understood, predating the arrival of the Spanish conquest.[9]

Schwatka was surprised at the extent of ruined buildings and houses, which exceeded one hundred, at times clustered together as villages. Many dwellings still retained pottery, utensils, and other relics, reflecting the once widespread and prosperous culture. With a melancholy heart, he pondered the mysterious fate of this once flourishing civilization. Now, a lone mountain lion passing through the ruins caused Schwatka to remark that "truly the wild beasts were wandering over the Toltec Babylon." Schwatka recognized that his trip was a sightseeing excursion, not a scientific endeavor, penning the forward-looking comment that "[t]here is an extensive field here for some special scientist skilled in archaeology." Backtracking from Juarez, Schwatka stopped at a large hacienda at Corralitos, an area well known for its lucrative silver mines. These had been worked by the Spanish centuries before, and were now operated by the Corralitos Company, an American-owned entity. Britton Davis, formerly a lieutenant in the Third Cavalry, and close friend of Schwatka, served as superintendent there. Having traversed about two hundred miles from the border and scouted the country, Schwatka concluded that crossing the Sierra Madre mountain range would be easier from the west side. Therefore, he and artist Landeau returned to Deming, and from there traveled west to Benson, Arizona, and southward to the city of Guaymas in Sonora, via the Mexican Central Railroad.[10]

The trip to Guaymas was a pleasant, but brief and largely unremarkable excursion that Schwatka's pen takes far too long to describe. The picturesque port city on the Gulf of California did not overly impress Schwatka, but he was pleased to see that in the seventeen years since his last visit, the bustling shipping commerce was now largely American in nature rather than European. For the scrupulous reporter, with an observant eye for even the smallest detail for his travelogue, Schwatka was unusually silent regarding a celebratory event near Guaymas in which he was a featured attendee. On April 6, at the invitation of Hüller's business partner, George Sisson, Schwatka boarded a special train with fifty political dignitaries, officers, and prominent citizens to travel six miles to the village of Batamatal. Here he attended a rousing celebration to mark the commencement of Hüller's railway line from Guaymas southward. Popping the cork and toasting to the success of the railway venture, which was expected to bring enormous prosperity to Mexico, a military band struck up lively music. The distinguished guests, including Frederick Schwatka and George Sisson, president of the railway company, gave patriotic toasts. Schwatka's normally productive pen ignored the event completely perhaps so as not to associate himself too closely with the railroad interests. Schwatka's letter to the *Inter-Ocean* on Guaymas did include a few carefully chosen words in support of the coming railways though.[11]

Having been informed by the local authorities that the Yaqui Indians, who were on Schwatka's route to the Sierra Madre mountain range, were restless at the moment and that the rivers were running dangerously high, Schwatka was advised to cross the mountains from the east. So, back again by rail to Deming, and then El Paso, he and Landeau made their way 250 miles south to the city of Chihuahua, the largest city in northern Mexico and capital of the province, with some 30,000 inhabitants. The seasoned traveler pushed on to the mining town of Cusihuiriachi, escorted by Don Augustin Becerra, whose enormously wealthy family held a land grant from the Mexican government in the rich Urique mining district.

Forty miles further, any semblance of a road ceased at the small village of Carichic, near the foothills of the Sierra Madre. Here, Schwatka first encountered a little-known Indigenous people living in this rugged and remote region of Mexico, the "Tarahumara" or "Rarámuri" as they call themselves. The shroud of isolation that cloaked these unassuming people was soon to be lifted by the pen of Frederick Schwatka. Within the village itself were a people Schwatka termed "civilized" Tarahumara, those that lived in stone or log huts and followed the "forms and duties of civilization," tending farms or working the mines or ranches. Sadly, these "civilized" Tarahumara had abandoned much of their traditional lifestyle under pressure of colonial rule. Their plight, like many others, was an all-too-common experience that followed the conquest and exploitation of the New World. Missionaries, soldiers, and government officials brought disease, death and disruption to their culture and way of life, and for many, a demoralizing loss of their own identity. That disruption was not limited to the effects of Spanish colonization. The disturbance continued after Mexican independence, which encouraged an influx of settlers to the Tarahumara homeland. Even as recently as the mining rush that Schwatka diligently chronicled, the introduction of a substantial Mexican labor force threatened to further disrupt the Tarahumara way of life. In contrast to Schwatka's "civilized" Tarahumara, some Tarahumara, the so-called "wild" Tarahumara, had retreated to hidden caves and caverns that offered a safe haven and refuge from the increasing turmoil and a preservation of their lifestyle.[12]

Faced with Spanish and Mexican dominance, Schwatka was impressed with how the reserved Tarahumara tenaciously sought to maintain their own culture, opining that even the "civilized" Tarahumara had only pretended to assimilate. He remarked that all of them operated independently from the Mexican Government to varying degrees, and except in cases of murder, they administered their own system of justice by officials of their own choosing and by their methods.

Despite acknowledging the obvious societal transformation wrought by the Spanish in their conquest of the New World, Schwatka could still praise the Spaniards enterprising spirit that unlocked the mineral wealth of the inaccessible Sierra Madre mountain range. Shaded by his own experience, Schwatka found the Apaches as the far greater invaders and disrupters, surmising that the Tarahumara were driven south from the cliffs of New Mexico and Arizona to the more remote regions of the Sierra Madre by the Apaches. To Schwatka, the Tarahumara were an anachronistic curiosity, truly a fascinating people, worthy of examination and understanding. Schwatka foreshadowed, and very likely stimulated, the later extensive work by the ethnologist Carl Lemholtz, when he remarked that "it would well pay someone to devote a few years to their thorough study...." The distinctive Tarahumara evoked Schwatka's admiration with their resilience and unbending independent lifestyle, but Schwatka recognized the impact precipitated by the commercial boom he advocated. He wrote that "since one of the richest mining districts of the world lies near the land I have briefly described, it will not be long before the age of steam and electricity will replace the age of stone."[13]

Schwatka could plainly see that the Tarahumara offered a more eye-catching feature for his readership than a plodding rundown of mines and railroads. His travelogue thus became the story of these unfamiliar people. With the assistance of his hosts, a window into their lifestyle was opened. With that entree, Schwatka succeeded in introducing the Tarahumara to the American people. "Rarámuri" means "foot-runner" and Schwatka was one of the first to recognize their running prowess, remarking that "their powers of endurance on the mountain trails are almost equally marvelous." He noted their great pleasure playing their "foot-ball" game, rarahipa, where endurance counted more than ball skills. At the village of Cusihuiriachi, Schwatka found to his disappointment that he had inadvertently left his Winchester rifle at an earlier station. He was astonished when a young Tarahumara boy who volunteered to retrieve it covered over 110 miles of rugged terrain in one night and half a day on his return. Schwatka also learned that another Tarahumara, a mail carrier on an assigned route, made a regular round trip of five hundred miles over the Sierra Madre range, which was accomplished in six days while carrying forty pounds of mail and provisions. Remarkably, after a one-day rest, he repeated the trip.[14]

As Schwatka correctly observed, the Tarahumara were inured to a highly aerobic lifestyle in the formidable mountains at an early age. Running games over long distances were a favorite pastime, with heavy betting of goats, sheep, and cattle. Although many Indians excelled in running endurance, according to Schwatka, the Tarahumara were the most prominent. Their running feats even brought them pop culture status in the running world during the 1990s. The best-selling book, "Born to Run," documented their performance in the Leadville 100, an ultramarathon event run over steep and rugged trails in the state of Colorado (the course rises and descends more than 15,000 feet). As recently as 1993, they finished first, second and fifth in the Leadville race. In 1994 a Tarahumara runner finished first, beating the course record by twenty-five minutes.[15]

Visiting their dwellings for a more intimate peek at their home life, Schwatka recognized that their implements were sparse but practical; a bow and arrows, a bench, a gourd for carrying water, a few dishes of baked pottery, in some cases a goat or deerskin for a bed. He was most impressed with the blankets and the loom used to fashion blankets from the wool of mountain sheep. Corn was their staple, and he recognized that they ferment corn into a form of beer, tesgüino.

After a delay in rounding up a group of motley and worn-out beasts

"Children of Cliff and Cave Dwellers Surprised in Sierra Madre."
Drawing by Sandor Landeau.

for transport that left them uneasy about reaching their destination safely, Schwatka's entourage made its way over rough and steep mountain trails. Here, he had his first glimpse of what he termed the reclusive "wild" Tarahumara, "of which the world has known comparatively nothing." Schwatka described them as dark skinned, tall, lean and muscular, with long hair, wearing only a breechcloth of animal skins and sandals. Little of their lifestyle was known. Schwatka claimed they were sun worshipers, with a superstitious fear of the owl; the "civilized" Tarahumara and the Mexicans looked down on them with contempt. Over the course of the trip, Schwatka claimed to have seen 300 to 500 individuals. Upon hearing the clanging mule team and falling rocks, the shy people had scurried away to the shelter of a large boulder. Schwatka's guide, Don Augustin Becerra, from whom Schwatka obtained much of his information about the Tarahumara, estimated the number of cave and cliff-dwellers at 20,000 (today the number is estimated at closer to 50,000 or more).[16]

Like most travel writers of the time, and in an effort to entertain his readers, Schwatka could be prone to exaggeration. This occasionally meant presenting particularly fascinating sights and events with some additional color and embellishment to make them seem more remarkable. Such was the case with the Tarahumara. Some Tarahumara, Schwatka's so-called "wild" Tarahumara did live in rock shelters, a more appropriate term than "caves" for their living areas located under natural overhangs, carve outs and rock strata that permeated their country. These "wild" Tarahumara were separated by Schwatka into either "cave-dwellers" or "cliff-dwellers," a distinction that reflected merely the location of their living quarters. Both groups of "wild" Tarahumara lived in "caves," but one upon ground level and the other in the cliffs of the cañons. The terms "cave-dweller" and "cliff-dweller" brought to mind a primitive society, lost to civilization, living an almost storybook existence, or as "children of nature" as Schwatka referred to them. Schwatka's writings maintained a marked distinction between the so-called "wild" and "civilized" Tarahumara (a suggestion encouraged by *Century* editor Clarence Buel), and highlighted in particular the "cliff-dwellers" as a culture that had chosen an almost tightrope existence.[17] To readers of the *Century Magazine*, Schwatka's "cliff-dwellers" took on a non-human character in precarious living spaces:

> So precipitous are some of the inclines leading to a few of these cliff-buildings that even these ape-like creatures cannot ascend them, and they pass from one bench in the rock, where they can get a foothold, to another directly overhead or underneath by means of a notched stick or log, which they climb like so many monkeys. Sometimes three or four of these are needed to reach a very high cliff-dwelling on a precipitous incline; for I have seen them living in cliffs so steep that I believe a stone tossed from the hand with ordinary force would reach the bottom of the cañon, two or three hundred feet below, before striking the walls of the cliff.[18]

Shortly after visiting the Tarahumara, at the nearby village of Urique, Don Augustin Becerra's home, Schwatka's entourage was welcomed with open arms, greeted by the entire village of almost two hundred Mexicans. Urique was a rich mining area and one of the first that had been colonized by the Spanish. The remote town itself was established in 1612, eight years before the arrival of the Pilgrims at Plymouth Rock. Don Jose Maria Becerra, brother of Don Augustin, treated them to a visit to the Cerro Colorado mine, said to be the richest gold mine in the world. Upon returning to his hacienda one afternoon, seeking to impress his visitor, Don Jose laid out on a chair four lumps of gold worth $70,000. The display astounded the wide-eyed Schwatka and left him envious of the mine owner's personal wealth. Mixing with the locals, who shared little in that wealth, Schwatka solicited their opinion of the foreign labor and capital incorporated into the mining production. He was surprised to gain an earful from the locals, who griped that they were opposed to outsiders "coming at all," and he found that "individually the Mexican is never so bitter against foreigners as the American...."[19]

Schwatka was a veteran of mule riding, but the experience in the steep and narrow trails of the cañons of the Sierra Madre, some of which were less than half a foot wide, left even the normally fearless ex-soldier skittish. Larger than the average Mexican or American, the plump Schwatka, now topping the scales at 267 pounds, needed a correspondingly weightier mount, which they found in "Old Steamboat," a one-eared mule. Although he was reassured by his hosts that Old Steamboat had never fallen, according to Schwatka "he [still] had an exasperating and blood-curdling way of stumbling along over [the trail] that would raise the hair on end of a bald-headed man." On the sheer edge of a dizzying switchback, he had a distinctive way of lurching slightly over the edge, perhaps purposefully, and to the terror of his rider.[20]

There were natural scenes to make even the moments of trepidation worthwhile. Schwatka had much to say about the beauty of the Grand Barranca of the Urique, or Urique Canyon, which he described as a cross between the Grand Cañon and Yosemite Valley, and "one of the most massive, stupendous pieces of nature's architecture that the word produces." This was an apt comparison, as the Urique Canyon is the most spectacular of six distinct canyons that make up the Copper Canyon region, a cañon system deeper and larger than the Grand Canyon. From his perch on the crest of the cañon, in the midst of a thick pine-oak forest that blanketed the plateau, he eyed the course of the river that had cut deep gorges in the volcanic rock, more than a mile below. The distant valley itself was a decidedly different eco-system, humid and hot, with scattered cactus, palms and tropical vegetation. From his viewpoint, as he scanned from plateau to valley, Schwatka could rightly survey a range of plant-life stretching from the equator to the pole.[21]

Schwatka was also impressed with the great coniferous forest of the northern part of the Sierra Madre, which he viewed as one of the largest in the world. Always commercially minded, he correctly predicted the logging boom of the 1920s as access to the remote region improved, a boom that brought with it deforestation and further intrusion to the Tarahumara lifestyle. Dropping almost a vertical mile, the men entered the Arroyo de las Iglesias (Cañon of Churches), a fairyland of wind and water sculpted rocks, pillars, spires, and formations of every shape and form to the imaginative eye, cast in shades of brown, red, and even blue and green in the setting sunlight. Also carved out of these rocks were a mixture of caves and caverns, among which Schwatka found more cliff-dwellers, some of whom lived in exceedingly high cliff-shelters, reachable only by a series of notched sticks or logs that offered a foothold for climbing. Schwatka was not shy about his inability or nerve to climb two or three hundred feet upwards, for he was "sorry to say that I am not sailor, a tightrope performer or a balloon professor."[22]

From here, Schwatka's journey came to a close. At the town of Batopilas, the two men were the guests of American Alexander Shepherd, a part owner of the Batopilas Mining Company, one of the most important silver mines in the region. Shepherd, also known as Boss Shepherd, had made a name for himself as head of the Public Works of the District of Columbia. He was later a governor of the district, undertaking massive public works projects that modernized the district, but at enormous cost. Personal bankruptcy led him to flee Washington, D.C. for Batopilas in 1876, where he made a fortune in silver mining. Spectacular views of the mile-high cliffs on both sides, a beautiful hacienda and a pleasant host made for a most enjoyable visit. Departing, Schwatka and Landeau tagged along with one of Shepherd's pack trains of eighty mules bound for Chihuahua, carrying a fortune in silver bricks. At Chihuahua, the two boarded a train back to the United States.

※ ※ ※ ※

After their three-month excursion through Mexico, Schwatka and Sandor Landeau returned to Deming on June 6. After an uneventful train ride north, they amicably parted ways. For Landeau, the Mexican trip was a pivotal event in his young career, a springboard that served as the impetus to widen his exposure beyond that of portrait artist to the local gentry. Landeau's sketches enlivened Schwatka's articles in the *Chicago Inter-Ocean,* one of the first newspapers to feature illustrations, and gave him nationwide recognition as an artist. With a portfolio of well executed watercolors depicting the people and places visited in Mexico, the young artist pedaled his works locally in La Crosse and to a larger market in Chicago. His work was taken notice of by the press, one newspaper remarking that "as a painter he has given evidence of wonderful conception and execution, and is undoubtedly destined for a bright career."[23]

Confident in his talent, and with financial backing from La Crosse benefactors, Landeau enthusiastically travelled to Paris for more formal studies, training at the Academie Julian. Ultimately, he gained an entry to the 1896 Salon de Paris, one of the most prestigious annual art exhibitions in the world. He gained further recognition and awards over the course of his career with a number of highly regarded works. One painting from

"A Halt in the Mesa." Painting by Sandor L. Landeau.

his Mexican travels is known to have survived, "A Halt in the Mesa," donated anonymously to the La Cross Public Library in 1890. Despite his professional success, his personal life remained shrouded in secrecy. After his initial move to La Crosse, he disowned his family, severed all contact with them and adopted a different name (Sandor instead of Samuel). His desperate parents, fearing he was dead, unsuccessfully attempted to locate him for more than twenty years. During that time, Landeau advanced his career, largely in Paris, married, and had one child, a daughter. In 1900, Landeau's sister Frances finally did establish contact with Landeau's wife and father-in-law. In regard to Landeau's unusual behavior, Frances told a reporter: "because he [Landeau] is ashamed of us, he told [his father-in-law] that all the members of his family were dead." Evidently, the contact failed to lead to a reconciliation, and the unusual story faded from the headlines. Sandor Landeau, who eventually separated from his wife, died alone and penniless in 1924. Such was the life of one of La Crosse's most important artists. Even today, his paintings are as difficult to find as the artist himself had been.[24]

For Schwatka and the *Chicago Inter-Ocean*, the Tarahumara were soon elevated to the status of an ancient "lost race" by the newspaper. Several days after Schwatka's June 2 letter detailing his first contact with the Tarahumara, the *Inter-Ocean* led with the headline, "THE CLIFF DWELLERS. THE RACE NOT EXTINCT AS REPORTED BY THE SMITHSONIAN INSTITUTION." Highlighting its importance, the *Inter-Ocean* boldly announced that Schwatka's discovery brought to light descendants of the ancient cliff-dwellers of the southern United States who had migrated to the mountain regions of northern Mexico. The *Inter-Ocean* claimed that "it will undoubtedly give Schwatka the credit, and make his expedition one of the most important in an archaeological sense, of any during the century."[25]

Interestingly, Schwatka himself had not conclusively asserted a relationship between the cliff-dwellers of the American Southwest and the Tarahumara of the Sierra Madre, though he believed that there likely was such a connection. He had offered a tantalizing opinion about the nature of the Tarahumara, which was enough for the *Inter-Ocean* to seize on as definitive fact. Not surprisingly, newspapers across the country sensationalized the story in bold headlines: "LIEUTENANT SCHWATKA LOCATES A RACE HITHERTO UNKNOWN"; "THOUSANDS OF CLIFF DWELLERS ARE STILL LIVING"; "CLIFF DWELLERS DISCOVERED"; and "THEY ARE NOT EXTINCT." There is no doubt that Schwatka's press reports reached a nationwide audience and brought widespread, and perhaps unwanted, public attention to the little known Tarahumara.[26]

Besides the coverage through the *Inter-Ocean*, Schwatka boasted in the journal *America* that eight or ten major metropolitan newspapers and more than twenty-five thousand smaller papers carried the full report of the expedition. As a subscriber to the various news clipping services of the time, Schwatka claimed that he was inundated with more than three thousand published reports on the Tarahumara. His typical bluster no doubt inflated the true numbers, but that it was a national sensation was certainly no exaggeration. Schwatka had availed himself, in a big way, with the growing use of syndication to extend his reach beyond the *Inter-Ocean's* audience. In the United States, organizations like the McClure Newspaper Syndicate were creating a full-blown industry by syndicating news, stories, and features with widespread appeal to numerous local and regional newspapers, and authors like Schwatka benefitted from additional royalty opportunities. Schwatka understood that his Tarahumara story was a "hot property." In 1892, the *Tacoma Ledger* quoted a report that the newspaper syndicate that had been formed for Schwatka's Tarahumara story was the largest ever assembled for one writer. This now long forgotten story contributed greatly to Schwatka's own public prominence. Overwhelmed with the coverage of his find, an elated Schwatka wrote to Clarence Buel at the *Century Magazine* that he has been "successful beyond my greatest expectations," and that the story of the Tarahumara, "has been more widely received by the press than my Arctic expedition...."[27]

Schwatka contributed to that coverage. For the *Century Magazine's* high-brow audience, already accustomed to his descriptions of Indigenous peoples, in June 1889, he published "Land of the Living Cliff-Dwellers," an informative article that described the Tarahumara in the context of his Mexico trip. His July article in the magazine *America, A Journal of the Americas*, gave a sense of the media flurry sparked by his find, noting that "a few hermit cave-dwellers would have caused no more attention than finding of one or two among our own people, …but the finding of them by hundreds, and hearing of them from good authority by the thousands, was certainly a revelation to all of *America's* party, and not much less of a surprise to the people of the United States, if general press comments can be taken as criterion." [28]

With the public desire for information about the Tarahumara at its peak, the resourceful Schwatka quickly realized there were still other opportunities of which he could avail himself. He was overwhelmed, almost blinded, by the frenzy of the Tarahumara craze and the enormous publicity it had showered upon him. Rather than seeking to temper the story he had set in motion, he became hell-bent to exploit it to the fullest. A message to Schwatka from the showman Buffalo Bill, then in Paris, set in motion his next decision (yes, the electrifying Tarahumara story had even reached an international audience). In July, half in jest, wholly in earnest, Bill had urged Schwatka to "come on at once with his cave-dwellers and claim the fortune that awaits their advent in the French capital." But Schwatka did not believe that he needed to cross the Atlantic to make that fortune, and his course would transform him from correspondent to gaudy showman.[29]

After a brief visit home to Chicago in late summer, without fanfare, Schwatka quietly returned to Mexico on behalf of another Chicago newspaper, the *Chicago Herald,* a well-regarded daily unrelated to the *New York Herald* of James Gordon Bennett, Jr. The *Chicago Herald* had undoubtedly watched closely as its local rival, the *Chicago Inter-Ocean*, reaped the benefit of the Tarahumara story. The competition between the two Chicago publications was not lost on Schwatka. Exploiting that rivalry, Schwatka worked an arrangement with the *Chicago Herald* to match the circulation boost achieved by the *Chicago Inter-Ocean* in its coverage of the Tarahumara. What better way to cover the sensational story of this "lost race" than by delivering them to civilization for all to see. Borrowing a page from its New York namesake and looking to create the news, the *Chicago Herald* agreed to back Schwatka on his trip to Mexico to do just that. For Schwatka, it was only the usual brief stay at home with Ada and his now three-year old daughter.

On his way to Mexico, Schwatka made a short stop at the cliff dwellings of the Southwest to compare for himself their possible connection with the

Tarahumara. Pushing his own narrative, he dispatched a special telegram to the *Chicago Inter-Ocean* confirming as fact what had previously been only a cautious opinion: "I have examined the cliff dwellings here and find them the same as those in Chihuahua. This supports the theory that the cliff-dwellers driven out of Arizona by the warlike tribes found safe refuge in the Sierra Madres, where I found thousands of them a few months since."[30]

Before trying to lure any Tarahumara from the Sierra Madre, Schwatka wisely requested and received permission from Lauro Carrillo, governor of Chihuahua, who laughed at the thought that any Tarahumara would consent. Carrillo was nearly proven correct. In the field, it proved to be no easy task to persuade the reclusive Tarahumara, as their characteristic timidity made them highly skeptical of leaving their homeland. The first three attempts to convince individuals to accompany Schwatka ended in utter failure before he could get them close to the trail. With the assistance of one Tarahumara with Mexican blood, an individual named Senor Luis Mesa who could speak the Tarahumara language as well as Spanish, a fourth group of eleven Tarahumara was delicately coaxed to leave. Although it is difficult to assess the nature and extent of the relationship between the Tarahumara and Schwatka, the Tarahumara had placed a considerable degree of trust in Schwatka for them to take such a monumental step. Schwatka promised some material consideration and a commitment to return any Tarahumara who desired to leave at any time, but it took more than promises to persuade the reclusive group.

The supportive words of Luis Mesa, one of the Tarahumara who was persuaded by Schwatka to go, would have carried some weight among the others. Mesa spoke from a position of authority, as he held a local Mexican political office and, just as important, he was married to one of the Tarahumara women. That Schwatka himself also provided needed reassurance and comfort came from a reporter who met the group as they changed trains in Kansas City. He noted that Schwatka always stayed near them and that the Tarahumara "grow restless and dispirited when [Schwatka] is not with them." The accommodating group of eleven was comprised of five men, three women, two boys and one baby; three were labelled "cliff-dwellers" and four were termed "cave-dwellers," and the remaining four "semi-civilized Mexican Indians but Tarahumara." They hailed twenty-five miles from the village of Yoquibo, sixty miles southwest of Batopilas.[31]

The trip to the metropolis of Chicago was an overwhelming cultural shock to the astonished Tarahumara, who had never travelled beyond their secluded canyons. After a one-hundred-mile trek by foot and by mule out of the mountains, they arrived at the village of Carichic for their next leg by coach. Never having seen a wheeled transport, and too fearful to enter the coach, Schwatka hit upon the idea of placing the women and children on top of the stage, while the men ran alongside. Remarkably, in a testament to their endurance, when they finally stopped seventy miles later, Schwatka remarked that the mules were played out, but he believed the men could have run another seventy miles.

At Chihuahua, the electric lights ("chained lightning" as the Tarahumara termed it), "nearly set the children of nature wild with terror." If press reports can be trusted, the frightened Tarahumara ran away, but were physically collared and held down. Despite their trepidation, Schwatka managed to somehow shuttle them into the caboose for a rather bumpy and unpleasant train ride, later switching to a passenger car at Kansas City. According to Schwatka, when the train departed, the men climbed up on the rafters of the car and the women crouched terror stricken in the corners. They were equally surprised when Schwatka imposed a dress code while they travelled. Reflecting his own cultural norms, the women uncomfortably donned skirts and blouses. At Fort Bliss, in El Paso, Texas, they were invited guests to military target practice, where in a rather cruel and callous display, a Gatling gun was fired towards the sun, an act that left them "flat on their bellies." Not surprisingly, their spirits were at a low ebb in El Paso, a likely combination of homesickness and the cultural shock.[32]

The city of Chicago itself was an eye-opener. Skyscrapers were just starting to dot the skyline. A myriad of retail stores, restaurants, banks, and newsstands crowded the streets that were filled with rushing omnibuses, trolleys and trains and a jostling crush of people. Their destination, or home away from home, was the newly constructed fourteen-story Owings building, a Gilded Age cliff-dwelling, an extravagant symbol of growing American corporate wealth and status; its bricks imitated those of ancient Rome. Believing they would be more comfortable one hundred and fifty feet above ground level, the Tarahumara were housed on the twelfth floor, that was only reached by a staircase (due to malfunctioning elevators), which they climbed "with the agility of cats." A *Herald* reporter noted that they are always glad to get back to their "high perch" again, evidently forgetting the fact that only three were so-called "cliff-dwellers." Awed by the surroundings, they spent long hours people watching from their windows. The *Herald* assured that they had food that mimicked availability in their homeland. Corn meal and deer meat were brought in regularly, but it was dryly noted that one of their favorite dishes became popcorn.[33]

What was Schwatka's motivation in bringing the Tarahumara to the United States? Although lip-service was paid to ethnographic examinations and making some interesting discoveries regarding their lifestyle, traditions and habits, the fact was that Schwatka sought to promote himself as the discoverer of the Tarahumara and to profit from that discovery, principally financially. Fame and wealth had become alluring pursuits for Frederick Schwatka and nowhere was it more apparent than with the Tarahumara. The entire experiment, rather than a scientific study, would become a sensational circus show, as ostentatious as that of the showman P.T. Barnum. In fact, Schwatka proudly boasted to a reporter that he had succeeded where Barnum had not, remarking that "many persons have attempted to get representatives of these people and have failed. Barnum's agent offered $20,000 to a half breed hunchback native and then failed to get him."[34]

Schwatka found a business partner with a speculative side, willing to share the risk associated with putting the Tarahumara on tour. William D. Boyce, born in Pennsylvania in 1858, was an entrepreneur and successful businessman involved in various publishing related ventures when he met Schwatka. Later, he became a multi-millionaire industrialist. About the time he partnered with Schwatka, his *Saturday Blade* was achieving the largest circulation of any weekly in America, making extensive use of newsboy agents for distribution in the backroads of small-town rural America. Boyce, however, is better known as the founder of the Boy Scouts of America, and as an advocate of progressive reform. That progressive-minded attitude made him an early supporter of unions and protector of labor rights of workers, including his own newsboys. Despite his concern for fair labor practices, Boyce had no qualms about profiting from an exhibition of the Tarahumara. The arrangement reached between the two was that Boyce was to contribute $3,000 and Schwatka $2,000 to bring the Tarahumara to the United States; they would each share profits from any lectures and exhibitions on a 50-50 basis, and of course Boyce would benefit from increased readership in his newspapers with the coverage.[35]

Like the lyceum and the lecture movement, the practice of exhibiting Indigenous peoples had gained popularity during the late nineteenth century; its demeaning aspects were not considerations. Exhibitions were thought to offer a more vivid educational or entertainment experience, in which the exotic peoples were placed before one's very eyes, rather than described vicariously through the lecturer. To a colonialist culture within America that had embraced industrial and technological progress, exhibitions of Indigenous people also offered a tangible measure of advancement over so-called "primitive" societies. Exhibitions reached a culmination at the World's Columbian Exposition in 1893, a display marking four hundred years of progress since the discovery of the New World. The Anthropology Building of the exposition represented more than forty different cultures, including handicrafts of the Tarahumara.[36]

Although the lines frequently blurred, the smaller, more common exhibitions of Indigenous peoples generally undertook one of two formats, and Schwatka had plans for exhibiting the Tarahumara in both. The first, billed as an educational or scientific lecture, was typically delivered in a civic venue. It featured an expert who spoke with an air of authority, be it the veteran explorer or the "professor" (a fictitious title). The second was the less profound "Barnum-type" sideshow event of human curiosities, frequently playing alongside other "sensations." Commencing the week of February 24, 1890, Chicago's Central Music Hall played host to an upscale "Popular Historical and Scientific Lecture" by Lieutenant Schwatka featuring the Tarahumara, the "strange beings" from his recent expedition serving as "living illustrations." Couched as an educational lecture, Schwatka, in a didactic touch, described their peculiarities and lifestyle to what the *Herald* characterized as a refined audience.[37]

Of course, the Tarahumara were the hit of the largely attended event. Ushered upon the stage at the later part of the first lecture on the evening of February 24, the guests and the Tarahumara looked upon each other in mutual wonder. The Tarahumara were quite the sensation, offending Victorian sensibilities in their native costume, "which was very scanty indeed," huffed one captivated *Herald* reporter. However, a raucous sideshow trumped the science lesson, with the Tarahumara delighting the audience with an impromptu bow and arrow exhibition, while the heartily amused crowd, casting aside their refinement, inundated the Tarahumara men with cigars and tossed coins to the women. For the benefit of ticket holders to the lecture, the Tarahumara could also be viewed at Chicago's Casino Gymnasium, an apropos venue where they would "give trials of their endurance in running for which they are remarkable."[38]

Meanwhile, stepping away from the more high-brow educational lecture circuit (and more costly admission), the Tarahumara were booked for a series of engagements at cheap entertainment venues, so-called "dime museums." Popular during the late 1800s, they featured a wide range of sensational amusements (so-called "freak shows"), including human curiosities, magicians, wax figures, vaudeville, and animal acts, to name a few. Looking to maximize financial return, the Tarahumara were separated into two groups, six remaining in Chicago at local venues with Schwatka, while the remaining five went on the road to various midwestern cities under the supervision of manager Frank O'Neill. In Chicago, through mid-March, Schwatka's group played at Kohl and Middleton's "Big Dime

Kohl & Middleton's Big Dime Museum broadside advertisement.

Museum," a very popular venue on Chicago's south side, sharing billing with "Capt. Paul Boynton's performing seals." During the last week of March, they exhibited at Epstean's New Dime Museum, described as "a museum of curiosities, waxworks, electric contrivances and natural human and animal freaks." The top billing for both the venues was "the Little Baby Cliff Dweller."[39]

The travelling group of Tarahumara were first featured at an exhibition at Robinson's Wonderland (Musee Theatre) in Buffalo, New York during the week of March 15. They shared the top billing with "The Rouclere's Rattlers," a renowned vaudeville company, and "Capt. Chittenden's exhibit of aboriginal life in British North America and Alaska." They played at another Wonderland venue in Detroit, and thereafter through April at Kohl and Middleton's dime museums in Cincinnati, St. Paul and Minneapolis. Sensational advertisements played up the cliff dwelling aspect, with images of loin-cloth-wearing Tarahumara swinging into cliff dwellings by means of vines, *a la* Tarzan. In the Wonderland venues, and likely others, the Tarahumara were displayed "in situ," wrapped in blankets within a representation of their homes in the Sierra Madre mountains arranged on stage, a two-tiered cliff that housed two Tarahumara in the lower cave and three perched in the upper. A museum lecturer, with a showman's cant, enlightened the audience about their journey to civilization as they disrobe their blankets and tantalizingly "disclose their nearly nude bodies."[40]

Kohl and Middleton had been so impressed with the Tarahumara exhibition that they had contracted for an eight-week tour at their venues. However, the tour quickly came to an abrupt end over a contract dispute between Schwatka and his business partner William Boyce. To his credit, Schwatka had already paid $1,000 for the return of six Tarahumara to their homeland in Mexico at their behest. The five remaining, then at Kohl's museum in Minneapolis, also had had enough and were also ready to return. Believing he had been shortchanged by his partner William Boyce, Schwatka filed an action in Superior Court in Chicago seeking an accounting of their business finances, claiming that Boyce had only contributed $2,000 of the $3,000 he had committed, whereas Schwatka was out of pocket $2,650 (including $1,000 to return the first six Tarahumara). Schwatka sought for Boyce to pay his remaining $1,000 share in order to return the remaining Tarahumara to Mexico, and to share an additional $1,280 Boyce had received from lectures and exhibitions.

In response to the filing, on April 29, Schwatka, together with the court appointed receiver and the five Tarahumara, made what must have been a rather sensational court appearance. A reporter noted that "the tribe was almost nude as far as clothing was concerned, having only a blanket thrown over their shoulders." Although there was a sexual aspect to the frequent references to their natural state, nudity (or near nudity) as a cultural matter characterized the Tarahumara as primitive. The result of the court appearance was that Judge Shepard assigned them all to a house on West Madison Street "where they board museum freaks" according to the reporter. Whether the court case was ultimately resolved is unclear. However, the Tarahumara made their way back to their home in the Sierra Madre. The circumstances surrounding the return are vague but reports out of Chihuahua were that Schwatka managed to arrange to transport them to El Paso, Texas. After their arrival, they presented themselves to the authorities looking for food and payment they claimed was still due from Schwatka. A generous benefactor, Mauro Candano Benitez, mayor of Ciudad Juárez, fed them and paid for their return.[41]

The contentious business of the Tarahumara must have been resolved amicably as the affair failed to dim the personal relationship between Schwatka and Boyce. Some years later, after Schwatka's death, Boyce fondly recalled the lieutenant as his "old friend" and contributor to the *Saturday Blade*, and as "endeared to readers of my [Boyce's] publications through the discovery of a race of people in Old Mexico, the cliff and cave dwellers...." Boyce was foremost a businessman, and he recognized that notwithstanding the dispute, the *Saturday Blade* and other Boyce publications had been beneficiaries of Schwatka's well publicized efforts in regard to the Tarahumara. While the tour was ongoing, Schwatka's Tarahumara writings included several timely-placed media pieces, including two lengthy articles in the periodical *The Independent* in April and May, 1890.[42]

Although his works are long forgotten today, Frederick Schwatka was the first to bring the reclusive Tarahumara to the attention of the general public in the United States and his popular writings inspired further scientific investigation. To a Gilded Age society that viewed itself at the apex of civilization, his "discovery" of living "cave-dwellers" and "cliff-dwellers" was a captivating story, and a chimerical tale, of an extinct civilization rediscovered. In fact, as one historian has noted, it is an imaginative tale that is still repeated even today; a 2009 bestseller refers to the Tarahumara as "'a near-mythical tribe of Stone Age superathletes' who 'live in the side of cliff's higher than a hawk's nest in a land that few have ever seen.'"[43]

Following in Schwatka's footsteps, in September 1890, the Norwegian ethnographer Carl Lumholtz began his extensive work in Mexico. Initially a botanist and zoologist, Lumholtz had recently completed a four-year period in Queensland, Australia, collecting not only botanical and natural history specimens but making detailed observations of the aboriginal people within the region. Curiously, in 1902, Lumholtz claimed that his idea of visiting Mexico was "first conceived" in 1887, as he pondered whether there could be cliff dwelling descendants of the people of the American southwest "yet in existence in the northwestern part of Mexico hitherto so little explored." Lumholtz makes no mention of the source of his 1887 inspiration that was only documented fifteen years later, but one might think it curious and perhaps even somewhat suspicious that his after-the-fact interest predates Schwatka's visit of 1889. Lumholtz's first definite steps were only initiated in 1890 during a lecture tour of the United States, a year after Schwatka's Tarahumara first made widely circulated headlines and the same year as Schwatka's exhibition tour. Interestingly, in a June 28, 1890 letter from W. P. Garrison, editor of the weekly publication *The Nation,* to the renowned archaeologist Adolph F. A. Bandelier, Garrison wrote: "His [Lumholtz's] book on the Cannibals of Queensland is just now the book of travel before the reading public. Primitive man is an obsession with him, and he [Lumholtz] has been attracted by Schwatka's late account of a new and wild people in your old stamping ground." Bandelier's "old stamping ground" was the

American Southwest and Mexico, and Bandelier was an acknowledged authority as to Indigenous peoples of those regions. It seems quite likely that Schwatka's well-publicized writings about the Tarahumara served as Lumholtz's inspiration, notwithstanding his unsupported 1887 assertion. If so, you would not know it from Lumholtz's persistent and rather nasty efforts to discredit Schwatka's writings.[44]

Lumholtz's first Mexican trip, between September 1890 and April 1891, had the backing and staffing of several scientific institutions. His large party spent six weeks examining the ancient ruins in the Piedras Verdes region previously visited by Schwatka, a trip likely also inspired by Schwatka's writings. Returning to Mexico in January 1892 on a second expedition, Lumholtz located the Tarahumara. Like Schwatka, Lumholtz had no hesitation headlighting them as "Cave-Dwellers," because, according to Lumholtz, they "live in caves to such an extent that they may properly be termed the American Cave-Dwellers of today." Lumholtz returned a third time, spending the three-year period between March 1894 and March 1897, while continuing his research in Mexico and immersion in Indigenous cultures. Coincidentally, Professor William Libbey, physical geographer on Schwatka's Mount St. Elias trek, was retained on Lumholtz's first expedition, perhaps through the efforts of one of the scientific institutions. However, the connection with Schwatka's Mexican expedition was more evident with Lumholtz's solicitation of Sandor Landeau, artist from Schwatka's Mexican journey, who was offered a position with Lumholtz in 1892, but evidently turned it down.[45]

Lumholtz deserves much credit for his extensive and groundbreaking work in regard to Mexican cultures, but his attacks on Schwatka's writings bear a particularly sharp edge. To an audience of scientists at the Congress of Anthropology in 1893 (part of the World's Columbian Exposition), in the opening sentence of his address (after Schwatka's death), in a sweeping statement he sought to debunk every aspect of Schwatka's narrative:

> I shall first have to say that the late Lieutenant Schwatka's writings about these people were a gross piece of humbug. *De mortuis nil nisi bonum* [Of the dead, [say] nothing but good]. But as I, on account of a prolonged stay of secluded life in the Mexican mountains, only recently came across a magazine article of his published last year, and as I fear that some scientists may have been led to believe in his so-called discoveries, I am in the name of truth bound to state:
>
> 1. His journey of discovery was to go by stage from

Chihuahua to Carichic; from there he took mules and went on the beaten track to Urique - five days' ordinary journey, - whence he returned by another beaten track through the well-known town Batopilas. I have ample proofs to show that he [Schwatka] never left this beaten track, the *camino real*, to examine a cave.

2. What he relates about "living cliff-dwellers," as he calls them, is what he has heard from others, supplanted by his own imagination.

3. He also brought back "cliff-dwellers" to Chicago. With the exception of a woman and child, who were pagans, and possibly may have been living in a cave, the "cliff-dwellers" were from a village, Yoquibo. To speak of these as cliff or cave-dwellers is ridiculous in the extreme to any one who knows the facts. I hardly think I need to waste my time by going farther into the subject of this kind of "cliff-dwellers." I shall now show that there are cave-dwellers in the Sierra Madre, but they are very different from those that the vivid imagination of the late Lieutenant Schwatka evolved.[46]

With the passage of time, Lumholtz seems to be protesting far too much and his acerbic comments as to Schwatka's methods sidestepped any criticisms of the substance of Schwatka's writings, which in many respects echoed Lumholtz's findings. Although far briefer, in light of his purpose, and on a more succinct timeframe, Schwatka's writings identified many of the same salient points regarding the Tarahumara as Lumholtz, such as their physical characteristics, diet and agricultural practices, clothing, governance, seasonal movements, running acumen, and even some specific customs. Schwatka was clear in stating that his work was not ethnographic research as such, but rather a popular travelogue written for the public at large. He also admitted that he did not visit a cliff dwelling, joking that his meaty frame could not make the climb and that some of his information came from informed third parties.

Schwatka did highlight the "cliff-dwellers" in his writings and even opined that they were descendants of those peoples that formerly inhabited the southwest (with which Lumholtz disagreed), perhaps the most legitimate criticism of Schwatka's Tarahumara writings. Interestingly though, even Lumholtz himself admitted that some Tarahumara live in what Schwatka characterized as "cliff-dwellings," when Lumholtz tersely reported that "if the [Tarahumara] caves are difficult of access, they are made accessible by one or two wooden ladders, or rather notched trunks of trees," coincidentally, the same means of access identified by Schwatka by his "cliff-dwellers." In the end, there were more similarities than differences between Schwatka's and Lumholtz's Tarahumara. Simple jealously over the widespread popularity of Schwatka's writings and, as importantly, Schwatka's priority in time with the Tarahumara may explain Lumholtz's caustic remarks and his efforts to discredit Schwatka. Certainly, like Schwatka, Lumholtz displayed his own cultural bias, even stating that the Tarahumara, "so far as their cave-dwelling habits, cannot be ranked above troglodytes," and more generally "the study of savage and barbaric races has since become my life's work."[47]

Lumholtz was preoccupied, and perhaps even obsessed, with establishing precedence as to the Tarahumara. Besides lambasting Schwatka's writings, Lumholtz shamefully sought to obscure the work of the renowned archaeologist Adolph Bandelier, but Bandelier was very much alive to set the record straight. A Lumholtz article in the November 1891 issue of *Scribner's Magazine* had insinuated that Bandelier had only been aware of the *former* existence of the Tarahumara, whereas Lumholtz was "satisfied that many of the tribe are still living." Bandalier bristled at Lumholtz's suggestion that Bandelier was unaware of their current existence, going so far as to publishing a rebuttal in the *Nation*, remarking that "Mr. Lumholtz knows better and should have stated it." Bandelier then quoted his own previously published report from 1890: "the Tarahumares are, at the present time, and in a few secluded localities, still the cave-dwellers of the American continent."[48]

The Tarahumara tour occupied a major portion of Schwatka's efforts in the spring of 1890. However, during this tour Schwatka struggled with an all too familiar demon. On St. Patrick's Day, he overdid it again by indulging in excessive drink. While incoherently wandering the streets of Chicago, he was arrested for disorderly conduct. When approached by a policeman on his beat at the intersection of Harrison and Michigan Avenues (not far from Schwatka's Chicago residence), Schwatka brazenly boasted in slurred speech that he knew every lieutenant in the force and labelled this officer a "fraud." Needless to say, his opinions didn't go over well with the officer. As he was booked, Schwatka even commented that "I have a little Irish blood in me." He spent the night drying out in a jail cell and was released the following day after reaching a semblance of sobriety. Embarrassed by the affair, he ducked a court appearance the following day.[49]

Although the road was not the best place for Frederick Schwatka under the circumstances, at the time it held more attraction than Chicago. Extremely pleased with the widespread Tarahumara coverage initiated by Schwatka's efforts, the *Chicago Herald* was open-minded about tasking Schwatka with another project, this one less sensational—the resources of the Black Hills. Schwatka was perfectly suited for the job, a correspondent playing up the natural resources of the West, in a region he knew extremely well. Although Schwatka met with several highly regarded scientists in the Black Hills region and visited a Sioux reservation, his journalistic output was modest. He had little to say about the Black Hills, beyond a long discussion of the bounteous artesian wells in the Woonsocket region, with which he was greatly impressed.

Perhaps Frederick Schwatka was distracted by other considerations during his trip. On his return to Chicago, Schwatka arranged for a lecture tour through Nebraska, a jaunt that enabled him to mix with old acquaintances, some dating back to his service at North Platte Station. Evidently, there were few bars in Omaha that he failed to patronize. A doctor and nurse called to his hotel room were forced to lock Schwatka inside to prevent him from continuing his uninterrupted binge. Nonetheless, he escaped the lockdown, and continued his erratic course through several more bars. His frantic nurse followed but was unable to apprehend him. Finally, he returned by taxi to his hotel dead drunk, with the angry driver demanding payment. The hotel was so disgusted with Schwatka's conduct that he was evicted. Moreover, when the taxi driver threatened legal action for nonpayment, Schwatka's friends intervened to "spirit him away" before he could be arrested. Ultimately, he made his way back to Chicago in disgrace.

Undaunted by his hair-raising escapades in Nebraska, the fall and winter lecture circuit of 1890-91 saw Frederick back on the road in the states of Iowa and Minnesota. For Ada Schwatka, who was never fully comfortable in their Chicago residence, her childhood home in Rock Island, Illinois, became a welcome refuge and place of retreat while the perennially absent Frederick was on tour or in the field. Her father Joseph Brackett, a well-respected citizen, and an energetic seventy-six-year-old, happily played the role of adoring grandfather to Frederika. Although dismayed by Frederick's alcoholic indiscretions, by all accounts Ada was a devoted and stoic wife who was supportive of Frederick Schwatka even under the most trying of circumstances. She would need to marshal all her strength in the coming days.

Perhaps it was a portent of things to come when a train wreck on the Illinois Central Railroad caused a cancellation of Schwatka's Dubuque event on January 22. Unfortunately, his lecture in the small town of Earlville the next night did not suffer the same fate. On the evening of January 23, after a laudatory introduction by a Baptist minister and temperance adherent who served as the lecture committee chairman, Schwatka opened with his customary thanks to the chairman and audience. Within moments however, Schwatka's slurred words and incoherent speech betrayed his apparent intoxication. The horrified clergyman leapt to the platform and charged Schwatka with drunkenness in front of the dumbstruck crowd. Taking to the pulpit and dispensing a damning temperance rebuke, he chastised Schwatka, telling him he had insulted his audience by appearing in that dreadful condition and advised the patrons that they would be refunded in full. Dismissed from the platform in disgrace, the lieutenant stood in utter silence, either too incoherent or too embarrassed to respond.

While in Mason City, Iowa, ironically a state at the forefront of the temperance movement, Schwatka's intoxication almost did him in for good. He arrived quite agitated, his friends remarking that he "did not possess that same calm and quiet frame of mind that marked his previous appearances." After spending the morning at the Park Hotel, a friend took Schwatka for a carriage ride, looking to calm his nerves, but hastily returned him to the hotel after Schwatka weakened and collapsed, nearly tumbling out of the carriage. In the evening, evidently experiencing an episode of alcohol-induced psychosis, he was in horrid fear of being left alone, and cried out for someone to remain with him.[50]

Delusions associated with alcoholic binges, known as *delirium tremens*, were well known by the late nineteenth century. Hallucinations could be both auditory and visual, in forms perceived as threatening to the individual, thus explaining Schwatka's fear of being left alone. Seeing his condition, several friends stayed until late in the evening. After they departed, Schwatka awoke several times and caused quite a commotion among the classy clientele when he stumbled through the foyer in his bed clothes (evidently, he had previously been known to have "paraded the rotunda without wearing apparel"). Despite his condition, the following day he continued to partake freely in his room, coaxed to leave only at the behest of well-meaning friends for a sleigh ride in the afternoon. Upon returning to the hotel, climbing the stairs and reaching the top, he lost his balance and stumbled, dropping like a load of bricks to the lobby. It was quite a fall, as he toppled over the railing and plunged eight feet to the ground floor. His nose struck a baggage trunk and was broken in two places, and he suffered three fractured ribs and severe bruises to his spine. In Rock Island, a telegram fortuitously reached Ada almost immediately about his state of affairs. Shocked and concerned by his injury, she hastily hired a special carriage and arrived at the Park Hotel at 2:00 a.m. the following morning, somewhat relieved to find him in a painful but otherwise stable condition. Ashamed and remorseful over the incident, Schwatka sulked in his room, avoiding his friends.[51]

At the time of his fall, the injuries appeared so severe that there was fear for his life. According to Schwatka, an Associated Press reporter anxiously hunting for information on Schwatka's condition was told in hushed tones by a hotel clerk seeking to impress the reporter that "Lieut. Schwatka will die in fifteen minutes." Running with the scoop, a special dispatch went immediately across the wire to hundreds of papers: "Mason City (Iowa), January 31 – Lieutenant Schwatka, who was fatally injured last night by falling over the bannister in a hotel, died this morning." Nowhere was the news more a sensation than in Rock Island where it reached Joseph Brackett. It wasn't until later in the day that Ada wired her father that the information was false.[52]

Nonetheless, the Associated Press had carried the report far and wide. With a nationwide reputation, the news of Schwatka's death generated an outpouring of sympathy and obituaries. Correcting the inaccuracy, one newspaper remarked that the rumor of Schwatka's death had been "exaggerated," a comment made six years before Samuel Clemens' similar humorous response to the reports of his own death. Despite the seriousness of his underlying condition, a jovial Schwatka, now in better spirits, laughed at receiving more than 1,500 obituaries, noting that he found information about himself that he would never otherwise have learned. There was something quite amusing about the publicity. One paper even noted that "Lieut. Schwatka, who was killed in western Iowa recently, lectures in Davenport on the 31st inst." Other reports had him crippled for life. Even his return to Rock Island was not taken lightly. It took four men to carry all of his 267 pounds to his carriage upon the arrival of his train.[53]

CHAPTER SEVENTEEN
THE LAST JOURNEY

ALASKA HAD NEVER BEEN FAR from Frederick Schwatka's thoughts as he continued to cross the country lecturing about its considerable resources. From a distance, he watched the ongoing attempts at its exploration with envy. That faraway view would soon change. Following Schwatka's 1883 reconnaissance, a determined General Miles had continued his low-key efforts to gain more knowledge of the region's interior. After Abercrombie's disappointing failure to ascend the Copper River in 1884, Lieutenant Henry T. Allen, a young West Pointer with an enthusiasm for Alaskan exploration as deep as Schwatka's, completed a brilliant expedition in one season. Allen explored lengthy sections of the Copper, Tanana and Koyukuk Rivers and traversed more than 1,500 miles of unknown territory. Allen's expedition and his official report received little fanfare and recognition beyond government circles but was proudly characterized by his commander General Miles as "exceed[ing] all explorations on the American continent since Lewis and Clark...." Ironically, Allen's Alaskan accomplishments competed with the popular accounts of Frederick Schwatka's own Alaskan efforts, his Yukon traverse, and his expedition to St. Elias, which were widely available to the general public.[1]

But Allen's achievement remained a high-water mark for the army in Alaska for some time. From 1886, activity by the United States government and its agencies in Alaska stalled due to political attention focused on internal affairs. At the same time private endeavors stepped in to fill the void, following the publicity success of Schwatka's activities. Although competitors had delighted in poking fun at the *New York Times* for its sponsorship of Schwatka's St. Elias expedition and the ensuing Jones River controversy, they could not ignore the circulation success the *Times* had gained. Schwatka's St. Elias attempt and its spotlight on the mountain were followed by the National Geographic Society's sponsorship of their joint expedition to Mount St. Elias with the U.S. Geological Survey in the spring of 1890. For the nascent geographic society (only two years old at the time), the St. Elias attempt was its first scientific field expedition and an opportunity to gain some publicity and recognition at a modest cost.

Also looking to profit from a good thing, *Frank Leslie's Illustrated Newspaper* sponsored a quite modestly staffed expedition to unexplored Alaska in 1890 in the same manner as the *Times*. *Frank Leslie's Illustrated Newspaper* had a long history of sensational reporting of accounts of travel and exploration and the benefit of impressive full-page illustrations. In fact, the cover of the magazine's first issue in 1855 pictured the fur-clad grizzled crew of the recently returned second Arctic expedition of Elisha Kent Kane, an image repeated in its 1000th issue in 1874. The magazine had changed course in 1889 after being sold, resulting in a dramatic drop in readership. Perhaps looking to recapture that excitement and gain a circulation boost, they sought more exciting and sensational copy. *Frank Leslie's* 1890 endeavor was led by E. Hazard Wells and included Edward James Glave, as artist and correspondent. It accomplished little beyond brief excursions into the Tanana and Alsek Rivers. Widespread publicity accomplished the magazine's purposes, however.

Schwatka again adroitly looked to profit from a spirit of competition among the private press and their desire for a circulation boost. In February 1891, prior to his fall in Iowa, he had approached the *New York Ledger* with a proposition that was near to his heart, the exploration of Alaska. Under the direction of Robert Bonner, who had acquired the publication in 1851, the *Ledger* was refashioned from a staid commercial publication into a fine weekly literary magazine, featuring serials, short stories, and poetry by recognized authors such as Alfred Lord Tennyson, Henry Ward Beecher and Henry Wadsworth Longfellow. A mix of fictional stories, from gripping adventures and thrillers to sentimental romances, had been the successful formula that captivated readers. By 1890 the magazine was tiring after Bonner's resignation in 1887, so Schwatka's real-life exploits, sure to be as exciting as the *Ledger's* imaginary tales, were sure to give a boost to the waning publication (it finally ceased publication in 1903). It certainly helped Schwatka's cause that *Frank Leslie's Illustrated Newspaper* already had one marketing success in Alaska and Glave was quickly preparing for another with *Century Magazine*. Although the *Ledger* had agreed to sponsor Schwatka's expedition in return for a series of articles, the ever-resourceful Schwatka had retained the right to syndicate his articles to as many as fifty regional and local papers. Those papers would hold exclusives in their respective circulation areas and would contribute between $100 and $500 towards expenses.[2]

For Schwatka, the Alaskan expedition would also serve as redemption for the disappointment over the Yellowstone fiasco and his own personal failings, and prove that he was still a true explorer in the strongest sense of the word. With a free hand to set his course, and unbridled authority, nothing could have pleased him more. It was his ideal situation. Remarkably, Schwatka shrugged off the effects of his near-fatal mishap in Mason City and kept to his timetable for the Alaskan expedition. At forty-one years of age, he was no indestructible youth. He still held a commanding presence, tall, broad shouldered and staunchly built, but perhaps too staunchly at 267 pounds, weakened by physical ailments and a drinking habit. Nonetheless, always the optimist, he believed that his iron constitution and fierce determination could overcome his shortcomings. Ada Schwatka surely had her reservations, but as usual any admonitions went unheeded.

Mobility and reliance upon local assistance, as usual, would dominate Schwatka's planning. Unexplored lands, "blank" spaces, were the objective of the expedition. For that Schwatka would need a qualified surveyor like Homan from his 1883 reconnaissance. On February 20, while on the road, Schwatka contacted John Wesley Powell, director of the U.S. Geological Survey, explaining his objectives and highlighting the need for an accurate survey of the unexplored reaches of Alaska:

> I intend to conduct an exploring expedition through that portion of the unknown parts of Alaska bounded, roughly speaking, by the Yukon and White Rivers on the east, the Copper or Atna River on the west and the headwaters of the Tanana River to the northward. I believe that this unexplored part of our country will be found of more than usual interest in a geological sense, and probably in economic phases that would lead to further developments of the country. It would connect the geographical and geological surveys of the great Yukon River with those of the Pacific Coast via Copper River, and would be the only connection so made on a point on the length of that long stream.[3]

Schwatka also petitioned for a competent geologist to accompany him to perform those surveying tasks. Apparently, his reputation still carried some influence within government circles. Powell ultimately recommended Charles Willard Hayes, known by his friends as "Willard," who would prove to be an excellent choice. Hayes possessed the necessary skills for a small-scale expedition: scientific competence, combined with a genial personality and an overall willingness to do whatever was necessary for the success of the mission. Born in Granville, Ohio in 1858, Hayes had graduated from Oberlin College in 1883. At Johns Hopkins University he earned a doctoral degree in chemistry with a minor in geology and mineralogy. Upon graduation, he joined the scientific staff of the U.S. Geological Survey. Working with Dr. Israel Russell, who led the National Geographic Society's St. Elias expedition of 1890, Hayes was engaged in a geologic survey of the southern Appalachians at the time. Despite never having travelled west of Ohio, an opportunity for scientific work in virgin territory and a love of the outdoors led the thirty-two-year-old Hayes to seize the opportunity to join Schwatka's expedition. Schwatka also negotiated a favorable arrangement with the geological survey, such that the survey would continue Hayes's salary and would have the benefit of any scientific work performed. Schwatka made it clear to Powell that Schwatka retained the right to his bread-and-butter, popular literary works.[4]

Accompanied by Ada and now five-year-old Frederika, who were travelling as far as Sitka, Schwatka and family started out from St. Paul and followed a zig-zag route north to Winnipeg, Canada and back through the Dakotas, Idaho and Washington. Schwatka was a one-man publicity campaign, providing interviews and whetting the appetites of readers of the participating journals in cities across the western portion of the continent. To reporters along the way he repeated a vague and open-ended response: "I expect to cover about 1,200 or 1,500 miles of unexplored country, but have not as yet made up my mind as to what direction will be taken.... The expedition is simply to open up an unexplored country...." He basked in the flattery and attention. His celebrity status was such that when spotted by bystanders upon the streets of Minneapolis, one reporter remarked that "he became the observed of all the observers."[5]

Arriving in Tacoma, the Schwatka family boarded the steamer *City of Topeka* for the journey to Juneau. As always, Schwatka left some flexibility in his plans, initially proposing to cross the Chilkoot Pass, as he had previously done, following what was now a well-worn and surveyed trail to the Yukon headwaters. From there, he would travel the Yukon River by compact folding boats (assembled on the spot) to some location between Fort Selkirk and the White River. There he hoped to obtain some local guides to assist in crossing 300 to 400 unexplored miles overland to the Copper River, and then follow that river or a branch to Prince William Sound.

During the trip to Juneau, Schwatka was persuaded by a commercially minded Judge Louis L. Williams, former district commissioner, to begin his trip from Juneau by following the deep inlet that extended into the interior along the Taku River to the Taku Trail. The Taku Trail was a longer march to the Yukon headwaters than from the Chilkoot Pass. However, information was spotty as to the character of the Taku Trail. Only the year before eight hardy prospectors had attempted the passage in late winter, and after an arduous eighty-day ordeal had stumbled onto Teslin Lake at the trail's end. Worn and dispirited by the trek, the following year they abandoned the approach for the Chilkoot Trail.

Juneau had only sprung up in the last decade on the heels of a gold strike in the fall of 1880. Its Treadwell mine complex had quickly become one of the world's most productive gold mines and a substantial employer. By 1890, an influx of two thousand five hundred persons had quickly established a modest town and the surrounding community of Douglas into a sprawling number of hotels and lodging houses, retail stores, pharmacies, laundries, barber shops, a slaughterhouse, and, of course, more than thirty ubiquitous bars and saloons. Prospectors looking to reach the Yukon gold fields typically stocked up in Juneau, then continued to Chilkoot Inlet for their start. Juneau merchants cheered Schwatka's decision to map the little used Taku Trail, as they believed that surveying the Taku Trail would increase their commercial opportunities by making Juneau a staging point for prospectors to the interior. The enthusiastic merchants even contributed several hundred dollars to support the effort, support they would later regret.[6]

Stepping off the steamer in Juneau, Schwatka breathed a heavy sigh of relief that his unfortunate injury had not delayed his start. The locals delivered the welcome news that the Taku River had not yet broken up. With time on his hands, Frederick and Ada were briefly tourists, this time with Frederika, sharing a pleasant memory of their 1883 visit. They remained aboard the *Topeka* which continued its journey along the now popular "Inside Passage," made famous by the eloquent and influential Alaskan writings of John Muir. They looked with wonder on the miles of spectacular scenery, arctic-like in its grandeur, massive glaciers stretching almost to the sea. Otters, seals and porpoises meandered in the icy waters, and birdlife by the millions covered the shores and rocky cliffs. They reveled again at Glacier Bay, still ice-choked, and were awestruck by the magnificent Muir Glacier, which they approached within a mile. With so much floating ice in the bay, Schwatka was reminded of his passage through Hudson Bay in 1878. From Sitka, the return was made to Juneau, and the all-too-short pleasure cruise was at an end. The parting with Ada and Frederika must have been a particularly heart-rending farewell. Ada certainly pondered whether her husband's constitution would stand up to the task. The wilds of Alaska were a far cry from Yellowstone National Park with its well-placed hotels.

In Juneau, Schwatka managed to retain the services of a Taku Tlingit, Kook-sáh'k, known as "Robert," a sub-chief who supplied a two-ton canoe for transport and helped arrange for six packers to carry supplies. The six Tlingit packers were not simply faceless assistants. Schwatka identified each by name and offered brief details on a few. One of them, Skeet-lah-káh ("Edward"), "a great raw-boned Chilkat young man," had been a fourteen-year-old packer during Schwatka's 1883 journey, hauling sixty-eight pounds more than thirty miles on the Chilkoot Trail. Shakqua-tãh, or "Sam," was educated in the mission school. The others, "Koolteén" or "Paddy"; Koo-nagh-ka-sáh or "Jim"; Tah-wõõt-z or "Barney," Kah-eé or "John," could speak English well enough to communicate. One additional white man was hired, Mark C. Russell. Little is known of Russell, either before or after the trip, other than he was a prospector, likely lured to the adventure to scout some unknown mineral deposits. He had been a member of the eight-man prospecting party that ventured down the Taku Trail the year before, so his knowledge about the country was invaluable. He proved to be an excellent frontiersman, a title that, in short, meant he was eminently resourceful in any circumstance. Efforts to secure a photographer failed when the would-be-cameraman could not get a release from grand jury duty. The task fell to Willard Hayes, who managed a collection of high-quality images with Schwatka's Anthony camera from the Mexico tour.

Their start on May 25 was rather inauspicious since Robert and one of the packers had overindulged themselves the evening before. Finally shoving off with three white men, seven Tlingit and their supplies in their two-ton transport, Schwatka laughingly noted for his first letter to the *New York Ledger* that "the commanding officer was the heaviest one of the party, and made excellent ballast in the rear part of the canoe. His avoirdupois surplus was not so beneficial, however, during other parts of the trip." Under a dreary and drizzling sky, they hoisted the American flag to the feeble waves of a small group of largely disinterested onlookers.[7]

The Taku River and Taku Trail combination proved no easy task. The craft was navigated over the forty-five-mile course of the river with sails, oars, and poles to its mouth and the end of canoe navigation. Impressed with the mile-wide river as he looked upstream at the start, Schwatka remarked that it is "one of great streams of Alaska and the British Columbian possessions." As they approached the river's mouth however, perhaps recalling his "Jones River" experience, he altered that opinion, as the river narrowed, and the swift current made forward progress difficult.

The New York Ledger Expedition. Photograph by C. Willard Hayes.

They made scant progress for several days, with hard poling and tracking over gravel bars, scraping the rocks and pebbles along the river bottom. Near the head of the inlet, weaving amongst progressively larger chunks of ice, Schwatka looked up in awe at the spectacular Taku Glacier, one of the thickest alpine glaciers in the world, over one mile thick from the ground to its upper surface.[8]

Leaving the inlet, the Taku Trail itself was a wild, rugged path of sorts that required sixteen backbreaking days to traverse its eighty or so miles to Teslin Lake. With only six packers and some 1,200 pounds of supplies and equipment, each packer's load of two hundred pounds was shuttled by means of two trips of one hundred pounds each, doubling back and adding exhausting miles to the trip. Schwatka, Hayes and Russell were not overtaxed though, as they each carried twenty to thirty pounds, mostly their meagre complement of scientific instruments (the prismatic compass, a sextant, and four aneroid barometers), photo equipment and clothing. Thick shrubbery and bushes impeded progress, as did quagmires of peat bogs and swamps. In higher elevations, the heavy-laden packers sank to their knees, and occasionally their armpits, in snowbanks. Much of the trail ran through wide valleys in the upper Taku basin from 3,500 to 5,000 feet above sea level, the last fifteen miles being heavily wooded with numerous lakes and streams. Thunderstorms and the bane of Schwatka's previous Alaska adventures, the ever-present mosquitoes, were rampant.

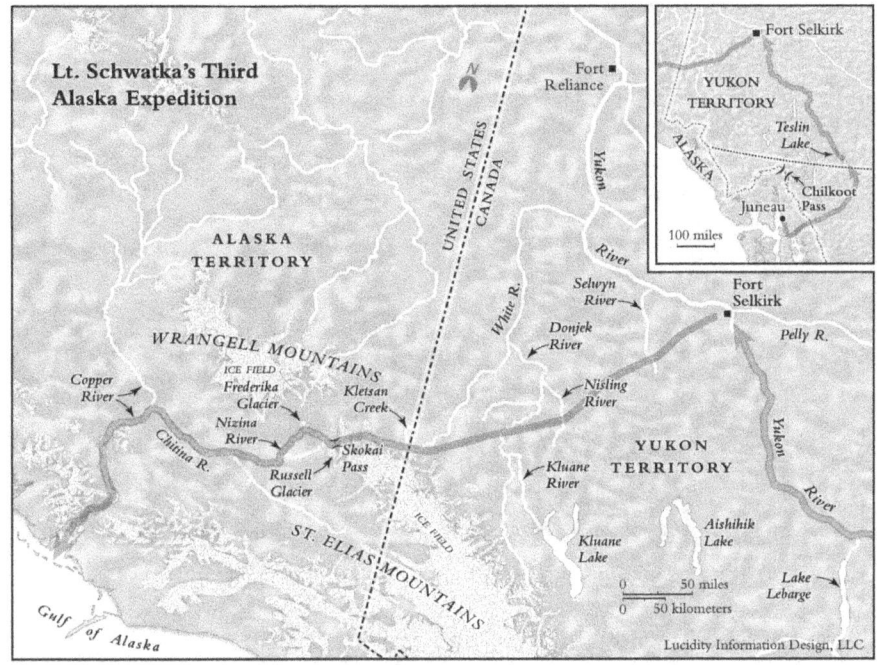

On June 16, much to their relief, the bank of Teslin Lake, was finally reached. Schwatka continued to adapt to his conditions and to draw from previous experience. To cross a series of five lakes on the approach to the Yukon, he had packed three ingenious folding boats weighing one hundred pounds each, manufactured by Charles W. King of The King Folding Boat Company in Kalamazoo, Michigan. Employing a waterproof outer covering, galvanized steel wire ribs, wooden cross pieces and floorboards, the folding boats were assembled in forty minutes and proved capable of ferrying most of their supplies across the lake system without incident, while Russell and the several Tlingit travelled overland. King's folding boats would later be used extensively during the Klondike Gold Rush and were so effective they were in use well into the 1970s.

At Teslin Lake, reminiscent of Schwatka's Yukon trip, the indefatigable packers dropped their packs, completed their duty, and quickly retreated, not resting for even a day to recover. No one was more pleased than Hayes on their departure. Perhaps unaccustomed to close contact with Indigenous peoples, he found his hard-working companions moody and grumpy complainers and offered little praise for their backbreaking labor. A more sympathetic Schwatka noted that their ankles "were black, bruised and swollen out of all shape, and it was evident that we were not reaching

Packers on the Taku Trail. Photograph by C. WIllard Hayes.

the end of their journey any too soon." Attentive to their physical condition from their start, he had provided for longer and more frequent rests. Schwatka could display cultural insensitivity in his writings, but he was also quick to acknowledge the skill and hard work provided by his Tlingit assistants. He relied heavily upon Robert's ability to handle the canoe and his thorough knowledge of the river. As for the packers, he understood the exasperating difficulties with which they contended, particularly the discouraging burden of doubling the trail by shuttling their heavy loads in two trips. Schwatka remarked that "they had performed a 'herculean task' indeed, and deserved well of the fruits of the undertaking whatever the future may show for this."[9]

Despite the difficulties, in a boost to the anxious Juneau merchants, Schwatka sent back an encouraging letter with the packers touting the potential of the Taku Trail to the Yukon, one that sounds far too optimistic in light of their experience. Schwatka ventured an opinion that the shallow Taku River was navigable by steamer most times of the year. From its headwaters, he was confident that the country was sufficiently open enough to build a wagon road or even a railroad. He believed that from Teslin Lake, a river steamer "can undoubtedly reach Bering's Sea and consequently the Yukon River." Despite Schwatka's positive acclaim for the route, the Juneau merchants would later gripe that Schwatka had not held up his end of the bargain. Evidently, the armchair businessmen expected that Schwatka would lead the way by somehow blazing an easier, improved trail.[10]

With makeshift sails, one hundred miles was made over the course of Teslin Lake in several days to the headwaters of a large river that would carry them to the Yukon. The river was commonly known as the Teslin River. With his usual naming flourish however, Schwatka had previously bestowed the name Newberry River, but Schwatka's designation never caught on. The fact that the Teslin River was located within British North America also did not concern Schwatka, since his expedition, as a purely private endeavor, would have avoided any international controversy. On June 24, Schwatka's group arrived at the convergence of the Teslin and the Yukon rivers. They were now crossing Schwatka's track of 1883.

As was his usual practice, Schwatka had committed to approximately fifteen letters for the *New York Ledger* and the syndicate. He never shortchanged his audience. Individually lengthy, typically filling two columns per issue and several thousand words each, together they would make a full-length narrative if published in book form. Filling those pages called for close observation and a breadth of detail, all the while maintaining a lively storyline. Unlike Hayes, the geologist, who focused on the physical properties of the surrounding country, Schwatka's observations touched on the life of the river, and the Indigenous people they encountered. Schwatka understood that the history of these people was interwoven with the river, noting that the river "bristles with picturesque graveyards and deserted or half-deserted buildings, until one is forced to acknowledge that it is a solemn and melancholy old stream."[11]

Schwatka painted a picture of life on the Yukon before the rush on the Klondike in 1896 changed everything. By 1891, there had been an increase in activity after gold was discovered on the Fortymile River, but the region was still largely the province of Indians, scattered miners, and a few traders. Schwatka offered a glimpse of routine of the river's First Nations peoples, and the developing economic system that was modifying their traditional lifestyle. Schwatka could see that their employment was becoming essential to extracting natural resources in the Yukon, much like Inuit labor had become essential to exploiting natural resources in Hudson Bay. When the Tlingit monopoly on the Chilkoot Pass was broken in 1882, Tlingit became contractors for incoming miners, packing supplies over the pass and into the mining country. On the river itself, Indigenous peoples worked the bars in summer, and hunted for those miners who overwintered. Over the course of the Taku Trail, Schwatka encountered several parties exiting the interior loaded with furs to trade at Juneau.

At the convergence of the Yukon and Pelly Rivers, Schwatka's group had come across the first of several mining camps. Schwatka likewise provided a thorough description of their arduous work at seasonal placer mining, conducted by several hundred miners on the bars of the Yukon and its tributaries. Among the prospectors and traders, Schwatka had earned respect through his own trailblazing adventures. Coupled with his easy temperament, those hardy men spoke freely to Schwatka while relaxing around the campfire, enabling him to gather stories, yarns, and human-interest features to enliven his narrative, interspersing them among his letters. About Fortymile River, believed by Schwatka to probably be the most isolated mining camp in the world, he wrote that news was received once a year and then "of a meagre character." [12]

Tall tales and exaggerated stories, like those from the American West, had their place in the similarly rugged and untamed Yukon, and Schwatka made a point of collecting them as well. No account of Alaska could ignore the singularly dreaded mosquito and the pesky bug provided some of his best wilderness humor:

> The miners have the usual grotesque frontier exaggeration to express their ideas of this numerous insect. One declared that he found them so thick between the Yukon and the Hotalingua rivers that he could make several sabre cuts through the dense swarm with his bowie-knife, and holding it aloft, see the blood trickle from the blade, while a tobacco-chewing companion asserted that at one locality on the Yukon he would have to thrust his Winchester rifle-barrel into the mass and withdraw it quickly to get a place to spit. On the lower river Esquimau dogs have been killed by them, and it asserted by some that bears, in crossing marshy districts swarming with them, have been known to stop and attempt to fight, rearing on their haunches bear-like, instead of retreating, and, after hours of combat, have their eyes so swollen with repeated attacks that they were closed, and often times wandered off, mired in the marsh and starved to death.[13]

From the Yukon River to Fort Selkirk, the only obstacle was the "Rink Rapids" (now the "Five Finger Rapids") that Schwatka had run on his 1883 journey. Outside of a touch of seasickness, this white-water trip was an exhilarating and almost enjoyable experience. At Selkirk, falling in with an Athabaskan party (Northern Tutchone) returning from the Pelly River, Schwatka had a difficult time negotiating to hire packers for the balance of his trip. Few of them cared to venture to the White or Copper River, although many were free with advice on how it could be reached. Copper served as a valuable resource, and it was used to fashion tools, musket balls, and arrowheads from the ore. The women used its deep blue powder,

First Nations Families at Fort Selkirk. Photograph by C. Willard Hayes.

made from azurite, for tattooing their cheeks and chins. The presence of the mineral quickly caught the attention of Schwatka and Hayes and only amplified their desire to visit the region. Claims of copper boulders the size of log-homes circulating among the group likewise piqued their interest. Even for Schwatka, a seasoned traveler possessed of infinite patience who was rarely despondent, his discouragement over his lack of recruiting success was palpable. Hayes bore witness to the frustration, remarking that he and Schwatka had "a few warm words," and the next day, that Schwatka "is awful glum, has nothing to say to me." Hayes on the other hand had begun to delight in the company, even teaching English to one determined boy and treating a woman with a stomach ailment.[14]

Fortunately, by happenstance, a miner from Fortymile River named Frank Bowker arrived by raft. With his assistance, Schwatka hired eight packers and eleven dogs, along with Bowker himself. Relying upon their guidance, Schwatka now revised his plans. He would follow the remnants of an old Indian trail towards the Copper River, rather than run the Yukon to its junction with the White River. Like his Barren Lands trek of 1879-80, this course, striking "across lots" rather than along rivers, ran southwest across the interior plateau between the Yukon River and the St. Elias range, an unexplored region that Schwatka believed "ought to give considerable novel information."[15]

At high noon on July 9, they started out, elated to be on the move again. Unlike the Taku Trail, their path reminded Schwatka of a walk through the woods and prairies of the far Northwest, a largely unobstructed trail through valleys of rolling hills of poplars and aspens with flowers blooming alongside adjacent numerous creeks. Ever on the lookout, Russell and Bowker made brief stops to look for placer gold along streambeds but found little of economic value. Food was more than ample. Graylings abounded in every stream. Caribou, moose, and mountain goats were spotted, and several caribou were taken. Geese, ptarmigans, and grouse were likewise abundant. There were some nuisances though. Schwatka wore out his hat swatting the swarming mosquitoes. Also, severe hornet stings left him grumbling that he wished he was "back in the land of rattlesnakes, centipedes and tarantulas."[16]

Travel soon became more troublesome, particularly for the low-to-the-ground pack dogs, as they waded across innumerable streams and through grass and moss carpeted valleys, overshadowed by rocky bluffs. Their course took them along a stretch of the Selwyn River, named by Schwatka in 1883, at its junction with the Yukon. On July 15, climbing a high ridge to up to 2,500 feet, they could see the main valley of the White River from which rose scattered smoke, a combination of natural fires and Indigenous campgrounds. Further in the distance they had their first view of the snow-clad mountains of the St. Elias range and the immense Kluane Lake, the largest in the Yukon Territory. Some ninety miles from Selkirk, according to the "doctor's" reckoning, i.e., Hayes, at the Nisling River they fell in with a camp of six families (fifteen to twenty persons) tending their fishing traps in preparation for the salmon run. Schwatka found the bustling encampment far too boisterous for his liking, but Hayes offered some observations. Hayes recognized that these people (Southern Tutchone) were closely related to the Northern Tutchone of Pelly River, with similarities in language, dress and lifestyle. He thought that no more than fifty or sixty lived throughout the White River region. Schwatka's interest was piqued more by their conspicuous display of many pieces of copper, a promising clue on the road to this veritable El Dorado in the wilderness. Disappointedly though, they advised Schwatka that a trip across the mountains to its source was impossible, and they refused to guide them. These people harbored a deep-set fear, perhaps not mistaken, that if misfortune befell Schwatka's group, white men would blame them. Undaunted, Schwatka convinced two of them to accompany him, and the party continued to the imposing Kluane River. The river proved too wide to ford on foot, but the group managed to cross by means of a raft purchased from a passing group of Tutchone. According to Hayes, they had never laid eyes on a white man. The Tutchone were astute business people who, holding all the proverbial cards, drove a hard bargain. According to Schwatka, "there were enough negotiations over [the raft] to have purchased the Cunard Line or the Canadian Pacific Railway...."[17]

Schwatka's group slowly worked their way toward the St. Elias range. Their raft took them down the Kluane River to its junction with the Donjek. They left the Donjek four miles later, following a rough trail to the west, thick with brush and dead timber, under a hot sun. Attention briefly turned to another attraction on the morning of July 24, as two caribou scampering through the camp triggered bedlam. According to Schwatka, between guns blazing and dogs howling, the camp "looked like a lunatic asylum after a broken-loose menagerie." Despite the activity, the no doubt confused and bewildered caribou escaped unharmed.

As the group continued, the landscape took on an alpine appearance, and at a slightly higher elevation it offered a picturesque view of the St. Elias range. They reached the glacier-fed Generc River, which also proved too wide to ford, leaving them faced with a challenging crossing of Klutlan Glacier and an even more difficult time persuading their packers. To Schwatka's men, their companions held some uncommon superstitions. Their "medicine man," named "Jackson," forbid frying grease that day, claiming that if they did so, they would fall into a crevasse. Schwatka sarcastically noted that they agreed "to forbear oleaginous condiments rather than have a ton of ice tumble in on us." On the glacier itself, they were in outright fear, racing across nonstop and avoiding even whispers. The imposing glaciers of the region, with their dynamic nature, invariably advancing, retreating, and surging, dominated the daily life of the Athabaskan and Tlingit. As the anthropologist Julie Cruikshank has noted the awe-inspiring phenomena were to them an ever-present, life-threatening danger that heavily influenced their oral traditions. In disregarding their beliefs, what the Euro-Americans failed to appreciate was the close relationship their companions shared with nature. To them, glaciers were sensitive to the human presence; loud voices, "oleaginous condiments" and imprudence could provoke a purposeful response.[18]

About twelve miles from the glacier, at what is now known as Kletsan Creek (wryly termed "False Copper Creek" by Schwatka), just west of the Alaskan-Canadian border, they reached the indigenous source of the mythical copper lode. For several hours, their companions worked the gravel bed to mine the numerous large nuggets, which amounted to about twenty to thirty pounds of copper. According to Schwatka, "to those who had hoped the oft-talked-of copper mine would amount to something lucrative, the realization was quite a disappointment." Hayes sardonically remarked that the promises of copper deposits as large as houses at Selkirk decreased as they approached the locality, down to mere ounces on their arrival. Having reached their objective, the packers had completed their task and refused to go any farther, claiming that the mountains were only passable in winter with snowshoes. With Bowker, they prepared to retreat, leaving Schwatka, Hayes, and Russell all alone. Schwatka settled up with the packers, $25 each, and after a swig of quinine they departed with Bowker.[19]

Schwatka now faced a dilemma. Schwatka, Hayes and Russell could retrace their steps, some 200 miles back to the Yukon River and then along a known track to the sea, or continue an uncertain route across the mountains to the St. Elias range and a village only vaguely described by the Indians. There was no hesitation on Schwatka's part. He was prepared to proceed through the unexplored territory with only fourteen days' supplies despite his own debilitating physical ailments and his excess weight. Inured to rough life in the outdoors, Russell likewise had no hesitation. Even Hayes, the novice Alaskan wilderness traveler, expressed unwavering support, remarking "it is hard work, but we will make it." Every aspect of the trip would now fall upon Schwatka, Hayes, and Russell, who dropped all nonessential items. This still left them with bulky seventy to eighty pounds packs for their arduous trek ahead. They were down to "'bed rock,' to use a miner's phrase" noted Schwatka.[20]

Firm in their resolve, they departed, following the White River to their right and steep mountains to their left. An incessant rain would make for miserable conditions for much of the way, exacerbated by the lack of a tent for shelter. The dense brush was so "wringing wet" that they found that following the gravel bed and wading hip-deep through glacial rivers and channels, soaked to the skin and numb, was less objectionable. Three days later they reached the mouth of the White River, behind which sat an immense wall of ice, Russell Glacier. They marched delicately across the glacier and pushed through the divide at Skolai Pass, marked by strong winds of almost gale force. For several days, they followed the canyon of the Skolai Creek toward the Nizina Glacier and its river. Though rough going along the floor of the canyon, through thick growth of alder and spruce, it offered a picturesque scene with glaciers extending inward from all sides of the pass. One particularly large glacier running into the valley left Schwatka longing for home and absent loved ones. With a surge of emotion, he named it Frederika after his young daughter.

On August 5, they faced one of their most memorable days, a litany of obstacles almost too unimaginable, that Schwatka described as "a fearful struggle with icy torrents, slippery rocks, hummocky glaciers, muddy moraines, willow and alder *chaparrals,* soft mountain turf knee deep, dizzy heights on rock slides and in every way one long to be remembered." For Schwatka, matters turned even worse. As they approached an exit in a narrow canyon, they were forced along a steep ridge overhanging the

Nizina River for a stretch of two to three miles. At one point, Schwatka slipped on a patch of moss and stumbled over the edge of the steep bluff. With his feet dangling over the side, he was only saved by his pack which luckily caught an overhanging tree limb. He finally managed to regain his footing and scramble back to the ridge. That evening represented the low point of their fortunes. Schwatka likely did not exaggerate their emotions when he stated that they were "tired, tattered, torn, dirty and dejected, and in some cases bloody. We had carried pack-mule pack loads for eighty-six miles through the only pass in the roughest range of North America, and our misery was getting monotonous and our whole natures cried out for a change of programme. We got it."[21]

Schwatka had proven himself a thoughtful leader and one prepared to take calculated risks. On August 8, as they rested on the Nizina River, he concluded that taking to the water would be a more preferable means of travel than "packing with almost shoeless feet." The situation was not yet critical, but provisions were nearly exhausted, game was scarce, and their overland travel was painfully slow. Harking back to the success of his 1883 Alaskan adventure, he decided that even though the Nizina River posed its own obstacles, a boat could descend the turbulent river far more rapidly. It was a daring choice, but Schwatka would be proven correct. Much of that success was attributable to the resourceful Russell, "a practical woodworker" remarked Schwatka, who managed to construct a sturdy raft from the primitive materials available in the short period of one day. Taking a page from *Robinson Crusoe*, the adroit frontiersman, using a dull axe, carved a keel, bow and stern from spruce and willow, ribs and a gunwale from black alder, and an outer skin from stretched and sewn bed covers using fishing line, all sealed with lard and spruce gum.[22]

The hastily crafted boat proved its seaworthiness, as the run down the Nizina River to the Chitina River was made in two days, sparing them formidable travel overland. Schwatka's bald-headed humor didn't understate the danger as he noted that on the first day on the water, they "cut through channels and dashed through breakers that were better than barbers' elixir for raising hair." They were thrown out of the boat on multiple occasions. At one stop for repairs, they threw up a smoke signal to alert any Indians in the area, a desperate but largely fruitless exercise. Even the second day was hair-raising at times, including a seven-mile run through a narrow rocky canyon with heavy rapids and tortuous curves wherein they came close to disaster on several occasions.[23]

Leaving the Nizina River, they traversed the Chitina River forty miles to its junction with the Copper River. Schwatka and Hayes openly praised Russell's talent in safely navigating the boat. Schwatka even humorously admitted that he played only a bit part in the entire affair, contributing his heavy weight, which was shifted like adjustable ballast, to stabilize the craft in the roaring torrent. Their descent from the plateau of the White River basin had been considerable, estimated at over 2,500 feet. To readers of the *Ledger*, the trip was a breathtaking experience, so palpable was Schwatka's description of the excitement and danger.

Though Schwatka's group was unaware at the time, they had actually been preceded by Lieutenant Allen, who had also travelled part of the Nizina River in 1885. By an overland route from the south, Allen had reached Nicolai, chief of the Copper River peoples, then at a camp along the Nizina River. While the Nizina was still partially ice-covered and the current far more tame, Nicolai had guided Lieutenant Allen's party down the Nizina River to the Chitina and Copper Rivers in a twenty-seven-foot boat constructed by Nicolai's people. Hayes was unable to link Schwatka's route to Allen's map until after reaching the Chitina River.

In far better spirits, Schwatka's group reached the junction of the Chitina and Copper Rivers. At the village of Taral, three miles further down the Copper River, which was reached fourteen days after leaving Bowker ("exactly on time" according to Schwatka), they were extremely pleased to find Chief Nicolai, whose "existence they had come to doubt." With Schwatka and his men down to only three pounds of flour and a handful of tea, it was an opportune meeting. Nicolai proved to be as generous a host as he had been to Lieutenant Henry Allen in 1885, offering bacon, bread and fish. With fresh salmon every day, Schwatka remarked that "we thought we had struck the Devonian period."

Although Schwatka failed to mention the size of the village, Taral was one of the larger villages along the Copper River valley, with multiple dwellings dotting the river and a gathering place. Nicolai's group were Ahtna, an Athabaskan people occupying the region, with an estimated population of about 330, according to Lieutenant Allen. Communication was carried on by means of a Chinook jargon that both parties understood. The incredulous chief was astounded that the three white men had traversed the Nizina River in Russell's modest craft. Schwatka's party agreed to accompany Nicolai and his contingent down the Copper River to their annual trading visit to the coast, but a few days recovery was in order. Schwatka's ankles and feet were swollen and black-and-blue, the effect of the ice water of the last two weeks.

With time on their hands, Hayes thoroughly immersed himself in the geology of the region. Both he and Schwatka were fascinated by Mt. Wrangell in the distance, as the stunning mountain appeared to be emitting smoke from its flat dome. After five days of rest, the group departed in

Nicolai's thirty-foot long sealskin boat, manned with ten of Nicolai's men and Schwatka's three-man group. The trip was by no means a pleasure journey. The Miles Glacier (previously named by Allen), reached to the river itself and discharged ice-mountains in front of it, posing a formidable challenge. Nicolai's men were dreadfully fearful of the three miles they ran across it, as the swells generated by falling ice and debris could swamp a boat of any size. The following morning, they reached the delta and the village of Alaganik, and were informed that white men were at Eyak, fifty miles further. That afternoon they arrived at the Peninsular Company cannery in the middle of the river delta, where Mike Duvall, an old Yukon prospector who knew Russell well, went out of his way to make his guests at home. Making their way to Eyak, the group was compelled to spend a month until the next ship arrived. On September 21, they finally reached Sitka.

Schwatka's third and final expedition in Alaska was a creditable endeavor, and provided a great deal of personal satisfaction, simply as a matter of geographical achievement. He had surveyed some 330 miles of blank territory on the map. The adventure reinforced the image he cultivated as a capable and efficient explorer, and certainly helped his marketability as a travel writer for hire. His eighteen letters for the *New York Ledger* (all told thirty columns), more than fulfilled his promise to the newspaper and delivered his usual spirited copy. With distribution through over forty syndicate newspapers regionally, coverage became widespread across the nation. Schwatka never managed to produce a full-length narrative before his death in 1892, a significant factor in the expedition's fade into obscurity after the more fleeting newspaper coverage ended. Moreover, the *Ledger* articles were published between March 19, 1892, and August 19, 1892, almost a year after the events they chronicled, thus losing much of their timeliness. The trip also did not have the same eye-catching appeal as his 1883 Yukon traverse or the press attention following his 1886 attempt on Mount St. Elias, followed by the Jones River controversy.

Schwatka's expedition was further overshadowed by the expedition of Edward James Glave to the southeastern corner of Alaska during the same summer. The adventurous Glave had gained his travelling experience in the sweltering jungles of equatorial Africa. Working on behalf of Belgian King Leopold's colonization efforts in the Congo, Glave impressed fellow explorer Henry Stanley with his pluck and enterprise, which Stanley put to use in establishing outposts while exploring the country. With six years of African pioneering experience, the hardy Glave turned his sights far north. During the summer of 1891, along with Jack Dalton, Glave tracked a more feasible and shorter route than Schwatka's to the Kluane Lake region. It started from Pyramid Harbor and veered southeast, following a route well known to the Tlingit. Glave's novel use of pack horses rather than man-hauling supplies also contributed to the route's practicability, and with it, wider public interest.

Exploration was a competitive enterprise, and it was not uncommon for explorers to be found seeking discoveries in similar locations at similar points in time. In the south polar regions, Robert Falcon Scott and Roald Amundsen converged on the South Pole at nearly identical dates, Amundsen arriving just a few weeks before Scott. Such was the case in this obscure corner of Southeastern Alaska in the summer of 1891. Edward Glave approached Kluane Lake from the south in August 1891, only several weeks after Schwatka had passed north of the lake. On August 8, a rather perplexed Glave was surprised to discover recent evidence of what looked to be white men having visited the region. Camped at a small lake near Kluane Lake, Glave hastily scribbled in his diary, "here we found some quite recent traces of people, prints of moccasins, probably Schwatka, plus with them is a clear sign of a whiteman['s] boots among the lot." On reconsideration, Glave struck the reference to Schwatka and "whiteman's boots," editing the phrase to read "here we found some quite recent traces of people, prints of moccasins," evidently not prepared to credit Schwatka at the moment. Over the next few days, Glave convinced himself that Schwatka had been an earlier visitor. In his journal entry for August 12, Glave conceded that, "we can be nearly certain that Lieut. Schwatka has visited this Lake. They were undoubtedly his tracks we saw at the small lake." Glave ultimately reconciled Schwatka's route as inferior to Glave's, a more round-about trail to their location. In the end, unwilling to share the limelight with Schwatka, Glave made no mention of Schwatka's earlier visit in Glave's published account of his journey in any of his detailed articles published in the *Century Magazine*. The specter of a visit to the lake by Schwatka in advance of Glave surely weighed heavily on his mind, even letting his imagination run away from him. Ironically, although Schwatka did visit the area north of Kluane Lake several weeks before Glave, the tracks spied by Glave closer to the southern edge of the lake were not those of Schwatka, as the paths of the two explorers never crossed.[24]

Schwatka's success was built upon his customary formula, that of a small cohesive group, combined with Indigenous peoples' assistance, sound decision-making, and calculated risk-taking. The mapping of the unexplored corridor between the Yukon River from Fort Selkirk to the junction of the Nizina and Chitina Rivers, thus linking to Allen's map, through exceedingly rough and rugged terrain, was a significant geographical accomplishment. Much of that credit belongs to Schwatka's recruitment of a competent scientific observer, in this case Willard Hayes, who would go on to a long and distinguished career at the U.S. Geological Survey, serving as chief geologist from 1905-1911. Hayes's 45-page report in the *National Geographic Magazine* has not received its full credit. Besides being an accurate survey, Hayes's report of the virtually unknown White River basin provided an accurate description of the region's mineral resources, its flora and fauna, and geological and glacial formations. Besides completing the geographical and geological survey of the unexplored area, Hayes performed the first geological assessment and survey of the Taku River region. Hayes also confirmed native copper deposits at Kletsan Creek, near the White River, previously reported by the Indians. In the long run, the White River region explored by Schwatka and Hayes never became the hoped-for bonanza of mineral wealth. The region on the east edge of the Kennicott Glacier west of the Nizina River, would prove viable for copper extraction after the turn of the century by the famous Kennecott mines. About Schwatka's last expedition, the noted Alaskan historian, Morgan Sherwood, concluded that "in terms of original discovery, natural obstacles and contributions to science, this 1891 expedition was the most notable journey Frederick Schwatka made in Alaska...." But that accomplishment was no walk in the park. The burly Schwatka was worn both mentally and physically, having shed thirty pounds during the difficult endeavor.[25]

CHAPTER EIGHTEEN
CONCLUSION

For Frederick Schwatka, recently returned from his third Alaskan adventure, there was little time for relaxation. Delaying his return to Chicago, he arranged an extensive tour through the province of Saskatchewan at the request of the Canadian Pacific Railway. Besides its core railroad franchise, the railway was a diverse and expansionist enterprise involved in land settlement, grand hotels, and luxury steamships. According to Schwatka, who was retained for his celebrity endorsement, he had visited this land of opportunity and was pleased to report that "there is much tillable land in the region, and he believes it is profitable for settlement." His own enthusiasm for potential rail lines continued to run unabated.[1]

Returning home in late 1891, he maintained an active writing schedule. Besides finishing the lengthy missives for the *New York Ledger*, he was still completing an article for *Century Magazine* on the cave-dwellers, and a variety of shorter pieces for newspapers. These included the pluck of Inuit dogs, the cold of the Far North, how to build a snow house, Christmas near the North Pole, and orienteering in the North. Despite his family ties to Chicago, Frederick Schwatka remained stubbornly determined to go his own way. The Northwest held an attraction for him, and he quickly returned there in April, much to Ada's consternation. For an undisclosed organization, likely a railroad interest, Schwatka conducted a survey of the coast from Yaquina, Oregon to Cape Flattery, Washington on the southwest side of the entrance to the Strait of Juan de Fuca. An air of secrecy tended to surround disclosures regarding his physical ailments, all intentionally avoiding disclosure of his drinking problem. In this most recent instance, while driving along the coast, it was reported that his stage overturned and he sustained a severe injury to his left arm, which was reported as being almost useless. With every injury now suffered by

Schwatka, questions swirled as to the cause. As always, he seemed to make a miraculous recovery, at least to outsiders.

The all-too-obvious truth was that Frederick Schwatka's alcoholism was affecting all aspects of his life. Regardless of the cause, Schwatka's drinking had become chronic, with episodes of extremely heavy binges marked by paranoia that were frightening and even dangerous. As a doctor, Schwatka was astute enough to self-diagnose his ailment, but slow to heed the physician's admonition to "heal thyself." As Schwatka progressed down this destructive path, Ada could see that the long-term effect of his habit was wreaking havoc both on himself and his family. By 1892, it had entered a phase in which his dependency was negatively impacting his professional occupations. The chronic drinking may have also contributed to mood swings and behavioral changes that were evidenced, at times, by a harsh and angry temperament and erratic conduct. Until then, he probably believed that he could handle it all.

It is generally accepted that the first step in treatment is to face the problem. Much to his credit, in the summer of 1892, Schwatka did admit to his addiction and took actionable steps on the road to recovery. He had already tried short rehabilitation periods in so-called "inebriate institutions." These hospitals simply offered a drying out without medication or behavioral modification, an ineffective approach that by 1890 was falling out of favor. One approach gaining widespread popularity at the same time was the one advocated by Doctor Leslie Keeley, whose methods were viewed with much skepticism by the medical profession. Keeley's simple premise was that "alcoholism is a disease and I can cure it." His theory was that alcohol impaired nerve function, thus undermining will power, thus leading to an inability to control the urge to drink and to alcohol dependency. In 1879, he opened his first "Keeley Institute" in Dwight, Illinois, and by 1890 he was franchising his approach across the United States. Keeley's cure was withdrawal in stages, reducing intake slowly over a period of days, coupled with support groups and with his medicine, the so-called "Gold Cure." The closely guarded concoction was subsequently found to include alcohol, opium and morphine by the government in 1905. Although the Keeley "cure" was deemed ineffective over time (the last institution closed in 1966), Keeley had approached alcoholism as a treatable disease, rather than a social condition.[2]

Schwatka voluntarily entered the recently opened Keeley Institute in Olympia, Washington, and completed the rigorous treatment regimen. As a prominent figure who had admitted to a dependence problem, Schwatka was asked to share his experience. Much to his credit, he summoned the courage to write publicly on the subject. On July 4, 1892 Schwatka offered some rational remarks in the *Tacoma Ledger* as to how his own problem had progressed to an illness:

> There has been a great deal said by all sides as to whether the liquor, opium and other similar habits can be called diseases...some extremists claiming that the subject is wholly one of morality and the others that it is wholly one of pathology, or purely a case of diseased conditions. Like a good many discussions, I think both sides are right in a greater or less degree. In the early part of acquiring any of these habits, there is no doubt more of the moral side to the subject and could the person concerned look ahead and truly comprehend the true effect of the habit, this fact alone would be sufficient to put a quietus to it. In its later stages it is as clearly a disease as any other morbid condition of the system or any of its parts have ever shown.[3]

He characterized drinking as a "moral" problem to start, which he began voluntarily, but it soon became a "pathological," i.e., addictive problem. He did not believe the Gold Cure had any particularly bad side effects, even the use of chinchona he had ingested that was evidently part of the cure. Although there were, of course, failures, he believed that a motivated patient who consciously attempted to affect a cure stood a high degree of success. In recounting his own Keeley treatment, he made the telling admission that he was heavier dosed than most patients. With his usual air of invincibility, Schwatka boasted that he was routinely dosed at levels considered lethal, remarking that "my constitutional aversion to medicine is great, having taken 180 grains of choral [chloral] to induce sleep, while forty grains have proved fatal; and also a hypodermic injection of morphine at five times past the fatal point, and other things in proportion." That belief in his own tolerance for higher dosages may ultimately be what led to his undoing.[4]

Having completed the treatment, at least to his own satisfaction, Schwatka looked at a busy balance of the year ahead of him. Commercial opportunities still beckoned. The lecture circuit was still a pleasing podium, and he did so in Portland, Olympia, Port Angeles, and Seattle. Evidently, he had made some positive strides with the Keeley regimen and was perhaps turning a corner on his lifelong struggle. In Seattle, a reporter who caught up with him found him looking to be "of powerful frame," and overall good health despite his recent experiences: "The hardships he has undergone have left so slight an impression on him that, though he was born in 1849, the casual observer would take him to be a man of

35 accustomed to an easy life." Even his lecture was well received, "an engaging recountal, enlivened with lively and humorous anecdote, of the longest sledge journey ever made." [5]

Another project that Schwatka pursued was the designation of Mount Rainier, then known as Mount Tacoma, as a national park. There were plenty of reasons to understand the designation. Commanding a spectacular presence sixty miles south of Seattle, at just above 14,000 feet, Mount Rainier is one of the most prominent mountains in the West, the highest peak in the Cascade Range. Still an active volcano, with more than twenty glaciers and snowfields, its distinctive snow and ice cap stands in sharp contrast above the surrounding dark green pines. The citizens of Tacoma were pushing the project and Schwatka reached an agreement with the Tacoma Commercial Club to ascend the mountain to make an exploration of its various parts. There was certainly a commercial angle to the project, which included improving the roads and entrances for tourists and, of course, a fee to Schwatka. Coincidentally, Schwatka was pursuing another fee-paying opportunity as a publicity hound. He had submitted a proposal to the Portland Chamber of Commerce to explore Mount Hood and publish a marketing piece for $500 (over $15,000 in today's money), with each member subscribing to purchase a copy. Ever resourceful, his more grandiose scheme was to land another sizable sponsorship. With interest developing in steamship lines to Alaska, China and Japan, Schwatka was pitching deals to the *Tacoma Ledger,* the Northern Pacific Railroad and Samuel S. McClure (then head of the McClure Syndicate, the first U.S. newspaper syndicate), to deliver a series of letters on a trip to Alaska and the Far East. Tellingly, he boasted to J. J. Hill, president of the Northern Pacific Railway, that he could command a syndicate of up to one hundred leading newspapers to furnish the "very best of advertising," or like his flashy "Wonderland" piece "[advertising] seemingly not intended as such."[6]

The evening of November 1 was a fairly typical one for Frederick Schwatka while away from home. Schwatka enjoyed a lunch with his friend Doctor David Walker, a local practicing physician. Walker's residence in Portland, Oregon was a fortuitous and pleasant circumstance for Schwatka as the men shared much in common. The two were linked by the search for Sir John Franklin and also frontier service. Walker had served as physician and naturalist on McClintock's expedition in the *Fox.* He was also a member of the crew on the *Florence* cruise in 1877 to Cumberland Sound, part of Henry Howgate's plan for an Arctic "colony" in advance of the Lady Franklin Bay Expedition. Like Schwatka, he was a man of many scientific interests, including botany and zoology, and was a prolific author on those subjects. A botanical excursion on behalf of the

British Government had initially led him to the Pacific Northwest, where he ultimately served the U.S. Army as a contract surgeon, a position he held for seventeen years, at times on the Plains, and occasionally at some of Schwatka's posts.

At 7:00 P.M., Schwatka enjoyed a pleasant dinner with a boyhood friend, Doctor T. L. Nicklin, a prominent Portland physician. Interviewed later, Nicklin recalled that Schwatka was far from despondent or depressed, rather in "his usual jovial mood, but complained some about pain in his stomach." With his usual enthusiasm for the next big bonanza, Schwatka advised Nicklin that he was close to finalizing arrangements for another trip to Mexico on business connected with a "gigantic land scheme." Evidently, he was still chasing the Palomas colony deal with his friends Cody and Powell but was now confident that the long delayed economic payoff would finally come to fruition. Closer to home, Schwatka was also pleased with his efforts regarding Mount Hood. To Dr. Nicklin, he was enthusiastic that both projects would be completed.[7]

Schwatka may have had his usual upbeat attitude with his intimate friend, but privately his chronic stomach ailment had exacerbated in its severity in recent months. No doubt the debilitating condition had been progressing, and it must have required every ounce of effort for him to maintain a regular schedule and a positive attitude. With his stomach still giving him much trouble, Schwatka visited a retail pharmacy, Woodard, Clark and Company, where he ordered two ounces of laudanum, his typical treatment for the disorder. Laudanum, a so-called tincture of opium, is a solution of alcohol with a ten percent opium powder by weight.

In use since at least the 1600s, laudanum was held out as a "cure all" treatment, a pain relief for a wide variety of conditions, including rheumatism, lung diseases, diarrhea, menstrual cramps, toothaches, and stomach ailments. Steady users could face serious side effects though, such as a propensity toward addiction and accidental death (or suicide) from overdose. The responsible pharmacist, not recognizing Schwatka, requested a prescription before he would dispense the narcotic to the explorer. When Schwatka advised him that he held a medical degree and could write the prescription, the pharmacist dropped with protocol and dispensed the drug. He confided to the pharmacist that he was used to taking fifteen to twenty drops when his stomach caused him discomfort. Shortly thereafter, a drug store clerk who spoke to Schwatka was told by Schwatka that he had taken the laudanum and that he was feeling much better. Later that evening, he had planned to speak at a political rally on behalf of President Grover Cleveland and Vice President Adlai Stevenson for the upcoming November 8 election, but Schwatka's appearance was cancelled, and he left at 9:00 p.m. He made a brief appearance at the local Pastime Club, a popular athletic facility, but left soon thereafter and was not heard from again.[8]

At about 3:00 A.M. Schwatka was found by a policeman slumped in the doorway of a furniture store, Forbes & Breedan, on First Street, in an apparent drunken stupor. The vial of laudanum, half empty, was found beside him. With some effort, the unconscious Schwatka was returned to the St. Charles Hotel. As his condition grew worse within the hour, in what appears a callous decision by today's standards, he was transported by paddy wagon to the city jail. The city physician, Doctor C. H. Wheeler, was hurriedly called by means of a newly installed telephone. Upon his arrival, Wheeler immediately diagnosed an overdose, and not intoxication, and had Schwatka hospitalized at Good Samaritan Hospital. Efforts to revive him at the hospital were unavailing and he died at 5:00 A.M. Sadly, it was little consolation for the grieving family to learn that Wheeler believed that had he been called as soon as Lieutenant Schwatka was discovered his life might have been saved.[9]

Under the circumstances, a postmortem was conducted by Doctor Wheeler the following day. Wheeler failed to find any evidence that Schwatka had been drinking that evening. His brain tissue appeared normal, but he found the cerebral meninges were slightly alcohol congested and there was a slight meningeal adhesion. Schwatka's friends vehemently asserted that the intrepid explorer had not touched a drop of liquor since completing his treatment at the Keeley center. Wheeler logically concluded that the cause of death was an overdose of laudanum taken to relieve his stomach pain. Schwatka's practice of heavier dosing may have increased this risk of overdose. Although initial reports suggested Schwatka had committed suicide, his upbeat demeanor and future planning negate the idea that he contemplated taking his own life. A few days before his death, Ada Schwatka had received a letter in which he expressed that he was anxiously awaiting tickets for a return home and looking forward with excitement to a new expedition.[10]

Back in Rock Island, Ada only learned of her husband's untimely death when a reporter from the *Rock Island Argus* suddenly appeared at the door of her residence at Joseph Brackett's home. Blurting out the circumstances of his death, the aggressive reporter pushed for a comment, leaving a shocked and surprised Ada incredulous at the news. She regained her composure over the next few days. In light of the distance, she and six-year-old Frederika elected to remain in Rock Island rather than attend the funeral in Salem.

The funeral ceremony was a fitting gathering of a close-knit group of Salem residents who came to pay their last respects to the local hero. A specially draped railroad car supplied by the Capital City Electric Railway carried the body from Portland to Salem, where it was met by a large delegation. The casket was carried by hearse to the Salem Pioneer Cemetery, followed by a parade of friends and relatives. Perhaps at no other location would Frederick Schwatka have received such an outpouring of mourners to pay their respects. Ironically, Schwatka maintained his connection to the Franklin search even upon his death, as Doctor David Walker was present at the ceremony. A few boyhood friends served as pall bearers. Although Schwatka held himself out as a Christian from a devout Christian family, his commitment had always been uncertain. The service was conducted by Reverend Plutarch S. Knight, himself a pioneer immigrant to Salem in 1857. After Reverend Knight read from scripture, a Baptist choir sang "Jesus, Lover of My Soul," at the closing and the casket was interred in the family plot beside his mother and father. A plain headstone reads "Lieut. F.G. Schwatka, 3rd Cav. Died November 2, 1892." Ironically, as if an afterthought, the word "EXPLORER" was chiseled on the timeworn stone at a much later date, and now stands out as the most prominent statement on the monument. Even in death, Schwatka could look toward the magnificence of the West which he loved so dearly. His headstone, carpeted by prairie grass, faces Mt. Hood, that iconic symbol of Oregon's pioneering spirit.

Newspapers nationwide ran his obituary, and on this occasion the reports of his death were not exaggerated. The obituaries were generally brief and factual, highlighting his Arctic journey of 1878-80 as his most significant geographic accomplishment. Proud of their local hero, the Oregonians were the most complimentary. The *Oregonian* (Portland), for example, praised his accomplishments and his heritage:

> In the death of Lieutenant Frederick Schwatka, which occurred at Portland a few weeks ago, America has lost one of her most daring explorers and one who achieved numerous successes on the Arctic waters and in the far northland. Lieutenant Schwatka was an Oregonian in perseverance, pluck and enterprise—everything but birth.[11]

But Schwatka had his detractors even upon his death. Never embraced by the scientific community or by the rival newspapers of his sponsors, their obituaries were lukewarm and even negative. The American Geographical Society could spare a mere ten sentences for the explorer who did much to further the society's purposes. Buried at the end of the fifty pages of "geographical notes" in the 1892 *Journal of the American Geographic Society* was a rather curt statement:

> Lieutenant Schwatka, who had achieved celebrity as an Arctic explorer, died suddenly at Portland, Oregon, on the 2d of November, 1892, from an overdose of morphine.... Accompanied by Mr. Wm. H. Gilder, Schwatka sailed for King's William Land in 1878, to search for traces of Sir John Franklin's party. The search was successful; many of the skeletons of Franklin's men were discovered and buried; the grave of Lieut. John Irving, of the Terror, was found, and also a copy of the Crozier record. The party made the longest known sledge journey, both in regard to time and distance, having been absent from its base eleven months and twenty days, and having travelled 3251 miles.[12]

The obituary lamented what Schwatka might have done, as much as what he did: "With his trained intelligence and his experience, his courage and great powers of endurance, he was fitted as few men were, to do excellent work in Arctic travel, and in the ordinary course of events there were many years of activity yet before him when he died." Certainly, it was not the greatest slight, nor was it the most flattering, but conspicuously absent from the obituary was any reference to the society's sponsorship of Schwatka's expedition, or even any mention of its primary purpose, the records of the Franklin expedition, or the confirmation of the destruction of those records. Schwatka's expedition had been one of the only Arctic expeditions actively endorsed and promoted by the society. In its success, it had raised the society's profile at a time when it sought to establish international stature and influence. The expedition also reflected well upon Charles Patrick Daly, president of the society, who still held that position in 1892. Daly's silence over Schwatka's death seems puzzling.[13]

By contrast, the British explorer, John Rae, merited three full pages in an "Obituary" section in the society's 1893 *Journal*. He was lauded for his admirable qualities and the successes of his various expeditions (described at some length) and it was noted that "[h]e had the gifts of the born explorer, the habit of exact observation, courage and fertility of resource, untiring energy, activity and strength; and with these a firmness and generosity of character that won the respect and affection of men." About his writings, the society added that "they testify to his thoroughness and accuracy." In the press, the *Sun*, bitter rival to Schwatka's Mount St. Elias sponsor, the *New York Times,* still clearly held a grudge that was apparent in its obituary. After acknowledging Schwatka's brilliant sledge journey to and from King William Island, the paper lodged a sweeping, but highly inaccurate, criticism of his geographical work, writing that "Schwatka entertained many readers with his stories of adventure, but unfortunately his researches were not sufficiently exact to win the confidence of geographers. His chart of the upper Yukon, for instance, was full of errors, as was proved later by Mr. Ogilvie. Schwatka made for himself some opportunities to visit some of the newer parts of the continent where good work awaited explorers. He cannot be said, however, to have improved the maps or added much of value to geographical knowledge." That same sentiment was communicated to a wider audience in the prominent *Dictionary of American Biography* (1935), which remarked that "his amazing and spectacular journeys, much as they appealed to the popular imagination, resulted in no great contributions to scientific knowledge...." As recently as 1999, the *Oregon Biographical Dictionary* repeated the statement. Other papers, like the *Chicago Inter-Ocean*, beneficiary of his widely popular Tarahumara account, devoted a column largely as to his failings with drink, noting "the Lieutenant was a hard drinker while in the army and his sprees would always be the talk of the regiment for days after. The drowsy life on the frontier post afforded him every opportunity for excess...." Similarly, the *New York Times* obituary obliquely noted that "his life had been marked by such a degree of convivialities that his stomach had of recent years given him much trouble...." Schwatka's very public drinking problem also tarnished his legacy, as did the unpleasant circumstances surrounding his death.[14]

Beyond his explorations, the full extent of Schwatka's literary and publicist career passed largely unnoticed, but it was those activities that served to diminish his geographic accomplishments and sparked the dour remarks of his detractors. Schwatka wrote for the entertainment of the general public, and it was the delivery of appealing content for the masses that most attracted his efforts. From his start as a tenderfoot apprentice on the hectic floor of the *Statesman's* newsroom, the newspaper would play an integral role throughout his life as he matured into the explorer-journalist wrapped in one. Invariably, his individualism led him to pursue his own course, and he found it in the press. His correspondence for the *Inter-Ocean* as a soldier on the Plains gave him a start as a writer. By the time of his death, he had become not just a prolific author, but a media property, a status that he shrewdly cultivated. During the decade before his death, he wrote and lectured extensively on the Arctic and Alaska, its people, features, and commercial possibilities, always in an entertaining fashion, skillfully maintaining an image as the authority on all aspects of the North. To his credit, his publicity for Alaska helped to shape our views of the possession and positioned it firmly in the American conscience. His works directed to juvenile audiences likewise introduced more than one generation to life in the Far North.

But there were other consequences to Schwatka's publicity efforts. The Franklin Records Search Expedition, sponsored in part by the enterprising Bennett, opened Schwatka's eyes to the power of the press and its desire for engaging, and at times sensational features. Gilder's cannibalism tale, one element in a broader storyline, generated a controversial sideshow stoked by Bennett. Schwatka was largely an observer as the struggle played out in the press, avoiding the controversy beyond a brief confirmation, but he quickly perceived how one slender thread or aspect of a story could become the centerpiece of an exciting attraction. In the 1870s, Bennett precipitated a momentous change in the popular press with his sensational reporting, and with it his dispatching of correspondents to bring back a story. But Schwatka took Bennett's approach a step further. Each of his private expeditions after his resignation from the military had followed a common theme. Schwatka managed to convince a potential newspaper sponsor that he could deliver them exciting copy and compete with the Bennett's of the world on the same basis. He was not simply a travel writer or correspondent hired by a publisher to view and report upon exotic places or events. Schwatka devised the adventure, and with the benefit of his exploration credentials and his own notoriety, recruited the publisher for his plans and served as an active participant, essentially an explorer with his pen for hire. Schwatka recognized that his relationships with the press served a mutually beneficial purpose, a symbiosis. The magazines and newspapers gained increased circulation and audience from his travels, particularly when that adventure included an aspect of "discovery." At the same time, Schwatka himself basked in the publicity that bolstered his professional writing and lecturing career, and as importantly, satisfied his own crave for fame. Those overwhelming motivations led Schwatka to sensationalize those travels.

In 1886, he managed to persuade the *New York Times*, which had never sponsored a discovery expedition, to back him on a trip to Mount St. Elias. Schwatka recognized that an attempt on what was viewed as the continent's highest mountain would have public appeal as a geographic "prize," but Schwatka also contributed his own piece of sensationalism with his discovery of the "Jones River," and delivered a windfall for the *Times*. Likewise, as Joseph Pulitzer looked to breathe new life into the *World*, Schwatka was there to promote another "exclusive," the first winter excursion through Yellowstone National Park. Schwatka's advocacy of an Alaskan trip on behalf of the *New York Ledger,* another neophyte to exploration sponsorship, played upon its journalistic competition with *Frank Leslie's Illustrated Newspaper*. Schwatka's Mexican venture, backed by the *Chicago Inter-Ocean*, originally intended as a descriptive visit to a little-known region, stoked a media frenzy over a "lost race," the Tarahumara, and their relation to the cliff-dwellers of the American Southwest. Schwatka's amplification of that story, highlighted by his crass exhibition of the Tarahumara in the United States, was itself supported through a sponsorship by the *Chicago Herald* and contributions from William Boyce that benefitted the *Saturday Blade*. The Tarahumara escapade became Schwatka's most exotic, most entertaining, and most sensational headliner, and one he carried too far. As popular as Schwatka's writings were with the general public, their embellishment and exaggeration undercut his credibility and legitimate accomplishments. One obituary made the telling comment that "latterly his [Schwatka's] writings for newspapers and periodicals have been of a more than semi-sensational character."[15]

Even two years after his death, the ethnographer Carl Lumholtz was still lambasting Schwatka's Tarahumara writings as the "reckless utterances of a traveler, lately deceased" in an address to the American Geographical Society. The geographical society's sentiment was openly expressed in a disparaging editorial footnote to Lumholtz's published remarks, stating that the "allusion is to Lieut. Schwatka, whose fantastic story of the cliff-dwellers, discovered by him on the well-beaten Urique and Batopilas road, received the unmerited honor of translation into German in *Globus* LXIII Band, S. 254-257, as a contribution to knowledge." In England, the Royal Geographical Society made no mention of Schwatka's death, and Markham's posthumously published *Lands of Silence* totally omitted Schwatka's 1878-80 expedition. Within the scientific establishment of the United States and England, Schwatka had few supporters by the time of his death.[16]

What Schwatka had exploited was the shady underside of self-promotion by explorers. What an explorer saw in the field didn't always accurately reflect what was set in print, and it was the print that shaped perceptions. The historian Beau Riffenburgh identified the reality that "the press was helpless in the hands of unscrupulous story-tellers." Certain later explorers grasped that reality and would push the limits of truthfulness much further in their quest for meaningful geographic firsts. In 1903, Frederick Cook claimed to have summited Denali (Mt. McKinley), the highest mountain in North America, a claim that has been discredited. Likewise, the later claims of the discovery of the North Pole by Cook in 1908 and by Peary in 1909 have also been called into question.[17]

The exploits of Frederick Cook, Robert Peary and later explorers who were darlings of the press had other effects; they overshadowed the earlier accomplishments of their predecessors, including those of Frederick Schwatka. In the midst of the rival claims of Peary and Cook to the discovery of the North Pole and the heated controversy that played out in the press, even the local Oregon papers had acknowledged Schwatka's fading glory. On September 6, 1909, as the competing claims of Peary and Cook crowded the front pages, an *Oregonian* editorial lamented that "in the chronology of polar expeditions, Oregon's explorer, Lieutenant Schwatka, has been lost sight of."[18]

Testimonials that more favorably reflected Schwatka's character and personality were offered by those hardnosed veterans of the Indian wars who actually knew him and had stood shoulder-to-shoulder with him under fire. George Hopkins, who served with Schwatka for four years on the Plains, stated that "a better or braver man never lived. He was kind hearted and generous to a fault." A captain who also served with Schwatka remarked that "the officers and men in the regiments in which he served loved him, and none more so than the lowliest private, for he was always kind and considerate and he never used a harsh word to any of them except his Irish body-servant, and this was always half-jocular.... He was long considered in the army to be one of its brightest officers...." Citizens of Omaha who knew him well noted that "everyone that knew him in Omaha has nothing but good words for him...." Perhaps the most heartfelt tribute, and the one that Frederick Schwatka would have most appreciated, came from the Brulé Sioux. Upon learning of Schwatka's untimely death, having been inducted in their tribe, and accepted by them, they chanted songs in their lodges, songs for their adopted brother, "Big Wolf." Schwatka's obituary in *Forest and Stream Magazine*, aptly summarized the vicissitudes of his life: "This ends the life of a fortunate and unfortunate man, a man brave and yet weak, a man who sufficiently well illustrates the continual contradictions of human life and human accomplishment."[19]

Ada Schwatka, his wife of ten years, became a longtime widow of thirty-seven years until her death in 1930 at the age of seventy-five. After Frederick's death, she returned to her family home in Rock Island, where she lived with her parents and widowed sister. Despite his failings, Ada had loved Frederick unconditionally. For a time, the dutiful widow, who admirably supported her husband's pursuits and his long absences in the

Ada Schwatka in the 1890s.

field and on the lecture circuit, faithfully continued her husband's work. In 1893, Ada managed to bring out *In the Land of Cave and Cliff Dwellers*, an assemblage in book form of Frederick's letters published in the *Chicago Inter-Ocean*, with an introduction under her husband's name. The work is a very readable and entertaining account of his Mexican tour, reflecting his usual sharp observations, lively descriptions, and his typical self-deprecating, comical side. It was reprinted by the Educational Publishing Company in 1899 as a descriptive piece on Mexico.[20]

In early 1895 Ada also stepped out to the lecture podium to continue the work of her husband, principally to local audiences in Rock Island and Peoria. On February 12, 1895, she addressed the cultured audience of the Peoria's women's club, which found her lecture on the cave-dwellers and cliff-dwellers "pleasing and no less instructive and interesting." More attention seemed to be paid to her stylish appearance though: "Mrs. Schwatka is tall in stature, with a pleasing countenance and dresses fashionably. Her costume was entirely of black, which was quite becoming with the tasteful dressing of her hair."[21]

Her heart was with Alaska however, where she had shared some of her happiest moments with Frederick, and the place that she knew had captivated him. During the Klondike Gold Rush, Ada Schwatka became a voice of concern over the fate of unprepared prospectors scrambling to the region, noting during an interview with a Chicago reporter that "the mountain passes are strewn with the skeletons of unfortunate miners, who perished from either cold, heat, malaria or starvation, while trying to reach the golden region." She called for government intervention to suspend the unchecked migration to the region. In several newspapers and magazines, she urged that a pack train route be established through the Taku Pass, to be linked to a steamer coming from the Taku River and Juneau, as Frederick had advocated. That approach she believed would reduce the danger to the miners. She was a knowledgeable contributor to one of many Klondike guides, *Alaska and the Klondike Gold Fields*, hastily published to cash in on the new El Dorado. She offered blunt advice to women who might be considering travelling there, echoing many of Frederick Schwatka's observations about the people and country. There were even various reports, seemingly farfetched, that Mrs. Schwatka might organize an exploring expedition to the Copper River in the footsteps of her husband.[22]

Ada had her share of difficult times after Frederick's death. With her modest pension, she and Frederika lived in Victorian fashion in Europe for ten years, where the dollar went further. Ada and her daughter Frederika were present in the city of San Francisco during the earthquake of 1906. While residing at the home of the French consul, she watched in horror as the business district burned and the blaze slowly crept towards the diplomat's residence. Escaping with just the baggage they could manage to carry bundled in bedsheets, they joined the fleeing masses. There was an air of entitlement about her, a product of her family position or perhaps her husband's notoriety. In a letter to her sister, Ada wrote that she "did not care to stay with the multitude," and demanded to meet General Frederick Funston, commander of Fort Mason on the city's waterfront, where she and Frederika turned for refuge. By virtue of her husband's stature, she was admitted to the post. There they remained as the guest of General Funston until a boat across San Francisco Bay to Fort Baker could be arranged. Sadly, among the personal effects lost in the disaster were Frederick Schwatka's manuscripts, journals, and papers which had been stored in the lock box of a bank razed during the firestorm. In 1908, Frederika married a young man, Edward Stafford, and returned to the family home in Rock Island with her mother. Sadly, Frederika predeceased Ada, dying in childbirth in 1915. In failing health, Ada Schwatka died on April 11, 1930 in Rock Island.[23]

CHAPTER NOTES

Abbreviations Used

AG	Adjutant General
AAG	Assistant Adjutant General
ACP	Appointment, Commission, Personnel
ASL	Alaska State Library and Historical Collections
DPL	Denver Public Library
GWB	G.W. Blunt White Library
MHS	Minnesota Historical Society
MSUL	Montana State University Library
NA	National Archives
NBWM	New Bedford Whaling Museum Research Library
NMM	National Maritime Museum, London
NYPL	New York Public Library
NYU	NYU Medical Archives
OHS	Oregon Historical Society
PPL	Providence Public Library
RICHS	Rock Island County Historical Society
SPRI	Scott Polar Research Institute
SI	Smithsonian Institution
UAF	University of Alaska Fairbanks
USMA	U.S. Military Academy Archives
UVA	University of Virginia, Clifton Waller Barrett Collection
WUA	Willamette University Archives and Special Collections

Chapter One – Pioneer Spirit [pages 1-22]

1. Brackett, "Memoir," 5. Brackett stated that August Schwatka (or Schwatke) emigrated to Baltimore from near Danzig (which had been annexed by Prussia). He did not identify August Schwatka's birthplace, though he stated that Frederick Schwatka's "ancestors" lived in "Northern Prussia" near the border with Poland; Nabrdalik, "How a Nation Outlived its State," 661.
2. *City of Baltimore Comprehensive Master Plan,* 27 (quoting A. T. Morison, *George Washington*); Stafford, *The Baltimore Directory for 1803,* 115.
3. Dennis Hockman, "Family Forges History at Baltimore Ironworks Shop," Chesapeake + Living, *Baltimore Sun,* August 11, 2011; Maryland SP Krug Iron Works, National Register, NA. The shop was sold to Andrew Merker in 1830 and then consolidated with Gustav Krug in 1851 to become A. Merker & Krug, and after Merker's death, G. Krug & Son. See G. Krug & Son official web site, https://gkrugandson.com/history/ (accessed January 20, 2022).
4. Henninghausen, *History of the German Society of Maryland,* 48. August Schwatka's membership in Baltimore's Zion Lutheran Church, a German congregation that conducted services in the German language, suggests that he and his wife had considerable German ties. Nabrdalik, "How a Nation Outlived its State," 661; Hofmann, *A History of Zion Church,* 31; Wust, *Zion in Baltimore 1755-1955,* 125.
5. Henninghausen, "The Germans in the Defense of Baltimore," 59 (quotation); "Called Higher," *Freeport Journal-Standard* (Freeport, IL), January 31, 1884 (notes that August Schwatka "was a soldier in the war of 1812").
6. "A Memento," *Oregon Statesman* (Salem, Ore.), January 20, 1888 (quotations).
7. "Obituary," *Oregon Statesman* (Salem, Ore.), January 3, 1885.
8. Best, "Cincinnati's German Community," 2, 20; Jakle, "Cincinnati in the 1830s," 4.
9. "An Ancient Odd Fellow," *The Weekly Enterprise* (Oregon City, Ore.), May 1, 1869; Wamsley, Brackett-Schwatka Papers.
10. "Death of Father Schwatka," *Oregon Statesman* (Salem, Ore.), January 13, 1888.
11. "Major William Williams' Journal," 246.
12. Steeves, *Book of Remembrance,* 202; "Death of Father Schwatka," *Oregon Statesman* (Salem, Ore.), January 13, 1888; "Death of Old Man Schwatka," *The Morning Astorian,* January 20, 1888.
13. McNeese, *The Oregon Trail,* 62-63.
14. *Annual Report of the Commissioner of Agriculture for the Year 1878,* 537.
15. Anderson to Hon. Joseph Lane, May 20, 1854 (quotation), Lane Papers, OHS. Frederick Schwatka Sr. was listed in the 1850 census of Clatsop County, Oregon, http://files.usgwarchives.net/or/clatsop/census/1850cens.txt (accessed January 20, 2022).
16. Deur, *Empires of the Turning Tide,* 18 (quotation); Thayer, "The Forest Hiker: The Clatsop Indians," http://www.foresthiker.com/?page_id=1956 (accessed July 20, 2021).

17. *Sailing Directions for the West Coast of North America*, 126 (quotation); Deur, "The Making of Seaside's 'Indian Place,'" 544; Ronda, *Finding the West,* 94.
18. Kortleever, *History of the Pacific Northwest,* 2:408, 570.
19. Deur, "The Making of Seaside's 'Indian Place,'" 545-46; Anderson to Lane, May 20, 1854, Lane Papers, OHS.
20. Deur, *Empires of the Turning Tide,* 222; Deur, "The Making of Seaside's 'Indian Place,'" 546-47; *The Douglas Independent* (Roseburg, Ore.), May 10, 1884; *Congressional Record* (House) 15 (April 24, 1884): 3349-50 (quotation); *Congressional Record* (Senate) 15 (January 9, 1884): 304-05. The delay in the government's award was due, in part, to Schwatka Sr.'s delay in filing a formal request for compensation until December 1870, a date outside the filing deadline. In defense of the late filing, Schwatka claimed that the delay was due to his suffering from intervals of mental depression during which he was unfit to work.
21. Schwatka, "Capturing a Herd of Buffalo," 103 (quotation).
22. Certificate of Death for Annie (Schwatka) Miller filed September 1, 1938, State of Oregon Archives, Salem, OR; "Obituary. Mrs. Annie S. Miller," *The Oregonian* (Portland, Ore.), September 7, 1938; Peters, *Seven Months to Oregon,* 300.
23. "Schwatka's Search," *Cumtux,* 34; *Genealogical Material,* 4:53; Anderson to Lane, May 20, 1854, Lane Papers, OHS.
24. Lockley, *History of the Columbia River Valley,* 1:269; Oswald West, "Lieut. Frederick Schwatka," *Capital Journal* (Salem, Ore.), September 17, 1952.
25. Hines, *Oregon and its Institutions,* 84 (quotation).
26. *State Rights Democrat* (Albany, Ore.), November 4, 1892 (quotation); Johnson, "Parties and Politics in Oregon History," 196; McLagan, "*The Black Laws of Oregon*"; Bancroft, *The History of Oregon,* 2:358-59.
27. Steeves, *Book of Remembrance,* 202 (quotations).
28. "Obituary," *Oregon Statesman* (Salem, Ore.), January 3, 1885 (quotation); "Personal," *State Rights Democrat* (Albany, Ore.), October 6, 1866; *Corvallis Gazette,* December 18, 1885; LaPlante, *Crater Lake National Park,* 13; "In memory of Mrs. A. C. Schwatka," *Oregon Statesman* (Salem, Ore.), February 8, 1875.
29. Branting, *Historic Firsts of Lewiston, Idaho,* 50-51.
30. Frederick Schwatka, "Hunters' Lucky Shots," *Chicago Inter-Ocean,* November 27, 1892.
31. Brackett, "Memoir," 5.
32. Ibid. (first four quotations); Schwatka, "Introduction," viii (fifth quotation).
33. Hodgkin, *Pen Pictures,* 65 (boyish prankster and leader); "The Statesman," *Oregon Statesman* (Salem, Ore.), January 1, 1887 ("inclined to mischief"); "Salem Explorer was Doctor, Lawyer, Soldier, and Author," *Oregon Statesman* (Salem, Ore.), April 15, 1991 (bright, ruddy-faced prankster, natural leader); "Retrospective," *Oregon Statesman* (Salem, Ore.), May 15, 1875; Oswald West, "Lieut. Frederick Schwatka," *Capital Journal* (Salem, Ore.), September 17, 1952.

34. *Catalogue of the Wallamet University for the Academical Year 1865-'66,* 12, WUA; *Catalogue of the Wallamet University for the Academical Year 1863-'64,* 7, WUA. Schwatka attended Willamette as a student for the academic years running from September 5, 1864 through July 20, 1865 (listed only as a student in the English Department), and from September 10, 1866 through July 25, 1867 (though he must have departed earlier than July 25 to arrive at the U.S. Military Academy by late June). The student listing for the academic year that ran from September 1865 through July 1866 is missing. However, Schwatka joined the Hesperian Society on September 8, 1865 which would suggest he was enrolled as a student for that year as well. "Living Celebrities of the Hesperian Society," *College Journal* 2, no. 4 (December 1881): 3, WUA.
35. Alfred Jones, "Hesperian Society was Salem's Spot for Heated Debates," *Oregon Statesman* (Salem, Ore.), April 22, 1991; Essay entitled "Latest by Telegraph - North Pole Feb. 7th," *Willamette Chronicle* 2, no. 1 (February 22, 1867), WUA.
36. Schwatka, Sr. to Williams, June 4, 1871 (quotations), Schwatka, ACP Files, NA; Gatch, et al. to Belknap, August 7, 1872, Schwatka, ACP Files, NA.
37. Schwatka to Stanton, January 23, 1865 (quotations), USMA Cadet Application Papers, NA.
38. Brackett, "Memoir," 5 (quotation).
39. "The Statesman," *Oregon Statesman* (Salem, Ore.), January 1, 1887 (quotations).
40. Hodgkin, *Pen Pictures,* 65 (quotation); Henderson, et al, to the President of the United States, January 25, 1865, USMA Cadet Application Papers, NA; Boynton, *The History of West Point,* 349.

Chapter Two - First Call [pages 23-49]

1. Crane, *West Point,* 234.
2. Kemble, *The Panama Route,* 147-48.
3. *Report of the Board of Visitors, July 1, 1871,* 443; *Oregon City Enterprise,* July 6, 1867.
4. Godson, *The History of West Point,* 32-33 (a railroad right of way and a wagon road were authorized in 1867 and 1868, respectively).
5. USMA Post Medical Record July 15, 1867, Schwatka, ACP Files, NA; Boynton, *The History of West Point,* 258-62.
6. Pappas, *To the Point,* 248; Newall, *Of Duty Well and Faithfully Done,* 304; Boynton, *The History of West Point,* 274-5; Weart, *USMA,* 10-11; Cunningham, "Recreant to his Trust," 6.
7. Phillips, "An Officer and a Scholar," 95 (quotation); Pappas, *To the Point,* 248.
8. Cunningham, "Recreant to his Trust," 6; Pappas, *To the Point,* 346-47.
9. *Report of the Board of Visitors, June 15, 1870,* 305; *Official Register of the Officers and Cadets of the U.S. Military Academy* (June, 1871): 22, USMA;

Records of the Academic Board, USMA; McCormick, *History of Foreign Language Teaching*, 321.
10. *Twenty-Fourth Annual Reunion*, 67-68 (quotation); Boynton, *The History of West Point*, 297; *Official Register of the Officers and Cadets of the U.S. Military Academy* (June, 1871): 22, USMA; Records of the Academic Board, USMA.
11. *Official Registers of the Officers and Cadets of the U.S. Military Academy* (June, 1869-1871), USMA; Records of the Academic Board, USMA.
12. "At West Point," *Oregon Statesman* (Salem, Ore.), March 4, 1870; "West Point," *New York Herald*, June 12, 1870.
13. "West Point," *New York Times*, June 13, 1871; "Threatened Insubordination at West Point," *New York Times*, June 20, 1871; Pappas, *To the Point*, 379-81.
14. *Twenty-Fourth Annual Reunion*, 67 (quotation).
15. "Gossip of the Day," *Kalamazoo Gazette*, October 21, 1880 (quotations).
16. Scheips, *Darkness and Light*, 282; Utley, *Frontier Regulars*, 15.
17. Schwatka, "Among the Apaches," 43 (quotation).
18. Schwatka, "Among the Apaches," 43 (first quotation), 49 (second quotation) 42 (third quotation). The information for Schwatka's Apache article was collected during his brief visit to the Arizona Territory in 1871 as well as another short visit in 1884.
19. Mills, *My Story*, 152 (quotation); Report of Captain and Asst. Surgeon F. W. Elbrey, Fort McPherson, March, 1872, Medical History of Posts, NA. Schwatka joined Mills at Fort McDowell, Arizona Territory in November 1871 and departed for Fort McPherson on December 1, 1871. Fort McDowell, December 1871, Post Returns, NA.
20. McDermott, Introduction to *My Story*, x.
21. Mills, *My Story*, 152 (quotation).
22. Buecker, "The Post of North Platte Station," 381.
23. Buecker, "The Post of North Platte Station," 389-90; "North Platte," *Western Nebraskan* (North Platte, Nebr.), January 13, 1875; "Hay Notice," *Western Nebraskan* (North Platte, Nebr.), July 16, 1875; Bonner, "Things Change," 18.
24. Webster, "The Last Romantic Buffalo Hunt," 329 (first quotation), 330 (second quotation); Cody, *Life and Adventures*, 256 (third quotation). Contrary to Webster's claim as to the group's hunting failure, Captain Joseph H. L. King, post surgeon at Fort McPherson, recorded that the group, which passed through Fort McPherson on their return, "had a very successful hunt, killing all the buffalo they wanted to." Report of Captain and Asst. Surgeon J. H. L. King, Fort McPherson, September 1872, Medical History of Posts, NA. Interestingly, Schwatka's hunting companions, Judge Dundy and John Lee Webster, would play prominent roles in advancing Indian rights. Judge Dundy presided in the landmark federal case *United States ex rel. Standing Bear v. Crook*, ruling in 1879 that Indians were deemed "persons" under federal law and therefore subject to the protection of habeas corpus. John Lee Webster and Andrew J. Poppleton represented Chief Standing Bear, the subject of the action.

25. Webster, "The Last Romantic Buffalo Hunt," 326 (first quotation), 331 (second quotation). Schwatka was so intrigued by the notion of lassoing buffalo, and had no lack of free time, that he set the Third Cavalry to work at the most effective methods of capture. Devising various contraptions, they succeeded in collaring more than fifty calves, nearly all of which died within hours. The survivors were sent to a park in Camden, N.J. *Wichita Daily Eagle*, June 24, 1888. He also sent eleven elk and two deer to a park in Cincinnati. "Local News," *North Platte Republican*, April 10, 1875.
26. Schwatka, "Buffalo Hunting," *The Times* (Philadelphia), April, 15, 1888 (quotation).
27. Mills, *My Story*, 153 (quotation); Schwatka, "Hunters' Lucky Shots," *Chicago Inter-Ocean*, November 27, 1892.
28. Schwatka, "Buffalo Hunting," *The Times* (Philadelphia), April 15, 1888 (first and second quotations); "Hunted with Schwatka," *Omaha Herald*, November 3, 1892 (third and fourth quotations); Schwatka, "Capturing a Herd of Buffalo," 103 (fifth quotation); "Tabular Statement of Expeditions, Fourth Quarter 1873," Adjutant General's Office Letters Received (Main Series) 1871-1880, NA; Buecker, "The Post of North Platte Station," 388; Hedren, *After Custer*, 110.
29. Nordin, "Dr. W. F. Carver," 344-49; Thorp, *Spirit Gun of the West*, 71 (quotations).
30. Bradley, *Dinosaurs and Indians*, 45; Mills Report, July 15, 1873, Adjutant General's Office Letters Received (Main Series), 1871-1880, NA (quotation).
31. Rosa, *They Called Him Wild Bill*, 207-09; Riley, "The Battle of Massacre Canyon," 228; Fort McPherson, January 1873, Post Returns, NA; Affadavit of S.S. Gast, witnessed by Schwatka, January 15, 1873, Adjutant General's Office Letters Received (Main Series), 1871-1880, NA.
32. Mills, *Big Horn Expedition*, 15 (quotation).
33. Buel, *Heroes of the Plains*, 415 (quotation).
34. Mahnken, "The Sidney-Black Hills Trail," 208.
35. "Hunted with Schwatka," *Omaha Herald*, November 3, 1892 (first quotation); "Pencil Paragraphs," *Queen City Mail* (Spearfish, S.Dak.), November 9, 1892 (second quotation); Buecker, "The Post of North Platte Station," 389.
36. "Local News," *North Platte Republican*, May 22, 1875; Bourke, *Diaries*, 4:113 (quotation).
37. Col. Reynolds to Brig. Gen. Ord, January 2, 1874, Adjutant General's Office Letters Received (Main Series), 1871-1880, NA (quotation); Agnew, *Medicine in the Old West*, 111-12. Drinking of course continued to plague the army, so much so that in February 1881 President Rutherford B. Hayes banned the sale of "intoxicating liquors" on military reservations. The prohibition had little effect as it continued to be freely available off post, and shortly thereafter, by order of the War Department, beer and wine were permitted on post.
38. Tate, "The Frontier Army," 180; "Arctic Exploration," *New York Herald*, April 12, 1878.

39. Hedren, "Camp Sheridan," 83.
40. Bourke, *On the Border*, 401 (quotation); Hedren, "Camp Sheridan," 88.
41. Bourke, *Diaries*, 2:243 (first quotation); Dodge, *The Black Hills Journals*, 239 (second quotation).
42. Mills, *My Story*, 156-57; Patrick, "To the Black Hills Gold Fields," 271-73; Hedren, "Camp Sheridan," 85; Special Order No. 50, June 22, 1875, Camp Sheridan, NA; Schwatka to Post Adjutant, July 1, 1875, Letters Received Camp Sheridan, NA.
43. *Bellevue Hospital Medical College: Annual Circular, 1875-76*, 002.A 1875-76a, 7, 10, NYU.
44. *Bellevue Hospital Medical College: Annual Circular, 1876-77*, 002.A 1876-77a, 14, NYU; Certificate of Study (twenty-three and one-half months)-Dr. J. B. Gardiner, January 1, 1876, 002.F 1875-76 .477, NYU; Certificate of Study (twelve and one-half months)-Dr. J. A. Gray, undated, 002.F 1875-76 .476, NYU.
45. Tate, *The Frontier Army*, 178-79; *A Report on the Hygiene of the United States Army*, 362.
46. *Bellevue Hospital Medical College: Annual Circular, 1876-77*, 002.A 1876-77a, 15, NYU. Schwatka left Camp Sheridan escorting several prisoners to Sidney, while surveying the road from Camp Sheridan to Sidney. Special Order No. 77, Sept. 6, 1875, Camp Sheridan, NA
47. Myers, "The Changing Face of Medical Education," 1; *Bellevue Hospital Medical College: Annual Circular 1875-76*, 002.A 1875-76a, 8, NYU.
48. Oshinsky, "Bellevue," 109, 113.
49. *Bellevue Hospital Medical College: Annual Circular 1875-76*, 002.A 1875-76a, 4-6, NYU; Mehta, "Austin Flint," 386-89; Zampini, "Lewis A. Sayre," 2263-67; Tickets for Dr. Flint Lectures, 002.F 1875-76 .520a (Principles and Practice of Medicine), 002.F 1875-76 .523a (Physiology and Physiological Anatomy), NYU; Ticket for Dr. Van Buren and Dr. Sayre Lectures, File 002.F 1875-76 .521a (Surgery), NYU; "Death of Professor A. B. Crosby," 165 (quotation); Ticket for Dr. Crosby Lecture, File 002.F 1875-76 .522a (Descriptive and Surgical Anatomy), NYU.
50. Mehta, "Austin Flint," 388; Schwatka, "An Inaugural Thesis on Diphtheria," 4 (first quotation), 7 (second quotation), Theses 1876, NYU; Richmond, "American Attitudes," 430; see also Flint, "Medical and Sanitary Progress," 83 ("the majority of medical thinkers" were of the opinion that "the demonstrative evidence is not considered as complete" that "specific organisms of microscopical minuteness" cause certain diseases).
51. "Arctic Expedition," *Breckenridge News*, July 17, 1878; Agnew, *Medicine in the Old West,* 32; "Records of Living Officers," 461 (notes rejection by medical examining board).

Chapter Three - The Battle of the Rosebud [pages 50-75]

1. AG to Schwatka, Special Order No. 56 (copy), March 21, 1876, Schwatka

Chapter Notes 409

Papers, ACP Files, NA; "Third Cavalry," *Army and Navy Journal*, 528.
2. Knight, *Following the Indian Wars*, 161.
3. Bourke, *On the Border with Crook*, 244 (quotation).
4. Knight, *Following the Indian Wars*, 43.
5. Schmitt, *General George Crook*, 213-14; Mangum, *Battle of the Rosebud*, 18.
6. Bourke, *On the Border with Crook*, 247.
7. Powers, *The Killing of Crazy Horse*, 145, 149-51. For more details of the abandonment of Private Ayers, see Hedren, *Powder River*, 183-93.
8. Bourke, *Diaries*, 1:265 (quotation). For his conduct at Powder River, Reynolds was court-martialed and suspended from command for one year (a sentence later sustained by President Grant).
9. Finerty, *War-Path and Bivouac*, 59 (quotation); Bourke, *On the Border with Crook*, 289-90; Hedren, *Rosebud*, 375-76; Abrams, "A Very Lively Little Affair," 9.
10. Finerty *War-Path and Bivouac*, 49 (quotations); Hedren, *John Finerty Reports the Sioux War*, 2; Knight, *Following the Indian Wars*, 173-74.
11. Powers, *The Killing of Crazy Horse*, 162; Knight, *Following the Indian Wars*, 172-73; "Recent Deaths," *Army and Navy Journal*, 194 (quotation).
12. Finerty, *War-Path and Bivouac*, 87 (first quotation); Bourke, *Diaries*, 1:294 (second quotation).
13. Finerty, *War-Path and Bivouac*, 90 (quotation).
14. "The Sioux War," *Chicago Tribune*, July 5, 1876 (first quotation); Abrams, *Sioux War Dispatches*, 71 (second quotation, reporter Charles St. George Stanley); Finerty, *War-Path and Bivouac*, 95 (third and fourth quotations); "The Sioux War," *New York Tribune*, July 1, 1876; Mangum, *Battle of the Rosebud*, 29, 39.
15. Finerty, *War-Path and Bivouac*, 95-96; Hedren, *Rosebud*, 97-98.
16. Finerty, *War-Path and Bivouac* 105 (quotation).
17. Mangum, *Battle of the Rosebud*, 46; Hedren, *Rosebud*, 178.
18. Vaughn, *With Crook at the Rosebud*, 51 (first quotation); Finerty, *War-Path and Bivouac*, 123 (second quotation); Mills, *My Story*, 405.
19. Mills, *My Story*, 405; Hedren, *Rosebud*, 199.
20. "Full Account of the Battle between Crook and the Sioux," *Black Hills Weekly Pioneer* (Deadwood, S.D.), July 22, 1876 (quotation).
21. Finerty, *War-Path and Bivouac*, 124 (quotation). Finerty stated that the Sioux broke and retreated at fifty paces, but Private Thomas Lloyd, E Company, Third Cavalry, stated that it was at one hundred yards. Finerty, *War-Path and Bivouac*, 125; Lloyd to Cousin Peter, January 20, 1877, MHS.
22. Mills, *My Story*, 406 (quotations); "Letter from Lieut. Schwatka," *Willamette Farmer*, August 11, 1876.
23. Finerty, *War-Path and Bivouac*, 126 (first, second and third quotations); Vaughn, *With Crook at the Rosebud*, 142; Lloyd to Cousin Peter, January 20, 1877, MHN (fourth quotation).
24. Hedren, *Rosebud*, 205.
25. Finerty, *War-Path and Bivouac*, 130 (first quotation); Bourke, *On the Border*, 315 (second quotation).

26. Mills, *My Story*, 408 (first quotation); Finerty, *War-Path and Bivouac* 133 (second quotation).
27. "Letter from Lieut. Schwatka," *Willamette Farmer*, August 11, 1876 (first quotation); "The Indians," *Minneapolis Messenger*, June 7, 1877 (second quotation); Mangum, *Battle of the Rosebud*, 87; Hedren, *Rosebud*, 350.
28. Bourke, *Diaries*, 1:329 (quotation); Hedren, *Rosebud*, 297.
29. Tate, *The Frontier Army*, 180-81.
30. Finerty, *War-Path and Bivouac*, 129-30 (quotations).
31. Finerty, *War-Path and Bivouac*, 138 (quotation).
32. Official Report of Augustus C. Paul, Co. M Third Cavalry, June 20, 1876 (first quotation, cited in Vaughn, *With Crook at the Rosebud*, 238); "Letter from Lieut. Schwatka," *Willamette Farmer*, August 11, 1876 (second quotation).
33. Finerty, *War-Path and Bivouac*, 144 (quotation).
34. Mills, *My Story*, 401 (quotation); Bourke, *On the Border with Crook*, 299-300.
35. Bourke, *On the Border with Crook*, 334 (quotation); Mills, *My Story*, 410.
36. Finerty, *War-Path and Bivouac*, 120 (quotation); Gray, *Centennial Campaign*, 198; Hedren, *Rosebud*, 318.
37. Stanley, *The Autobiography of Henry Morton Stanley*, 228.
38. Hedren, *Rosebud*, 81, 318. The *Chicago Inter-Ocean* dispatches from Schwatka were published on the dates indicated under the respective headings: "The Indian War," August 3, 1876; "The Sioux War," August 16, 1876; "The Bloody 'Ingines,'" September 11, 1876; "Struggles of the Sioux," September 26, 1876; "The Sioux War," October 4, 1876; "The Black Hills," October 11, 1876; "Crook's Campaign," October 24, 1876; "Crook's Expedition," November 2, 1876.
39. "Struggles of the Sioux," *Chicago Inter-Ocean*, September 26, 1876 (first quotation); "The Sioux War," *Chicago Inter-Ocean*, October 4, 1876 (second quotation); "The Indian War," *Chicago Inter-Ocean*, August 3, 1876.
40. "The Indian War," *Chicago Inter-Ocean*, August 3, 1876 (first and third quotations); "Struggles of the Sioux," *Chicago Inter-Ocean*, September 26, 1876 (second quotation).
41. "The Sioux War," *Chicago Inter-Ocean*, August 16, 1876 (quotations).
42. "The Bloody 'Ingines,'" *Chicago Inter-Ocean*, September 11, 1876; Schwatka, "The Sun-Dance of the Sioux," 753-59.
43. Hollabaugh, *The Spirit and the Sky*, 140, 149; Holler, *Black Elk's Religion*, 58.
44. "The Bloody 'Ingines,'" *Chicago Inter-Ocean*, September 11, 1876 (quotations). In his *Century* account, Schwatka mentions only one circle of stakes, not two, and therefore no "inner ring." Interestingly, in the *Century* article, he also wrote that his friend Chief Spotted Tail and warrior Standing Elk permitted him full access to the event, though neither were mentioned in the *Inter-Ocean*.
45. Ibid. (quotation).
46. Ibid. (quotations); Hollabaugh, *The Spirit and the Sky*, 138; Holler, *Black Hawk's Religion*, 52.
47. Finerty, *War-Path and Bivouac*, 106-07. Finerty never seems to have modified

his views over time. See Hedren, *John Finerty Reports the Sioux War*, 18-19.
48. Powers, *The Killing of Crazy Horse*, 162-63; Knight, *Following the Indian Wars*, 172-73; "The Gold Seekers," *New York Herald*, August 26, 1875.
49. Schwatka, "The Sun-Dance of the Sioux," 753-59; "The Sun Dance," Fletcher Papers, Smithsonian (quotation).

Chapter Four – The Battle of Slim Buttes and the Starvation March [pages 76-100]

1. "Crook's Campaign," *Omaha Bee*, September 22, 1876 (quoted in Hedren, *Ho! For the Black Hills*, 222).
2. Greene, *Slim Buttes*, 8-9, 15; Bourke, *On the Border with Crook*, 342.
3. Finerty, *War-Path and Bivouac*, 213 (quotation).
4. "The Bloody 'Ingines,'" *Chicago Inter-Ocean*, September 11, 1876 (quotations).
5. Finerty, *War-Path and Bivouac*, 242 (quotation).
6. "Crook's Campaign," *New York Herald*, October 2, 1876 (quotation).
7. "Battle of Slim Buttes Interview Notes," Walter Camp Papers, DPL (first quotation); Schmitt, *General George Crook*, 206 (second quotation).
8. Finerty, *War-Path and Bivouac*, 260.
9. "Battle of Slim Buttes Interview Notes," Walter Camp Papers, DPL (first quotation, interview of Mills); Mills, *My Story*, 170 (second quotation); "Crook's Victory," *New York Herald*, September 17, 1876 (third quotation); Greene, *Slim Buttes*, 54. In his autobiography, Grouard claimed to have entered the village and assessed its size. De Barthe, *Life and Adventures of Frank Grouard*, 303.
10. Powers, *The Killing of Crazy Horse*, 212; "The Battle of Slim Buttes," *Journal of the United States Cavalry Association*, 402; Greene, *Slim Buttes*, 56-57.
11. "Crooks Campaign," *New York Herald*, October 2, 1876 (first quotation); Mills, Official Report, 133 (second quotation).
12. Mills, Official Report, 133 (quotation); "The Sioux War," *Chicago Inter-Ocean*, October 4, 1876.
13. "Letter from Lieut. Schwatka," *Willamette Farmer*, October 27, 1876 (quotation).
14. "The Sioux War," *Chicago Inter-Ocean*, October 4, 1876 (quotation).
15. "Crook's Campaign," *New York Herald*, October 2, 1876.
16. "Crook's Victory," *New York Herald*, September 17, 1876 (quotation). Two soldiers were awarded Medals of Honor for their actions in the ravine. Greene, *Slim Buttes*, 111.
17. Finerty, *War-Path and Bivouac*, 254.
18. Finerty, *War-Path and Bivouac*, 255 (quotation); Schmitt, *General George Crook*, 208n.6
19. Mills, *My Story*, 171.

20. Finerty, *War-Path and Bivouac*, 258 (first quotation), 257 (second quotation); Mills, *My Story*, 172. Davenport claimed that about forty Indians had been killed and twenty-one were captured. "Crook's Victory," *New York Herald*, September 17, 1876.
21. Bourke, *Diaries*, 2:108; De Barthe, *Life and Adventures of Frank Grouard*, 306; Finerty, *War-Path and Bivouac*, 252.
22. Dary, *Frontier Medicine*, 143; Tate, *The Frontier Army*, 179.
23. Bourke, *Diaries*, 2:117 (first quotation); "The Sioux War," *Chicago Inter-Ocean*, October 4, 1876 (second quotation).
24. Schmitt, *General George Crook*, 209 (first quotation); "The Sioux War," *Chicago Inter-Ocean*, October 4, 1876 (second and third quotations).
25. Finerty, *War-Path and Bivouac*, 252 (first quotation); "The Story of the Scout Bearing Herald Despatches," *New York Herald*, September 18, 1876 (second quotation); Mills, *Official Report*, 134-35 (third quotation).
26. "Struggles of the Sioux," *Chicago Inter-Ocean*, September 26, 1876 (quotation).
27. "Recent Deaths," *Army and Navy Journal*, 194.
28. "A Munchausen Reporter Corrected," *Army and Navy Journal* 14, no. 14 (November 11, 1876): 218 (quotation); See also Abrams, *Sioux War Dispatches*, 242-43, 387n.34. Davenport had also reported that Mills had contemplated attacking the village immediately after it was spotted, but was talked out of the action by Crawford and Schwatka. "Crook's Campaign," *New York Herald*, October 2, 1876. These comments were also refuted by Schwatka and other officers and retracted.
29. King, *Campaigning with Crook*, 154 (first quotation); *Army and Navy Journal* 28, no. 19 (January 3, 1891): 317 (remaining quotations); See also Anderson, "Some Footnotes," 18.
30. Reuben Briggs Davenport, *The Death-Blow to Spiritualism* (New York: G. W. Dillingham, 1888).
31. Lloyd to Cousin Peter, January 20, 1877, MHS (quotation).
32. Finerty, *War-Path and Bivouac*, 280 (first quotation); "A Distinguished Visitor," *Black Hills Weekly Times* (Deadwood, S.D.), May 17, 1890 (second quotation).
33. Mills, *My Story*, 174; Schwatka, "The New York Ledger Expedition," *New York Ledger*, May 14, 1892 (quotations).
34. Bourke, *On the Border*, 411 (quotation); 395.
35. Porter, *Paper Medicine Man*, xiii (quotation).
36. Bourke, *Diaries* 4:113 (quotations).
37. Schwatka to Editor, July 20, 1884, Century Papers, NYPL (quotations).
38. Schmitt, *General George Crook*, 301; Ellis, "The Humanitarian Soldiers," 59.
39. Brackett, "Memoir," 5 (quotation).
40. Brackett, "Memoir," 5 (quotations); "Lieut. Schwatka," *Davenport Morning Star*, February 12, 1891.
41. Schwatka, *Among the Apaches*, 45, 48 (quotations).
42. Schwatka, "The Sun-Dance of the Sioux," 759 (first quotation); Schwatka, "How A Great Chief was Named," 298 (second quotation); David, *The Arctic*

in the British Imagination," 208-09.
43. Schwatka, "Among the Natives of the North," *Harper's Monthly Magazine* 14, no. 4 (October 1883): 404 (first quotation); Murphy, "First Among Savages," 536 (second quotation);
44. Noonan, *Reading the Century Illustrated Magazine,* xix, 87. Schwatka cited Sir Daniel Wilson in his writings, who like Lewis Henry Morgan, was a proponent of the theory of cultural hierarchy in which civilizations progress through stages of social development from "savage" or "primitive" to "advanced." For articles expressing that view in *Century Magazine,* see for example, Eggleston, "The Aborigines and the Colonists," 104-14 and Munger, "Immigration by Passport," 792-93.
45. Post Returns, May-October, 1877, Camp Sheridan, NA.
46. Schwatka Report July 9, 1877, Office of Indian Affairs Letters Received, NA (quotation).
47. Schwatka, "Ho Wash-Tay," 250; Anderson, "Gilbert C. Fosdick II." The story as told by Schwatka in *The Youth's Companion,* twelve years after the event, differs slightly from Schwatka's original reports from 1877, but the principal deductions by Good Voice confirming Hardenburg's guilt are largely consistent. The highly regarded Good Voice would continue to be active in Indian affairs. The indefatigable tracker was one of several scouts tasked to keep a watchful eye over Crazy Horse after the great Sioux leader arrived at the Spotted Tail Agency prior to his fateful removal to Camp Robinson and his death on September 5, 1877. Later in 1877, Good Voice would accompany the Sioux delegation to Washington, D.C. to protest the removal of the agencies to the Missouri River. Powers, *The Killing of Crazy Horse,* 396, 402-03.
48. Hedren, "Camp Sheridan," 89; "Spotted Tail's Mission," *New York Herald,* February 23, 1877; Fred [Schwatka] to Father [Frederick G. Schwatka Sr.], February 5, 1877 (quotations), GLI.
49. Gillett, *Six Years with the Texas Rangers,* 155-82.
50. "Spotted Tail Agency," *The Daily Press and Dakotaian* (Yankton, S.D.), January 28, 1878 (quotation). In 1878, the Brulés and Oglalas were subsequently moved to what became the Rosebud Agency and the Pine Ridge Agency, respectively, in South Dakota.
51. "From the North Pole," *Ann Arbor Democrat,* December 20, 1889 (first quotation); "After Crazy Horse," *Pittsburgh Dispatch,* April 14, 1889 (second quotation). The failure of Congress to approve an appropriation to pay army officers after June 30, 1887, which was only rectified in late November 1877, could have added to Schwatka's discontentment.
52. Vaughn, *Then and Now,* 308 (quoting Strahorn letter to Vaughn from 1878).

Chapter Five – Arctic Fever [pages 101-120]

1. Levere, *Science and the Canadian Arctic,* 41-42.

2. Potter, *Finding Franklin*, 5.
3. Owen, *The Fate of Franklin*, 26-27.
4. Ibid., 34 (quotation); Godwin, *The Ships of Trafalgar*, 69.
5. Franklin to Beaufort, February 10, 1836, in "Communications on a North-West Passage," 46 (first quotation); Parry, *Memoirs*, 367 (second quotation).
6. "Another Arctic Expedition," *The Times* (London), November 27, 1852 (quotation).
7. Rae to the Secretary of the Admiralty, July 29, 1854, in Rae, "Proceedings," 831.
8. Ibid. (quotation); Richards, *Dr. John Rae*, 100.
9. McClintock, *The Voyage of the Fox* (1859), 232-34, 251-52; Woodman, *Unravelling the Franklin Mystery*, 248.
10. McClintock, *The Voyage of the Fox* (1859), 262 (quotation)(itals in original). The identification of the skeleton as that of Peglar has been subject to question based on a number of factors, including the uniform and the writings found on the remains. Stein, *Scattered Memories*, 229.
11. McClintock, *The Voyage of the Fox* (1859), 296 (quotation).
12. "Are there Survivors of Sir John Franklin's Expedition?," *Cincinnati Daily Gazette*, February 7, 1860.
13. Hall, *Narrative*, 64, 108; Loomis, *Weird and Tragic Shores*, 190.
14. Hall, *Narrative*, 274 (first quotation); 360 (second quotation); Loomis, *Weird and Tragic Shores*, 218.
15. Hall, *Narrative*, 393 (quotation), 398.
16. Ibid., 405 (quotations).
17. Ibid., 401. Based on the use, in part, of forensic technology, the attribution to Le Vescount has been concluded as unlikely. Mays, et al, "New Light," 1571.

Chapter Six – In the Land of the Midnight Sun [pages 121-146]

1. "Arctic Exploration," *New York Herald*, April 12, 1878; "Sir John Franklin," *New York Herald*, January 23, 1878.
2. Ross, "Commercial Whaling in Hudson Bay," 544-46, 551; Eber, *When the Whalers were Up North*, 23 (quotation).
3. Daly, "Chief Daly's Introductory Address," 238 (quotation). Barry stated that two Inuit families arrived while the *Glacier* wintered at Repulse Bay and "stayed only about a month. It was in the month of February, 1872." Barry, "Thomas Barry's Statement," 276 (quotation). Barry may have been confused as to the year. The *Glacier* was wintering at Marble Island in February 1872, and its logbook records no arrivals of the Nattilingmiut that winter. The winter of 1872-73 was spent by *Glacier* at Repulse Bay. The logbook records a visit by several Nattilingmiut on January 6, 1873, and a visit by several more on March 18, 1873. Logbook of the *Glacier*, PPL.
4. "Sir John Franklin," *New York Herald*, October 11, 1873 (first quotation); Logbook of the *Glacier*, August 17, 1872 (second quotation), PPL. Potter's

account also included additional assertions, such as Franklin's men disagreeing over the route to follow after abandoning the *Erebus* and *Terror*. Potter's informants may have been correct. Not all of the retreating men continued to the Back River; larger parties from the the Franklin expedition may have split into smaller groups and traveled in various directions due to disagreements over the best route to safety or to maximize the likelihood of rescue. David Woodman, personal communication; see also Hall, *Narrative*, 334, 348.

5. Barry, "Thomas F. Barry's Statement," 277-78; "The Region of Ice," *Stark County Democrat* (Canton, Ohio), October 11, 1877;
6. Cyriax, *Sir John Franklin's Last Arctic Expedition*, 97 (citing publication notice in *The Times* (London), January 24, 1872); "Editor's Historical Record: Europe," *Harpers New Monthly Magazine* 44, no. 263 (April 1872): 794 (£2000 reward). Morison's manuscript instructions dated June 19, 1878 only instructed Schwatka to return the remains of Franklin. However, those instructions as published in the *Herald* on June 29, 1878, instructed Schwatka to return the remains of Franklin or any of those of "his unfortunate party." Morison to Schwatka, June 19, 1878, Small Manuscript Collections, Chicago History Museum, Chicago, IL; "Franklin Search Party," *New York Herald*, June 29, 1878.
7. Wright, *Geography in the Making*, 76, 101 (quotation).
8. "The Franklin Search," *New York Herald*, May 3, 1878 (quotation).
9. Maria Lydig Daly, Diaries, vol. 27, June 13, 1870 (first quotation), September 13, 1870 (second quotation), Daly Papers, NYPL; Morin, *Civic Discipline*, 151. In her diary, Mrs. Daly mistakenly referred to Ebierbing as "Hans," likely Hans Hendrik who had served with Kane, Hall and Nares.
10. Ebierbing, "Joseph Eberling's [sic] Statement," 280 (quotation); Kenn Harper, personal communication (re: whalers' jargon).
11. Ebierbing, "Joseph Eberling's [sic] Statement," 281 (quotations); Wright, *Geography in the Making*, 101. Barry's statement, transcribed in reply to Daly's questions and corroborated by Ebierbing, is presumed to be the most accurate version of Barry's account of his 1876 meeting with the Nattilingmiut. It was not however Barry's only statement. On October 6, 1877, immediately upon Barry's arrival in New York City (and before the Daly interview), the *New York Herald* carried an interview with Barry in which Barry provided some additional details he had received about the destruction of Franklin's ships and its crew. In his *Herald* interview, Barry stated that in 1876 he obtained the Franklin spoon "from one of a party of fifteen Esquimaux *who came from Cape Englefield*" (itals added). Barry pointed out that these men had made their way from Cape Englefield by way of Melville Peninsula to Barry's location. He was told by some of these men (who were at least seventy-years-old) that these men had also seen Franklin's ship stove in and assisted the beleaguered crews to shore. Franklin and his men later died. Barry surmised that Franklin reached

Cape Englefield by way of Davis Strait, then through Lancaster Sound or Eclipse Sound. "Relics of Sir John Franklin," *New York Herald*, October 6, 1877. Could Barry have misunderstood the Inuit testimony as to Cape Englefield for events that actually occurred near King William Island?

12. McClintock, "Letter of Admiral Sir Leopold McClintock," 282 (quotation).
13. Rae, "Letter of Dr. John Rae," 288 (quotation). Despite Rae's rather forceful belief that Hall's and Barry's Melville Peninsula stories were simply a retelling of Rae's earlier sojourn and not evidence of Franklin's men, the historian David Woodman has identified numerous discrepancies between the specifics of Rae's journey and the facts and accounts gathered by Hall and Barry. See Woodman, *Strangers Among Us*, 19-48. Cape Englefield was named by Parry in 1822 after the scientist Sir Henry Charles Englefield. Rae, who referred to the cape as Cape Inglefield, may have confused Englefield's name with the naval officer and Arctic explorer, Edward A. Inglefield.
14. "Franklin Expedition Relics," *Buffalo Commercial*, March 2, 1878.
15. "The Arctic Regions," *New York Herald*, April 13, 1878 (quotation).
16. Schwatka, "Among the Natives of the North," *Frank Leslie's Sunday Magazine* 14, no. 1 (July 1883): 31 (quotation); "Some Personal Items," *Army and Navy Journal* 18, no. 11 (October 16, 1880): 204.
17. "The Arctic Regions," *New York Herald*, April 13, 1878 (quotations).
18. Daly to Sherman, March 16, 1878, Schwatka Papers, ACP Files, NA (quotation).
19. Stewart, *American Military History*, 317 (first quotation); Memorandum of Sherman May 5, 1880, Gustavus C. Doane Papers, MSU (second quotation).
20. Sherman to the AAG, March 19, 1878, Schwatka Papers, ACP Files, NA (quotation).
21. Sherman to the AAG, undated, Schwatka Papers, ACP Files, NA (quotation); Schwatka, "In the Land of the Midnight Sun, Part III," 7, nos. 19-20 (March-April, 1881): 13.
22. Riffenburgh, *The Myth of the Explorer*, 57-58, 72.
23. Woodward, *Portrait of Jane*, 363; Riffenburgh, *The Myth of the Explorer*, 74.
24. Morin, *Civic Discipline*, 131 (first quotation); Daly, "Annual Address (1878)," 45 (second and third quotations); "A Year's Explorations," *New York Herald*, February 28, 1878.
25. "Arctic Exploration," *New York Herald*, April 12, 1878 (quotations).
26. Ebierling, "Joseph Eberling's [*sic*] Statement," 279 (first quotation); "Relics of the Franklin Expedition," *New York Tribune*, February 28, 1878 (second quotation).
27. Klutschak, *Overland to Starvation Cove*, 14; Schwatka, "In the Land of the Midnight Sun, Part III," 7, nos. 19-20 (March-April 1881): 13 (quotation). Klutschak stated that $450 in cash contributions was received and that the expedition was furnished at a "total outlay of barely $5000," by which presumably Klutschak meant the total value of all goods and the $450 cash contributed. Klutschak, *Overland to Starvation Cove*, 16 (quotation).

Daly stated that money was contributed by four individuals, Judge Daly, and Messrs. Brevoort, Hermann, and Bernheimer. Wright, *Geography in the Making*, 102; Klutschak, *Overland to Starvation Cove*, 14-16. Additional minor cash contributions were apparently later received. "Franklin Search Party," *New York Herald*, June 29, 1878.

28. "The Franklin Search Party," *New York Herald*, June 5, 1878; "The Franklin Search Party," *New York Herald*, May 5, 1878; "The Franklin Arctic Search," *New York Herald*, May 20, 1878. The specific weaponry was as follows: two repeating Winchester carbines, two Remington breech-loading muskets, one breech-loading Sharp's sporting rifle, one heavy breech-loading Whitney (Creedmore model) rifle, one Evans' 26-shot repeating sporting rifle, two Smith & Wesson revolvers, two shotguns, and six muzzle-loading muskets (the last to be used for trading purposes). Also included were 4,000 rounds of ammunition, additional percussion caps, and large quantities of powder and lead. Schwatka, Manuscript, 44, GWB.
29. "Franklin Search Party," *New York Herald*, June 29, 1878 (quotations).
30. Schwatka, "In the Land of the Midnight Sun, Part III," 7, nos. 19-20 (March-April 1881): 13 (first quotation); "Franklin Search Party," *New York Herald*, June 29, 1878 (second quotation); "A Winter in the North," *Milwaukee Sentinel*, October 8, 1879 (third quotation).
31. Barr, "To the North Pole from York Factory," 36 (quotation); "Obituary. William Henry Gilder," *New York Tribune*, Feb. 6, 1900; Adelman, *Devil's Den*, 134.
32. "The Ice-Bound Ocean," *Milwaukee Sentinel*, September 17, 1882 (quotation); American Whalebook Logbook Data, https://whalinghistory.org/wri/AE071821017, NBWM (accessed September 30, 2021); "Gravely Speaking: C.T. Melms, Milwaukee's First Beer Baron" https://gravelyspeaking.com/2017/09/12/c-t-melms-milwaukees-first-beer-baron/ (accessed September 1, 2021).
33. Klutschak, *Overland to Starvation Cove*, xxvi-xxvii; Kim; "The Mimicry of Empire," 132-33; Traeger, "Heinrich W. Klutschak," in Feest and Traeger, *Eskimo*, 157; Traeger, "Heinrich Wenzel Klutschak," in Nuttal, *Encyclopedia of the Arctic*, 1099; American Whaling Logbook Data, https://whalinghistory.org/wri/AC057881, NBWM (Klutschak's name is misspelled as "Harry Klutzchack")(accessed November 17, 2020).
34. Schwatka, "In the Land of Midnight Sun, Part III," 7, nos. 19-20 (March-April 1881): 13 (quotation); "The Franklin Search Party," *New York Herald*, June 11, 1878; "The Eothen's Whaling Voyage," *New York Times*, June 18, 1878.

Chapter Seven – To the North [pages 147-163]

1. "Toward the North Pole," *The Sun* (N.Y.), June 3, 1878.
2. For the account published in *Good Company*, see Schwatka, "In the Land of

the Midnight Sun," and for the 1968 publication of the Marine Historical Association of Mystic Seaport Museum, see Schwatka, *The Long Arctic Search: The Narrative of Lieutenant Frederick Schwatka*. It should be noted that, for unexplained reasons, *The Long Arctic Search* is not a completely faithful transcription of Schwatka's original manuscript in several instances. Besides omitting sections from the original, *The Long Arctic Search* includes several entries attributed to Schwatka that do not appear in Schwatka's original manuscript. For example, the following powerful statements of Schwatka in *The Long Arctic Search* do not appear in the original manuscript: "It was a nightmarish time. What this ancient hag told us became the most important link in our chain of evidence in the trail of the Franklin party ..Tuktoocheeah's account proved that there had been a central place, or last resting place, in which the vital records of the Franklin Expedition had been placed by the last survivors." Schwatka, *The Long Arctic Search*, 74. Another example: "We questioned her several times on the one fact which had claimed all our attention. Was there a box, containing books of white man's writings? – Her answers were always the same - without hesitation." Schwatka, *The Long Arctic Search*, 75. The original manuscript and a complete transcript of the original manuscript have now been made available on the website of Mystic Seaport Museum, see https://research.mysticseaport.org/item/l040026/.
3. Schwatka, Manuscript, 72-3, GWB (quotation).
4. Schwatka, Manuscript, 74, GWB (quotation).
5. Schwatka, Manuscript, 82, GWB (quotations); see also Savitt, "Frederick Schwatka," 195 (fair and just treatment).
6. Klutschak, *Overland to Starvation Cove*, 22 (quotation).
7. "Schwatka's Search," *New York Herald*, September 5, 1879; "Schwatka's Search," *New York Herald*, September 5, 1879.
8. Klutschak, *Overland to Starvation Cove*, 29 (quotation).
9. Ibid. (quotation).
10. Ibid., 32 (first quotation); "Winter in the North," *Milwaukee Sentinel*, October 8, 1879 (remaining quotations).
11. Schwatka, Manuscript, 146-47, GWB (quotation); Phinney, "Ketogenic Diets," 2-3, 6.
12. "Schwatka's Search," *New York Herald*, September 6, 1879 (quotation). Rasmussen had adopted an all-encompassing designation of all the Inuit of the southern Kivalliq Region (then Keewatin) as "Caribou Eskimos" (later "Caribou Inuit"). Burch, "Knud Rasmussen," 87.
13. "Christmas, Cold and Hot: Near the North Pole" *Sioux Valley News* (Correctionville, Iowa), December 24, 1891 (quotation).
14. Schwatka, "Among the Natives of the North," 13, no. 5 (May, 1883): 474-75 (first two quotations); "Inuit Philology," *New York Herald*, March 13, 1881 (Inuit names for Schwatka and Gilder). For Schwatka's adoption of the word "Inuit" in place of "Esquimaux" see Schwatka, "Among the Natives of the

North," 13, no. 6 (June, 1883): 583.
15. Schwatka, Manuscript, 97, GWB (first quotation); "Schwatka's Search." *New York Herald*, September 3, 1879 (second quotation), "Schwatka's Search," *New York Herald*, September 5, 1879 (third quotations).
16. Schwatka, Manuscript, 96, GWB (first quotation); Schwatka, "In the Land of the Midnight Sun, Part V," 7, no. 21 (May 1881): 210 (second quotation).
17. "The Secrets of the Cairn," *New York Times*, June 11, 1878.
18. "Schwatka's Search," *New York Herald*, September 6, 1879; "Schwatka's Search," *New York Herald,* September 24, 1880; Schwatka, Manuscript, 105, GWB; Schwatka to Daly, March 31, 1879, in Daly, "Annual Address (1880)," 105-06. There were some differences in the testimony of Nutokecak as recorded by Schwatka and Gilder. Schwatka recorded in his manuscript *In the Land of the Midnight Sun* that a cairn was found by Nutokecak on the south side of the island, containing a paper that was lost. Schwatka, Manuscript, 105, GWB. In a letter to Daly on March 31, 1879, Schwatka added more details, stating that the note was in a tin box and that a second cairn lying over a flat slab was located on the north shore of Washington Bay as Gilder had similarly remarked. Although it was not clear from Gilder's report, Schwatka noted that Nutokecak had actually visited the location of the second cairn, but his small party could not lift the heavy slab. Schwatka to Daly, March 31, 1879, in Daly, "Annual Address (1880)," 105-06.
19. "Schwatka's Search," *New York Herald*, September 24, 1880 (quotation). About the trip to Marble Island, Schwatka only recorded that Gilder went to transact "some minor business for the Search Party" and to obtain dogs. Schwatka, Manuscript, 104, GWB. One of the perplexing unanswered questions was why Gilder didn't question Barry about Gilder's conversation with Potter, as Barry was present on the *Eothen* at Marble Island at the time. Barry even made that point in an interview after the return of the *Eothen*. When pressed by a *Herald* reporter, Barry angrily remarked that he wanted to address Potter's account of how Barry came by his spoon. Barry claimed that he had received his spoon from an Inuk after being cast away at Cape Fullerton in 1877. He went on to add that Potter's "accusation should have been made in Hudson's Bay in presence of Captain Potter when we were all there together. I got the spoon, as I have stated before, from a native in exchange for an iron one in the spring of 1877 while cast away near Cape Fullerton." He concluded that "I do know that any story of how the spoon came into my possession different from the way I have stated is a lie." "Captain Barry's explanation how he failed to reach Depot Island," *New York Herald*, September 25, 1880 (quotations). In yet a further inconsistency, Barry had previously stated in his Daly interview that he claimed he received the spoon in the Fall of 1876 while at Whale Point, not in the spring of 1877.
20. Gilder, *Schwatka's Search*, 39 (quotation)(the quote was not in the original

Herald article). For the presentation of the spoon to Miss Cracroft see, Hall, *Narrative,* xxiii. The spoon is labelled N(980(b)) in the collection of the Scott Polar Research Institute. Two other spoons (one bearing the initials "J.G.F." and the other bearing Franklin's crest and an English crown and stamp) were purchased from Barry by Thomas N. Molloy, U.S. consul at St. John's, in September 1877 and also presented to Miss Cracroft by Rear Admiral John Rogers, Superintendant of the U.S. Naval Observatory. See Cracroft note dated May 1882 among the Cracroft Papers, SPRI; "Personal," *Chicago Tribune,* October 4, 1877.

21. Klutschak, *Overland to Starvation Cove,* 33.
22. Ibid. (quotation). Though dismissed as completely untrue, historian David Woodman has suggested that aspects of Barry's Melville Peninsula story can be found in earlier Inuit testimony as told to Hall. See Woodman, *Strangers Among Us,* 104-05.
23. Schwatka, Manuscript, 96, GWB (quotation); Schwatka, "Arctic Experiences," 321.
24. Schwatka, *Nimrod in the North,* 88 (quotation).
25. Schwatka, Manuscript, 103, GWB (quotation); Pelly, *Ukkusiksalik,* 141-42.

Chapter Eight – Franklin Records Search [pages 164-184]

1. Schwatka, Manuscript, 113, GWB. Schwatka, Gilder and Klutschak spelled the names of the various Inuit in their party differently. Schwatka's spellings are used throughout except for two persons, whose names are supplied by Gilder: Kutcheenuark and Karleko. Gilder, *Schwatka's Search,* 58. At the start, according to Klutschak, their food comprised 1,000 pounds of walrus meat and hide for man and dogs (though Schwatka recorded 2,000 pounds), 1,000 pounds of biscuits (though Gilder recorded 500 pounds), 200 pounds of salt pork, 200 pounds of canned corn beef, and much smaller quantities of margarine, cornstarch, coffee, condensed milk and salt. Their plan was to ration the prepared foods over the length of the journey.
2. Gilder, *Schwatka's Search,* 137 (quotation).
3. Schwatka, Manuscript, 97, GWB (quotation). Gilder echoed the sentiment, stating that "the most unpleasant feature of winter travelling is the waiting for an igloo to be built." Gilder, *Schwatka's Search,* 204.
4. Schwatka, *Nimrod in the North,* 157 (quotations); Klutschak, *Overland to Starvation Cove,* 41; Oswalt, *Eskimos and Explorers,* 126, 176.
5. Schwatka, Manuscript, 96, GWB (quotation).
6. "Schwatka's Search," *New York Herald,* September 24, 1880 (quotations). McClintock carried the Minié rifle, a single shot, rifled musket with a large caliber shot that could produce devastating wounds. McClintock, *The Voyage of the 'Fox'* (1859), 213.
7. Klutschak, *Overland to Starvation Cove,* 169; Schwatka, "*Arctic Experiences,*" 312-14.

8. Schwatka, Manuscript, 114, GWB (quotation).
9. Klutschak, *Overland to Starvation Cove*, 56 (first quotation), 57 (second quotation).
10. Zaslow, *The Opening of the Canadian North*, 251-52. American whaling activities in Hudson Bay, and mineral prospecting by Americans in Cumberland Sound, did raise greater sovereignty concerns for the Canadians however. Ibid., 251.
11. "Schwatka's Search," *New York Herald*, September 24, 1880; Klutschak, *Overland to Starvation Cove*, 65 (quotation).
12. Klutschak, *Overland to Starvation Cove*, 64 (first quotation); Schwatka, Manuscript, 124, GWB (second quotation); "Schwatka's Search," *New York Herald*, September 24, 1880. Although Gilder recorded that the Nattilingmiut had forced out the Ugjulingmiut, Schwatka identified both the Nattilingmiut and the Inuinnait as occupying the former Ugjulingmiut lands of King William Island and Adelaide Peninsula. Schwatka noted that the Ugjulingmiut had mistaken Schwatka's expedition for the Inuinnait of whom they were in great fear. Schwatka, Manuscript, 124, GWB. Schwatka would later note that the Inuinnait are a "more belligerent tribe than usual ... with a pertinacity bordering upon open hostility by their Netchilluk [Nattilingmiut] and Ookjoolik [Ugjulingmiut] neighbors." Schwatka, Manuscript, 157-58, GWB. There was some further evidence of Inuinnait aggressiveness towards other Inuit groups. During the Fifth Thule Expedition, Knud Rasmussen was told by the Nattilingmiut of King William Island that the Inuinnait were "dangerous people," whom the Nattilingmiut "seemed to fear." Rasmussen, "The Netsilik Eskimo," 50 (quotations). For his part, Klutschak stated that he heard that the Ugjulingmiut and Nattilingmiut drove out the Utkuhiksalingmiut from the western coast of the Adelaide Peninsula, which is inconsistent with Gilder's and Schwatka's account. Klutschak, *Overland to Starvation Cove*, 64.
13. Rasmussen, *The Netsilik Eskimos*, 120-21 (first and second quotations); Alt, et al, "Arctic Climate during the Franklin Era," 69 (third quotation); 74-75; Savelle, "Effects of Nineteenth Century European Exploration," 204-05; Fossett, *In Order to Live Untroubled*, 149-53. Rasmussen wrote that he was told that famine had driven the beleaguered Ugjulingmiut to the mouth of the Back River before the Nattilingmiut occupation of the territory of the Ugjulingmiut, whereas both Savelle and Fossett believed that they were forcibly displaced by the Nattilingmiut, with Savelle noting that the Ugjulingmiut were still on Adelaide Peninsula when they collected relics from one of Franklin's ships. Rasmussen, *The Netsilik Eskimos*, 121; Savelle, "Effects of Nineteenth Century European Exploration," 205.
14. Schwatka, Manuscript, 125-26, GWB. Both Gilder and Schwatka recorded the travelers were in one boat. "Schwatka's Search," *New York Herald*, September 24, 1880. Pe-ro-wat, Puhtoorak's son-in-law, also interviewed, stated that he saw two boats and that the men may have stopped at Montreal Island and

left a cairn. Schwatka, Manuscript, 126, GWB. Klutschak also recorded two boats and ten men, which could have been the expedition of James Anderson and James Stewart sent by the Hudson's Bay Company which travelled in two canoes to the Back River in 1855. Klutschak, *Overland to Starvation Cove*, 65-6, 230n3.

15. Schwatka, Manuscript, 126, GWB. Gilder recorded that the ship was frozen in the ice near an island five miles due west of Grant Point and that Puhtoorak walked three miles across the ice to reach the ship. "Schwatka's Search," *New York Herald*, September 24, 1880. Klutschak simply stated the beset ship had "drifted with wind and current to a spot west of Grant Point on Adelaide Peninsula, where some islands halted its drift." Klutschak, *Overland to Starvation Cove*, 65. Only Schwatka mentioned that some books ended up on shore. McClintock was also told of a body on board the ship, which required five men to lift and had long teeth. McClintock, *Voyage of the Fox* (1859), 252.

16. Woodman, *Unravelling the Franklin Mystery*, 248-51 (citing Hall's field notes); Schwatka, Manuscript, 125, GWB (first quotation); "Schwatka's Search," September 24, 1880, *New York Herald* (second quotation); Pelly, *Ukkusiksalik*, 163.

17. "Schwatka's Search," *New York Herald*, September 24, 1880 (first quotation); Schwatka, Manuscript, 129, GWB (second quotation). The trepidation on the part of the Nattilingmiut lends credibility that the Inuinnait had visited this region, and had been aggressors. See note 12 above. Evidently, Ebierbing still believed that the Nattilik men were preparing to fight. Gilder stated that they had a custom of killing the first stranger who arrived after the death of one of their group, a circumstance that had recently occurred, but no violence was recorded. "Schwatka's Search," *New York Herald*, September 24, 1880.

18. Schwatka, Manuscript, 129-30, GWB; Klutschak, *Overland to Starvation Cove*, 76; Walpole, *Relics of the Franklin Expedition*, 94. The *Herald* correspondent, Januarius A. MacGahan, who accompanied Ebierbing on the voyage of the *Pandora* in 1875, had a much more critical opinion of Ebierbing's interpreting skills. Although Ebierbing was fluent in several Inuit dialects, MacGahan found that Ebierbing had little knowledge of the English language, thus making it difficult to understand his translations. MacGahan, *Under the Northern Lights*, 137-38.

19. "The Fate of Franklin," *New York Tribune*, October 6, 1880 (quotations). Schwatka's original journal has not been located. Klutschak referenced Schwatka's journal on June 7, 1880, while they awaited their departure at Depot Island: "Schwatka reworked and completed his journal, which he had kept only in the form of key phrases during the cold weather." Klutschak, *Overland to Starvation Cove*, 195.

20. Schwatka, Manuscript, 129 (first quotation), 130 (second quotation), GWB; Klutschak, *Overland to Starvation Cove*, 72 (third, fourth and fifth quotations); "Schwatka's Search," *New York Herald*, September 24, 1880. The statement that one of the Inuit men pointed out the location of the boat, the tent and

three "canoes" was only recorded in Schwatka's journal read to the *Tribune* reporter on October 5. "The Fate of Franklin," *New York Tribune*, October 6, 1880. The Nattilik Toolooah also claimed to have visited Grant Point and identified on a map the location eight miles west of Grant Point where a ship was sunk based on information given to him by another Ugjulingmiut. "Schwatka's Search," *New York Herald*, September 24, 1880; Schwatka, Manuscript, 130, GWB.

21. Stenton, "Finding the Dead," 204; "Schwatka's Search," September 24, 1880, *New York Herald* (quotation).
22. Klutschak, *Overland to Starvation Cove*, 75. The historian R.J. Cyriax pointed out that the letters "L.F." did not match any of the crew of Franklin's *Erebus* or *Terror*, George Back's HMS *Terror*, Robert McClure's HMS *Investigator* or John Ross's *Victory*. Historian David Woodman has suggested that the initials may originally have represented "R.I.P.," with the "R" lost and the "I" misread as the letter "L". Woodman, *Unravelling the Franklin Mystery*, 254-55.
23. Schwatka, Manuscript, 132, GWB (quotations); Stenton, "Finding the Dead," 202-03 (Fig. 1, site no. 24).
24. "Schwatka's Search," September 25, 1880 (first quotation); Schwatka, "In the Land of the Midnight Sun, Part V," 7, no. 21 (May 1881): 220 (second quotation); Hall, *Narrative*, 607. Schwatka had some of his strongest words for this angakkuq, labelling him "the most obnoxious of these sarcophagous [sic] humans," and "a pot-marked brute with an appetite as unlimited as his ideas of soap and society were deficient." Schwatka, Manuscript, 154, GWB. Ahgekshewah would later so spook Ebierbing with murderous exhortations that Ebierbing moved his camp to avoid him. Schwatka was more skeptical of any danger, believing the medicine man, for whom he had nothing but contempt, was simply prone to verbose exaggeration. Schwatka, Manuscript, 158, GWB. Klutschak later found him to be involved in the only case of "deception" by the Inuit. Understanding that items with the embossed stamp of the Queen's broad arrow would be purchased by Schwatka, Ahgekshewah presented a knife with the broad arrow scratched into the blade rather than stamped. Klutschak, *Overland to Starvation Cove*, 124.
25. "Schwatka's Search," *New York Herald*, September 25, 1880 (quotations); Klutschak, *Overland to Starvation Cove*, 73. About Tuktoocheeah's interview, Klutschak recorded that she stated that when accompanied by her husband and seven Inuit, she found skeletons and a body "near the beach in a small inlet," a vague description that might correspond to Starvation Cove. Klutschak, *Overland to Starvation Cove*," 73.
26. Schwatka, Manuscript, 133, GWB (quotation). Interestingly, this was not the first mention of a tin box. At Camp Daly, Nutokecak had previously told Gilder of a tin box at Washington Bay containing papers. "Schwatka's Search," *New York Herald*, September 6, 1879. For an analysis of Inuit testimony that posits that the tragedy believed to have occurred at Starvation Cove may have occurred at a different location, such as Erebus Bay, see Woodman,

Unravelling the Franklin Mystery, 184-93.
27. "Schwatka's Search, *New York Herald*, September 25, 1880 (first quotation); Schwatka, Manuscript, 134, GWB (second quotation); "The Fate of Franklin," *New York Tribune*, October 6, 1880 (third quotation).
28. Klutschak, *Overland to Starvation Cove*, 73 (first quotation), 133-34 (second and third quotations).
29. Schwatka, "Address of Lieutenant Frederick Schwatka" (quotation), in "Arctic Meeting at Chickering Hall," 251-52. Gilder and Klutschak also reported that the tin box was two-feet long and a foot square. "Schwatka's Search," September 25, 1880, *New York Herald*; Klutschak, *Overland to Starvation Cove*, 73.
30. "Schwatka's Search," New York Herald, September 25, 1880 (quotations). Schwatka and Gilder also reported the odd statement by Ahgekshewah that one body, with flesh on it, had a gold chain, fastened to gold earrings and a gold watch was attached to the chain. Schwatka, Manuscript, 133-34, GWB; "Schwatka's Search," *New York Herald*, September 25, 1880. Gilder remarked that when he pulled the chain it pulled the head up by the ears. Gilder thought it strange, but he claimed that he had reported it as he heard it, as did Schwatka. Gilder surmised the chain may have been attached to the ear someway, or that the wearer was simply eccentric and had simply worn it that way. Klutschak noted that statements about a watch attached by a chain to earrings were reported "variously and ambiguously." Klutschak, *Overland to Starvation Cove*, 73.
31. Rae, "Proceedings," 839 (first quotation); "To the Editor of the Times," October 23, 1854, *The Times* (London) (second quotation); "The Schwatka Search," *New York Herald*, October 16, 1880 (third, fourth and fifth quotations).
32. Klutschak, *Overland to Starvation Cove*, 73 note (first quotation); "Schwatka's Search," *New York Herald*, September 25, 1880 (second and third quotations). In his *Tribune* interview and in the *Midnight Sun* manuscript at Mystic, Schwatka also stated that it was the opinion of the Inuit that Franklin's men "were eating each other" because some of the bones had been sawed in two. Schwatka, Manuscript, 133, GWB. "The Fate of Franklin," *New York Tribune*. October 6, 1880. Interestingly, Klutschak did note that "a small saw" was among the articles found in the boat. Klutschak, *Overland to Starvation Cove*, 73 (Gilder and Schwatka mentioned two saws).
33. "Schwatka's Search," *New York Herald*, September 25, 1880 (quotation); Riffenburgh, *The Myth of the Explorer*, 135 (Gilder's reporting accuracy).
34. Schwatka, Manuscript, 130-31, GWB. Gilder stated that although there were a great many articles lying around, "the books were not taken notice of." "Schwatka's Search," *New York Herald*, September 24, 1880. Klutschak also mentions many articles but no books. Klutschak, *Overland to Starvation Cove*, 74. In 1948, a skull and bones were found by L. A. Learmonth on the east side of Washington Bay. Stenton, "Finding the Dead," 205 (citing Learmonth,

L. "Notes on Franklin Relics," *Arctic* 1 (1948), 122-23)).
35. Wamsley, "Albert L. Operti," *Polar Record*, 281.

Chapter Nine – King William Island and Return [pages 185-209]

1. Cooper, *Island of the Lost*, 11-14; Balikci, *The Netsilik Eskimo*, xviii-xix.
2. Klutschak, *Overland to Starvation Cove*, 77 (quotation).
3. Schwatka, Manuscript, 135, GWB (quotations).
4. Klutschak, *Overland to Starvation Cove*, 81-83; Schwatka's Search, *New York Herald*, September 25, 1880; Schwatka, Manuscript, 136, GWB. Although Toolooah claimed it was a white man's skull, Schwatka claimed that "there was no other confirmatory proof." Schwatka, Manuscript, 137, GWB. Klutschak's narrative differs in that he claimed that Schwatka "immediately identified [the skull] as that of a white man." Klutschak, *Overland to Starvation Cove*, 83 (quotation). Gilder stated that the skull was reinterred and marked by a monument on July 13 on their return from Cape Felix. "Schwatka's Search," *New York Herald*, September 25, 1880. The remains at this location have not been located. Stenton, "Finding the Dead," 200, 205, 207 (Franklin Point (Fig. 1, site No. 4)).
5. Schwatka, Manuscript, 137-38, GWB; Klutschak, *Overland to Starvation Cove*, 83-4; "Schwatka's Search," *New York Herald*, September 25, 1880; Stenton, et al, "A Franklin Expedition Officer's Burial," 3. Gilder stated the medal was found on a stone at the foot of the grave. A monument was erected on the grave site on July 13 on the return from Cape Felix. Subsequent investigations have found no other human remains at this site. Stenton, "Finding the Dead," 198-99 (Crozier Camp (NjLg-1) (Fig. 1, site no. 2)).
6. "Schwatka's Franklin Relics," *New York Herald*, October 6, 1880 (quotation).
7. Bell, *Lieut. John Irving*, 75 (quotation).
8. Klutschak, *Overland to Starvation Cove*, 87 (quotation); "Schwatka's Search, *New York Herald*, September 25, 1880; Schwatka, Manuscript, 138, GWB; Stenton, "Finding the Dead," 198 (Cape Felix (NlLf-7) (Fig. 1, site no. 1)). Although the Schwatka expedition did not locate any graves or remains at the site, in 1949, R.C.M.P. Inspector Henry Larsen found skull fragments and a leg bone believed to be of a Franklin expedition member. Stenton, "Finding the Dead," 198.
9. Schwatka, "In the Land of the Midnight Sun, Part V" 7, no. 21 (May, 1881): 218 (quotation).
10. Schwatka, Manuscript, 140, GWB (quotation).
11. Ibid., 141 (quotation); Klutschak, *Overland to Starvation Cove*, 93; "Schwatka's Search," *New York Herald*, September 26, 1880. The descriptions by Schwatka, Klutschak and Gilder are confusing as to the actual locations of the graves and their distances from one another. See Stenton, "Finding the Dead," 201-02 (Le Vesconte Point)(Fig. 1, site no. 5)) and (Two Grave Bay)(Fig. 1, site no. 6)). An investigation in 2018

located the first grave referenced by Schwatka, which contained human remains and clothing apparel and accessories, both within and outside the grave. Stenton, et al, "A Franklin Expedition Officer's Burial," 3.
12. Klutschak, *Overland to Starvation Cove*, 94-96; Schwatka, Manuscript, 142, GWB; "Schwatka's Search," September 26, 1880; Stenton, "Finding the Dead," 202 (Erebus Bay (Fig. 1, sites no. 7-11)); Stenton, et al, "DNA Identification."; Stenton, et al, "The 'Boat Place' Burial," 32.
13. Schwatka, Manuscript, 145, GWB (quotation).
14. Ibid., 150 (first quotation); "Schwatka's Search," *New York Herald*, September 26, 1880 (second quotation). The skeletal remains near Cape Crozier were reinterred and a monument erected. Schwatka, Manuscript, 146; Stenton, "Finding the Dead," 205 (Cape Crozier site (Fig. 1, site no. 12)). Modern surveys have not located the grave.
15. Schwatka, Manuscript, 147, GWB (quotation).
16. Klutschak, *Overland to Starvation Cove*, 110; "Schwatka's Search," September 26, 1880. For more detail as to archaeological work performed at this site see Stenton, "Finding the Dead," 204, 210 (Starvation Cove Boat Site)(Fig. 1 site no. 31)). Hall surmised that as many as twenty-five men had died at the site, but Schwatka suggested at most ten and likely closer to four. In 1949, Inspector Henry Larsen conducted a survey and found no human remains, and a survey in 2015 also failed to locate any. Stenton, "Finding the Dead," 204. In 1923, Rasmussen stated that on the east coast of Adelaide Peninsula "near Starvation Cove" he had found and buried some bones and clothing of some of Franklin's men. Rasmussen, *The Netsilik Eskimos*, 131, 440 (quotation).
17. Schwatka, Manuscript, 154, GWB (quotation); Stenton, "Finding the Dead," 206 (Tulloch Point (Fig. 1, site no. 21)); Beattie and Savelle, "Discovery of Human Remains," 104.
18. Klutschak, *Overland to Starvation Cove*, 117 (quotation); McClintock, *Fate of Sir John Franklin*, [75]. By the 1930s, the seasonal caribou migration to King William Island had almost ceased, possibly attributable to hunting, severe weather conditions or caribou population dynamics. Ljubicic, et al, "The Curious Case of King William Island," 112.
19. Klutschak, *Overland to Starvation Cove*, 135-36.
20. Ibid., 135 (quotation).
21. Ibid., 130 (first and second quotations); "Schwatka's Return," September 27, 1880, *New York Herald* (third quotation).
22. Schwatka, Manuscript, 156, GWB (first quotation), 157 (second quotation); "Schwatka's Return," September 27, 1880, *New York Herald* (third quotation). Gilder reported that the Inuit were planning to kill "all of our party except the women." "Schwatka's Return," *New York Herald*, September 27, 1880. Schwatka remarked that the various Inuit groups "very seldom indeed war against each other," and none had occurred in the "memory of the oldest inhabitant." Schwatka, Manuscript, 157, GWB.

23. Schwatka, Manuscript, 159, GWB (quotation).
24. Klutschak, *Overland to Starvation Cove,* 148 (first two quotations), 133 (third quotation); Schwatka, "Address of Lieutenant Frederick Schwatka," 255; "Schwatka's Return," *New York Herald*, September 27, 1880. According to Schwatka and Gilder, but not mentioned by Klutschak, the skeleton was of a white man whose clothing was not that of an officer. For a description of the site where the remains were located, see Stenton, "Finding the Dead," 204 (Hill South of Starvation Cove (Fig.1, site no. 32)).
25. Klutschak, *Overland to Starvation Cove*, 153, 146 (first and third quotations), Schwatka, Manuscript, 161, GWB (second and fourth quotations).
26. Klutschak, *Overland to Starvation Cove*, 156 (quotation).
27. Ibid., 157-58 (first quotation); Schwatka, Manuscript, 164, GWB (second quotation).
28. Ross, "Nineteenth Century Exploration of the Arctic," 308. The Schwatka expedition's low temperatures were by no means the lowest ever recorded. A temperature of -89.9F was reached at Oymyakon in Eastern Siberia in February 1933. The Northern Forum, "Amazing Facts about the Arctic" (published October 12, 2017), https://www.northernforum.org/en/news/309-amazing-facts-about-the-arctic (accessed November 10, 2020).
29. Tom Spears, "Science in Winter: Why your Voice carries Farther on a Cold Morning," *Ottawa Citizen,* February 1, 2017 (quoting David Phillips, Environment Canada, senior climatologist).
30. Schwatka, Manuscript, 161, GWB. (quotation).
31. Ibid., 502 (quotations).
32. "Schwatka's Return," September 27, 1880, *New York Herald* (first quotation); Schwatka, Manuscript, 503, GWB (second quotation).
33. "Schwatka's Adieu*,"* October 25, 1880, *New York Herald* (first, third, and fourth quotations); Klutschak, *Overland to Starvation Cove*, 197 (second quotation).
34. "Schwatka's Adieu," *New York Herald*, October 25, 1880 (quotations).
35. Ibid.
36. "Schwatka's Search*,"* *New York Herald* September 25, 1880 (quotation).

Chapter Ten – The Traveler at Home [pages 210-225]

1. Riffenburgh, *The Myth of the Explorer*, 75-76. Gilder's letters were published in the September 23, 24, 25, 26, 27 and 28, 1880 and October 2, 16 and 25, 1880 issues of the *Herald* although coverage of the expedition was extensive throughout that period. Earlier letters had been published on September 3, 5 and 6, 1879. A letter published in the *Herald* on March 13, 1881 in the third person on Inuit language and a vocabulary was included as an Appendix to

"Schwatka's Search." "Inuit Philology," *New York Herald*, March 13, 1881.
2. "The Fate of Franklin," *New York Tribune*, October 6, 1880 (quotations).
3. "Schwatka's Search," *New York Herald*, September 25, 1880 (quotations). Schwatka stated that the provisions left behind with the *Eothen* by his party included more than 1,000 pounds of bread, as well as goods to trade with the Inuit and a number of muskox and polar bear skins. Schwatka, Manuscript, 241, GWB. Though catches were hard to come by during the 1878-79 season, in contrast to the empty *Eothen*, the New Bedford whalers, *Abbie Bradford, Abbott Lawrence* and *Isabella,* returned with modest quantities of whale bone and oil. "Whalemen," *New York Herald*, August 26, 1879 ("Arrived at St. John's, NF, *Eothen,* from Hudson's Bay, clean"). Whether the *Eothen* logbook could have exonerated Barry is unclear; only entries for the first three months of the voyage are known to have survived, and offer no clarification. *Eothen* logbook 1878, NBWM.
4. Schwatka to Drum, September 29, 1880, Schwatka Papers, ACP Files, NA; Drum to Schwatka, October 6, 1880, Schwatka Papers, ACP Files, NA.
5. "Schwatka's Search," September 26, 1880, *New York Herald* (first quotation); "Schwatka's Journey," October 23, 1880, *New York Herald* (second quotation) (republished from *The Times* (London), October 8, 1880); "Arctic Explorers," September 28, 1880, *New York Herald* (third quotation).
6. "Sir John Franklin," *Christian Herald,* November 11, 1880 (first quotation); Editorial, *The Times* (London), September 25, 1880 (second quotation); "Weyprecht on the *Jeannette*," *New York Herald,* November 11, 1880 (third quotation).
7. McClintock, "Letter of Admiral Sir Leopold McClintock," 245 (first quotation); Hall, *Narrative*, xxi (second quotation); see also McClintock's interview quoted in "Schwatka's Search," *New York Herald,* September 26, 1880 (Schwatka's "report is a confirmation of mine [McClintock].").
8. "Schwatka's Journey," *New York Herald,* October 23, 1880 (quotations) (republished from *The Times* (London), October 8, 1880); "The Schwatka Search," *New York Herald*, October 16, 1880.
9. "Arctic Amenities," *New York Herald,* September 26, 1880 (quoting *The Chronicle*)(first quotation); W. Parker Snow, "The Franklin Expedition-To the Editor of the Times," *The Times* (London), September 25, 1880 (second quotation).
10. "Schwatka's Great Sledge Journey," *New York Herald*, September 24, 1880; "The Schwatka Expedition," *New York Herald*, September 27, 1880; Markham to McClintock, November 5, 1880, McClintock Papers, NMM (quotation).
11. "Schwatka's Search," *New York Herald*, September 29, 1880 (quotations); Cavell, "Publishing Sir John Franklin's Fate," 174 (Bennett motivated by desire to sell newspapers, among other reasons). Bennett and Jane Franklin were the principal backers of Young's 1875 *Pandora* expedition. Woodward, *Portrait of Jane*, 363.
12. Bell, *Lieut. John Irving*, 162-65; "Lieut. Schwatka's Reception," *New York*

Herald, October 25, 1880; Irving to the Secretary of State for Foreign Affairs, September 26, 1880 (copy), Adjutant General's Office Letters Received (Main Series), 1871-1880, NA.
13. Schwatka to McClintock, September 29, 1880, McClintock Papers, NMM (first and second quotations); McClintock to Schwatka, October 2, 1880, McClintock Papers, NMM (third and fourth quotations). The last sentence in McClintock's letter quoted above appears to have been crossed out in McClintock's draft, evidently reflecting second thoughts on acknowledging the fact of cannibalism. McClintock confirmed having sent the October 2 letter to Schwatka in a letter to Judge Daly. McClintock to Daly, October 2, 1880, McClintock Papers, NMM.
14. The Fate of Franklin, *New York Tribune*, October 6, 1880 (first quotation); "Incidents of the Franklin Search," *New York Tribune*, October 7, 1880 (second quotation).
15. "Schwatka's Journey," *New York Herald,* October 23, 1880; "A Deplorable Discussion," *New York Herald*, October 23, 1880 (quotation).
16. "The Schwatka Expedition," October 27, 1880 (quotation); Hall, *Narrative*, 420, 595, 608.
17. "Honor to Schwatka," *New York Herald*, October 29, 1880 (first quotation); "The Fate of Franklin," *New York Tribune*, October 6, 1880 (second quotation).
18. Schwatka, Manuscript, 116, GWB; Klutschak, *Overland to Starvation Cove*, 166, 175 (5,287.5 km per Klutschak).
19. Schwatka, "Address by Lieutenant Frederick Schwatka," in "Arctic Meeting at Chickering Hall, October 28th, 1880," 256 (quotation); [Rae, J.], *Voyages and Travels*, 4, 7.
20. Stefansson, *Discovery,* 7 (first three quotations); Weems, "Peary's Long Quest," 31 (fourth quotation, from Peary's papers in the possession of Peary's daughter Marie); Savitt, "Frederick Schwatka," 208.
21. Tyrrell, *Across the Sub-Arctics of Canada,* 9 (first quotation); Hanbury, *Sport and Travel*, 20 (second quotation), 108 (third quotation).
22. Pelly, "Ukkusiksalik," 186-88; Pelly, "Wager Bay," 17-18.
23. Pelly, "Wager Bay," 20 (quoting HBC Post Journal, Tasiujaq, November 8, 1929).
24. Eber, *Encounters on the Passage*, 107 (quotation).
25. Stenton, et al., "A Franklin Expedition Officer's Burial," 3. Schwatka's party reinterred remains at six locations on King William Island and two on Adelaide Peninsula. As to five of those locations, the previous attribution to Franklin expedition members is now considered "doubtful," and one has been determined to be incorrect. Ibid. For a description and photographs of the relics recovered by Schwatka, see https://www.rmg.co.uk/collections/objects/search/schwatka (accessed February 5, 2022)
26. Klutschak, *Overland to Starvation Cove*, 218-19 (first quotation); Stefansson, *My Life with the Eskimo*, 43 (second quotation).
27. Gilder, *Schwatka's Search*, 240 (first quotation), xii (second quotation);

Klutschak, *Overland to Starvation Cove*, 13 (third and fourth quotations); "Address of Frederick Schwatka," 257-58 (fifth quotation).
28. Potter, "Finding Franklin," 221-32 (list of Franklin searches). For an excellent summary of the history of discoveries of remains of Franklin expedition members, as well as the results of recent archaeological work, see Stenton, et al., "Finding the Dead, 197-212."

Chapter Eleven – New Horizons [pages 226-248]

1. Markham to McClintock, October 12, 1880, McClintock Papers, NMM (first and second quotations); Markham to McClintock, November 5, 1880 (third quotation), McClintock Papers, NMM; Markham to McClintock, October 14, 1880 (fourth and fifth quotations), McClintock Papers, NMM.
2. McClintock, *Fate of Sir John Franklin*, [54].
3. Ibid., [71] (quotations).
4. Ibid., [77-8] (quotation). McClintock's comment also clarified his statement of September 26, 1880 when he was quoted as stating that all explorers prior to Schwatka "have relied chiefly on the supplies carried with them." "Schwatka's Search," *New York Herald*, September 23, 1880.
5. Klutschak, *Overland to Starvation Cove*, 161 (first quotation); McClintock, *Fate of Sir John Franklin*, [77] (second quotation). Contrary to McClintock's comment, Schwatka did note that the intense cold is normally accompanied by no wind or light winds. Schwatka, Manuscript, 164, GWB.
6. Gilder, *Schwatka's Search*, viii (quotation); Back, *Narrative of the Arctic Land Expedition*, 568; Markham, *The Great Frozen Sea*, 252.
7. Schwatka, "Address to the Geographical Society," 256 (first quotation); Markham, *The Lands of Silence*, 356 (second quotation); McClintock, "On Arctic Sledge-Travelling," 467-68. In McClintock's 1875 article, "On Arctic-Sledge Travelling," he wrote that a journey of 1400 miles (McClintock's journey) and another of 1350 miles (by Lieutenant George M. Mecham), "have not yet been surpassed." McClintock, "On Arctic Sledge-Travelling," 467-68. Interestingly, McClintock's 1875 article was reprinted in 1901 in the *Antarctic Manual for Use of the Expedition of 1901*, without mention of Schwatka's sledge journey. The historian Ronald Savitt has remarked that a 1995 analysis of nineteenth-century sledge journeys in the Arctic and Antarctic regions noted Schwatka's "extensive sledging," but omitted any reference to his journey (or its time or distance), in a detailed comparative chart of polar journeys. Pearson, "Sledges and Sledge Journeys," 3-24; Savitt, "Frederick Schwatka," 196.
8. Dorn, "Sunday Afternoon," 238, 241; see Schwatka, "In the Land of the Midnight Sun."
9. Schwatka, Manuscript, 120, GWB (quotation).
10. "What People Read," *New York Times*, January 22, 1882 (first quotation); Gilder, *Schwatka's Search*, ix (second and third quotations); Markham,

"Expedition of Lieutenant F. Schwatka," 659 (fourth quotation); Markham, *Life of Sir Admiral Leopold McClintock,* 284 (fifth quotation); "British Tribute to the Schwatka Expedition," *New York Herald,* November 18, 1880. The final publication of *Schwatka's Search* was completed by a ghost-writer, as Gilder had taken leave to join the U.S.S. *Rodgers* in search of the missing *Jeannette.* The introduction states that "beyond a mere concatenation of the chapters it has been nowhere altered with a view to literary effect or sensational color." Gilder, *Schwatka's Search,* viii (quotation). Gilder's letters are reproduced rather faithfully, and additional descriptions of the Inuit were incorporated to complete the full work.

11. Klutschak, *Als Eskimo unter den Eskimo,* [v] (quotation); Klutschak, *Overland to Starvation Cove,* [3]; Kim, "The Mimicry of Empire," 134.
12. "The Franklin Search Expedition," *Illustrated London News* (Supplement), January 1, 1881, 18 (quotation); David, *The Arctic in the British Imagination,* 17; Barr, "Klutschak," 14; Craciun, *Writing Arctic Disaster,* 73 (noting the discrepancy between the original drawing and the published image in ILN). For a full analysis of Klutschak's illustrations within the context of Inuit and European relationships, see Cracuin, *Writing Arctic Disaster,* 66-81.
13. Franz Boas to Marie Krackowizer, February 15, 1884, quoted in Boas, *Franz Boas among the Inuit of Baffin Island,* 17.
14. Schwatka, "Among the Natives of the North," 13, no. 5 (May 1883): 475 (first four quotations), 476 (fifth quotation).
15. Schwatka, "Among the Natives of the North," 13, no. 5 (May 1883): 474 (quotations).
16. Schwatka, "Among the Natives of the North," 14, no. 1 (July 1883), 27 (first and second quotations); 13, no. 5 (May 1883), 474 (third and fourth quotations).
17. Schwatka, "Among the Natives of the North," 14, no. 1 (July 1883), 27 (quotation).
18. Caswell, *The Utilization of Scientific Reports,* 172; Krupnik, "Coming Home," 22-24.
19. Lawrence, *Classified Reading,* 101 (first quotation); *Documents of the School Committee,* 36, 50, 62, 78; Schwatka, "The Intelligence of Eskimo Children," *The Independent* (N.Y.), October 7, 1887 (second quotation).
20. Pelly, *Ukkusiksalik,* 157 (quotation). Bruce stated that Ujaralaaq was her grandmother, and that her father (Maliki) and another relative (Tasiuq), were also on the Schwatka expedition. Unfortunately, the names are not identifiable to names identified by Schwatka, Gilder or Klutschak.
21. Pelly, *Ukkusiksalik,* 158 (quotation).
22. Ibid., 159 (quotations).
23. Ibid. (quotations).
24. Ananguaq, "The Schwatka Expedition," 8 (first and third quotations), 9 (second quotation).
25. Rasmussen, "The Netsilik Eskimos," 29 (quotation). Ananguaq stated that his

mother was Ujaralaaq. Guy Mary-Rouseliére suggested that Ujaralaaq may not have been a participant in the Schwatka expedition, but had met the expedition members at Camp Daly. Ananguaq, "The Schwatka Expedition," 9–10.
26. Schwatka to Drum, November 4, 1880, Schwatka Papers, ACP Files, NA (quotation); "Arctic Explorers at Home," *Northern Pacific Farmer* (Wadena, Minn.), January 6, 1881; John Metcalfe, "When Lager Reigned," *CityLab*, February 20, 2017, citylab.com (accessed February 5, 2022).
27. "Frank Melms Insane," *Milwaukee Daily Journal*, September 13, 1883 (quotations).
28. "A Checkered Career," *New York Times*, March 27, 1890 (quotation).
29. Frederick Schwatka to August Schwatka, January 10, 1881, quoted in "Lieutenant Schwatka," *Oregonian* (Portland, Ore.), February 2, 1881.
30. Drum to Sherman, June 19, 1881, Schwatka Papers, ACP Files, NA.
31. Report of Post Surgeon, Fort D. A. Russell May 26, 1881, Schwatka Papers, ACP Files, NA (first and second quotations); Drum to Sherman June 19, 1881, Schwatka Papers, ACP Files, NA (third quotation); Sherman Memorandum, June 20, 1881, Schwatka Papers, ACP Files, NA (fourth quotation).
32. "Lieutenant Schwatka," *San Francisco Chronicle*, July 24, 1881 (quotations).

Chapter Twelve – Down the Yukon - Part I [pages 249-271]

1. Thayer, Earhart, et al September 14, 1881 to Lincoln, Schwatka Papers, ACP Files, NA (quotation).
2. Drum to Sherman, September 16, 1881, Schwatka Papers, ACP Files, NA (first quotation); Sherman to Drum, September 17, 1881, Schwatka Papers, ACP Files, NA (second quotation).
3. Sherman to Drum, [September 17, 1881], Schwatka Papers, ACP Files, NA.
4. Charlton, "Our Ice Islands," 25.
5. Schwatka to Miles October 26, 1881, Adjutant General's Office Letters Received (Main Series), 1881-1889, NA; Miles to the AAG, November 2, 1881, Adjutant General's Office Letters Received (Main Series), 1881-1889; *Congressional Record* 13 (December 12, 1881): 68 (Senate); *Congressional Record* 13 (December 16, 1881): 175 (House)(introduction of bills (S. No. 360 and H.R. 1363) for a scientific exploration of Alaska)); "Exploration of Alaska," *Oregonian* (Portland, Oreg.), November 21, 1881.
6. "Congress and Alaska," *New York Times*, July 29, 1882 (quotation); "Good Choice," *Daily Astorian*, December 11, 1881 ("Lieut. Schwatka is the very man to head the expedition").
7. "Personal," *Cleveland Leader*, December 24, 1881; "Personal," *Rock Island Argus*, January 6, 1882.
8. "Schwatka-Brackett," *The Moline-Review Dispatch*, January 27, 1882 (quotation); *Historic Rock Island County*, pt. 2, 160; "Rock Island Homes

of the 1850s," *Rock Island Argus*, April 29, 1941; Ada Schwatka Interview, RICHS; Wamsley, Brackett-Schwatka Papers.
9. *Congressional Record* 13 (December 12, 1881): 69 (Senate); *Congressional Record* 13 (February 20, 1882): 1303 (House).
10. "Personal," *Evening Star* (Washington, D.C.), July 27, 1882.
11. Schwatka to Drum, August 6, 1882, Schwatka Papers, ACP Files, NA (first quotation); Drum to Schwatka, August, 1882, Schwatka Papers, ACP Files, NA (second quotation); "Lieutenant Schwatka Swindled," *New York Tribune*, September 1, 1882.
12. "An Explorer," *Rock Island Argus*, September 4, 1882; "Married," *Rock Island Argus*, September 6, 1882; Kelly, "The Story of Peoria's Grand Opera House"; Bishop, "Peoria's Grand Opera House"; "Peoria's New Opera House," *Chicago Tribune*, September 8, 1882.
13. AG to Miles, December 1, 1881, Adjutant General's Office Letters Received (Main Series), 1881-1889, NA; AG to Miles, January 12, 1882, Adjutant General's Office Letters Received (Main Series), 1881-1889; "The Pacific Coast," *New York Herald*, May 13, 1882; "A Survey of Alaska," *Reno Gazette-Journal*, May 3, 1882.
14. Miles to Schwatka, April 7, 1883, in Schwatka, *Report,* 119 (quotations). Curiously, the only potential sign of hostility, which was more in the nature of dissatisfaction, might be the surrender by the Tlingit people of their monopoly over the Chilkoot Trail. Sherwood, *Exploration of Alaska*, 99; Bearss, *Proposed Klondike Gold Rush National Historic Park,* 11n. 7.
15. Miles to Schwatka, April 7, 1883, in Schwatka, *Report,* 119 (quotation).
16. Schwatka, *Along Alaska's Great River*, 11 (quotation).
17. Schwatka, *Report*, 9 (quotation); Waterbury, "Tlingit Potlatches."
18. Schwatka, *Report*, 13. Reverend Willard and his family departed soon thereafter after the child of a Tlingit chief died of pneumonia at the mission, and the Willards feared reprisal against Willard's two children. Ogilvie, *The Klondike Official Guide*, 16; Jackson, "Presbyterian Missions in Alaska in 1885," 400.
19. Schwatka, *Along Alaska's Great River*, 189 (first quotation); Schwatka, *Report*, 15 (second quotation); McClellan, *My Old People Say*, pt.1, 4-5, 38; McClellan, "Tagish," 482-83, 489-90.
20. Schwatka, *Report*, 13. The Chilkoot Trail ran some thirty-three miles and ended at Lake Bennett. A second trail, the White Pass Trail, completed in 1878, ran about forty-five miles but was less steep at 2,865 feet, and likewise ended at Lake Bennett. Both presented difficulties traveling with heavy packs and gear. The writer Tappan Adney heard one traveler state that "whichever way you go, you will wish you had gone the other." Tappan Adney, "News from the Klondike," *Harper's Weekly* 41, no. 2130 (October 16, 1897): 1030 (quotation). In July 1899, after a railway was completed from Skagway through the White Pass Trail to Lake Bennett traffic on the Chilkoot Trail dropped significantly.

21. *Hearing before the Subcommittee*, 83 (citing 22,000 men crossing the pass in the winter of 1897-98).
22. Schwatka, *Along Alaska's Great River*, 83, (quotation).
23. Ibid., 104 (quotations).
24. Ibid., 61 (quotation); *Hearing before the Subcommittee*, 83; The Historic Chilkoot Trail https://www.nps.gov/klgo/learn/historyculture/historic-chilkoot-trail.htm (accessed July 12, 2021). Schwatka claimed that he later learned that the idea of rafting the headwaters of the Yukon had been done before his expedition. Schwatka, *Along Alaska's Great River*, 116.
25. Schwatka, *Along Alaska's Great River*, 172 (first quotation); 125 (second quotation).
26. Ibid., 165-66 (quotation).
27. Ibid., 166 (first quotation), 167 (second and third quotations).
28. McIntosh, *Diary*, July 2, ASL. In a *Forest and Stream* article, Schwatka was more forthcoming, stating that both Billy and Indianne canoed out to the raft in the cascades. Schwatka, "Down the Yukon on a Raft, Seventh Paper," 123.
29. Schwatka, *Along Alaska's Great River*, 187 (quotation).
30. Wright, *Prelude to Bonanza*, 154n.66; see also, Lundberg, "Five Finger Rapids, Yukon." In 1887, after Schwatka's "Rink Rapids" were renamed "Five Finger Rapids," the name "Rink Rapids" was given to a set of rapids twelve miles further downstream. Harris, *Schwatka's Last Search*, 118n43 and 120n44.
31. Copland, "The White River Ash"; Capps, "An Ancient Volcanic Eruption," 62.
32. Schwatka, *Along Alaska's Great River*, 204 (quotation). Schwatka stated that the Tlingit burned the post at the time of the attack. McIntosh noted that his Tlingit companions told him that the post was not destroyed in August 1851, "but caught fire by other means some time in 1853." McIntosh, *Diary*, July 14, ASL.

Chapter Thirteen – Down the Yukon - Part II [pages 272-289]

1. Schwatka, *Report*, 33 (quotations).
2. Sir L. S. Sackville West to Mr. Bayard, September 14, 1887, in *Papers Relating to the Foreign Relations*, 768 (quotation).
3. Miles's Report, May 14, 1884, in Schwatka, *Report*, 121 (first quotation); "British Columbia and Alaska," *Indianapolis Journal*, March 25, 1885 (second quotation).
4. Schwatka, *Along Alaska's Great River*, 190 (first quotation); McIntosh, *Diary*, July 13, ASL (second quotation), July 14, ASL (third quotation).
5. McIntosh, *Diary*, July 15, ASL (quotation); Schwatka, *Along Alaska's Great River*, 224-234; McClellan, "Tutchone," 495-96, 503.
6. Schwatka, *Report*, 40 (quotation); Crow and Obley, "Han," 513.

Chapter Notes 435

7. Schwatka, *Along Alaska's Great River*, 248 (quotation).
8. Ibid., 256 (quotation); Crow and Obley, "Han," 509-13.
9. McIntosh, *Diary*, July 23 (quotation), ASL.
10. McIntosh, *Diary*, August 5 (quotation), ASL.
11. Schwatka, *Along Alaska's Great River*, 309 (first quotation), 310 (second quotation); McIntosh, *Diary*, August 7, ASL (third and fourth quotation).
12. Collinson, *Journal of HMS Enterprise*, 130. Collinson's brother (editor of Richard Collinson's published journal) noted that Barnard's death was "one of the heaviest of all the misfortunes experienced by the *Enterprise*, and, perhaps the most depressing to its commander." Ibid.
13. McIntosh, *Diary*, August 22 (quotation), ASL.
14. McIntosh, *Diary*, September 8 (quotation), ASL.
15. Schwatka, *Report*, 9 (quotations); Brown, *The History of the Brooks Range*, 33.
16. Dawson, *Report on an Exploration in the Yukon District*, 1898, 142 (first quotation); see also Dawson, *Historical Notes on the Yukon District*, 11 (Lieut. Schwatka "crossed the Chilkoot pass and descended by the Lewes and Yukon to the sea, making a fairly correct sketch of his route."); Foley, *Field Surveying and Topographic Mapping in Alaska*, 122 (second quotation).
17. "Lieutenant Frederick Schwatka," *The Pathfinder*, 16 (quotations); Bearss, *Proposed Klondike Gold Rush National Historic Park*, 17; Sherwood, *Exploration of Alaska*, 100.
18. Dawson, *Report on the Exploration of the Yukon*, 12, 142; Sherwood, *Exploration of Alaska*, 101; Wright, *Prelude to Bonanza*, 164 (quoting MacBride, "Schwatka's Northern Expeditions," *Whitehorse Star*). In an 1885 letter to the anthropologist Franz Boas, Schwatka remarked that he ignored "native names" in places mapped unless they were easy to pronounce by Euro-Americans because in his experience, such names "will not remain." The fanciful names invented by miners, such as "Broken Bottle Rock," were treated similarly, but he preferred to retain those of Lindeman. Schwatka to Boas, August 16, 1885, Boas-Rukyser Collection, American Philosophical Society, Philadelphia, PA.
19. Schwatka, *Along Alaska's Great River*, 180 (quotations).
20. Dall, "Schwatka's 'Along Alaska's Great River,'" 308 (quotation).
21. Molnia, *Glaciers of North America-Glaciers of Alaska*, K28; Hakonson, *Most Distant Fastnesses*, 19-20. The photographic plates (five by eight inches) were too large for the camera and were trimmed, likely leading to the defects in the images. Schwatka, *Report*, 18. Homan was not the earliest photographer in Alaska. At least one photograph of Alaska by Charles Ryder, working with the Western Union Telegraph Expedition in 1866, has survived, and in 1868 Eadweard Muybridge had taken photographs in Southeast Alaska on behalf of the U.S. Army.
22. Goetzmann, *New Lands*, 429 (quotation). For Schwatka's views on shamans, see for example, Schwatka, "The Thlinkets of Alaska," *New York Times*, November 8, 1886.

23. "Alaska Exploration," *New York Times*, October 10, 1883 (quotation).
24. Schwatka, "Down the Yukon on a Raft: Fifth Paper," 4 (quotation); see also "The Yukon River," *San Francisco Chronicle,* January 20, 1884.
25. Miles to Pope, May 15, 1884 (quotation), in Schwatka, *Report*, 121; "The Yukon River," *San Francisco Chronicle,* January 20, 1884; "Alaska," *San Francisco Examiner* April 20, 1884.
26. *Congressional Record* (Senate) 16 (January 22, 1885): 541 (quotations); *Congressional Record* (House) 16 (February 7, 1885): 1392; *Congressional Record* (Senate) 16 (February 16, 1885): 1730; *Annual Report of the Public Printer*, 31. The final report was not delivered to the Senate until December 1, 1885, due to a delay in procuring the photographic illustrations used in the report. Schwatka, *Report*, 1.
27. "The Evening Lamp: A Summer in Alaska," *The Christian Union,* 33, no. 4 (January 28, 1886): 28 (quotation); see also "Books: Along Alaska's Great River," *The Nassau Literary Magazine* 41, no. 7 (January 1886): 364; "Review: Along Alaska's Great River," *The Eclectic Magazine of Foreign Literature* 43, no. 1 (January 1886): 137.
28. Editorial, "An Important Bill," *Daily State Journal* (Richmond, Va.), February 9, 1874 ("we have not yet had a popular book on Alaska"); Buske, "The Wilderness," vi, 21-24 (noting also that more than fifty articles were published on Alaska from 1868 and 1888). In comparing Dall's work and Whymper's, one reviewer stated that Whymper's was read more frequently "it being in a more lighter and discursive vein." "Unexplored Alaska," *Evening Star* (Washington, D.C.), September 12, 1883.
29. Murray, "Introduction," 7; Hayrock, *Alaska*, 197.
30. Schwatka, "The New York Ledger Expedition," *New York Ledger*, March 19, 1892 (first quotation); Higginson, *Alaska*, 1 (second quotation); Haycock, *Alaska*, 197-98.
31. "Literary Notes," *The Sunday Herald*, January 3, 1886 (first quotation); "The Resources of Alaska," *New York Times*, September 21, 1886 (second quotation).
32. *Arizona Champion* (Peach Springs, A.T.), January 3, 1885 (quotation); Schwatka, "The Resources of Alaska," 7920; Schwatka, "Benefits Accruing," 1-2; see also Campbell, *In Darkest Alaska*, 23. One prominent prospector remarked in 1893 that "among the travelers of the present day, who have added to our store of knowledge regarding this wonderful region, Lieutenant Frederick Schwatka is one of the foremost." Downie, *Hunting for Gold*, 336

Chapter Fourteen- To the Top of the Continent [pages 290-320]

1. "Personal Notes and Comments," *Frank Leslie's Sunday Magazine* 14, no. 1 (July 1883): 102 (quotation); "Schwatka on Greely," *New York Times*, August 17, 1884 (Russian award).
2. Worcester, *The Apaches,* 263 (quotation).
3. Ibid., 258-62.

4. "Frederick Schwatka on the Indian Question," *Brooklyn Times Union*, February 8, 1886 (quotation).
5. Schwatka, "Among the Apaches," 42 (quotation); Sweeney, *From Cochise to Geronimo*, 62-63.
6. Schwatka to AG, May 16, 1884, Schwatka Papers, ACP Files, NA (first quotation); "Schwatka's resignation," *New York Times*, February 16, 1885 (second and third quotations).
7. Sheridan to AG, May 27, 1884, Schwatka Papers, ACP Files, NA (quotation).
8. "Schwatka's resignation," *Daily Chronicle*, September 11, 1884 (first and third quotation); "Out of the Wilds," *St. Louis Globe*, July 14, 1887 (second quotation).
9. *San Francisco Examiner*, April 20, 1884 (quotations); Abercrombie, *Report of Explorations in Alaska*, 392-93; Reedy, "Kelp-Fed Beef," 7, 9; "The Yukon Valley," *Plain Dealer* (Cleveland, Ohio), May 8, 1884.
10. Post Medical Records, Fort Grant, June 12, 1884 and July 5, 1884, Schwatka Papers, ACP Files, NA; *Portage Daily Register* (Portage, Wis.), April 13, 1886 (quotation).
11. Agnew, *Medicine in the Old West*, 112; Flint, *Treatise*, 395, 404, 411.
12. Schwatka to AG, June 21, 1884, Schwatka Papers, ACP Files, NA (first quotation); Schwatka to AAG, June 1884 (copy), Schwatka Papers, ACP Files, NA (second quotation); Mrs. Schwatka to AG July 11, 1884, Schwatka Papers, ACP Files, NA (third quotation).
13. Brackett to Logan, July 9, 1884, Schwatka Papers, ACP Files, NA (quotations).
14. Mrs. Schwatka to AG, July 17, 1884, Schwatka Papers, ACP Files, NA (quotation).
15. Dolph and Logan to Sheridan December 16, 1884, Schwatka Papers, ACP Files, NA (first quotation); Lincoln to Logan, December 27, 1884, Schwatka Papers, ACP Files, NA (second quotation).
16. "Schwatka's Resignation," *New York Times*, February 16, 1885 (quotation); "Lieutenant Schwatka's Reported Resignation," *New York Times*, January 25, 1885; "Lieut. Schwatka and the Army," *New York Tribune*, January 21, 1885.
17. Schwatka, "Schwatka in Mexico," *Chicago Inter-Ocean*, April 21, 1889 (quotation).
18. Harper, *West Chester to 1865*, 446 (quotation).
19. "Down the Yukon on a Raft," *New York Times*, December 13, 1884 (first quotation); *Arizona Champion* (Peach Springs, A.T.), January 3, 1885 (second quotation); *Omaha Daily Bee*, December 18, 1884 (third quotation); *Sacramento Daily Record*, February 19, 1884 (fourth quotation); "Lieut. Schwatka on the Yukon," *Connecticut Western News* (Canaan, Conn.), December 24, 1884 (fifth quotation); "The Monthly Concert," *Presbyterian Home Missionary*, February 1, 1885 (sixth quotation).
20. "An Arctic Journey," *Rock Island Argus*, March 9, 1885 (first quotation); "Eating Dead Comrades," *The World* (N.Y.), August 15, 1884 (second quotation); "Were they Cannibals?," *New York Herald*, August 14, 1884 (third

quotation); "'Cannibalism'!," *Buffalo Morning Express*, August 14, 1884; Riffenburgh, *The Myth of the Explorer*, 126-27.
21. *Morning Star* (Rockford, Ill.), December 6, 1888 (first quotation); *Owosso Times* (Owosso, Mich.), April 16, 1886 (second quotation); "Talk About People," *The Macon Telegraph* (Macon, Ga.), October 23, 1885 (third quotation).
22. "Nimrod in the North," *The Critic* 85 (August 15, 1885): 75 (quotation)
23. Schwatka, "Mineral Resources of Alaska," in *Bradstreet's: A Journal of Trade, Finance and Public Economy* (quoted in *The West Shore*, February 1, 1886).
24. Deur, et al, "Yakutat Tlingit," 1.
25. Frost, *Bering*, 144.
26. Smith, "The Trials and Triumphs of the Editor," 2 (quotations); "Ups and Downs of an Editor," *Omaha Daily Bee*, December 28, 1889.
27. Schwatka, "'The *Times's'* Alaska Expedition," *New York Times*, June 21, 1886 (quotation). Schwatka's interest in Mount St. Elias likely stems from an 1882 article by C. W. Woods in the *Century Magazine* in which he tells of his aborted attempt in 1877 to climb the mountain, starting from Sitka, a location well known to Schwatka. Wood, "Among the Tlinkits of Alaska," 323-38.
28. Schwatka, "The Secrets of Alaska," *New York Times*, June 21, 1886 (quotation).
29. "'The *Times's'* Alaska Expedition," *New York Times*, June 24, 1886 (quoting the *Home Sentinel*, June 22, 1886).
30. Koelsch, "William Libbey of Princeton," 1-3.
31. Schwatka, "On the Way to Alaska," *New York Times*, June 27, 1886 (quotations).
32. Schwatka "Nearing Mount St. Elias," *New York Times*, August 9, 1886 (quotation).
33. Mulligan John, "Jack Dalton. Alaska Mining Hall of Fame Foundation," https://alaskamininghalloffame.org/inductees/dalton.php (accessed Feb. 11, 2022).
34. Schwatka, "Nearing Mt. St. Elias," *New York Times*, August 9, 1886 (quotation).
35. De Laguna, *Under Mt. St. Elias*, Part 3, 181-82; Deur, "Yakutat Tlingit," 100-01; 109-114.
36. Schwatka, "Nearing Mt. St. Elias," *New York Times*, August 9, 1886 (quotation); Deur, "Yakutat Tlingit," 58-59; de Laguna, *Under Mount St. Elias*," Part 3, 187-88.
37. Seton-Karr, *Shore and Alps,* 59 (quotation); Conrad, "Emmons of Alaska," 51; Seaton, "The Native Collector," 44; Schwatka, "The Thlinkets of Alaska," *New York Times*, November 8, 1886. Libbey's Tlingit materials form an important collection of Northwest Coast materials at Princeton University. Baird, "Tlingit treasures," 6-17. Lieutenant Emmons developed a deep interest in the Tlingit and made extensive studies of their culture. His acquisitions at Yakutat Bay set him on a path to systematic collecting of cultural artifacts. By virtue of his travels along the Northwest Coast

during the 1880s and 1890s, Emmons was extremely well positioned to amass an enormous collection of Indigenous handicrafts. Recognizing that institutions would be eager to acquire the curiosities, he sold his finds to several of them. Conrad, "Emmons of Alaska," 51.
38. Libbey, "Some of the Geographical Features," 281-82 (quotation).
39. Schwatka, "The Greatest Altitudes," *New York Times*, August 16, 1886 (quotation).
40. Schwatka, "In the Surf at Icy Bay," *New York Times*, October 4, 1886 (first quotation); Seton-Karr, *Shores and Alps*, vi (second quotation); Schwatka, "Nearing Mt. St. Elias," August 9, 1886 (third quotation).
41. Schwatka, "Up the Saint Elias Alps," *New York Times*, September 20, 1886 (quotations). Karr wrote that "it was a large river, but not larger than one might expect, as forming one of the many streams which drain the vast expanse of snow and ice which covers and encircles the St. Elias range." Seton-Karr, *Shores and Alps*, 75. While in San Francisco after his return, Karr advised a reporter for the *San Francisco Chronicle* that "the stream [Jones River] is nothing more than an assemblage of small glacial flows." "Seton Karr," *San Francisco Chronicle*, November 16, 1886. Upon his return to New York however, the *New York Times* remarked that Karr "corroborates Schwatka's account of the discovery of Jones River." "Seton Karr's return," *The New York Times*, November 16, 1886. See also "Professor Libbey's Research," *New York Times*, October 22, 1886 (Libbey states "the river is an enormous one, as Schwatka described . . ."). For the change in size of the river, see Harris, *Schwatka's Last Search*, 8 and Orth, *Dictionary of Alaska Place Names*, 442 and 1063.
42. Seton-Karr, *Shores and Alps*, 93 (quotations).
43. Schwatka, "The Loneliest Place in the United States," 23 (first quotation), 25 (second quotation); Seton-Karr, *Shores and Alps*, 99 (third quotation).
44. Schwatka, "Cloud-Capped St. Elias," *New York Times*, October 7, 1886 (quotations); Karr stated that they started for the summit at 4:30 am with three days of provisions, and roped together at 6:00 am. Karr, *Shores and Alps*, 101. Schwatka stated they started for the summit at 6:00 am. Schwatka, "Up the Saint Elias Alps," *New York Times*, September 20, 1886.
45. Schwatka, "Cloud-capped St. Elias," *New York Times*, October 7, 1886 (first quotation); Seton-Karr, *Shores and Alps*, 103 (second quotation).
46. Seton-Karr, "Explorations in Alaska," 65 (quotations).
47. Seton-Karr, *Shores and Alps*, 105 (quotations); Schwatka, "*King of the Continent*," October 19, 1886.
48. "Up the Saint Elias Alps," *New York Times*, September 20, 1886 (first three quotations); "Lieut. Schwatka's Discoveries," *New York Times*, September 23, 1886 (fourth quotation).
49. "An envious contemporary," *New York Times*, September 24, 1886 (first and second quotations); "Fresh Fields for Explorer Jones," *The Sun* (N.Y.), September 27, 1886 (third quotation).

50. "George Jones' River," *Chicago Tribune*, October 22, 1886 (quotation).
51. Schwatka, "The Thlinkets of Alaska," *New York Times*, November 8, 1886. The *Globe* correspondent stationed in Sitka claimed that during a drunken frenzy by the expedition members after their unsuccessful attempt to climb Mount St. Elias, a case of arsenic was flung out their tent and picked up by a Tlingit man on which he and his family made a meal. *The Sun* itself doubted the report, but had no problems touting it, noting that "the innuendoes conveyed in this narrative seem to us to bear the marks of malice and intentional exaggeration," and that the story told in the *Globe's* letter "does not impress the reader with confidence in its truthfulness." "New York Times's Arsenic," *The Sun* (N.Y.), November 15, 1886. The *Sun's* questioning of the credibility of the letter, embroiled the *Sun* its own controversy with the *Globe*. "More News from Icy Bay," *The Sun* (N.Y.), November 25, 1886.
52. Schwatka, "The Thlinkets of Alaska, *New York Times*, November 8, 1886 (quotations); "Superstitious Neglect- Killed by the Treatment of the Medicine Man," *New York Times*, November 16, 1886. Interestingly, Seton-Karr, in his *Shores and Alps of Alaska*, later recalled the facts of the affair slightly differently than Schwatka and Libbey, placing more of the failed responsibility on Dalton. Seton-Karr remarked that after Libbey had seized the tainted can from Kernuk, Libbey had not instructed Kernuk to dispose of the poison. Rather, Libbey directed Dalton to destroy the material, which Dalton neglected to do, simply hiding it until it was retrieved by Kernuk.
53. Schwatka, "Mountaineering in Alaska," 89-93; Broke, *With Sack and Stock, Longmans*, 1-2.
54. Tenderini and Shandrick, *The Duke of the Abruzzi*, 35.
55. Schwatka, "Up the St. Elias Alps," *New York Times*, September 20, 1886 (first quotation); Molnia, "Glaciers of North America-Glaciers of Alaska," K29 (second quotation). In the *Century Magazine* article, Schwatka suggested that the necessity of taking barometer readings over a one-hour period compelled him to remain at 5,800 feet, while Seton-Karr and Wood continued the ascent. Schwatka, "Two Expeditions," 872.
56. Seton-Karr, "The Alpine Regions of Alaska," 274, 282, 283 (first and second quotations); "King of the Continent," *New York Times*, October 19, 1886 (third and fourth quotations).
57. *Chattanooga Daily Times*, September 30, 1886 (first quotation); "The Resources of Alaska," *New York Times*, September 21, 1886 (second quotation); Sherwood, *Exploration of Alaska*, 79.

Chapter Fifteen - Thro' the Wonderland [pages 321-339]

1. Seitz, *Joseph Pulitzer*, 16 (quotation); Riffenburgh, *The Myth of the Explorer*, 92.
2. Schwatka, "The Yellowstone Park," *New York Times*, July 5, 1886 (quotation);

Lang, "At the Greatest Personal Peril," 19.
3. Schwatka to Buel, October 16, 1886, Century Records, NYPL (quotation).
4. Ibid. (quotation).
5. Fee to Haynes, December 8, 1886, Haynes Papers, MSU (quotation).
6. "Lieut. Schwatka's Expedition," *Livingstone Enterprise*, January 1, 1887.
7. Schwatka, *Wonderland*, 20 (quotation); Whittlesey, *Gateway to Yellowstone*, xiii. The Yellowstone Park Association was the owner of the Mammoth Springs Hotel. The association's majority stockholders were also stockholders of the Northern Pacific Railroad. *Annual Report of the Superintendent*, 8-9.
8. "Bitter Weather in Montana," *The Indianapolis Journal*, February 10, 1887; Henry, *Snowshoes, Coaches, and Cross Country Skis*, 46.
9. "Two Weeks on Snow Shoes," *St. Paul Globe*, December 29, 1886.
10. Schwatka, "A Midwinter Wonderland," *The World* (N.Y.), December 29, 1886; Schwatka, "Our Snowshoe Expedition," *The World* (N.Y.), February 13, 1887.
11. "Local Lay-out," *The Livingston Enterprise*, January 8, 1887 (quotation); Henry, *Snowshoes, Coaches and Cross Country Skis*, 47; Haynes to Lily, January 5, 1887, Haynes Papers, MSU. The skis used by Schwatka's group were typical of the time; made of pine and ash, secured to the foot by a three or four-inch leather band. Schwatka noted that the bottoms were "toasted" to the point of charring, and some skiers applied wax so they were "smooth as the ice itself." Schwatka, "Our Snowshoe Expedition," *The World* (N.Y.), February 13, 1887.
12. Lang, "At the Greatest Peril," 20. Schwatka had made his request for army assistance through Brigadier General Thomas H. Ruger, commander of the Department of the Dakota, stationed in St. Paul. Schwatka, "Our Snowshoe Expedition," *The World* (N.Y.), February 13, 1887.
13. Schwatka, "A Midwinter Wonderland," *The World* (N.Y.), December 29, 1886.
14. "Yellowstone Park Party," *Rock Island Argus*, January 19, 1886 (first quotation); Hofer, "Winter in Wonderland," 28, no. 12 (April 14, 1887): 246 (second quotation).
15. "Mr. Bosse's Experience," *Rock Island Argus*, February 1, 1887 (quotation).
16. "A Trip Full of Peril," *Chicago Tribune*, March 5, 1887; Henry, *Snowshoes, Coaches and Cross Country Skis*, 47-49; Culpin, *"For the Benefit and Enjoyment of the People,"* 1.
17. "Haynes Winter Expedition," *Helena Independent*, February 6, 1887 (quotation).
18. "Yellowstone Park Party, *Rock Island Argus*, January 19, 1887.
19. "Haynes Winter Expedition," *Helena Independent*, February 6, 1887 (first three quotations); Editorial, *Helena Independent*, February 6, 1887 (fourth quotation); Henderson to Haynes February 14, 1887, Haynes Papers, MSU (fifth quotation).
20. Whittlesey, "Storytelling in Yellowstone," 119-28, 119 (quoting G.L. Henderson).
21. "A Trip Full of Peril," *Chicago Tribune*, March 5, 1887 (quotations).
22. Fee to Haynes, February 12, 1887, Haynes Papers, MSU (first quotation);

Schwatka to Buel, March 14, 1887, Century Records, NYPL (second and third quotations). Within the Haynes family circle, Schwatka was labelled "a fraud," certainly an opinion that originated from F. J. Haynes. Haynes went so far as to press Baronette as to whether Schwatka had honored his payment obligations to Goddard (which Schwatka had). See Loa Snyder (Haynes's sister-in-law) to May & Dot, January 30, 1887; Goddard to Haynes, 1887, Haynes Papers, MSU.
23. Schwatka to Buel, March 14, 1887, Century Papers, NYPL (quotations).
24. Hofer, "Winter in Wonderland," 28, no. 11 (April 7, 1887): 221 (quotation).
25. Ibid., 223 (quotations); Henry, *Snowshoes, Coaches and Cross Country Skis*, 55. Hofer's full story was published in multiple issues of *Forest and Stream*. See Hofer, "Winter in Wonderland."
26. *Ann Arbor Democrat*, December 20, 1889 (quotation).
27. "American Authors for a Library," *Chicago Inter-Ocean*, August 4, 1888 (first quotation); "The Youth's Companion Announcements for 1890," *Freeland Tribune* (Freeland Pa.), October 24, 1889 (second quotation); Schwatka, "Tight Pinches in the Arctic," *Youth's Companion*, December 12, 1888.
28. "Lieutenant Schwatka as a Lecturer," *The Times* (Philadelphia), September 23, 1888 (quotations); "The Chautauqua Building, Grounds and Programme," *Atlanta Constitution*, June 17, 1888.

Chapter Sixteen- South of the Border [pages 340-367]

1. Hebberd, "Notes on Dr. David Franklin Powell," 308 (quotation).
2. Id.; Sorg, "Doctor, Lawyer, Indian Chief," 42; Hardy, "The Sonora, Sinaloa and Chihuahua Railroad," 262, 254 (quoting Andersen, Alexander, *Mexico from the Material Stand-Point*, Washington, D.C.: 1884, 6); Dormady and Tamez, *Just South of Zion*, 165.
3. "Lieutenant Frederick Schwatka," *Chicago Inter-Ocean*, February 9, 1889 (quotation).
4. Mark Strong, "Sandor Leopold Landeau 1864-1924." https://wolfsgallery.com/artists/sandor-leopold-landeau (accessed May 6, 2020). The *Inter-Ocean* reported that Landeau had studied under the prominent landscape artist, Henry Elkins, and that Elkins died in Sandor's arms in 1884 in Colorado. "Bloomington," *Chicago Inter-Ocean*, April 14, 1889.
5. Schwatka, "Schwatka in Mexico," *Chicago Inter-Ocean*, April 21, 1889 (quotation); Hardy, "The Sonora, Sinaloa and Chihuahua Railroad," 254; Hebberd, "Notes on Dr. David Franklin Powell," 308.
6. Schwatka, "America's Expedition," 517 (quotation).
7. Schwatka, "Schwatka in Mexico," *Chicago Inter-Ocean*, April 21, 1889 (quotation). The Mormon settlers, who were originally encouraged and welcomed by President Porfirio Diaz, fled Mexico following Diaz's removal from office in 1911 and the violence caused by the Mexican Revolution. Fontana, "Introduction," 17.

8. Schwatka, *In the Land of the Cave and Cliff Dwellers*, 73 (quotation).
9. Phillips, "The End of Casas Grandes"; "Archaeological Zone of Paquimé, Casas Grandes," http://whc.unesco.org/en/list/560 (accessed May 14, 2020).
10. Schwatka, "Schwatka in Mexico," *Chicago Inter-Ocean*, April 21, 1889 (first quotation); Schwatka, "America's Expedition," *America*, 519 (second quotation).
11. Schwatka, "Schwatka in Mexico," *Chicago Inter-Ocean*, May 5, 1889; "Work Commences," *Deming Headlight*, April 26, 1889.
12. Schwatka, "Schwatka in Mexico," *Chicago Inter-Ocean*, June 2, 1889.
13. Ibid., (first quotation); Schwatka, "Land of the Living Cliff-Dwellers," 276 (second quotation).
14. Schwatka, "Schwatka in Mexico," *Chicago Inter-Ocean*, June 30, 1889 (quotation).
15. McDougall, "Secrets of the Tarahumara," 65, 104. The American botanist Edward Palmer had visited the region in 1885 in his quest for botanical specimens for the Smithsonian, but failed to report on the Tarahumara. Before Palmer, only a few Spanish accounts touched on the Tarahumara. Fontana, "Introduction," 18.
16. Schwatka, *In the Land of the Cave and Cliff Dwellers*, 171 (quotation); Schwatka, "Land of the Living Cliff-Dwellers," 276.
17. "They Dwell in Caves," *Chicago Herald*, February 9, 1890 (quotation); Wyndham, "The Semiotics of Powerful Places," 408.
18. Schwatka, "Land of the Living Cliff-Dwellers," 276 (quotation); Schwatka to Buel, April 1, 1890, Century Country Archives, NYPL.
19. Schwatka, "Schwatka in Mexico," *Chicago Inter-Ocean*, July 7, 1889 (quotation).
20. Schwatka, "Schwatka in Mexico," *Chicago Inter-Ocean*, June 9, 1889 (quotation).
21. Schwatka, "Schwatka in Mexico," *Chicago Inter-Ocean*, June 23, 1889 (quotation).
22. Schwatka, "Schwatka in Mexico," *Chicago Inter-Ocean*, July 21, 1889 (quotation).
23. "Beautiful Pictures," *The Pantagraph*, October 28, 1889 (quotation); *Chicago Inter-Ocean*, October 20, 1889 ("he has discovered a grand field for his genius . . .").
24. "Artist Son Found at Last," *New York Times*, August 15, 1900 (quotation); Boudreau, *National Attention*," 23-25; "Sandor Leopold Landeau 1864-1924." https://wolfsgallery.com/artists/sandor-leopold-landeau (accessed May 6, 2020).
25. "The Cliff Dwellers," *Chicago Inter-Ocean*, June 7, 1889 (quotations).
26. Schwatka, "Schwatka in Mexico," *Chicago Inter-Ocean*, June 2, 1889; "Cliff Dwellers in Mexico: Lieutenant Schwatka Locates a Race Hitherto Unknown," *The Inquirer* (Lancaster, Pa.), June 15, 1889 (first quotation); "Vouched for by Schwatka, Thousands of the Cliff Dwellers are Still Living," *Macon Telegraph* (Macon, Ga.), June 10, 1889 (second quotation); "Cliff Dwellers Discovered," *Sturgis Advertiser*, June 26, 1889 (third quotation); "They are Not Extinct," *Chicago Tribune*, February 9, 1890 (fourth quotation);
27. Schwatka, "America's Expedition," 517; "The Largest Newspaper Syndicate,"

Tacoma Daily Ledger, August 27, 1892; Schwatka to Buel, June 26, 1889, Century Company Archives, NYPL (quotations).
28. Schwatka, "America's Expedition," 519 (quotation).
29. *Chicago Inter-Ocean*, July 26, 1889 (quotation).
30. "The Cliff Dwellers," *Chicago Inter-Ocean*, August 29, 1889 (quotation).
31. "Men of a Strange Race," *Memphis Daily Commercial*, February 10, 1890 (quotation).
32. "They Dwell in Caves," *Chicago Herald*, February 9, 1890 (first quotation); "Captured Cliff Dwellers," *The Washington Critic* (Washington, D.C.), February 11, 1890 (second quotation).
33. "They Dwell in Caves," *Chicago Herald*, February 10, 1890; Korom, *The American Skyscraper*, 135; Chicagology, https://chicagology.com/goldenage/goldenage029/ (accessed Feb. 8, 2022).
34. "A Weird Race," *Greenville Times*, February 15, 1890 (quotation).
35. Petterchak, *Lone Scout*, 8-11.
36. Hinsley, *The World Marketplace*, 345-46.
37. Id., 346; "Central Music Hall," *Chicago Inter-Ocean*, February 16, 1890 (Central Music Hall).
38. "Schwatka's Odd Find," *Chicago Herald*, February 25, 1890 (first quotation); "Items," *Chicago Tribune*, February 16, 1890 (second quotation).
39. Banks, *The Artistic Guide to Chicago*, 124 (quotation).
40. "The Cliff Dwellers," *Buffalo Weekly Express*, March 20, 1890 (quotation). At the Wonderland Buffalo venue, women attendees also received a photograph of the "two-headed baby."
41. "Indians in Court," *Chicago Inter-Ocean*, April 30, 1890 (quotations).
42. Boyce, *Alaska and the Panama Canal*, 78 (quotations).
43. Wyndham, "The Semiotics of Powerful Places," 408 (quoting the 2009 bestseller McDonald, *Born to Run*, 4).
44. Lumholtz, *Unknown Mexico*, vii (first and second quotations); "Saturday Small Talk," *Santa Fe New Mexican*, June 28, 1890 (third quotation).
45. Lumholtz, *Unknown Mexico*, xii (quotation); *Oshkosh Northwestern*, April 21, 1892.
46. Lumholtz, "Cave-Dwellers of the Sierra Madre," 100 (quotation).
47. Lumholtz, "The American Cave Dwellers," 306 (first quotation), 308 (second quotation); Lumholtz, *Unknown Mexico*, vii (third quotation).
48. "Existing Cave-Dwellers," *The Nation* 53, no. 1378 (November 26, 1891): 408 (quotations). Interestingly, Bandelier had his own interest in establishing priority, claiming that he had been advised as to the existence of the "cave-dwellers" before Schwatka published the fact. Id.
49. "Schwatka on a Toot," *Plain Dealer* (Cleveland, Ohio), March 18, 1890 (quotation).
50. "Lieut. Schwatka's Fall," *The Algona Upper Des Moines*, February 11, 1891 (quotation).
51. "Lieutenant Schwatka, *The St. Joseph Herald*, January 31, 1891 (quotation).

52. "Lieut. Schwatka at New York," *Boston Daily Advertiser*, February 24, 1891 (first quotation); "Schwatka Dead," *The Evening Bee* (Sacramento, Calif.), January 31, 1891 (second quotation).
53. "The Famous Explorer," *Evening Journal* (Wilmington, Del.), February 4, 1891 (first quotation); *Muscatine News-Tribune* (Muscatine, Iowa), March 13, 1891 (second quotation).

Chapter Seventeen – The Last Journey pages [368-387]

1. Isserman, *Exploring North America*, 121 (quotation); Sherwood, *Exploration of Alaska*, 116.
2. Mott, *A History of American Magazines*, vol. II, 357-58. Before his successful pitch to the *Ledger*, Schwatka had also proposed Alaskan sponsorship with two other New York publications, *The Cosmopolitan* and *The Illustrated American*, both of which declined. In those failed efforts, he was even assisted by his old companion William Gilder. During 1890 and 1891, the two explorers also unsuccessfully attempted to court investors and raise capital for mining and commodity schemes. Gilder-Mss., Rauner Special Collections Library, Dartmouth College, Hanover, N. H.
3. Schwatka to Powell, February 20, 1891, Letters Received, USGS (quotation).
4. Ibid.; White, "Charles Willard Hayes," *Science*, 125-26.
5. "Off for Alaska," *Star Tribune* (Minneapolis, Minn.), April 17, 1891 (quotations).
6. Haycock, *Alaska*, 189.
7. Schwatka, "The New York Ledger Expedition," *New York Ledger*, March 19, 1892 (quotation).
8. Schwatka, "The New York Ledger Expedition," *New York Ledger*, March 26, 1892 (quotation). The distinctive blue-tinged glacier had been an anomaly in a world of rapidly retreating glaciers. Until about 2014, the glacier was the only one in the massive Juneau Icefield that was still advancing. Since that time, its course has reversed and it is now melting faster than its advancement, impacted by rising global temperatures. Doyle Rice, "'This is a Big Deal:' Mighty Glacier finally succumbs to Climate Change," *Sydney Morning Herald*, November 8, 2019.
9. Schwatka, "The New York Ledger Expedition," *New York Ledger*, April 16, 1892 (quotations).
10. "Day's Doings on the Coast," *San Francisco Examiner*, July 4, 1891 (quoting Schwatka letter of June 16 at "Great Lake").
11. Schwatka, "The New York Ledger Expedition," *New York Ledger*, March 26, 1892 (quotation).
12. Schwatka, "The New York Ledger Expedition," *New York Ledger*, June 11, 1892 (quotation).
13. Schwatka, "The New York Ledger Expedition," *New York Ledger*, April 30, 1892 (quotation).

446   Chapter Notes

14. Hayes, Field Notebook, July 4, 1891 (first quotation); July 5, 1891 (second quotation), USGS.
15. Schwatka, "The New York Ledger Expedition," *New York Ledger*, June 11, 1892 (quotation).
16. Schwatka, "The New York Ledger Expedition," *New York Ledger*, July 16, 1892 (quotation).
17. Schwatka, "The New York Ledger Expedition," *New York Ledger*, July 23, 1892 (quotation)
18. Ibid. (quotation); Cruikshank, "Glaciers and Climate Change," 378, 388-89; Cruikshank, *Do Glaciers Listen*, 19.
19. Schwatka, "The New York Ledger Expedition," *New York Ledger*, July 30, 1892 (quotation); Hayes, "An Expedition through the Yukon District," 143.
20. Hayes, Field Notebook, July 30, 1891, USGS (first quotation); Schwatka, "The New York Ledger Expedition," *New York Ledger*, July 30, 1892 (second quotation).
21. Schwatka, "The New York Ledger Expedition," *New York Ledger*, July 30, 1892 (quotations).
22. Schwatka, "The New York Ledger Expedition," *New York Ledger*, August 6, 1892 (quotation).
23. Ibid., (quotation).
24. Glave Diary, August 8, 1891 (first quotation), August 12, 1891 (second quotation), Glave Papers, UAF. For more of Glave's consideration and omission of Schwatka's visit, see Gates, *History Hunting in the Yukon,* 76-77; Michael Gates, "Frederick Schwatka's Forgotten Expedition," *Yukon News*," June 25, 2010; Cruikshank, *Do Glaciers Listen*, 193; Glave, *Travels to the Alseck*, 265-67.
25. Sherwood, *Exploration of Alaska*, 143 (quotation); Gates, *History Hunting,* 76; Brooks, "The Copper Deposits," 13. Jack Dalton would be the prime beneficiary of the 1891 Glave expedition and the brainchild of pack horse transport to the interior. Over several years, starting from Pyramid Harbor (Glave's starting point), Dalton established the toll road known as the "Dalton Trail" to the Yukon which enabled stampeders as well as pack horses, cattle and sheep to reach the Yukon and Dawson City.

Conclusion [pages 388-401]

1. "Sketched at the Hotels," *Star Tribune* (Minneapolis, Minn.), November 19, 1891 (quotation).
2. Hanson, "'Alcoholism is a Disease,'" 1 (quotation).
3. "Drink and its Cure," *Tacoma Daily Ledger*, July 25, 1892 (quotation).
4. Ibid.
5. "The Passing Throng," *Daily Intelligencer* (Seattle, Wash.), August 6, 1892 (first and second quotations); "Lieut. Schwatka's Lecture," *Daily Intelligencer* (Seattle, Wash.), August 16, 1892 (third quotation).

6. "Brief Tacoma News," *Daily Intelligencer* (Seattle, Wash.), September 15, 1892; "News of the Northwest," *Oregonian* (Portland, Ore.), September 14, 1892; Schwatka to Hill, September 2, 1892, MN State Archives, Great Northern Railway Company Files, Minneapolis, MN (quotations); Schwatka to McClure, July 31, 1892, McClure Papers, UVA.
7. "Lt. Schwatka Dead," *Oregonian* (Portland, Ore.), November 3, 1892 (quotations).
8. "Schwatka is Dead," *Daily Intelligencer* (Seattle, Wash.), November 3, 1892.
9. Ibid.
10. Ibid.
11. "Life of Adventure," *Oregonian* (Portland, Ore.), April 22, 1893 (first quotation).
12. Hurlbut, "Lieutenant Schwatka," 619 (quotation).
13. Ibid., 619–20 (quotation).
14. [Rae, John] "Obituary," 481 (first and second quotations); *Oregon Statesman*, November 11, 1892 (third quotation, from the *New York Sun*); Malone, *Dictionary of American Biography*, 482 (fourth quotation); "Had One Deadly Foe," *Chicago Inter-Ocean*, November 11, 1892 (fifth quotation); "Lieut. Schwatka is Dead," *New York Times*, November 3, 1892 (sixth quotation).
15. "Schwatka Dead," *Rock Island Argus*, November 2, 1892 (quotation).
16. Lumholtz, "The American Cave-Dwellers," 300 and note (quotations).
17. Riffenburgh, *The Myth of the Explorer*, 137 (quotation).
18. *Oregonian* (Portland, Ore.), September 6, 1909 (quotation). The sentiment had been raised as early as his death. See *The Gazette* (Montreal, Que.), November 3, 1892 ("Lieut. Schwatka's fame as an Arctic explorer has been somewhat dimmed by the achievements of more recent visitors to the frozen zone.").
19. *Queen City Mail* (Spearfish, S.D.), November 9, 1892 (first quotation); "Had One Deadly Foe," *Chicago Inter-Ocean*, November 11, 1892 (second quotation); "Hunted with Schwatka," *Omaha-World Herald*, November 3, 1892, (third quotation); Hough, "Death of Lieut. Schwatka," 402 (fourth quotation); Brackett, "Memoir of Fred'k Schwatka," 5.
20. Schwatka, *In the Land of the Cave and Cliff Dwellers*. That Ada had a hand in the introduction may be reflected in the rather conspicuous error incorrectly identifying the journal *America* as the sponsor of Schwatka's first Mexican trip when in fact it was the *Chicago Inter-Ocean*.
21. "Mrs. Schwatka," *Rock Island Argus*, February 12, 1895 (quotation).
22. "Strewn with Skeletons," *Rock Island Argus*, July 30, 1897 (quotation).
23. "Tells of Flight," *Rock Island Argus*, April 28, 1906 (quotation); Wamsley, Brackett-Schwatka Papers.

BIBLIOGRAPHY

Manuscripts and Archival Collections

Alaska State Library, Historical Collections, Juneau, Alaska
    McIntosh, J. B., Diary
    Gloster, Charles, Files
Denver Public Library, Western History Collection, Denver Colorado
    Ellison, Robert S., Walter Camp Papers
The Gilder Lehrman Institute of American History, New York, New York
    Schwatka, Frederick, Letter
G. W. Blunt White Library, Mystic Seaport, Mystic, Connecticut
    Schwatka, Frederick, Manuscript, 1878-1880
    Cobb, Wendell, Papers
Minnesota Historical Society, St. Paul, Minnesota
    Lloyd, Thomas, Letter
Montana State University Library, Merrill G. Burlingame Special Collections, Helena, Montana
    Doane, Gustavus C., Papers
    Haynes, F. Jay, Papers
National Archives, Washington, District of Columbia
    Adjutant General's Office Letters Received (Main Series), 1871-1880, Microcopy 666
    Adjutant General's Office Letters Received (Main Series), 1881-1889, Microcopy 689
    Camp Sheridan General Orders, Special Orders and Circulars, 2/1874-7/1876, Record Group 393
    Medical History of Posts, 7/1868-1913, Record Group 94, Entry 547
    National Register of Historic Places and National Historic Landmarks Program, Record Group 74
    North Platte Station Letters and Endorsements Sent, 7/1867-1878, Record Group 393

Office of Indian Affairs Letters Received 1824-1881, M234 (Spotted Tail Agency), Record Group 75
Returns from U.S. Military Posts, 1800-1916, Microform 617
Schwatka, Ada, Widow's Pension, No. 427087, Bureau of Pensions
Schwatka, Frederick, Appointment, Commission, Personnel File, 234 ACP 1876, Record Group 94
Schwatka, Frederick, USMA Cadet Application Papers, 1814-1866, 1865 File 256-360, Record Group 94

National Maritime Museum, London, England
McClintock, Leopold, Papers

New Bedford Whaling Museum Research Library, New Bedford, Massachusetts
Eothen, Logbook, 1878-79
George and Mary, Logbook, 1879-80

New York Public Library, Archive Division, New York, New York
Century Company, Records
Daly, Charles and Maria Patrick, Diaries

NYU School of Medicine, Lillian and Clarence de la Chapelle Medical Archives, New York, New York
Bellevue Medical College, Papers

Oregon Historical Society, Research Library, Portland, Oregon
Lane, Joseph, Papers

Providence Public Library, Nicholson Whaling Collection, Providence, Rhode Island
Glacier, Logbook, 1871-73

Rock Island County Historical Society, Moline, IL
Brackett, Ada, Papers

Scott Polar Research Institute, Cambridge, England
Cracroft, Sophia, Papers

Smithsonian Institution, National Anthropological Archives, Washington, District of Columbia
Baird, Spencer Fullerton, Correspondence
Fletcher, Alice Cunningham and Francis La Flesche, Papers, NAA MS 4558

University of Alaska Fairbanks, Elmer E. Rasmuson Library, Fairbanks, Alaska
Glave, Edward, Notebooks

U.S. Military Academy Archives, Pershing Building, West Point, New York
Records of the Office of the Dean of the Academic Board, Record Group 404.3
Records of the Academic Board, Proceedings (Staff Records), 1866-1872, Record Group 404.3.2
Records of the Office of the Commandant, Record Group 404.4
General Records, Record Group 404.4.1

U.S. Geological Survey, Alaska Science Center, Anchorage, Alabama
Hayes, Charles Willard, Field Notebook 1891
Letters Received, USGS 1879-1901, Record Group 57

University of Virginia, Clifton Waller Collection, Richmond, Virginia
    McClure, S. S., Letters
Wamsley, Douglas W.
    Brackett-Schwatka, Papers
Willamette University Archives and Special Collections, Salem, Oregon
    Willamette University Publications, Catalogs and Bulletins

Books and Articles

Abercrombie, W. R. "The Copper River Country, Alaska." *Journal of the Franklin Institute* 158, no. 4 (October-November 1904): 289-310, 353-66.

Abercrombie, W. R. "Supplementary Expedition into the Copper River Valley, Alaska." In *Compilation of Narratives of Explorations in Alaska*, 383-408. Washington, D.C.: GPO, 1900.

Abram, Marc H. "'A Very Lively Affair': The Skirmish at Tongue River Heights, 6 June 1876." *The Crow's Nest* 13, no. 2 (Autumn/Winter 2013): 7-17.

Abrams, Marc H., ed. *Sioux War Dispatches: Reports from the Field, 1876-1877*. Yardley, Pa.: Westholm Publishing, 2012.

Abrams, Marc H., ed. *"Crying for Scalps": St. George Stanley's Sioux War Narrative*. Brooklyn: Abrams Publications, 2010.

Adelman, Garry E. and Timothy H. Smith. *Devil's Den: A History and Guide*. Gettysburg, Pa.: Thomas Publications, 1997.

Agnew, Jeremy. *Medicine in the Old West: A History, 1850-1900*. Jefferson, N.C.: McFarland, 2010.

Alt, B. T., R. M. Koerner, D. A. Fisher, and J. C. Bourgeois. "Arctic Climate During the Franklin Era, as Deduced from Ice Cores." In *The Franklin Era in Canadian Arctic History 1845-59*. Edited by Patricia D. Sutherland, 69-92. Ottawa: National Museum of Canada, 1985.

Ananguaq, J. M. and Guy Mary-Rousselière. "The Schwatka Expedition as seen by the Inuit." *Eskimo* 38-39 (Fall 1989-Summer 1990): 8-10.

Anderson, Harry. "Some Footnotes to Charles King's 'Campaigning with Crook.'" *Historical Messenger: Milwaukee County Historical Society* 29, no. 1 (1973): 2-25.

Anderson, Mardi. "Gilbert C. Fosdick II, Stagecoach Driver." *Buffalo Tales: Buffalo County Historical Society* 25, no. 3 (May-June 2002).

Annual Report of the Commissioner of Agriculture for the Year 1878. Washington, D.C.: GPO, 1879.

Annual Report of the Public Printer for the Fiscal Year Ended June 30, 1885. Washington, D.C.: GPO, 1886.

Annual Report of the Superintendent of the Yellowstone National Park to the Secretary of the Interior: 1888. Washington, D.C.: GPO, 1888.

Back, George. *Narrative of the Arctic Land Expedition*. London: John Murray, 1836.

Baird, Donald. "Tlingit Treasures: How an Important Collection came to Princeton." *Princeton Alumni Weekly* 65, no. 17 (February 18, 1965): 6-11, 17.

Balikci, Asen. *The Netsilik Eskimo*. Long Grove, Ill: Wave Press, 1970.

Bancroft, Hubert Howe. *The History of Oregon, Vol. Two, 1848-1888*. Vol. 30 of *The Works of Hubert Howe Bancroft*. San Francisco: History Company, 1888.
Banks, Charles Eugene. *The Artistic Guide to Chicago and the World's Columbian Exposition*. Chicago: Peale, 1893.
Barr, William. "Klutschak: An Artist in Search of Franklin." *Beaver* 71, no. 3 (1991): 12-25.
Barr, William. "To the North Pole from York Factory: Col. W. H. Gilder's Last Expedition to the Canadian Arctic, 1886-1887." *Beaver* 68, no. 2 (April-May 1988): 34-45.
Barry, Thomas F. "Thomas F. Barry's Statement." In "Arctic Meeting at Chickering Hall." *Journal of the American Geographical Society* 12 (1880): 275-79.
"The Battle of Slim Buttes." *Journal of the United States Cavalry Association* 28 (1918): 399-408.
Bearss, Edwin C. *Proposed Klondike Gold Rush National Historic Park: Historic Resource Study*. Washington, D.C.: U.S. Office of History and Historic Architecture, 1970.
Beattie, Owen B. and James M. Savelle. "Discovery of Human Remains from Sir John Franklin's Last Expedition." *Historical Archaeology* 17, no. 2 (1983): 100-05.
Bell, Benjamin, ed. *Lieut. John Irving, R.N. of HMS "Terror," in Sir John Franklin's Last Expedition to the Arctic Regions: A Memorial Sketch with Letters*. Edinburgh: David Douglas, 1881.
Biggers, Jeff. *In the Sierra Madre*. Urbana: University of Illinois Press, 2007.
Bishop, Molly Crusen. "Peoria's Grand Opera House." *Peoria Magazine*, November 2019.
Boas, Franz. *Franz Boas Among the Inuit of Baffin Island, 1883-1884: Journals and letters*. Edited by Ludger Müller-Wille and Trans. by William Barr. Toronto: University of Toronto Press, 1998.
Bonner, Etta. "Things Change in Ninety Years: North Platte in 1873." In *Fort McPherson Centennial, 1863-1963*. North Platte, 1963.
Bourke, John G. *The Diaries of John Gregory Bourke, Vol. One, November 20, 1872- July 28, 1876*. Edited by Charles Robinson III. Denton: University of North Texas Press, 2003.
Bourke, John G. *The Diaries of John Gregory Bourke, Vol. Two, July 29, 1876-April 7, 1878*. Edited by Charles M. Robinson III. Denton: University of Texas Press, 2005.
Bourke, John G. *The Diaries of John Gregory Bourke, Vol. Four, July 3, 1880-May 22, 1881*. Edited by Charles Robinson III. Denton: University of North Texas Press, 2009.
Bourke, John G. *On the Border with Crook*. Lincoln: Charles Scribner's Sons, 1891.
Boyce, William D. *Alaska and the Panama Canal*. Chicago: Rand McNally, 1914.
Boynton, Edward C. *The History of West Point and its Military Importance during*

the American Revolution; and the Origin and Progress of the United States Military Academy. New York: D. Van Nostrand, 1864.
Brackett, William S. "Memoir of Fred'k Schwatka." *The Peoria Journal* 28, no. 267 (March 6, 1894): 3, 5.
Bradley, Lawrence W. *Dinosaurs and Indians: Paleontology Resource Dispossession from Sioux Lands.* Parker, Co.: Outskirts Press, 2014.
Branting, Stephen D. *Historic Firsts of Lewiston, Idaho: Unintended Greatness.* Charleston, S.C.: History Press, 2013.
Broke, George. *With Sack and Stock in Alaska.* London: Longmans, Green, 1891.
Brooks, Albert H. "The Copper Deposits of the White, Tanana and Copper Rivers Regions of Alaska." *Engineering and Mining Journal* 74 (1902): 13-15.
Brown, William E. *The History of the Brooks Range: Gaunt Beauty, Tenuous Life.* Fairbanks: University of Alaska Press, 2007.
Buecker, Thomas R. *A Brave Soldier & Honest Gentleman: Lt. James E.H. Foster in the West, 1873-1881.* Lincoln: Nebraska State Historical Society Books, 2015.
Buecker, Thomas R. "History of Camp Sheridan, Nebraska." *Journal of America's Military Past* 22 (1995): 55-73
Buecker, Thomas R. "The Post of North Platte Station, 1867-1878." *Nebraska History* 63 (1982): 381-98.
Buel, James W. *Heroes of the Plains.* St. Louis: Historical Publishing Company, 1883.
Burch, Ernest S., Jr. "Knud Rasmussen and the Original 'Inland' Eskimos of Southern Keewatin." *Etudes Inuit Studies* 12, nos. 1-2 (1988): 81-100.
Campbell, Robert. *In Darkest Alaska: Travels and Empire Along the Inside Passage.* Philadelphia: University of Pennsylvania Press, 2007.
Cavell, Janice. "Publishing Sir John Franklin's Fate: Cannibalism, Journalism, and the 1881 Edition of Leopold McClintock's *The Voyage of the 'Fox' in the Arctic Seas.*" *Book History* 16 (2013): 155–84.
Charlton, Ryan. "'Our Ice Islands': Images of Alaska in the Reconstruction Era." *Journal of Transnational American Studies* 10, no. 1 (2019): 23-46.
City of Baltimore Comprehensive Master Plan 2007-2012: A Business Plan for a World-Class City. Baltimore: City of Baltimore Planning Commission, July 9, 2009.
Cody, William F. *Life and Adventures of "Buffalo Bill."* Chicago: John R. Stanton, 1917.
Collinson, Richard. *Journal of HMS Enterprise on the Expedition in Search of Sir John Franklin's Ships in Behring Strait.* Edited by T.B. Collinson. London: Sampson Low, Marston, Searle and Rivington, 1889.
"Communications on a North-West Passage." *Journal of the Royal Geographical Society* 6 (1836): 34-50.
Conrad, David E. "Emmons of Alaska." *Pacific Northwest Quarterly* 69, no. 2 (1978): 49-60.
Cook, James. *A Voyage to the Pacific Ocean undertaken, by the Command of His Majesty, for making Discoveries in the Northern Hemisphere.* 2nd ed. London: H. Hughs, 1785.
Cooper, Paul F. *Island of the Lost.* New York: G.P. Putnam's Sons, 1961.

Copland, Hugh. *The White River Ash, the Mega Eruption Next Door.* https://whatsupyukon.com/Yukon%20Outside/the-white-river-ash-the-mega-eruption-next-door/ (accessed April 4, 2020).

Corbusier, Fanny Dunbar. *Recollections of her Army Life, 1869-1908.* Edited by Patricia Stallard. Norman: University of Oklahoma Press, 2003.

Craciun, Adriana. *Writing Arctic Disaster: Authorship and Exploration.* Cambridge: Cambridge University Press, 2016.

Crane, John and James F. Kieley. *West Point: "The Key to America."* New York: McGraw-Hill, 1947.

Crow, John R. and Philip R. Obley. "Han." In *Handbook of the North American Indians.* Vol. 6, *Subarctic.* Edited by Julie Helm, 506-13. Washington, D.C.: Smithsonian Institution, 1981.

Cruikshank, Julie. *Do Glaciers Listen? Local Knowledge, Colonial Encounters and Social Imagination.* Vancouver and Toronto: University of British Columbia Press, and Seattle: University of Washington Press, 2005.

Cruikshank, Julie. "Glaciers and Climate Change: Perspectives from Oral Tradition." *Arctic* 54, no. 4 (December, 2001): 377-93.

Culpin, Mary Shivers. *"For the Benefit and Enjoyment of the People": A History of Concession Development in Yellowstone National Park, 1872-1966.* YCR-CR-2003-01. Yellowstone National Park, WY.: National Park Service, 2003.

Cunningham, Roger D. "'Recreant to his Trust': The Disappointing Career of Major James Wasson." *Professional Bulletin of Army History* 60 (Winter-Spring 2004): 4-22.

Cyriax, Richard. *Sir John Franklin's Last Arctic Expedition.* London: Methuen, 1939.

Dall, William. *Alaska and its Resources.* Boston: Lee and Shepard, 1870.

Dall, William. "Schwatka's 'Along Alaska's Great River.'" *Science* 7, no. 165 (April 2, 1886): 308.

Daly, Charles P. "Annual Address of Chief Justice Daly, LL.D., President." *Journal of the American Geographical Society* 10 (1878): 1-76.

Daly, Charles P. "Annual Address of Chief Justice Daly, LL.D., President." *Journal of the American Geographical Society* 12 (1880): 1-107.

Daly, Charles P. "Chief-Justice Daly's Introductory Address." In "Arctic Meeting at Chickering Hall." *Journal of the American Geographical Society* 12 (1880): 237-243.

Danby, Ryan K., David S. Hik, D. Scott Slocombe and Andrew Williams. "Science and the St. Elias: An Evolving Framework for Sustainability in North America's Highest Mountains." *Geographical Journal* 169, no. 3 (Sept. 2003): 191-204.

Dary, David. *Frontier Medicine: 1492-1941.* New York: Alfred A. Knopf, 2008.

David, Robert G. *The Arctic in the British Imagination, 1818-1914.* Manchester: Manchester University Press, 2000.

Dawson, George. *Historical Notes on the Yukon District.* Toronto: University of Toronto, 1898.

Dawson, George. *Report on an Exploration in the Yukon District, N.W.T. and Adjacent*

Northern Portion of British Columbia, 1887. Ottawa: S.E. Dawson, 1898.

"Death of Professor A. B. Crosby." *Journal of Materia Medica* 15, no. 8 (August 15, 1877); 165.

De Barthe, Joe. *The Life and Adventures of Frank Grouard, Chief of Scouts, U.S.A.* St. Joseph, Mo.: Combe Printing, 1894.

de Laguna, Frederica. *Under Mount Saint Elias: The History and Culture of the Yakutat Tlingit.* Smithsonian Contributions to Anthropology. Vol. 7 (In three parts). Washington, DC: Smithsonian Institution Press, 1972.

Deur, Douglas. *Empires of the Turning Tide: A History of the Lewis and Clark National and State Historic Parks and the Columbia-Pacific Region.* Pacific West Region: Social Science Series No. 2016-001. Washington, D.C.: U.S. Department of the Interior, 2016.

Deur, Douglas, "The Making of Seaside's 'Indian Place': Contested and Enduring Native Spaces on the Nineteenth Century Oregon Coast." *Oregon Historical Quarterly* 117, no. 4 (Winter 2016): 536-73.

Deur, Douglas, Thomas Thornton, Rachel Lahoff and Jamie Hebert. "Yakutat Tlingit and Wrangell-Mt. St. Elias National Park and Reserve: An Ethnographic Overview and Assessment." Anthropology Faculty Publications Presentations 99. U.S. Department of the Interior: National Park Service, 2015.

Documents of the School Committee for the City of Boston 1913. Boston: Printing Committee, 1913.

Dodge, Richard Irving. *The Black Hills Journals of Colonel Richard Irving Dodge.* Edited by Wayne R. Kime. Norman: Oklahoma University Press, 1966.

Dormady, Jason H. and Jared M. Tamez, eds. *Just South of Zion: The Mormons in Mexico and its Borderlands.* Albuquerque, N.Mex.: University of New Mexico Press, 2015.

Dorn, Jacob H. "Sunday Afternoon: The Early Social Gospel in Journalism." *The New England Quarterly* 44, no. 21 (June 1971): 238-58.

Downie, William. *Hunting for Gold: Reminiscences of Personal Experience and Research in the Early Days of the Pacific Coast from Alaska to Panama.* San Francisco: California Publishing, 1893.

Eber, Dorothy Harley. *Encounters on the Passage: Inuit Meet the Explorers.* Toronto: University of Toronto Press, 2008.

Eber, Dorothy Harley. *When the Whalers were Up North: Inuit Memories from the Eastern Arctic.* Norman: University of Oklahoma Press, 1989.

Ebierbing, "Joseph Eberling's [sic] Statement." In "Arctic Meeting at Chickering Hall." *Journal of the American Geographical Society* 12 (1880): 279-81.

Eggleston, Edward. "The Aborigines and the Colonists." *Century Magazine* 26, no. 1 (May 1883): 96-114.

Ellis, Richard N. "The Humanitarian Soldiers." *The Journal of Arizona History* 10, no. 2 (Summer 1969): 53-66.

Emmons, George Thornton. *The Tlingit Indians.* Vol. 70, *Anthropological Papers of the American Museum of Natural History.* Edited by Frederica de Leguna with a biography by Jean Low. Seattle: University of Washington Press, and New York: American Museum of Natural History, 1991.

Finerty, John F. *War-Path and Bivouac, or the Conquest of the Sioux*. Chicago: Donohue & Henneberry, 1890.

Fitzpatrick, Mike. "A Volunteer joins the Regulars." *Military Images* 24, no. 1 (July-Aug. 2002): 10-13.

Flint, Austin. *A Treatise on the Principles and Practice of Medicine*. 4th ed. Philadelphia: Henry C. Lea, 1873.

Flint, Austin. "Medical and Sanitary Progress." *Harper's New Monthly Magazine* 53, no. 313 (June 1876): 70-84.

Fontana, Bernard L. Introduction to *In the Land of the Cave and Cliff Dwellers* by Frederick Schwatka, 13-20. Glorieta, N.Mex.: Rio Grande Press, 1977.

Fontana, Bernard L., with photographs by John P. Schaefer. *Tarahumara: Where Night is the Day of the Moon*. Tucson: University of Arizona Press, 1979.

Fossett, Renée. *In Order to Live Untroubled: Inuit in the Central Arctic, 1550 to 1940*. Winnipeg: University of Manitoba Press, 2011.

Freebairn, Alison. "The Pointing Hand of King William Island." September 30, 2020. https://finger-post.blog/2020/09/30/the-pointing-hand-of-king-william-island/ (accessed November 17, 2020).

Frost, Orcutt. *Bering: The Russian Discovery of America*. New Haven: Yale University Press, 2003.

Gaston, Joseph. *Portland, Oregon: Its History and Builders*. Vol. 1. Chicago: S.J. Clarke Publishing Company, 1911.

Gates, Michael. *Gold at Fortymile Creek: Early Days in the Yukon*. Vancouver, B.C.: UBC Press, 1994.

Gates, Michael. *History Hunting in the Yukon*. Madeira Park, B.C.: Harbour Publishing, 2010.

Genealogical Material in Oregon Donation Land Claims: Abstracted from Rejected Applications filed in the Oregon City, Roseburg and the Dalles Land Offices. Portland: Genealogical Forum of Oregon, 1967.

Gilder, William H. "Among the Esquimaux with Schwatka." *Scribner's Monthly* 22, no. 1 (1881): 76-88.

Gilder, William H. *Schwatka's Search: Sledging in the Arctic in Quest of the Franklin Records*. New York: Charles Scribner's Sons, 1881.

Gillett, James B. *Six Years with the Texas Rangers: 1875-1881*. Austin, Tex.: Von Boeckmann-Jones, 1921.

Glave, Edward J. *Travels to the Alseck: Edward Glave's Reports from Southwest Yukon and Southeast Alaska, 1890-91*. Edited by Julie Cruikshank, Doug Hitch and John Ritter. Whitehorse: Yukon Native Language Centre, 2013.

Godson, William F. H. *The History of West Point: 1852-1902*. Philadelphia: Temple University, 1934.

Godwin, Peter. *The Ships of Trafalgar: The British, French and Spanish Fleets, October 1805*. London: Conway Maritime Press, 2005.

Goetzmann, William H. *New Lands, New Men: America and the Second Great Age of*

Discovery. New York: Viking, 1986.

Gray, John Stephens. *Centennial Campaign: The Sioux War of 1876*. Norman: University of Oklahoma Press, 1998.

Greene, Jerome A. *Slim Buttes, 1876: An Episode of the Great Sioux War*. Norman: University of Oklahoma Press, 1982.

Greene, Jerome A., comp. and ed. *Indian War Veterans: Memories of Army Life and Campaigns in the West*. New York: Savas Beatie, 2007.

Hall, Charles Francis. *Narrative of the Second Arctic Expedition made by Charles Francis Hall*. Edited by Professor Joseph E. Nourse. Washington, D.C.: GPO, 1879.

Hanbury, David T. *Sport and Travel in the Northland of Canada*. London: Edward Arnold, 1904.

Hanson, David J. "'Alcoholism is a Disease and I can cure it,' Dr. Leslie Keeley and the Keeley Institutes." In *Alcohol Problems and Solutions* https://www.alcoholproblemsandsolutions.org/alcoholism-is-a-disease-and-i-can-cure-it-dr-leslie-keeley-and-the-keeley-institutes/ (accessed May 31, 2020).

Hardy, B. Carman. "The Sonora, Sinaloa and Chihuahua Railroad." *Jahrbuch für Geschichte Lateinamerikas* 12, no. 1 (1975): 253-83.

Harper, Douglas R. *West Chester to 1865: That Elegant and Notorious Place*. West Chester, Pa.: Chester County Historical Society, 1999.

Harper, Francis. *The Barren Ground Caribou of Keewatin*. Lawrence: University of Kansas, 1955.

Harper, Kenn. *Give Me My Father's Body: The Life of Minik the New York Eskimo*. South Royalton, Vt.: Steerforth Press, 2000.

Harris, Arland S. *Schwatka's Last Search: The New York Ledger Expedition through Unknown Alaska and British America*. Fairbanks: University of Alaska Press, 1996.

Haycock, Stephen. *Alaska: An American Colony*. Seattle: University of Washington Press, 2002.

Hayes, Charles W. "The Journal of Charles Willard Hayes, 1891." In Harris, *Schwatka's Last Search*, 207-58.

Hayes, Charles W. "An Expedition through the Yukon District." *National Geographic Magazine* 4 (May 15, 1892): 117-62.

Hearing before the Subcommittee on National Parks and Recreation of the Committee on Interior and Insular Affairs on . . . a Bill to Establish the Klondike Gold Rush Park: Washington, D.C.: Committee on the Interior and Insular Affairs, May 12, 1975.

Hebberd, M. H. "Notes on Dr. David Franklin Powell, Known as White Beaver." *Wisconsin Magazine of History* 35, no. 4 (Summer 1952), 306-09.

Hedren, Paul L. *After Custer: Loss and Transformation in Sioux Country*. Norman: University of Oklahoma Press, 2011.

Hedren, Paul L. "Camp Sheridan, Nebraska: The Uncommonly Quiet Post on Beaver Creek." *Nebraska History* 91 (2010): 80-93.

Hedren, Paul L., ed. "*Ho! For the Black Hills: Captain Jack Crawford Reports the Black Hills Gold Rush and Great Sioux War*. Pierre: South Dakota State Historical Society Press, 2012.

Hedren, Paul L., ed. *John Finerty Reports the Sioux War*. Norman: University of Oklahoma Press, 2020.

Hedren, Paul L. *Powder River: Disastrous Opening of the Great Sioux War.* Norman: University of Oklahoma Press, 2016.
Hedren, Paul L. *Rosebud June 17, 1876: Prelude to the Little Big Horn.* Norman: University of Oklahoma Press, 2019.
Heitman, Francis B. *Historical Register and Dictionary of the United States Army, from Its Inception, September 29, 1789, to March 2, 1903.* 2 vols. Washington, D.C.: GPO, 1903.
Henninghausen, Louis P., comp. *History of the German Society of Maryland.* Baltimore: W.E.C. Harrison & Sons, 1909.
Henninghausen, Louis P. "The Germans in the Defense of Baltimore in the War of 1812 to 1814." In *Sixteenth Annual Report of the Society for the History of Germans in Maryland.* Baltimore: Schneidereith and Sons, 1907: 55-60.
Henry, Jeff. *Snowshoes, Coaches, and Cross Country Skis: A Brief History of Yellowstone Winters.* Emigrant, Mont.: Roche Jaune Pictures, 2011.
Higginson, Ella. *Alaska: The Great Country.* New York: The MacMillan Company, 1909.
Hines, Rev. Gustavus. *Oregon and its Institutions.* New York: Carleton and Porter, 1868.
Hinsley, Curtis M. "The World Marketplace: Commodification of the Exotic at the World's Columbian Exposition, 1893." Chap. 18 in *Exhibiting Cultures: The Poetics and Politics of Museum Display.* Edited by Ivan Karp and Steven D. Levine, 344-65. Washington, D.C. and London: Smithsonian Institution Press, 1991.
Historic Rock Island County. Rock Island, Ill.: Kramer and Company, 1908.
Hodgkin, Frank E. and J.J. Galvin. *Pen Pictures of Representative Men of Oregon.* Portland, Ore.: Farmer and Dairyman Publishing House, 1882.
Hofer, Elwood. "Winter in Wonderland." *Forest and Stream* 28, no. 11 (April 7, 1887), 222-23; 28, no. 12 (April 14, 1887), 246-47; 28, no. 13 (April 21, 1887), 270-71; and 28, no. 14 (April 28, 1887), 294-95.
Hofmann, Julius. *A History of Zion Church of the City of Baltimore.* Baltimore: C.W. Schneidereith & Sons, 1905.
Hollabaugh, Mark. *The Spirit and the Sky: Lakota Visions of the Cosmos.* Lincoln: University of Nebraska Press, 2007.
Holland, Clive. *Arctic Exploration and Development c. 500 b.c. to 1915: An Encyclopedia.* New York: Garland, 1994.
Holler, Clyde. *Black Elk's Religion: The Sun Dance and Lakota Catholicism.* Syracuse: Syracuse University Press, 1995.
Holmes, Louisa A. *Fort McPherson, Nebraska: Fort Cottonwood, N.T, Guardian of the Tracks and Rails.* Lincoln: Johnsen Publishing Company, 1963.
Hough, E. "Death of Lieut. Schwatka." *Forest and Stream* 39, no. 19 (November 10, 1892): 404.
Hunt, William R. *Mountain Wilderness: An Illustrated History of Wrangell-St. Elias National Park and Preserve, Alaska.* Anchorage: Alaska Natural History Association, 1996.

Hurlbut, George C. "Lieut. Frederick Schwatka." In "Geographical Notes." *Journal of the American Geographic Society* 24 (1892): 618-20.
Isserman, Maurice. *Exploring North America: 1800-1900*. Rev. ed. New York, Chelsea House, 2010.
Jackson, Sheldon. *Alaska and the North Pacific Coast*. New York: Dodd, Mead, 1880.
Jackson, Sheldon. "Presbyterian Missions in Alaska in 1885." *The Gospel in All Lands* (September, 1886): 398-402.
Jakle, John A. "Cincinnati in the 1830s: A Cognitive Map of Traveler's Landscape Impressions." *Environmental Review* 3, no. 3 (Spring 1979): 2-10.
Johnson, Robert D. "Parties and Politics in Oregon History." *Oregon History Quarterly* 110, no. 2 (Summer, 2009), 194-201.
Johnson, Robert E., Margaret H. Johnson, Harriet S. Jeanes and Susan M. Deaver. *Schwatka: The Life of Frederick Schwatka (1849-1892), M.D., Arctic Explorer, Cavalry Officer; A Précis*. South Burlington, Vt.: Horn of the Moon Enterprises, 1984.
Keely, Robert N., Jr. and G. G. Davis. *In Arctic Seas: Voyage of the "Kite."* Philadelphia: Thompson Publishing, 1893.
Kelly, Norman V. "The Story of Peoria's Grand Opera House." *Peoria Magazine*, May/June 2010.
Kemble, John Haskell. *The Panama Route, 1848-1869*. Vol. 29, *University of California Publications in History*. Berkeley: University of California Press, 1942.
Kim, David D. "The Mimicry of Empire: Reinventing Autobiography in the Arctic." *Austrian Studies* 20 (2012): 129-41.
King, Charles. *Campaigning with Crook and Stories of Army Life*. New York: Harper & Brothers, 1890.
Klutschak, Heinrich W. *Als Eskimo Unter den Eskimos: Eine Schilderung der Erlebnisse der Schwatka'schen Franklin-Aufsuchungs-Expedition in den Jahren 1878-1880*. Wein: A. Hartleben, 1881.
Klutschak, Heinrich W. *Overland to Starvation Cove: With the Inuit in Search of Franklin, 1878-1880*. Trans. and ed. William Barr. Toronto: University of Toronto Press, 1987.
Knight, Oliver. *Following the Indian Wars: The Story of the Newspaper Correspondents among the Indian Campaigners*. Norman: University of Oklahoma Press, 1960.
Koelsch, William A. "William Libbey of Princeton: A Forgotten Geographer." *Middle States Geographer* 49 (2016): 1-8.
Korom, Joseph J. *The American Skyscraper 1850-1940: A Celebration of Height*. Wellesley, Mass.: Braneon Books, 2008.
Kortleever, Maaike, transcriber. *History of the Pacific Northwest: Oregon and Washington*. 2 vols. Portland: North Pacific History Company, 1889.
Krupnik, Igor. "'Coming Home' after 130 years: Lt. Frederick Schwatka's Aivilingmiut Vocabulary Returns to Smithsonian." *Arctic Studies Newsletter* 21 (April 2014): 22-24.
Lang, William L. "'At the Greatest Personal Peril to the Photographer': The Schwatka-Haynes Winter Expedition in Yellowstone, 1887." *Montana: The Magazine of Western History* 33, no. 4 (Winter 1983), 14-29.

LaPlante, Margaret. *Crater Lake National Park*. Charleston, S.C.: Arcadia Publishing, 2013.
Lawrence, Isabel. *Classified Reading: Books for the School, the Library, and the Home with a Full Bibliography of Education*. St. Cloud, Minn.: Normal St. School, 1898.
Levere, Trevor H. *Science and the Canadian Arctic: A Century of Exploration, 1818-1918*. Cambridge University Press, Cambridge, 1993.
Libbey, William, Jr. "Some of the Geographical Features of Southeastern Alaska." *Journal of the American Geographical Society* 18 (1886): 279-300.
"Lieutenant Frederick Schwatka." *The Pathfinder: Devoted to the Welfare of the Pioneers of Alaska* 1, no. 8 (June, 1920).
Ljubicic, Gita, Erica Oberndorfer and Glenda Smith. "The Curious Case of King William Island, Nunavut: An Island Overlooked in Caribou Research." *Arctic* 70, no. 1 (March 2017), 107-17.
Lockley, Fred. *History of the Columbia River Valley from The Dalles to the Sea*. 2 vols. Chicago: S. J. Clark Publishing Company, 1928.
Loomis, Chauncey C. *Weird and Tragic Shores: The Story of Charles Francis Hall, Explorer*. New York: Alfred A. Knopf, 1971.
Lumholtz, Carl. "The American Cave-Dwellers: The Tarahumaris of the Sierra Madre." *Journal of the American Geographical Society* 26, no. 3 (1894): 299-325.
Lumholtz, Carl. "Cave-Dwellers of the Sierra Madre." In *Memoirs of the International Congress of Anthropology*. Edited by C. Staniland Wake, 100-12. Chicago: Schulte Publishing, 1894.
Lumholtz, Carl *Unknown Mexico: A Record of Five Years' Explorations among the Tribes of the Western Sierra Madre*. New York: Charles Scribner's Sons, 1902.
Lundberg, Murray. "Five Finger Rapids, Yukon." *Explore North: An Explorer's Guide to the North*. http://www.explorenorth.com/campgrounds/five_finger_rapids.html (accessed April 4, 2020).
Mahnken, Norbert R. "The Sidney-Black Hills Trail." *Nebraska History* 30 (1949), 203-25.
MacGahan, J. A. *Under the Northern Lights*. London: Sampson Low, Marston, Searle, & Rivington, 1876.
"Major William Williams' Journal of a Trip to Iowa in 1849." Edited by Mrs. John F. Duncombe. *Annals of Iowa*. 3rd. ser., 12, no. 4 (April 1920): 242-81.
Malone, Dumas, ed. *Dictionary of American Biography, Volume 16*. New York: Charles Scribner's Sons, 1935.
Mangum, Neil C. *Battle of the Rosebud: Prelude to the Little Bighorn*. El Segundo, Calif.: Upton & Sons, 1987.
Markham, Albert Hastings. *The Great Frozen Sea: A Personal Narrative of the Voyage of the "Alert" during the Arctic Expedition of 1875-76*. London: Daldy, Isbister, 1878.
Markham, Clements R. "Expedition of Lieutenant F. Schwatka to King William Land." *Proceedings of the Royal Geographical Society* 2, no. 11 (Nov. 1880): 657-62.

Markham, Clements R. *The Lands of Silence: A History of Arctic and Antarctic Exploration*. Cambridge: Cambridge University Press, 1921.

Markham, Clements R. *The Life of Admiral Sir Leopold McClintock*. London: John Murray, 1909.

Mays, S., A. Ogden, J. Montgomery, S. Vincent, W. Battersby and G. M. Taylor. "New Light on the Identification of a Member of Sir John Franklin's last expedition to the Arctic." *Journal of Archaeological Science* 38, no. 7 (July 2011): 1571-82.

McCandless, Barbara and John Rohrbach. *Singular Moments: Photographs from the Amon Carter Museum*. Fort Worth, Tex.: Amon Carter Museum of Western Art, 2001.

McLagan, Elizabeth. "*The Black Laws of Oregon, 1844-1857*" (March 30, 2009), https://www.blackpast.org/african-american-history/black-laws-oregon-1844-1857/_(accessed April 20, 2019).

McClellan, Catherine. "History of Research in the Subarctic Cordillera." In *Handbook of the North American Indians*. Vol. 6, *Subarctic*. Edited by Julie Helm, 35-42. Washington, D.C.: Smithsonian Institution, 1981.

McClellan, Catherine. *My Old People Say: An Ethnographic Survey of the Southern Yukon Territory*. Part 1. Mercury Series. Paper 137. Ottawa: Canadian Museum of Civilization, 2001.

McClellan, Catharine. "Tagish." In *Handbook of the North American Indians*, Vol. 6, *Subarctic*. Edited by Julie Helm, 481-92. Washington, D.C.: Smithsonian Institution, 1981.

McClellan, Catharine. "Tutchone." In *Handbook of the North American Indians*, Vol. 6, *Subarctic*. Edited by Julie Helm, 493-505. Washington, D.C.: Smithsonian Institution, 1981.

McClintock, Francis Leopold. *Fate of Sir John Franklin: The Voyage of the 'Fox' in the Arctic Seas in Search of Sir John Franklin and his Companions*. 5th ed. London: John Murray, 1881.

McClintock, Francis Leopold. "Letter of Admiral Sir Leopold McClintock to the British Admiralty, 19th December, 1872." In "Arctic Meeting at Chickering Hall." *Journal of the American Geographic Society* 12 (1880): 282-83.

McClintock, Francis Leopold. "On Arctic Sledge-Travelling." *Proceedings of the Royal Geographical Society* 19, no. 7 (June 1875), 464-79.

McClintock, Francis Leopold. "On Arctic Sledge-Travelling." In *The Antarctic Manual for the Use of the Expedition of 1901*. Edited by George Murray, 293-304. London: Royal Geographical Society, 1901.

McClintock, Francis Leopold. "Reminiscences of Arctic Ice-Travel in Search of Sir John Franklin and his Companions." *Journal of the Royal Dublin Society* 1 (1857): 1-68.

McClintock, Francis Leopold. *The Voyage of the "Fox" in the Arctic Seas: A Narrative of the Discovery of the Fate of Sir John Franklin and his Companions*. London: John Murray, 1859.

McCormick, John R. "History of Foreign Language Teaching at the United States

Military Academy." *Modern Language Journal* 54, no. 5 (May 1970): 319-23.

McDermott, John. Introduction to *My Story* by Anson Mills. Edited by C. H. Claudy, vii-xxiii. Mechanicsburg, Pa.: Stackpole Books, 2003.

McDougall, Christopher. *Born to Run: A Hidden Tribe, Superathletes, and the Greatest Race the World has Never Seen.* New York: Alfred A. Knopf, 2010.

McNeese, Tim. *The Oregon Trail: Pathway to the West.* NY: Chelsea House, 2009.

Mehta, Nirav J., Rajal N. Mehta, and Ijaz A. Khan. "Austin Flint: Clinician, Teacher and Visionary." *Texas Heart Institute Journal* 27, no. 4 (2000): 386-89.

Miles, Nelson A. *Personal Recollections and Observations of General Nelson A. Miles.* Chicago: Werner Company, 1897.

Mills, Anson. *Big Horn Expedition: August 15 to September 30, 1874.* N.d., n.p. (copy at NYPL).

Mills, Anson. *My Story.* Edited by C. H. Claudy. Washington, D.C.: By the Author, 1918.

Mills, Anson. *Official Report of Captain Anson Mills on Slim Buttes Battle.* In Greene, *Slim Buttes, 1876: An Episode of the Great Sioux War*, 132-35. Norman: University of Oklahoma Press, 1982.

Molnia, Bruce F. "Glaciers of North America-Glaciers of Alaska." Chap. K in *Satellite Image Atlas of Glaciers of the World: Alaska.* Edited by Richard S. Williams, Jr. and Jane G. Ferrigno. U.S. Geological Survey Professional Paper 1386-K. Washington, D.C.: GPO, 2008.

Morin, Karin M. *Civic Discipline: Geography in America, 1860-1890.* Surrey, UK: Ashgate Publishing, 2011.

Mott, Frank Luther. *A History of American Magazines, Volume 2, 1850-1865.* Cambridge: Harvard University Press, 1938.

Munger, T. T. "Immigration by Passport." *Century Magazine* 35, no. 5 (March 1888): 791-99.

Murphy, David Thomas. "'First Among Savages': The German Romance of the Eskimo from the Enlightenment to National Socialism." *German Studies Review* 25, no. 3 (Oct. 2002): 533-50.

Murray, John A. Introduction to *A Republic of Rivers.* Edited by John A. Murray, 3-19. Oxford: Oxford University Press, 1990.

Myers, Steven R. "The Changing Face of Medical Education." *Journal of Medical Education and Curricular Development* 1 (2014): 1–3. doi:10.4137/JMECD.S17270.

Nabrdalik, Bartosz. "How a Nation Outlived its State: Polish Partitions and their Impact on the Former Citizens of the Commonwealth." *Journal of Slavic Military Studies* 20, no. 4 (September 2007): 653-78.

Neuzil, Mark. *Views on the Mississippi: The Photographs of Henry Philip Bosse.* Minneapolis: University of Minnesota Press, 2002.

Newall, Clayton R. and Charles R. Shrader. *Of Duty Well and Faithfully Done: A History of the Regular Army in the Civil War.* Lincoln: University of Nebraska Press, 2011.

Noonan, Mark J. *Reading the Century Illustrated Monthly Magazine: American Literature and Culture, 1870-1893.* Kent, Ohio: Kent State University Press, 2010.

Nordin, Charles R. "Dr. W. F. Carver, 'Evil Spirit of the Plains.'" *Nebraska Historical Magazine* 10, no. 4 (Oct.-Dec. 1927): 344-52.

Ogilvie, William. *Early Days on the Yukon and the Story of its Gold Fields*. Ottawa: Thorburn & Abbott, 1913.

Ogilvie, William. *The Klondike Official Guide: Canada's Great Gold Field, The Yukon District*. Toronto: Hunter, Rose, 1898.

Olsen, Jerry C. "Charles A. Homan (1847-1918)," Olsen Engineering, Vancouver, WA, https://www.olsonengr.com/download/globios/homancharlesabio.pdf (accessed June 4, 2021).

Orth, Donald J. *Dictionary of Alaska Place Names*. Geological Survey Professional Paper 567. Washington, D.C.: GPO, 1971.

Osgood, Cornelius. *The Han Indians: A Compilation of Ethnographic and Historical Data on the Alaska-Yukon Boundary Area*. New Haven, Conn.: Department of Anthropology Yale University, 1971.

Oshinsky, David. *Bellevue: Three Centuries of Medicine and Mayhem at America's Most Storied Hospital*. New York: Anchor Books, 2017.

Oswalt, Wendell H. *Eskimos and Explorers*. Novato: Chandler & Sharp, 1979.

Owen, Roderick. *The Fate of Franklin*. London: Hutchison, 1978.

Papers relating to the Foreign Relations of the United States, Transmitted to Congress, with the Annual Message of the President, December 3, 1888. Part I. Wash., D.C.: GPO, 1889.

Pappas, George S. *To the Point: The United States Military Academy, 1802-1902*. Westport, Conn.: Praeger Publishers, 1993.

Parry, Rev. Edward. *Memoirs of Rear-Admiral Sir W. Edward Parry, Kt*. London: Longman, Brown, Green, Longmans and Roberts, 1857.

Patrick, Jeffrey L. "To the Black Hills Gold Fields: The Letters of Samuel M. Zent, Hoosier Prospector, 1875-6." *Indian Magazine of History* 91, no. 3 (September 1995): 262-87.

Pearson, Michael. "Sledges and Sledging in the Polar Regions." *Polar Record* 31, no. 176 (1995): 3-24.

Peary, Robert E. *Northward over the Great Ice*. New York: Frederick A. Stokes, 1908.

Pelly, David F. *Ukkusiksalik: The People's Story*. Toronto: Dundurn, 2016.

Pelly, David F. "Wager Bay, a History and a Future." *The Beaver* 67, no. 5 (Oct.-Nov., 1987) 16-25.

Peters, Harold J., ed. *Seven Months to Oregon, 1853: Diaries, Letters and Reminiscent Accounts*. Tooele, Utah: The Patrice Press, 2008.

Petterchak, Janice A. *Lone Scout: W. D. Boyce and American Boy Scouting*. Rochester, Ill.: Legacy Press, 2003.

Phillips, Christopher J. "An Officer and a Scholar: Nineteenth Century West Point and the Invention of the Blackboard." *History of Education Quarterly* 55, no. 1 (February 2015): 82-108.

Phinney, Stephen D. "Ketogenic Diets and Physical Performance." *Nutrition and Metabolism* 1, no. 2 (2004): 1-7.

Porter, Joseph C. *Paper Medicine Man: John Gregory Bourke and his American West.* Norman: University of Oklahoma Press, 1986.

Potter, Russell A. *Finding Franklin: The Untold Story of a 165-year Search.* Montreal: McGill Queen's University Press, 2016.

Powers, Thomas. *The Killing of Crazy Horse.* New York: Vintage Books, 2010.

Rae, John. "Letter of Dr. John Rae to the British Admiralty, 15th Dec., 1877." In "Arctic Meeting at Chickering Hall." *Journal of the American Geographical Society* 12 (1880): 284-88.

Rae, John. *Narrative of an Expedition to the Shores of the Arctic Sea in 1846 and 1847.* London, T. & W. Boone, 1850.

Rae, John. "Obituary, Dr. John Rae, M.D., F.R.S." In *Journal of the American Geographic Society,* 25 (1893): 479-81.

Rae, John. "Proceedings of Dr. Rae, Chief Factor, Hudson's Bay Company." In *Further Papers relative to the Recent Arctic Expeditions in Search of Sir John Franklin, and the Crews of HMS "Erebus" and "Terror,"* 831-44. London: George Edward Eyre and William Spottiswoode, 1855.

Rae, John. *Voyages and Travels of Dr. Rae in the Arctic Regions.* N.p., n.p., 1856.

Rasmussen, Knud. *The Netsilik Eskimos: Social and Spiritual Culture.* Vol. 8, nos. 1-2. *Report of the Fifth Thule Expedition 1921-24.* Copenhagen: Boghandel, 1931.

Raymond, Charles. "Reconnaissance of the Yukon River," 19-41. In *Compilation of Narratives of Explorations in Alaska.* Washington, D.C.: GPO, 1900.

"Recent Deaths." *The United States Army and Navy Journal and Gazette of the Regular and Volunteer Forces* 30 (November 12, 1892): 194.

Records of Living Officers of the United States Army. Philadelphia: Hamersly, 1884.

Reedy, Katherine L. "Kelp-Fed Beef, Swimming Caribou, Feral Reindeer and their Hunters: Island Mammals in a Marine Economy." *Sustainability* 8, no. 113 (2016): 1-25.

Report of the Board of Visitors, July 1, 1871. In *Annual Report of the Secretary of War, Vol. 1.* H. Rep., 42nd Cong., 2nd sess., Ex. Doc. 1, Part 2. Washington, D.C.: GPO, 1871.

Report of the Board of Visitors, June 15, 1870. In *Annual Report of the Secretary of War, Vol. 1,* H. Rep., 41st Cong., 3rd sess., Ex. Doc. 1, Part 2. Washington, D.C.: GPO, 1870.

A Report on the Hygiene of the United States Army, with Descriptions of Military Posts. Washington, D.C.: GPO, 1875.

Richards, Robert L. *Dr. John Rae.* Whitby: Caedmon of Whitby, 1985.

Richmond, Phyllis Allen. "American Attitudes toward the Germ Theory of Disease (1860-1880)." *Journal of the History of Medicine and Allied Sciences* 9, no. 4 (Oct. 1954): 428-54.

Riffenburgh, Beau. *The Myth of the Explorer: The Press, Sensationalism and Geographical Discovery.* Oxford: Oxford University Press, 1994.

Riley, Paul D. "The Battle of Massacre Canyon." *Nebraska History* 54 (1973): 220-49.

Roberts, David. *Great Exploration Hoaxes.* New York: The Modern Library, 2001.

Robinson, Michael. *The Coldest Crucible: Arctic Exploration and American Culture.*

Chicago: University of Chicago Press, 2010.

Ronda, James P. *Finding the West: Explorations with Lewis and Clark*. Albuquerque: University of New Mexico Press, 2001

Rosa, Joseph G. *They Called Him Wild Bill: The Life and Adventures of James Butler Hitchcock*. 2nd ed. Norman: University of Oklahoma Press, 1974.

Ross, W. Gillies. "Commercial Whaling in Hudson Bay." In *The Bowhead Whale*. Edited by John J. Burns, Jerome Montague and Cleveland J. Cowles, 511-61. Lawrence, Kans.: Society for Marine Mammalogy, 1993.

Ross, W. Gillies. "Nineteenth Century Exploration of the Arctic." In *North American Exploration*. Edited by John Allen, 244-331. Lincoln: University of Nebraska Press, 1997.

Sailing directions for the West Coast of North America. London: James Imray, 1853.

Savelle, James M. "Effects of Nineteenth Century European Exploration on the Development of the Netsilik Inuit Culture." In *The Franklin Era in Canadian Arctic History, 1845-1859*. Edited by Patricia D. Sutherland, 192-214. Ottawa: National Museum of Canada, 1985.

Savitt, Ronald. "Frederick Schwatka and the Search for the Franklin Expedition Records." *Polar Record* 44, no. 3 (July 2008): 193-210.

Savitt, Ronald. "F. G. Schwatka's Headstone." *Polar Record* 43, no. 226 (February 2007): 271-72.

Savours, Ann. *The Search for the Northwest Passage*. London: Chatham Publishing, 1999.

Scheips, Paul. "Darkness and Light: The Interwar Years, 1865-1898." Chap. 13 in *American Military History: Army Historical Series*. Washington, D.C: Office of the Chief of Military History, U.S. Army, 1989.

Schmidt, Martin F., ed. *General George Crook: His Autobiography*. New ed. Norman: University of Oklahoma Press, 1960.

Schuricht, Hermann. *Thirteenth and Fourteenth Annual Reports of the Society for the History of Germans in Maryland*. 2 vols. Baltimore: Theo. Kroh & Sons, 1900.

Schwatka, Mrs. Frederick. "A New Route to Alaska's Eldorado." *The Midland Monthly* 8, no. 5 (November 1897): 395-401.

Schwatka, Mrs. Frederick. "Around about Alaska's Metropolis." *The Midland Monthly* 8, no. 4 (October 1897): 553-60.

Schwatka, Frederick. "Address of Lieutenant Frederick Schwatka." In "Arctic Meeting at Chickering Hall, October 28th, 1880," 237-96. *Journal of the American Geographical Society* 12 (1880).

Schwatka, Frederick. *Along Alaska's Great River*. New York: Cassell, 1885.

Schwatka, Frederick. "America's Expedition." *America: A Journal for Americans* 2, no. 69 (July 25, 1889): 517-20.

Schwatka, Frederick. "Among the Apaches." *Century Magazine* 34, no. 1 (May-Oct., 1887): 41-52.

Schwatka, Frederick. "Among the Natives of the North." *Frank Leslie's Sunday Magazine* 13, no. 5 (May 1883): 473-79; 13, no. 6 (June 1883): 582-90; 14, no. 1 (July 1883): 25-31; 14, no. 2 (August 1883): 25-30; 14, no. 3 (September

1883): 234-40; 14, no. 4 (October 1883): 401-08.

Schwatka, Frederick. "An Elk Hunt on the Plains." *Century Magazine* 35, no. 3 (January 1888): 447-56.

Schwatka, Frederick. "Arctic Experiences." *Journal of the Military Service Institution of the United States* 2 (1881): 304-22.

Schwatka, Frederick. "Benefits Accruing to the United States from the Possession of Alaska." *America: A Journal for Americans* 1, no. 51 (March 21, 1889): 1-2.

Schwatka, Frederick. "Capturing a Herd of Buffalo." *The Golden Rule* 9, no. 5 (November 1, 1894): 103.

Schwatka, Frederick. *Children of the Cold*. New York: Cassell, 1886.

Schwatka, Frederick. "Down the Yukon on a Raft: Part 1-Introductory." *Forest and Stream* 21, no. 21 (December 20, 1883), 402-03; "Part 1-Introductory Concluded." 21, no. 22 (December 27, 1883): 432-33; "Third Paper." 21, no. 24 (January 10, 1884), 471-72; "Fourth Paper." 21, no. 26 (January 24, 1884): 513-14; "Fifth Paper." 22, no. 1 (January 31, 1884): 4-5; "Sixth Paper." 22, no. 4 (February 21, 1884): 64; "Seventh Paper." 22, no. 7 (March 13, 1884): 122-23; "Eighth Paper." 22, no. 10 (April 3, 1884): 182-83; "Ninth Paper." 22, no. 12 (April 17, 1884): 222-23; "Tenth Paper." 22, no. 13 (April 24, 1884): 242-43.

Schwatka, Frederick. "Exploration of the Yukon River in 1883." *Journal of the American Geographical Society* 16 (1884): 45-82.

Schwatka, Frederick. "The Great River of Alaska. Exploring the Upper Yukon." *Century Magazine* 30, no. 5 (Sept. 1885): 738-51.

Schwatka, Frederick. "The Great River of Alaska. II. Exploring the Middle and Lower Yukon." *Century Magazine* 30, no. 6 (Oct. 1885): 819-29.

Schwatka, Frederick. "Ho Wash-Tay." *The Youth's Companion* 62, no. 19 (May 9, 1889), 249-50.

Schwatka, Frederick. "How A Great Sioux Chief was Named." *St. Nicholas Magazine* 15 (February 1888): 296-98.

Schwatka, Frederick. "A Hunt for a Young Antelope." *Harper's Young People* 7, no. 380 (February 8, 1887): 235-36.

Schwatka, Frederick. "Hunting Buffalo Calves with a Lasso." In *Boy's Book of Cowboys. Stories of Ranch, Indian and Mine*. Edited by Til Tilford, Paul Hull, W. O. Stoddard and others, 181-89. New York: Harper & Brothers, 1910.

Schwatka, Frederick. "Hunting Buffalo Calves with a Lasso." *Harper's Young People* 6, no. 311 (October 13, 1885): 788-80.

Schwatka, Frederick. "The Igloo of the Inuit." *Science* 2, no. 28 (August 17, 1883), 182-84; 2, no. 29 (August 24, 1883), 216-18; 2, no. 30 (August 31, 1883), 259-62; 2, no. 31 (September 7, 1883), 304-06; 2, no. 32 (September 14, 1883), 347-49.

Schwatka, Frederick. "The Implements of the Igloo." *Science* 4 (July 25, 1884): 81-85.

Schwatka, Frederick. *In the Land of the Cave and Cliff Dwellers*. New York: Cassell Publishing, 1893.

Schwatka, Frederick. "In the Land of the Midnight Sun." *Good Company* 6, no. 18, pt. 1 (Feb. 1881): 550-60; 7, nos. 19-20, pts. 2 and 3 (March-April, 1881): 1-21; 7, no. 21, pts. 4 and 5 (May 1881): 202-22; 7, no. 22, pt. 6 (June, 1881): 306-18.

Schwatka, Frederick. Introduction in Lauridsen, Peter. *Vitus Bering: The Discoverer of Bering Strait, translated from the Danish by Julius E. Olson*, vii-xi. Chicago: S. C. Griggs, 1889.

Schwatka, Frederick. "Land of the Living Cliff-Dwellers." *Century Magazine* 44, no. 2 (June 1892): 271-76.

Schwatka, Frederick. *The Long Arctic Search. The Narrative of Lieutenant Frederick Schwatka, U.S.A. 1878-1880 Seeking the Records of the Lost Franklin Expedition.* Edited by Edouard A. Stackpole. Mystic, CT: Marine Historical Association, Inc., 1965.

Schwatka, Frederick. "The Loneliest Place in the United States." In *In Alaska: Selections from the Youth's Companion*, 21-25. Boston, Mass.: Perry Mason, 1897.

Schwatka, Frederick. "Mountaineering in Alaska." *Alpine Journal* 13, no. 94 (Nov. 1886): 89-93.

Schwatka, Frederick. "The Neitschilluk [sic] Innuit." *Science* 4 (1884): 543-44.

Schwatka, Frederick. "The New York Ledger Expedition through Unknown Alaska and British America," *New York Ledger*, March 19, and 26, 1892; April 2, 9, 16, 23 and 30, 1892; May 14 and 28, 1892; June 4, 11 and 18, 1892; July 9, 16, 23, and 30, 1892; August 6 and 13, 1892.

Schwatka, Frederick. *Nimrod in the North, or Hunting and Fishing Adventures in the Arctic Regions*. New York: Cassell, 1885.

Schwatka, Frederick. *Report of a Military Reconnaissance made in Alaska in 1883.* Washington, D.C.: GPO, 1885.

Schwatka, Frederick. "The Resources of Alaska." *Scientific American Supplement* 20, no. 496 (July 4, 1885), 7919-21.

Schwatka, Frederick. "Schwatka in Mexico." *Chicago Inter-Ocean*, April 7, 14, 21 and 28, 1889; May 5, 12 and 26, 1889; June 2, 9, 16, 23 and 30, 1889; July 7, 14, and 21, 1889.

Schwatka, Frederick. "The Sun-Dance of the Sioux." *Century Magazine* 39, no. 5 (March 1890): 753-59.

Schwatka, Frederick. "Tight Pinches in the Arctic." *Youth's Companion*. December 12, 1888.

Schwatka, Frederick. "The *Times's* Alaska Expedition." *New York Times*, June 21 and 27, 1886; July 4, 5, 13, 14, 18, 26 and 30, 1886; August 9 and 16, 1886; September 20, 1886; October 3, 4, 5, 6, 7, 9, 17, 20 and 26, 1886; November 8, 1886.

Schwatka, Frederick. "Two Expeditions to Mount St. Elias: I. The Expedition of 'The New York Times,'" *Century Magazine* 41, no. 114 (1886), 865-72.

Schwatka, Frederick. "Wintering in the White Zone." *Cosmopolitan* 4, no. 6 (February 1888): 478-85

Schwatka, Frederick and John Hyde. *Wonderland: or Alaska and the Inland Passage, with a Description of the Country Traversed by the Northern Pacific Railroad*. St. Paul: Northern Pacific Railroad, 1886.

"Schwatka's Search." *Cumtux: Clatsop County Historical Society Quarterly* 18, no. 4 (Fall 1998): 34-35.

Seaton, Elizabeth P. "The Native Collector: Louis Shotridge and the Contests of Possession." *Ethnology* 2, no. 1 (March 2001): 35-61.

Seitz, Don C. *Joseph Pulitzer: His life and Letters*. New York: Simon & Schuster, 1924.

Sessional Papers. Fourth Session of the Ninth Parliament of the Dominion of Canada Session 1904. Ottawa, 1898.

Seton-Karr, H.W. "The Alpine Regions of Alaska." *Proceedings of the Royal Geographical Society* 9, no. 5 (May 1887): 269-85.

Seton-Karr, H.W. "Explorations of Alaska and North-west British Columbia." *Proceedings of the Royal Geographical Society* 13 n.s., no. 2 (Feb. 1891): 65-86.

Seton-Karr, H.W. *Shores and Alps of Alaska*. London: Sampson Low, Marston, Searle & Rivington, 1887.

Seton-Karr, H.W. *Ten Years Sport & Travel in Foreign Lands*. 2nd ed. London: Chapman & Hall Limited, 1890.

Sherwood, Morgan. *Exploration of Alaska: 1865-1900*. Fairbanks: University of Alaska Press, 1992.

Smith, Charles Emory. "The Trials and Triumphs of the Editor." *The Independent* 41, no. 2140 (December 5, 1889): 1-2.

Sorg, Eric V. "Doctor, Lawyer, Indian Chief: The life of Frank Powell, Medicine Man." *Wyoming History Journal* 67, no. 1 (Summer 1995): 32-47.

Stafford, Cornelius William. *The Baltimore Directory for 1803*. Baltimore: John W. Butler, 1804.

Stanley, Henry Morton. *The Autobiography of Henry Morton Stanley*. Edited by his wife Dorothy Stanley. Boston: Houghton Mifflin, 1909.

Steeves, Sarah Hunt. *Book of Remembrance of Marion County, Oregon, Pioneers 1840-1860*. Portland: The Berncliff Press, 1927.

Stefansson, Vilhjámur. *Discovery: The Autobiography of Vilhjámur Stefansson*. New York: McGraw-Hill, 1964.

Stefansson, Vilhjálmur. *My Life with the Eskimo*. London: Macmillan, 1913.

Stein, Glenn M. "Scattered Memories and Frozen Bones: Revealing a Sailor of the Franklin Expedition, 1845-48. *Orders of Medals and Research Society Journal* 46, no. 4 (2007): 224-32.

Stenton, Douglas R. "Finding the Dead: Bodies, Bones and Burials from the 1845 Franklin Northwest Passage Expedition." *Polar Record* 54, no. 3 (May 2018): 197-212.

Stenton, Douglas R., Anne Keenleyside and Robert W. Park. "The 'Boat Place' Burial: New Skeletal Evidence from the 1845 Franklin Expedition." *Arctic* 68, no. 1 (March 2015): 32-44.

Stenton, Douglas R., Anne Keenleyside, Philippe Froesch and Robert W. Park. "A Franklin Expedition Officer's Burial at Two Grave Bay, King William Island,

Nunavut." *Journal of Archaeological Science: Reports* 35 (2021): 1-14.
Stenton, Douglas R., Stephen Fratpietro, Anne Keenleyside and Robert W. Park. "DNA Identification of a Sailor from the 1845 Franklin Northwest Passage Expedition." *Polar Record* 57, E14 (April 2021). doi:10.1017/S0032247421000061.
Stenton, Douglas R. and Robert W. Park. "History, Oral History and Archaeology: Reinterpreting the 'Boat Places' of Erebus Bay." *Arctic* 70, no. 2 (June 2017), 203-17.
Stewart, Richard W. ed. *American Military History*. Vol. 1, *The U.S. Army and the Forging of a Nation, 1775-1917*. 2nd. ed. Washington, D.C.: Center of Military History, U.S. Army, 2009.
Sweeney, Edwin R. *From Cochise to Geronimo: The Chiricahua Apaches, 1874-1886*. Norman: University of Oklahoma Press, 2020.
Tate, Michael L. *The Frontier Army in the Settlement of the West*. Norman: University of Oklahoma Press, 1999.
Tenderini, Mirella and Michael Shandrick. *The Duke of the Abruzzi: An Explorer's Life*. Seattle: Mountaineers, 1997.
Thayer, Jim. "The Forest Hiker: The Clatsop Indians." http://www.foresthiker.com/?page_id=1956 (accessed June 5, 2020).
"Third Cavalry." *The United States Army and Navy Journal and Gazette of the Regular and Volunteer Forces* 13, no. 33 (March 25, 1876): 528.
Thorp, Raymond W. *Spirit Gun of the West: The Story of Doc W. F. Carver*. Glendale, Calif.: Arthur H. Clark, 1957.
Traeger, Verena. "Heinrich Wenzel Klutschak." In *Encyclopedia of the Arctic*. Vol. 2. Edited by Mark Nuttall, 1099-1101. New York: Routledge, 2005.
Traeger, Verena. "Heinrich W. Klutschak." In *Eskimo: Am Nordrand Der Welt, Schwerpunkt Grönland*. Edited by Christian F. Feest and Verena Traeger, 157-60. Wien: Museum für Völkerkunde, 1991.
Twenty-Fourth Annual Reunion of the Association of Graduates of the United States Military Academy at West Point, New York, June 9, 1893. Saginaw, Mich.: Seeman & Peters, 1893.
Tyrrell, James W. *Across the Sub-Arctics of Canada*. 3rd ed. Toronto: William Briggs, 1908.
United States Army and Navy Journal and Gazette of the Regular and Volunteer Forces 13, no. 33 (March 25, 1876): 528.
Utley, Robert M. *Frontier Regulars: The United States Army and the Indian: 1866-1891*. New York: MacMillan, 1973.
Vaughn, J. W. *With Crook at the Rosebud*. Harrisburg: Stackpole, 1956.
Vaughn, Robert. *Then and Now; or Thirty-Six Years in the Rockies*. Minneapolis: Tribune Printing, 1900.
Walpole, Garth. *Relics of the Franklin Expedition: Discovering Artifacts from the Doomed Arctic Voyage of 1845*. Edited by Russell Potter. Jefferson: McFarland, 2017.
Wamsley, Douglas W. "Albert L. Operti: Chronicler of Arctic Exploration." *Polar Record* 52, no. 3 (December 2015): 276-93.

Wamsley, Douglas W. "'We Are Fully in the Expedition': Philadelphia's Support for the North Greenland Expeditions of Robert E. Peary, 1891-1895." *Geographical Review* 107, no. 1 (2017): 207-35.

Warshaw, Leon. *Malaria: The Biography of a Killer*. New York: Rinehart, 1949.

Waterbury, Barbara. "Tlingit Potlatches." (revised by Blythe Carter, 2013) https://www.sheldonmuseum.org/vignettes/tlingit-potlatches (accessed March 27, 2021).

Webster, John Lee. "The Last Romantic Buffalo Hunt on the Plains of Nebraska." In *Collection of Nebraska Pioneer Reminiscences: Issued by the Nebraska Society of the Daughters of the American Revolution*, 326-32. Cedar Rapids, Iowa: Torch Press, 1916.

Weems, John Edward. "Peary's Long Quest for Fame and the North Pole." *Polar Notes*, 9 (May 1969): 26-34.

White, David. "Charles Willard Hayes." *Science* 44, 1126 (July 28, 1916): 124-26.

Whittlesey, Lee. *Storytelling in Yellowstone: Horse and Buggy Tour Guides*. Albuquerque: University of New Mexico, 2007.

Whittlesey, Lee. *Gateway to Yellowstone: The Raucous Town of Cinnabar on the Montana Frontier*. Guildford, Conn.: Twodor, 2015.

Whymper, Frederick. *Travel and Adventure in the Territory of Alaska*. London: John Murray, 1868.

Wisener, Kathy. "Big Train, Nebraska Train Robbery." https://www.legendsofamerica.com/ne-bigspringsrobbery/ (accessed March 3, 2021).

Wood, C. E. S. "Among the Tlinkits of Alaska." *Century Magazine* 24, no. 3 (July 1882): 328-29.

Woodman, David C. *Strangers Among Us*. Montreal: McGill-Queens's University Press, 1995.

Woodman, David C. *Unravelling the Franklin Mystery: Inuit Testimony*. Montreal: McGill-Queen's University Press, 1991.

Woodward, Frances J. *Portrait of Jane: A Life of Lady Franklin*. London: Hodder and Stoughton, 1951.

Worcester, Donald E. *The Apaches: Eagles of the Southwest*. Norman: University of Oklahoma Press, 1979.

Wright, Allen A. *Prelude to Bonanza: The Discovery and Exploration of the Yukon*. Sidney, B.C.: Gray's Publishing Company, 1976.

Wright, John Kirkland. *Geography in the Making: The American Geographical Society 1851-1951*. New York: American Geographical Society, 1952.

Wust, Klaus G. *Zion in Baltimore 1755-1955: The Bicentennial History of the Earliest German-American Church in Baltimore, Maryland*. Baltimore: The Zion Church of the City of Baltimore, 1955.

Wyndham, Felice. "The Semiotics of Powerful Places: Rock Art and Landscape Relations in the Sierra Tarahumara, Mexico." *Journal of Anthropological Research* 67, no. 3 (Fall 2011): 387-420.

Zampini, Jay M. and Henry H. Sherk. "Lewis Sayre. The First Professor of Orthopaedic Surgery in America." *Clinical Orthopaedics and Related Research*

466, no. 9 (Sept. 2008): 2263–67.

Zaslow, Morris. *The Opening of the Canadian North, 1870-1914*. Toronto and Montreal: McClelland and Stewart, 1971.

Special Reports

Barnwell, Allison. *Summiting in the Last Wilderness: A Cultural and Environmental History of Mountaineering in Alaska*. CMC Senior Theses. Paper 858. http://scholarship.claremont.edu/cmc_theses/858 (accessed November 23, 2020).

Best, Tiffany. "Cincinnati's German Community: Mid-1800s to World War 1." Honors College Capstone Experience/Thesis Projects, Paper 173, 2004. https://digitalcommons.wku.edu/stu_hon_theses/173 (accessed July 15, 2019).

Boudreau, Richard, comp. *National Attention: Local Connection; La Crosse's Contributions to the Arts and Entertainments in America*. La Crosse, Wis.: UW-La Crosse, 2013. https://www.lacrossehistory.org/collections/literature (accessed July 3, 2020).

Buske, Frank E. "The Wilderness, the Frontier and the Literature of Alaska to 1914: John Muir, Jack London and Rex Beach." PhD diss., University of California, Davis, 1976.

Capps, Stephen R. *An Ancient Volcanic Eruption in the Upper Yukon Basin*. U.S. Geological Survey. Professional Paper 95-D. Washington D.C.: Dept. of the Interior, 1917.

Caswell, J.E. *The Utilization of Scientific Reports of United States Arctic Expeditions 1850-1909*. Technical Report II. Stanford: Stanford University, 1951.

Dredge, L.A. and I. McMartin. "Glacial Lakes in the Wager Bay Area, Kivallik, Nunavut." Current Research 2005-B1. Ottawa: Geological Survey of Canada, January 2005.

Foley, Robert C. *Field Surveying and Topographic Mapping in Alaska: 1947-83*. U.S. Geological Survey Circular 991. Washington, D.C.: Dept. of the Interior, 1987.

Hakonson, Alexander Leif. *Most Distant Fastnesses: The Photography of the 1887 Yukon Expedition*. Thesis, Ryerson University, 2016.

Phillips, David. "The End of Casas Grandes." Paper presented at the 73rd annual meeting of the Society of American Archaeology, Vancouver, BC, March 27, 2008.

Weart, Jeffrey M. *USMA: Seedbed for American Military Thought 1865-1881*. HI 600 Research Project. 7 December 1988.

ILLUSTRATION CREDITS

Front cover. Portrait of Frederick Schwatka. Courtesy of Bibliothéque nationale de France.
Rear cover. "Franklin Arctic Search Party in Winter Quarters Hudson Bay. 1878-79," by Heinrich Klutschak. Oil on board. Mystic Seaport Library and Museum.
Page 4: Frederick G. Schwatka, Sr. and Amelia Hukill Schwatka. Author's collection.
Page 25: Frederick G. Schwatka. USMA Archives and Special Collections.
Page 36: The Post at North Platte Station. Union Pacific Railroad Museum.
Page 72. "The Charge of the Sun-Pole." Frederic Remington, 1890, oil on board. Museum purchase. National Cowboy & Western Heritage Museum. 1979-07.
Page 82. "Lt. Schwatka's Charge at Slim Buttes." Library of Congress.
Page 85. Buckskin lodge and guidon of Seventh Cavalry. Denver Public Library, Special Collections.
Page 86. Officers of the Third Cavalry. Denver Public Library, Special Collections.
Page 106. Portrait of Sir John Franklin, by Louis Haghe. Rex Nan Kivell Collection. National Library of Australia.
Page 117. Ebierbing and Tooktoolito. Hall, *Narrative of the Second Arctic Expedition*.
Page 133. Second Lieutenant Frederick G. Schwatka, April 1878. Paul L. Hedren.
Page 143. William H. Gilder. Courtesy Lilly Library, Indiana University, Bloomington, Indiana.
Page 145. Heinrick Klutschak and Frank Melms. The Explorer's Club.
Page 150. Camp Daly from Observatory Point. American Geographical Society of New York.
Page 159. Whaleships at Marble Island. Library and Archives Canada, Acc. No. 1993-447-9.
Page 182. "The Last Franklin Search," by Abert Operti. American Geographical Society of New York.
Page 254. Ada Josephine Brackett and Lieutenant Frederick Schwatka. Author's collection.
Page 265. "In the Chilkoot Pass," drawing by Charles Gloster. Rock Island County Historical Society.

Illustration Credits

Page 267. "Prying the Raft off a Bar," drawing by Charles Gloster. Alaska State Museum: 2006-6-4.

Page 276. "Near Entrance to Klondyke on the Yukon River," drawing by Charles Gloster. Rock Island County Historical Society.

Page 298. Portrait of Frederick Schwatka. Courtesy of Bibliothéque nationale de France.

Page 307. Members of the *Times*'s expedition. Richard Alan Wood Collection.

Page 309. Chief Yen-at-set'l. Libbey Slide Collection, Clark University Archives and Special Collections.

Page 312. "Mt. Elias (20,000 ft.) from Yakutat." Alaska State Library, Heywood W. Seton-Karr Sketchbook, 1886, 1887, ASL-MS201-054.

Page 328. The Schwatka expedition passes Obsidian Cliff. Photograph by F. J. Haynes. Montana Historical Society Research Center.

Page 330. Members of the expedition outside Norris Hotel. Photograph by F. J. Haynes. Montana Historical Society Research Center.

Page 332. Henry Bosse at the Norris Geyser Basin. Photograph by F. J. Haynes. Montana Historical Society Research Center.

Page 333. Lower Falls of the Grand Canyon of the Yellowstone. Photograph by F. J. Haynes. Montana Historical Society Research Center.

Page 348. "Children of the Cave and Cliff Dwellers," by Sandor L. Landeau. Author's collection.

Page 352. "A Halt in the Mesa." La Crosse Public Library.

Page 374. The *New York Ledger* expedition. Photograph by C. Willard Hayes. Department of the Interior, U.S. Geological Survey.

Page 376. Packers on the Taku Trail. Photograph by C. Willard Hayes. Department of the Interior, U.S. Geological Survey.

Page 379. First Nations Families at Fort Selkirk. Photograph by C. Willard Hayes. Department of the Interior, U.S. Geological Survey.

Page 400. Ada Schwatka. Author's collection.

INDEX

"A Halt in the Mesa" (Landau), 352
A. J. Ross (whaleship), 157, 159
Abbie Bradford (whaleship), 157-59
Abbott Lawrence (whaleship), 159
Abercrombie, William, 290, 297, 368
Abernathy, Thomas, 108-09
Adelaide Peninsula, 112, 122, 171, 173, 175-78, 182-83, 187, 195-98, 200, 221, 227, 421nn12-13, 422n15, 426n16, 429n25
Agassiz Glacier, 313
Aglooka, 120
Agriculturalist and Plowman, 15, 21
Ahdlekok, 178
Ahgekshewah, 176, 178-80, 182-83, 423n24, 424n30
Ahlangnyuck, 183-84, 195
Ahmow, 155, 207
Ahtna, 384
Aivilingmiut, 122, 126-27, 149-50, 155-56, 158, 161-63, 168, 198, 206, 232, 234-35, 237, 239
Akkolear (station), 209
Alaganik, Alaska, 385
Alaska and its Resources (Dall), 282, 287, 436n28
Alaska and the Klondike Gold Fields (Harris), 401
Alaska Commercial Company, 278-79
Albany Medical College, 46
Albany, Oregon, 13
Alert (British ship), 132
Aleutian Islands, 18, 286, 293-94
Alexander II, Emperor of Russia, 37
Alexandre Brothers Company, 211-12
Alexis, Grand Duke, 37
Allen, Henry T., 368, 384-85
Along Alaska's Great River (FGS, Jr.), 269, 282-84, 286-88, 288, 300
Alpine Club of London, 305
Alpine Journal, 318
Alsek River, 369

America, A Journal of the Americas (FGS, Jr.), 353-54
America (merchant ship), 8
America's Expedition, 343
American bison, extermination of, 11, 38
American Civil War, 14, 22-23, 26, 28-29, 33, 46, 49, 51, 67-68, 84, 142, 166, 245, 247, 250, 253, 258, 338
American Geographical Society, 100, 121, 125-28, 135, 137-40, 181, 184, 212, 217-19, 223-24, 229, 243, 285, 298-99, 319, 394-95, 398
American Revolutionary War, 23, 26
"Among the Apaches" (FGS, Jr.), 32, 92-93, 292
"Among the Natives of the North," 95, 234-36
Amundsen, Roald, 386
"An Elk Hunt on the Plains" (FGS, Jr.), 337
Ananguaq, Jean-Marie, 242, 431n25
Anderson, Butler P., 8
Anderson, James, 113, 421n14
Anguttitauruq, Thomas, 222
Ann Houghton (whaleship), 124-25, 153
Anson Mills Building, 33
Anvic, Alaska, 279
Apache Indians, 32, 51, 92-94, 291-92, 335, 341, 346
Arctic Explorations (Kane), 152
Arctic Fever, 116, 130-31
Arctic Highlanders (Polar Eskimos or Inughuit), 104
Army and Navy Journal, 89
Arroyo de las Iglesias (Cañon of Churches), 350
Arthur, Chester A., 255, 324
Assistance (British ship), 214
Astor, John Jacob, 5, 7, 135
Astoria, or Anecdotes of an Enterprise beyond the Rocky Mountains (Irving), 7
Astoria, Oregon, 7-8, 13
Atchison, Topeka and Santa Fe Railway, 342

Athabaskans, 262, 271, 274, 276, 279, 378, 381, 384
Atlin Lake, 265
Atna River, 370
Awanak (brother of Ikqueesik), 164, 187, 195
Ayers, Lorenzo, 52, 409n7
Back River, 109, 112-15, 149, 161-62, 170-74, 181, 199, 201-05, 221-22, 229, 236, 239-40, 414n4, 421nn13-14
Back, George, 107, 109, 173, 233, 253
  expedition of 1833-1835, 109, 173, 229
Badger, 40
Baffin Island, 101-02, 116
Baffin, William, 102, 104
Baird Glacier, 262, 283
Baird, Spencer Fullerton, 145
Baker Lake, 221-22
Baker, Captain Michael, 208-09
Baltimore, Maryland, 1-5, 24
Bandelier, Adolph F. A., 361-62, 364, 444n48
Banks, Sir Joseph, 104
Barnard, John, 279, 435n12
Barnum, P. T., 357-58
Baronette, C. J., 324, 330
Barren Lands (barrens), 107, 161, 197, 203, 219, 221, 228-29, 379
Barrow Strait, 111
Barrow, Sir John, 103-05, 109-10
Barry, Thomas
  Inuit cairn testimony, 121-30, 137-38, 144-45, 149-50, 157-60, 414n3, 415n11, 416n13, 419n19
  selected as captain of *Eothen*, 134, 142
  supplies at Depot Island, 151, 207, 211-12, 242, 419n19, 428n3
Batopilas Mining Company, 351
Batopilas, Mexico, 351, 355, 363, 398
Bayard, Thomas F., 272
Beaver Creek, 44, 99
Becerra, Don Augustin, 345, 348-49
Becerra, Don Jose Maria, 349
Bedford (British warship), 106
Beechey Island, 111, 115
Beechey, Frederick William, 107
Beehive Geyser, Yellowstone, 331
Belknap, William W., 29
Belle Island, 276-77
Bellerophon (British warship), 106
Bellevue Hospital Medical College, 46-50, 245
Benicia Barracks (Cal.), 31
Benitez, Mauro Candano, 360
Bennett, James Gordon, Jr., 54, 68, 137-38, 140, 142, 183, 214, 243, 266, 302, 354, 397, 428n11

Bennett, James Gordon, Sr., 137
Bering Glacier, 319
Bering Sea, 104, 259
Bering Strait, 17, 107, 111, 279
Bering, Dane Vitus, 17-18, 134, 301, 303, 307
Berry, Robert, 243
Bessels, Emil, 131, 233
Big Horn and Yellowstone Expedition, 53, 68, 76, 89-90, 93, 291, 322
Big Horn Mountains, 57, 67-69
Big Springs, Nebraska, 99
Big Wolf (FGS, Jr. Sioux name), 94, 399
Bismarck, North Dakota, 42, 53
Black Hills, 41-42, 44-46, 50, 53, 69, 74, 78, 82, 96, 273, 365
  Bandits, 99
  Expedition of 1874 (Custer), 42
Blakely, James A., 324
Blue Water Creek, battle of, 45
Board of Geographic Names, 282
Boas, Franz, 234, 435n18
Bohemia (newspaper), 144
Bonanza Creek, 263
Bonaparte, Napoleon, 103
Bonner, Robert, 369
Booth Point, 179
Booth, Felix, 108-09
Boothia Peninsula, 108-09, 112, 114, 116, 118-19, 141, 172, 219
Bosse, Henry P., 323, 329, 331, 335
Boundary Butte (Eagle Bluff), 277
Bourke, John Gregory, 45, 51, 53, 55, 62, 64, 67, 86, 91-93
Bowker, Frank, 379, 380, 382, 384
Boyce, William D., 357, 360-61, 398
Bozeman Trail, 50, 52
Bozeman, Montana, 53
Brackett, Ada Josephine. *See* Ada Brackett Schwatka
Brackett, Albert Gallatin, 247, 253, 296
Brackett, James, 253
Brackett, Joseph, 247, 253, 295, 297, 324, 331, 334, 365, 367, 393
Brackett, William (nephew of FGS, Jr.), 18, 21, 93-94, 131, 404n1
Bradstreet's: A Journal of Trade, Finance and Public Economy, 300
Bremen Geographical Society, 265
Bridger, Jim, 322
British Arctic Expedition of 1875-76, 132, 228-29
Broke, George, 318
Brooklyn Times Union, 292

Index 475

Bruce, Tuinnaq Kanayuk, 240-42, 431n20
Brulé Sioux Indians, 44, 71, 79, 97, 99, 399
Bubb, John W., 76, 78-80, 88
Buchan, David, 104, 106
Buel, Clarence, 322, 335-36, 349, 353
Buffalo Bill's Wild West Show, 340, 342
Buffalo Snow Shoe Club, 324
Bureau of Ethnology, 92
Bureau of Indian Affairs, 292
Burlington, Iowa, 5, 7
Bush, Asahel, 21
Caetani, Onorato, 313
cairn (possible site of the Franklin records), 123-25, 128-30, 135, 139, 141, 144, 150, 157-58, 175, 178, 222-23, 419n18, 421n14
Calamity Jane. *See* Canary, Martha Jane
California Academy of Sciences, 247
Camp Daly, 151-57, 161-64, 187, 197-98, 201-03, 206-08, 219, 221-22, 228-29, 239-42
Camp Robinson (later Fort Robinson), 44-45, 91, 98, 413n47
Camp Sheridan (Neb.), 44-46, 91, 95, 98-99, 131
Camp Sheridan (Yellowstone), 327-28
Campbell, Robert, 271, 274
Canadian Geological Survey, 221, 281
Canadian Pacific Railway, 380, 388
Canary, Martha Jane, 66
cannibalism, stories of, 107, 112-14, 118-19, 126, 182-83, 200, 214-18, 226-27, 232, 241-42, 299, 302, 397, 429n13
Canyon Hotel, Yellowstone, 331-32
Cape Crozier, 115, 194-95, 426n14
Cape Englefield, 118, 123, 125, 127-28, 141, 149-50, 161, 415n11, 416n13
Cape Felix, 108, 114, 187, 190-92, 218-19, 425nn4-5
Cape Fullerton, 124, 157, 221, 240, 419n19
Cape Geddes, 178
Cape Herschel, 114-15, 187-88
Cape Victoria, 114
Cape Walker, 111
Cape York, 104
Carichic, Mexico, 345, 356, 363
Carrillo, Lauro, 355
Carver, William Frank, "Doc," 38-39
Casas Grande River, 343
Cassell & Co., 286, 300
Castina Lake, 313, 316
Castle Geyser, Yellowstone, 331
Castor and Pollux River, 109, 112
cave-dwellers, 349, 354-55, 361-64, 388, 400
Cavell, Janice, 214

Central Eskimo, The (Boas), 234
Century Magazine, 32, 71, 74-75, 92-95, 142, 286, 292, 300, 319, 322-23, 335-37, 349, 353, 369, 386, 388, 410n44, 413n44, 438n28, 440n55
Cerro Colorado Mine, 349
Chadron Creek, 71
Chaix Hills, 313
Chambers, Alexander, 53
Chantrey Inlet, 222
Charley's Village, 277
Chase, George F., 78
Chautauqua Circuit, 338
Chautauqua Lake, New York, 338
Chautauqua, Piedmont, 338
Chesterfield Inlet, 161, 169, 203, 207, 229
Cheyenne Indians, 52, 56, 59, 62-65, 76, 79, 251
Cheyenne, Wyoming, 42, 50
Chicago Herald, 354, 356, 358, 365, 398
Chicago Inter-Ocean, 67-74, 77, 81, 87-88, 95, 338, 341-42, 345, 351-55, 396, 398, 400, 447n20
Chicago Times, 54
Chicago Tribune, 68, 334
Chicago, Illinois, 337, 340-41, 351, 354-56, 358-60, 363-65, 388
Chihuahua, Mexico, 343, 345, 351, 355-56, 360, 363
Children of the Cold (FGS, Jr.), 237-38, 300
Chilkat Inlet, 260-61, 278
Chilkoot Inlet, 261-63, 272, 285, 372
Chilkoot Pass, 259, 261-64, 275, 281-82, 371-72, 377, 435n16
Chilkoot Trail, 261-65, 273, 281, 372-73, 433nn14, 20
Chiricahua Apache Indians, 292
Chitina River, 383-84, 386
Churchill-Bona massif, 271
Cincinnati, Ohio, 3-5, 116, 342, 359, 407n25
Cinnabar, Montana, 323-24, 332
City of Rome (ocean liner), 295
City of Topeka (steam ship), 371
Clark, William (explorer), 6, 17
Clark, William P. (soldier), 92
Clatsop Indians, 9-10
Clemens, Samuel, "Mark Twain," 21, 367
Cleveland, Grover, 392
cliff-dwellers, 348-50, 352-56, 361, 363-64, 398, 400
Cody, William F., "Buffalo Bill," 36-39, 41-42, 340-42, 354, 392
Coho, J. W., 324, 330
Coleman, Patrick, 118
Collinson Inlet, 187-89

Index

Collinson, Richard, 129, 279, 435n12
Colonia Diáz, 343
Colonia Juarez, 343
Columbia River, 6-10, 12-13, 250
Cone-Hill River (Fortymile River), 276
Congress of Anthropology (1893), 362
Connery River, 161-62, 169, 221
Cook, Frederick, 107, 398-99
Cook, James, 301
Cope, Edward Drinker, 39
Copper River, 290, 368, 370-71, 378-79, 383-84, 401
Coppermine River, 103, 105-07, 109
Cornwallis Island, 115
Corps of Discovery, 13
Corralitos Company, 344
Cosmopolitan (magazine), 338, 445n2
Cottage Hotel, 334
Cracroft, Sophia, 129-30, 160, 243, 419n20
Crawford, Emmet, 76, 78-79, 81, 87-88, 93, 412n28
Crawford, Jack, 76, 82, 87
Crazy Horse (chief), 61, 64, 66, 79, 83-84, 98
  death of, 99, 413n47
Croker Mountains, 104-05, 108
Crook, George, 32, 45, 51-59, 62-69, 74, 76-79, 82-86, 88, 90, 92-93, 98 133-34, 165, 246, 250, 291-92, 406n24
Crosby, Alpheus B., 48
Crow Indians, 53, 57-59, 63, 65, 69, 326, 336
Crown Prince Frederik Island, 127
Crozier, Francis, 110, 120, 189, 192, 395
Crozier's Camp, 189
Cruikshank, Julie, 381
Cumberland Sound, 144, 149, 391, 421n10
Curley, Buffalo, 39
Cusihuiriachi, Mexico, 345, 347
Custer, George A., 37, 42, 53, 55, 62, 64, 66-67, 76, 79, 81, 84, 87, 94, 98, 138, 273
D'Abbadie River, 273-74
D'Abbadie, M. Antoine, 273
Dall, William, 282-83, 287, 300, 436n28
Dalles, The, Oregon, 12-13, 15
Dalton Trail, 306, 446n25
Dalton, John, "Jack," 306, 311, 317, 385, 440n53, 446n25
Daly, Maria, 126, 135, 415n9
Daly, Charles Patrick, 125-28, 130, 134-40, 146, 148, 151, 160, 168, 184, 213, 218, 243-44, 395, 415n11, 416n27, 419nn18-19
Dangerous Rapids, 199-202
Danzig (Gdańsk) Poland, 1
Dart, Anson, 10

Davenport, Reuben Briggs, 54, 74, 78-81, 88-89, 100
Davis Strait, 144
Davis, Britton, 93, 344
Davis, John, 101, 116
Dawson City, Yukon, Canada 264, 270, 275, 446n25
Dawson, George M., 281-82
De Long, Emma, 248
De Long, George W., 223
Dead Cañon (aka Rosebud Narrows), 58, 62, 64, 69, 77
Deadwood, 69, 77, 85-87, 90, 275
Dease, Peter Warren, 109, 112, 185, 187, 198
Death-Blow to Spiritualism (Davenport), 89
Deer River, 275
Deming, New Mexico, 341-43, 345, 351
Denali (Mt. McKinley), 398
Department of the Arizona, 32
Department of the Columbia, 250-51
Department of the Platte, 34, 50-51
Depot Island, 122, 149-50, 155-58, 164, 168, 206-09, 211, 419n19, 422n19
di Savoia, Luigi Amedeo, 318
Diáz, Porfirio, 341, 344
Dickens, Charles, 113, 126
Dickinson, Billy, 264, 269, 273, 434n28
Dictionary of American Biography (1935), 396
Discovery (British ship), 132
Doane, Gustavus C., 136
Dobbs, Arthur, 102
Dodge, Richard Irving, 45
Dolph, Joseph, 296
Donation Land Claim Act (1850), 7, 9, 13
Donjek River, 381
Donner Party (1846/1847), 11
Dorothea (British ship), 104
Douglas Bay, 197
Douglas, Alaska, 372
Down the Yukon on a Raft (FGS, Jr.), 285
Drum, Richard C., 212, 243, 246-47, 249-50, 255, 295-96
Dundy, Elmer Scipio, 36, 38, 42, 406n24
Duvall, Mike, 385
Eagle, Alaska, 277
Ebierbing (Ipiirvik), 127-28, 138-39, 141-42, 149, 155-56, 160, 164, 167-68, 178, 187, 195-96, 199-200, 415nn9, 11, 422nn17-18, 423n24
  interpreter on Schwatka expedition, 164, 173, 175
  interviews Thomas Barry, 126
  later years and death, 209

Index

leads detached group to Adelaide Peninsula from KWI, 187, 195-96
marries Nipschark (daughter of Ishoowark), 156
serves with Hall, 116-17
saves *Polaris* crew, 126, 131
Educational Publishing Company, 400
Eeglee-leock, 207
Eelanak, 222
Egede, Hans, 235
El Dorado, 6-7, 42, 53, 341, 380, 401
El Paso, Texas, 33, 345, 356, 360
Elizabeth I, Queen of England, 101
Ellesmere Island, 280
Elliott, Henry Wood, 287
Emmons, George Thornton, 309-10, 438n38
Enterprise (British ship), 279
Eothen (whaleship), 140-42, 145-49, 151, 159, 207, 211, 419n19, 428n3
Epstean's New Dime Museum, 359
Erebus Bay, 178, 188, 193, 195, 423n26
Erebus (British ship), 110, 113, 120, 172, 174, 199, 215, 223, 225, 239, 414n4, 423n22
Etah, North Greenland, 220
Eyak, Alaska, 385
Fairholme, James Walter, 215
Fairholme, Lady Elizabeth Marjory, 215
False Copper Creek, 381
Far West (steam ship), 77
Fargo, North Dakota, 304
Fee, Charles S., 323, 335
Feigenspan & Co. (brewery), 140
Felix Harbor, 108-09
Fetterman, William, 54
Fifth Cavalry, 76, 85, 89
Fifth Thule Expedition, 242, 421n12
Fillmore, Millard, 10
Finerty, John, 53-62, 65-67, 74, 77-78, 83-84, 87, 90, 410n47
Firehole Hotel, Yellowstone, 330
First International Polar Year, 280
First Cavalry, 257, 327
First Sioux War, 45
Fisher, Elnathan B., 157
Fitzjames, James, 111, 192
Five Finger Rapids, 270, 378, 434n30
Fletcher (tug boat), 146
Fletcher, Alice Cunningham, 75
Flinders, Matthew, 105
Flint, Austin, Sr., 48, 49
Florence (ship), 391
Forbes & Breedan Furniture Co., 393
Forest and Stream (magazine), 284, 300, 336, 399

Fort Abraham Lincoln, 53
Fort Baker, 401
Fort Bliss, 356
Fort Bridger, 12
Fort Clatsop, 13, 17
Fort Conger, 243
Fort D. A. Russell, 50, 65, 246-47, 253
Fort Ellis, 53
Fort Fetterman, 52-55
Fort Grant, 294
Fort Laramie, 12
Fort Laramie Treaty of 1851, 12
Fort Laramie Treaty of 1868, 44, 50
Fort Leavenworth, 45
Fort Mason, 401
Fort McDowell, 31-32, 406n19
Fort McPherson, 33-34, 36-37, 39-40, 406nn19, 24
Fort Reliance (Great Slave Lake), 229
Fort Reliance (Yukon), 275-76
Fort Reno, 52, 54
Fort Robinson. *See* Camp Robinson
Fort Selkirk, 259, 263, 270-75, 282-85, 306, 371, 378, 380-81, 386
Fort Stevens, 8, 10
Fort Stevens State Park, 8
Fort Sumter, 14
Fort Thomas, 291-92, 294-96
Fort Yukon, 259, 277
Fortymile River, 276-77, 377-79
Fosdick, Gilbert C., II, 96-97
Foster, E. H., 55, 68
Fox (ship), 114, 116, 132, 212, 391
Fox, Maggie, 89
Foxe, Luke, 102
Frank Leslie's Illustrated Newspaper, 369, 398
Frank Leslie's Sunday Magazine, 243
Franklin expedition (1845), 34, 110-21, 124-28, 132, 135, 157-58, 171-202, 212-31, 240-42, 278-79, 299, 395, 414-15nn4, 6, 11, 417n2, 422nn15, 20, 424nn30, 32, 425nn4, 5, 8, 429n25
Franklin Point, 188
Franklin Record Book, 129
Franklin, Eleanor (nee Porden), 107
Franklin, Lady Jane (nee Griffin), 107-08, 110, 113, 125, 129, 213-15, 217, 428n1
Franklin, Sir John, 66, 105-21, 123-30, 135-37, 141, 157-58, 161, 171-84, 188-98, 200-202, 212-18, 222-27, 231-33, 240-43, 247, 266, 278-79, 299, 391, 394-95, 415nn6, 11, 419n20
   birth and early years, 105-06

commands last expedition (1845), 110
death on last expedition, 115
first and second land expeditions, 106-07
Frederick (Kersunk), 306, 314
Frederika Glacier, 382
Freshfield, Douglas, 319
Frobisher, Martin, 101, 116
Funston, Frederick, 401
Fury and Hecla Strait, 123
Fury Beach, 109
G. Krug & Son Ironworks, 2, 403n3
G.W. Blunt Library. *See* Mystic Seaport Museum
Galena, Illinois, 5-7, 11
Gardiner, J. Burrows, 46
Garfield, James, 211
Garrison, W. P., 361
Gatch, Thomas M., 20, 22
Generc River, 381
Geographical Society of Paris, 291
George and Mary (whaleship), 208-10
George IV, King of England, 189
George, Melvin, 254
Geronimo, 251, 291, 342
 surrender of, 291
Giantess Geyser, 331
Gibbon, John, 53
Gibbs, Addison C., 22
Gilder, Jeanette Leonard, 142
Gilder, Richard Watson, 95, 142, 286
Gilder, William Henry, 95, 148, 154-56, 164-65, 167, 171-72, 187, 189, 192, 194-96, 199-200, 203-04, 207-12, 218, 224, 229, 231-34, 239, 242-43, 286, 395, 419nn18-19, 420n1, 421n12, 422n17, 425nn4-5, 11, 426n22, 427n24, 445n2
 birth and early years, 142-43
 cannibalism reports in *New York Herald*, 183, 214-15
 interview of Ahlangnyuck, 183-84
 interview of Puhtoorak, 173-74, 422n15
 interviews of Seotitechung, Tuktoocheeah, Ahgekshewah, 175-83, 423n26, 424nn29-30, 34
 later years and death, 243-44
 efforts to verify Barry's story, 157-62
 publishes *Schwatka's Search, Sledging in the Arctic in Quest of the Franklin Records,* 232, 239, 431n10
Gjoa Haven, 241
Glacier (whaleship), 122-25, 144-45, 159-60, 414n3
Glacier Bay, 287, 372
Gladman Point, 197

Glave, Edward James, 369, 385-86
Globus LXIII Band (Lumholtz), 398
Gloster, Charles A., 257, 283
Good Company, 148, 230, 246, 417n2
Good Voice ("Ho Wash-Tay"), 97-98, 413n47
Good Will, 94
Goose Creek, 57, 66, 69
Gordon, David, 273
Gould, Jay, 321
Grady, Henry, 338
Graham Gore Peninsula, 194-95
Grand Geyser, 331
Grand Barranca of the Urique, 350
Grand Canyon of the Yellowstone, 326, 331
Grand Opera House (Peoria, Illinois), 256
Grande Ronde Valley, 12
Grant Point, 173, 199, 221, 227, 422nn15, 20
Grant, Frederick Dent, 27, 30, 92
Grant, Ulysses S., 27, 29, 51, 250, 409n8
Gray, Adoniram Judson, 46
Gray, Robert, 8
Great Bear Lake, 221
Great Britain (British ship), 196
Great Northern Expedition (Velikaya Severnaya Ekspeditsiya), 17-18, 301
Great River of Alaska, The (FGS, Jr.), 286, 300
Great Sioux Reservation, 50-51
Great Sioux War, 45, 50, 52, 78, 95, 98-99
Great Slave Lake, 109, 229
Greely, Adolphus W., 223, 243, 280, 299, 302
Greenland, 102, 104, 111, 114, 137, 167, 220, 235, 304
Gregory, John, 194, 225
Griffin, Jane. *See* Franklin, Lady Jane
Grinnell, Henry, 116, 125, 213
Grouard, Frank, 78-79
Grover, La Fayette, 254
Gulf of Boothia, 123, 135
Guyot Glacier, 311, 313, 319
Guyot, Arnold Henry, 303
Haddington, Lord Thomas, 110
Haines Mission, 262, 264, 269
Hall, Charles Francis, 116-21, 124-31, 139, 141, 152, 154, 156-58, 161, 167, 174, 176-79, 192-93, 197, 213, 217-19, 222-23, 227, 232-34, 416n13, 420n22, 426n16
Han Indians, 262, 275-77, 283
Hanbury, David T., 221
Hancock, Winfield Scott, 245
Handsmeller, 40
Hanscom, William, 255
Hardenburg, Mr., 97
Harper, Arthur, 284

Index 479

Harper's Young People, 338
Harper's Magazine, 233, 246
Hartsuff, Albert, 64-65
Hawley, Joseph Roswell, 286
Hayes River, 170-71, 174, 221-22
Hayes, Charles Willard, 370-87
Hayes, Isaac Israel, 125, 152, 203, 220, 231, 297
Hayes, Rutherford B., 82, 99, 135-37, 170, 407n37
Haynes, Frank Jay, 323, 326, 329-36, 441nn11, 22
Hazard Hills, 162, 169, 221
Hearne, Samuel, 103
Helena Independent, 333-34
Henderson, George Legg, 333-34
Henderson, James H. D., 22
Hendrik, Hans, 131, 415n9
Henry, Guy V., 58, 65
Hickok, James Butler, "Wild Bill," 40, 90
Higginson, Ella Rhoades, 288
Hill, J. J., 391
"Ho Wash-Tay" (FGS, Jr.), 98. *See also* Good Voice
Hobson, William, 114-16, 119, 191-92, 213
Hofer, Thomas Elwood, 336-37
Holmes, Sherlock, 96
Homan, Charles A., 257-58, 265, 272, 274, 278, 280-81, 283, 370
Hood, Robert, 107
Hooper, William Hulme, 235
Hopkins, George, 43, 399
Hotalingua River, 378
"How a Great Sioux Chief was Named" (FGS, Jr.), 94
Howgate, Henry, 136, 391
Hudson Bay, 102-03, 105, 112, 117, 122, 124, 126, 140, 147, 149, 157, 160-61, 169, 177, 201, 204, 206, 208-09, 211, 221-22, 263, 279, 372, 377, 421n10
Hudson River, 23
Hudson Strait, 102, 149, 209
Hudson, Henry, 102
Hudson's Bay Company, 9, 102-03, 109, 111-13, 149, 185, 221-22, 259, 271, 277, 282, 419n19, 421n14, 428n3
Hüller, Luis, 341-43, 345
Hyde, John, 304
Icy Bay, 309-10, 312, 316-17, 319
Icy Cape, 107
Igeark-too-aloo (Inuit name for FGS, Jr.), 156
Ik-kin-nil-lik Puh-too-rak. *See* Puhtoorak
Ikqueesik, 156-57, 164, 167, 171, 175, 195, 205-06, 240
Illustrated London News, 233

In the Land of the Cave and Cliff Dwellers (FGS, Jr.), 400
In the Land of the Midnight Sun (FGS, Jr.), 148, 158, 160, 180, 217, 230-31, 246, 417n2, 419n18, 424n32
Independent Order of Odd Fellows (I.O.O.F.), 4-5, 14
Indian Creek, 328
Indianne, 264, 273, 434n28
Inglefield, Edward, 128, 217, 416n13
Innookpoozhejook, 112, 119
Inside Passage of Alaska, 260, 288, 305, 372
Inughuit (Polar Eskimos), 104, 220
Inuinnait, 175, 421n12, 422n17
Inuit testimony as to the Franklin expedition, 112-14, 117-20, 123-31, 157-60, 168, 171-84, 195, 199-201, 213-18, 222-23, 226-27, 232, 239-43, 299, 397, 415n11, 416n13, 417n2, 419n18, 420n22, 421n14, 422nn15, 20, 423nn25-26, 424nn29-30, 32, 34. *See also* Ahgekshewah, Ahlangnyuck, Seotitecheung, Tuktoocheeah, Tuinnaq Kanayuk Bruce, Ujaralaaq
Inuktitut (language), 112, 123, 127, 144, 152, 159, 279
Investigator (British ship), 105, 423n22
Iqungajuq, 222
Iron Plume, 79, 83-84
Irving Bay, 190, 192-93
Irving, Alexander, 215
Irving, John, 189-90, 192, 215, 223, 226-27, 241, 243, 395
Irving, Washington, 7
Isabella (Ross ship), 109
Isabella (whaleship), 144, 159
Isedlak, 206
Ishoowark, 156, 164, 167-68, 178
Iyawkawauk, 164
Jackson (medicine man), 381
Jackson, Sheldon, 287
Janeway, Edward, 245
Jeannette (US ship), 218, 243, 247, 280, 302, 430n10
Johnnie Bull, 209
Johnson, John B., 66
Jones River, "Yas´ei Héen," Yahtse River, 312-13, 316-17, 320, 368, 373, 385, 397, 439n42
Jones Sound, 102, 104
Jones, George, 302, 312, 316
Jones, William Gore, 125, 130
Joseph (chief), 99, 138, 251-52
Joseph, Franz, Emperor of Austria, 233
Juneau, Alaska, 288, 371-73, 376-77, 401

Index

Kabloona (Oallunaat), 119, 175, 195
Kah-eé, "John," 373
Kalaallisut (Greenlandic), 114
Kamiakin (chief), 17
Kane, Elisha Kent, 89, 116, 125, 152, 213, 220, 231, 369
Karleko, 164, 420n1
Kayak Island, Alaska, 18
Kearney and Black Hills Stage, 96
Kearney, Nebraska, 96-97
Keeley Gold Cure, 389-90
Keeley Institute, 389, 393
Keeley, Leslie, 389
Kennecott Mines, 387
Kennicott Glacier, 387
Keogh, Myles W., 85
Kernuk, 317-18, 440n53
Ker-Sunk (Kersunk). *See* Frederick
Key, Francis Scott, 2
King Folding Boat Company, 375
King William (infant), 118
King William Island (King Wiliam Land), 108-09, 111-23, 127, 132, 141, 149-50, 156, 158, 161-64, 171-72, 176-79, 182-98, 200, 212, 215, 219, 227, 240, 396, 421n12, 426n18, 429n25
King, Albert Freeman Africanus, 255
King, Charles W., 89, 100
Kivalliq (Keewatin) barrens, 161, 219, 221, 418n12
Klat-ol-kin (Johnny's Village), 276-77
Kletsan Creek, 381, 387
Klondike Gold Rush, 263-65, 269, 275-76, 281, 300, 306, 375, 377, 400
Klondike River, 263, 275
Kluane Lake, 380, 385, 386
Kluane River, 380-81
Klutlan Glacier, 381
Klutschak, Franz, 144
Klutschak, Heinrich (Henry), 151-55, 157-60, 162, 164, 167-68, 170-71, 187, 193, 201-08, 219, 221, 224, 228, 234, 239, 241, 244, 416n27, 420n1, 421nN12, 14, 422n19, 423n24, 425nn4, 11, 427n24
   adoption of Inuit lifestyle, 151-53, 191
   birth, early years and background, 142, 144-45
   death of, 244
   interview of Puhtoorak, 173-74, 422n15
   interviews of Seotitechung, Tuktoocheeah, Ahgekshewah, 175-83, 423n25, 424nn29-30, 32, 34
   leads detached group from KWI to Adelaide Peninsula and back, 194-97
   leads detached group from KWI to Dangerous Rapids, 199, 201
   locates grave of Irving, 189
   mate on board *Glacier* 1871-73, 144, 160
   mediates reconciliation between Aivilingmiut and Nattilingmiut, 198
   publishes *Als Eskimo unter den Eskimos*, 232-33
Knight, Rev. Plutarch S., 394
Kodiak, Alaska, 316
Kohl and Middleton's Big Dime Museum, 358-59
Kollmar Creek, 63-64
Kook-sáh'k, "Robert," 373
Kool-teén, "Paddy," 373
Koomawnah, 164
Koo-nagh-ka-sáh, "Jim," 373
Koyukuk River, 368
Krause, Arthur, 265
Krause, Aurel, 265
Kress, Mortimer Newton, "Wild Bill," 40
Krusenstern (ship), 172
Kuro-Siwo (Kurishio Current), 280, 294
Kutcheenuark, 164, 206, 420n1
L'Aigle (French ship), 106
La Crosse, Wisconsin, 340, 342, 351-52
La Perouse, Jean François de Galaup, 301
Ladue, Joseph, "Jo", 275
Lady Franklin Bay, 136, 280
Lady Franklin Bay Expedition (Greely expedition), 223, 280, 299, 302, 391
Lake Bennett, 261, 433n20
Lake Borgne, battle of, 106
Lake Lebarge, 269
Lake Lindeman, 265, 270-71
Lake Tanganyika, 137
Lancaster Sound, 102, 104-05, 108-09, 111, 114, 415n11
"Land of the Living Cliff-Dwellers" (FGS, Jr.), 354
Land of the Midnight Sun. See In the Land of the Midnight Sun
Landeau, Frances, 352
Landeau, Samuel (Sandor) Leopold, 342-43, 345, 351-52, 362
   death of, 352
Lands of Silence, A History of Arctic and Antarctic Exploration (Markham), 232, 398
Las Palomas, Mexico, 341, 343
laudanum, 392-93
Lauridsen, Peter, 18
Le Vesconte, Henry, 120
Leo (steam ship), 279-80
Leopold II, King of Belgium, 385

Index 481

Lewes River, 270-72, 282, 435n16
Lewis and Clark River, 13
Lewis, Meriwether, 6, 17
Libbey, William, 303, 305, 308-13, 316-19, 362, 438n38, 439n42, 440n53
Lincoln, Robert Todd, 249, 252, 256, 296-97
Little Big Horn, battle of, 64, 67, 81, 87, 98
Little Big Horn River, 64
Livingston, Montana, 322, 324, 332
Livingstone, David, 137, 302
Lloyd, Thomas, 61, 90, 409n21
Logan, John, 296
Lone Elk, 91
Long Arctic Search: The Narrative of Lieutenant Frederick Schwatka, (FGS, Jr.), 148, 230, 417n2
Longfellow, Henry Wadsworth, 4, 369
Lorillard Company, 140
Lorillard River, 162, 169, 221
Loup Fork, 11
Lower Falls of the Yellowstone River, 331
Lumholtz, Carl, 361-64, 398
Lyceum Bureau, Oregon and Washington, 246
Lynn Channel, 261
Lyon Inlet, 122
M'Donald, Alexander, 114
MacGahan, Januarius A., 137, 422n18
Mackenzie River, 107, 109
Mackenzie, Alexander, 103
MacMillan, Thomas C., 67
Mahan, Dennis Hart, 25
Malaspina Glacier, 313, 319
Malaspina, Alejandro, 301
Mammoth Hot Springs, 323-24, 326-27, 331-32, 334-35
Mammoth Hot Springs Hotel, 324, 330, 441n7
Marble Island, 122, 127, 152, 155, 157-59, 162, 207-08, 211, 221, 414n3, 419n19
Markham, Albert Hastings, 128
Markham, Clements R., 214, 226-27, 230, 232, 398
Marsh, Othniel Charles, 39, 266, 303
Martin, Captain (whaleman), 111
Mary-Rousselière, Father Guy, 242, 431n25
Mason City, Iowa, 366-67, 370
Matonabbee, 103
Matty Island, 108, 184
Maudslay, Sons & Field, 194
McCall, Jack, 90
McClintock, Sir Francis Leopold, 113-16, 121, 127-32, 141, 158, 166, 174, 176, 178, 187, 189, 192-93, 198, 212-17, 223, 226-30, 232, 241, 391, 420n6, 422n15, 429n13, 430nn, 4, 7

McClure Newspaper Syndicate, 353, 391
McClure, Samuel S., 391
McDowell, Irvin, 252
McIntosh, J. B., 258, 268, 273-74, 277-80, 434n32
McQuesten, Jack, 275, 284
Meinhold, Charles, 40
Melms, Carl T., 143-44
Melms, Frank, 142-44, 153-54, 164, 167, 187, 189, 195, 201, 207-08, 243-44
  early years and background, 142-44
  death of, 244
  Jeannette relief expedition, 243
Melville Bay, 104, 114
Melville Island, 105
Melville Peninsula, 118, 123-24, 130, 149, 219, 415n11, 416n13, 420n22
Melville, George, 243
Melville, Lord (Henry Dundas, 1st Viscount Melville), 104
Merriam, Edward F., 230
Merriam, George, 230
Merritt, Wesley, 76
Mesa, Senor Luis, 355
Mexican-American War, 23, 27, 247, 250
Midnight Sun. See In the Land of the Midnight Sun
Miles Cañon, 267-270, 283-84
Miles Glacier, 385
Miles, Nelson A., 99, 250-52, 256-58, 259, 267, 272-73, 280, 285-86, 290-91, 368
Milkolilluk (brother of Ikqueesik), 162, 164, 167, 195
Mills, Anson, 30, 32-35, 39-42, 44-45, 52-53, 56-64, 66-68, 76-91, 96, 99, 134, 218, 412n28
Mills, Nannie, 91
Mills, Sebastian Bach, 141
Milwaukee Asylum for the Insane, 244
Minneconjou Indians, 79, 83, 91
Mississippi River, 5, 19, 253, 266, 299, 312, 323, 340
Missouri River, 6, 50, 99, 100, 413n47
Monarch Geyser, Yellowstone, 336
Montreal Island, 112-14, 175, 421n14
Montreal Snow Shoe Club, 324
Morgan, Edwin, 135
Morison & Brown, 125, 135, 147, 160, 211
Morison, John C., 125, 127-30, 134-35, 138-42, 144-47, 160, 189, 215, 244, 415n6
Mount Hood, 256, 391-92, 394
Mount Princeton, 304
Mount Rainier, 391
Mount St. Elias, 301-08, 310-20, 322, 327, 330, 335, 362, 368-69, 371, 379-82, 385, 395,

397, 438n28, 439nn42, 45, 440n52
Mount St. Helens, 256
Mount Tacoma, 391
Mount Washburn, 326, 331
Mount Wrangell, 271, 301, 303, 384
Muir Glacier, 287, 372
Muir, John, 287-89, 372
Mystic Seaport Museum, 147, 176, 230, 417n2, 424n32
Nanook, 207
Nansen, Fridtjof, 220
Nares, George, 132, 148, 212, 266, 415n9
Narrative of the Second Arctic Expedition made by Charles F. Hall (Nourse), 218
Nation (journal), 361, 364
National Academy of Sciences, 244
National Geographic Magazine, 387
National Geographic Society, 318, 369, 371
National Maritime Museum, 223
Nattilingmiut (Nattilik), 117-20, 122-25, 127, 134-35, 138-40, 150, 157-58, 162-63, 171-72, 175-78, 183, 185, 195-99, 201, 222, 232, 234-36, 239-42, 414n3, 415n11, 421nn12, 13, 422n17
Neville, James, 36-37
New Bedford, Massachusetts, 122, 210, 216, 428n3
New London, Connecticut, 122, 144
New York Academy of Music, 49
New York Academy of Sciences, 244
New York Herald, 15, 54, 67-68, 74, 87, 89, 100, 121, 124, 130, 137-39, 141-42, 148, 160, 181, 183, 209-18, 226, 243-44, 302, 354, 415nn6, 11, 419n19, 427n1
New York Ledger, 369, 373, 377, 384-85, 388, 397, 445n2
New York Sun, 316-18, 395, 440n52
New York Times, 145, 232, 252, 284, 288, 297, 301-05, 308, 310-12, 315-22, 368-69, 395-97, 439n32
New York Tribune, 139, 176, 180, 217, 297, 422n20, 424n32
New York World, 321-23, 327, 336, 397
Newark Register, 142
Newberry River, 377
Newton-Jenney Expedition, 74
Nez Perce Indians, 99, 251
Niak'ilaki (Clatsop village), 9
Nichols, Henry Ezra, 306
Nickerson, Azor H., 59, 63
Nicklin, T. L., 392
Nicolai (chief), 384
Nimrod in the North (FGS, Jr.), 300

Nipschark (daughter of Ishoowark), 156, 164
Nisling River, 380
Nizina Glacier, 382
Nizina River, 383-84, 386-87
Noo-klak-ó (Nuclaco), 275
Nordenskiöld, Adolf Erik, 291
Norris Geyser Basin, 329
Norris Hotel, 327, 329-32, 335
North American Review, 338
North Bay, 209
North Magnetic Pole, 109, 188
North Platte River, 34, 53
North Platte Station, 34, 38-40, 42-44, 46, 96, 365
North Platte, Nebraska, 34-35, 41-42
North Pole (geographic), 20, 66, 102, 104, 106, 131-32, 137, 220, 223, 233, 243, 301, 303, 321, 333, 337, 350, 388, 398-99
Northern Pacific Railway, 69, 304-05, 322-24, 332, 335, 391, 441n7
Northwest Passage, 101-05, 108-10, 132, 136
Norton Sound, 259, 279
Nourse River, 262
Nourse, Joseph E., 129-30, 160, 217-18
Novaya Zemlya, 132
Nowleyout, 174, 202
Noyes, Henry E., 58
Nuklukayet, Alaska, 278
Nulato, Alaska, 278-79
Nutokecak, 158, 419n18, 423n26
O'Reilly Island, 117, 119
Ogallala, Nebraska, 99
Ogilvie, William, 277, 281, 283, 281, 396
Oglala Sioux Indians, 40, 44, 52, 79
Old Faithful Geyser, 327, 331
Olympia, Washington, 247, 389-90
Omaha Bee, 82
Omaha, Nebraska, 37, 43, 365, 399
Ommanney, Erasmus, 214
Ook-joo-lik. *See* Oot-loo-lik
Oot-loo-lik, 114, 117, 174
Operti, Albert, 184
Oregon Biographical Dictionary, 396
Oregon City, Oregon, 13
Oregon Institute. *See* Willamette University
Oregon Statesman (newspaper), 15, 21-22, 396
Oregon Trail, 6, 12, 16, 20, 23, 30, 34, 304
Oregonian (newspaper), 394, 399
Palmer, Edward, 443n15
Palmer, Henry, 144
Palomas Tract, 341
Panama Route, 23
Pandora (yacht), 132, 137, 214, 422n18, 428n11

Index

Panorama des Universums, 144
Paquimé, Casas Grandes, 344
Parry, Sir William Edward, 105, 110, 120, 228, 233, 416n13
Paso del Norte and Ciudad Juarez, 360
Patzki, Julius, 64
Paul, August C., 53, 66, 96
Pawnee Indians, 39-40
Payer Pass, 169
Peary, Robert, 167, 220, 304, 398-99
Peel Sound, 132
Peffer River, 120, 178
Peglar, Henry, 115, 414n10
Pelly Bay, 112, 117-18, 178
Pelly River, 259, 270-71, 274, 377-78, 380
Pelly, David, 240
Peninsular Company, 385
Peoria Journal, 18
Peoria, Illinois, 256, 400
Perrier Pass, 282
Petersen, Carl, 114
Petersen, Captain, 277-78
Petropavlovsk-Kamchatskiy, Russia, 18
Phillip Best Beer Brewery (Pabst Brewery), 144
Philosophical Society of Washington, 255
Phipps, Constantine John, 104
Piedras Verdes region, 343, 362
Piedras Verdes River, 343
Pinta (US ship), 306, 309-11, 316
Platte River, 11-12, 34, 53
Point Adams, Oregon, 8-10, 13
Point Barrow, 107, 109, 279-80, 286
Point Le Vesconte, 193
Point Ogle, 112
Point Turnagain, 107-09
Polaris (US ship), 126, 131, 137, 167
Polyphemus (British ship), 104
Pooyetta, 179
Pope, John, 286, 296
Porcupine River, 277
Porden, Eleanor Anne. *See* Eleanor Franklin
Port Angeles, Washington, 390
Portland Chamber of Commerce, 385
Portland, Oregon, 15, 247, 258-59, 280, 285, 292-93, 390-92, 394-95
Potter, Edwin, 121, 123-24, 127, 144, 158-60, 414n4, 419n19
Powder River, 50, 52-53, 68, 409n8
Powell, David Franklin, 340-42, 392
Powell, John Wesley, 92, 237, 370-71
Prairie Dog Creek, 55
Prince Regent Inlet, 108, 114
Prince William Sound, 371

Princeton University, 303-04, 310, 438n38
Princeton University Art Museum, 319
Puhtoorak (Ik-kin-nil-lik Puh-too-rak), 173-74, 175-76, 421n14, 422n15
Pulitzer, Joseph, 321, 323, 327, 397
Punch (magazine), 132
Pyramid Harbor, 261, 263, 306, 386, 446n25
Qikiqtaq (a big island), 185
Quinn, James, 82
Quoich River, 229
Rae Strait, 109
Rae, John, 111-14, 118-19, 127-28, 141, 152, 158, 161, 176, 181-82, 213, 215, 217, 219-20, 226, 228-30, 395, 416n13
  Inuit cannibalism testimony, 112-13, 215, 217
  obituary of, 395
Rainbow (British ship), 108
Rasmussen, Knud, 127, 172, 243, 418n12, 421nn12, 13, 426n16
Ray, Patrick Henry, 280, 282, 286
Raymond, Charles, 278, 282
Red Cloud (chief), 44, 51, 98
Red Cloud Indian Agency, 44-45, 64, 71, 76, 79, 98-99
Red Cloud's War, 50
Reid, William "Scotch," 293
Remington, Frederic, 74, 95
Report of a Military Reconnaissance (FGS, Jr.), 258, 263, 272, 281, 283-86
Repulse Bay, 112, 117-18, 120, 122-24, 126-27, 135, 140-42, 144, 149, 156, 161, 219, 229, 242, 414n3,
Resolute (raft), 266, 278
Revillon Frères, 221
Reynolds, Joseph, 52-53, 409n8
Richards, Sir George Henry, 129, 218
Richardson Point, 113, 119-20, 175, 177, 179
Richardson, John, 107, 112
Riffenburgh, Beau, 210-11, 398
Rime of the Ancient Mariner (Coleridge), 102
Rink Rapids. *See* Five Finger Rapids
Rink, Henrik Johannes, 235, 270
Robinson's Wonderland (Musee Theatre), 359
Rock Island Argus, 253, 393
Rock Island, Illinois, 247, 253, 255-56, 260, 262, 294-95, 303, 323, 335, 365-67, 393, 399-401
Rocky Mountains, 7, 12, 247
Rodgers (rescue ship), 243-44, 430n10
Roes Welcome Sound, 122
Rogue River Wars, 16
Rosebud Creek, 57-59, 63-64, 66, 68, 77
Rosebud Narrows (cañon), 58, 62, 64, 69
Rosebud, battle of, 57, 59, 61-70, 77, 94, 138

484 Index

Rosebud, village, 57-58, 62-64, 67, 77
Ross, James G., 324, 331, 333, 335-36
Ross, John, 104-05, 108-09, 172, 178, 228-29, 233, 423n22
Ross, Sir James Clark, 108-10, 178, 185, 188
Roth, John, 257
Royal Geographical Society, 109, 214-15, 319, 398
Royal Society, 104, 215
Royall, William B., 53, 63
Russell Glacier, 382
Russell, Israel C., 318, 371
Russell, Mark C., 373-75, 380, 382-85
Russian American Company, 278
Sackville-West, Lionel, 272-73
Sailor's Snug House, 244
Salem, Oregon, 13-17, 19-22, 31, 211, 250, 393-94
Salt Lake City, Utah, 34, 299
San Carlos Apache Indian Reservation, 292
San Francisco Chronicle, 15, 285, 439n42
San Francisco, California, 15, 23, 33, 247, 252, 280, 284-85, 287, 294, 299, 401, 439n42
  earthquake (1906), 401
Sand Hills, 40
Saturday Blade, 357, 360-61, 398
Saussure Glacier, 283
Sayre, Lewis A., 48, 245
Schuyler, Walter S., 78
Schwatka Lake, 269
Schwatka, Ada Brackett (wife of FGS, Jr.), 247, 253-54, 256, 260-62, 294-96, 303, 328, 331, 337, 354, 365-67, 370-72, 388-89, 393, 399-401, 447n20
  birth of daughter, 303
  death of, 399, 401
  intervenes to prevent Schwatka's army resignation, 295
  introduced to Schwatka at Fort D. A. Russell, 247
  learns of husband's death, 393
  writings, 400-401
Schwatka, Amelia, Jr. (sister of FGS, Jr.), 4, 15-16
Schwatka, Amelia Hukill (mother of FGS Jr.), 3-4, 7, 11-15, 394
Schwatka, Annie (sister of FGS, Jr.), 12, 15
Schwatka, Annie Gaines (wife of ACS, Jr.), 15
Schwatka, August C. (brother of FGS, Jr.), 5, 15
Schwatka, August (gr.father of FGS, Jr.), 1-3, 403n1
Schwatka, Catherine (sister of FGS, Jr.), 4, 15
Schwatka, Catherine Geissendörfer (gr.mother of FGS, Jr.), 2-3

Schwatka, Frederick Gustave, Jr.
  1878-1880 Franklin Records Search Expedition, 144-209
  1883 The Yukon (Alaskan Reconnaissance) expedition, 257-80
  1886 The *Times's* expedition to Mount St. Elias, 303-20
  1887 The *World's* expedition to Yellowstone, 327-337
  1889 The *Inter-Ocean* journey to Mexico, 342-51
  1891 The *Ledger* expedition to Alaska, 372-85
  Army experience
    appointed to U.S. Third Cavalry, Company M, 30
    commands train robbery manhunt, 99
    commissioned as second lieutenant, 30
    duties at Camp Sheridan, 95-96
    escort and scouting duties, 31, 36-40, 46, 50
    Gen. Miles aide-de-camp, 250, 290
    investigative duties (Sioux murders), 40
    promoted to first lieutenant, 191
    requests for leave of absense and extensions from U.S. Army
      for Arctic expedition, 135-36
      for injuries, 246
      for private purposes, 212, 243, 249, 254-55, 292, 295-96
      rejected by U.S. Army, 246, 249-50, 293
      approved by U.S. Army with resignation, 296
    resigns from U.S. Army, 297
    service with Buffalo Bill, 36-38, 41
  soldier, at
    Tongue River Heights, 55-57
    Rosebud, 59-64
    Slim Buttes, 79-85
  soldier-scientist, 49, 91-92
  sportsman/hunter, 38, 407n25
  Starvation March, 85-86
  suffers from depression, 88
  survey map to Black Hills, creation of, 42
  tends to wounded after Rosebud, battle of, 64
  accomplishments
    military, 66, 81-82, 87-88, 138
    Arctic exp., 219-24
    Yukon exp., 281-89
    Mount St. Elias exp., 320
    final Alaska exp., 386-87
  alcoholism, 42-43, 88, 294-95, 365-67, 370,

Index 485

388-90
    seeks treatment for, 389-90
    spends night in jail for drunkenness, 364
    suffers alcohol-induced psychosis, 366
appearance, 29, 133-34, 295, 390
    excessive weight, 295, 311, 314-15, 350, 367, 370, 373
application to government for Arctic exploring, 131
as advocate for fair treatment of native peoples, 32, 149, 236, 238-39, 292, 344
as blood brother to his Inuit companions, 156
as *Inter-Ocean* Indian wars correspondent, 68-75, 81, 87-88, 95, 396
as leader, 18, 81-82, 134, 167-68, 224, 383
as lecturer, 244-48, 252-53, 297-99, 337-39, 357-58, 365-66, 390-91, 397
as writer, 92-94, 70-73, 230-31, 234-39, 269, 284-89, 297-301, 320-21, 337-38, 341-42, 348-49, 353-54, 362-64, 369-70, 385, 391, 396-99. *See also Along Alaska's Great River,* "Among the Apaches," "Among the Natives of the North," *Children of the Cold, In the Land of the Midnight Sun, In the Land of the Cave and Cliff Dwellers, Nimrod in the North,* "Sun Dance of the Sioux. *See also* Schwatka, as *Inter-Ocean* correspondent
sensationalism in writings, 74, 268-69, 311-12, 319, 348-49, 352-54, 397-99
attorney misappropriates salary, 255
awards, 291
birth of, 6
birth of daughter, 303
business schemes
    Aleutian cattle, 280, 293-94
    mining and commodity schemes, 445n2
    Palomas colony, 340-41, 392
    "Schwatka" building, 35
    Tarahumara exhibition, 354-61
collects Aivilingmiut vocabulary, 237
criticisms of, 75, 94-95, 236, 272-73, 281-83, 328-29, 362-63, 394-99
death of, 393
    false report of, 367
dispute with Haynes and Fee, 333-36
early years, 11-12, 16-19
educational experience
    attends Willamette 19-20, 405n34
    legal apprenticeship, 43
    medical apprenticeship, 46
    attends U.S.M.A. (West Point), 24-30
    attends Bellevue Hospital Medical College, 46-49

engagement and marriage to Ada Brackett, 253, 255-56, 260, 295-96, 303, 337, 354, 365, 371, 399-400
fractures ribs and nose at Park Hotel, 366
fractures radial bone at Occidental Hotel, 294
fractures leg at Sturtevant Hotel, 245-46
friend to Chief Spotted Tail, 45
    named Big Wolf by Sioux, 94, 399
funeral of, 393-94
illnesses
    chronic stomach, 24-25, 295, 392, 396
    hospitalized with malaria, 255
    Yellowstone exp., 329-30
    Mt. St. Elias exp., 313, 315-16
investigates murder of Fosdick, 96-98
journal during Arctic expedition, 147-48, 422n19
laudanum overdose, 393
learns from his Indian and Inuit companions, 32, 92-94, 100, 133-34, 151-53, 162-63
lives amongst Sioux tribe, 92
lives amongst Inuit in the Arctic, 92
manuscripts, journals, papers destroyed by fire, 401
praises skills and character of his Inuit and Indian counterparts, 32, 165-66, 188, 193, 195, 209, 234-39, 264, 274-75, 277, 284, 376
religious beliefs of, 236
reports Barry to U.S. Marshall's office, 211
returns to Mexico as *Herald* journalist, 354
speaks at Chickering Hall about Franklin Search, 218
Senator Hawley recommends publication of Alaskan report, 286
Schwatka, Frederick Gustave, Sr. (father of FGS, Jr.), 3-15, 20-21, 64, 66, 80-81, 98, 245, 394
    anti-slavery stance, 14
    Clatsop relations, 9-10
    Oregon homesteading, 8-9, 13
Schwatka, Frederika (daughter of FGS, Jr.), 303, 354, 365, 371-72, 382, 393, 401
    dies in childbirth, 401
    marries Edward Stafford, 401
Schwatka, Helena (sister of FGS, Jr), 4
Schwatka, Josephine (sister of FGS, Jr), 6
Schwatka, Laura (sister of FGS, Jr), 5
Schwatka's Search (Gilder). *See* Gilder
Science (magazine), 236, 285
Scoresby, William, 104, 233
Scott, Robert Falcon, 386
Scribner's Magazine, 364
Seattle, Washington, 247, 288, 390-91
Selwyn River, 380

Index

Second Cavalry, 41, 46, 55-56, 58-59, 62, 64, 77, 92, 136
Seotitecheung, 176-77, 182-83
Seton-Karr, Heywood Walter, 305-06, 308-19, 313-20, 439nn42, 45, 440nn53, 55
Seventh Cavalry, 53, 66, 79, 84, 85, 87, 218
Seward, William, 320
Seward's Folly, 251
Shak-qua-tăh, "Sam," 373
Sheperd, Alexander, "Boss", 351
Sheridan, Philip, 36-37, 39, 250, 291, 293, 296-97
Sheridan, Wyoming, 66
Sherman Basin. *See* Sherman Inlet
Sherman Inlet, 199-200, 221
Sherman, Mary Hoyt, 251
Sherman, William Tecumseh, 26, 46, 76, 135-38, 246-47, 249-51, 254, 256, 291
Sherwood, Morgan, 387
Shircliff, William H., 257
Shores and Alps of Alaska (Seton-Karr), 313, 318
Shoshone Indians, 53, 57-59, 63, 65, 69, 70, 76
Sibley, Frederick W., 46
Sidney, Nebraska, 42, 408n46
Sierra Madre Mountains, 291-92, 341-47, 350, 353, 355, 359-60, 363
Simpson Strait, 177, 185, 187, 193, 195-98
Simpson, George, 112
Simpson, Thomas, 109, 185, 187, 198
Sinuksook, 158
Sioux Indians, 36, 39-41, 44, 50-52, 56, 58-63, 65-66, 70-71, 74-77, 81, 83-84, 88, 91, 93-98, 304, 365, 399, 413n47
Sisson, George, 345
Sitka, Alaska, 251, 260, 288, 305-07, 309, 316-17, 371-72, 385, 438n28, 440n52
Sitting Bull (chief), 57-58, 60-62, 64, 66-67, 77, 79, 98, 252
Sitting Bull's Sun Dance, 58
Skagway, 283, 288, 433n20
Skeet-lah-káh "Edward," 373
Skolai Creek, 382
Skolai Pass, 382
Slim Buttes, battle of, 69, 78, 80-89, 93, 138
Smith Sound, 102, 104, 132
Smithsonian Institution, 145, 237, 352, 443n15
Snake River, 12
Snow, Elmer A., 61-62, 66
Snow, William Parker, 214
South Platte River, 34
Southern Pacific Railroad, 342
Southwest Pass, 221
Spanish-American War, 65
Spleen Lake, 316

Spotted Tail Indian Agency (Beaver Creek), 44-45, 71, 92, 94-95, 96, 98-99, 413n47
Spotted Tail Indian Agency (Missouri River), 99-100, 121, 130
Spotted Tail (chief), 44-45, 51, 74, 91, 94, 98, 152, 410n44
Spuhn, Carl, 261
St. Charles Hotel, 393
St. Lawrence Bay, 243
St. Michael, 259, 266, 278-79
St. Michael (steam ship), 279
St. Nicholas Magazine, 237, 300
St. Paul Globe, 317, 440n52
St. Paul, Minnesota, 5, 304-05, 323, 326, 359, 371
St. Peter (ship), 301
Stables, William Gordon, 237
Stafford, Edward, 401
Stanley, Henry Morton, 68, 137, 302, 338, 385
Stanley, Stephen S., 112
Stanton, Edwin M., 21
Starvation Cove, 113, 119-20, 175, 177-84, 196, 199-201, 227, 423nn25, 26, 426n16
Starvation March (Horsemeat March), 77, 85-87, 90, 134, 205, 275
Stefansson, Vilhjamur, 220, 224
Stein, Robert, 244
Stephens, Charles (also spelled as Stevens), 64, 70
Stevenson, Adlai, 392
Stewart River, 275
Stewart, James, 113, 421n14
Stewart, Reid T., 171
Stewart's Monument, 171, 221
Stoddard, Charles A., 324, 331
Stoney, George, 282
Strahorn, Robert E., 100
Strang, Frederick (nephew of FGS, Jr.), 16
Strang, Thomas, 16
Stratton, David, 324, 331, 334
Sturtevant House, 145, 243, 245
Sun Dance, 58, 70-75, 94-95
"Sun-Dance of the Sioux" (FGS, Jr.), 74-75, 94-95
Sunday Afternoon, a Magazine for the Household. See *Good Company*
Sutorius, Alexander, 62
Sutter's Mill, 8, 42
Summer in Alaska, A (FGS, Jr.), 287
Sweetwater Park Hotel, 338
Sweetwater River, 41
Swineford, Alfred, 305-06
Tacoma Commercial Club, 391
Tacoma Ledger, 353, 390-91
Tacoma, Washington, 304-05, 371, 391

Index

Tagish Indians, 262-65, 267, 283
Tagliabue, C. J., 139
Tah-wŏŏt-z, "Barney," 373
Taiya Inlet, 261-62, 283
Taku Glacier, 374, 445n8
Taku Pass, 401
Taku River, 372-73, 376, 387, 401
Taku Trail, 372-74, 376-77, 379
Talapus (wolf-spirit), 9
Tanana River, 278, 368-70
Tanana, Alaska, 278
Tansey, Jack, 336-37
Tarahumara Indians, "Rarámurí," 345-65, 396, 398, 443n15
Taral, Alaska, 384
Tasiujaq, 222
Taylor, Bayard, 338
Taylor, Charles H., 324
Tegethoff (ship), 132
Tennyson, Alfred Lord, 369
Tenth Cavalry, 134, 218
Terohaute, Michel, 107
Terror Bay, 119-20, 184, 194-95
Terror (British ship), 110, 113-15, 172, 189-90, 194-95, 199, 215, 225, 395, 414n4, 423n22
Terry, Alfred H., 53, 66-67, 76-77
Teslin Lake, 372, 374-77
Teslin River, 377
Thayer, Sylvanus, 25
Thayer, William W., 249
Third Cavalry, 20, 30-34, 36, 38-41, 44-45, 50, 53-54, 56, 58-59, 62, 64, 66, 68-69, 77-78, 82, 84, 88, 90-93, 99, 136, 218, 247, 253, 291, 338, 342, 344, 407n25, 409n21
Thomas Corwin (cutter), 278-79
Thunder Cove, 178
Tierney, Francis, 55
Times, The (London), 181, 213, 218
Tiringaneak, Matthew, 222-23
Tlingit Indians, 261-64, 269, 271, 284, 306-10, 312-15, 317-19, 337, 373, 375-77, 381, 386, 433nn14, 18, 434n32, 438n38, 440n52
Todd Islands, 119-20
Tongue River, 52-53, 55-57, 68-69
Too-ah-de-ah-rak, "Lieut Back," 173
Tookoolito, "Taqulittuq," 116-18, 156
Toolooah, 156, 164, 166-69, 171, 177-78, 187, 193, 196-96, 198-200, 203, 205-06, 425n4
    hunting prowess, 174, 195, 203, 209
    parting with Schwatka and Gilder, 208-09
    scouts route to Back River, 161-63
    sledging skills, 188
Toolooahalek (wife of Toolooah), 164

Topham, Edwin, 318
Topham, Harold W., 318
Touch-the-Clouds (chief), 91, 94
Tower Fall, 326
Tr'ondëk, "Klondike," 275
Trafton, Stephen J., 191
Travel and Adventure in the Territory of Alaska (Whymper), 287, 436n28
Treadwell gold mine, 372
Trent (British ship), 104
Tuktoocheeah, 176, 178-79, 182-83, 417n2, 423n25
Tulloch Point, 197
Tuniit, 185
Tutchone Indians, 262, 274, 283, 378, 380
Tutherly, Herbert, 327-28
Two Grave Bay, 223, 425n11
Tyndall Glacier, 313-15
Tyrrell, James W., 221
Tyrrell, Joseph B., 221
U.S. Army Corps of Engineers, 27, 30, 323
U.S. Coast and Geodetic Survey, 306
U.S. Exploring Expedition (1838-1842), 310
U.S. Geological Survey, 74, 257, 281, 318-19, 369-71, 387
U.S. International Polar Year Expedition, 280
U.S. Military Academy (West Point), 20-30, 33, 43, 49, 51, 92, 171, 249, 322
U.S. Naval Academy, 16, 306, 310
U.S. Naval Observatory, 129, 160, 419n20
Ugjulingmiut, 171-74, 199-202, 233, 239-40, 421nn12-13, 422n20
Ujaralaaq, 240, 242, 431nn20, 25
Ukkusiksalik. *See* Wager Bay
Umnak, Alaska, 294
Unalaska, Alaska, 280, 294
Union Pacific Railroad, 34, 42, 50, 99
United States Coast Pilot (1853), 9
University Medical College of New York University, 46
Upper Geyser Basin, 331, 336
Urique Canyon, 350
Urique, Mexico, 345, 349, 363, 398
Ute John, 84
Utkuhiksalingmiut, 163, 172, 222, 239, 421n12
van Buren, William Holme, 48
Van Diemen's Land (Tasmania), 110
Van Vliet, Frederick, 58
Vancouver Barracks, 250-51, 254, 256, 258, 291, 293
Vancouver, George, 8, 301
Vancouver, Washington, 250, 258
Vermillion, John Wilson, "Texas Jack," 145

488 Index

Victoria (US ship), 259-60
Victoria Strait, 188
Victory (Nelson's ship), 106
Victory (Ross's ship), 108-09, 172, 423n22
Victory Point, 108-09, 115, 189, 192-93
Victory Point record, 115, 224, 241
Von Luettwitz, Adolphus H., 78-79, 80-81, 84, 86, 88
Voyage of the 'Fox' in the Arctic Seas (McClintock), 226-30
Wadsworth, Henry C., 324, 331, 333
Wager Bay (Ukkusiksalik), 161-62, 169-70, 221-22, 229, 240, 242
Wager Plateau, 170
Walker, David, 391, 394
Walker, Fergus, 45
War Department, 6, 10, 34, 45, 286, 407n37
Washington Bay, 158, 183, 187, 196, 227, 419n18, 423n26, 424n34
Washington, D.C., 28, 36, 51, 212, 255, 296, 351, 413n47
Washington, George, 1, 23
Wasson, James R., 27
Webster, Daniel, 253
Webster, John Lee, 37, 406n24
Wellington Channel, 111
Wells, E. Hazard, 369
West, W. W., 324
Western Union Telegraph Company, 259, 435n21
Weyprecht, Karl, 213
Whale Fish Islands, 111
Whale Point, 125, 149, 156, 419n19
whaler's pidgin, 126-27, 152, 160
Wheeler Peak, 162
Wheeler, C. H., 393
Whistler, 40
Whistling Elk, 72
White Horse Rapids, 269
White River (Yukon tributary), 371, 379-80, 382, 384, 387
White River (Missouri River tributary), 44, 99
White, Charley, "Buffalo Chip," 84
Whitehorse, Yukon, Canada, 269-70
Whitewood Creek, 90
Whitman, Walt, 298
Whitney, William Collins, 306
Whymper, Frederick, 287, 436n28
Wilkes, Charles, 310
Wilks, Henry, 189
Willamette Chronicle, 20
Willamette Farmer, 68
Willamette River, 7, 13-14

Willamette University, 19-22, 49, 405n34
Willamette Valley, 6-7, 13, 17, 20
Willard, Rev. Eugene, 262, 433n18
William and Ann (HBC ship), 9
Williams, George H., 21
Williams, Louis L., 371
Willow Creek Park, Yellowstone, 328
Wilmot and Crampton Bay, 174, 198
Wilson, Ed, 324, 331
Wilson, George F., 257-58, 262, 283
"Wintering in the White Zone" (FGS, Jr.), 338
Woodman, David, 416n13, 420n22, 423n22
Woods, C. W., 438n28
Woods, Joseph, 306, 314-15
World's Columbian Exposition (1893), 357, 362
Wrangell Mountains, 271, 301, 303
Wrangell, Alaska, 260, 288
Wyndham-Quin, Windham Thomas, 37
Yahtse, "Yas´ei Héen" River. *See* Jones River
Yakima War, 17
Yakutat Bay, 306-07, 309-10, 316-19, 438n38
Yakutat Tlingit, 307-10, 313-15, 317-19
Yale University, 39, 303
Yancey's Hotel, 326-27, 331
Yaqui Indians, 345
Yellowstone
 National Park, 275, 304, 321-37, 373, 397
 River, 55, 57, 69, 77, 250
Yen-at-set'l (chief), 307
Yoquibo, Mexico, 355, 363
York Factory, 219, 243
Young, S. Hall, 287
Young, Sir Allen, 129, 132, 137, 212-14, 217
Youth's Companion, The, 98, 338, 413n47
Yukon (steam ship), 277-79

ABOUT THE AUTHOR

Douglas W. Wamsley, an attorney by profession, is an independent researcher and scholar who has written extensively on the history of nineteenth-century Arctic exploration and its participants. He is the author of numerous publications that examine individual contributions to our knowledge and perceptions of the far northern regions, including *Polar Hayes, The Life and Contributions of Isaac Israel Hayes, M.D.* published by the American Philosophical Society.

www.ingramcontent.com/pod-product-compliance
Lightning Source LLC
Chambersburg PA
CBHW052230230426
43666CB00035B/2594